Nothing in this world happens in isolation.
Everything is connected to everything else.
Analysis is finding those connections.

Disclaimer

All information in this book taken from other sources is assumed to fit within the "fair use" provisions of the copyright law. This book attempts to explain what has become one of the most controversial issues in America in this century, an issue that has haunted the families of all of the people who died on 9/11: Why did the intelligence agencies in the US fail to prevent the attacks on 9/11? This book represents over five years of research and is intended to bring to the American people an account of these failures in a form that is as comprehensive as possible. All analysis and conclusions in this book should be considered to be the sole and expressed "opinions of the author."

I again repeat here the statement I made in writing when sending the FBI in e-mail the summaries of the interviews I had with them on several occasions.

"Since I believe all of this information in this letter (account of 9/11) to be true and accurate, to the best of my ability, I will willingly agree to submit to a polygraph test given by any official government agency, with their own people, to answer any questions, to eliminate any doubt whatsoever as to the truth of what I believed to be the facts with regard to the information concerning this event (and my analysis of this event prior to 9/11)."

Prior Knowledge of 9/11

Robert Schopmeyer

Prior Knowledge of 9/11

Published by:
Palo Alto Publishing
459 Hamilton Ave., Suite 201
Palo Alto, CA 94301

www.prior-knowledge-of-9/11.com

www.priorknowledgeof911.com

www.eventson911.com

Library of Congress Cataloging-in-Publishing Data

Prior Knowledge of 9/11

ISBN-13 978-0-9791060-0-2
ISBN-10 0-9791060-0-1

Printed in the United Sates of America

First Edition August 09, 2007

Table of Contents

Appendix: The 9/11 Letters

Letter to 9/11 Commission

Summary FBI Interview September 19, 2001

Letter to Joint Senate-House Intelligence Committee

Replies from Joint Committee

Letter to Bob Kerrey, 9/11 Commission

Introduction

Of all of the stories on 9/11, this story is unique. It is unique because I had known about the events of 9/11, and the attack on the World Trade Center Towers, seven months prior to these events taking place. In what can be called a hideous chain of events, I had uncovered the plans for the attacks that were to occur on 9/11, on a flight from San Francisco to Newark on February 11, 2001. This book is the story of how I had discovered the plan for this attack and why I was not able to do anything in order to prevent these horrific attacks from taking place.

I wrote this book in order to put this story on paper. I also felt this information might be useful sometime in the future for someone at one of the intelligence agencies to get a better understanding of how the next terrorist event can be anticipated before it takes place.

I also thought writing this book would bring a measure of closure to what I thought had been my fault by not preventing these attacks in the first place. Every day since these events occurred, I have gone over in my mind a hundred thousand times what I could have done differently to have prevented the events of 9/11 from occurring. There is no way to go back in time. All of the "what if" rethinking of an event will never make this event go away. No amount of reliving a horrific event can ever bring it back in order to change the outcome in any way. This book in fact was written with the hope that writing it would be somehow like a sort of catharsis and finally put this whole thing behind me.

I had found out on this flight to Newark that the al Qaeda terrorists had publicly declared war against the United States in February 1998, and were determined to mount a massive attack inside of the US. Knowing this, I was able to discover the following additional information:

The targets of this attack were going to be the World Trade Center Towers.

The terrorists were going to hijack four large US airliners in flight to carry out this attack and intended to fly these aircraft directly into the sides of these towers in order to cause these towers to collapse.

They would hijack planes departing from eastern airports using four to five terrorists, armed with four-inch knives.

This attack would most likely take place during the first two weeks of September 2001.

Not only was there an extremely high probability this attack would take place, it was inconceivable that this attack would not occur.

The FAA, the FBI and the CIA would do absolutely nothing at all to prevent these attacks from taking place, even if I provided them with the information I had.

This was the nightmare I lived with for seven months. I was literally consumed with the thought of what I could do to prevent these attacks from taking place. Every single day I went over in my mind, how was it going to be possible to go to the FAA or the FBI and be believed and then have them take what I thought would be the appropriate action to prevent these attacks? I came up with roadblock after roadblock in my mind as to why the people I was going to have to talk to at these agencies were never going to accept my input or do anything with my information. I ultimately came to the conclusion that unless I was able to get credible information on this attack or the people who were determined to carry out this attack, information that could be corroborated by the FBI, there was going to be no one at any of these agencies who would ever accept what I had to say and do what I thought was necessary to prevent these attacks from occurring.

On the day this attack occurred, just after these events took place on 9/11, I came to the conclusion this event had been largely my fault, and in fact my fault alone. I could not see myself at first blaming the intelligence agencies since I had concluded these agencies were huge bureaucracies with layers of brain-dead, clueless bureaucrats. It was my opinion at the time that they probably had not even been aware this huge disaster was about to occur, even though this had been their job.

Immediately after the events of 9/11, I went to the FBI and in a sit-down interview explained to the FBI agent doing the interview

2

how I had known about these events beforehand. I had actually gone to the FBI with one single goal, to ask them if they thought this disaster was my fault, and could this event have been prevented had I come to them in February when I first found out the details of this attack.

The FBI agent who interviewed me said that it was not my fault. I accept this as the official view of the FBI. The agent said that if I had come to them with this information in February 2001, they would have done nothing with it. He told me that I did not have the exact flight numbers of the aircraft that were to be hijacked, the names of the hijackers, or any other information they would normally use to prevent an attack. Prior to 9/11, I had no real proof for any of this information that I had, proof the FBI would have required in order to start an investigation.

In the period after 9/11, I was never able to understand why the large intelligence agencies had not done what I had done to uncover the events of 9/11. This just did not make any sense. As more information came out after 9/11 from the Joint Inquiry Committee and then the 9/11 Commission, I began to feel more and more that there had indeed been significant information these agencies could have used in order to anticipate and then prevent the attacks on 9/11.

I eventually sent e-mails to the investigators on the Joint Senate/House Inquiry Committee explaining in detail how I had uncovered the events of 9/11. I also phoned them directly and had a long conversation with Michael Jacobson, one of the investigators for this Committee. I sent the Joint Inquiry Committee investigators summaries of all of the FBI reports I had, with detailed explanations how it was possible to know how these attacks were going to occur. On April 13, 2004, I personally presented summaries of all of the FBI reports and the material I had sent to the Joint Inquiry Committee to members of the 9/11 Commission.

This book describes the experiences I had with the FBI and both the Joint Inquiry Committee investigators and the 9/11 Commission members.

The Joint Inquiry Committee investigators said they agreed with the FBI, that this disaster was not my fault. The 9/11 Commission members were curious as to how I had known about this event in the first place and in particular how I had known the World Trade Center Towers would be the particular target for this attack. One member of the 9/11 Commission even inquired as to why I was not currently working for the CTC section of the CIA. I thank all of them for their understanding and support. Not a single person with whom I talked or otherwise communicated thought this had been my fault in any way.

After attending the 9/11 Commission hearings on April 13-14, 2004, I became more and more perplexed over the reasons the intelligence agencies had given for not anticipating and then preventing the events of 9/11. With their multi-billion-dollar budgets and tens of thousands of employees, this did not make any sense. In order to get to the bottom of this, I decided to carefully go through all of the testimony that had been given in both investigations, and to go over the FBI Inspector General's report when it was released later in 2005.

The Joint Inquiry Committee stated these intelligence agencies had been surprised by the attack on 9/11, and wanted to know why. What did these agencies know before 9/11 and what did they do with this information?

After one and one-half years of investigation and testimony, the 9/11 Commission said the failure to stop the events of 9/11 was due to the lack of imagination at these agencies. They also concluded that their report would not place blame on any individual or agency; that this task was better left to the Inspector General for each agency. They further said that they were not going to definitively conclude one way or the other whether the events on 9/11 could have been anticipated beforehand and prevented. These investigations had found numerous "dots," but for some reasons unexplained even to this day, these dots had not been connected by these huge agencies with their multi-billion-dollar budgets. Now this just did not make any sense. If I was able to discover the plan for the attack against the World Trade Center Towers several months beforehand, it made no sense that these agencies with multi-billion-dollar budgets and tens of thousands of employees could not have done the same thing. They not only had significantly more information than I had, but numerous opportunities to do what would have been required to anticipate these events ahead of time.

As more information was described in the media from both of these investigations, a more complete picture of exactly what went wrong began to emerge. The FBI Inspector General's report, even though much of it had been originally redacted, provided more insight into who at these agencies had caused their efforts to fall short.

To get a final complete picture of the events that took place prior to 9/11 required an exhaustive search through hundreds and hundreds of pages of government investigation reports, many completely and apparently deliberately obtuse, direct interviews with investigators on the Joint Inquiry Committee, Commissioners on the 9/11 Commission, and numerous FBI agents. Much of this documentation is in this book and it was intentionally left in so the reader could actually feel the frustration I had felt of having to read hundreds of pages of obtuse government reports, and almost getting the full picture, but finding at each point as the facts were coming out, critical information was either left out, missing, or just never fully investigated and explained. It was only after the account of FBI Agent Ali Soufan came out was it finally possible to see the whole picture of what had gone wrong on 9/11, a picture that the American people are unaware of even today.

It was not simple mistakes that had allowed the events on 9/11 to take place as had been described by the directors and managers at these agencies, or a lack of manpower and financial resources but something entirely different. This book describes in detail what it was exactly that had gone wrong at these agencies to allow the attacks on 9/11 to be successfully carried out by a group of religious fanatics from a far-off country most Americans barely knew even existed.

Every effort was applied to take out the immense emotions I had felt after having been caught up in this horrible tragedy, a tragedy that should have been prevented with even the most minimal of effort by the US intelligence agencies. This book, one story amongst thousands of stories from 9/11, was written in the hope something can be learned from this so that the American people can be kept safer and more secure in the future.

Chapter 1

Trip to New York

Although it has been over five years, it still feels as if it had all happened just yesterday. For me, the nightmare began seven months before the events of 9/11, on a Sunday morning, February 11, 2001.

I was about to catch a flight on United Airlines, from San Francisco to Newark, New Jersey, on what seemed to be in every way a very ordinary day. (Looking back at what had started out as merely just another day, little did I know at that time that I was about to experience what can only be described as the ultimate horror story. A horror story from which I would never really recover.)

I had just returned to the US from a business trip in Japan late the day before. In my carry-on bag was a magazine I had just recently purchased at the Narita Airport in Japan. I had briefly glanced through this magazine on the flight from Japan, and saw that most of the articles in it had been in large part devoted to Usama bin Laden.

Since I was running very late, I realized I was not going to have enough time to be able to stop at a newsstand on the way to the gate. On long flights, I always purchase at least five or six magazines prior to the flight. As I ran past the magazine stand I thought, "Damn it, there is just not enough time to stop for magazines without missing my flight. How am I going to keep from being completely bored on this flight, with just one single magazine? This flight has to be at least five to six hours. And why in the world would I want to read about Usama bin Laden, which is what most of the only magazine I have is devoted to? DAMN!"

Bin Laden seemed to me like a religious nut case holed up in a cave somewhere in Afghanistan, venting his hatred at the rest of the non-Muslim world. Why in the world would anyone want to waste valuable time reading about this person? In my opinion he had absolutely nothing to contribute to the rest of the world with his hatred for the West, infidels, and the US in particular.

After the flight took off, I started to read this magazine for the complete lack of anything else to do. While I was very familiar with much of the information in this magazine already, having read about this group previously in many newspaper articles, some of what I read was entirely new. As I continued to read more about bin Laden, I started to become somewhat fascinated but at the same time increasingly uneasy and concerned over some of the information I was reading.

In particular, the fact bin Laden had built over 20 training camps in Afghanistan was not only shocking but also puzzling at the very same time.

Why in the world did Usama bin Laden need 20 training camps in Afghanistan?

This did not make any sense, maybe one or two, but 20 training camps? What in the world did he need with 20 training camps, especially when each one would, without a doubt, have cost a significant amount of money? This made absolutely no sense at the time.

When the article stated that over 20,000 terrorists had gone through training at these camps, I was really concerned. This obviously explained why he had built so many camps in Afghanistan. But then in my mind, how was this even possible? Over 20,000 people had gone through these training camps for no other purpose than to train to become terrorists. Up to this point, based on reading the mainstream media in the US, I had thought maybe at the outset bin Laden had just a few hundred followers.

Over 20,000 terrorists trained at his camps was just a stunning number. What was even more stunning and I mean stunning, was the fact he had 10,000 of his followers go through what they called "martyrdom training," and these future martyrs were going to be focused on attacks against the United States.

GOOD GOD ALMIGHTY!

This was just stunning. Why had the mainstream media not alerted everyone in then US to these facts? Having such a large number of trained terrorists at this time was completely outside my scope of understanding, in spite of the fact I usually read at least three or four newspapers each day in addition to reading many magazines each week and consider myself to be very well-read on current events.

After reading this information on this organization, I went from having no interest at all in learning anything about bin Laden, to being concerned enough I wanted to get a more in-depth understanding not only about him, but his entire al Qaeda movement. With that many trained terrorists, then it was going to be important to learn as much about them as I possibly could, if for no other reason than just to keep my family and myself safe from ever encountering a terrorist event.

The most disturbing point raised in these articles was the extremely large number of people who had actually trained for martyrdom missions. And what was this ultimately going to mean for the US?

These people had training for no other reason than to ultimately carry out suicide missions against the US. With this many trained terrorists running around the world, I was puzzled over why had no major attacks had been committed in the US up to now by these al Qaeda terrorists? This seemed a bit odd.

If what I read was true, then sometime in the future the US surely would then be on the receiving end of many significant terrorist events, perhaps right inside of our own borders. It would just be a matter of time.

How were the US authorities ever going to be able to stop and keep out of the US, perhaps thousands of potential terrorists trying to enter the US in preparation for carrying out some future terrorist attack? Certainly they could stop some, but with this many potential terrorists, it was inconceivable they would be able to stop them all as they tried to enter the US.

Americans traveling abroad were also now no longer going to be safe or at least as safe as we had expected. Since I was traveling extensively all over the world at this time, this was not good news. Now, as I traveled outside the US, I would have to be constantly on the lookout for potentially dangerous situations.

Sitting down to have a cup of coffee at an outdoor cafe, getting on an airplane, or traveling by train, any of these could be subject to some possible terrorist event and would require being especially vigilant.

As president of my own small software company, I had to deal with many issues, but what a major burden this was going to be, trying to remain vigilant all of the time, always watching out for a dangerous situation involving these al Qaeda terrorists. But it was obvious a lack of vigilance here could prove to be deadly, so from now on there appeared to be no other way.

In hindsight, it is clear that I was now being sucked into what would shortly become a horrific sequence of events. It was at this point that I was passing the point of no return. Trying to solve this puzzle was so profound, that I had no way out. I did not realize at the time that I was now on a one-way street and there was no way back.

It was as if I were floating down a river and in the distance I could see a huge vortex off to the side and in front of me and as I got closer, it pull\ed me around and around and then eventually pulled me down, under water, into complete inky black darkness. I was to walk onto this flight as myself and then walk off of this flight as someone entirely different, a person I would never have recognized prior to boarding this flight.

Chapter 2

The Fatwa and Declaration of Jihad

"The al Qaeda Code"

While the information about the terrorist training camps was disturbing enough, as I continued to read further, I came upon even more alarming information, information up to this point I had never seen before. In this magazine were two statements actually written by the terrorists themselves. One was a declaration called the "Jihad Against Jews and Crusaders," and the other statement, which was part of this Declaration, was referred to as the "Fatwa." The Fatwa was an edict that purportedly had been issued by bin Laden himself, calling for the killing of Americans:

Published in Al-Quds al-'Arabi on February 23, 1998.

> *"To kill Americans and their Allies, both civil and military, is an individual duty of every Muslim, who is able, in any country where this is possible... By God's leave, we call on every Muslim who believes in God and hopes for reward to obey God's command to kill Americans and plunder their possessions wherever he finds them and whenever he can."*

Jihad Against Jews and Crusaders
World Islamic Front Statement

Statement signed by

> Shaykh Usamah Bin-Muhammad Bin-Laden
> Ayman al-Zawahiri, amir of the Jihad Group in Egypt
> Abu-Yasir Rifa'i Ahmad Taha, Egyptian Islamic Group
> Shaykh Mir Hamzah, secretary of the Jamiat-ul-Ulema-e-Pakistan
> Fazlur Rahman, amir of the Jihad Movement in Bangladesh

Praise be to God, who revealed the Book, controls the clouds, defeats factionalism, and says in His Book "But when the forbidden months are past, then fight and slay the pagans wherever ye find them, seize them, beleaguer them, and lie in wait for them in every stratagem (of war)"; and peace be upon our Prophet, Muhammad Bin-'Abdallah, who said "I have been sent with the sword between my hands to ensure that no one but God is worshipped, God who put my livelihood under the shadow of my spear and who inflicts humiliation and scorn on those who disobey my orders." The Arabian Peninsula has never – since God made it flat, created its desert, and encircled it with seas – been stormed by any forces like the crusader armies now spreading in it like locusts, consuming its riches and destroying its plantations. All this is happening at a time when nations are attacking Muslims like people fighting over a plate of food. In the light of the grave situation and the lack of support, we and you are obliged to discuss current events, and we should all agree on how to settle the matter.

No one argues today about three facts that are known to everyone; we will list them, in order to remind everyone:

First, for over seven years the United States has been occupying the lands of Islam in the holiest of places, the Arabian Peninsula, plundering its riches, dictating to its rulers, humiliating its people, terrorizing its neighbors, and turning its bases in the Peninsula into a spearhead through which to fight the neighboring Muslim peoples.

If some people have formerly debated the fact of the occupation, all the people of the Peninsula have now acknowledged it.

The best proof of this is the Americans' continuing aggression against the Iraqi people using the Peninsula as a staging post, even though all its rulers are against their territories being used to that end, still they are helpless. Second, despite the great devastation inflicted on the Iraqi people by the crusader-Zionist alliance, and despite the huge number of those killed, in excess of 1 million... despite all this, the Americans are once against trying to repeat the horrific massacres, as though they are not content with the protracted blockade imposed after the ferocious war or the fragmentation and devastation.

So now they come to annihilate what is left of this people and to humiliate their Muslim neighbors.

Third, if the Americans' aims behind these wars are religious and economic, the aim is also to serve the Jews' petty state and divert attention from its occupation of Jerusalem and murder of Muslims there.

The best proof of this is their eagerness to destroy Iraq, the strongest neighboring Arab state, and their endeavor to fragment all the states of the region such as Iraq, Saudi Arabia, Egypt, and Sudan into paper statelets and through their disunion and weakness to guarantee Israel's survival and the continuation of the brutal crusade occupation of the Peninsula.

All these crimes and sins committed by the Americans are a clear declaration of war on God, his messenger, and Muslims. And ulema have throughout Islamic history unanimously agreed that the Jihad is an individual duty if the enemy destroys the Muslim countries. This was revealed by Imam Bin-Qadamah in "Al-Mughni," Imam al-Kisa'i in "Al-Bada'i," al-Qurtubi in his interpretation, and the shaykh of al-Islam in his books, where he said "As for the militant struggle, it is aimed at defending sanctity and religion, and it is a duty as agreed. Nothing is more sacred than belief except repulsing an enemy who is attacking religion and life."

On that basis, and in compliance with God's order, we issue the following fatwa to all Muslims:

The ruling to kill the Americans and their allies – civilians and military – is an individual duty for every Muslim who can do it in any country in which it is possible to do it, in order to liberate the al-Aqsa Mosque and the holy mosque from their grip, and in order for their armies to move out of all the lands of Islam, defeated and unable to threaten any Muslim. This is in accordance with the words of Almighty God, "and fight the pagans all together as they fight you all together," and "fight them until there is no more tumult or oppression, and there prevail justice and faith in God."

This is in addition to the words of Almighty God "And why should ye not fight in the cause of God and of those who, being weak, are ill-treated and oppressed – women and children, whose cry is 'Our Lord, rescue us from this town, whose people are oppressors; and raise for us from thee one who will help!'"

We – with God's help – call on every Muslim who believes in God and wishes to be rewarded to comply with God's order to kill the Americans and plunder their money wherever and whenever they find it. We also call on Muslim ulema, leaders, youths, and soldiers to launch the raid on Satan's US troops and the devil's supporters allying with them, and to displace those who are behind them so that they may learn a lesson.

Almighty God said "O ye who believe, give your response to God and His Apostle, when He calleth you to that which will give you life. And know that God cometh between a man and his heart, and that it is He to whom ye shall all be gathered."

Almighty God also says "O ye who believe, what is the matter with you, that when ye are asked to go forth in the cause of God, ye cling so heavily to the earth! Do ye prefer the life of

13

this world to the hereafter? But little is the comfort of this life, as compared with the hereafter. Unless ye go forth, He will punish you with a grievous penalty, and put others in your place; but Him ye would not harm in the least. For God hath power over all things."

Almighty God also says "So lose no heart, nor fall into despair. For ye must gain mastery if ye are true in faith.

As I read over the Declaration of Jihad, it was obvious this Declaration was in reality something you might expect to see written by a leader of a Muslim terrorist organization. It stated Americans should leave the Saudi Peninsula and the Muslim temples in Medina and Mecca should be returned to the "true" Muslims. It was not hard to see how a very intensely religious person, a leader of a terrorist organization, could come up with the Declaration of Jihad Against Jews and Crusaders.

They felt Americans, the vast majority being non-Muslims, supported and protected the corrupt regimes in possession of the sacred territory in the Muslim country where the most important Islamic shrines were located. They felt the Americans (particularly the US military) who were located inside of Saudi Arabia were despoiling this holy ground, since they were infidels. They clearly wanted to see all Americans and all Westerners leave the Saudi Peninsula with their holy shrines returned to very strict Muslim regimes.

The Fatwa was a whole different matter. When I first read the text of this Fatwa, I was instantly stunned!

I kept saying under my breath over and over, "This is not possible, this text cannot possibly be printed here in this magazine, and especially a magazine an American could read. This is not possible." I must have read this statement 10 or 20 times, thinking each time I read this statement, the text would somehow say something entirely different. But it didn't. No matter how many times I read this statement, it always said exactly the same thing.

This text called for the killing of Americans both military and civilian in whatever country they were found. This meant that I should be killed since I was an American civilian.

As I read this statement over and over, the very fact this statement could appear in any magazine an American could read appeared to create an absolutely enormous and insurmountable paradox.

Terrorists are secret by their very nature; this is how they carry out their most horrendous acts of terrorism, sneaking into position, committing some terrorist act and then sneaking away or just dying in an act of suicide.

What terrorist leader or terrorist organization would ever allow a statement like the Fatwa to get out from their organization with their closely held secrets?

And how in the world did it end up in a magazine an American might read? This made no sense. This meant they now would have a bulls-eye placed right on their foreheads.

The Americans, particularly the American military would have every justification to kill terrorists from this organization anywhere they could be found, after they read this Fatwa. The Fatwa had exposed this whole terrorist organization to massive and potentially deadly bombing by the Americans at a time of their choosing. All of the money and work that had gone into their 20 terrorist training camps could be destroyed at any moment if the Americans decided to bring in waves of B52s and flatten these camps. A 2,000-pound bomb would kill almost anything or anyone in a 100-yard radius of where it landed. If the Americans carpet-bombed these camps with hundreds of these 2,000-pound bombs, these camps would be obliterated along with most of the recruits and other al Qaeda terrorists present at these sites.

As I was mulling over the words of this text, I looked over to the empty seat to my right, and began to see in my imagination, a Middle Eastern person sitting in this seat. This person was about 30-32 years of age, 180-190 pounds in weight, and about 5 feet 7-8 inches in height. He had black hair cut short, a neatly trimmed three to four day old beard and mustache, and was wearing an expensive yellowish silk suit with a black T-shirt.

At first I thought to myself he looked just like an ordinary Persian rug salesman. But I noticed he had a small caliber pistol in his right hand, which he raised, placed against my temple and pulled the trigger. After I was shot and sitting there bleeding, I turned in his direction and said, "Now why in the world did you do that, what have I ever done to you to have made you do this?" He put the pistol down and with the index finger on his right hand reached over and touched the text right in this magazine in my lap, pointing at the text for this Fatwa and said.

"See, it says right here I should do this."

And as he pointed at the Fatwa, he continued, "It says right here it is the duty of all Muslims to kill Americans both military and civilian, and you are a civilian. And because I am a good Muslim, I am just doing what this text says I should do." I had to agree with him, he was just doing exactly what the text was telling him to do.

Because of what he had said, I reread the text of the Fatwa again, in fact, I reread this text over several more times, and indeed he was correct. It clearly stated it was the duty of all Muslims worldwide to kill Americans both military and civilian. The interpretation I had the first time I read this was in fact the same interpretation I had when I read it for the nth time. I had not been mistaken. This is exactly what it said. Rereading these words over and over did not change their meaning in any way.

I began to think how unusual it is, when something appears in print, it somehow gains a strange undeniable aura of authority, of correctness, even when you totally disagree with what the text says. It was starting to become obvious this statement was going to have an enormous and profound and perhaps even horrific implication for me in the coming months.

I had been planning a trip to Germany in March, about one month out. I was going to fly to Frankfort and then take a train to Düsseldorf and another train over to Hanover. I realized I would have to be especially careful because of what I had just read.

On a trip to Germany the prior summer, I had an unusually disturbing experience. As I was walking through the Düsseldorf train station, I had noticed a group of four or five Middle Eastern men sitting at one of the cafés that are located right in the station. I had on very dark sunglasses. The lenses are so dark no one can see exactly what you are looking at as long as you keep you head pointed straight ahead.

As I was going through the station, I noticed these men were glaring intensely right at me. When I walked past where they were sitting they continued to glare right at me.

Their looks were terrifying. If looks alone could kill, I would have been dead.

At first I thought I looked like an American and they were angry with all Americans. However when I looked down at the way I was dressed, I appeared just like any German businessperson. The only thing that made any sense after trying to analyze this behavior was these people were displaying anger at Germans and in fact all Westerners.

Trying to analyze this further, I concluded they must have been Middle Eastern students, studying in Germany at the invitation of the German government. They must have encountered a great deal of hostility by the ordinary citizens, who were not as accepting of outside cultures as the government. This caused these students to become very alienated and disenfranchised by this process, and they had become extremely bitter and hostile towards all Westerners.

Since I had not seen this type of hostility in Munich, I concluded the hostility these students faced was a function of where in Germany they were located. The further north they went, the more hostility they faced and the more these students had become alienated with the whole system. I had come to the conclusion this disenfranchisement process was enabling a situation where Germany was now becoming a terrorist incubator.

However, if these same students undertook some terrorist act, it certainly would not be in Germany since Germany was still somewhat like a police state. But in the US, the more open nature of the society would allow them to operate with more impunity.

Once I was aware the Fatwa was a potential spark that could ignite an easily influenced Muslim into an act of violence against Westerners, and me in particular, and there were many people in Germany who had already become polarized against Westerners, I concluded it was important to be doubly careful when I traveled to Germany. I was going to be especially careful whom I sat next to, especially in the outdoor cafés in Germany. And I was determined more than ever to solve this puzzle of how this statement could ever have appeared in this magazine.

After further researching the origin of this statement, I found in the footnotes that the al Qaeda leadership had deliberately released this statement in February 1998. [Note: They later publicly proclaimed this Fatwa at a press conference on May 28, 1998.] They had released this statement so it would be published worldwide in Muslim newspapers.

Now this was beginning to become an even bigger puzzle. This information had not secretly leaked out of their organization as I had originally thought. They had released this statement to the whole world. Now, this really made no sense. Not only had terrorists placed a bulls-eye on their foreheads, they had deliberately done this themselves. The puzzle as to why they had allowed this information to get out had now become a puzzle of what exactly had motivated them to do this, when the negative impact of doing this was horrific.

I was immediately aware that publishing this statement violated what I considered "the immutable law of positives and negatives."

The law of positives and negatives says for every action taken to eliminate a negative of a certain size, there has to be a corresponding positive resulting from this action, which is at least equal to or greater than the negative. What looked like an enormous negative, which was the result of publishing this Fatwa, the destruction of their terrorist training camps by the Americans with the massive B52 bombers, had absolutely no conceivable corresponding positive of any size I could see. A single large bombing raid by the Americans would destroy the investment the terrorists had made in their Afghanistan training camps in just a few minutes. I just could not figure out what in their minds had represented the positive that was equal to or greater than this negative.

They either were crazy, which I had doubted, or they had some other unknown reason or motivation for having done this, and I was determined to find out what had motivated them to do this.

Chapter 3
The plan to analyze
the thinking of al Qaeda

After puzzling over this for several minutes, with no reasonable answer, I decided to try a different approach to answer this question.

I had come to the conclusion that you can find answers to these types of questions using a right-brained or intellectual approach, which I had been doing, with no success. Or you can use an emotional approach, using the left-brain to answer the question. In the intellectual approach you carefully analyze all of the information on the person or the organization you are trying to understand, including their thinking, and then go through a lengthy step-by-step question-and-answer process to get the correct answer.

In the emotional analysis approach using the left-brain you again start with a careful analysis of the thinking of the person or the organization you want to understand. Then you build in your head the emotional framework of the person or organization you are trying to understand. When you have a reasonable facsimile of their thinking, you then switch on their thinking, ask the questions you are attempting to answer, and instantly you will feel the right answer, if your emotional model is reasonably accurate. You are attempting to see the world through their eyes.

You are getting into their head and seeing the world through their eyes

It wasn't that I thought an intellectual approach would not get the right answer eventually; it was that the emotional approach would produce the right answer much faster and with less effort. I had vowed when I was on this flight to Newark on Sunday that I was just going to sit back and relax. The last thing I wanted to do was any real intense thinking. And I had come to the conclusion the emotional approach would be the fastest way solve this puzzle, to understand what exactly had motivated the al Qaeda terrorists to publish this Fatwa.

The first step in this approach was to gain a complete and thorough understanding of the thinking of the top leadership of al Qaeda, and Usama bin Laden in particular. To do this, I had to get a quick overview of the Islam religion, the family background of Usama bin Laden, as he was growing up and his life experiences in adulthood, which eventually led him in becoming the leader of the al Qaeda terrorist organization.

Then I would go to a point in his life where I could basically understand his thinking; and then relive his life experiences, from this point on, until at least February 1998, to get to a point where I would be able to write down the words in the Declaration of Jihad, word for word, just as it had been written by bin Laden in the first place.

The second part of this plan was to refine my understanding of his thinking, by reviewing the attacks the al Qaeda organization had mounted to this date, February 11, 2001, to see either if I could understand the reasons for these attacks, or to further refine my view of his thinking. After this second step I would be ready to use this understanding of his thinking to finally figure out what had actually motivated him to publish this horrific statement, the Fatwa.

The first step of this plan was to try to understand the Muslim religion. What was there about this religion, which caused the most devout Muslims to hate infidels and the US in particular?

Many Muslims, in this part of the world had been indoctrinated by religious schools from a very early age in the Islamic religion, but it was very hard for me to see how even a lifelong indoctrination could have generated hatred so intense for Americans they would state in a Fatwa a desire to kill American civilians.

It was important to find out where this hatred came from, how intense it was and more important, how was I going to internalize it so that I could start to see the world from their point of view. What was important in this search for the source of this hatred was not to find the most accurate reason for the hatred, but rather to identify a credible enough reason to enable me to internalize this hatred in my mind.

It was obvious that it was the most devout Muslims who were part of al Qaeda and its affiliates, and it was these same people who had the greatest hatred of Americans.

The word "Jihad", and its historical transformation was important in understanding Islam. The word Jihad in my opinion originally meant the struggle to "find the way." "Jihad" described the process whereby a very devout Muslim would spend his life in a struggle to finding the "true way, the way of Mohammed," in effect the way Mohammed had lived his life 1,300 years ago.

Muslims were trying to live their lives as Mohammed had. The search for "finding the way" appeared to be related to what would become one's "place" in the afterlife. Depending on how close one had come to actually living according to the original Jihad, by their degree of Islamic piety, Muslims could improve their place or position in the hereafter, a position that was to be fixed for eternity. NOTE: It is this extreme focus on their life in the hereafter that distinguishes the thinking of Muslims from the thinking of Western peoples and makes their actions seem many times almost incomprehensible to the Western mind.

The upbringing of Muslim males (in very large extended Arab families with lots of males) would reinforce this concept. For male children, brought up in large Arab families where there were a large number of wives and male children, their place in the family depended on their position with respect to their father.

This position was determined by how close the male child's mother was to her husband. In Arab families with many male children and many wives, the position of male children were determined by forces outside of their control. This must have been especially true for older males who felt passed over by younger male siblings because their younger mothers were considered more desirable. It was easy to see how this type of reinforcement of "position" in the family would cause a passed-over son to conclude that from now on he would never allow this to happen again.

From their religious training, male children were taught that their position in the next world would be determined by how closely they adhered to a devout life. Their position was now in their own hands, under their control, and would be unaffected by forces outside of their control. The extreme focus on the afterlife in the

Islamic religion, especially by radical Muslims makes them very hard to understand by western values.

To a devout Muslim, issues like having lands they lived in that held their most sacred shrines governed by the Shariah, and under a devout Muslim Caliph, free from corrupt western influence became all-important. Replacing what they considered to be corrupt regimes with a Caliphate made up of esteemed Muslim imams became important goals.

In addition to understanding how this struggle, this Jihad could become so consuming, it was obvious these Muslims had an uncanny ability to morph their thinking of this Jihad. This struggle, which originally described a personal religious obligation, morphed into a political statement. Originally describing a personal obligation, it would come to describe what someone could force others to do.

Jihad, which had started out as an individual and personal struggle for a devout life, came to mean "in the defense of Islam." In defense of Islam morphed further to mean not only defending Islam but since Islam was in their view the only true religion carrying out offensive military operations against infidels, anyone who was non-Muslim, in Muslim countries.

[Note: It was this final morphing that ultimately characterizes the beliefs of what are now called "radical Muslims."]

Jihad became a call for holy war, the killing of infidels and ultimately the killing of American civilians, since it was the belief of radical Muslims that American civilians were financing the American military troops positioned on Saudi soil who were despoiling this holy place with its major Muslim shrines. Jihad also came to mean attacking and killing even moderate Muslims, those Muslims who did not believe or accept this radical definition of Jihad.

These terrorists in effect had their most intense hatred for moderate Muslims, while professing initially their intent to include them as part of their Islamic community.

From this analysis, it was easy to see what gave rise to this intense hatred for infidels, and Americans in particular. With this understanding, the plan to understand their motivation was to use the Declaration of Jihad as the template for the thinking of the persons who had written the Fatwa. This page of text was a complete and accurate view of the thinking of the persons who had actually written the text. In fact, the actual writing of the text was just a mechanical rendering of their thinking onto a piece of paper. The plan was to understand their thinking to such an extent that I would be able to write word for word the Declaration itself.

First, I put myself in the place of bin Laden himself, living in Saudi Arabia starting from an early point in his life. From this point on, I tried to imagine his life experiences from this point to the time he became leader of the al Qaeda movement. Bin Laden had been an extremely devout Muslim at an early age while growing up in Saudi Arabia. He had been part of a large family with many sons. His mother had died while he was quite young, leaving him with no support inside this large family. His place in this family would have remained much better had his mother lived.

After his religious schooling, bin Laden joined the successful effort against the Soviet Union in Afghanistan. When he returned from Afghanistan, his thinking was influenced by the knowledge that the group he had been part of in Afghanistan had defeated a super-power. This reinforced in his thinking the concept that even a poorly equipped army could defeat a super-power, if they were sufficiently motivated by their cause.

From his Afghanistan experience, bin Laden felt it was now possible to ultimately replace the rulers of Saudi Arabia with a religious Caliph governed by the law of the Shariah. These leaders were considered corrupt and not sufficiently religious to be worthy of being leaders in lands where the holiest shrines in the Islamic religion were located. To remove these leaders, what was needed was an army of very devout and highly motivated followers

The invasion of Kuwait by Iraq altered with his plans. When the United States came to rescue the state of Kuwait after it had been invaded by Iraq, and placed military troops on Saudi Arabian soil, bin Laden was greatly incensed. Not only were infidels defending corrupt leaders of a Muslim country; they were even corrupting the Muslim religion itself with their western culture.

Bin Laden realized that replacing the current leadership of Saudi Arabia would first require the expulsion of the US forces. His initial immense hatred for the corrupt Saudi leadership transferred itself to an immense hatred of the US itself and eventually to an immense hatred of the people of the US. Bin Laden reasoned even civilians should become legitimate targets since they were the ones financing the US troops on the Saudi Peninsula with their tax payments.

The fact that bin Laden was expelled from Saudi Arabia and forced to live in the Sudan, is a clear indication of his intense feeling against the ruling class in Saudi Arabi. He clearly had been openly advocating the overthrow of the leaders in Saudi Arabia, the House of Saud.

Bin Laden was then eventually expelled from Sudan and relocated to Afghanistan in 1996. In Afghanistan, he linked up again with Amen Al-Zawahiri again, a leader of the Egyptian Jihad, whom he had come in contact with in the original war in Afghanistan against the Soviet Union. By then he was thinking in terms not only of a religious theocracy for Saudi Arabia, but had adopted a pan-Islam point of view. He had come to feel that a religious Caliph should rule not only Saudi Arabia, but also all of the Islamic areas, from Morocco to Indonesia.

After getting a reasonably complete view of bin Laden's thinking, I next tested it by reviewing the attacks that had occurred up to this point, to see if they made sense.

From what I had read, al Qaeda, or a closely aligned group, had carried out the attack on the Khobar Towers in Saudi Arabia with a huge truck bomb (the evidence for who was really responsible for this attack was not entirely conclusive). They had also carried out an attack on the US embassies in Tanzania and Kenya, again with huge truck bombs. In October 2000, they had been responsible for the bombing of the USS Cole in Yemen.

The attack on the Khobar Towers made perfect sense. Bin Laden, or radicals connected to like mined groups were sending a message to the US to get out of Saudi Arabia. This was the message in the Declaration of Jihad.

The attacks on the embassies in Tanzania and Kenya were a bit different. In analyzing the thinking of the leadership of al Qaeda, I had come to the conclusion bin Laden and the rest of al Qaeda wanted to see the entire Middle East governed by a single Caliphate that would include all of the current countries, where the majority of the population was Muslim. This was the area from Morocco along North Africa, all of the way over to Pakistan and perhaps even including Malaysia and Indonesia. The attack on the embassies at first made very little sense or no sense, in my view, since Tanzania and Kenya were out of the area to be governed by this single Caliph. These countries were not in this area where the clear majority of people are Muslim.

The leadership of the al Qaeda terrorists saw the world as made up of two separate regions. The area inside of the Caliphate they assumed was temporarily under the control of the secular and corrupt governments, which they were going to replace.

The region outside of the Caliphate was populated by a majority of infidels and was viewed by the leadership of al Qaeda, and other Islamic radicals, as an amorphous black space with almost no detail. Only the faintest of detail indicated the location of the largest cities, such as Paris, London, New York, and Washington DC. The immense hatred for the people who inhabit a region outside of their immediate interest prevented radical Muslims from seeing any sort of detail in these areas.

The major decision the leadership of al Qaeda had to make when considering attacking a target, was first, not what target they were going to hit, but whether to plan an attack on a target inside the region to be governed by the Caliph or outside of this region. Then once they decided to go outside of this region, to them, there was not much difference between the different targets with one major exception. If they were to plan an attack on a target inside of an imaginary boundary drawn around Washington DC and New York City, this attack would have to be a "signature event" of titanic proportions. Any attack in the US would be an attack that would reverberate around the world to all of their followers and to all of the other Muslims in the world. The first and initial attack directly on the US was going to establish or destroy their reputation for years, perhaps hundreds of years to come.

Once they had decided to attack a target outside of the area governed by the Caliph, the attack on the East African embassies, it was clear New York and Washington DC were now also vulnerable to an attack. The attacks against the American embassies in Kenya and Tanzania meant bin Laden had an enormous enmity for the US and its people unrelated to the reasons in the Declaration of Jihad but described in the Fatwa. He really did mean what had been written in the Fatwa. And the only difference between an attack on Tanzania and Kenya instead of New York and Washington DC was nothing more than sitting a few more hours on an airplane.

The analysis of the *USS Cole* attack provided the clearest view of al Qaeda's thinking. A small boat loaded with high explosives is driven alongside the most modern warship in the US arsenal, and blows a giant whole in the side of this warship. *The weapons they had used in this attack were secrecy, surprise, suicide and psychology to attack this ship. They had absolutely no fear of even a four-inch cannon mounted on the bow of this ship.*

The attack on the *Cole* made sense in light of what had been written in the Fatwa, and even answered one more significant question with regard to bin Laden's thinking and the targets he must have been planning to attack. If he felt he could attack the *USS Cole* armed with a large gun mounted on the deck of this ship, bin Laden must have felt he literally could attack and destroy any target any where in the world. What building comes with a four-inch cannon mounted on the roof?

All he had to do to destroy any target in the world was pick a target and his fanatical followers would literally fall all over them selves to be part of a suicide attack to carry out his plans.

Prior to the *Cole* attack, bin Laden must have come to the conclusion he could select and destroy any target in the world. "Prior to" had to mean at least a year prior to January 2000. This was the date of the attack on the *USS The Sullivans*, the ship he had tried but failed to attack in January 2000 before the attack on the *USS Cole*. "Prior to" had to mean at least by February or March of 1999, when the terrorists left Afghanistan for Yemen in preparation for the attack on the *USS The Sullivans*. But if the al Qaeda terrorists planned each attack in Afganistan for about one year before sending terrorists to the country where an attack was to take place, 'prior to' had to mean one year prior to the terrorists leaving Afganistan, or February 1998, the date of the Fatwa.

This meant that now all large buildings in any US city were now potential targets. The largest and most important buildings in the US, in particular in Washington DC and New York, were now vulnerable to future attacks. What was most disturbing was the fact that the Americans seemed to be oblivious to what these previous attacks actually meant, and what these attacks could tell them about the thinking of the leadership of al Qaeda. The investigations of each attack had focused on finding evidence of exactly who had been involved in the attack, but had not considered what these attacks meant for the long-range implications of the US. The FBI investigators were focused on the minutiae and apparently just could not see the big picture, the strategic importance of what each these attacks really meant.

The Americans did not seem to even begin to grasp at what a clear understanding of these attacks from the terrorists' perspective could mean with respect to understanding and anticipating their future plans against the United States.

The Americans seemed to be especially oblivious to the terrible vulnerability of their largest buildings and to the damage this group and their leadership could inflict in both material and human toll if they decided to undertake a plan for a major attack inside of the US.

In fact after I understood the lessons from the *Cole* attack and the East African bombings, I had come to the conclusion that the very largest structures in the US and in particular New York and Washington DC were the most vulnerable targets. Why would al Qaeda terrorists attack a small target when they felt they could attack the biggest buildings? The Cole attack in fact must have been bin Laden's conformation to his own people that he could pick and destroy any target any where in the world. After this very simple analysis, I kept repeating over and over, "Didn't anyone in the US government see this, and see how vulnerable the largest buildings in the largest US cities had become? What were the CIA and the FBI doing when they did their

27

investigations of these attacks? How could they have missed this absolutely critical point?"

How was it even remotely possible that these huge intelligence organizations had apparently completely missed the most important and critical lesson from these attacks?

Chapter 4

Attack on America

After analyzing the attacks al Qaeda had carried out against the US, I went back to see if I could answer the original question. "Why did al Qaeda publish the Fatwa? What was their motivation for doing this?"

Even with a relatively complete view of their thinking, I first attempted to answer this question as an American, without using the understanding I had just gained on the thinking of bin Laden. If I were able to answer this question as an American, then the follow-up process, to re-analyze the answer in order to reconfirm my analysis, would not take as long.

In doing this analysis I came up with the concept that I would call "distance." Distance is defined as the gap between the emotional framework I had and the emotional framework of the terrorists I was trying to understand. For an answer to have validity when you use an emotional process to answer a question, you have to at some point close this distance. The emotional process can rapidly sort through millions and millions of answers and quickly find the right one. But before you can accept this answer as the correct answer, you have to go back and use the intellectual process to re-analyze this answer from your perspective, to ensure in your own mind that this is the right answer. This process closes this space or "distance". And unfortunately, I knew doing this would require an exhausting analysis by the intellectual portion of the brain. The bigger the distance to be closed, the more exhausting this process was going to be.

If I could, however, analyze and then figure this question out as an American, then I would need only a very short process or no additional process to re-analyze this answer in order to determine that this was indeed the correct answer.

Unfortunately, as I went over this question as an American, I was not able to even come close to figuring this out. This action, the worldwide publishing of the Fatwa, simply made no sense whatsoever. The only explanation from an intellectual point of view was that they had gone crazy, and I knew that this was most likely not the right answer.

This is when I decided to switch on the thinking of bin Laden. To do this, I first imagined myself as bin Laden, presenting this Fatwa to a large audience of terrorists from his organization and journalists. This must have been done at a press conference, in a primitive building somewhere in Afghanistan. This was the image in my mind as I started sounding out the words to the Fatwa:

"...to kill the Americans and their allies – civil and military – is an individual duty for every Muslim..."

It was at this point I stopped, and asked, "Why am I doing this?"

Just as soon as I did this, I suddenly realized exactly why bin Laden had issued this Fatwa. The first thing I said to myself was:

"OH MY GOD, OH MY GOD, OH MY GOD!"

It was instantly obvious why bin Laden had issued this Fatwa. He had just publicly declared war on the US. But this Fatwa had been issued 10 years after bin Laden had started the al Qaeda organization. This now had to mean that they were going to be planning and carrying out a monumental increase in the level and ferocity of attacks against the US. And this could mean only one thing.

The al Qaeda terrorists were going to mount a titanic attack at a target inside of the US. Nothing else represented a monumental increase in the level of their attacks, nothing else made any sense. All I could think was:

"OH MY GOD"

There was no other reasonable explanation. This had to be the positive in their minds that would be as big as the negative from the potential risks to their training camps from a bombing attack by the Americans. Issuing the Fatwa with this suggestion of a huge attack directly in the US would send a message throughout the Muslim world that al Qaeda was in fact the premiere terrorist organization acting "in the defense of Islam," attracting additional young recruits and funding from Saudi Arabia.

The first thought I had once I realized this Fatwa was a public declaration of war against the US was: "Why had the media, in particular the largest newspapers in the largest US cities, not alerted us, all of the people in the US, to this huge danger?"

When the Fatwa had been printed in Muslim newspapers worldwide in February 1998, the people at the large newspapers in the US must have read this in a translated form. They must have seen this statement for what it was, a public declaration of war against the US.

Why had they not put eight-inch headlines on their front pages, "WAR," with a subtitle that would have read, "Most dangerous terrorist group in world declares war on the US"?

This is what was required to motivate the big intelligence agencies enough so they proactively would do something about this threat. The intelligence agencies were not going to proactively do anything to stop whatever attacks the al Qaeda terrorist organization was planning. These agencies are simply not proactive, particularly the FBI. They do not do the kind of proactive prevention that would have been necessary to stop this sort of attack.

The FBI is a criminal investigation agency. They use multiple occurrences of criminal events to establish a pattern they can use to anticipate and stop further criminal events. They normally never even start a criminal investigation without a crime being committed or without ironclad proof that this is about to happen.

The CIA uses only information that has been properly vetted. This is information obtained from overheard conversations, intelligence from other intelligence agencies on terrorist organizations, or spy satellite data to establish that some terrorist event is going to happen. The terrorists were going to use extreme secrecy to keep their plans unknown to the US. Without estimating what these groups were capable of doing and then proactively trying to stop them, there was no hope in my opinion that potential terrorist attacks in the US could be prevented. It was going to take an aroused US public to light a big enough fire under these agencies so that they would do what was required to stop future al Qaeda terrorist attacks inside the US.

When bin Laden and al Qaeda had issued this Fatwa, it was in the face of what was an absolutely massive and major negative. Bin Laden was inviting massive attacks by the Americans with

B52 bombers and cruise missiles. He had to have had an equally major and massive positive for doing this. The reason had to be to signal to all of his followers around the world, that they were now going to now ratchet up the war with the US to a much higher level and this now had to mean attacks against targets inside the US. There was simply no other reasonable explanation that made any sense.

After issuing this Fatwa, if al Qaeda did not carry out attacks in the US, they would have looked weak, and like fools to their own followers. This would have been the end of the al Qaeda organization. Bin Laden had often said: "People are attracted to the strong horse." By issuing this Fatwa, and publishing it worldwide, they were now forced to plan and to carry out attacks directly inside the US. It appeared that they had no other option.

I went back to the footnotes to see exactly when this Declaration and Fatwa had been issued and published. The footnotes indicated it had been published in February 1998, almost three years earlier. After a delay of three years, I could not figure out why this attack had not already taken place. This made absolutely no sense. There must have been hundreds of possible targets he could have attacked in this three-year time period.

The next question I had was, "If we are going to be attacked, what targets are the al Qaeda terrorists most likely going after?"

In order to answer this I went back to analyze the people who actually would put these plans together and select the targets. I had come to the belief that these targets were selected at the very highest levels of the al Qaeda leadership. These people were relatively uneducated, and lived in primitive conditions in Afghanistan. They had a very limited view of the US.

They would only focus on what might be called the "most obvious targets."

Even if at first others selected little-known targets in the al Qaeda organization, it would be bin Laden who would ultimately make the final selection of the targets. And with his limited knowledge of the US, he would select targets that were only the most well known buildings.

I had come to the conclusion that when I finally figured out what the targets were going to be, I was going to find that they were buildings that could be considered as "almost too obvious." The buildings he selected had to be huge symbolic targets, targets that would result in large numbers of civilian casualties.

Since there is little communication for extended periods of time between the leadership of al Qaeda and the people who will ultimately execute their plans, the plans they came up with had to be extremely simple. I came to the conclusion their plans had to be so simple, a third grader could hear and understand it, and then recount it back in every detail. In order to find the targets, I was going to have to dumb down my thinking to the level of a third grader!

The three-year delay from the date the Fatwa had been issued meant that whatever target they selected had to be enormous. They just would never take this much time on a small insignificant target.

As I sat there and puzzled over this for at least three-quarters of an hour, I was completely unable to get any picture at all in my mind of what the target was going to be. As I continued to analyze this over and over, nothing appeared obvious. No building even came close to standing out as the obvious target. I completely failed to come up with the "obvious target." And I was tired and exhausted from all of the thought I had put into this. Because I had made up my mind when I had originally gotten on this flight that I was going to use this time for nothing but relaxation and because I had now become exhausted trying to uncover what could be the target, I decided to give up continuing to look for the target. Trying to figure out the target of this al Qaeda attack was going to be way too hard, and it was going to take far too much thinking in a very exhaustive process.

Chapter 5

Realizing the targets were the
World Trade Center Towers

I put down the magazine and to get some lighter reading material and I pulled out a travel brochure from the seat pocket in front of my seat. Right on the front cover of this brochure was the picture of the World Trade Center Towers. The photograph appeared to have been taken from a position high over the Statue of Liberty.

When I looked at this cover and it first came into clear focus, I was instantly and completely stunned.

I sat there just frozen. Every synapse in my brain had fired all at the same time. It felt just like I had been sitting in an electric chair, and had been jolted with several hundred million volts of electricity. I was so stunned at first I was not able to move. I was not able to breathe. I was totally paralyzed.

When this image of the World Trade Center Towers came into focus, though I did not realize it at this time, my life would never be the same again. It would be changed forever. I continued to sit there numbed by the sight of this one picture. To me, it seemed time had almost come to a stop, or to go in slow motion. Fractions of seconds turned into seconds, seconds turned into minutes.

As soon as I was first able to move, I leaned my head back, looked up at the ceiling of this aircraft, and started to yell at the very top of my voice:

"OH MY GOD, OH MY GOD, I KNOW WHAT THAT BASTARD IS GOING TO DO NEXT!"

As I was doing this, a small voice in my head said, "What in the world are you doing? You are yelling at the top of your voice on an airplane. Do you want to get arrested?" Then another small voice said, "But this is going to be your one and only chance to save all of those people in those buildings. In a few seconds you will be too terrified to be able to say anything to anyone. You must let other people know what you have just found out. This is your one and only chance."

When I realized what I had just done, I looked around carefully to see how the other passengers might be reacting. There were only about a three of four people in my visual vicinity. And they were being extremely cautious. None of them even dared to look in my direction. Almost all, however, were giving very subtle glances in my direction to see what the hell had just happened.

The flight attendant got up from her seat in the front of the aircraft, about 15 rows away, and started coming down the aisle to see what was going on. My first thought was, "Oh my God! What am I going to say?" "What was I going to say when she reached my seat, and asked me what had just happened? If I tell her I have just come to the conclusion that the al Qaeda terrorists are going to destroy the World Trade Center Towers, she is going to think I have just gone nuts." I immediately tried to figure out what I was going to do in order to get rid of her without even talking to her at all.

Just before she reached my seat, I started to shake my head, and banging my forehead with the palm of my hand and at the same time muttered in a loud voice, "Good grief, I must have just had a nightmare." When she had gotten to within two rows from where I was sitting, I looked up right at her, and gave her meanest stare I could muster to indicate I absolutely did not want to be disturbed.

I was amazed when it worked just as I had thought. It was just exactly the right thing to do. She turned right around and went back to her seat without even asking me what had happened.

As I continued to I sit there and look at this one picture, it was obvious. Bin Laden and rest of the leadership of the al Qaeda organization must have had 100 percent of their thinking focused on these two buildings, the World Trade Center Towers. They must have already been working on a plan to destroy these structures. This was the only thing that could explain this three-year delay since they had released the Fatwa. The target was simply so big that the plan would take a considerable amount of time. Spending three years or even more on this plan was acceptable to them due to the immense size of this target.

I realized that these structures were also the targets that I had been searching for, the targets that were "almost too obvious." These buildings were the huge symbolic targets whose destruction would result in thousands of civilian casualties. Destroying these structures, which had both US and worldwide visibility and importance, would deal a major psychological blow to almost everyone in the US and even much of the world. This was exactly what I had felt the terrorists must have wanted to do when they had issued the Fatwa.

But I remembered that terrorists had tried to attack the World Trade Center Towers before, in 1993 with a truck bomb. The security of the WTC Towers would surely be looking for exactly this type of attack. Since there was no way to destroy these towers with a truck bomb in any future attack, it had to be with some other way. Since I was sitting on a larger airliner, in fact a Boeing 757, I immediately came to the conclusion that the only way these terrorists could completely destroy these buildings was through the use of several hijacked aircraft. There appeared to be no other way that would be as simple. The security people at the WTC Towers would never expect hijacked aircraft used in an attack on these buildings. The terrorists would hijack several large airliners in flight and then drive these planes right into the sides of these buildings.

From the photograph on the travel brochure cover, these buildings looked like ordinary steel-frame structures with box-like steel frames. The frames inside of a typical steel structure are normally vertical supporting steel columns, placed at approximately 15-20 foot centers throughout the interior of this building. For a building 200 feet wide in a square box-like structure, this would have meant many vertical supporting columns spread evenly across the width of this structure on each floor providing the internal vertical support. With this type of structure, it did not appear that a single aircraft would have had any where near enough force to collapse a single tower. It was clear that to collapse these structures it was going to take two aircraft attacking the each tower. The intention of the al Qaeda terrorists had to be the collapse of these buildings with everyone still inside. They hated the people in the US. They had said so right in the Fatwa. This had to have been their motivation for publishing this Fatwa, to destroying these buildings, and kill as many American civilians as possible in this attack.

If they were going to use hijacked aircraft, then it was obvious the terrorists would hijack commercial planes while they were in flight, with weapons they could easily bring on board these aircraft.

I had been aware since the mid-1990s of a change to the FAA rules allowing passengers to legally carry knives onto US airliners, knives with blades that did not exceed four inches. In fact, when I heard this change to the FAA rules announced on a nightly newscast in the mid-1990s, I almost had a heart attack. A single person with a four-inch knife would not be much of a threat; but four or five terrorists with four-inch knives would be unstoppable. They would cut the throat of the first person who stood up to them and the other passengers would be too terrified at that point to do anything in their own defense.

Because of this rule, four or five terrorists could just walk onto any airliner with knives and take this plane over. They would then disable the pilot and copilot, and take over the controls using one of their team members who had undergone pilot training. These planes would then be flown down to the World Trade Center Towers in New York City, and driven right into the sides of these buildings. There was no other way I could see as simple as this. The objective of the terrorists was to collapse these structures with almost everyone still inside of these buildings, and this had to mean at least 30,000 people.

From their monumental determination and hatred of the US, this had to be their plan. They must have had at least 100 people working directly on this plan at this very moment. This number would include the 16-20 terrorists who would actually be sent to the US to carry out this plan, in addition to al least another 80 support people outside the US who would select the terrorists, train them prior to sending them to the US, and handle the financial details of moving money around to fund this plan. As this picture became clearer, all I could think over and over was:

"OH MY GOD, OH MY GOD, all of those people.
What in the world am I going to do to stop this?"

Chapter 6

Estimating the timing for this attack

At this point, I was wondering if it was even possible to determine approximately when this attack was going to occur. I thought it was best to start with the following information.

First, the attacks from al Qaeda up to this point seemed to occur at approximately two-year intervals, the Khobar Towers attack in 1996 (although this attack had still not definitively been blamed on bin Laden), the embassy bombings in 1998, and the attack on the *USS Cole* in 2000. On the Khobar Towers attack, even though the evidence had not been finalized on who actually had done this, it was inconceivable to me bin Laden had not somehow been involved, especially when Saudi Arabia was his home country.

Second, the al Qaeda terrorists seemed to prefer the fall for launching their latest attacks. The prior two attacks that had successfully been carried out had taken place in August 1998 and in October 2000.

Third, because of the substantial amount of time between all of their attacks, the leadership of al Qaeda seemed to be capable of planning only one attack at a time. They did not have two major attacks occur close together in time.

Because of this, I came to the conclusion al Qaeda directed these attacks from the top of the organization, at least in the initial planning phases. And they were only able to focus on a single plan at a time from the time they actually initiated the plan to the point where they sent the attackers off to execute the plan in the country where the attack was to take place. Once the attackers were sent to their country of destination, the top leadership of al Qaeda was again free to start planning an attack on their next target.

After a quick estimate of the time-line for this plan, I came to the conclusion that the final planning phase would take about a year and one half after the terrorists first started to enter the US to carry out this attack. This was based on an analysis of the steps in their plan.

First I estimated the terrorists who would be trained as pilots would need at least three months prior to starting their flight training to enter the US, find appropriate flight schools and then enroll into these schools.

Second, in order to get sufficient flight training to fly large airliners to their final destination from the point where they were hijacked, four teams of pilots would require at least one year of calendar time, in my estimation.

Third, they would require about three months after the flight training was complete to bring in the non-pilot terrorists. To bring in the non-pilot terrorists earlier would not only be too expensive but also be too risky, increasing the likelihood that the whole plan could be exposed.

I finally estimated it would take them about one month to integrate all of these teams together and be ready to carry out this attack.

To get a final estimate on when this attack was to be carried out I had to get some estimate of when this final phase of their planning had actually started. I knew I was a novice when it came to matters regarding terrorism. If I had just figured out this plan, and I was a complete novice at analyzing terrorists' plans, then it stood to reason the terrorists must have been already working on this plan for a considerable period prior to my finding out. It was just inconceivable that I had found out their plans just after they had started on this final phase. In addition, because the Fatwa had been issued three years earlier, it was inconceivable they had not been working on the final phase of the plan long before I had figured it out.

I had also come to the conclusion it would be hard to estimate any of their planning steps that actually took place outside the US. During this phase of their planning, they would be under less pressure to complete these tasks in a timely manner. They could take their time for this early phase of their planning. However, once they sent al Qaeda terrorists into the US, they would be under enormous pressure to move their plan forward at a predictable and methodical pace. This is because they would now be spending substantial sums of money to support the plan and also during this phase they would be subject to discovery at any time.

I quickly determined that the last phase of their plan could not have started anywhere near February 1998, when the Fatwa had been released. Although I assumed this date was the first indication this attack was going to take place, if the last phase of their plans had been underway on this date, the World Trade Center Towers would already have been destroyed at least a year before my flight from San Francisco to Newark. This is because this last phase of their plans was going to take just over 18 months. Bringing in the pilots by February 1998 meant the World Trade Center buildings would have been destroyed no later than September 1999, over one year prior to my flight.

Since I could not use February 1998 or even any date close to this date, I next decided to move the start date for their final plans in the other direction, out as far as possible, as far as I could logically see this start date happening. For lack of any *a' priori* way to determine this date, and for simplicity, I decided to initially use one year from my flight in February 2001. To keep my analysis as simple as possible, I was using round numbers for these estimates, one-month, three-months, one-year, etc. in my starting estimate. This made the start date February 2000 as the date when I estimated al Qaeda must have first started sending terrorists into the US to be trained as pilots.

I could not use a date later than this and be consistent with my belief that the last phase of this plan had to have been in operation for a considerable time prior to my finding out. I had assumed this estimate for the start date for this plan was, again, going to be nothing but just another guess. If further analysis deemed it way off, I could go back and change it again. As I started to put more and more of the pieces of this next puzzle together, I could even modify it drastically if the analysis showed that this was the appropriate thing to do.

I next added in the three months to get all of the pilots into the US prior to them starting their flight training. This would have been the months of February, March and April. During these three months, the terrorists would find and select appropriate flight schools, and then get enrolled for flight training.

I then added approximately one year for the four teams of terrorists to start and complete their flight training. This is the time period from May 2000 to April 2001.

I was estimating the timing for this plan assuming they had four teams of hijackers; each team would have four to five members, with only one or two of the members having to get proficient at flying large airliners. I assumed when estimating these dates that the dates for each team and each pilot going through training could vary considerably among the teams.

The activity that was to have the greatest variability was the time the terrorists actually spent in flight training. Some of the terrorists would be highly educated and would be fluent in English; others would not be highly educated and would be almost non-conversant in English.

In my opinion, the most well educated terrorists would be able to get a private license in about two or three months, and a commercial rating with some instrument time in another three to four months. A private pilot's license requires at least 40 hours of flight time. A commercial rating with instrument time and multi-engine time requires at least another 200 hours of flight time. This works out to be a total of six to seven months if they worked at it full-time. Their ultimate goal had to be to get air transport time on a simulator designed for a large multi-engine jet aircraft. Without this type of training, they would never have even the minimum skills to take over and fly a huge aircraft, and fly it hundreds of miles into the side of a large building. Without a commercial license with multi-engine time, it is hard to see how any company selling simulator time on a large airliner simulator would not suspect immediately the person taking the simulator training was potentially a terrorist.

The terrorists who had virtually no or little Western education and very poor English skills would require, in my estimation, at least six to seven months just for a private license and an additional four to five months or longer for a commercial license with multi-engine time, if they could get one at all. They would have to have a very good command of English even before they would be allowed to start flight training. In fact, the first and most important skill each pilot would need would be a good command of the English language. They would have to be able to hear and understand commands in English issued by an airport control tower. Even persons who have spoken English all of their lives can find it very difficult to understand control tower commands, particularly when spoken rapidly by controllers at busy airports.

I had estimated a single pilot would take about six months to obtain all of his training, if he worked at it full-time. Because they had, from my estimation, four sets of pilots, each pilot would have his six months or more of training somewhere within this one-year window.

The one-year to get flight training was also aimed at attempting to estimate the flight training time for the least educated and least fluent in English of the terrorist pilots. The terrorists least proficient in English would most likely be the terrorist pilots whose flight training would ultimately determine the timing for this phase of the plan.

I had estimated the first pilots would start their training by about May 2000 and the last pilots would be finishing their training by April 2001. The calendar time of about one year would ensure that the slowest and least skilled pilots would be finished with their training by the end of this one-year window. This also took into account the fact that the al Qaeda terrorists are extremely meticulous in their planning and preparation for each attack. They take as much time as they need. And it was not the pilots who were the fastest to complete their training who would gate this project, but the slowest.

After their flight training, which would end in April 2001, I had estimated it would take another three months, from May through July, to bring the non-pilot terrorists to the US. The final date for this phase of their plan came out to the first of August 2001.

From this estimate, they would be ready to start practicing as whole teams by August 1, 2001. I could not see how they could have been ready to go as integrated teams without al least one month for final integration as teams and last-minute preparations. During this time, they would book seats on the flights they were going to hijack and familiarize themselves with all of the security procedures they could expect on these flights and at the boarding areas. If this last phase took a month, this would mean that they would be ready to complete the final step in their plan, the actual execution of this plan, by the first of September.

From looking at the attack on the USS Cole, once the al Qaeda terrorists are ready, they do not wait. They would schedule their flights for sometime in the first two weeks of September and it would all be over. They were obviously aware that unnecessary delays after this point would expose them to arrest and capture. To me it was inconceivable that this plan would not be completed in the two-week period after they were ready on the 1st of September. All that remained for them to do would be to schedule their fights with takeoffs that could be synchronized to within 30 or 45 minutes of each other.

From looking at past attacks, it was obvious that they do not prolong this last phase. They plan, they practice, they pick the final date and then it is all over. When the final date came out to be the middle of September, I was sure I had estimated this as accurately as was possible with the information I had at this time. This date fell right between the dates for the last two al Qaeda attacks. The attack on the East African embassies had occurred in August, and the USS *Cole* attack had occurred in October. After I had put these dates in a time-line, and reviewed this time-line again, there was absolutely no doubt in my mind that I had calculated the dates as accurately as was humanly possible.

Estimating the time-line for this attack was very similar to adding links to a chain. You have as your starting point the last link in the chain, and you have to find the next date that logically connects the last link to a new point in this chain. You are looking for at least one and if possible two corroborating elements to make the new link in the chain connect at both points. When the date for the attack fell right between the dates for the prior two attacks, I knew I had the piece of corroborating evidence that made this estimate work.

At this time I still felt I was going to go to the FBI's Manhattan office to tell them about what I had just pieced together. As I thought about this date, I was concerned that in fact the September 15 date would become a significant liability in stopping this attack. What if bad weather delayed the attack to some later date? I could not in any way see how they would be able to fly these huge airliners in any kind of IFR (Instrument Flight Rules) weather. Even if they had instrument time, flying a large airliner with which you are barely familiar in clouds at any point on their route or at their final destination would be an impossible task in my opinion.

If they did not have absolutely clear VFR (Visual Flight Rules) weather, in fact have VFR weather from the point where they where going to hijack these airliners, all of the way along their intended flight path and at their final target destinations, they would just reschedule their flights to a later date, hoping for better weather on that date. If I went to the Manhattan FBI office and told them that this attack would take place before the middle of September and it did not due to bad weather or some other reason, I would look like an idiot. The FBI might then let down their guard, and take their focus off of trying to foil this plan. The hijackers would then be free to walk onto their next flight with absolutely no opposition.

I decided the best approach was to tell the FBI I thought the attack would take place between September 1 and the end of October. I would keep the fact I felt this September 15 date was in fact the final date for this attack to myself as a complete secret. In my opinion, by expanding this time out to the end of October, I would lose nothing in my attempt to stop this attack.

I had come to the conclusion that the aircraft the terrorists would hijack had to be type 767 and 757. The plane I was flying out to Newark on was, in fact, a United 757. The 757 is easily distinguished by having a single aisle down the middle of the aircraft for use by passengers. It is one of the most common types of commercial aircraft in use. There were a smaller number of 767s in regular service. The 767 is larger and heavier, and is easily distinguished by the fact it has two aisles down the length of the aircraft for use by passengers.

I had known from the mid-1990s that an important characteristic of the 767 and 757 aircraft was the fact they both had had the exact same cockpit layout. I had remembered this fact after reading an article in an aviation magazine because Boeing had claimed in this article they had saved $4.5 billion by having these two cockpits identical. What caught my interest in this article was not the fact that these aircraft had the exact same cockpit layout, but how could a company save $4.5 billion by making the cockpits identical? A new mechanical design surely would not cost more than a few hundred million dollars, new tools another several hundred million. I could not see how they would save $4.5 billion by making the two cockpits identical.

If the hijackers were do their final training on large airliner simulators five to seven months in advance of the actual hijackings and if they were going to select the aircraft to be hijacked just a few weeks prior to the attack, then they would have to train on aircraft that had the same cockpit layout. Anything else would be inconceivable, and the 767 and the 757 type aircraft were the only type of American aircraft I was aware of that had identical cockpits.

I had come to the conclusion that the terrorists would most likely select flights departing from eastern airports. This would give them the shortest time in the air after the hijacking to fly to the target.

This attack was going to take place in the first two weeks of September 2001, by al Qaeda terrorists, who would hijack 767s and 757s out of eastern airports. They would take over these flights in midair, using four teams of hijackers with four to five members on each team carrying four-inch knives. Each team would have at least one terrorist trained as a pilot. The three to four other terrorists would storm the cockpit, take over the plane in midair, and then keep the passengers in check. As long as they kept quiet and stayed out of trouble prior to boarding the flights they were about to hijack, they would not be stopped.

Once they had published the Fatwa worldwide in newspapers you could come to no other possible conclusion. Nothing else made any sense.

All that I needed to come to these conclusions was a belief the terrorists actually meant what they said in the Fatwa when they wrote it down for all the world to see.

Using a careful and logical analysis of this document and the information on the other attacks the terrorists had previously carried out, I could come to no other conclusion. I further came to the conclusion that the FBI and CIA were going to do nothing to stop this attack. The FBI was simply not set up to proactively stop this type of attack. Whatever information they were going to ultimately obtain was going to be buried deep in their bureaucracy. The American media was asleep at the switch. They had alerted no one to this impending disaster.

I could not believe I was the only one who had caught on to this and had figured this out. The Fatwa has right there in public view and must have been seen by the people at the FBI the CIA and the large news media. How would they not have picked up on this? And yet, as I was thinking about this, I started to come to a horrible conclusion. If I went to the FBI, and gave them what I thought I knew, they were going to look at me like I was a space alien who had just come from Mars. I had no proof, no corroborating evidence of any kind. The FBI always requires, and in fact demands, a high level of proof prior to launching any investigation. This would be particularly true if this information came from someone outside of the FBI. If I went down to the FBI I thought:

"Good God almighty! What are they going to think? Who at the FBI is ever going to believe me?"

Chapter 7

Reevaluating the analysis

After I had a moment to reflect on what I had actually done, I realized I had gone through this entire analysis without really recognizing exactly what I was doing. I had, in fact, just frantically gone from one horrific thought to the next. I was absolutely horrified when I realized what conclusions I had just reached. My first reaction was, "How was it possible that after you find two sentences in a magazine that were extremely puzzling, the only thing that made any sense out of this and would explain this was the conclusion that the World Trade Center Towers were going to be totally destroyed by al Qaeda terrorists in the first two weeks of September? How was this even remotely possible?"

And I had come to these conclusions doing nothing more than just trying to understand the thinking of the top people at al Qaeda in order to answer one question. What had motivated them to publish the Fatwa worldwide in Muslim newspapers in the first place? And in doing this, I had come up with these absolutely horrific conclusions. I kept thinking how in the world do you come to these sorts of conclusions after reading just two sentences in a single magazine? And, was it possible no one else aware of this?

As it started to dawn on me the conclusions I had just come to, and the fact I was convinced I was right, all I could say was:

"Oh my God, Oh my God, Oh my God," if I am right, all of those people who work in these buildings are going to be at a terrible risk. This attack could result in the deaths of thousands and thousands of Americans.

This plan was just too simple and obvious. At this point, I was hoping beyond hope that somehow I had done something dreadfully wrong in my analysis and therefore my conclusions were wrong. Perhaps I had taken a wrong turn in my analysis at some point. If I went back over the analysis I had done with a very critical eye, reexamining every minute detail, perhaps I could come to the conclusion that this attack was not going to take place after all. Or perhaps I could come to the conclusion that the al Qaeda terrorists were going to attack an entirely different target with far fewer casualties.

At this point I had concluded that the World Trade Center Towers were going to be attacked in such a way it would cause them to collapse with everyone still inside the buildings. I had come to the conclusion that bin Laden was intent on killing as many people as possible, and in my mind this meant at least 30,000 people in this attack.

I gave this reexamination of the analysis only a slight chance of finding anything wrong. I began with what had been the starting point of my analysis, the analysis of the Fatwa. What had motivated al Qaeda and bin Laden to publish this Fatwa worldwide in the first place?

In reviewing my analysis, I came to the exact same conclusion again that I had come to the first time. This document, published, as it was, worldwide in Muslim newspapers, had to be a public declaration of war against the United States. I could not see how it could have been issued for any other purpose. This declaration of war, nine years after al Qaeda had been formed, had to mean the al Qaeda terrorist organization was going to mount a monumental increase in the level of their attacks on the US. And this could only mean just one thing, a titanic attack inside of the US. Nothing else could possibly represent a monumental increase in the level of attacks against the US. Nothing else could even begin to explain why they had published this Fatwa! There appeared to be no other even semi-reasonable explanation for both writing down this statement and then publishing it worldwide. Bin Laden had unmistakably declared war on the United States with this statement. I not only could feel the hatred and venom he must have had for the US, but could feel the monumental determination he must have had to want to strike a titanic and horrific blow at the entire country.

This would be the first major attack inside the US, directed by the leadership of al Qaeda. The al Qaeda organization was going to be identified with this attack for the next 100 years. Therefore it had to be a massive attack against a major symbolic target. The target would be selected in order for this attack to deliver a massive psychological blow to the entire US population. There was just no other reasonable conclusion you could reach.

In fact, the conclusion I came to again was that after bin Laden issued this Fatwa in front of his own followers, and published it worldwide in Muslim newspapers, he was now forced to go through with a direct attack on the US. If he did not, his credibility would have gone to zero, and his whole organization would have gone defunct. Even his own people would have labeled him a weakling and a complete fool. I came to the exact same conclusions I had come to the first time. It was now obvious that once he issued this Fatwa, he would carry out a horrific attack directly inside the US.

The top leadership of this organization maintained its self-appointed position of leadership in the worldwide radical Muslim movement by creating an "aura of authority." They stated their goals in Fatwas and declarations, and then carried out attacks that were suggested by these statements. Had they not carried out the attacks their statements had suggested, they would have looked weak and foolish in the eyes of their followers. Not carrying out an attack directly inside the US would have destroyed bin Laden's "aura of authority" and his whole organization would have disintegrated.

Prior to even discovering what the targets were going to ultimately be, my analysis of the USS Cole attack convinced me that even before the attack on the Cole, bin Laden had assumed he could attack and destroy any target anywhere in the world using secrecy, suicide, surprise and psychology as weapons. "Any target" clearly included the biggest buildings in the US, and in particular, in New York City and Washington DC. The three-year delay from the time they had issued the Fatwa indicated this group was going to select a huge target, a target that would fully justify this long delay. Both the reexamination of the Cole attack and the three-year delay pointed right at the World Trade Center Towers as the target.

I had come to the conclusion that all of the plans for al Qaeda had to be approved by bin Laden himself. Because of his extremely limited view of the US, whatever target he ultimately selected had to be well known worldwide. I had even come to the conclusion in my original analysis, that when I finally discovered the target, it was going to be a target that was "almost too obvious." The World Trade Center Towers certainly were targets that were "almost too obvious." The most dangerous terrorist

51

organization in the world had focused on what had to be the most important targets in the world. It was my conclusion they would never go after a lesser target when in their minds they thought they could successfully attack and destroy the world's biggest targets.

When I realized the target had to be the World Trade Center Towers, the only conceivable way I could see how this terrorist group could destroy these buildings was by using hijacked aircraft. There appeared to be literally no other way as simple as this to successfully attack these buildings. If you assumed their goal was to collapse these buildings, then it looked as if they would need at least four large aircraft. These buildings, viewed from their photographs, appeared to be just too strong to be collapsed by a single aircraft, even a large airliner. With the complete lack of any real security for US aircraft, the terrorists could literally walk right onto the aircraft they were going to hijack carrying four-inch knives, and take over these aircraft in mid-flight, almost unopposed. Once they were on board the aircraft they were going to hijack with their weapons, I could see no way they could be prevented from successfully carrying out this attack.

I reviewed again the estimated time-line of when I thought this attack might occur. I had originally concluded this attack would require at least one and possibly two of the hijackers from each team to get sufficient pilot training to be able to fly hijacked aircraft from the initial point of the hijacking to the intended targets.

Since I assumed these planes would be taken over in mid-flight, I concluded they most likely would use "dead reckoning" along with perhaps the use of their compass to navigate these hijacked aircraft to their intended targets. Dead reckoning means the pilot follows a major landmark on the ground, a river, or a coastline, until they get to their destination. It was inconceivable they would use the complicated navigation computers on board or even the navigation radios to fly these huge aircraft hundreds of miles to their final target. They would be under way too much stress. The stress level would be way too high to perform even the most basic tasks needed to navigate these aircraft using the complex navigation systems.

I went back over again what I thought it would take in calendar time to get four teams of pilots enough training to carry out this plan. The estimate it would require at least one year of calendar time was as good an estimate as I could possibly come up with. One year, in fact, was twice the time period of the six months it would take to get a highly motivated, well-educated person, who worked at their training full-time, sufficient skills to pilot a large airliner.

The most important training they would need in order to pilot a large airliner and the key to this whole plan would be getting actual time on large aircraft simulators. The terrorists were going to have to get several hours of "air transport time." To be able to obtain air transport time, the pilots who were going to get this training would have to get, at the very least, a private pilot's license, most likely a commercial license, and time toward an IFR rating or even an IFR rating itself. If they did not have this type of training prior to starting air transport training, alarm bells would have gone off immediately at the training schools that something was dreadfully wrong. A reasonable person was not going to spend thousands and thousands of dollars on this type of training if they eventually could not use this in a job or other commercial activity. The original estimate it would require at least one year of calendar time to get the four pilots through all of this training was as good an estimate as I could possibly come to at this time.

In order to get the hijackers into the US, select their flight schools, apply to the selected schools and get accepted, the best estimate I could come up with was three months. The three-month estimate to get the non-pilot hijackers into the US, after the pilots had been trained, again seemed to be just about right.

The most difficult part of this entire estimate had been finding the starting date for this final phase. I had no known a' priori way to actually estimate accurately this starting date. My original estimate for a starting date had been February 1998, which I quickly found did not work at all. The second estimate for a start date, February 2000, one year prior to my flight, seemed to fit all of the criteria I was using to find this date, the fact the plan had to have been in operation for a substantial period of time prior to February 2001, the use of round numbers, until the round number was shown not to work and would need revision, and this date along with the time-line providing additional corroboration to the dates for prior attacks. Using the estimate for the final phase of their plan of 1½ years, plus one month for final preparation, the date for the attack came to the time period between September 1 and September 15. This time period fell right between the dates of the last two attacks, the East African bombings in August 1998 and the *Cole* attack in October 2000. Again, when I saw the relationship between the dates of the prior attacks and the estimated date for this attack, I felt I had found the corroboration I was looking for. There was simply no other information I had that would lead me to estimate any different date for this attack.

While this analysis reconfirmed February 2000 as the most likely start date for the final phase of the al Qaeda plan (when al Qaeda first sent the terrorists to be trained as pilots to the US), and reconfirmed the time estimates as well, once I had the date for the attack, the starting time and time-line dates became irrelevant since I was only using these intermediate dates to find the estimated date of the attack on the World Trade Center Towers. They would be potentially useful only if I could reconfirm these dates somehow with another totally independent process.

After reviewing all of my original analysis, I came to the conclusion that I had done nothing obviously wrong. My reexamination could come up with no other target and no other time-line for this attack. I was now more convinced than ever that the World Trade Center Towers were completely doomed and by mid-September they would be obliterated along with every single person in these buildings.

There was no other conclusion that could be drawn from the analysis of the thinking of the people who had written the Fatwa. You read two sentences in one single magazine and the only thing that would even begin to explain this is that the World Trade Center Towers were going to be obliterated by the al Qaeda organization by no later than the middle of September.

Again, all I could think of was, "OH MY GOD!"

I just continued to sit there stunned and horrified at the numbers of deaths and injuries these attacks were going to cause.

After a few minutes, I decided I still had to attempt one last time to prove this attack was not going to happen. If I could not prove this, then I had to prove the attack was going to be directed at some target other than the World Trade Center Towers. I felt at the very minimum, I had to prove this attack was going to be directed at some other target with far fewer casualties. Perhaps the target was going to be the Pentagon. Or perhaps the target was going to be the US Capitol Building or even some other less well-known building. In spite of the original analysis and the review of this analysis, I was now more determined than ever to prove to myself there was not going to be an attack on the World Trade Center Towers. It was simply too horrible for me to contemplate an attack against these buildings. In order to disprove my original thinking, I decided to throw several arguments I considered to be 500-pound cannon balls right at these conclusions, in order to find at least one argument that would literally smash apart the original analysis and the conclusions. I was going to find at least one argument that I hoped would disprove these building were the targets. I decided to go back through all of the analysis I had done in much greater detail and also re-analyze my thinking and conclusions by adding in several additional and independent new ways of looking at it.

General review of al Qaeda motivation and resources

From a general review of their motivation and capabilities, it was obvious the leadership of al Qaeda hated the US with a tremendous intensity. They had issued an edict publicly to kill Americans, and had even directly targeted American civilians. They had trained 20,000 terrorists in their training camps and half of these had gone through martyrdom training, training to attack enemies of Islam with suicide attacks. The enemy in their eyes was the United States.

Bin Laden had large monetary resources and al Qaeda was obtaining more and more financial resources from sympathizers in the Muslim world, and especially Saudi Arabia. They had the motivation, the resources and the recruits. Over 10,000 of these recruits had already gone through martyrdom training. Al Qaeda was utterly determined to ultimately attack directly inside the US.

When I first realized they were going to attack a target inside the US, I came to the conclusion because they had already waited three years; it had to be an enormous target and a target that was "almost too obvious." Going back and reviewing these arguments all over again indicated the most obvious target had to be the World Trade Center Towers. A general review not only did not eliminate these buildings as the most obvious target, but also reconfirmed all over again that they were indeed the targets. These towers had to be al Qaeda's first choice.

Magnification

A terrorist organization like al Qaeda is run almost like a corporation. Instead of sales they have contributions, and instead of employees, they have mostly unpaid or low-paid recruits. Instead if press releases, they use terrorist events to present their views to the world. These terrorist events are used to attract additional contributions and additional recruits. The terrorists are focused on what might be referred to as a concept called "magnification" in these events.

Magnification refers to the ultimate goal of the terrorists, to take a small team of people, do a terrorist event, and then have this event magnified in the newspapers around the world, in particular in Europe and the Middle East. Magnification can be measured in two ways, by the length of these articles and by the length of time these articles stay on the front pages of these major newspapers. In order to come up with a quantitative rather than a qualitative measure of magnification, I created a point system to measure magnification. One point would be added for each target for each thousand people killed, and one point added for each building destroyed.

For the World Trade Center Towers, the magnification came to 30 points for the 30,000 people I had estimated would be killed by this attack, and two points for the two buildings which would be destroyed. This came to a total of 32 points if the al Qaeda terrorists attacked this target. The Capitol Building came to ¼ point for the 250 people killed and ½ point for destruction of a portion of this building. It was too low to be knocked down completely. A large aircraft would only destroy one-third to one-half of this building at most, for a total of about ¾ point.

For an attack on the Pentagon, the points came to ¼ point for 250 people killed and ⅕ point for the one wedge of the Pentagon that would be destroyed. This building was too low to collapse completely. The number of 32 for the World Trade Center Towers compared with ¾ point for the Capitol Building and ½ point for the Pentagon again confirmed that the WTC Towers were the target. This exercise to try to find targets that could prove that the World Trade Center Towers were not the target only confirmed what I already thought, and which were my worst fears. There was no other target that even came close to the WTC Towers as a target in the eyes of the al Qaeda terrorists.

Chance of Success (COS)

In my original analysis, I had used a version of what I would call "chance of success" analysis. Chance of success analysis is almost like the analysis done by a rat in a maze. At each intersection in the maze where the rat has to decide to go left or right, it is attempting to pick the direction that will lead to the cheese. Terrorists do a similar sort of analysis. At each decision-point in their plans, it was obvious these terrorists had spent a great deal of time on deciding the ultimate details of each plan of the attack in order to achieve the highest possible "chance of success."

Their planning was in a word, meticulous, and never rushed. For each detail in their attack plan, they would go over each point many times to figure out what was needed in order to achieve the highest possible chance of success for the mission.

In fact, they must have gone over their plans using this method of analysis literally hundreds of times, to make sure the selection of every single detail had given them the highest possible chance of success. Even after they had selected a target, they would go over every other possible target to make sure they had selected the target with the highest possible chance of success consistent with achieving the highest magnitude. Using this analysis, I selected each building that appeared in the photograph that included the World Trade Center buildings and as I pointed to different buildings, asked, "How did this affect their estimate for the ultimate 'chance of success' of this mission? Did it make the chance of success higher, or did it make it lower, or did it have no effect on the ultimate chance of success of this mission?"

As I selected each new alternate building, once you knew they were going to use hijacked aircraft to attack these structures, it was obvious every alternative structure had either no effect on the chance of success or because the alternate building was significantly smaller and better integrated with the surrounding structures actually lowered the chance of success. From this analysis, the analysis the terrorists must have done years earlier, it was obvious that the World Trade Center Towers had to be their primary targets.

Repeating a target they had missed once

After reading about the *USS Cole* attack, and the attack on the *USS The Sullivans*, a failed attack that had taken place nine months earlier, I came to the conclusion terrorists never give up on a target once they have it in mind. If they or a closely aligned group missed destroying a target the first time, they simply regroup and go right back after the target they had missed. This made complete sense. An unsuccessful attack on any target would leave this target foremost in their consciousness.

They had attempted to attack the *USS The Sullivans* in January 2000. When their attack failed because their rubber boat sank from the weight of the explosives, they did not give up but went after the *USS Cole* nine months later. Both US warships were docked at the exact same place in Yemen. From a base in Afghanistan, the al Qaeda terrorists had carefully planned this attack over a period of many months and even years, carefully choosing this target as the best that they could find. With an expenditure of this much effort on this target, they were just unprepared to give up since they have had invested so much time and effort in their planning.

Al Qaeda or a closely related organization had attacked the World Trade Center in 1993, and failed to destroy these buildings. The fact that Ramzi Yousef had been arrested at an al Qaeda safe house was proof in my mind that even if the original attack in 1993 had not been an al Qaeda operation, because of the worldwide notoriety that he had generated from this 1993 attack, these buildings certainly would have become foremost in the consciousness of al Qaeda, particularly when it was clear Ramzi Yousef had become involved with al Qaeda. These buildings now had to be right at the top of their target list. *If a destroyed target is ever rebuilt, the new structure will certainly become the focus of their attention.*

The attack on the East Africa embassies

I had concluded after analyzing the attack on the embassies that any attack by al Qaeda in the US would be directed at the biggest buildings in the biggest US cities. This analysis had been done prior to even knowing the Fatwa was a declaration of war on the US, and that the terrorists were determined to hit the US directly. I had concluded from my original analysis that the leadership of the al Qaeda organization viewed the area outside of the region that was to be governed by an Islamic Caliphate as an amorphous black space with almost no detail. The terrorists viewed all of the cities – London, Paris, New York, and Washington DC – that could have been possible targets as equal with one major exception. The area including New York and Washington DC was encircled by an imaginary boundary I would call the "signature boundary." These were the major cities in the US, the primary enemy of the al Qaeda terrorists. Any attack that crossed this imaginary boundary would have to be a "signature event," an attack so large and spectacular that it would establish the reputation of bin Laden and his al Qaeda organization for the next 100 years. This attack would be focused on only the biggest buildings in the biggest cities on the East Coast, New York or Washington DC. The biggest buildings in the biggest US cities were the World Trade Center Towers, the Pentagon, and the Capitol Building.

The magnification analysis I had done ultimately ruled out the Pentagon and the Capitol Building. This could only mean this attack was going to be directed at the World Trade Center Towers. After reviewing the original analysis of the attack on the embassies in Tanzania and Kenya, it was obvious any attack inside of the US was going to be directed at the World Trade Center Towers as the primary targets in the future plans of al Qaeda.

The attack on the *USS Cole*

I went back and reviewed the original analysis I had done on the *USS Cole* bombing.

In this attack, the terrorists had used as weapons secrecy, surprise, suicide and psychology to ensure this attack would be successful. I had come to the conclusion that the leadership of al Qaeda felt by using these weapons, they would be able to attack and destroy any target in the world. And this included the biggest buildings in the largest US cities.

If they felt they could successfully attack the most modern warship in the US Navy – a ship with a four-inch cannon mounted right on the deck – then they must have felt they could successfully attack any building anywhere in the world. If they felt they could successfully attack and destroy the biggest buildings given the right plan, then why would they ever attack a smaller building? The reevaluation of this analysis on the attack on the *USS Cole* reconfirmed that any attack by al Qaeda in the US had to be directed at the World Trade Center Towers. In effect the attack on the *Cole* pointed unmistakably right at the World Trade Center Towers as the most likely targets in the minds of the terrorists.

Straight line on a log scale graph

Terrorists, and in particular the Muslim extremists who had carried out several successful attacks against US interests overseas, were like drug addicts. They needed ever-increasing numbers of casualties from their acts of terror to achieve the same effect as from their previous attacks. The best evidence for this was from the history of their prior attacks. The Khobar Towers attack in 1996 had killed about 20 people; the attack on the embassies in 1998 had killed over 200. The attack on the east African embassies had resulted in 10 times as many deaths as the Khobar Towers attack.

But the *Cole* attack had only killed 17. How did this attack fit their pattern? It didn't. The reason I came to for this was, in my opinion, that the *Cole* attack was not a "signature event." It was an attack on a target that can be described as "a target of opportunity." A signature event is an event planned over several years by the top leadership of al Qaeda, perhaps bin Laden himself. These attacks were carried out in order to build the reputation of al Qaeda, get new funds from contributors in Saudi Arabia and attract new recruits.

A target of opportunity was a terrorist attack that simply happened because some target presented itself, perhaps by accident, and the leadership of al Qaeda had nothing better to do. An attack on a target of opportunity would keep the image of al Qaeda alive even if the attack did not fit their main intentions for a signature event. It would also send a message to the US: "We are still here."

If you plotted the signature events on a log graph, and drew a straight line connecting the number of people killed in the Khobar Towers attack (20 killed in 1996) and the East Africa bombings (200 killed in 1998), this line could be extended out to 2002 and 2004. Looking at this graph plotted at two-year intervals and continuing out along this straight line, a signature event should have occurred in the year 2000. From the graph, this attack should have resulted in 2,000 casualties. But the *Cole* attack was their focus in 2000, and hence they had not planned any signature event for that year.

If you follow the straight line out in time, to 2001 and 2002, these dates would indicate if attacks occurred at these time-points, the resulting casualties would be approximately 3,000-plus in 2001 and 20,000 in 2002. As I was reevaluating the attacks on the World Trade Center Towers, and trying to see if they fit the pattern for what I had called their signature events, I came to the conclusion that the attack on the World Trade Center Towers did generally fit the pattern for the next attack by al Qaeda.

Focus of attention

At first I felt it was not going to be possible to estimate the timing for the planning of the World Trade Center attack that took place inside Afghanistan. It looked as if there was no way to accurately analyze this time period with the information I had. However, as I looked over this planning phase, I ultimately saw a way that this time could be estimated based on what I would call the "focus of attention" and an analysis process based on reduction. This analysis process subtracts out all of the time the al Qaeda terrorists must have devoted to planning for their previous attacks and attempted to see if they had an opportunity to "focus their attention" on planning for the attack on the World Trade Center Towers.

This process is different from the logic process of deduction. Deduction takes a number of facts and attempts to generate new facts by connecting them together with a logical process. Reduction takes away everything that is known and sees what is left. In this case, reduction takes away all of the time the leadership of al Qaeda would have been focused on planning prior attacks on other targets, the embassy bombings, the *USS Cole*, and the *USS The Sullivans* attacks, and then estimates the time the leadership of al Qaeda would have had to focus on the attack on the World Trade Center Towers.

I had assumed the planning in Afghanistan for the attacks they had already carried out, in general, took approximately one year. Since I had originally calculated the timing for the plan for the attack on the World Trade Center Towers using "magic" numbers (round numbers such as one year, three months, one month used in a time-line), this was an attempt to reconfirm the results of this analysis, by confirming the original estimate for when the execution phase of their plan had started. This is the phase of their plan that started when these terrorists first entered the United States to train as pilots in preparation for this attack.

When I looked at the timing for the attacks on the Khobar Towers in June 1996, the embassy attacks in August 1998, and the *USS Cole* attack in October 2000, it was obvious that there had to be some reason for the date of the attacks coming every two years. I had concluded that this two-year interval was due in some measure to these attacks being planned by the al Qaeda organization at the highest levels, and that at the very highest leadership levels, they only had the bandwidth for planning one significant attack at a time.

I had also concluded that the planning for each attack was also broken down into two phases. The planning that was taking place in Afghanistan, which I estimated took about one year was the first phase. This was followed by the execution phase of each plan, when the terrorists were sent into the country where the attack was to be carried out. I had estimated from prior attacks by al Qaeda that the people sent to carry out these attacks would take at least one year to 18 months in order to put the plan into place.

Once the members of the terrorist team were sent to the country where the attack would occur, the leadership of the al Qaeda organization would be free to start planning the next attack. Since the attack on the *USS The Sullivans* had occurred in January of 2000, this meant that the terrorists must have left Afghanistan by February or March of 1999. After this point in time, the leadership of al Qaeda would be free to plan the next attack. If the al Qaeda leadership had started planning the attack on the World Trade Center Towers in February or March of 1999, and this planning took approximately one year, they would

62

have completed this phase by about January or February of 2000.

The January-February 2000 date for the finish of the planning in Afghanistan dovetailed almost exactly with the prior estimate that the hijackers must have started coming into the US by February of 2000 for the execution phase of their plan. Now I not only had an estimate with a final date that fell right between their prior two attacks, but that had a starting date that began just as soon as their planning had ended in Afghanistan. This reconfirmed the original time-line for the final phase of their operation, the phase that was to take place in the US. They would plan this attack on the World Trade Center Towers from February or March 1999 to approximately January 2000 in Afghanistan, and then start sending the terrorist hijackers into the US just after this planning phase had ended.

If I had thought of this plan, then these terrorists must also have thought of this plan.

If the major details of this plan were obvious after just a few hours of analysis, while sitting on an airplane, with nothing more the material from a single magazine, then it was inconceivable the terrorists had not also thought of this same plan. They were just too smart and too aggressive. They are very entrepreneurial and had put together many plans to attack US interests outside the US.

It was also inconceivable to me that the terrorists had not seen the gigantic hole in the security of US airliners. There were no real security checks for passengers getting on board US aircraft. There was no background check of passenger lists to reconfirm exactly who was getting on board US airliners. There was an almost insane disregard for any type of profiling, which could have spotted suspicious persons getting on board aircraft or getting reservations, in particular those who were easily identifiable as possible al Qaeda terrorists.

Then the huge monster of an issue: FAA rules allowing passengers to get on board US aircraft with four-inch knives. In my opinion, this amounted to a complete lack of any real security that bordered on utter and total insanity.

The system created to protect the US from aircraft hijackings was so full of holes that determined teams of terrorists could easily hijack a number of US aircraft with almost no opposition. All they had to do was get flight training, which was not hard, and keep their plans absolutely secret. These terrorists were very determined. They would test and retest US airline security until they were sure they could get on board US airliners with these four-inch knives. Once they were on board the aircraft they were going to hijack, it was all over. No one would be able to stop them. No power on earth would be able to stop them at that point.

The 100,000-pound gorilla

Once I realized that bin Laden had become focused on the World Trade Center Towers, I came to the conclusion he must have had every brain cell in his head trained on how to obliterate these buildings and kill as many people as possible. The world's most maniacal and dangerous terrorist had become focused on the world's largest target. All he would have to do is point at a target and his fanatical supporters would line up and in fact fall all over themselves to commit suicide in order to destroy this target.

This was the thought that I could never get out of my head. This was the 100,000-pound gorilla that meant these building were doomed. Their huge height and resulting worldwide symbolic status had simply doomed these structures to that of the "ultimate" target in the eyes of the world's most dangerous terrorist, and his organization. And this would result in their complete and total destruction.

I had thrown argument after argument at my thinking and resulting conclusions and had not been able to dent even one of my original conclusions. The original conclusions I had come to were like a huge bank vault door that had been closed.

Each new argument I had thrown at this door with the hope of breaking it open had not only not broken it open, but was like a another huge pin that had come down and further locked this door into place.

These arguments had not changed my conclusions in any way. In fact these arguments had only further reinforced the same conclusions I had originally reached.

When I originally had come to the conclusion the World Trade Center Towers were going to be obliterated in an attack by the al Qaeda terrorists, I had estimated the chance of this not happening as one chance in 100,000. After the first review of my analysis, the conclusion I came to was that the chances of the al Qaeda terrorists not attacking the WTC Towers as one chance in a million.

After going through all of these arguments, the chance of this not happening was now one chance in 100 million, billion, trillion.

There was no way the al Qaeda terrorists were not going to attempt to get on board US aircraft with weapons to carry out this plan, and once they were aboard, along with their weapons, there was in fact going to be no way of stopping them from successfully carrying out this attack.

I further came to the conclusion this had actually not been that hard to figure out in the first place. It required no real intense thinking, just the use of plain simple common sense. After realizing the al Qaeda terrorists were determined to attack in the US, and that their plan had to be in active operation for a considerable amount of time, it took just a very simple step-by-step approach with common sense to find the target, the method of attack, and even the timing for the attack. No real intense intellectual thinking of any kind was required to figure out almost every important detail.

At this point, what I found to be extremely puzzling was: Why had the FBI not picked up on this, when this was so obvious? A completely untrained person in a few hours on a flight from San Francisco to Newark, reading a single magazine, and finding two sentences that were extremely puzzling, could come to no other conclusion than there was going to be an attack against the World Trade Center Towers, using four teams of hijackers with four to five members each, armed with nothing but four-inch knives to take over these airliners in midair. This attack would take place in the first two weeks in September of 2001. Not only was it highly probable this attack would take place, there appeared to be no conceivable way this attack would not occur.

I could just not even begin to understand how the FBI would not be aware of this plan. But I knew that the FBI was not proactive, which was what was needed to figure out and prevent this attack. In fact, I could not see any government agency that was set up in such a way they would proactively do what was necessary to anticipate and prevent this attack.

What could stop this attack?

The next thought I had was if this is the plan, then what in the world can be done to stop this attack from succeeding. If FBI agents were riding on the airplane that was to be hijacked, and if they stopped these terrorists one second before they were going to hijack these aircraft, could they arrest and charge the terrorists with a crime?

I came to the conclusion at this point that the FBI would have had no probable cause to arrest these people or even search their possessions. The terrorists would maintain the highest possible secrecy regarding their plans, in order to give this plan the highest possible chance for success. As long as the terrorists kept their plans secret, the FBI would be unable to do anything at all until after the hijacking actually took place.

They would be able to do nothing at all unless they were actually on the planes that would be hijacked and then only after the hijacking was in progress. Because of this, I could not see how anyone, including the FBI, would be able to do anything to stop these attacks. The only thing I could see that would maybe prevent this attack was to make the cockpit doors solid enough so no one could ever penetrate these doors. Even then the airlines would have to have armed guards on board the airliners in case the terrorists tried kicking down the doors.

Next, I asked myself exactly who these people were who were going to hijack these aircraft. All of the hijackers, in my opinion, had to be from the middle class. It was also inconceivable to me that the four terrorists would train for over a year to become pilots and would be equally motivated to go through this training to learn flight skills, just to kill themselves. I came to the conclusion that one of these terrorists, the person I called the "ramrod," was going to lead this attack. This person would have undergone a lengthy period of extremely high emotional stress in his life, six or seven years at least, which would put him in his early 30s. The al Qaeda recruiters must have caught up with this person at his local mosque at a point where he was searching for some sort of meaning in his life. The al Qaeda recruiters must have offered him what amounted to an escape from this stress. This person was told he would become part of the worldwide Jihad "in the defense of Islam" by crashing a large airliner into a building in the US. His failed life on earth would be rescued with this one glorious act. His place in heaven would be assured for eternity by this one single act.

The other three pilots had to be in their mid-20s, plus or minus a few years, and were going to fall under the domination of this key organizer. The 12-16 final non-pilot hijackers were most likely in their early 20s, plus or minus a few years. They were going to be young Muslims, educated from an early age in the Koran and a hatred for the West. They would have been recruited from Middle Eastern countries and then would have gone through martyrdom training at one of bin Laden's training camps. This training combined with their prior heavy religious indoctrination would have been enough to motivate these people to die in a suicide attack "in the defense of Islam."

The person who had assumed the role of "ramrod," and who would lead this attack, was going to hold the pilots together for over a year while they were training in the US. He would then organize the attack teams when the non-pilot team members came to the US, after the pilots had been trained. I had come to the conclusion that this "ramrod" would be the only one who knew all of the information about this attack, and would determine the final date for the execution for the plan.

The people being recruited for this plan, and particularly the pilots, were obviously going to be selected for one outstanding characteristic, enormous stability. No one who was considered unstable, and who had quick flashes of anger, particularly during the stress of pilot training, would ever be allowed to be part of this group. Just this alone would raise suspicions enough to give away the whole group. All of these people had to be significantly religious, and had to have a significant hatred of the US and the West, which would have been an outcome of their religious education. While they were in the US, training as pilots or doing other things to further this plan, they could never express this hatred for the US openly or they would give the whole plan away.

My next thought was: "If I went to the FAA and told them this, what would they do?" I could not see how they were going to do anything. The FAA was so large and bureaucratic; I could not see how they would ever listen to an outsider in the first place. And second, even if they did believe me, making the cockpit doors much stronger would never happen in the time needed to prevent a terrorist attack. The more solid doors would have to be in place by August 1, 2001 at the latest, in case the terrorists launched their attack early, in order to stop this attack. This would be an impossible task.

While this plan was extremely simple and I thought there was perhaps even an outside chance the FBI might pick up on this plan, I came up with other al Qaeda plans I thought might take place after the attack on the World Trade Center Towers had occurred. The next plan would rely on the fact the FBI is always looking at the past to anticipate the future. They just do not try to anticipate future attacks that might be different from the attacks that had already been carried out.

The FBI after this first attack would be focused on plans where four or five young Muslim men from Middle Eastern countries were trying to bring small knives on board US aircraft for another hijacking. All the al Qaeda terrorists would have to do to completely overcome the FBI would be to recruit Muslim men with English-sounding names (I thought of John Smith or Robert Reid as possible good English-sounding names) to carry out their next set of attacks. Because the FBI would not be looking at each and every passenger as they actually boarded their flights at the boarding gates, the terrorists could remain completely undetected since their names would not give them away. Instead of bringing knives on board US airliners, they would have explosives in their shoes or on their persons.

[Note: After the attacks of 9/11, I was so concerned about the prospect of this type of attack that in mid-September 2001, when I gave the FBI a written summary of my analysis, I carefully pointed out that airline security absolutely must use nitrogen-detection devices to keep bombs hidden in shoes from ever coming on board US aircraft. I had also sent this same information to the *Wall Street Journal* in October 2001, hoping that printing this story and my warning to a wider audience would focus attention on this security issue. This information is included in the appendix of this book. See "Letter to the *Wall Street Journal*." The *Wall Street Journal* in fact did not print my story or even the warning I had sent them. What would they have thought if Richard Reid had actually set off the bomb in his shoe and 200 or 300 people had been killed on the flight he was on in December 2001, and they knew they had been given this warning ahead of time?]

At the end of this flight, as I walked off the aircraft, I passed by the two pilots at the front of the aircraft. They had come out of the cockpit and were standing at the front of the first-class section of the aircraft. As I was walking past them, I was about to tell them what I had just discovered. I had intended to say:

"Gentlemen, I have just finished reading material on the al Qaeda terrorist organization during this flight and I have spent several hours analyzing this information because it just did not make any sense. The al Qaeda terrorists had published a document in 1998 called a Fatwa, which is a declaration of war against the United States. After analyzing why these terrorists had published this document, the only conclusion I can come to is the al Qaeda terrorists are going to hit the US with a horrific attack, and this attack will most likely take place in the first weeks of September.

The plan from what I have figured out will be to hijack four large US airliners and then fly these planes into the sides of the World Trade Center Towers. I am convinced at this point these towers will collapse as a result of this attack and everyone in the buildings will be killed. After racking my brain over and over for several hours, I could come up with absolutely no other explanation that even begins to explain why the terrorists had published this document. I could come to absolutely no other conclusion."

Before I even had a chance to say this, I realized if you say, "hijack," "bomb," or "gun" on a commercial aircraft, you are immediately arrested on the spot. No further explanation is even considered. Right then and there I had this image in my mind of being escorted off of the aircraft bound in chains.

I walked past the pilots without saying even one word. I had came to the realization, on this flight, after reading nothing more than one or two sentences in this magazine, that I had turned into a combination of a secret agent and a space alien, the kind of space alien who at one minute looks human and the next minute looks like a monster.

The thing that was starting to really make me angry was the realization I had now become a secret agent in my own country, in the country where I had been born.

How was this even possible, especially when I had been born in the US and had lived in this country my entire life? But I was becoming aware that if I said the wrong thing at the wrong time to the wrong people, they were going to think I had gone completely crazy. I might even be arrested.

From this moment on, I was going to have to live in a secret world, almost like a world in another dimension that only I would be able to understand.

What a horrible turnabout. What a complete disaster. My life had changed forever and not for the better.

I also came to the realization that I had to somehow, some way, stop this attack. This was now going to be my life's goal.

Chapter 8
February 14, 2001
Standing in front of the
World Trade Center Towers

I was on this flight to New Jersey to exhibit my software at a small EDA software conference held at Holmdel, NJ. This conference lasted three days, Monday, Tuesday and Wednesday. After this conference was over, on the afternoon of February 14, 2001, I took down my booth, placed all of the material I had at this conference into shipping containers, and added shipping labels to the containers to be air-freighted back to California. At about 6:00 pm on Wednesday, I left Holmdel to drive to New York City. I had wanted to get up to New York City as fast as I could in order to view the World Trade Center buildings up close. All during this conference, I had been telling myself that when I saw these huge buildings up close, I would realize they were just too huge to collapse, even after getting hit by several large airliners.

I arrived in downtown Manhattan at about 9:30 pm. After checking in to my hotel, I left my room in lower Manhattan by about 11:00 pm, and then walked down about one mile to these buildings. By 11:30 pm, I was standing right in front of these huge buildings.

As I walked up to these building at night, and was able to see these structures for the first time up close, I was just mortified. I stood there completely stunned, almost in a state of total disbelief. These buildings were doomed. They were just way, way too tall for their dimensions from side to side.

These buildings were about 200 feet across from side to side. But they were around 1,400 feet tall. There was no way I could see they would ever be able to withstand a collision with large aircraft without collapsing. If the collision did not knock them down, the resultant fire would cause them to collapse.

71

The entire structure of each building appeared to be supported by extremely long steel beams running down the outside from the top to the bottom of these buildings. All of the support for these buildings came from these outside beams and from beams inside of a central core located in the middle of each floor. The small central core in the center on each floor must have held not only some supporting beams, but also elevator shafts, and the emergency stairwells. Outside of these beams, there was no other support for these buildings. All of the floor space was wide open with no other visible support at all.

The beams on the outsides of these buildings appeared to be about 1,400 feet in length. At night you could see a 2½-foot black space between each floor, where very long spans or floor trusses must have been located to hold up the weight of each floor. This allowed the buildings to have no visible internal beams in the floor area at all. Because of the height of the buildings, the compression forces on these vertical beams must have been tremendous.

I estimated there must been al least one to two million pounds of compression force on each beam. What obviously kept these very long vertical columns from deforming under this tremendous load were the trusses at each floor that in my opinion must have been welded to these beams. This compression force was constrained by the welds at each floor in such a way that no column had more than about a 12-foot distance before these welds would keep the massive compression force from deflecting the column. If the force of the collision with the aircraft knocked out even one set of welds, or the resultant fire caused the floors to sag and pull apart the welds from the outside columns to the trusses, this compression force would be acting over 24 feet; if two sets of welds were broken, this would be 36 feet, etc.

Even worse, if the welds held and the fire from the fuel on board each aircraft caused these very long floor trusses to sag, then the welds would pull the outside columns into the building. The huge weight of the building was then going to be directed not downward, but laterally into the floors, above where the fire occurred, causing these floors to bend down even faster.

Once two floors came together for either reason, it was over. The weight from the hundreds of thousands of tons of material in the building above this point would snap off these welds instantly and the buildings would just pancake down as this weight came in contact with each floor below it. In my opinion, the long floor trusses in effect doomed these buildings to failure, regardless of whether or not the welds to the outside long columns failed.

[Note: in civil engineering postmortems of structural failures, the analysis always starts by "looking at the long spans first."]

This means in any failure of a structure, engineers first look at the long spans as the source of the failure. In this case, the very long floor trusses were, in my opinion, the long spans. This is where the failure – in my opinion, and the opinion of the civil engineering profession – would be most likely to occur first. It was obvious that if the impact of the collision from the aircraft did not bring these buildings down, the very long trusses were going to be the first point where these buildings would fail. The heat from the fire would cause these long trusses to sag from the enormous weight of each floor. Since a straight line is the shortest distance between two points, this sag would have to be made up somewhere, either by pulling the long outside beams in, or by breaking off the welds connecting the long floor trusses to the outside beams.

In fact, looking at these buildings at night, it was obvious that a blow from even a single large aircraft would most likely bring down each building. These towers in my opinion were doomed. Their huge size would not save them from collapsing as I had originally hoped. There was so much weight on the supporting columns that in my opinion any disturbance at all to these structures would bring them crashing down in a classic tent-pole type of accident.

I could not believe why the city officials or the building owners ever allowed this structure to keep standing, when the threat of terrorists had become obvious after the mid-1990s. Literally thousands of people were depending for their very lives on the integrity of the structure of this building. Perhaps this building was justified in the late 1960s when it was first built, but not after information on the al Qaeda terrorists became widely known.

What did the New York City officials think they could do to protect the people in these building in the face of a terrorist attack? These same buildings had been attacked once before, so it was well known that they had been the focus of terrorist organizations in the past. They were obvious targets.

Standing there in the darkness, and looking at these structures, I could not see how they were going to get everyone out in time. It looked as if there would be a huge jam-up in the stairwells at the lower floors, the bottom third of this building, as everyone came together at this point, all trying to get out of these buildings at the same time.

As I was staring at these structures, up close, in a kind of stunned silence, it seemed even then, that what these city officials should have done was remove at least 60 floors from the top of these structures. First, this would have made these structures much less inviting targets, and second, it would have positioned the entire structure and all of the occupants much closer to the ground. This would not only have lowered the mammoth stresses on the building, but ensured that everyone could escape in the event of any catastrophe. These huge structures seemed to be just inviting terrorists who wanted to harm the US to attack them. The people in these buildings in my opinion were at monumental risk. This should have been obvious to everyone. While I was standing in front of these building I keep repeating.

"I cannot believe I am the only person in the world (outside of the terrorists) who knows these huge buildings are going to be obliterated. The FBI has to know this; this is simply too GOD-DAMN obvious."

"The FBI has 18,000 employees and 11,000 agents. How would it be even possible that 16 to 20 hijackers could come to the US in full view and the FBI not even know it? These terrorists are going to be hiding in plain sight. How would this even be possible?"

This is when I raised my right hand in front of my face and said. "The problem is that the FBI is so big, that when they have information on this plot, this FBI agent will know this," touching my index finger to my thumb, "this FBI agent will know this," touching my middle finger to my thumb, "and this FBI agent will know this," touching my ring finger to my thumb. And as I put all of my fingers together, "They will never get this information all together in one place." "This information will stick like flies on flypaper at different points in their bureaucracy." "They will never get all of this information together in one single place in order to be able to connect all of the dots."

"OH MY GOD!"

This is when I bowed my head in front of these buildings and started to weep. How in the world was I going to stop this attack? If I went down to the Manhattan FBI Field Office and told the FBI this huge plot was in progress to destroy the World Trade Center Towers, they would surely think I must have lost a few screws. I had absolutely nothing to corroborate this story at all, no real physical evidence of any kind.

I had read some magazine articles and I had looked at a single picture in a travel brochure, and had put this plan together from an analysis of this information. I had absolutely no corroborating information of any kind to prove my theory was correct. Even if the agent who interviewed me believed my story, he would never be inclined to take this story to his boss, when there was absolutely no way I or he could corroborate any of this. If he did, his boss would surely think he was just as crazy as he would think I was.

I came to believe this meant that the FBI was going to do absolutely nothing with my information. It didn't make any difference in my knowing what I was sure was true, I had no known way I could see to convince the FBI of this.

As I was standing there thinking this over, I came to the conclusion that in order for the FBI to be able to stop this attack, they were going to have to figure this out by themselves or I was going to have to come up with additional corroborating information. They would never listen to or believe an outsider, particularly an outsider who had never had any contact with counterterrorism issues before, telling professional FBI agents that he knew more about how to do their job then they did, unless I could substantiate the conclusions I had come to.

It was obvious there would be well-defined points in the terrorists' attack plan where it would be the most likely that the FBI would detect that this plan was in operation. The time and place where the FBI would be most likely to uncover this plan was when the terrorists were going through flight training. Terrorists sending messages back and forth over the Internet in the Internet cafés would never generate enough suspicion to be discovered. But when they went through flight training, surely that would the most likely place where their lack of prior training, or lack of skills in English or flying, or even just their angry attitude and hatred of Americans, would give them away.

And when the FBI found out that young Arabs, who could possibly be al Qaeda terrorists, were getting flight training on large airliners, surely this information would immediately go right through the FBI organization, right directly to the very top of the FBI and even to the top of the US government. But even then as I pondered this further, I was starting to become more and more concerned that even horrific information about al Qaeda terrorists getting flight training might simply just get stuck somewhere inside of the huge FBI bureaucracy and might not ever get to the appropriate point where this information could be acted upon in a timely fashion. The FBI is a huge agency. Information is like straw; it is soft, and the FBI bureaucracy is like a block of cement. How were you ever going to be able to drive straw through this block of cement? In fact, how was anyone going to be able to do this?

In a huge bureaucracy, there are always a thousand people who can and will stop information from going anywhere in the organization. This is how these people maintain their power, by stopping information from going past their position in the bureaucratic hierarchy. There is almost no one whose job it is to make sure information is passed up the chain of command, except the people at the very top of the organization. But they are never going to be aware if critical information has gotten stuck somewhere in the bureaucracy. This meant there was a large possibility the FBI would never uncover this plan, or even if they did, this information would not go to the appropriate place in the FBI where it could be acted upon in time. This is not to criticize the FBI. All large bureaucracies work like this, they all work in almost the same way. All of this meant in the end that these huge buildings were doomed.

I was going back to California on Sunday, and the knowledge these building were going to be destroyed was going to be an unacceptable and monumental burden. I knew I just could not go back to California knowing these buildings were going to be destroyed.

This is when I came up with a plan to prove, at least in my mind, that even if large aircraft hit these towers during this attack, they would not collapse. This plan was to visualize in my imagination these huge buildings getting hit with huge aircraft. I assumed that I was going to see they would just shudder from the collision with large airliners but remain standing. The buildings would absorb the huge force of this collision and remain upright and intact. The collision would take out three to four floors and perhaps kill 250 to 375 people in each tower, but it would not kill 30,000 people, the number of casualties I had estimated if the buildings collapsed.

I was standing to the north of the South Tower. I could see clearly the complete north face of the South Tower. My plan was to imagine a large airliner crashing into the south wall of the South Tower. I turned in the direction of the North Tower and said:

"OK this is it. I will imagine a large airliner hitting this tower." At the same time I also said to myself:

"I am going to take my hands completely off of my imagination, and provide absolutely no guidance of any kind. This way my imagination will show me an accurate and complete picture of this event without my influence or any preconceived notion on my part of what is going to occur affecting the mental image of this in anyway. This is the only way I will accurately see exactly what is going to happen when a large aircraft hits one of these towers."

I looked over in the direction of the North Tower. I first visualized a large airliner flying above the Hudson River, coming from the north at about the 1,000-1,200 foot level. I followed it down the river until it passed behind the North Tower. When it reappeared from behind the North Tower, it continued down the Hudson River into the New York Harbor, and then swung around with a 180-degree turn, coming right over the top of the Statue of Liberty. It continued on over the southern end of Manhattan, and then slammed into the south wall of the South Tower. I imagined it hitting the tower about 25 percent of the way down from the top of this building, approximately 1,000 feet above the ground. This was in the middle of the distance between the highest buildings in the immediate vicinity and the top of this tower. The south wall was the wall of the South Tower hidden from my view since I was standing just to the north of the north wall of this tower.

What I imagined next was the sound of this horrendous crash. Then a huge fireball followed this crash almost immediately, within a fraction of a second, literally exploding out from of the east wall of this tower. Almost immediately another fireball exploded out of the north wall of this building, right over my head. What was so startling to me was the speed at which these explosions took place after the sound of the collision. These explosions took place just fractions of a second after the original sound of the collision. At first I was just stunned. I was shattered by this image. As I stood there stunned, my first thought was to minimize what I had just seen. I said to myself: "But what new information do I actually know now that I did not already know on the flight from San Francisco? I already knew large airliners were going to crash into these towers. I already knew that, so realistically why should I be so stunned by this image?"

I was stunned because I did not realize, or had not been able to visualize on that flight, the fact these planes would be traveling 500 to 600 miles per hour when they hit the towers. When they hit these buildings with 100,000 pounds of fuel, the fuel was going to shoot across the wide-open floor spaces at hundreds of miles per hour with nothing to stop it. And it was becoming clear this was going to result in yet the cause of another disaster. The stairwells could not possibly have been built with doors that were watertight. The fuel was going to flow under these doors right into the stairwells, trapping all the occupants on the floors above where the planes hit these buildings.

I kept repeating over and over to myself:

"Good God almighty, all of those people, they are all just going to be trapped until these buildings collapse, good God almighty!"

I had come down to the World Trade Center Towers in the hope that when I viewed these building up close and actually saw how big they were, I would be able to go back to California with the realization they were not going to collapse, and now I had seen this!

"GOOD GOD ALMIGHTY!"

As soon as I recovered from the shock, I turned around and headed across the plaza at the bottom of the World Trade Center, in order to go back to my hotel. Just as I had gotten a short distance across the plaza, I could see a police officer coming down Church Street. My first reaction was to run over to him and say, "Officer, please help me stop this huge attack, please help me stop this attack on the World Trade Center Towers."

But then I immediately stopped in my tracks. I realized, if I did that, he would most likely think I had completely lost my mind. His job was not stopping an attack on the World Trade Center; his job was stopping ordinary street crime.

That's when I turned around again, to run over to alert the night watchmen who were working in the bottom of the World Trade Center Towers. I wanted to let them know this huge attack against these towers was in progress and going to happen. Again I stopped even before I had advanced in their direction. I realized these guards are $10-per-hour night watchmen. They would not be able to comprehend what I was telling them. What would they do with this information? I finally turned around again and ran back to my hotel, in a state of pure shock. As I left the ground level plaza of the World Trade Center Towers, I was focused on trying to figure out what I was going to be able to do in order to stop this huge attack.

Chapter 9

Back in California

On both Thursday and Friday while I was in New York City, I still had in the back of my mind the possibility of going to the FBI offices in Manhattan to let them know what I believed to be the al Qaeda plan against the World Trade Center Towers. After visually imaging what was going to take place at this interview, I concluded again that if I went to the FBI, they would do nothing with my information. I knew that the FBI is just not proactive. I would be an outsider with no experience in counterterrorism at all, and they would never start an investigation without significant proof this attack was in progress and was actually going to take place.

In my mind I could just see the expression on the face of the FBI agent doing the interview. After I went through what I thought was the al Qaeda plot against the World Trade Center Towers, the first thing he would say would be: "This is a very interesting story. But just how did you come up with all this information and the plan against the World Trade Center Towers?" At this point, I would tell him I had read a magazine and looked at a photograph, a photograph that had the picture of the World Trade Center Towers on it. And I had basically put this together from analyzing two sentences in this one magazine.

I could literally see him slowly go into a rage or at the very least a slow burn after I told him this. I could even imagine the scowl on his face and his desire to reach across the table and strangle me for wasting his valuable time with this ridiculous story. My story was based on speculation. I had no credible facts of any kind that could be corroborated by the FBI. This information and the process this information could be used to stop these attacks also had one very disagreeable aspect that I could not see how I was going to overcome.

In order to use this information to thwart an attack, airport security people and the FBI would have be on the lookout for four or five young Middle Eastern people getting onto the same aircraft carrying four-inch knives, at eastern airports in the first two or three weeks of September. I was convinced this type of racial profiling could hit a sensitive nerve at the FBI. It was highly likely they would think this was just too much of a hot potato. I literally could see the FBI agent who would be interviewing me, looking right at me with a horrified expression saying, "None of this is of any use to us. Are you actually asking us to racially profile passengers getting on board US airliners? That will never fly, not in today's FBI. If we were ever to get caught racially profiling anybody, we would be crucified. The newspapers would have a field day. Are you aware that every single agent in the FBI connected with this would face a career-ending reprimand? Your story is no good to us at all, and can never be used here under any circumstances. It is absolutely abhorrent to us and our whole organization that you would suggest we use racial profiling for any FBI investigation."

After finally coming to the conclusion that going to the Manhattan office of the FBI was going to get me nowhere, I flew back to California on Sunday, February 18, 2001. Starting on Monday, February 19, and over the next week, I told almost every single one of my employees, one at a time, in private, out of earshot from anyone else, what conclusions I had come to in New York. I even tried to soften this information so it did not come off sounding so horrific. The first person I told was Alina, one of sales persons I rely on to be both a sales person and as an all-around jack-of-all-trades.

I said "Alina," when I was able to talk to her by herself, "you will not believe the conclusions I came to after reading a magazine on that flight last week to Newark. I have come to the conclusion the al Qaeda terrorists are going to hijack four large airliners. They will use four to five of their recruits per plane armed with four-inch knives to take over these planes. They will drive these planes into the walls of the World Trade Center Towers and collapse these structures with everyone still in these buildings. I am convinced they intend to kill every single person working in these buildings. I feel these buildings will be obliterated no later than by the end of October 2001. Not only is there an enormous probability this will happen, I can see absolutely no way this huge attack will not happen, it is inevitable. I feel that I have to go to the FBI with this information. I absolutely must go to the FBI with this information."

Her reaction was worse than anything I could have ever imagined. She just stood there frozen stiff, mouth wide open, eyes bulging right out of her head, staring directly right at me. She did not move or speak for at least what felt like two or three solid minutes. I had never in my life seen anything like it. It was just as though she thought I must had turned into some kind of Frankenstein's monster as I stood right in front of her. My own employee was thinking this. I was even stunned myself at her reaction. As soon as she recovered, I again said I feel that I absolutely have to go to the FBI with this information. She said, "Bob, you go down to the FBI and tell them that, they are going to just lock you up and you aren't ever going to get out of there. They will just throw away the key. You just can't go to the FBI and tell them that."

I went over in my mind what she had just said, and after thinking about it for a short time I came to the same conclusion she had. Without some evidence of some kind that the FBI could corroborate and deem credible, I would get absolutely nowhere. In fact, if I went to the FBI with this story, it is conceivable they might blackball me from then ever contacting them in the future, when I might really have some credible information that really could be corroborated.

The people to whom I confided this information over the next week were almost everyone in sales at my company, about five or six people who were working at my company in sales in February 2001.

After talking to Alina, I decided the best thing to do was to carefully and thoroughly read the daily newspapers every single day and find that missing piece of corroborating information. That was the only way I could see where I would then have enough credible information that would allow me to contact the FBI with information on the upcoming attack on the World Trade Center Towers. At that point I could go down to the FBI and say, "Here are my conclusions on an attack on the World Trade Center Towers, and here is the information right in the newspaper that now confirms my thinking on what I believe to be an upcoming terrorist attack. Here are the most important details of how this attack will take place." With no corroborating information of any kind, I was never going to get anywhere with the FBI or any other government organization.

Despite meticulously reading the daily newspapers every single day, I never found the one piece of credible information I was looking for. The FBI had Zacarias Moussaoui in custody from the middle of August, and they were convinced he was a terrorist learning to fly large airliners. When he refused to cooperate they were absolutely sure he was a terrorist. The FBI and the CIA had the names of two al Qaeda terrorists who had entered the country. They knew that these two al Qaeda terrorists had been connected with people who were responsible for the horrific attacks on the US embassies and the *USS Cole*. The CIA had even been aware of these two terrorists and the fact that at least one of them had entered the US 18 months earlier. None of this information ever got into the newspapers.

All of the people at the top of the executive branch were in a complete panic in the summer of 2001, concerned that a massive attack by al Qaeda was imminent. They knew that this attack would be catastrophic and would result in possibly thousands of US casualties. Why did they not put this information in the newspapers, announce this to the general public, and warn the American people of this attack? Why did they not ask the general population of the US for information or help that they might provide that could be used to stop this attack? This was all kept secret from the American people. At the same time I was desperately looking for just such information, they kept this information completely secret. They claimed they could not uncover what the target of this attack was ultimately going to be. What was their purpose in keeping this information secret? They must have known that an informed public was their best defense against this impending attack and yet they kept completely quiet. The public was never informed that this huge attack was about to take place.

Chapter 10

The Trip to Las Vegas

As we were getting ready for a large software show in Las Vegas that was taking place during the second week of June 2001, one of the sales persons was so concerned over the possibility of having al Qaeda terrorists being on her flight that she came to me and asked, "What are we going to do if the al Qaeda terrorists (who are going to attack the World Trade Center) get on board our aircraft flying (from San Francisco) to Las Vegas?"

I said, "Tina, terrorists don't go to Las Vegas, they are all devout Muslims. They would not be caught dead in Las Vegas. Las Vegas is sin city. Devout Muslims do not go to sin city. But just in case you see them on your flight (the World Trade Center hijackers),

"JUST GET THE HELL OFF THE AIRPLANE IMMEDIATELY!"

"They will very easy to spot, four to five young Arabs, all sitting in first class or business class in groups of twos or threes. They hate Americans so they will not be talking to any of the American passengers sitting next to them, but will be huddled down quietly whispering to each other. They will never give you eye contact. So when you see them, just get the hell off of the airplane, throw away your ticket and I will buy you a brand new ticket, no questions asked.

DO NOT TRY TO GET A REFUND!

They will ask you why you are getting a refund. Just keep your mouth shut. Do not say anything to anyone. If you say anything they will not arrest the terrorists, they will arrest you and my company will get sued. In fact, I will do you one better, I will make this exact same announcement to the whole company, to every single person going to Las Vegas for the Design Automation Conference."

We had a company meeting that was held in the first week of June 2001, to go over the details for this DAC conference. I started off this meeting with the following announcement to the whole company:

"*Everyone knows that I have been talking about the World Trade Center terrorists and this big attack on the WTC Towers coming up this fall since February of this year. Some of the sales people are so concerned about this they have contacted me, and asked what should they do if these terrorists are on board their flight from San Francisco to Las Vegas.*

There is only a very small probability that these terrorists will be on board your flight. However, if these terrorists are on your flight, get the hell off of your flight immediately. Do not say anything to anyone. They will arrest you if you do and if the people you think are terrorists are not terrorists, they will sue us.

THE LAWS OF THIS COUNTRY HAVE BEEN DESIGNED TO LET THESE TERRORISTS GET ON FLIGHTS (IN THE US) TOTALLY UNMOLESTED.

These terrorists will be extremely easy to spot. They are all young Arabs, all sitting together in twos and threes in first class and in business class. They will never give you eye contact. They will not be talking to the Americans passengers sitting next to them. They hate Americans. If you see them, just get the hell off of the flight immediately. Do not even try to get a refund for your ticket. If you ask for a refund they will ask you why, and what are you going to say? I will buy you a new ticket, no questions asked. Everyone working here is worth far more than the price of an airline ticket. Again, remember:

KEEP YOUR MOUTH SHUT! DO NOT SAY ANYTHING TO ANYONE OR YOU WILL BE ARRESTED AND WE WILL BE SUED!"

I never really felt that the terrorists were actually going to be on these flights, but I wanted to make all my employees know they did not have to ever worry about getting on any flight they were required to take for company business and that might be hijacked. Otherwise they simply would not have flown to Las Vegas.

After setting up our booth and computers at the Las Vegas DAC Conference, and returning back to my room at the Belagio, I had decided to see some other casinos. After leaving the Belagio, I was standing at the edge of the street in order to cross Las Vegas Boulevard, which is at least 100-200 feet across at this point. I was facing a very large crowd gathered on the other side of the street. As I scanned this group, I saw four or five young Arabs gathered on the left side of this crowd. I was just frozen in pure terror. My first thought was, these could possibly be the terrorists who were going to attack the World Trade Center Towers later this fall. I even said under my breath:

"OH MY GOD, THEY COULD BE
THE WORLD TRADE CENTER HIJACKERS."

When you looked at them, they were all dressed like Americans; and they blended right in perfectly with the rest of this crowd. Then I saw another group of young Arabs right in the center of this crowd and again got the exact same terrified reaction all over again. And then I saw a third group off to the right of this crowd and had again the same reaction.

After I recovered from my shock, I realized it wasn't that I actually thought these people were the World Trade Center hijackers, but I was struck by the fact if they were, how would you ever know? Even if I walked across the street and was standing right next to and up close to them up, looking right directly at them, how would you know? Even if you were looking right at them, up close, you could not see into their brains. In fact I had this terrifying thought. You were never going to be able to tell if these people, or any other group of people, were the World Trade Center terrorists until they actually were in the process of hijacking the flights they planned to hijack.

Even one second before the hijacking took place, as long as they stayed above the law and did nothing wrong to bring suspicion to themselves, no one would ever know they were hijackers. In fact, how would anyone know until the hijackings were actually taking place?

[Note: In hindsight, and to explain this, I was at this point literally consumed night and day with the thought of these horrific attacks about to take place on the WTC Towers I was absolutely sure was coming up in September and of the terrorists who were going to carry out these hijackings. I literally must have had thought about these upcoming hijacking and these hijackers a hundred thousand times a day. In my mind I probably killed them a million times on the aircraft they were going to hijack, when they carried out these hijackings. I was even contemplating concealing a 12-inch knife in a compartment below my laptop.

Knowing they were only going to have four-inch knives, I was going to operate off the principle that in the land of the blind the one-eyed man is king, a 12-inch knife would clearly trump a four-inch knife, particularly when both parties are in a narrow aircraft aisle.]

Chapter 11

Trip to Boston
and September 11, 2001

I was in Boston when the horrific events of 9/11 took place. I was attending an EDA software show that was scheduled for the evening of September the 10th at the Marriott in Newton, MA. I had flown from San Francisco to Boston on the 8th of September 2001, on UAL 170, and passed through Logan Airport at my destination. I was going to return to San Francisco on the September 13 on UAL 173.

I arrived in Boston on the 8th and immediately went to the UAL security checkpoint at Logan Airport to see if I could spot the terrorists. I knew the week before the attack on the World Trade Center Towers that they would be intensely surveying the security checkpoints at the airports where they were going to board the flights they were going to hijack. I knew the biggest concern the al Qaeda terrorists had was how to get the four-inch knives through security and on board the aircraft they were about to hijack without setting off alarms with airport security people. In my mind, this had to be their main concern. Discovery at this point would have stopped their plans completely and would have been catastrophic for them.

I had come to the conclusion that the hijackers would wait until the actual date of the hijacking before trying to get the knives with four-inch blades onto the aircraft they were going to hijack. It was my opinion that they would never try to get these knives through airport security before the day of the actual hijacking. If they had gotten caught attempting to board aircraft in possession of these knives prior to the actual hijacking, they knew this would have tipped off the authorities and thwarted their whole plan.

On September 8, I felt the hijacking would occur in one of two time periods, either the first two weeks of September, or a few weeks later, in the second or third week of October, about four to five weeks out. If the hijacking had been moved to October, there would have been only a very small probability the terrorists would be out at the airport security checkpoints this far ahead of their October flights. I did not know what airports they would use, but assumed they would use several of the biggest airports on the East Coast, and, in my mind Logan Airport was as a good possibility as any of the other big eastern airports. I landed at Logan Airport at about 6:00 pm.

I knew exactly what I was going to be looking for, young Middle Eastern males, positioned right at the airport security checkpoints carefully surveying the security procedures for every detail. According to newspaper reports, the terrorists had apparently been there earlier in the day, intensely checking airport security. From news accounts printed right after the attack of 9/11, they had been surveying these checkpoints for a week ahead of this attack, from September 5. Perhaps one question still remains. Even if I had seen the terrorists, even then would I have been able to get anyone else to believe my description of what I thought was going to happen? On the 8th of September, two of the hijackers (Flight 175 hijackers Mohand al-Shehri, Fayez Ahmed (Banihammad)) actually landed at Logan Airport in preparation for the hijacking on September 11.

All day Sunday, September 9, I sat in my hotel room at the Newton Marriott, mulling over if I should go out to Logan again on Sunday to see if I could spot the terrorists. (I was unaware that four of the hijackers of American Airlines Flight 11 – Waleed al Shehri, Satam al Sugami, Wail al Shehri and Abdul Aziz al Omari – were actually staying at the Park Inn in Newton, just a short distance from my hotel.)

I came to the conclusion it would be very unlikely for the terrorists to be out at the airport on Sunday since they would know Sunday was not a typical day for airport security and whatever information they uncovered might be very misleading.

On Tuesday, September 11, after the hotel had given me a wakeup call, I got up and prepared for the demo later that morning. I left the hotel around 6:00 am to travel to Lowell, MA, for a demo of my company's software, which was to start at 9:00 am. When the attack happened on September 11, I was in the middle of giving this demo. The order to evacuate the building came at 10:00 am. Someone came running into the room where the demo was being held and said there had been a problem in New York City and everyone was required to evacuate the building right away. Because the demo was canceled, I invited everyone to breakfast at a restaurant across the street. There was a TV monitor in the corner of the restaurant about 15 feet away from where we were sitting. Just as soon as the waitress brought the breakfast, the South Tower collapse was shown on the TV monitor. As soon as I saw the South Tower fall, I became very sick to my stomach, announced that I had no appetite any more, paid the bill and left to drive back to my hotel in Newton. As I was leaving, I just had a thought, which kept going over and over in my mind:

"MY GOD, THE HORSES ARE OUT OF THE BARN,
AND I DID NOT CLOSE THE BARN DOOR IN TIME.
MY GOD, THIS DISASTER IS MY FAULT."

I drove back to my hotel in Newton, about 40 miles away, as fast as I could, almost in a state of shock. As soon as I got to my room, I turned on the TV to see what going to be said about this event, particularly on the 24-hour news channels. I was concerned as to what had happened to all of those people in the South Tower. Did they escape in time, or was this the disaster I had known about all along?

When Mayor Giuliani came on TV, he announced that he thought 6,500 people had been killed when the towers collapsed. I was just absolutely stunned, and my first thought was:

"OH MY GOD, I JUST KILLED 6,500 AMERICANS.
GOOD GOD ALMIGHTY, HOW IS THIS EVEN POSSIBLE?
OH MY GOD!"

As I was sitting on the edge of the bed just stunned by these events, I thought, "But why do I think I am the only person who is solely responsible for this huge disaster? There are 280 million other people in this country. With all of these people, why is this all my fault alone? Don't the FBI and CIA feel partly responsible for this Goddamn disaster? Aren't they also partly to blame? Isn't some of this their fault? Why is this all my fault?"

As I continued to reflect on this, I realized these huge bureaucratic organizations are so completely clueless, they probably were not even aware this huge attack was about to happen. Even had they been given an infinite amount of time, they probably still would have never figured this out. Perhaps some of the people in these agencies were aware of some of the details of this attack, but apparently the people who could have stopped this attack were not aware. How can you blame a bunch of clueless idiots for this disaster? How do you blame huge organizations when these whole organizations are full of just clueless bureaucrats? Even if the people at the bottom are good, and concerned, they will never be able to do anything with the huge impenetrable monolithic bureaucracy over their heads.

Even after hours and hours of going over these events, I was not able to get the thought out of my head that this whole catastrophe had been my fault. Again and again I went over how I could have approached the FBI and have them believe me. Could I have convinced them somehow to stop this tragedy?

At times it seemed if only I had gone to the FBI beforehand and told them my supposition, they would have listened to me and stopped this attack. But I realized this was exactly like pushing on the side of Mount Everest and expecting the mountain to move one inch. At first you think that it only has to move one inch. Surely a person could do that. But then you realize that no amount of pushing will ever get Mount Everest to move even one-thousandth of an inch. Getting the FBI to listen and then do the right thing to stop this attack was like thinking you were going to move Mount Everest one inch. It was just not going to happen. Information, in fact information based on speculation, coming from a person outside of the FBI without any corroboration, would have gotten nowhere at the FBI.

At about 2:00 pm on the 11th, I called the FBI Boston Field Office and told them I had known about the attack on the World Trade Center Towers since February 11, 2001. I wanted to ask them if they thought this was my fault. Had I come to the FBI in February, would they have been able to stop this? The FBI office in Boston took down my name and phone number and said they would call me back, but they never did. When I got back to San Francisco, I immediately had to fly out to Dallas for another software demo. When I finally got back to San Francisco I called the FBI office in San Francisco. The agent who talked to me on the phone was Agent Robert Stow. When I explained that I had known about the events of 9/11 seven months prior to this event happening, he went ballistic and started to scream over the phone:

"HOW DID YOU KNOW THIS?
HOW COULD YOU POSSIBLY HAVE KNOWN THIS?
YOU TELL ME NOW RIGHT NOW HOW YOU KNEW THIS?
YOU TELL ME RIGHT NOW!"

He just kept up screaming and screaming at me at the top of his voice, which made it impossible to even get a word in edgewise. Finally, I told him, in between his screams, that it was going to be very difficult to explain this over the phone in a few minutes, and it would be better if I came in for a short sit-down interview. He then calmed down, or at least stopped screaming, and said they were way too busy to have anyone come to the FBI San Francisco office. I should contact the San Jose FBI office. That is when I called the San Jose FBI office and arranged to go in for an interview.

The FBI agent I was able to see was Agent Vince Tagleari. I went through the story of how I had found out about the attack on the World Trade Center and after I was finished explaining this, I said:

"I am in here for one reason and one reason only and I want your best and your completely honest answer on this. Do you think I killed all of those people who died at the World Trade Center? Is this disaster all my fault? Do you blame me, am I to blame for this disaster?"

Vince replied: "Bob, don't blame yourself. If you had come in February (2001), we would have done nothing. You did not know the flights. You did not know the names of the people behind this. You did not have anything we would normally use. Do not blame yourself. You are not to blame. There was nothing we could have done with your information at that time."

In hindsight, figuring out 9/11 before it happened was not that hard. The big issue was: What were you going to be able to do with this information? How were you going to get anyone else to believe you, especially the FBI? How was I going to be able to use this information to stop this attack? If I was to stop this attack, I would have to get the people at the FBI to believe me and then work on stopping this attack and how was I going to do that? How was I ever going to get the necessary people at the FBI to believe me when I had no credible evidence of any kind?

Even in hindsight, I cannot see any way I could have done this prior to 9/11.

At that time the FBI would not even start a real (criminal) investigation until a crime had actually been committed. They were never going to investigate this until it was all over. At that point, they would start an investigation, but there would be nothing left to investigate but small bits of DNA. Only after this attack was all over, and it was obvious a crime had been committed, would the FBI authorize the start of a criminal investigation.

With large bureaucracies, the longer they exist, the more rules they have made for everyone to follow based on past incidents that have happened. As they get more and more rules, these very rules ultimately tie the whole organization up in such a knot that no one can do anything or even function. Their rules create a kind of maze trapping the entire organization, with every path for investigations stopping at a dead end. These organizations ultimately become completely dysfunctional. That is unfortunately the nature of all large bureaucracies.

An untrained person reading a single magazine in a few hours on a flight to Newark could figure out the details for the events of 9/11 in every important detail, and in such a way they would know not only was there a high probability this attack was going to take place, but know there was no possible way this attack was not going to occur. This analysis had been based almost entirely on the words contained in two sentences. I never even went back to analyze what these sentences actually meant. All that I had actually analyzed was what had motivated the leadership of the al Qaeda organization to publish these two sentences in the Fatwa in the first place. I never spent more than a few minutes attempting to analyze the sentences themselves.

Not only had it been possible to figure out these events in every detail, it was even possible to get a reasonably accurate estimate for the date of the attack to within a one- to two-week window based on a single date, the date for the publication of this statement, February 1998, and the dates for their prior attacks.

Was the Fatwa, in fact, a coded message? In fact, in the final analysis it was. It was a coded message but not in the normal concept of a code, where the deciphering takes place using a one-to-one correlation for each word in the message. This code had to be deciphered in an entirely different way, by using the entire message as the code. The only way you could decode the message contained within the Fatwa was by analyzing it in the context of the Declaration of Jihad. The Declaration of Jihad was the cipher for the Fatwa. With this document, nothing else but simple common-sense steps were needed to decipher and understand the ultimate and horrific message inside of the Fatwa.

Both the Declaration of Jihad and Fatwa were in the public domain, and had been published worldwide available for all to see and analyze.

From a careful analysis of these documents, you could come to no other conclusion. Once the al Qaeda terrorists had issued the Fatwa, they had unmistakably signaled they were going to hit the US directly with a massive attack. This attack from even the most primitive analysis of this organization had to be directed against the largest symbolic targets they could identify. And this had to be the World Trade Center Towers. Once these buildings were identified as the targets, it was obvious the only conceivable method of attack had to be with the use of hijacked US airliners. There was no other way this huge attack could be successfully carried out. Analyzing what had motivated the al Qaeda terrorists to publish these documents quite possibly had been the one and only way this plan could have been figured out ahead of time.

Why hadn't any of the US intelligence agencies done this analysis? This statement was there for all to see. The terrorists had made this statement widely known so no one could possibly miss seeing it. This statement alone gave the clearest possible view into the thinking of the leadership at the top of al Qaeda. And why had the large American newspapers not alerted us to this unmistakable declaration of war, and the possible horrific consequences this meant?

Chapter 12
The Postmortem

Exactly how was it possible that an untrained person in a few hours sitting on a US airliner could put the most important details of this attack plan together with no more information than the information contained in a single magazine? Looking back, there were three very important assumptions made, which in the end were critical in doing this analysis.

Figure this puzzle out without having to think

The first decision I made, after attempting to figure out why the al Qaeda organization had published the Fatwa, with absolutely no success, was the decision to find a technique that would allow me to do this analysis without having to think. This is not as unusual as at first it might appear. This, in fact, probably was the key to solving the puzzle of 9/11.

After I spent at least 30 minutes of very intense and exhausting thinking, which had yielded absolutely no results whatsoever trying to figure out this strange puzzle (why the al Qaeda leadership had published the Fatwa), I came up with a different process altogether. I felt this new approach would yield results much faster, but what was even better, in my opinion, this approach was going to require no real intense thinking on my part.

Instead of using my intellectual brain, the right-brain, and a huge amount of energy to do this analysis, I was going to use my emotional brain, what is called in popular terms the left-brain. First I had to come up with a scheme that would allow this problem to be solved using the left-brain. To be able do this, I decided I was going to build a copy of bin Laden's thinking process in my head. Once I had a reasonable facsimile of his thinking process, I could switch on his thinking, and at this point I could simply ask the question, "What was the motivation for publishing the Fatwa in the first place?" And I would instantly feel the right answer.

To build the thinking process of bin Laden in my head, I decided to use the Declaration of Jihad Against Crusaders and Jews, a document he had written as the template for his thinking. In my opinion, this Declaration of Jihad was in fact nothing more than his deepest thoughts recorded on paper. In fact, the actual document was just a mechanical rendering of his thoughts. To start this process, I did a quick review of the basics of Islam. Then I imagined myself, as bin Laden, growing up in a devout Muslim family with lots of male children, in Saudi Arabia, and worked this image back and forth until I felt I was at the point where I would be able to write the words in this Declaration of Jihad, word for word.

Could I have figured out this puzzle with just a pure analysis approach using nothing but intellectual thought? I had tried that and gave up eventually after I found this approach way too hard, and required way too much intense, exhaustive thought. This approach yielded no results at all. I was not able to even begin to understand what had motivated bin Laden to publish this Fatwa. It made no sense from any perspective.

In hindsight it is obvious now that using the left-brain for this analysis was in fact a very important component in being able to figure out this puzzle and ultimately the al Qaeda plan to attack the World Trade Center Towers. After carefully reviewing this entire analysis process I have come to the following conclusions.

First, I originally had thought that given enough time, I could analyze this with an approach using a pure intellectual thinking process. I am now sure this could not have been possible. The thinking process has, in my opinion, two distinct ways in order to do analysis. The first way is a pure intellectual process, using the right-brain. When you add one plus one you are using this process. You visualize first a one and then visualize another one and then count them up and get two. No emotions are involved; just a simple one plus one equals two. This thinking process is based on pure logic. This process is unique to humans, and developed because other types of thinking processes were not adequate when confronting new situations. It has some important and serious limitations. Since this process has only been part of the way humans think for the last two or three million years, it is still very primitive compared to other types of thinking. This process also has one important component missing; it has no emotional component. There is no amplitude with any answer. You get an answer and that is it. There is no way to know exactly how correct or incorrect an answer is; there is just the answer.

The second way to do analysis is by using an emotional process, or more accurately, the emotional-visual-auditory process with the left-brain. This is the thinking process that is extremely well developed in almost all animals, and has been part of the evolution of thinking processes for several hundred million years. This process relies on pattern-matching logic to do two things. First determine the closest match to a visual or auditory pattern, even when this pattern is enormously complex, and has never even been observed before, and second, produce a response to this pattern.

This response has two elements, an action or answer as a result of the pattern match and a second-order effect, which can be best be described as "amplitude," along with this action or answer. This amplitude depends on some characteristic of the match, in most cases on the closeness of the match to characteristics that indicate an increasing degree of danger.

This process is best explained in the following way. An animal on the African plains at dusk sees a movement in the brush, and sees nothing more than the dark shape of the top of a predator's head and ears. This image is immediately compared in a pattern-matching process in the animal's brain. The resultant response is an indication of the degree of danger. In this case, this is based on the perceived distance to the image, and the amplitude for this response is generated. If the image is 500 feet away, the amplitude indicates no real concern. If the image is 20 feet away, the amplitude will be much greater, immediately indicating a real and significant danger. In this case, the animal in reaction to the closeness of this danger instantly turns around 180 degrees from the direction of the image and starts moving away at top speed. One of the most important components of this type of thinking is the speed at which the reaction is generated. The image is viewed, the brain using this pattern-matching logic decides how to react, and reaction occurs in just fractions of a second.

In humans, using the left-brain allows you to visualize and even feel the thousands of nuances in an answer to a question, which the right-brain would never even begin to see. It would be as if you were looking at an answer in three dimensions in color instead of in two dimensions in black-and-white. This was the approach that allowed me to answer the question: What had motivated the al Qaeda terrorists to publish the Fatwa in the first place? Using this approach it was obvious the al Qaeda terrorists were determined to attack inside the US, in fact with an attack that would be a massive blow to the US. You could feel this enormous determination bin Laden felt for carrying out this attack. This meant the attack had to be directed at a target in the US, resulting in many casualties to American civilians and an attack that would deal a massive psychological blow to the whole country. Knowing this, it was absolutely inconceivable that after three years this plan had not already been put into operation.

Dumb down my thinking

After I had come to the conclusion that this Fatwa meant bin Laden had publicly declared war on the US and he now must be planning a huge attack directly in the US, I tried to figure out what the target was going to be. I first started with the concept that this plan had been put together under very primitive conditions in Afghanistan, and had to have been put together largely by bin Laden himself. He was ultimately going to direct and personally approve the selection of the targets. This plan was to be carried out with people who would have no or little communications for months with the people who were directing and financing this plan in Afghanistan. Hence, whatever plans the al Qaeda terrorists came up with had to be "extremely simple," focused on only the most obvious targets. The terrorists would never devise a complex plan when a simple plan would do. In fact they would be focused on finding the absolute simplest plan they could to attack the targets they were interested in.

Therefore, I came to the conclusion that I had to dumb down my thinking as far as possible, to a level no higher than the level of a second- or third-grader, in order to figure out their plans. After I had dumbed down my thinking to this level, I continued my analysis. I was aware the target was going to be one that could be described as almost too obvious. It had to be a target that was huge and would result in massive civilian casualties. The al Qaeda terrorists had already waited three years from the date the Fatwa had been published. In my opinion, they would never spend this much time on a minor target.

After all of this analysis, I was still not able to figure out what the target was going to be. However I had put together enough of the details of the target and their plans, so that when I gave up and picked up the travel brochure with the picture of the World Trade Center Towers on it, I knew immediately this had to be what the al Qaeda terrorists had focused on.

Long after the fact, I have figured out why, when I had all of the information right at my fingertips, I was not able originally to put this all together at that time. I had been attempting to use an intellectual approach to find the target, the right-brain, and at the same time, I was trying to feel the right answer. This is not possible. This is not even remotely possible. The intellectual thinking process has no emotional component at all. It is in effect a dead brain. It cannot feel anything. It can give you answers but it will never give you any feeling at all whether this answer is correct or incorrect. It is simply not capable of doing this. Using an intellectual process was never going to even begin to work and produce an answer that would feel like the right answer.

When the picture of the WTC Towers came into focus, I was instantly just completely stunned. This was exactly the target I had been searching for. I had been looking for a target that would feel like the target the terrorists were going to attack. These buildings matched exactly the target I had been searching for. A pure intellectual process with exactly the same information failed to produce any result at all. The nonintellectual, emotional portion of the brain produced the correct result almost instantly. It also produced enormous amplitude, meaning to me that this answer had to be the right answer.

Assume I am new at counterterrorism

Next, I had asked: "When is this attack going to take place?" To answer this question, I started with the premise I was new at counterterrorism. I considered myself new to counterterrorism because after years of reading many magazines and newspapers on terrorism, I had never been aware bin Laden had 20 training camps in Afghanistan or had over 20,000 people go through these camps. Considering myself an untrained person on issues of terrorism was a key decision. This was the major decision, which resulted in an accurate time-line of this attack. The major implication of this decision was the conclusion this attack plan must have started long before I figured it out. It was then only a matter of time using trial and error until I had figured out the dates for the attack. With the bounding dates of February 1998 for the publishing of the Fatwa, and February 2001 (the date of my flight) for the estimate of the start of the execution phase of their plan, the phase where they started sending the al Qaeda terrorists into the US for pilot training, it was just a matter of time to calculate the calendar time-line for this attack, which would correlate to dates of their prior attacks. This estimated date might have been wrong, but I at the time I had no other information to use to produce a different estimate.

According to the 9/11 Commission, the primary failure of the intelligence organizations was a failure in having no imagination at these large agencies. Yet as shown from the description of the process I had used, no real imagination was required to put these events of 9/11 together, months prior to it happening. What was required was a creative approach to thinking about the problem, combined with a determined step-by-step, logical, common-sense analysis of each problem until they were solved one by one. The most critical first step was having enough confidence that these horrific and difficult puzzles could actually be solved in the first place. What was needed next was innovative ways to solve each problem, combined with the persistence to keep trying even after failing many times during trial-and-error attempts to find a solution.

What was also important, even before starting, was a complete understanding of the thinking of the top people at al Qaeda. And in particular not only an understanding of the almost unimaginable hatred bin Laden had for the US, but an internalization of this hatred, in the person doing the analysis.

Only by internalizing this hatred could you begin to understand his thinking and see the world through his eyes.

It is in fact this step that allowed the analysis to quickly figure out and see what apparently the intelligence agencies could not. Step by step, with nothing but plain common sense, each answer following each question came from the last step. No imagination was required, just a dogged determination to find the final answer through a number of very logical steps regardless of where they led, and the willingness to think the unthinkable. You had to be able to think the unthinkable if you were ever going to stop it from taking place.

Chapter 13

New information
that has come out since 9/11

The analysis done on the flight from San Francisco to Newark was triggered by my puzzlement over why the terrorists had published the Declaration of Jihad and the Fatwa. After considerable analysis at this time, I had concluded these documents, and the way they had been presented to the world, meant a huge attack against the US was in progress. This statement had in fact triggered the entire analysis. One could argue, however, that the interpretation of these documents was wrong. It could be argued the terrorists were in fact just venting their hatred of the US in these documents and when they were published worldwide, it meant nothing. This must have been the conclusion the CIA and the FBI had both come to, in view of their taking no serious notice of these statements.

This would imply that my analysis was faulty in spite of the fact it had resulted in determining almost every single detail of this attack of 9/11, even the week of the attack. It could further be argued that this was nothing more than a huge coincidence. Information since the events of 9/11 tends to confirm my original analysis.

A tape of the press conference that took place on May 28, 1998, where the Declaration of Jihad and the Fatwa were issued, was found by CNN after the fall of the Taliban in Afghanistan. This tape shows what occurred in this press conference. With Muslim journalists and terrorists in attendance, bin Laden presented his Declaration of Jihad and proclaimed this Fatwa. After his presentation one journalist, in perfect English, asked; "How could you (al Qaeda), declare war on the US, when the US is so big and you are such a small group?"

Bin Laden's answer, given in a barely audible monotone delivery was that every major movement in history had been started by a small number of dedicated people, and al Qaeda was just such a group. At this press conference, this journalist, along with most of the other people present, had determined almost immediately that the presentation of this Declaration of Jihad was in fact a public declaration of war against the US, a conclusion I had only come to after several hours of analyzing the thinking of these terrorists.

Next, as the camera panned around the room, sitting to the immediate right of bin Laden was Aymen Al-Zawahiri, and to his immediate right, Mohamed Atef. Sitting to the immediate left of bin Laden right at this press conference on May 28, 1998 were the two sons of Sheikh Omar Rahman, the blind cleric who had been the mastermind behind the 1993 attack on the World Trade Center.

When these al Qaeda terrorists put on a news conference, everything they do is symbolic. The two sons of Sheikh Omar Rahman, sitting to his immediate left could mean only one thing: bin Laden had again focused on the World Trade Center Towers.

What is even more prophetic is that this Fatwa being declared worldwide by bin Laden had actually been written by Sheikh Omar Rahman himself. The very person who had attacked the World Trade Center Towers in 1993 had written a Fatwa that was presented at this press conference by bin Laden as a public declaration of war against the US.

They literally could not have made it more obvious to the whole world that they were again going after the World Trade Center Towers at this point, if they had put this up in bright neon lights!

What had taken this journalist perhaps a few minutes had taken me several hours – just getting to this same point. Since I was not at this conference, I first had to understand the mindset of the top people in the leadership positions in al Qaeda, and then had to walk through the exact sequence bin Laden had followed in writing down and then presenting this Declaration to this news conference, in my mind.

Since September 11, 2001 other people have commented on this Fatwa. They have stated it had to be a declaration of war, and this was the signal the al Qaeda terrorists were possibly going to attack a target in the US. Even the President of the United States, in 1999, said this Fatwa issued in February 1998 had to be a de facto declaration of war against the US. What is so strange when so many people had come to this conclusion, why was this not made public?

If you went through this press conference, in your mind, and you could feel the hatred implied by these words, there was no other conclusion you could come to other than they were determined to attack inside of the US with some sort of terrorist attack. I had come to the conclusion this attack had to be of massive proportions intended to cause a huge psychological blow to the entire US. Bin Laden was going to settle some score against the US for what he thought were past injustices, which the US was possibly not even aware of. Perhaps the biggest injustice in his mind had been stationing of American military forces in Saudi Arabia.

What, however, the journalists at this press conference apparently did not picked up on was the fact this Fatwa had to be an indication bin Laden was now determined to attack inside the US. I had come to the conclusion that if he did not follow through on this attack, his whole organization would look foolish and weak, and al Qaeda would have then gone out of existence. Bin Laden had no way out after publishing this Fatwa in Muslim newspapers and this press conference. After this public news conference he was forced to proceed with his plans, or look like a complete fool to his followers.

What was different between the image I had had of this press conference, on the flight on February 11, 2001, and the actual videotape of this conference? It was bin Laden's tone of delivery. I had imagined a fairly animated delivery. Instead it was given with an almost inaudible monotone style of delivery without an ounce of emotion or even the slightest change of tone.

What can be said is his style of delivery fit the message, which itself appeared to be almost devoid of any emotion.

> **We – with God's help –-call on every Muslim who believes in God and wishes to be rewarded to comply with God's order to kill the Americans and plunder their money wherever and whenever they find it.**

One additional piece of information came out in the Joint Inquiry Committee sessions, in the testimony by George Tenet, on June 20, 2002, when he was explaining what the CIA knew about the plan for the attack on the World Trade Center Towers.

> *Bin Laden's determination to strike America at home increased with the issuance of the February 1998 fatwa*

targeting all Americans, both military and civilian. The ideas about destroying commercial airliners that had been circulating in al Qaeda leadership circles for several years appear to have been revived after that fatwa.

Although we lack details on exactly when the plan was formulated and received bin Laden's approval, we know that the planning for the attacks began three years before 11 September.

If there had been any doubt at all remaining that this Fatwa issued in February 1998 was the genesis for this huge attack on the World Trade Center Towers with hijacked aircraft, this was the key piece of intelligence indicating this plan went into operation soon after the issuance of this Fatwa. This was the key apparently missed by every single intelligence agency in the United States and missed by the entire US media, in spite of the fact these statements had been published worldwide in full view by both Muslim and non-Muslim newspapers.

An interview with two of the terrorists, Ramzi Bin al-Shibh and Khalid Shaikh Mohammed, on October 9, 2002, also confirms my original analysis, that the initiation or genesis for the attack on the World Trade Center Towers stemmed from the February 1998 press conference. This interview illustrates in almost unmistakable detail, the process al Qaeda went through for planning the attacks on 9/11.

The Plot, Oct. 9, 2002

Ramzi bin al-Shibh (CBS)

"They decided that the goal was to cause as many deaths as possible, to direct a big slap to America on American soil, in front of the world." Aljazeera *reporter Yosri Fouda (CBS)*

Khalid Shaikh Mohammed

(CBS/AP)

(CBS) Khalid Shaikh Mohammed, who bills himself as the mastermind of Sept. 11, has his own name for the attacks on America: "Holy Tuesday."

That is among the details emerging from a never-before-seen-in-America interview that Mohammed gave late last spring in Karachi to *Aljazeera* reporter Yosri Fouda, *60 Minutes II* correspondent Bob Simon reports.

Not only did Fouda interview Mohammed, whose role in the plot only became clear to American intelligence last spring, but he also spoke with Ramzi bin al-Shibh, Mohamed Atta's Hamburg roommate who was originally slated to be one of the four pilots leading the attack.

Invited to Karachi by al Qaeda, Fouda was driven blindfolded – with several changes of cars – to an apartment where he met the two men.

"Immediately Khalid introduces himself as head of the military committee of al Qaeda," said Fouda of Mohammed, a Kuwaiti of Pakistani descent who has terrorized Americans since 1993.

According to Khalid, that committee actually was the arm of al Qaeda that decided to strike America inside America, and also chose the targets that were actually hit on Sept. 11.

As Fouda described it, Osama bin Laden is the chairman of the board, and Khalid Shaikh Mohammed is the CEO, who gets things done.

Unlike Mohammed, bin al-Shibh was ready to do an interview for broadcast. In it, he said, "I do not regret any of this whatsoever, for this is our path and the end is best for the righteous, Allah willing. We will persevere with this until Allah the Almighty, grants us victory, or takes us to him as martyrs."

Intelligence sources say Mohammed directed the first World Trade Center bombing, as well as a 1995 plot to down a dozen American airliners in the Pacific and crash a plane into the CIA Headquarters. His operative in those plots was his nephew: Ramzi Yousef. But those attacks failed.

When Yousef was captured and jailed, Mohammed needed a new blueprint and a new master terrorist.

"You need a perfectionist if you are playing with America," Fouda told Simon. "And I think Khalid, for this reason, was lucky to find someone like Atta. With these qualities and at the same time with a lot of black smoke inside him."

The smoke had not turned black yet when a preppy-looking teenager known then as Mohamed El-Amir went to the American University in Cairo to learn English. The smoke started appearing in Hamburg, where the man we know as Mohamed Atta came to study city planning at a technical university. He was becoming increasingly religious and increasingly frustrated: he wanted to go back home to Cairo and get a job but saw few prospects.

Atta grew a beard to show solidarity with Muslim fundamentalists in Egypt. He was looking for a cause, and Khalid Shaikh Mohammed was looking for a candidate. It was a perfect match.

Atta was recruited by al Qaeda at the Al Quds mosque, hidden in a nondescript building in downtown Hamburg. So was a Yemeni student, Ramzi bin al-Shibh. In 1998, Atta and bin al-Shibh became roommates in Hamburg. The cell was forming, and the nucleus was Mohamed Atta.

"This brother was amazing, extremely amazing," bin al-Shibh is heard telling Fouda. "I have never come across anyone from among the brothers that I know who was more eager than him to perform the night prayers, to the point where I remember the neighbors complain about his reading of the Koran at night."

By the end of November 1999, Atta, bin al-Shibh and two other future pilots were sent to Afghanistan to an elite al Qaeda camp. Khalid Shaikh Mohammed and his military committee had drawn up a new plan for America.

"The first thing that jumped into their minds, according to Khalid, was striking at a couple of nuclear facilities in America," said Fouda. "That, according to him, was later taken off the list for fear it might get out hand."

When he pressed them on this, Fouda said, they said they were unwilling to take that much risk "for now."

Instead, the operation would strike at symbols of America's military, political and economic power. When Atta arrived in New York in June 2000, he carried with him a report on potential targets made by reconnaissance teams that had been sent to the US a year earlier.

"The White House, at that time, was on the list," Fouda said. "But one of the reconnaissance units went back and recommended that it should be taken out of the list for navigation reasons."

The Capitol took its place. At the top of the list was a site Khalid Shaikh Mohammed wanted to revisit with a vengeance: The Twin Towers. His new plan took elements of the World Trade Center bombing in 1993 and mixed them with the failed '95 operation to use American airliners as weapons.

"He said that during the meeting of his committee," Fouda reported, "they decided that the goal was to cause as many deaths as possible, to direct a big slap to America on American soil, in front of the world."

To deliver the slap, terrorists had to learn how to fly. By the summer of 2000, Atta and two of his comrades were looking for flight schools. Bin al-Shibh reveals why they chose Florida.

"The prices in America were convenient and the weather was ideal for more flying hours, especially in the coastal states like Florida," bin al-Shibh said. "And the term of study wouldn't take long."

Bin al-Shibh was supposed to join them, to become one of the four pilots. He applied for a US visa four times, and was turned down four times. Kept off the front line, bin al-Shibh stayed behind in Hamburg and became the link between Atta in Florida and Khalid Shaikh Mohammed in Afghanistan. Atta often used hard-to-trace Internet chat rooms to send messages to bin al-Shibh in Hamburg.

Atta posed as a student writing to his girlfriend Jenny, code for bin al-Shibh. The targets were given code names, too. The Twin Towers were called the "faculty of city planning," Atta's major at the university. Reflecting a hatred of skyscrapers, he decided to make the World Trade Center target his very own.

"It's very ironic, very bitter. And in some ways, of course, very sick," said Fouda.

Atta and his two comrades had their pilot's licenses. According to bin al-Shibh, their studies were almost complete: "All that was left for them to do was master flying in simulators of big jumbo jets. Also, to study the security arrangements at the airports, like John Kennedy Airport, for instance."

In early 2001, a fourth pilot, a Saudi, was found to replace bin al-Shibh. Then, it was time to choose the hijackers, those who would actually take over the planes.

"About five months before the zero hour, the foot soldiers, or so-called muscles, were chosen," Fouda said.

Khalid Shaikh Mohammed said his problem was that he had too many volunteers.

Mohammed told Fouda he plucked more than a dozen Saudis out of what he called the Department of Martyrs in Afghanistan. Each recorded a video before leaving for the US. The Saudis knew they were going to die; they just didn't know how.

"It was unwise for a brother to know all the details of the operation while he was still in Afghanistan," bin al-Shibh was heard saying. "Too much information would be a security disaster."

As the Saudis were arriving in the US in July, Atta was taking off, flying into Madrid and driving 500 miles to a Spanish coastal resort for a working vacation. Joining him was bin al-Shibh with a message from Khalid Shaikh Mohammed. The final date for the operation was in Atta's hands. Atta had Shaikh Mohammed's complete trust.

"I think Atta, as far as Khalid is concerned, was the perfect soldier," said Fouda. "He's highly educated, he's sophisticated. He's very organized."

As the summer wore on, intelligence services around the world detected increased chatter from al Qaeda.

Just days after Atta returned to the US from Spain, Egyptian intelligence in Cairo says it received a report from one of its operatives in Afghanistan that 20 al Qaeda members had slipped into the US and four of them had received flight training on Cessnas.

To the Egyptians, pilots of small planes didn't sound terribly alarming, but they passed on the message to the CIA anyway, fully expecting Washington to request information. The request never came.

That wouldn't have surprised Mohamed Atta. Bin al-Shibh says Atta had very little respect for the CIA or the FBI: "Mohamed used to belittle the security services and he never used to give them much thought."

In the States, Atta and pilots Marwan Al-Shehhi and Ziad Jarrah began taking cross-country flights to check things out. They usually treated themselves to first class. The hijackers determined that the best time to attack the cockpit was during the 15 minutes after takeoff.

"The group storming the cockpit is formed of two persons," bin al-Shibh is heard saying. "It would be the nearest group to the cockpit, in order to seize the opportunity when the door is opened and enter into it swiftly, take it over and slaughter those inside completely. And then the brother pilot comes very quickly to assume the rest of the mission and guide the aircraft."

In August, Atta and the other pilots wanted a closer look at their targets. "This was the phase for studying the targets, whether from the ground or the air, be it from normal travel by plane or by renting planes and flying over these targets from a close range," bin al-Shibh said.

Mohamed Atta had rented a plane for a final peek at the World Trade Center. Then, on August 29, the phone rang in bin al-Shibh's Hamburg apartment at three in the morning.

It was Atta with an important, but cryptic message: "He said to me, 'One of my friends related a riddle to me and I cannot solve it, and I called you so that you can solve it for me,'" bin al-Shibh is heard saying.

Atta goes, "Two sticks, a dash and a cake with a stick down."

Bin al-Shibh said, "I said to him, 'is this the riddle? You wake me from a deep sleep to tell me this riddle? Two sticks and I do not know what?'"

Eventually, Fouda says, bin al-Shibh realized what Atta meant. So he says to him, "OK. Tell your friend, he has nothing to worry about. It's such a sweet riddle."

Bin al-Shibh explained it: "The two sticks represent the number 11, then the dash, and then the cake from which a stick dangles represents number nine. Thus, the picture becomes complete: the 11th of September."

Bin al-Shibh left Hamburg on Wednesday, September 5, for Pakistan. From there, he sent a messenger into Afghanistan with news for Khalid Shaikh Mohammed and Osama bin Laden: Tuesday, September 11, would be the day.

In America, Atta, the city planner, was getting ready to destroy a city, getting ready to finish the job Khalid Shaikh Mohammed had started years before.

Even when he saw the carnage, bin al-Shibh, in Pakistan, felt no remorse: "No sane Muslim doubts that the operations of the blessed day of Tuesday, on the 11th of September in Washington and New York, was one of the glorious days of the Muslims," he said.

In fact, both bin al-Shibh and Shaikh Mohammed had hoped for a much higher death toll. Even so, they want history to record what they did accomplish.

Bin al-Shibh gave Fouda a manifesto justifying the attacks in the name of Allah, and asked him to hand it over to the Library of Congress.

Now, it seems, bin al-Shibh will get all the recognition he wants – in an interrogation room.

His brazenness caught up with him and, on September 11, 2002, his voice on the audiotaped interview was matched to a phone call.

A year to the day after he helped murder thousands, he was captured in Karachi, the same city where he had granted the interview to Fouda.

Khalid Shaikh Mohammed, the mastermind, with a $25 million reward on his head, remains at large.

American intelligence sources admitted to *60 Minutes II* they've lost his trail. All they have is a chilling question: After orchestrating the '93 World Trade Center bombing and September 11, what's next?

Another rendition of this same interview added the following information:

At the end of 1998, Fouda says, Atta and several other planners moved to 54 Marienstrasse in Hamburg, which he describes as "the kitchen of the September 11 operation."

Khalid Shaikh Mohammed says, "We had a large surplus of brothers willing to die as martyrs. As we studied various targets, nuclear facilities arose as a key option." Fouda says nuclear targets were dropped for fear they could "get out of hand."

Bin al-Shibh and Mohammed say that when al Qaeda forces attacked the *USS Cole* in Yemen in October 12, 2000, leaders of the organization were already preparing for a larger operation they knew would kill large numbers of civilians.

In that year, some of the hijackers began taking flight lessons in Florida and Arizona, acquiring just enough training to fly large planes into their targets.

Security breakdowns

At this point in the documentary, Fouda discusses security breakdowns, including one that allowed Khalid Al-Mihdhar, a Kuwaiti who was on the US "most wanted" terrorist list, to enter the country two months before the attacks. He was on the plane that crashed into the Pentagon.

He also describes the failed efforts by an FBI agent in Minneapolis to alert her superiors to accused terrorist Zacarias Moussaoui, and a memo from an Arizona agent who reported an unusual number of Arabs taking flying lessons, which was not acted upon.

About three weeks before September 11, targets were assigned to four teams, with three of them bearing a code name: The US Capitol was called "The Faculty of Law;" the Pentagon became "The Faculty of Fine Arts;" and the North Tower of the World Trade Center was code-named by Atta as "The Faculty of Town Planning."

One of the terrorists, Abu Abdul Rahman, pretended to send a love message via an Internet chat room to his German girlfriend, who was actually bin al-Shibh. It contained more code for the attacks:

"The first semester commences in three weeks. Two high schools and two universities.... This summer will surely be hot ...19 [the eventual number of hijackers] certificates for private education and four exams. Regards to the professor. Goodbye."

Soon after, Fouda says, the hijackers began "moving fast," picking the flights to be hijacked, choosing ones involving large planes with "maximum volume of fuel and best punctuality."

Seats in business class were chosen for some to allow for "mobility and maneuverability," according to bin al-Shibh.

Atta calls with a puzzle

Bin al-Shibh gives an account of an early morning phone call from Mohammad Atta, who said he needed help solving a puzzle:

"He [Atta] said, 'Two sticks, a dash and a cake with a stick down. What is it?' I said, 'Did you wake me up to tell me this puzzle?' As it turns out, two sticks is the number 11, and a dash is a dash and a cake with a stick down is the number 9. And that was September 11."

At this point, over graphic images of the September 11 attacks and related events, the documentary has quotations from some of the hijackers bolstering their courage with quotes from the

Quran and expressing assurances that they will be rewarded as martyrs.

Bin al-Shibh describes watching the attacks with others: "The brothers shouted, Allah-u-Akbar, thanks to God, and cried. Everyone thought that this was the only operation. We said to them, 'Wait, wait.'"

"Suddenly our brother Marwan was violently ramming the plane into the [World Trade Center] in an unbelievable manner! We were watching live and praying: God ... aim ... aim ... aim."

At the close, Professor Dittmar Machule, a former teacher of Atta, says, "The first thing I would say to Mohammed: 'Why?'"

The question is followed by a quote attributed to Osama bin Laden: "We treat them in the same way. Those who kill our women and innocent, we kill their women and innocent, until they refrain."

Finally, Fouda appears on camera saying: "Westerners, Americans in particular... should now question what would drive a group of young men, some of them highly educated... some among the richest of Arabs, and all in their youth, to voluntarily throw themselves into what Americans see as perishment, but to them is paradise."

And parts of a version from the Australian, of September 9, 2002

Now it was clear. Khalid and Ramzi were the two master planners of 9/11 – relaxed, calm and willing to speak. For the first time the men behind the Twin Towers operation had decided to break their silence.

They swiftly began to explain the planning and execution of "Holy Tuesday" – or the Manhattan and Washington raids, as they also call them, using an old Arabic word, ghazwah, which refers to a raid against enemies of the prophet.

"About 2½ years prior to the holy raids on Washington and New York," said Khalid, "the military committee held a meeting during which we decided to start planning for a martyrdom operation inside America."

He continued: "As we were discussing targets, we first thought of striking at a couple of nuclear facilities but decided against it for fear it would go out of control."

It was Khalid, as chairman of the al-Qa'ida military committee, who had come up with the proposal that the "martyrdom operation" in the US should target prominent buildings.

Superficially his plan was similar to an earlier one to send 12 airliners simultaneously into US landmarks.

Intelligence agencies know about this previous Bojinka plot, as they call it, because it went disastrously wrong. Khalid had worked on it in 1994-95 with his nephew Ramzi Yousef, who was on the run after the first World Trade Centre bombing. Hiding in Manila, Yousef had worked on bomb designs and initial logistics. Fleeing when bomb chemicals in his apartment caught fire, he left behind a laptop containing details and was arrested within months in Pakistan.

There has been much conjecture over the past year about when Atta and the other key figures were first recruited. Khalid's story confirmed that, working and studying in Hamburg as a town planner since 1992, Atta was an al Qaeda sleeper. During 1999 he and other sleepers were earmarked by the military committee as pilots for the death flights.

Late that year they got together to start detailed planning. They met in the dust and dirt of Kandahar in southern Afghanistan, the effective capital of the Taliban. Their gathering place was a building often used by volunteers from Saudi Arabia. It was even known as al-Ghumad House, after the Saudi al-Ghamdi clan – four of whose young members would be foot soldiers in the hijackings.

"There was a shura [council] consisting of the four pilots, as well as Khalid al-Mihdar and Atta's deputy, Nawaf al-Hazemi," said Ramzi, naming other key figures. It had never been revealed before that al-Hazemi was Atta's second-in-command. He was with Hani Hanjour on American Airlines Flight 77, which crashed into the Pentagon.

Khalid revealed: "After the shura we sent at least four reconnaissance units to America in pairs or singles over the space of five to six months." Also shortly after the shura, Atta left for Germany – where, to avoid questioning over the Pakistani visas that his passport contained, he reported it stolen.

Two of the other young men at the shura – Marwan al-Shehhi, who was to pilot United Airlines Flight 175 into the South Tower of the World Trade Centre, and Ziad Jarrah, who flew UA Flight 93, which crashed in Pennsylvania – reported their passports stolen, too.

The next stage was to learn the rudiments of flying. In the summer of 2000 Atta entered the US and began flying lessons in Venice, Florida, along with al-Shehhi. Jarrah was nearby in another training school. Hanjour, already a trained pilot, was undergoing further training in Arizona.

In July, Atta flew from the US to Madrid, where he met Ramzi and other al-Qa'ida operatives to finalise details. It was agreed Atta would have full control over the choice of targets and the timing of the attacks. An elaborate code was agreed so that Atta could keep in touch with his al-Qa'ida commanders via e-mail and Internet chat rooms.

What is revealed in this interview confirms many of the details of the plan of 9/11 I had come to on the flight on February 11, 2001:

> Bin al-Shibh says Atta had very little respect for the CIA or the FBI: "Mohamed used to belittle the security services and he never used to give them much thought."

I had come to the conclusion the FBI and CIA would do nothing to stop this attack. In my opinion, they were just not proactive in trying to either understand the al Qaeda organization, or in attempting to figure out beforehand what they may have been up to. I also felt that as long as the terrorists kept their plans secret they would be in very little danger of discovery and arrest.

> The Saudis knew they were going to die; they just didn't know how.

> "It was unwise for a brother to know all the details of the operation while he was still in Afghanistan," bin al-Shibh was heard saying. "Too much information would be a security disaster."

It was clear secrecy was going to be one of their most important weapons. They would do everything they could to limit the information on their plan to just the people who needed to know it. Why was it not obvious to the large security agencies? If they were going to stop any attack, they would have to become proactive to figure out what the terrorist organization was up to.

> Instead, the operation would strike at symbols of America's military, political and economic power. When Atta arrived in New York in June 2000, he carried with him a report on potential targets made by reconnaissance teams that had been sent to the US a year earlier.

"The White House, at that time, was on the list," Fouda said. "But one of the reconnaissance units went back and recommended that it should be taken out of the list for navigation reasons."

The Capitol took its place. At the top of the list was a site Khalid Shaikh Mohammed wanted to revisit with a vengeance: The Twin Towers. His new plan took elements of the World Trade Center bombing in 1993 and mixed them with the failed '95 operation to use American airliners as weapons.

The target they were going to attack had to have a great deal of symbolic importance. Attacking such a target would deal a huge psychological blow to all of America. It was clear why the World Trade Center Towers were at the top of their list of targets. As I was trying to list the targets, I had come to the conclusion the White House was a target that was too hard to hit; it was simply too small. I had come to the conclusion, based on the magnification analysis, that the terrorists would not attack the Pentagon or the Capitol Building since the magnification factor for these two buildings was so much lower than for the World Trade Center Towers.

"He said that during the meeting of his committee," Fouda reported, "they decided that the goal was to cause as many deaths as possible, to direct a big slap to America on American soil, in front of the world."

To deliver the slap, terrorists had to learn how to fly. By the summer of 2000, Atta and two of his comrades were looking for flight schools. Bin al-Shibh reveals why they chose Florida.

"The prices in America were convenient and the weather was ideal for more flying hours, especially in the coastal states like Florida," bin al-Shibh said. "And the term of study wouldn't take long."

It was clear why the terrorists would use hijacked aircraft to attack the World Trade Center Towers. There was simply no other way this attack could be carried out as far as I could see. In order to use hijacked airliners, the terrorists would have to learn how to fly large US aircraft. I had further concluded the terrorists would start coming into the US as early as February 2000 in order to select and then attend flight schools. I had estimated that they would start taking their flight training by May 2000, three months after first entering the US. In the interview, it says they started looking for flight schools in the summer of 2000. Mohammed Atta had written to a number of flight schools from Germany in March 2000, in order to select schools for the terrorists coming from Hamburg.

Atta was recruited by al Qaeda at the Al Quds mosque, hidden in a nondescript building in downtown Hamburg. So was a Yemeni student, Ramzi bin al-Shibh. In 1998, Atta and bin al-Shibh became roommates in Hamburg. The cell was forming, and the nucleus was Mohamed Atta.

I had come to the conclusion this plan was being run by a single person, the person I would call the "ramrod." In order for this person to go through flight school, I had come to the conclusion they would have to have been well educated and to possess a good command of the English language. When I was trying to figure out why a highly educated person would want to commit suicide, I had come to the conclusion that this person must have undergone years under very high stress (bin al-Shibh refers to this as "smoke inside of him"), and hence would have to have been in his early 30s. It was this stress that I felt would tip him over the edge and make him vulnerable to al Qaeda recruiters searching for recruits in European mosques.

It is clear, after the fact, the years Mohamed Atta had spent to pursue a career in city planning and architecture created an enormous stress within him. The stress would have come from not knowing if it was going to be possible to get a job in his profession once he went back to Egypt. It would have been almost unimaginably humiliating for him to undergo years of expensive training in Germany and then to go back to Egypt and find no jobs in his chosen profession. When his worst fears were realized and he found it impossible to get work back in Egypt, Atta was transformed into a person who started to drift into radical Muslim philosophies. This made him vulnerable to the efforts of the al Qaeda recruiters. If he could not succeed in life, he would succeed in death, in one spectacular glorious event, as what must have been described by the words of the al Qaeda recruiter, "in the defense of Islam." This is the argument the al Qaeda recruiters must have used to lure him and ultimately his friends into their plan.

It is clear that once the "ramrod" (Atta) had been recruited, he would bring the other recruits into this plan by the strength of his personality to be trained as pilots and then keep them in line until the hijacking actually took place. It was inconceivable to me that four or more very well educated people would spend at least one year getting flight training and then they would all be equally willing to commit suicide in one horrendous act. This person would also ensure that all four teams of terrorists would come together at the right time in the US for the ultimate attacks on 9/11.

> "About 2½ years prior to the holy raids on Washington and New York," said Khalid, "the military committee held a meeting during which we decided to start planning for a martyrdom operation inside America."

This works out to be February or March 1999, the exact month I had estimated they had started their planning in Afghanistan. I had used a process of reduction to find what I had called the time for their "focus of attention," the one year I had estimated they needed in Afghanistan to plan for this attack prior to sending the pilots into the US.

> It was Khalid, as chairman of the al-Qa'ida military committee, who had come up with the proposal that the "martyrdom operation" in the US should target prominent buildings. Superficially his plan was similar to an earlier one to send 12 airliners simultaneously into US landmarks.

This clearly says that the Bojinka plot was the precursor for the attack on 9/11. Both the FBI and the CIA had been aware of the Bojinka plan and Khalid Shaikh Mohammed's involvement with this plan since 1995.

> Khalid revealed: "After the shura we sent at least four reconnaissance units to America in pairs or singles over the space of five to six months."

The PDB (President's Daily Brief) sent to the President of the United States on August 6, 2001 makes the following statement:

Nevertheless, FBI information since that time indicates patterns of suspicious activity in this country consistent with preparations for hijackings or other types of attacks, including recent surveillance of federal buildings in New York.

Was this what Khalid Shaikh Mohammed referred to when he says "we sent at least four reconnaissance units to America" in 1999?

In hindsight I had made a major mistake in my analysis

There was at least one enormous error in my analysis. The mistake I made was due to the fact that the analysis I had done required all three parts of the brain and not two as I had first assumed.

In trying to come up with a reasonably quick method to analyze the thinking of al Qaeda and understand the message in the Fatwa, I had concluded the human brain had two parts: the intellectual part, the right-brain, and the emotional part, the left-brain. I had concluded it was going to be too hard to do a quick analysis of how the terrorists think using the intellectual part of the brain. In fact I had come to the conclusion, after getting nowhere with the intellectual approach, that this analysis could only be done quickly using the left side or the emotional part of the brain.

What I did not realize at the time was the fact the brain does not have two distinct parts when doing analysis. It has three distinct parts. The third part is the knowledge base. I had not even been aware, as I was doing the analysis on the thinking of the terrorists, that I was using knowledge based on my own thinking and the knowledge of the terrorists could be significantly different. After standing in front of the World Trade Center Towers on February 14, 2001, I had concluded each tower would surely collapse even from the collision with a single large airliner. If the collision itself did not bring them down, the resulting fire would certainly cause these buildings to collapse. You could come to no other conclusion after viewing these building up close at night.

I had assumed the terrorists must also have been in front of these towers at night, and must have seen the same thing. They would have seen these buildings were not built like ordinary steel towers, but were built with almost no internal steel beams for vertical support outside of a central core.

However, instead of concluding these building would collapse, the terrorists must have assumed that after being hit with a large airliner, several floors would be destroyed from the collision, but the building would basically remain standing. When you do a magnification analysis with this scenario, and you conclude most of the buildings' occupants would escape, the attacks on the

Pentagon and the Capitol would then have approximately the same relative magnitude as the attacks on the WTC Towers.

I had never come to this conclusion. It was inconceivable to me these structures would not collapse and I could never have even imagined the terrorists not thinking the same thing.

The major problem with the type of analysis is you are completely unaware of how your own knowledge has affected your analysis, and it becomes difficult to go back and say others might have come to a different conclusion because they had a different knowledge base.

Chapter 14

9/11 Commission hearings

How could we have been so surprised?

The big question is not how I figured this all out, when in the final analysis it was not all that hard but why had the FBI and CIA not done the same type of analysis? When I was originally trying to answer this question, it appeared there were several reasons for this.

One reason could have been that while virtually my entire analysis had relied on publicly available information, the US intelligence agencies might view this type of information with complete disdain. Having been in the intelligence business for years, they might have felt that valuable and useful information came only from uncovering secrets. If indeed they had actually ignored publicly available information, then they had cut themselves off from perhaps the most voluminous and valuable information that had been available. It was my opinion, at the time I had done my analysis that in particular printed materials actually written by the top people at al Qaeda was absolutely essential when attempting to understand their mindset. Without actually seeing this information for the value it had and then using it to do their analysis, these intelligence agencies had in effect severely crippled their entire analysis efforts from the start.

Another reason might have been that large bureaucracies, once a direction has been picked for their organizations, have a very hard time redirecting their activities in a different direction, or even to changing their way of thinking, their mindset. Once set in a given direction based on their current mindset, everyone will have been given a job or assignment, and redirecting people to completely new activities becomes very difficult.

In addition, a criminal investigating organization like the FBI can in most cases never use speculation. They require hard facts, facts that can be verified, and will lead down a trail to find even more facts. Indeed, this is how the FBI does its most important investigations. After being trained from day one on getting and using hard verifiable facts, since criminal trials require impeccable fact-finding and multiple ways to verify these facts in court, FBI investigators would be trained to avoid putting much weight on speculation, especially speculation done by persons outside of the FBI itself.

An intelligence organization such as the CIA uses only information that has been properly vetted, information from satellites, or from other intelligence agencies, or from their own covert field agents. They apparently do not start with speculation, but only from vetted information. Unfortunately, the terrorists must have known this also. As long as they remained completely secret with their plans, they knew no one was set up to stop them.

As the Joint Inquiry Committee of the Senate and House went forward with their investigation and hearings, and then the 9/11 Commission undertook an investigation, it was becoming more and more apparent the CIA and the FBI did have significant information on a number of these terrorists prior to 9/11. However, according to the heads and managers of these agencies, even with this information, they all claimed there was absolutely no way to figure out the events of 9/11, in effect connect the dots, ahead of time. America was told that 19 mostly high school graduates with a budget of few hundred thousand dollars were in effect either so smart or so lucky that they had outwitted the 11,000 agents of the FBI and the 5,000 officers of the CIA with their multi-billion-dollar budgets. The staff statement of the Joint Inquiry Committee described the activity of the large US intelligence agencies in the following way:

> As the horror and sheer inhumanity of that day engulfed this nation, all of us struggled with the shock, the utter disbelief, and the inevitable search for answers. The questions, if not the answers, were obvious: How could we have been so surprised? What did our government, especially our intelligence agencies, know before September 11, 2001? Why didn't they know more? What can we do to strengthen and improve the capabilities of our intelligence agencies and, as a result, help save ourselves, and our children, from ever having to face this again?

Much of the Joint Inquiry Committee investigation was going to focus on the same questions I had. To provide insights, which perhaps even the Joint Inquiry Committee was not aware of, I called their office in the fall of 2002, and offered to provide both direct testimony under oath, and summaries of the FBI interviews I had given to the FBI on how it was possible to figure out the events of 9/11, seven months prior to the actual events taking place.

I called the office of the Joint Inquiry Committee, and was able to talk to a Joint Inquiry Committees investigator, a Michael Jacobson. I went over orally in almost every single detail on how I been able to figure out the events of 9/11 on the flight in February of 2001. He directed me to send the FBI reports to another person on this committee, a Richard Cinquegrana. I forwarded the several FBI reports I had to Rick Cinquegrana, and with the exchange of several e-mails provided all of the information I had at that time. Rick agreed with the FBI agent who first interviewed me, that I should not feel guilty about not preventing this disaster. He said he felt the same way the FBI did, that if I had gone to the FBI in February with the information I had, they would not have done anything to stop this attack. I just had no way to corroborate my information; furthermore, the FBI had even more compelling information than I had. They had arrested a terrorist trying to obtain flight training on large US type aircraft in August 2001, and he had no reasonable explanation as to why he was doing this, nor could he explain the $32,000 in his bank account.

Even after closely following news reports of this investigation, it was not clear exactly what had gone wrong at these agencies or at the National Security Council, the agency most responsible for ultimately protecting the American people from terrorist attacks.

After the Joint Inquiry Committee report was published, the 9/11 Commission was formed and started its investigation of the intelligence agencies, the FAA, the NSC and the military to answer the broader question of what had gone wrong at all of these agencies. I called the 9/11 Commission in the winter of 2003-2004 as they were scheduling their remaining public hearings, and offered to give the same FBI summaries to them I had given to the Joint Inquiry Committee. Their web page had directed me to call a person named Al Felzenberg. When I called Mr. Felzenberg, and offered to send him all of this information, he said he would discuss this with the different Commissioners and then get back to me.

After a week went by, and I had not heard from him, I called his office. When I asked him again if they were interested in receiving information, and summaries of FBI reports on how it had been possible to figure out the details of the events of 9/11 prior to it taking place, he replied as follows:

"I have talked to the members on the 9/11 Commission and they have said they are not interested in knowing how anyone could have figured out the events of 9/11 ahead of time. Don't bother to send the summary of FBI interviews or the information you provided to the Joint Inquiry Committee. None of the 9/11 Commissioners has any interest at all at looking at these reports or knowing how someone could have figured this all out ahead of time."

Now this was truly amazing. I was getting this reply from the spokesman for the group chartered to figure why the intelligence agencies had been so surprised by the events of 9/11, and why these agencies had not been able to anticipate or prevent the events on 9/11. And yet, according to Al Felzenberg, none of the 9/11 Commissioners wanted to know how it could have been possible to figure out and prevent the events on 9/11 ahead of time. And I had thought all along this was exactly what they had wanted to find out.

This was probably the most dumbfounding thing I had ever heard. Here was the one independent commission assembled to find out why the FBI and CIA had been so surprised by these attacks and why they had not figured out what the terrorists were up to prior to this attack on 9/11, and here were summaries of FBI reports explaining in every single bitter detail exactly how these events could have been figured out ahead of time from just carefully analyzing material the terrorists had written down and published worldwide themselves, and yet the spokesman for the 9/11 Commission said they had no interest in this information at all. Had the FBI and CIA done the same type of analysis they might possibly have prevented the attack on 9/11. According to Al Felzenberg, the 9/11 Commission members were not at all interested in knowing how these events could have been uncovered ahead of time. This just did not make any sense to me at all. What a stunning and totally unexpected revelation.

In fact as I thought about this, I was curious how the 9/11 Commissioners were going to know if this information would be of interest unless they actually had a chance to review it? Was Al Felzenberg, who worked under the direction of Philip Zelikow (executive director of the 9/11 Commission) preventing what might be important information from reaching the 9/11 Commissioners? Was he spiking the information that went to the 9/11 Commissioners without the Commissioners even knowing it? The thought came up if Al Felzenberg was deliberately preventing the information I had from being considered by the 9/11 Commission, then what other possibly important information might he have kept from this group of Commissioners?

To find out if Al Felzenberg was indeed telling the truth, and whether the 9/11 Commission members really did not want to know how the events of 9/11 could have been uncovered ahead of time, I decided to fly out to Washington DC and attend the 9/11 Commission hearings scheduled for April 13-14, 2004.

Prior to going to the 9/11 hearings I dropped off a copy of the "9/11 Letters," which are included at the back of this book, at the office of Representative Anne Eshoo (D-CA). She was a member of the House of Representatives who happened to have an office not more than five blocks from my company's office in Palo Alto, CA. I dropped off all of the material I had, mostly e-mail correspondence and summaries of FBI interviews over 2½ years, from 9/11 to the spring of 2004, and said I would be in Washington DC for the 9/11 hearings on April 13-14. If they had any questions at all on any of the material and on any of the FBI reports, I would be more than happy to go over it when I was out there.

Two days later I got a call from a person who described herself on the phone as a House investigator. She said neither Anne Eshoo nor her office could help me in any way, and I should under no circumstances go to her office in Washington DC. I got the sense that I would not be welcome to visit her office in Washington DC. I informed the investigator that I was about to leave on a flight to Washington DC in order to attend the 9/11 hearings and had offered to go over the same material I was presenting to the 9/11 Commission with Anna Eshoo or her staff at her office if they so desired. I had offered to help them if they required it so they could also understand the material in the FBI reports, describing how it had been possible to figure out the events of 9/11 ahead of time.

All I can add is this experience was very enlightening. It was now becoming abundantly clear why the entire US government had so completely failed the country on 9/11, and allowed 3,000 innocent Americans to be murdered by religious fanatics. It was now obvious why the government had been so surprised by the events of 9/11. It can be best summed up with the following:

Ignorance, incompetence, failure, and even a complete lack of common sense ruled the day in Washington DC. It was almost as if Washington DC was surrounded by a high wall, with an arched entry way that had inscribed in the arch over this portal;

***To all those who would pass through this entryway,
You are now entering the land of the stupids.***

These people just simply did not care that 3,000 Americans had died on September 11, 2001. They had absolutely no interest at all in knowing how the deaths of 3,000 people who were murdered by religious fanatics could have been prevented. The House investigator had made this quite clear.

When an agency failed, all they had to do is go back to the same incomprehensibly incompetent politicians who had not only appropriated their funding in the first place and who had continually overlooked their obvious incompetence, and say the reason they had failed was they just did not have enough money or manpower. What a perfect excuse. The agencies in Washington DC never had to do what they had been chartered to do in the first place in order to keep Americans safe and secure. When they failed all they had to do was say they did not have the actual details of the attack because they did not have enough money and manpower, and this was why they failed. Failure in effect became the perfect excuse to ask for an increased level of funding.

And in the end, the politicians were going to keep relying on the same intelligence agencies that had failed them so completely in the past. These same agencies had failed them in the Bay of Pigs invasion, when the Soviet Union collapsed, when India and Pakistan tested nuclear weapons, when the Marine barracks had been blown up in Beirut, when the attack on Khobar Towers occurred, when the attack on the *USS Cole* occurred, when the events of 9/11 unfolded, and even when they said Iraq had weapons of mass destruction.

These agencies had failed in almost every way for any number of years with respect to forecasting and anticipating any of these events. And yet the politicians, regardless of these monumental failures, were going to rely on the CIA and the FBI and other dysfunctional agencies that had failed so many times in the past for intelligence.

The politicians now had the perfect excuse for failure. They could always say the intelligence was wrong or could have been better.

And the intelligence agencies had an equally good excuse for failure. They could just say the politicians had just not given them enough money.

It did not make any difference at all. In the case of the events on 9/11 the intelligence it was about to happen was overwhelming. In the case of weapons of mass destruction in Iraq, there actually was no intelligence. It made no difference in the slightest that the politicians or intelligence agencies didn't even believe what they themselves had said. They just assumed there were sufficiently large numbers of gullible Americans and dimwitted journalists who they could give them cover and keep their jobs. They had in fact raised failure and incompetence to a new art form.

This was a monumental revelation. Not only were these huge agencies incompetent, the congressional people were going to continue to rely on their erroneous input. It was obvious now that the most basic and simple form of common sense was never going to have any place in Washington DC.

On April 12, I flew out to Washington DC to attend the 9/11 hearing scheduled on April 13-14. I got to the hearing room at the Hart Senate Office Building early, in order to get a place close to the speakers, just behind the seats reserved for the many relatives who had lost family members on that horrific day. As I sat there listening to the testimony of George Tenet, James Pavitt, Louis Freeh, Tom Pickard, I was absolutely dumbfounded. The only word to describe it was dumbfounded. Speaker after speaker said they were very sorry, but they had failed. But the reason they had failed was their multi-billion-dollar budgets were simply way too small to have successfully combated these terrorists. And the thousands and thousands of employees they had were simply insufficient to do the job. They were simply overwhelmed and undermanned and the way to fix this was by greatly increasing their budget. These "heroes" (as they were described by Cofer Black) were simply inundated and overwhelmed by the huge volume of information they had to sort through.

And yet the thought kept crossing my mind, if a single person with absolutely no training or background at all in counterterrorism – in fact a person who had given this not one second's thought prior to this flight to Newark – could figure out the events of 9/11 in almost ever single detail in a few hours on this flight from San Francisco to Newark by reading and analyzing information from a single magazine, why could these agencies not have done the same thing with their tens of thousands of employees and multi-billion-dollar budgets? This just didn't seem to make any sense. In fact, this was just incomprehensible. Were all of the employees at these agencies just completely incompetent, or had the bureaucracy at these agencies stifled them to such an extent they could get nothing accomplished? Were these agencies so severely dysfunctional nothing could get done?

Incredibly, at these 9/11 hearings, the managers and directors of these agencies all said the reason they had failed was they were under funded and overworked. No mention at all on how close they had actually come to figuring out the events of 9/11 ahead of time. No testimony at all on how they had done their analysis, and then pointing out what had gone right in their analysis and what had gone wrong. No, they had just failed because "mistakes were made." According to George Tenet, there was just not enough "redundancy or fusion to overcome errors, errors that will happen in any human endeavor." Almost 3,000 Americans are murdered and this is attributed to simply that "mistakes were made."

When the testimony came to a breaking point, and I was sure Al Felzenberg had left the room, I went directly to several of the 9/11 Commission members and gave each of them a copy of the "9/11 Letters," the 100-page *dossier* I had compiled, with all of the summaries of the FBI interviews and the correspondence with the investigators on the Joint Inquiry Committee (this *dossier* is at the back of this book).

I gave the first copy to Robert Kerrey, one of the Commissioners I thought up to that point had asked the most intelligent and probing questions. From his probing questions to the managers of the intelligence agencies, it really appeared that he was desperately trying to understand what actually had gone wrong at these huge agencies. He looked through it briefly, read the introduction and conclusions I had come to. When he looked up, I explained I had figured out the events of 9/11 seven months beforehand, and these were the summaries given to the FBI and the Senate-House Joint Inquiry Committee investigators on how this had been done. Bob Kerrey looked at me and said, "You look like an upstanding person in the community, why aren't you working for the CTC (at the CIA)?"

At the time I was not familiar with the acronym CTC. However it was obvious this group had to be part of the government, so I replied, "Do you think if had I been working in the government, anyone would have believed me? I don't believe independent thought is tolerated at large government agencies. I would have been considered as a rogue or a maverick and gotten nowhere. This type of independent thinking is never tolerated in a large organization."

Then I asked him, "Did you get the e-mail I had sent earlier in the week to the New School, in New York City?" He replied he rarely had the time to look at his e-mail since he had such a large volume. So I pointed out the e-mail letter I had sent him, which was included at the back of the "9/11 Letters" and said, "This has to be the first time in history a hand-delivered letter has gotten to the destination before the actual e-mail." Mr. Kerrey said he would read over this material, turned around and went back to his seat for the continuance of the Commission hearings.

Since the hearings were not going to resume for a few minutes, I next went over to Tim Roemer, who was just about to sit down to resume the hearings, and I handed him the *dossier*. I then asked if he had a minute or two, I would explain what was in these papers. I explained I had known about the events of 9/11 approximately seven months before they occurred, and these were summaries of the several FBI reports of interviews I had given, along with e-mail correspondence I had with the Joint Inquiry investigators, with a step-by-step description of the analysis I had done to reach these conclusions. I asked him if he could read through this material when he had the time.

Finally at the end of the hearings for this day, as everyone was getting up top leave, I went over to Richard Ben-Veniste, just as he was getting up to leave, and handed him a copy of this material. I asked him if he had time so I could explain what was in this material. He said he was too busy and was late for another engagement. But he took the *dossier*, turned and left the hearing room.

The next day, as I was in the hallway leading into the hearing room in the process of picking up the staff statements and the written statements from the witnesses who were to present at the hearings, Tim Roemer passed by. As soon as he saw me, he came over, put his hand on my shoulder and asked, "How did you know the al Qaeda attack on 9/11 was specifically going to be directed at the World Trade Center Towers?"

At first I was just flabbergasted. My initial reaction was one of dumbstruck disbelief. How was it possible to have been involved on the 9/11 Commission for over a year and one half and still not know how the terrorists thought and how they picked their targets? Certainly the CIA must have told them before now how the terrorists actually thought. This was apparently not the case. So unprepared as I was, I tried my best to answer this question in terms I thought he could understand. I first said the analysis of the magnification of different targets had pointed out that this was indeed the target with the largest magnification. Magnification in this context meant the duration and extent of the headlines in European and Middle Eastern newspapers. And secondly, the COS (chance of success) analysis showed the many smaller target buildings that were possible targets would have a lower chance of success, while at the same time producing a lesser magnification.

In retrospect, had I thought about it beforehand, I would have answered as follows:

Tim, from the analysis I had done during a flight from San Francisco in February 2001, I concluded that the Fatwa bin Laden had issued in February 1998 was a nothing less than a public declaration of war against the US. I was convinced that after the top people at al Qaeda had released this document to the whole world, they were now determined to attack directly inside of the US. Nothing else I could think of made any sense at all other than this conclusion, for the motivation of these terrorists in publicly issuing this Fatwa.

From the attack on the East African embassies in August of 1998, I had concluded an attack on the US would have to be a signature event, meaning any attack inside the US would be focused on the biggest buildings located in the biggest US cities.

From the analysis of the attack on the Cole, I had concluded the terrorists had used as weapons secrecy, surprise, suicide and psychology. I further concluded they felt by using those weapons, they could successfully attack any target in the world.

In addition, the three-year delay from the publication of the Fatwa to the date of my flight without any attack inside the US convinced me the target had to be huge. They would, in my opinion, not waste this much time on a small target. The target also had to have great symbolic importance, which would immediately give the terrorists enormous worldwide press coverage. The attack itself had to result in a large numbers of civilian casualties. This in fact had to be one of their main objectives.

I was convinced the long intervals between their prior attacks, and the media exposure bin Laden had been courting, meant all of targets were either directly selected by him, or were in the final analysis directly approved by him. Since I had come to the conclusion that he had only a very limited knowledge of the US, the targets he selected had to have worldwide recognition and importance. He would simply not be aware of the many smaller buildings in the US. Hence when I went looking for the target of his next attack, after the Cole bombing, I felt the target he was going to select had to be a building that would be described as huge and "simply too obvious."

With all of this information, I still was not able figure this out. I was unable to come up with any suitable target at all, even after 45 minutes of intense concentration. At that point I put down the magazine I was reading and picked up a travel brochure, which happened to have a picture of the World Trade Center buildings right on the cover.

When I saw the picture of those towers, I knew immediately this had to be the target I had been looking for. All of the pieces of the puzzle fit perfectly at this point. In the final analysis, I had not figured this out with analytical thinking. I had figured this out through this hideous accident.

After attending the 9/11 hearings on April 14, 2004, I flew back to California. Even after the 9/11 Commission concluded their hearings in the summer of 2004 and released their report, it was not obvious why the intelligence agencies had failed. The huge amount of information these agencies actually had, which had come out during the 9/11 Commission and Joint Inquiry Committee hearings, their huge budgets, their thousands of employees, all indicated that they should have been able to have anticipated these terrorists and been able to prevent the events on 9/11. None this made any sense. After the release of the 9/11 Commission report, I was becoming more determined then ever to really find out what actually had gone wrong at these huge agencies.

All of the testimony in front of these commissions and committees seemed like nothing more than pathetic excuses for their failures. From the information that had come out of these investigations, it appeared these agencies had just not done the type of analysis required to uncover this plan ahead of time. These agencies had significant information prior to the events on 9/11, and had this information been followed up in a timely fashion, it seemed that these attacks should have been prevented.

In order to find out, and understand in my own mind exactly why these agencies had failed so badly and exactly what had gone wrong, I decided to go back over the testimony from both the Joint Inquiry Committee and the 9/11 Commission in great detail. When the redacted report from the office of the FBI Inspector General was released to the public, I went over this also, after first spending a day or two un-redacting the parts of the FBI Inspector General report that had been redacted.

Since I felt neither the Joint Inquiry Committee nor the 9/11 Commission had fully and adequately explained the failure of the intelligence agencies, my analysis of this information was going to be specifically addressed at understanding exactly this one question.

Why did these agencies so completely fail to anticipate and prevent the attacks on 9/11?

If one single person with a $10.00 magazine could put all of the important details of the attack on 9/11 together in two to three hours, literally sitting on an airplane, then why could the thousands of people at these agencies with their multi-billion-dollar budgets not have done the same thing? This just did not make any sense.

After going back over all of the incomprehensible testimony that I had heard at these hearings, I made a promise to myself to go over this information from these investigations until I was able to put all of this together and make some sense out of it. Even if all of the information was not available from these investigations at first, and it was not possible to put all of this together, time has a way of uncovering information. Even the most closely guarded secrets have a way of eventually leaking out of even the most secret organizations. I was convinced that with enough persistence and time I would ultimately find all of the answers and what was indeed the truth.

I was now on a mission, a mission that might even take years. This was now going to be my life's work. I was never going to give up until I was able to understand in every single bitter detail the reasons for the failures at these agencies, failures I was sure had directly contributed to making me feel that I had been the one directly responsible for the disaster on 9/11. And I had every possible motivation for doing this, immense anger, indescribable bitterness, but ultimately the hope that I could eventually feel that there was no way I could ever have prevented the events of 9/11.

Chapter 15

Joint Inquiry Committee testimony

The Joint Inquiry Committee of the Senate and the House investigated the intelligence agencies and issued its first set of findings in September 2002. This is the information gathered for the Joint Inquiry Committee that the investigators for this Committee had obtained by the fall of 2002. The entire Part 1 of this staff statement follows.

The questions, if not the answers, were obvious: How could we have been so surprised? What did our government, especially our intelligence agencies, know before September 11, 2001? Why didn't they know more?

Joint Inquiry Staff Statement, Part 1
Eleanor Hill, Staff Director
September 18, 2002

Introduction

Chairman Graham, Chairman Goss, members of this Joint Committee, good morning. I appreciate the opportunity to appear here today to advise the Committees, and the American public, on the progress to date of the Joint Inquiry Staff's review of the activities of the US Intelligence Community in connection with the September 11 terrorist attacks on the United States. As the horror and sheer inhumanity of that day engulfed this nation, all of us struggled with the shock, the utter disbelief, and the inevitable search for answers.

The questions, if not the answers, were obvious: How could we have been so surprised? What did our government, especially our intelligence agencies, know before September 11, 2001? Why didn't they know more? What can we do to strengthen and improve the capabilities of our intelligence agencies and, as a result, help save ourselves, and our children, from ever having to face this again?

On February 14, 2002, the leadership of these two Committees announced their resolve to come together to find credible answers to those sobering, but critically important questions. The Committees joined in an unprecedented, bicameral, and bipartisan Joint Inquiry effort to meet that challenge. With the support of the Senate and House leadership and the White

House, the Joint Inquiry focused its work on seven areas of investigation:

What the Intelligence Community knew prior to September 11 about the scope and nature of any possible terrorist attacks against the US or US interests by international terrorists, including by any of the hijackers or their associates, and what was done with that information;

Whether any information developed before or after September 11 indicates systemic problems that may have impeded the Intelligence Community from learning of or preventing the attacks in advance, or that, if remedied, could help the Community identify and prevent such attacks in the future.

My purpose today is to report to you on the results of the Joint Inquiry Staff efforts to date.

Any information obtained before September 11 suggesting that an attack on the US was imminent and what was done with it.

Any information obtained before September 11 that should have alerted the Intelligence Community to this kind of attack, i.e., using airplanes to attack buildings, and what was done with it.

Any information obtained before about the 19 dead hijackers, as well as Zacarias Moussaoui, and what was done with it; and

Any information obtained after September 11 about the hijackers and their background (including their involvement with al Qaeda), entry into this country and activities while in this country, and activities while in this country, as well as why they never came to the attention of the US government.

Many people instantly associate the term "Intelligence Community" with the CIA. When we use the term "Intelligence Community" we are referring to the group of 14 government agencies and organizations that, either whole or in part, conduct the intelligence activities of the US government:

Central Intelligence Agency (CIA)
Department of the Treasury
Department of Energy
Department of State
Defense Intelligence Agency (DIA)
Federal Bureau of Investigation (FBI)
National Imagery and Mapping Office (NIMA)
National Reconnaissance Office (NRO)
National Security Agency (NSA)

US Air Force Intelligence
US Army Intelligence
US Coast Guard Intelligence
US Navy Intelligence
US Marine Corps Intelligence

The Intelligence Community has multiple responsibilities with respect to counterterrorism, all of which are relevant to this Inquiry. Among the most important are:

Collecting, analyzing, and disseminating information regarding terrorist incidents and groups that perpetrate terrorism, including such things as how these groups are organized, who their leaders are, what their objectives are, their weapons and tactics, and whether they are receiving any support from any state sponsors.

Issuing warnings to policymakers to counter potential terrorist threats.

Preventing, preempting, and disrupting terrorist operations.

Supporting diplomatic, legal, and military operations against terrorism.

The Joint Inquiry is examining the Intelligence Community's performance to all these responsibilities as they relate to the attacks of September 11, 2001… With respect to the Intelligence Community's role in warning of impending terrorist operations, our review has focused on both strategic and tactical warning capability.

"Strategic Warning" is used to describe instances in which the Intelligence Community has very broad indications that an attack may occur but does not have the specifics as to where, when, or how the attack will be carried out.

"Tactical Warning" may be issued when the Intelligence Community has not only broad indications of an impending attack but also more detailed information on where, when, or how the attack might be carried out. Tactical warning enables policymakers and government decision-makers to direct preventive action against specific individuals who may be involved in the planned attack and to implement appropriate protective action for specific targets. Ideally, such action occurs before the attack ever gets underway.

The distinction is important because, so far as the Inquiry has been able to determine to date, the Intelligence Community did have general indications of a possible terrorist attack against the United States or US interests overseas in the spring and summer of 2001 and promulgated strategic warnings. However, it does not appear to date that the Intelligence Community had information prior to September 11 that identified precisely where, when and how the attacks were to be carried out.

From 1994 through as late as August 2001, the Intelligence Community had received information indicating that international terrorists had seriously considered the use of airplanes as a means of carrying out terrorist attacks. While this method of attack had clearly been discussed in terrorist circles, there was apparently little, if any, effort by Intelligence Community analysts to produce any strategic assessments of terrorists using aircraft as weapons.

Bin Laden's own words indicated a steadily escalating threat. In August 1996, Usama bin Laden issued a public fatwa, or religious decree, authorizing attacks on Western military targets in the Arabian Peninsula.

In February 1998, bin Laden issued another public fatwa authorizing and promoting attacks on US civilians and military personnel anywhere in the world. Following the August 1998 bombings of two US embassies in East Africa, Intelligence Community leadership recognized how dangerous bin Laden's network was. In December 1998, DCI George Tenet provided written guidance to his deputies at the CIA, declaring, in effect, "war" with bin Laden. By late 1998, the Intelligence Community had amassed a growing body of information, though general in nature and lacking specific details on time and place, indicating that bin Laden and the al Qaeda network intended to strike within the United States;

Concern about bin Laden continued to grow over time and reached peak levels in the spring and summer of 2001, as the Intelligence Community faced increasing numbers of reports of imminent al Qaeda attacks against US interests.

In July and August 2001, that rise in intelligence reporting began to decrease, just as three additional developments occurred in the United States: the Phoenix memo; the detention of Zacarias Moussaoui; and the Intelligence Community's realization that two individuals with ties to Usama bin Laden's network – Khalid al-Mihdhar and Nawaf al-Hazmi – were possibly in the United States. The two individuals turned out to be two of the 19 hijackers on September 11, 2001. The Intelligence Community apparently had not connected these individual warning flags to each other, to the "drumbeat" of threat reporting that had just occurred, or to the urgency of the "war" effort against Usama bin Laden.

The first World Trade Center bombing, the New York City landmarks plot, and the Bojinka Plot are significant, in terms of this inquiry, for several reasons:

- They indicated a growing threat from individuals who ascribed to a radical interpretation of Sunni Islam. Usama bin Laden emerged in this same time-frame as a promoter of this ideology.

- These plots involved efforts to inflict mass casualties.

- The incidents confirmed that international terrorists were interested in attacking symbolic targets within the United States, including the World Trade Center.

- Compounding the resource problems, the staff has been told by numerous individuals that al Qaeda proved an exceptionally difficult target for US intelligence. Details of major terrorist plots were not widely shared in the al Qaeda organization, making it hard to develop the necessary intelligence to preempt or disrupt an attack. In addition, senior al Qaeda officials were very sensitive to the need for operational security.

Central to the September 11 plot was Usama bin Laden's idea of carrying out a terrorist operation inside the United States. It has been suggested, both in published reports and in interviews, that prior to September 11, 2001, information available to the Intelligence Community had, for the most part, pointed to a terrorist threat against US interests abroad:

The Joint Inquiry Staff therefore requested and reviewed reports the Intelligence Community had prior to September 11, 2001 suggesting that an attack within the United States was a possibility. Our review confirmed that, shortly after Usama bin Laden's May 1998 press conference, the Intelligence Community began to acquire intelligence information indicating that bin Laden's network intended to strike inside the United States.

Several of these reports are summarized below:

In June 1998, the Intelligence Community obtained information from several sources that Usama bin Laden was considering attacks in the US, including Washington

DC and New York. This information was provided to senior US government officials in July 1998.

In the fall of 1998, the Intelligence Community received information concerning a bin Laden plot involving aircraft in the New York and Washington DC areas.

In April 2001, the Intelligence Community obtained information from a source with terrorist connections who speculated that bin Laden would be interested in commercial pilots as potential terrorists.

Usama bin Laden's declaration of war in February 1998 and intelligence reports indicating possible terrorist plots inside the United States did not go unnoticed by the Intelligence Community, which, in turn, advised senior officials in the US government of the serious nature of the threat.

Many individuals in the National Security Council staff and at the DCI's CTC interviewed by the Joint Inquiry Staff in the course of this Inquiry pointed to the August 1998 bombings of the US embassies in Africa as the moment in time when they recognized that bin Laden was waging war on the United States.

The Joint Inquiry Staff has also reviewed documents, other than individual intelligence reports, that demonstrate that, at least at senior levels, the Intelligence Community understood that bin Laden posed a serious threat to the domestic United States. Here are five examples of what we have found in our Inquiry thus far:

A December 1, 1998 Intelligence Community assessment of Usama bin Laden read in part: "UBL is actively planning against US targets... Multiple reports indicate UBL is keenly interested in striking the US on its own soil... Al Qaeda is recruiting operatives for attacks in the US but has not yet identified potential targets;"

In June 1999 testimony before the Senate Select Committee on Intelligence and in a July 1999 briefing to House Permanent Select Committee on Intelligence staffers, the chief of the CTC described reports that bin Laden and his associates were planning attacks in the United States; and

A classified document signed by a senior US government official in July 1999 characterized bin Laden's February

1998 statement as a "de facto declaration of war" on the United States.

What is less clear is the extent to which other parts of the government, as well as the American people, understood and fully appreciated the gravity and immediacy of the threat.

While the FBI's New York office was the lead office in the vast majority of counterterrorism investigations concerning Usama bin Laden, many other FBI offices around the country were unaware of the magnitude of the threat.

On a broader scale, our review has found little evidence, prior to September 11, of a sustained national effort to mobilize public awareness and to "harden" the homeland against a potential assault by bin Laden within the United States with the possible exception of heightened focus on weapons of mass destruction.

On August 20, 1998, in his address to the nation on military action against terrorist sites in Afghanistan and Sudan, President Clinton said: "A few months ago, and again this week, bin Laden publicly vowed to wage a terrorist war against America."

On July 6, 1999, in a Presidential statement on the national emergency with respect to the Taliban, President Clinton said: "To this day, bin Laden and his network continue to plan new attacks against Americans, without regard for the innocence of their intended victims or for those non-Americans who might get in the way of his attack."

On August 29, 2001, in remarks at the American Legion's 83rd Annual Convention, President Bush said: "We recognize it's a dangerous world. I know this nation still has enemies, and we cannot expect them to be idle. And that's why security is my first responsibility. And I will not permit any course that leaves America undefended."

Our focus in this section, however, is on what we have found regarding the level and nature of threat information that was obtained by the Intelligence Community during the spring and summer of 2001. Our review has confirmed that, at least in the eyes of the Intelligence Community, the world did appear increasingly dangerous for Americans in the spring and summer of 2001.

During that time period the Intelligence Community experienced a significant rise in information indicating that bin Laden and al Qaeda intended to strike against United States interests in the very near future. Some individuals Within the Intelligence Community have suggested that the increase in threat reporting was unprecedented, at least in terms of their own experience. While the reporting repeatedly predicted dire consequences for Americans, it did not provide actionable detail on when, where and how specific attacks would occur.

Between late March and September 2001, the Intelligence Community detected numerous indicators of an impending terrorist attack, some of which pointed specifically to the United States as a possible target:

Between May and July, the National Security Agency reported at least 33 communications indicating a possible, imminent terrorist attack. None of these reports provided any specific information on where, when, or how an attack might occur, nor was it clear that any of the individuals involved in these intercepted communications bad any first-hand knowledge of where, when, or how an attack might occur. If they did know, it was not evident in the intercepts. These reports were widely disseminated within the Intelligence Community.

In July 2001, the DCI's CTC was aware of an individual who had recently been in Afghanistan who had reported, "Everyone is talking about an impending attack." The Intelligence Community was also aware that bin Laden had stepped up his propaganda efforts in the preceding months.

On August 16, 2001, in Minneapolis, MN, the INS detained Zacarias Moussaoui. Prior to that date, in August 2001, Mr. Moussaoui's conduct had aroused suspicions about why he was learning to fly large commercial aircraft and had prompted the flight school he was attending in Minneapolis to contact the local FBI Field Office.

The events surrounding Mr. Moussaoui's detention will be discussed in greater detail in a future statement.

On August 23, 2001, the Intelligence Community requested that two individuals, Khalid al-Mihdhar and Nawaf al-Hazmi, who had first come to the attention of the Intelligence Community in 1999 as possible associates of Usama bin Laden's terrorist network, be added to the US

Department of State's watchlist for denying visas to individuals attempting to enter the United States.

Working levels of INS and US Customs Service had determined that at least one of them was likely in the United States, prompting FBI Headquarters to request searches for them in both New York and Los Angeles. The FBI's New York Field Office unsuccessfully searched for al-Mihdhar and al-Hazmi. The FBI's Los Angeles Field Office received the search request on September 11, 2001. On September 11, 2001, these two individuals were part of the team that hijacked United Airlines Flight 77 and crashed it into the Pentagon. We will examine in greater detail all of the Intelligence Community's actions regarding al-Mihdhar and al-Hazmi in a later statement.

On September 10, 2001, NSA intercepted two communications between individuals abroad suggesting imminent terrorist activity. These communications were not translated into English and disseminated until September 12, 2001. These intercepts did not provide any indication of where, when, or what activities might occur. Taken in their entirety, it is unclear whether they were referring to the September 11 attacks.

In June 2001, the Intelligence Community issued a terrorist threat advisory warning US government agencies that there was a high probability of an imminent terrorist attack against US interests by Sunni extremists associated with Usama bin Laden's al Qaeda organization. The advisory mentioned the Arabian Peninsula, Israel, and Italy as possible locations where an attack might occur. According to the advisory, the Intelligence Community continued to believe that "Sunni extremists associated with al Qaeda are most likely to attempt spectacular attacks resulting in numerous casualties."

Subsequently, intelligence information provided to senior US government leaders indicated that Usama bin Laden's organization expected near-term attacks to have dramatic consequences on governments or cause major casualties.

A briefing prepared for senior government officials at the beginning of July 2001 contained the following language: "Based on a review of all-source reporting over the last five months, we believe that UBL will launch a significant terrorist attack against US and/or Israeli interests in the coming weeks. The attack will be spectacular and designed to inflict mass casualties against US facilities or interests. Attack preparations have been made. Attack will occur with little or no warning."

On September 4, 2001, the FBI sent a lengthy teletype to the FAA and key components of the Intelligence Community setting forth facts about Moussaoui. The teletype noted that Moussaoui was being held in custody but did not describe any particular threat that the FBI thought he posed. The teletype also did not recommend that the addressees take any action or look for any additional indicators of a terrorist attack.

Intelligence Information on Possible Terrorist Use of Airplanes as Weapons

Central to the September 11 attacks was the terrorists' use of airplanes as weapons. In the aftermath of the terrorist attacks, there was much discussion about the extent to which our government was, or could have been, aware of the threat of terrorist attacks of this type and the extent to which adequate precautions were taken to address that threat. We therefore asked the question: Did the Intelligence Community have any information in its possession prior to September 11, 2001 indicating that terrorists were contemplating using airplanes as weapons?

Despite these reports, the Intelligence Community did not produce any specific assessments of the likelihood that terrorists would use airplanes as weapons.

While focused strategic analysis was lacking, the subject of aviation-related terrorism was included in some broader terrorist threat assessments, such as the National Intelligence Estimates (NIE) on terrorism. For example, the 1995 NIE on terrorism mentioned the plot to down 12 US-owned airliners. The NIE also cited the consideration the Bojinka conspirators gave to attacking CIA Headquarters using an aircraft loaded with explosives.

The FAA worked with the Intelligence Community on this analysis and actually drafted the section of the NIE addressing the threat to civil aviation. That section contained the following language:

"Our review of the evidence.. suggests the conspirators were guided in their selection of the method and venue of attack by carefully studying security procedures in place in the region. If terrorists operating in this country [the United States] are similarly methodical, they will identify serious vulnerabilities in the security system for domestic flights."

As a result of the increasing threats to aviation, Congress passed Section 310 of the Federal Aviation Reauthorization Act of 1996, requiring the FAA and the FBI to conduct joint threat and vulnerability assessments of security at select 'high risk" US airports and to provide Congress with an annual report. In the December 2000 report, the FBI and FAA published a classified assessment that suggested less concern about the threat to domestic aviation:

After September 11, 2001, the CIA belatedly acknowledged some of the information that was available regarding the use of airplanes as weapons. A draft analysis dated November 19, 2001, "The 11 September Attacks: A Preliminary Assessment," states:

"We do not know the process by which bin Laden and his lieutenants decided to hijack planes with the idea of flying them into buildings in the United States, but the idea of hijacking planes for suicide attacks had long been current in jihadist circles.

For example, GIA terrorists from Algeria had planned to crash an Air France jet into the Eiffel Tower in December 1994, and Ramzi Yousef – a participant in the 1993 World Trade Center bombing – planned to explode 12 US jetliners in midair over the Pacific in the mid-1990s. Likewise the World Trade Center had long been a target of terrorist bombers."

Despite the intelligence available in recent years, our review to date has found no indications that, prior to September 11, analysts in the Intelligence Community were:

Cataloguing information regarding the use of airplanes as weapons as a terrorist tactic;

Sending requirements to collectors to look for additional information on this threat; or

Considering the likelihood that Usama bin Laden, al Qaeda, or any other terrorist group, would attack the United States or US interests in this way.

We also have come to know – from our review of the intelligence reporting – the depth and intensity of the enemy's hatred for this country and the relentless zeal with which it targeted American lives. We understand not only the importance, but also the enormity of the task facing the Intelligence Community. As my statement this morning suggests, the Community made mistakes prior to September 11 and the problems that led to those mistakes need to be addressed and to be fixed.

Statement of Kristen Breitweiser
September 18, 2002

I would like to thank the families of the 3,000 victims for allowing me to represent them, here today, before the Joint Intelligence Committee. It is a tremendous honor. Testifying before this Committee is a privilege and an enormous responsibility that I do not take lightly. I will do my best not to disappoint the families or the memories of their loved ones.

Toward that end, I ask the members present here today to find in my voice the voices of all' of the family members of the 3,000 victims of September 11th. I would also ask for you to see in my eyes, the eyes of the more than 10,000 children who are now forced to grow up without the love, affection, and guidance of a mother or a father who was tragically killed on September 11.

My three-year-old daughter's most enduring memory of her father will be placing flowers on his empty grave. My most enduring memory of my husband, Ronald Breitweiser, will be his final words to me, "Sweets, I'm fine, I don't want you to worry, I love you." Ron uttered those words while he was watching men and women jump to their deaths from the top of Tower One. Four minutes later, his Tower was hit by United Flight 175. I never spoke to my husband, Ron, again.

I don't really know what happened to him. I don't know whether he jumped or he choked to death on smoke. I don't know whether he sat curled up in a corner watching the carpet melt in front of him, knowing that his own death was soon to come or if he was alive long enough to be crushed by the buildings when they collapsed. These are the images that haunt me at night when I put my head to rest on his pillow.

September 11th was the devastating result of a catalogue of failures on behalf of our government and its agencies. My husband and the approximately 3,000 others like him went to work and never came home. But, were any of our governmental agencies doing their job on that fateful morning? Perhaps the carnage and devastation of September 11th speaks for itself in answering this question.

Our intelligence agencies suffered an utter collapse in their duties and responsibilities leading up to and on

September 11th. But their negligence does not stand alone. Agencies like the Port Authority, the City of NY, the FAA, the INS, the Secret Service, NORAD, the Air Force, and the airlines also failed our nation that morning.

In closing, I would like to add one thought. Undoubtedly, each of you here today, because you live and work in Washington DC, must have felt that you were in the bull's-eye on September 11th. For most of you, there was a relief at the end of that day; a relief that you and your loved ones were in safe hands. You were the lucky ones. In your continuing investigation, please, do not forget those of us who did not share in your good fate.

Statement of Stephen Push
September 18, 2002

Chairmen Graham and Goss, Ranking Minority Members Shelby and Pelosi, and members of the Senate and House Intelligence Committees, my name is Stephen Push. I am a co-founder and Treasurer of Families of September 11, a nonprofit organization that represents 1,300 family members of victims murdered in the 9/11 terrorist attacks. On that day my wife, Lisa Raines, was a passenger on American Airlines Flight 77, the plane that crashed into the Pentagon.

First, I would like to thank you and the Joint 9/11 Inquiry staff for the vital work you are doing to understand the problems of the intelligence agencies and take steps to correct them. I appreciate the hard work you and the staff are doing to ensure that our loved ones will not have died in vain.

Second, I would like to thank you for inviting Kristen Breitweiser and me to testify today. I realize that your decision was not popular with bureaucrats in the Intelligence Community. But the victims' families greatly appreciate the opportunity to have their voices heard on the important work of your inquiry. Our loved ones paid the ultimate price for the worst American intelligence failure since Pearl Harbor. I hope that Kristen and I can do justice to their sacrifice and contribute in some small way to preventing other families from experiencing the immeasurable pain that accompanies such tragic loss.

While I eagerly await the final report of your inquiry, one thing is already clear to me based on news reports about the intelligence failures that led to the attacks: If the Intelligence Community had been doing its job, my wife would be alive today.

I realize that preventing terrorism is a difficult task and that we will never achieve absolute safety. But a series of missteps that defy common sense made the attack on the Pentagon possible.

In January 2000 the Central Intelligence Agency (CIA) learned that two Saudi nationals, Nawaf al-Hazmi and Khalid al-Mihdhar, attended an al Qaeda meeting in Kuala Lumpur. Thanks to the infamous "stovepiping" of information in the Intelligence Community, these two men, who were to become two of the hijackers of Flight 77, were not immediately placed on the terrorist watchlist and were allowed to enter the United States.

Shortly after the bombing of the USS Cole in October 2000, the CIA discovered that one of the men photographed with al-Hazmi and al-Mihdhar in Kuala Lumpur was a suspect in the Cole attack. But still the two suspected terrorists in the United States did not appear on the watchlist. The Federal Bureau of Investigation (FBI) seems to have been unaware of them, even though they lived with an FBI informant during part of their time in this country.

The two suspects were finally added to the watchlist on August 23, 2001. But on September 11 they were able to board Flight 77 using their own names. I don't know why it was called a watchlist; apparently no one was watching it.

After the Kuala Lumpur meeting, al-Hazmi had at least three meetings with Hani Hanjour, the terrorist believed to have piloted Flight 77. 1 am convinced that, had the CIA and FBI displayed any initiative, al-Hazmi, al-Mihdhar, and Hanjour could have been apprehended. With the loss of three of the hijackers, including the pilot, Flight 77 would not have been hijacked and the lives of the 184 people killed in the Pentagon attack would have been saved.

What's more, Mohammed Atta, the ringleader of the 9/11 conspiracy and pilot of the first plane to hit the World Trade Center, attended one of the meetings between al-Hazmi and Hanjour. Thus it's possible, if not likely, that surveillance of al-Hazmi could have led to surveillance of Atta and discovery of the other terrorists involved in the conspiracy. In fact the FBI, in an apparent attempt to pin the blame for 9/11 on the CIA, reportedly developed a chart that showed how timely access to the information about al-Hazmi and al-Mihdhar would have enabled the FBI to foil the entire 9/11 plot.

I won't belabor the argument about the possibility of preventing the 9/11 attacks. A number of intelligence experts have said that such preventive work is easier said than done. I don't know if that's a fair excuse, but one conclusion is incontestable: The 9/11 attacks exposed serious shortcomings in the American Intelligence Community.

Or to state this fact more precisely: The attacks exposed these flaws to the wider public. Many of the flaws had been know to intelligence professionals, to your two committees, and to a succession of commissions for years.

In voicing these complaints, it is not my intention to malign the Field Officers, agents, analysts, and technicians serving their country in the intelligence agencies. I'm sure most of them are competent and dedicated. But in many cases they seem to be stymied by a bloated, risk-averse, politicized intelligence bureaucracy that is more interested in protecting its turf than protecting America.

Initially I thought 9/11 would be a wakeup call for the Intelligence Community. But I was mistaken. The intelligence agencies and the White House have asserted that no mistakes had been made. That they couldn't possibly have conceived that anyone would use commercial jets in suicide attacks on buildings. That al Qaeda is impossible to penetrate. Such a "can't do" attitude is profoundly un-American. It also raises the question of why taxpayers should continue to provide the Intelligence Community with tens of billions of dollars annually if it cannot protect us.

In conclusion, I would like to thank you again for offering the 9/11 families this opportunity to have our voices – and the voices of our loved ones – heard on these important questions.

This is the unclassified testimony given to the Joint Inquiry Committee in June of 2002.

Testimony of George J. Tenet, Director CIA
Joint Inquiry Committee

Before Director Mueller and I focus on the 9/11 plot, as you've asked us to do Mr. Chairman, I would like to begin with some remarks on the context in which the attacks occurred. There are two key points:

- First, we had followed bin Laden for many years and had no doubt that he intended a major attack.

- Second, the 18 months prior to 9/11 were a period of intense CIA-FBI efforts to thwart dramatically heightened UBL operational activity.

We first locked onto bin Laden in the period from 1991 to 1996 when he was in Sudan.

- *Bin Laden jumped right to the top of our list with his move to Afghanistan in 1996 and his drive to build the sanctuary that subsequently enabled his most spectacular attacks. This focus resulted in the establishment within CTC of a bin Laden-dedicated Issue Station staffed by CIA, FBI, DOD, and NSA officers.*

- *Bin Laden showed his hand clearly that year when he said that the June bombing of Khobar Towers marked the beginning of the war between Muslims and the United States.*

- *Two years later, he issued a fatwa stating that all Muslims have a religious duty "to kill Americans and their allies, both civilian and military worldwide."*

- *He then attacked our East African embassies in 1998 and said that an attack in the US was his highest priority.*

- *We took this as his unequivocal declaration of war, and we in turn declared war on him, inaugurating an intensive period of counterterrorist activity that filled the months running up to 9/11.*

There were three broad phases in that struggle before 9/11 and I want to set the stage for the 9/11 plot by telling you about them:

- *And finally, the Pre-9/11 Period.* Starting in the spring and continuing through the summer of 2001 we saw a significant increase in the level of threat reporting. Again, working with the FBI and foreign liaison services, we thwarted attacks against US facilities and persons in Europe and in the Middle East.

- *Bin Laden himself – in a candid videotape found in Afghanistan after the attacks – said even some members of his inner circle were unaware of the plot.*

- *He also indicated that some of the hijackers themselves never knew the targets.*

- *Based on what we know today, the investigation of the 9/11 attacks has revealed no major slip in the conspirators' operational security.*

Let me start with what we knew before the 9/11 attacks:

- We knew, and warned, that Usama bin Laden and his al Qaeda organization were "the most immediate and serious" terrorist threat to the US. We said that in several ways, including in my statement to the SSCI in February 2001.

- In the months prior to 11 September, we alerted policymakers that operations that al Qaeda had in motion were likely to cause large-scale loss of life and be spectacular in nature.

- Beginning in June 2001, we received a barrage of intelligence indicating that al Qaeda associates in Afghanistan and abroad expected imminent attacks against unspecified US interests.

- Over the summer of 2001, it became evident that multiple attacks were in the works, especially abroad. Some of these were interdicted, such as planned attacks against US targets in Europe and the Middle East – successes for US intelligence.

- Finally, we knew – and warned – of bin Laden's desire to strike inside the US.

Malaysia

A major question surrounding the 9/11 investigation is how the United States government was able to identify two of the hijackers as al Qaeda but not uncover the plot they were part of. To explain how the intelligence case against Nawaf al-Hazmi (#14) and Khalid al-Mihdhar (#12) developed, I'll walk you through the case.

- We had learned in late 1999 that two suspect bin Laden operatives, "Nawaf" and "Khaled," were planning to travel to Malaysia. At that point we only knew of their first names, and only suspected that they might be bin Laden operatives because of a link between them and a facility known to be connected to al Qaeda and Egyptian Islamic Jihad operatives.

- Based solely on this tenuous link, the CIA initiated an operation to place "Khaled" under surveillance. Recall that we did not know either "Khaled's" or Nawaf's true identities at this time. The subsequent operation to learn more involved eight stations and bases and a half-dozen liaison services.

- Our interest in monitoring the meeting was based on our suspicion that "Khaled's" travel to Malaysia was associated with supporting regional terrorist plans or operations. We believed that the meeting was likely for discussion of regrouping from extensive disruptions around the world that the CIA had engaged in.

- In early 2000, just before he arrived in Malaysia, we acquired a copy of "Khaled's" passport, which showed a US multiple-entry visa issued in Jeddah in April 1999 and expiring on 6 April 2000.

- It is at this point that we learned that "Khaled's" name was Khalid bin Muhammad bin Abdallah al-Mihdhar (#12). This was the first point at which CIA had complete biographic information on al-Mihdhar.

- On 5 January 2000, the US Intelligence Community widely disseminated an information report advising that "Khaled," identified as an individual with ties to members of the bin Laden organization, had arrived in Malaysia.

- It was not until 5 March 2000 that we obtained information from one of our overseas stations that enabled us to identify "Nawaf" as Nawaf al-Hazmi (#14). This was the earliest time that CIA had full biographic information on al-Hazmi (#14). By that time, both al-Hazmi (#14) and al-Mihdhar (#12) had entered the US, arriving on 15 January 2000 in Los Angeles.

The Malaysia meeting took on greater significance in December 2000 when the investigation of the October 2000 *USS Cole* bombing linked some of Khalid al-Mihdhar's Malaysia connections with *Cole* bombing suspects. We further confirmed the suspected link between al-Mihdhar and al-Hazmi and an individual thought to be one of the chief planners of the *Cole* attack, via a joint FBI-CIA HUMINT asset. This was the first time that CIA could definitively place al-Hazmi and al-Mihdhar with a known al Qaeda operative.

In August 2001, because CIA had become increasingly concerned about a major attack in the United States, we reviewed all of our relevant holdings. During that review, it was determined that al-Mihdhar (#12) and al-Hazmi (#14) had entered the US on 15 January 2000, that al-Mihdhar had left the US on 10 June 2000 and returned on 4 July 2001, and that there was no record of al-Hazmi leaving the country. On 23 August 2001, CIA sent a Central Intelligence Report to the Department of State, FBI, INS, and other US government agencies requesting that al-Hazmi and al-Mihdhar be entered into VISA/VIPER, TIPOFF, and TECS (Treasury Enforcement Communication System). The message said that CIA recommends that the two men be watchlisted immediately and denied entry into the US.

The fact that earlier we did not recommend al-Hazmi (#14) and al-Mihdhar (#12) for watchlisting is not attributable to a single point of failure. There were opportunities, both in the field and at Headquarters, to act on developing information. The fact that this did not happen – aside from questions of CTC workload, particularly around the period of the disrupted Millennium plots – pointed out that a whole new system, rather than a fix at a single point in the system, was needed.

Conceptualization

We now believe that a common thread runs between the first attack on the World Trade Center in February 1993 and the 11 September attacks. We also know that a high-ranking al Qaeda member was either the mastermind or one of the key planners of the 11 September operation.

- Mukhtar is the uncle of Ramzi Yousef, who masterminded the 1993 bombing plot against the World Trade Center.

- Following the 1993 attack, Yousef and Mukhtar plotted in 1995 to blow up US planes flying East Asian routes – for which Mukhtar was indicted in 1996. Philippine authorities uncovered the plot in January 1995 and Yousef was apprehended the following month, but Mukhtar escaped.

- Yousef also considered flying a plane into CIA Headquarters, according to one of his co-conspirators [Murad], who was interrogated by Philippine authorities in 1995.

Bin Laden's determination to strike America at home increased with the issuance of the February 1998 fatwa targeting all Americans, both military and civilian. The ideas about destroying commercial airliners that had been circulating in al Qaeda leadership circles for several years appear to have been revived after that fatwa.

- Although we lack details on exactly when the plan was formulated and received bin Laden's approval, we know that the planning for the attacks began three years before 11 September.

- We understand that when one of bin Laden's associates proposed that the World Trade Center be targeted by small aircraft packed with explosives, bin Laden reportedly suggested using even larger planes.

In December 1999, the plot moved from conceptualization to preparation, with the arrival in Afghanistan of three young Arab men from Hamburg, Germany, who would become pilot-hijackers on 11 September.

Preparation

The men selected to carry out the 11 September attacks largely fall into three overall categories:

- the three pilots from Hamburg I just mentioned

- al Qaeda veterans

- and young Saudis.

The Hamburg cell

The men from Hamburg were Muhammad Atta (#1), Marwan al-Shehhi (#6), and Ziad Jarrah (#16), on whom the US held no derogatory information prior to 11 September 2001.

- They were part of a group of young Muslim men in Hamburg, Germany, who came from different countries and backgrounds, but attended the same mosques, shared common acquaintances, and were drawn together by their increasingly extreme Islamist views and disenchantment with the West.

- They were intelligent, English-speaking, and familiar with Western society – traits crucial to carrying out the 11 September plot.

- They were well suited – educated, including in technical subjects, and proficient in several languages – to mastering the skills they would need to pilot three of the four planes on September 11.

Future hijacker-pilot **Marwan al-Shehhi (#6)** came to Germany from the United Arab Emirates in April 1996 on a UAE military scholarship.

- We believe he lived in Bonn through early 1999, when he passed a German proficiency exam, but apparently was a visitor to Hamburg before 1999.

- Al-Shehhi gave power of attorney in July 1998 to Mounir Motassadeq, a Moroccan living in Hamburg who in 1996 was one of two witnesses to Atta's will and is currently being detained by German authorities.

- Marwan Al-Shehhi moved to Hamburg in 1999 and enrolled at the Hamburg-Harburg Technical University where Atta studied.

Ziad Jarrah (#16), *like Atta, came from a middle-class family*.

- Having dreamed of becoming a pilot since childhood, Jarrah traveled from his home in Lebanon to Germany to study in 1996.

- At some point during the time he spent in Greifswald from 1996 to 1997, Jarrah appears to have come in contact with Abdulrahman al-Makhadi, an imam at a Greifswald mosque suspected of having terrorist connections.

- Jarrah moved to Hamburg in August 1997, where he began studies in aircraft construction at Hamburg's School of Applied Sciences.

Atta's (#1) relationship with his roommate, Yemeni Ramzi bin al-Shibh, may also have been crucial in focusing the Islamist beliefs of the Hamburg circle on al Qaeda. Since 11 September, we have received a variety of reports identifying bin al-Shibh as an important al Qaeda operative and we suspect that, unlike the three Hamburg pilots, he may have been associated with al Qaeda even before moving to Germany in 1995.

The al Qaeda veterans

We now know that two of the hijackers had been involved with al Qaeda for several years before 11 September 2001.

• They were Saudis Nawaf al-Hazmi (#14) and Khalid al-Mihdhar (#12), who on 11 September would help to hijack American Airlines Flight 77 that crashed into the Pentagon. We have learned a great deal about these men since 11 September

• The two men grew up together in Mecca.

• In the mid 1990s, al-Hazmi (#14) and al-Mihdhar (#12) traveled to Bosnia.

• Afterward their involvement with al Qaeda strengthened. Al-Hazmi traveled to Afghanistan sometime before 1998 and swore loyalty to bin Laden. Later, al-Mihdhar (#12) also traveled to Afghanistan and swore his allegiance to bin Laden.

• Al-Hazmi (#14) and al-Mihdhar (#12) returned to Saudi Arabia in early 1999. In April, both men obtained visas from the US consulate in Jeddah.

The young Saudis

The young Saudi men who made up the bulk of the support hijackers became involved with al Qaeda in the late 1990s, we have learned since 11 September.

• Many, like veterans al-Hazmi (#14) and al-Mihdhar (#12), knew each other before they traveled to Afghanistan and became involved in the 11 September operation.

• Investigative efforts have uncovered two sets of brothers – the al-Hazmis (#14 and #15) and al-Shehris (#4 and #5) – as well as small networks of friends and acquaintances among the young Saudi hijackers, many of whom came from southwest Saudi Arabia.

• They came from a variety of backgrounds – their families came from different parts of the socioeconomic spectrum, and a few had higher education while others had little at all. Some had struggled with depression or alcohol abuse, or simply seemed to be drifting in search of purpose.

• Some of these young men had reportedly never exhibited much religious fervor, before apparent exposure to extremist ideas – through family members, friends, or clerics – led to an abrupt radicalization and separation from their families.

As part of their commitment to militant Islam, these young Saudis traveled to Afghanistan to train in the camps of their exiled countryman Usama bin Laden.

- An analysis of travel data acquired since 11 September suggests that most went to Afghanistan for the first time in 1999 or 2000, traveling through one or more other countries before entering Afghanistan to disguise their destination.

- Although their early travel to Afghanistan added these young men to the ranks of operatives that al Qaeda could call upon to carry out future missions, we do not believe that they became involved in the 11 September plot until late 2000 [we don't believe the al Qaeda leadership would have wanted them knowing about a plot in the US any sooner than necessary given the conspiracy's compartmentation]. Even then, they probably were told little more than that they were headed for a suicide mission inside the United States.

Saudi Hani Hanjour (#11), the fourth pilot, is similar to the other young Saudi hijackers in some ways, yet stands out because of:

- His probable role as a pilot on 11 September, given that he had far greater flying experience than Flight 77 co-hijackers Nawaf al-Hazmi and Khalid al-Mihdhar.

Hani Hanjour (#11) expressed an early wish to participate in a Jihad conflict, but did not appear to experience a sudden increase in his religious fervor until 1992. In April 1996, Hanjour returned to the US.

The Hamburg pilots traveled to Afghanistan in late 1999, at which time they were likely selected for and briefed on the 11 September plot.

- Atta (#1) flew from Hamburg to Istanbul in late 1999, then on to Karachi, Pakistan. After that, he evidently traveled into Afghanistan.

- According to information acquired after the 11 September attacks, Atta (#1) and al-Shehhi (#6) were both present at bin Laden facilities in Afghanistan in late 1999; Atta's presence has been corroborated by a separate source.

- Al-Shehhi (#6) likely left Hamburg at roughly the same time as Atta (#1), since he granted power of attorney over his German bank account to another member of the Hamburg cell beginning November 1999.

- Jarrah's (#16) travel at this time mirrored Atta's, flying from Hamburg to Istanbul and then on to Karachi in late 1999.

Since 11 September we have also obtained information on which al Qaeda leaders were involved in planning the attacks during this crucial late-1999 period in Afghanistan.

- We know that bin Laden deputy Muhammad Atif deliberately chose the hijackers from young Arab men who had no previous terrorist activities.

- The hijackers were also chosen on the basis of nationality so that they would not have trouble obtaining US visas. Another senior bin Laden lieutenant then arranged for them to get pilot training.

- A key planner of the 2000 attack on the *USS Cole* was also in Afghanistan at this time.

- We also now believe that bin Laden's security chief, Sayf al-Adl, played a key role in the 11 September plot, and Abu Zubaydah was supportive and aware of the operation and its stages.

When they left Afghanistan at the end of 1999 and early 2000, the Hamburg hijackers immediately began to prepare for their mission.

- They began by acquiring new passports that would show no sign of travel to Afghanistan when they applied for US visas.

Al-Shehhi (#6), Atta (#1), and Jarrah (#16) entered the US on different dates in May and June 2000, from three different European cities, possibly to mislead authorities as to their common purpose.

- Al-Shehhi (#6) flew from Brussels to Newark on 29 May 2000.

- Atta (#1) traveled by bus to Prague, entering the city on 2 June 2000, and flew to Newark the next day.

- Jarrah (#16) flew from Düsseldorf to Newark, and then on to Venice, Florida, on 27 June 2000.

While the Hamburg pilots were wrapping up their training in Afghanistan and returning to Germany in late 1999 and early 2000, halfway around the world the al Qaeda veterans, Nawaf al-Hazmi (#14) and Khalid al-Mihdhar (#12), prepared to enter the US.

- After receiving US visas in April 1999, both men had traveled to Afghanistan and participated in special training in the latter half of 1999. This training may have been facilitated by a key al Qaeda operative.

- After the January 2000 Malaysia meeting outlined earlier, they entered the US on 15 January.

As you may have already noticed, the inclusion of al-Hazmi (#14) and al-Mihdhar (#12) in the plot seems to violate one of the conspiracy's most successful tactics: the use of untainted operatives. Unlike the other hijackers, al-Hazmi (#14) and al-Mihdhar (#12) had years of involvement with al Qaeda – to such an extent that they had already come to our attention before 11 September. Without the inclusion of al-Hazmi (#14) and al-Mihdhar (#12) in the plot, we would have had none of the hijackers who died on 11 September in our sights prior to the attacks. We speculate that this difference may be explained by the possibility that the two men originally entered the US to carry out a different terrorist operation prior to being folded into the 9/11 plot. I'll briefly outline the factors, other than their long track record with al Qaeda, that have led us to consider this possibility.

- Al-Hazmi (#14) and al-Mihdhar (#12) obtained US visas far earlier than the other hijackers – in April 1999, while the Hamburg pilots didn't begin getting US visas until early 2000.

- As noted above, al-Hazmi (#14) and al-Mihdhar (#12) received special training in Afghanistan in the latter half of 1999, along with USS Cole suicide bomber al-Nibras and a key planner of the Cole attack

- Pilots Atta (#1), al-Shehhi (#6), Jarrah (#16), and later Hanjour (#11) all began flight training quite soon after arriving in the US, while al-Hazmi (#14) and al-Mihdhar (#12) did not engage in flight training activity until April 2000 – approximately three months after coming to this country.

As mentioned earlier, it appears that at least one other member of the Hamburg cell – and possibly two – intended to participate in the 11 September attacks as a pilot.

• Yemeni Ramzi bin al-Shibh, a close associate and roommate of Atta (#1) in Germany, failed on multiple occasions in 2000 to obtain a US visa and even sent a deposit to the flight school where Jarrah (#16) was training.

• Both men displayed the same tradecraft that characterized the other hijackers: persistence in the face of obstacles, an evident decision to enter the country legally and under true name, and flexibility regarding their roles in the plot. Bin al-Shibh, for instance, transferred money to Marwan al-Shehhi (#6) in 2000 while still attempting to acquire a US visa.

As training for the pilot-hijackers proceeded in the US through the latter half of 2000, al Qaeda leaders turned their attention to bringing into the plot the young men who would support the pilots.

• Most of the young Saudis obtained their US visas in the fall of 2000. The State Department did not have a policy to stringently examine Saudis seeking visas prior to 11 September because there was virtually no risk that Saudis would attempt to reside or work illegally in the US after their visas expired. US Embassy and consular officials do cursory searches on Saudis who apply for visas, but if they do not appear on criminal or terrorist watchlists they are granted a visa. Thousands of Saudis every year are granted visas as a routine – most of whom are not even interviewed. The vast majority of Saudis study, vacation, or do business in the US and return to the kingdom.

• Reporting suggests that all of them – possibly including pilot Hani Hanjour (#11) – then traveled to Afghanistan at some point in late 2000 or early 2001.

Khalid al-Mihdhar (#12) returned to the US on 4 July 2001 after nearly a year out of the country. He had spent the past year traveling between Yemen and Afghanistan, with occasional trips to Saudi Arabia.

• Al-Mihdhar (#12) returned to Saudi Arabia in June and on 13 June obtained a US visa in Jeddah.

• In July 2001, Atta (#1) returned to Spain. On 7 July, he flew from Miami to Zurich, then on to Madrid.

Conclusion

By 5 August 2001, all of the hijackers are in the United States to stay.

The lessons of 11 September have not just been learned, but acted on.

- And our support to watchlisting is being revamped. Standardized guidance has been distributed to CTC officers on watchlist procedures, reminding them to err on the side of reporting when sending names to the Department of State.

- However, al Qaeda is known for changing its tactics, and a determined group of terrorists, using a slightly different approach, could succeed if they used much of the resilient tradecraft employed by the 11 September hijackers.

- Al Qaeda's tradecraft, combined with the enormous volume of travelers entering the US every year, will make it impossible to guarantee that no terrorists will enter the country.

- Based on what we have learned about the 11 September plot, an attempt to conduct another attack on US soil is certain.

- Even with the increased government and public vigilance employed against terrorism since 11 September, the danger is still great.

Statement for the Record
FBI Director Robert S. Mueller III
Joint Intelligence Committee Inquiry

Introductory Remarks

Mr. Chairman, members of the Committee, I am pleased to appear before you today with my colleague, George Tenet, to describe the hijackers' activities once they arrived in the United States. Director Tenet has provided you with an overview of how this plot came to fruition, the preparations conducted abroad, and the intelligence available at the time indicating that Usama bin Laden and al Qaeda desired to strike the United States.

My testimony will cover what our investigation indicates happened once these terrorists arrived on US soil and how they executed their plans. I have not included a discussion of Zacarias Moussaoui and any connection to the hijackers, and all of my statements should be understood as excepting those topics. That is because of the pending capital case against Moussaoui.

None of the 19 suicide hijackers are known to have had computers, laptops, or storage media of any kind, although they are known to have used publicly accessible Internet connections at various locations. They used 133 different prepaid calling cards to call from various pay phones, cell phones, and landlines.

The 19 suicide hijackers used US checking accounts accessed with debit cards to conduct the majority of financial activity during the course of this conspiracy.

Meetings and communications between the hijackers were done without detection, apparent surveillance flights were taken, and nothing illegal was detected through airport security screening.

In short, the terrorists had managed very effectively to exploit loopholes and vulnerabilities in our systems. To this day we have found no one in the United States except the actual hijackers who knew of the plot and we have found nothing they did while in the United States that triggered a specific response about them.

Khalid al-Mihdhar and Nawaf al-Hazmi (American Airlines Flight 77 – pilot-trained, but not believed to have piloted this flight)

Khalid al-Mihdhar and Nawaf al-Hazmi arrived in Los Angeles, California on January 15, 2000. On April 10, 2000, al-Hazmi took a one-hour introductory lesson at the National Air College in San Diego.

On May 5, 2000 and May 10, 2000, al-Mihdhar and al-Hazmi each took introductory flying lessons and bought a Jeppesen flight training kit. During this time-frame, al-Hazmi was also enrolled in English classes. On June 10, 2000, al-Mihdhar left the United States en route to Kuwait, transiting Frankfurt, Germany. Al-Mihdhar is then believed to have returned to Saudi Arabia. Al-Hazmi, however, remained in the San Diego area.

Khalid al-Mihdhar arrived back in New York from Saudi Arabia on July 4, 2001 after spending over a year out of the country. Al-Mihdhar's role in the September 11 plot between June 2000 and July 2001 – before his reentry into the United States – may well have been that of the coordinator and organizer of the movements of the non-pilot hijackers. This is supported by his apparent lengthy stay in Saudi Arabia and his arriving back in the United States only after the arrival of all the hijackers.

Mohamed Atta (American Airlines Flight 11 suicide pilot) and Marwan al-Shehhi (United Airlines Flight 175 suicide pilot)

Mohamed Atta is known to have inquired about flight training in the United States as early as March 2000, when he made e-mail Internet inquiries from Germany to several flight schools in the United States. In May of that year Atta was issued an Egyptian passport in Hamburg, Germany, replacing one, which he claimed, had been lost.

On May 29, 2000, Marwan al-Shehhi arrived in Newark, New Jersey from Brussels, Belgium.

On June 3, 2000, Atta arrived in Newark from Prague, Czechoslovakia and hooked up with al-Shehhi. They remained in the New York area through July 2, 2000. While in New York, al-Shehhi was enrolled in an English language school.

Exactly one month after his arrival in the United States, al-Shehhi received from UAE a $5,000 Western Union transfer from Isam Mansar, an alias for Ali Abdul Aziz Ali, the same person in UAE who sent funds to Atta and al-Hazmi.

Atta and al-Shehhi both obtained pilot's licenses, instrument certifications, and commercial pilot certificates in the fall and winter of 2000 at Huffman Aviation.

In September 2000, al-Shehhi and Atta continued their flight training at Jones Aviation in Sarasota, Florida, but failed their Stage I flight test. From December 29, 2000 through December 31, 2000, al-Shehhi and Atta took flight simulator lessons at Sim Center and Pan Am International. Both signed up for time on a Boeing 727 and a Boeing 767 simulator.

Ziad Samir Jarrah (United Airlines Flight 93 suicide pilot)

From abroad, Ziad Jarrah applied to the Florida Flight Training Center in Venice, Florida on March 2, 2000. On May 25, 2000, Jarrah received a Bl/B2 multiple-entry visa to enter the United States. On June 27, 2000, Jarrah arrived in the country (Atlanta, Georgia) and began his training at the Florida Flight Training Center on June 28, 2000. His training ended in December 2000. From December 15-18, 2000 and again on January 8, 2001, Jarrah took flight simulator lessons at Aeroservice Aviation in Miami, Florida on Boeing 727 and Boeing 737 simulators.

The Florida Flight Training Center is significant for another reason as well. On May 17, 2400 (sic) 2000, 1 day(s) after the last known flight lessons for al-Mihdhar and al-Hazmi, an individual identified as Ramzi bin al-Shibh made his first application for a US visa, which was denied. Bin al-Shibh reapplied for a US visa on June 15, 2000, but again was denied. We know that bin al-Shibh attempted to enroll in the Florida Flight Training Center (FFTC), the facility where Ziad Jarrah was training at the time.

In August of 2000, bin al-Shibh wired $2,200 as a deposit to this flight training center in Florida. Bin al-Shibh tried twice more to obtain a visa to travel into the United States – in Yemen on September 15, 2000, and again on October 25, 2000. However, these requests were also denied. Bin al-Shibh would later become a significant money person.

With their training complete, it appears that the pilots began conducting possible surveillance flights as passengers aboard cross-country flights transiting between the Northeast United States and California. *On each flight, the pilots were seated in the first-class section of the plane. The first of these flights occurred on May 24, 2001, when Marwan al-Shehhi flew from JFK Airport to San Francisco.*

Ziad Jarrah flew from Baltimore-Washington International to Los Angeles in early June 2001. Later that month, Mohammed Atta flew from Boston Logan Airport to San Francisco.

In August 2001, Nawaf al-Hazmi and Hani Hanjour flew from Dulles International Airport to Los Angeles.

Each of the return flights for these hijackers had layovers in Las Vegas. To date, the purpose of these 1-2 day layovers is not known. However, with respect to travel to Las Vegas, we know that at least one hijacker on each of the four hijacked airplanes traveled to Las Vegas, Nevada sometime between May and August of 2001. *This travel consisted of an initial transcontinental trip from an East Coast city to a West Coast city, and a connection in that West Coast city to a Las Vegas-bound flight.*

Arrival of Non-Pilots into the United States

Now, let me turn to the remaining hijackers, the individuals we believe were the "muscle" on the flights, responsible for keeping the passengers under control.

The first pair arrived on April 23, 2001 and the last pair arrived on June 29, 2001. Each of these hijackers traveled with at least one other hijacker and each transited through the UAE prior to arriving in the United States.

During the summer of 2001, some of the hijackers, specifically Mohamed Atta and Nawaf al-Hazmi, appear to have met face-to-face on a monthly basis to discuss the status of the operation, and ultimately the final preparations for the attack.

In July 2001, Mohamed Atta, Abdul Aziz al Omari, Nawaf al-Hazmi, Salem al-Hazmi, Khalid al-Mihdhar, Ahmed Al-Ghamdi, and Majed Moqed purchased personal identification cards at Apollo Travel in Paterson, New Jersey. Atta purchased a Florida identification card, while the others purchased New Jersey identification cards.

In August, the hijackers began purchasing tickets for the flights they intended to hijack. Al-Mihdhar and Moqed ultimately purchased their tickets with cash on September 5 at the American Airlines counter at Baltimore-Washington International Airport.

On August 28, Marwan al-Shehhi purchased his ticket for Flight 175 at the Miami International Airport. The next day, Mohand al-Shehri and Fayez Banihammad bought two one-way first-class tickets for Flight 175.

On August 27, 2001, Nawaf al-Hazmi and Salem al-Hazmi purchased their tickets through the website Travelocity.com using a VISA debit card in name of Nawaf M. al-Hazmi.

A few days later, Hani Hanjour attempted to purchase his ticket with a VISA debit card at Advanced Travel Services, in Totowa, New Jersey. After the card was rejected because the cost of the ticket exceeded the card's credit limit, Hanjour paid for the ticket with cash.

Hamza Al-Ghamdi purchased his ticket for Flight 175 through the Internet on August 29, 2001, using his Florida SunTrust Visa debit card. He also purchased an e-ticket for United Airlines Flight 7950, flying from Los Angeles to San Francisco, at the same time. Hamza Al-Ghamdi's SunTrust Visa debit card was also used the following day to purchase a business class e-ticket for Ahmed Al-Ghamdi for Flight 175. Also that day, Hamza Al-Ghamdi purchased two one-way tickets for himself and Ahmed Al-Ghamdi to fly AirTran from Fort Lauderdale, Florida, to Boston, Massachusetts, on September 7.

Just days before the attacks, the hijackers began arranging to assemble in their final departure cities. On September 5, 2001, Mohamed Atta and Marwan al-Shehhi booked airline flights at a travel agency in Boca Raton, Florida. Atta booked a US Airways flight from Fort Lauderdale, Florida, to Baltimore-Washington International Airport, and al-Shehhi booked a reservation on Delta Airlines from Fort Lauderdale, Florida, to Boston, Massachusetts. That same day, al-Shehhi and Banihammad made their reservations for September 8, 2001, to travel from Fort Lauderdale, Florida, to Boston, Massachusetts, on AirTran.

In the days just prior to the September 11 attacks, several of the suicide hijackers of American Airlines Flight 11 and United Airlines Flight 175 were in Boston. Once they arrived in that city, the hijackers stayed in their established groups, lodging in different hotels. Hamza Al-Ghamdi and Ahmed Al-Ghamdi stayed at the Charles Hotel. On September 8, the two checked out of the Charles Hotel and moved to the Days Hotel in Boston.

Flight 11 hijackers Waleed al Shehri, Satam al Sugami, and Wail al Shehri are believed to have shared a room at the Park Inn in Newton, Massachusetts beginning on September 5. The room was registered to Waleed al Shehri. Abdul Aziz al Omari is also believed to have stayed at this same hotel.

Flight 175 hijackers Mohand al-Shehri, Fayez Ahmed (Banihammad), and Marwan al-Shehhi stayed at the Milner Hotel in Boston. On September 9, Mohamed Atta also checked into the Milner Hotel, staying that night where he met with Marwan al-Shehhi. A telephonic message on that same day recovered from Atta's cellular telephone has Ziad Jarrah referring to Atta as "boss."

Shortly after noon on the day before the attacks, Mohamed Atta left the Miler Hotel, picked up Abdul Aziz al Omari at the Park Inn, and drove to Portland, Maine. They checked into the Comfort Inn in South Portland. Atta and al Omari were seen together on several occasions in the Portland area later that evening but their reason for going there, to date, remains unclear.

That same day in Maryland, Flight 77 hijackers Majed Moqed and Hani Hanjour checked out of the Budget Host Valencia Hotel in Laurel, Maryland.

Finally, on September 7, Saeed Al-Ghamdi, Ziad Jarrah, Ahmed al Haznawi, and Ahmed Alnami, the four Flight 93 hijackers, arrived in New Jersey on a Spirit Airlines flight from Fort Lauderdale, Florida.

September 11 – suicide hijackers' activities hours preceding the attacks

On September 11, at 6:00 am, Mohamed Atta and Abdul Aziz al Omari boarded a US Airways flight leaving Portland, Maine en route to Boston's Logan Airport. They were both carrying black shoulder bags when they passed through security. When Atta arrived at Logan Airport, he received a telephone call on his cellular telephone from a pay phone located inside Terminal C. This call is believed to have originated from one of the Flight 175 hijackers who were waiting to board Flight 175, which was boarding in Terminal C.

Early that same morning, Hamza Al-Ghamdi checked out of the Days Hotel in Boston and with Ahmed Al-Ghamdi took a taxi to the airport.

Fayez Banihammad and Mohand al-Shehri, also booked on Flight 175, checked out of the Milner Hotel in the Boston area and drove a rental car to the airport, where they returned the car to the rental company.

Marwan al-Shehhi, who had received a cell phone call from Ziad Jarrah in the morning, also arrived at the airport, resulting in the Boston teams being in place.

On September 11, Nawaf al-Hazmi, along with three others [believed to have been three of the other Flight 77 hijackers], left the Marriott Residence Inn in Herndon, Virginia and was later seen with Salem al-Hazmi approaching the American Airlines ticket counter at Dulles.

Execution of the Attacks

American Airlines Flight 11

At approximately 7:59 am, American Airlines Flight 11, a Boeing 767, left Logan International Airport, Boston, Massachusetts, bound for Los Angeles, California, with 81 passengers and 11 crewmembers on board. Five hijackers, apparently using commonly available box cutters, hijacked the aircraft approximately 14 minutes into the flight. The five hijackers aboard Flight 11 were Mohamed Atta; Abdul Aziz al Omari; Satam al Suqami; Waleed al Shehri; and Wail al Shehri.

The hijackers from Flight 11 all purchased one-way tickets in either first class or business class. Each of their seats on the plane had a direct line of sight of one another and with the cockpit door. Brothers Waleed al Shehri and Wail al Shehri sat in the first two seats in first class – the cockpit doors were easily accessible from these seats. Atta, who we believe was the pilot (he is the only hijacker on this flight known to have formally received flight training), and al Omari occupied the two middle seats of the second row in business class. Al Suqami sat in the aisle seat in the next to last row in business class.

Flight 11 was cleared for takeoff at 7:59 am and diverted course at 8:13 am. Twenty-two minutes later, the flight crashed into the North Tower of the World Trade Center.

As you will recall, earlier that morning, Atta and al Omari had flown from Portland, Maine, to Logan Airport. Following the crash of Flight 11, authorities recovered two pieces of luggage in the name of Mohamed Atta that had not been loaded onto that flight. A search of this baggage revealed a three-page letter handwritten in Arabic which, upon translation, was found to contain instructions on how to prepare for a mission applicable, but not specific, to the September 11 operation. Copies of this letter were also recovered at the crash site of Flight 93 and in the car registered to Nawaf al-Hazmi that was found at Dulles International Airport.

United Airlines Flight 175

At approximately 7:58 am, United Airlines (UA) Flight 175, a Boeing 767, left Logan International Airport, Boston, Massachusetts, bound for Los Angeles, California, with 61 passengers and 11 crewmembers on board. Shortly after takeoff, the plane was hijacked by Marwan al-Shehhi; Fayez Ahmed (Banihammad); Ahmed Al-Ghamdi; Hamza Al-Ghamdi; and Mohand al-Shehri. Two of the hijackers on this flight sat in first class, two others sat in economy class, while Marwan al-Shehhi sat in business class.

Marwan al-Shehhi, who was flight trained, is believed to have been the suicide pilot on this hijacked flight.

At 9:05 am, Flight 175 crashed into the South Tower of the World Trade Center.

American Airlines Flight 77

American Airlines Flight 77, a Boeing 757, left Dulles International Airport at 8:20 am enroute to Los Angeles with 58 passengers and six crewmembers on board. At 8:50 am, the last routine radio contact with the aircraft was made. Four minutes later, the aircraft began an unauthorized turn to the south and shortly thereafter, radar contact was lost. *At 9:39 am, Flight 77 crashed into the southwest side of the Pentagon in Arlington, Virginia.*

Flight 77 was hijacked by five individuals – Khalid al-Mihdhar, Nawaf al-Hazmi, Hani Hanjour, Salem al-Hazmi; and Majed Moqed. Three of the hijackers were seated in first class and two were seated in economy class.

The lengthy and extensive flight training obtained by Hani Hanjour throughout his years in the United States makes it reasonable to believe that he was the pilot of Flight 77 on September 11. We know that Hanjour was seated in Seat 1B, the first row aisle seat of the first-class section. The other hijackers on this flight were seated in pairs further back in the airplane.

On September 12, 2001, a 1988 Toyota Corolla registered to Nawaf al-Hazmi was found in a parking lot at Dulles International Airport. A subsequent search of this vehicle revealed many documents and other items associated with the hijackers, including a three-page letter handwritten in Arabic. This letter was identical to those found in luggage belonging to Atta and at the crash site of United Airlines Flight 93 in Pennsylvania.

United Airlines Flight 93

At approximately 8:42 am, United Airlines (UA) Flight 93, a Boeing 757, left Newark International Airport enroute to San Francisco with 37 passengers and seven crewmembers on board. At approximately 10:03 am, the plane hit the ground in Stoney Creek Township, in southwestern Pennsylvania. Flight data recovered from the "black box" indicated that Flight 93 was heading east at the time of the crash.

The hijackers of this flight, Ziad Samir Jarrah, Saeed Al-Ghamdi, Ahmad Ibrahim A. al Haznawi, and Ahmed Alnami were all seated in first class and sat in rows 1, 3 and 6, respectively. Jarrah is the presumed suicide pilot of this flight since he was the only hijacker known to have a pilot's license and flight simulator time.

Conclusion

What I have just provided is an overview of what we have learned about the US activities of the hijackers before and during the attacks.

Clearly, these 19 terrorists were not supermen using extraordinarily sophisticated techniques. They came armed with simple box cutters. But they also came armed with sophisticated knowledge about how to plan these attacks abroad without discovery, how to finance their activities from overseas without alarm, how to communicate both here and abroad without detection, and how to exploit the vulnerabilities inherent in our free society.

There were no slip-ups. Discipline never broke down. They gave no hint to those around them what they were about. They came lawfully. They lived lawfully. They trained lawfully. They boarded the aircraft lawfully. They simply relied upon everything from the vastness of the Internet to the openness of our society to do what they wanted to do without detection.

And just like the CIA, we do not think the threat has subsided.

These realities to me mean we need a different FBI, one that does not just think in terms of cases and prosecutions. *We need new structures, new training, new levels of cooperation, new technologies, more analytical capacity, and a different mindset.* All of these things are being put in place. Nothing can be paramount to preventing the next attack.

When we looked back, there were clearly things we should have done better or differently. But there are also many things we have done quite well and things we should do more of.

Since September 11, we have taken dozens of significant steps to improve the FBI. Some of those allowed us to unravel what happened on September 11. And even though more needs to be done, especially with technology, I am extraordinarily proud of the men and women of the FBI, CIA and NSA who made sacrifices and did the work that led us to knowing those responsible and who have kept us safe in the post-September 11 environment. We are working hand-in-hand toward that goal every minute of every day, seven days a week.

Statement of Louis J. Freeh, Former FBI Director, Joint Intelligence Committee October 8, 2002, 10:00 am

Introduction

I want to begin by expressing my prayers and condolences for the victims, and to the families and loved ones who have been devastated by terrorism, in all of its destructive forms. I spent 26 years in public service as an FBI Agent, prosecutor, Army Officer, judge and FBI Director, striving every day, as did my colleagues, to protect both people and the Rule of Law.

The Intelligence Community and the FBI does not appear to have had sufficient information to prevent the September 11th attacks

What has been stated recently to this Committee by FBI Director Robert S. Mueller III includes the following:

"The plans for the September 11th attacks "were hatched and financed overseas over a several year period.

"Each of the hijackers, apparently purposely selected to avoid notice, came easily and lawfully from abroad ...

"While here, the hijackers effectively operated without suspicion, triggering nothing that alerted law enforcement and doing nothing that exposed them to domestic coverage. As far as we know, they contacted no known terrorist sympathizers in the United States. They committed no crimes with the exception of minor traffic violations. They dressed and acted like Americans, shopping and eating at places like Wal-Mart and Pizza Hut.

To this day we have found no one in the United States except the actual hijackers who knew of the plot and we have found nothing they did while in the United States that triggered a specific response about them."

We have read and heard much about the July 2001 memo by a Phoenix special agent, the Minnesota arrest and investigation of Moussaoui in August, and the information, which the CIA obtained regarding two of the 19 hijackers relating to a Kuala Lumpur meeting in 2000.

It is very important in hindsight to segregate this relevant information and put it into a dedicated time-line. However, the predictive value of these diverse facts at the time that they were being received must be evaluated. Analyzing intelligence information can be like trying to take a sip of water coming out of a fire hydrant. The several bits of information clearly connected and predictive after the fact need to be viewed in real time. The reality is that these unquestionably important bits have been plucked from a sea of thousands and thousands of such bits at the time. Additionally, as this Committee well knows, the difference between strategic and tactical intelligence is critically important to keep in mind.

Although not privy to all the relevant information known to this Committee, I am aware of nothing that to me demonstrates that the FBI and the Intelligence Community had the type of information or tactical intelligence which could have prevented September 11. In terms of the FBI's capability to identify, investigate and prevent the 19 hijackers from carrying out their attacks, the facts so far on the public record do not support the conclusion that these tragic events could have been prevented by the FBI and Intelligence Community acting by themselves.

That is not to say things could not have been done better or that more resources or authorities would not have helped. It is only to say I have not seen a reporting of facts that leads to that conclusion, with one important caveat, however. Because of the narrow focus of this inquiry, I leave aside any view of the larger but very relevant issues like foreign policy, military might, airline safety, national commitment, etc.

Law Enforcement's ability to act against entrenched terrorists in overseas sanctuaries is very limited

The FBI and CIA can devise and implement a very effective counterterrorism strategy both inside the United States and overseas. However, often a greater involvement of national resources is required.

And I particularly want to commend George Tenet and the courageous men and women of the CIA for fighting bravely on the front lines of this war for many years. Under Mr. Tenet's sound leadership, dedication and vision, the CIA has achieved great successes in rolling up major terrorist plots in Albania, Jordan, Southeast Asia and many other places. Importantly, the CIA and FBI have been fully cooperating and jointly carrying out America's counterterrorism war for many years – forming the first joint FBI-CIA group dedicated to al Qaeda/ Usama bin Laden a year prior to the August 1998 East African embassy attacks.

But the fact is that working at their best and highest levels of efficiency and cooperation, the FBI and CIA together will still fall short of a total war against terrorism.

I realize that your Committees' efforts have publicly focused for the most part on the Intelligence Community and the FBI. And I'm confident that the upcoming Commission, should there be one, will more fully examine these broader issues with a global view. It should be obvious, for instance, that the FBI with about 3.5 percent of the country's counterterrorism budget and the CIA with their share comprise but pieces of a mosaic of a total government commitment to the war on terrorism.

US airlines and aviation have long been known as a major target for terrorist attacks

Aviation and airplanes have long been known to be preferred targets of terrorist hijackers. Protecting civil aviation from a terrorist attack has for years been an urgent national issue. A September 1996 GAO Report concluded that "nearly every major aspect of the system ranging from the screening of passengers, checked and carry-on baggage, mail and cargo as well as access to secured areas within airports and aircraft – has weaknesses that terrorists could exploit."

In the aftermath of the tragedy of TWA Flight 800 in New York City, the White House Commission on Aviation Safety and Security was formed. I along with New York City Police Department Commissioner Ray Kelly, Bill Coleman, Franklin Raines, Jim Hall, and other distinguished Americans served as commissioners appointed by President Clinton. The Chairman of the Commission was Vice President Al Gore, who did an excellent job leading the effort and making much-needed recommendations. Known as the Gore Commission, the panel made its final report and recommendations on February 12, 1997. For example, Recommendation 3.19, entitled "Complement Technology with Automated Passenger Profiling," contemplated the development of a passenger profiling system wherein law enforcement and intelligence information on known or suspected terrorists would be used in passenger profiling.

The critical issue of terrorism directed against our aviation security was well known for many years prior to September 11th. As this Committee knows, the FBI conveyed repeated warnings to the FAA and the airline industry regarding terrorism, right up to September 11, 2001. Efforts by the government and the airline industry to implement these and other recommendations deserve intensive and careful study, and, most likely, massive resources.

This is not to criticize the FAA, which does a difficult job very well. Rather, the point is that while the CIA and the FBI should be intensely examined regarding September 11 – they should not be examined in a vacuum. The Executive and the Congress, the various government agencies with primary responsibility for public safety and national security, foreign policy, technologies, as well as the private sector and the international community are all components in whether or not terrorism is addressed with the vigor it so deserves.

Resources

You have asked me to talk about resource allocation and whether sufficient resources were allocated to and within the FBI for fighting terrorism. The short answer is that the allocations were insufficient to maintain the critical growth and priority of the FBI's counterterrorism program.

"Strategic Goal: Prevent, disrupt, and defeat terrorist operations before they occur.

"Terrorism, is both international and domestic, poses arguably the most complex and difficult threat of any of the threats for which the FBI has a major responsibility. State-sponsored terrorism, though still of concern, is no longer the only terrorist problem. New perpetrators – loosely organized groups and ad hoc coalitions of foreigners motivated by perceived injustices, along with domestic groups and disgruntled individual American citizens – have attacked United States interests at home and abroad. They have chosen nontraditional targets and increasingly have employed no conventional weapons. The dilemma, of course, is that the new perpetrators, targets, and weapons exist in almost unlimited numbers, while the law enforcement resources arrayed against them are finite." (emphasis added)

In my report to the American people on the work of the FBI 1993-1998, entitled "Ensuring Public Safety and National Security Under the Rule of Law," I wrote:

"One of my major priorities has been to seek increased funding for the FBI's counterterrorism programs. The Congress has shown great foresight in strengthening this vital work. For example, the counterterrorism budget for Fiscal Year 1996 was

$97 million. The FY 1999 budget contains $301 million for counterterrorism efforts."

"Some terrorism now comes from abroad. Some terrorism is homegrown. But whatever its origin, terrorism is deadly and the FBI has no higher priority than to combat terrorism; to prevent it where possible; and where prevention fails, to apprehend the terrorists and to do everything within the law to work for conviction and the most severe sentences. Our goal is to prevent, detect and deter."

"Foreign Terrorists in US"

"Terrorism can be carried out by US citizens or by persons from other countries. At one time, with these crimes erupting in much of the world, many Americans felt we were immune from terrorism with foreign links. All of that ended in 1993." (emphasis added)

"The type of terrorism which had previously occurred far from our shores was brought home in a shocking manner when in February a massive explosion occurred in the parking garage at the World Trade Center complex in New York City."

The 1998-2000 period was critical and unprecedented regarding both the changes in and the demands on the FBI's counterterrorism program and its domestic and international responsibilities.

As examples, we indicted Usama bin Laden in June 1998 and again in November 1998. We put bin Laden and al Qaeda on the FBI's Top Ten list, in April 1999, making them our number one counterterrorism priority. Also in 1999, we set up a dedicated Usama Bin Laden Unit at FBI Headquarters.

We doubled and tripled the number of Joint Terrorism Task Forces (JTTFs) around the United States so we could multiply our forces and coordinate intelligence and counterterrorism operations with the FBI's federal, state and local law enforcement partners. Thirty-four of these JTTFs were in operation by 2001.

The FBI was given national responsibility for coordinating the protection of the Nation's critical infrastructure. As a result, we created the National Infrastructure Protection Center (NIPC) at FBI Headquarters, which had critical responsibilities regarding terrorist threats and cyberattacks.

The FBI was also tasked to set up the National Domestic Preparedness Office to counterterrorist threats and to enhance homeland security.

At the same time, we were conducting major terrorism investigations leading up to the successful prosecution in New York City of the al Qaeda members who attacked our embassies in Africa.

We stood up the massive Strategic Information Operations Center (SIOC) at FBI Headquarters whose main purpose was to give us the capability to work several major and simultaneous terrorist matters at the same time.

We established the FBI's Counterterrorist Center at FBI Headquarters, which was coordinated with the CIA's Center by communications, information exchange, and personnel staffing.

We instituted MAX CAP O5 in July 2000 to enable each of the FBI's 56 Field Offices and their Special Agents in Charge (SAC) to improve our counterterrorism efforts, analyze threats and develop capabilities and strategies throughout the United States. Regional SAC Conferences were held during the summer of 2000 to roll out the MAX CAP O5 strategy.

We set up a national threat warning system in order to disseminate terrorism-related information to state and local authorities around the country. We organized and carried out a significant number of national, regional and local practical exercises to help the country prepare for terrorist attacks. The Attorney General and I conducted regular meetings with the National Security Advisor and the Secretary of State dedicated to terrorism issues, cases and threats.

I met with dozens of Presidents, Prime Ministers, Kings, Emirs, law enforcement, intelligence and security chiefs around the world. The primary reason for these contacts was to pursue and enhance the FBI's counterterrorism program by forging an international network of cooperation. We were not an island. It had to be done.

We proposed and briefly received from Congress the authority to hire critical scientists, linguists and computer specialists without the salary restrictions of Title V. This flexibility is critical to fighting terrorism.

The DOJ and the FBI prepared hundreds of FISA Court applications in counterterrorism matters where electronic surveillance or legal assistance was required from the Court.

I regularly met and discussed counterterrorism issues, intelligence and force protection issues with the Attorney General, the National Security Advisor, United States Attorneys, the Secretaries of State and Defense, our Ambassadors and the Joint Chiefs of Staff.

Perhaps, most significantly as to the issue of the FBI's focus on the terrorist threat, in November 1999, I created a new FBI Counterterrorism Division. Nobody in the Executive or the Congress suggested that this step be taken. I took it because I firmly believed that it was necessary to expand and enhance the FBI's counterterrorism capability. Dale Watson was elevated to run this new Division and develop our new strategies. We enhanced and reorganized the entire FBI Counterterrorism Program.

At the same time, I proposed the creation of a new Investigative Services Division to support the new Counterterrorism Division as well as the Criminal and National Security Divisions. My purpose in doing so was to put together all of the FBI's analytical and support assets in order to better prevent terrorism and enhance our intelligence bases with the resources that we had available.

Nine months later, this reorganization was approved and the FBI for the first time consolidated its counterterrorism program assets with the support of a greater analytical engine. Ultimately, history has shown that more was needed on every front, ours included.

Thus, at the most critical time, the available resources for counterterrorism did not address the known critical needs.

A final note on FBI resources to carry out its critical mission, including waging war against terrorists. To win a war it takes soldiers. Front line troops, as you know, each require several more soldiers to support them. I don't know if the Joint Staff has advised you, but even after September 11th, the FBI has less FBI Agents today – 11, 516 Special Agents – than it had in 1999 – when the number was 11,681.

We need to support the brave men and women whom we ask to take great risks for our nation's safety.

The FBI was focused both on preventing domestic and foreign terrorist attacks

As I stated earlier and as reflected in the FBI's 1998 Strategic Plan and Five-Year Report, the 1993 bombing of the World Trade Center by foreign terrorists clearly demonstrated the effort to target America and Americans. Usama bin Laden's fatwa calling for the deaths of Americans anywhere left no doubt that terrorist attacks within the United States were as likely as those in Saudi Arabia, East Africa, Yemen and elsewhere.

More convincingly, the failed efforts by Ressam and his New York City based co-conspirators to carry out a major terrorist attack within the United States at the end of 1999 made the FBI focus intently on protecting homeland security. Indeed, the FBI investigation of the *USS Cole* attack and CIA efforts overseas led to our conclusion that the millennium attacks by Ressam on the West Coast were planned to coincide with other al Qaeda-sponsored terrorism in Jordan and in Yemen. The al Qaeda suicide bombers of the *USS Cole* had previously planned to attack another United States warship – *USS The Sullivans* – which was docked at the same fuel pod the *USS Cole* used in October 2000. The earlier attack was postponed because the bomb-laden attack boat sunk when it was launched.

So before the end of 1999, the FBI and the Intelligence Community clearly understood the foreign-based al Qaeda threat regarding targets within the United States. Congress and the Executive were fully briefed as to this threat analysis.

The notion that the FBI, other law enforcement agencies and the Intelligence Community were not focused on homeland threats is not accurate and belied by many factors.

Modern information technology is necessary to combat terrorism

When I left office in June 2001, the FBI was just beginning to get back on track in upgrading its information technology. In fact, just one month prior to my departure, the FBI was finally able to award the first contract for the Trilogy initiative, a three-year program to upgrade the FBI's aging information technology infrastructure.

The FBI and CIA have fully cooperated and worked side-by-side fighting terrorism

During my tenure as FBI Director, I was immensely proud of the cooperation and integration of FBI and CIA efforts to combat terrorism. Myself and recent DCIs, particularly George Tenet, have taken bold and unprecedented steps to work together and forge an effective FBI-CIA partnership to combat terrorism. Exchanging senior officers, standing up the joint Usama bin Laden/al Qaeda operations and intelligence center, fully coordinating our Legat and Station Chiefs, cross-training and many additional measures were taken to integrate our counterterrorism resources and capabilities. Our joint efforts in the East African bombings is a template for how successful we were in working together. Some of these efforts cannot be described in this session.

This historical and successful integration does not mean that on every possible point of intersection, a lapse did not occur. But to focus on those isolated instances while ignoring the huge successes of this top-down directed integration is misplaced. I personally credit George Tenet with making this happen and winning the trust and respect of the entire FBI in the process.

Conclusion

The FBI and CIA working together have accomplished much in fighting terrorism at home and abroad but it is a constant and continuing battle. These agencies should remain the primary counterterrorism agencies for this mission. The DCI's authority for coordinating and implementing government-wide efforts in this regard should be expanded. The war against terrorism must be waged relentlessly. It will require that significantly more resources be allocated to the FBI and CIA. These fine agencies and the brave men and women who fight this war cannot defeat some forms of terrorism without total government intervention no matter how great and heroic their efforts. Al Qaeda-type organizations, state sponsors of terrorism like Iran, and the threats they pose to America are beyond the competence of the FBI and the CIA to address. America must maintain the will in some cases to use its political, military and economic power in response when acts of war are threatened or committed against our nation by terrorists or their state sponsors.

Finally, however treacherous the enemy, the FBI must fight this war as a law enforcement agency of the Department of Justice governed by the Rule of Law and the Constitution. The rules, statutes and guidelines which establish the legal authorities of the FBI may change – as they did after September 11th – as long as those changes are clearly defined and understood. Its adherence to the Constitution and the Rule of Law must not change. We do not have sacrifice our freedom to protect it. So before the end of 1999, the FBI and the Intelligence Community clearly understood the foreign-based al Qaeda threat regarding targets within the United States. Congress and the Executive were fully briefed as to this threat analysis.

Analysis of the testimony of Louis Freeh

The Intelligence Community and the FBI does not appear to have had sufficient information to prevent the September 11th attacks.

What has been stated recently to this Committee by FBI Director Robert S. Mueller III includes the following:

"The plans for the September 11th attacks were hatched and financed overseas over a several year period.

"Each of the hijackers, apparently purposely selected to avoid notice, came easily and lawfully from abroad.

"While here, the hijackers effectively operated without suspicion, triggering nothing that alerted law enforcement and doing nothing that exposed them to domestic coverage. As far as we know, they contacted no known terrorist sympathizers in the United States. They committed no crimes with the exception of minor traffic violations. They dressed and acted like Americans.

It is clear that the FBI and the other agencies had more information than they needed to prevent the attack on 9/11. What the FBI and the other agencies did not have was an organizational structure, procedures, and mindset that would have allowed them to fully exploit this information.

They knew that bin Laden wanted to strike in the US and a huge attack was imminent in the summer of 2001. They knew this attack could kill thousands of Americans and would come without warning. The FBI even knew al-Mihdhar and al-Hazmi were in the US and they could have connected them with the warnings they received in the summer of 2001. They could have connected Zacarias Moussaoui, a terrorist wanting to fly a large airliner, to the warnings of the summer of 2001. Why they could nor connect an al Qaeda terrorist taking flying lesions on a Boeing 747, or the two al Qaeda terrorists inside of the US, Mihdhar and Hazmi to the huge al Qaeda attack they knew was about to occur inside of the US has never been explained.

As I stated earlier and as reflected in the FBI's 1998 Strategic Plan and Five-Year Report, the 1993 bombing of the World Trade Center by foreign terrorists clearly demonstrated the effort to target America and Americans. Usama bin Laden's fatwa calling for the deaths of Americans anywhere left no doubt that terrorist attacks within the United States were as likely as those in Saudi Arabia, East Africa, Yemen and elsewhere.

So before the end of 1999, the FBI and the Intelligence Community clearly understood the foreign-based al Qaeda threat regarding targets within the United States. Congress and the Executive were fully briefed as to this threat analysis.

The notion that the FBI, other law enforcement agencies and the Intelligence Community were not focused on homeland threats is not accurate and belied by many factors.

Although not privy to all the relevant information known to this Committee, I am aware of nothing that to me demonstrates that the FBI and the Intelligence Community had the type of information or tactical intelligence which could have prevented September 11th. In terms of the FBI's capability to identify, investigate and prevent the 19 hijackers from carrying out their attacks, the facts so far on the public record do not support the conclusion that these tragic events could have been prevented by the FBI and Intelligence Community acting by themselves.

Louis Freeh gave this statement in sworn testimony to the Joint Inquiry Committee on October 8, 2002. By this time the FBI had extensively searched all of the items in the possession of Zacarias Moussaoui. On March 7, 2006, court testimony was presented by the prosecutor at the Zacarias Moussaoui trial, Assistant US Attorney Robert A. Spencer, and is described below:

Hoping to put to death the only man charged in the September 11 conspiracy, federal prosecutors opened the sentencing trial for Zacarias Moussaoui on Monday by revealing that documents linking him to the hijacked jets were in his possession when he was arrested three weeks before the attacks. If Moussaoui, then in custody on a visa infraction, had told FBI agents about his phone calls and two lists of flight schools hidden in his duffel bag, the government could have prevented the deadliest terrorist attack in US history.

"The FBI would have quickly been on to all four pilots of the hijacked planes," according" to Spencer. "But Moussaoui lied so his brothers could go forward. He lied and nearly 3,000 people perished."

Spencer said that the FBI would have contacted the flight schools to immediately locate and arrest the four pilots; if that failed, he continued, agents would have alerted airport officials to keep the hijackers from approaching security gates or boarding planes [*LA Times*, March 7, 2006].

But FBI agents in Minnesota had Moussaoui's duffel bag and phone number for Ramzi bin al-Shibh, roommate of three of the 9/11 pilots, right on it. What prevented the Minnesota agents from looking in his duffel bag was the fact that his FISA search warrant required was blocked No reasonable explanation has ever been produced why FBI agents at the RFU at FBI Headquarters blocked this search warrant. They had even been told by the Minnesota agents that Zacarias Moussaoui was a terrorist that they thought wanted to fly a large airliner into the World Trade Center Towers.

In over 18,300 FISA applications for a search warrant, only five requests have ever been denied since 1978, when the requirement for this warrant first became law. It was the deliberate sabotaging of this investigation and ignoring the frantic pleas for assistance from the Minnesota agents by the RFU section at FBI Headquarters that blocked this investigation until it was too late to uncover the plans for the attacks on 9/11.

Dale L. Watson, Executive Assistant Director
Counterterrorism and Counterintelligence, FBI
Statement for the Record
September 26, 2002

Introduction

Good morning Messrs. Chairmen and members of the Committees. I am Dale Watson, the FBI's Executive Assistant

Director for Counterterrorism and Counterintelligence and I am pleased to appear before you today with my colleague Cofer Black from the CIA. I plan to describe to you the FBI's counterterrorism role within the Intelligence Community prior to September 11, 2001, and to provide my observations of the changes made since then to better enable the Intelligence Community to detect and prevent future attacks.

FBI relationship with the CIA

Much has been made during these hearings about the relationship between the FBI and the CIA, and not without cause. There is a long history between these two proud organizations and I am pleased to be seated with Cofer Black during this hearing today to discuss the changes which have occurred from my perspective.

In 1996, as a result of an exchange program initiated by FBI Director Freeh and Director of Central Intelligence Deutch, I was the first Bureau official to participate in an exchange of senior personnel between the FBI and CIA in the Counter-terrorism arena. I was assigned as the Deputy Chief with line authority to the Counterterrorist Center (CTC), and a senior CIA officer was assigned as the Deputy Section Chief in the Counterterrorism Section at FBI HQ. This exchange provided a foundation to solidify our future coordinated efforts and was extremely beneficial as it was top-down-driven.

Since that time and continuing today, the interaction between and the exchange of personnel, both agent and analytical, has increased significantly, particularly since September 11, 2001. While there might be individual examples where information was not shared, institutionally the barriers have come down and we are currently exchanging information daily, if not hourly, with our colleagues at the CIA.

The FBI is taking a leadership role in enhancing interagency cooperation and communication through utilization of a proactive threat warning system. The National Threat Warning System (NTWS) ensures vital information regarding terrorism reaches those in the US Intelligence and Law Enforcement Communities responsible for countering terrorist threats. The NTWS provides warnings to US government components and law enforcement agencies in the United States and Canada via the National Law Enforcement Telecommunications System. The FBI also provides warnings to private security personnel via the "Awareness of National Security Issues and Response" Program.

There are currently over 56 established Joint Terrorism Task Forces (JTTFs) in operation, an increase of 45 since 1996. By integrating the investigative abilities of the FBI and local law enforcement agencies, these JTTFs represent an effective response to the threats posed to US communities by domestic and international terrorists.

Within the FBI, the FBI's Counterterrorist Center was established in 1996 and is designed to combat terrorism on three fronts: international terrorism operations; within the United States and in support of extraterritorial investigations; domestic terrorism operations; and countermeasures, pertaining to both international and domestic terrorism. Through the FBI's Counterterrorist Center, the FBI has enhanced cooperation with other US government agencies. An exchange of working-level personnel and senior managers at the Headquarters level has also strengthened cooperation between the FBI and other agencies.

Prior to September 11, 2001, the FBI worked closely with all of the US government through efforts of the National Security Council. Regular, if not daily meetings were held to discuss counterterrorism matters. The core group participating in these meetings were the CIA, Department of Defense, Department of State, Department of Justice and other Federal agencies as needed to discuss and coordinate counterterrorism issues in the US government.

Conclusion

The continuing threat and the ever-present reminder of the events since September 11, 2001 have reconfirmed my belief that the FBI and our partners in the Intelligence Community must continue to aggressively develop the capacity to identify, penetrate and prevent terrorist activities worldwide.

The FBI must be ready, in concert with our Intelligence Community partners and foreign services to respond to terrorism issues as they present themselves. In order to do this, we must:

1) Develop a strategic analysis program to recognize trends aimed at identifying and preventing terrorists activities;

2) Develop a coordination program within the United States Intelligence Community and foreign services to identify persons who have attended the terrorist training camps in Afghanistan;

3) Improve information sharing capabilities with State and local law enforcement;

4) Improve methods and capabilities to track and remove terrorists from within our borders;

5) Increase and improve the technology to obtain and analyze information; and

6) Increase the number of analysts assigned and trained in terrorism matters.

In closing, let me stress – terrorism matters are the number one priority of the FBI. The FBI, along with the CIA and other members of the Intelligence Community, are working to coordinate multi-divisional and multi-agency investigations to establish a robust intelligence base, with adequate and ongoing analysis to identify and stop any future terrorist acts and strengthen our abilities to safeguard the American people and our interests, both at home and abroad.

Dale Watson was the person responsible for counterterrorism at the FBI. His testimony did not explain why his group failed on 9/11. Prior to 9/11, according to Dale Watson, they and the FBI were doing everything right.

Prior to September 11, 2001, the FBI worked closely with all of the US government through efforts of the National Security Council. Regular, if not daily meetings were held to discuss counterterrorism matters. The core group participating in these meetings were the CIA, Department of Defense, Department of State, Department of Justice and other Federal agencies as needed to discuss and coordinate counterterrorism issues in the US government.

Organizations don't fail because they make a thousand mistakes, they fail because they do not do a thousand things right they are required to do. They had never prepared a complete strategic analysis, even after Congress had asked for one. They gave the investigation of al-Hazmi and al-Mihdhar no sense of urgency, when they knew these al Qaeda terrorists had entered the US just after attending an al Qaeda terrorist-planning meeting. They did not start an investigation when they received the Williams memo detailing the fact al Qaeda terrorists were known to be attending flight training schools in Arizona. FBI Headquarters delayed the investigation of Zacarias Moussaoui with a bogus request for additional information the Minnesota agents were required to get in order to complete an application for a FISA search warrant. When the Minnesota agents obtained this information, FBI Headquarters sabotaged the application by removing this information from the search warrant. Even the terrorists themselves had no regard for the FBI or their ability to stop them from carrying out the attacks on 9/11. And even to this day none of this has been explained.

Cofer Black
Director Counterterrorist Center, CIA
Joint Inquiry Committee, Statement for the Record
September 26, 2000

Mr. Chairman, I am honored to be here. I appreciate your offer for me to speak from behind a screen in order to protect me. Normally, I would have accepted. This hearing is more important. I do not want to be only a voice. The American people need to see my face. I want to look the American people in the eye.

Introduction

My name is Cofer Black. I served as the Director of the CIA's Counterterrorist Center from 1999 until May of 2002. I hope these proceedings provide the relatives and loved ones of those lost some of the answers they seek. We are meeting here today because of the murder of more than 3,000 innocents on 9/11. We provided strategic warning. Despite our intense efforts we were unable to provide tactical warning on 9/11.

CTC

Everything we do in this global war and the very real risks of our work have only one objective: to protect America, to protect innocent people. In this long fight, my CIA colleagues operating with me in Khartoum, Sudan in 1995 preempted preparations of Usama bin Laden's thugs to kill me. The same Usama bin Laden and his al Qaeda are the killers of 9/11.

When you look at our counterterrorism programs, you need to fully appreciate choices in three areas. These were choices made for us. Made for the CIA and made for my Counterterrorist Center. These involved numbers of people, finances, and operational flexibility.

People: Before 9/11, the CIA's Counterterrorist Center had as many people as three infantry companies. Three infantry companies can be expected to cover a front of a few kilometers: Our Counterterrorist Center has worldwide responsibilities for all terrorist threats. It was not only al Qaeda we had to engage... Prior to my arrival, the Director had increased our personnel nearly 100 percent. The DCI and the Deputy Director of Operations struggled with real shortages. While all the other operating components were being cut, counterterrorism received what small increases were available.

Cash: This is what we use to pay for operations. At the beginning of each of my three fiscal years as Chief, the Counterterrorist Center had enough money to purchase about two modern jet fighter aircraft.

Operational flexibility: This is a highly classified area. All I want to say is that there was "before" 9/11 and "after" 9/11. After 9/11 the gloves come off.

Nearly 3,000 al Qaeda terrorists and their supporters have been detained. In Afghanistan the al Qaeda who refused to surrender have been killed. The hunt is on.

At your hearing last Friday my colleague (referred to only as "CIA Officer") was a witness before you and spoke from behind a screen. The significant point of his remarks was the unprepared statement that he had been "over-whelmed" by the limitless work of counterterrorism and the lack of resources. We can now see why he said this. However even a fully staffed and supported effort will not provide 100 percent defense. We must go on the offense and stay there.

Working with the FBI

I am very concerned that your hearings last week left you with a substantial misunderstanding about communications between the CIA and the FBI during the investigation of the attack on the *USS Cole*. In that case, we were supporting the FBI's investigation. Both agencies wanted to find out who killed our sailors. Both agencies were working to bring those terrorists to justice. We were in the business of providing information to the FBI, not withholding it.

I want to be as clear as I can be that FBI agents and analysts had full access to information we acquired about the **Cole** *attack. For example, we ran a joint operation with the FBI to determine if a* **Cole** *suspect was it a Kuala Lumpur surveillance photo. I want to repeat – it was a joint operation. The FBI had access to that information from the beginning. More specifically, our records establish that the*

Special Agents from the FBI's New York Field Office who were investigating the USS Cole attack reviewed the information about the Kuala Lumpur photo in late January 2001.

I also want to be clear that, according the CTC analyst who attended the June 2001 FBI-CIA meeting in New York City, an FBI employee brought the photos to New York and showed them to FBI agents at the meeting. I want to repeat that. An FBI employee brought the photos to New York. Furthermore, the CIA analyst was not able to provide all of the information FBI criminal investigators wanted because of laws and rules against contaminating criminal investigators with intelligence information. As your staff has pointed out, there are laws that complicate our work.

The men and women of CTC and those in CIA who work counterterrorism are the finest Americans this country can produce. They are highly professional, smart, hard working, brave and have an unbelievable work ethic working 14-18 hour days, seven days a week, month after month for my entire three years...

I want to thank all in the Intelligence Community and in CIA who work counterterrorism particularly our field personnel.

Bin Laden declares war

(U) From 1996 on, bin Laden's threats against Americans increased dramatically.

- In 1996 his allies issued a fatwa authorizing attacks against Western military targets on the Arabian Peninsula.

- *In 1998, just before the East African embassy bombings, his clerics issued another fatwa stating that Muslims have a religious obligation to kill military and civilian Americans worldwide.*

Kuala Lumpur

(U) The January 2000 operation to learn what a group of suspected al Qaeda-associated men were doing in Kuala Lumpur is a case where our procedures were inadequate. The first part of that operation was successful. We picked up on intelligence developed during the FBI's investigation of the 1998 Nairobi attack to identify two suspected al Qaeda men. We tracked them to a meeting in Kuala Lumpur where they met with other terrorist operatives. We were not able to learn what the men did during that

meeting, but we were able to identify other participants. That information continues to be operationally useful today.

(U) While the meeting was in progress, CTC officers detailed to the FBI kept the FBI updated through verbal briefings. Where we fell short was in our not informing the Department of State that we had identified two al Qaeda men so that the Department could decide whether to place them on the watchlist. Nearly two years later, those two men, al-Mihdhar and al-Hazmi, were hijackers on Flight 77.

(U) Last week, you discussed that issue at length so I won't repeat the details. In my judgment, we should have watchlisted both. That we did not do so was, in part, the result of insufficient training for our officers. But mainly, it was due to the extraordinary pace of our operations during that period. We worked on high numbers of operations simultaneously constantly adding ever more operations – all with the objective of defeating terrorist attacks and defending our country.

(U) I identified the source of the problem and moved to fix it. We improved training for our officers and established a more comprehensive program for using intelligence to support watchlists.

Threats in 2001

(U) I want to turn to the period leading up to the September 11 attacks. During the spring and summer of 2001, I became convinced that al Qaeda was going to strike hard. We did not know where but the Arabian Peninsula and Israel were the most likely targets. By late summer, I was growing more concerned about a potential attack on the United States. However, I knew that we needed very specific information about an attack if anyone was going to pay attention to us and facilitate action. Warning is one of our most important functions; translating warning into effective, specific homeland defense defensive action is hard. As an example, I concluded my briefing of 15 August 2001 to the Department of Defense's Annual Convention on Counterterrorism that "…we are going to be struck soon, many Americans are going to die, and it could be in the US." However, the DCI and the President of the United States need exacting intelligence in order to take effective, selective defensive action. They need to know such things as – the attack is coming within the next few days and here is what they are going to hit. I regret that we did not have

191

specific, actionable intelligence before the September 11, 2001 attacks as we had provided many times before.

Pre-attack capabilities

(U) You have asked for an assessment of our capabilities before and after the September 11 attacks. While the DCI and the intelligence Committees worked hard to provide additional resources – we had to deal with 10 years of decline in the Directorate of Operations generally, and in our overseas capabilities in particular. At the most fundamental level, the answer to both questions is simple – before September 11, we did not have enough people, money, or sufficiently flexible rules of engagement. After September 11, we did.

Final thoughts

(U) As the Committee conducts its work, I want to reflect for a moment on my service as Chief of CTC. We are at WAR. We in CTC were aware of this fact. We gave it all we had. We, CIA, are this country's primary offense abroad against the terrorist threat. We willingly accept this tough job. I know that some Americans are alive today because of our efforts. And the same for citizens of other countries.

Nobody regrets more that we did not stop the attacks on September 11 than the officers of CTC or their former Chief.

I know that we are on the right track today and as a result we are safer as a nation. Lastly, I was proud of them then, am now, and will be until I die...

Analysis of the testimony of Cofer Black

At your hearing last Friday my colleague (referred to only as "CIA Officer") was a witness before you and spoke from behind a screen. The significant point of his remarks was the unprepared statement that he had been "overwhelmed" by the limitless work of counterterrorism and the lack of resources.

From this testimony, we are told officers at the CIA CTC were undermanned and overworked.

"'Overwhelmed' by the limitless work of counterterrorism and the lack of resources."

But only three terrorists from overseas were known to have entered the US, Khalid al-Mihdhar, Nawaf al-Hazmi, and Zacarias Moussaoui. Moussaoui was already in custody by the time the CIA was informed about him. It is hard to see how hundreds of employees with multi-billion-dollar budgets were so overworked keeping track of the other two al Qaeda terrorists who had entered the US.

> I am very concerned that your hearings last week left you with a substantial misunderstanding about communications between the CIA and the FBI during the investigation of the attack on the *USS Cole*. In that case, we were supporting the FBI's investigation. Both agencies wanted to find out who killed our sailors. Both agencies were working to bring those terrorists to justice. We were in the business of providing information to the FBI, not withholding it.

Additional facts that surfaced after this testimony show that on numerous occasions the CIA did not provide information to the FBI in a timely fashion and in fact had kept important information hidden from the FBI.

Working with the FBI

> (U) The January 2000 operation to learn what a group of suspected al Qaeda associated men were doing in Kuala Lumpur is a case where our procedures were – inadequate. The first part of that operation was successful. We picked up on intelligence developed during the FBI's investigation of the 1998 Nairobi attack to identify two suspected al Qaeda men. We tracked them to a meeting in Kuala Lumpur where they met with other terrorist operatives. We were not able to learn what the men did during that meeting, but we were able to identify other participants. That information continues to be operationally useful today.

> (U) While the meeting was in. progress, CTC officers detailed to the FBI kept the FBI updated through verbal briefings. Where we fell short was in our not informing the Department of State that we had identified two al Qaeda men so that the Department could decide whether to place them on the watchlist. Nearly two years later, those two men, al-Mihdhar and al-Hazmi, were hijackers on Flight 77.

According to the testimony of Cofer Black, people at this meeting had been identified as having been al Qaeda terrorists, and had been connected with other al Qaeda terrorists involved with the East Africa embassy bombings by the FBI in a prior investigation. The participants of this meeting were photographed and videotaped by Malaysian intelligence. These photographs were then sent to the CIA, but inexplicably not turned over to the FBI for 21 months, not until August 23, 2001.

I want to be as clear as I can be that FBI agents and analysts had full access to information we acquired about the Cole attack. For example, we ran a joint operation with the FBI to determine if a Cole suspect was it a Kuala Lumpur surveillance photo. I want to repeat – it was a joint operation. The FBI had access to that information from the beginning. More specifically, our records establish that the Special Agents from the FBI's New York Field Office who were investigating the USS Cole attack reviewed the information about the Kuala Lumpur photo in late January 2001.

Cofer Black said FBI agents had access to the information the CIA had on the *Cole* attack "from the beginning," and in fact the FBI worked in a joint operation with the CIA to determine whether a *Cole* suspect was in the Kuala Lumpur photo in January 2001. "Specifically our (CIA) records establish that the Special Agents from the FBI's New York Field Office who were investigating the *USS Cole* attack reviewed the information about the Kuala Lumpur photo in late January 2001."

And yet information available at the time of this testimony shows that the CIA did not give the FBI this information and the photographs from Kuala Lumpur on Mihdhar until August 23, 2001, and on Khallad bin Attash until August 30, 2001. If they had given the FBI this information from the beginning, why did they specially transfer these photos over to the FBI in August 2001? This shows Cofer Black's testimony was misleading and false.

Information that came out later if the FBI IG report contradicts the testimony Cofer Black gave to the Joint Inquiry Committee.

I also want to be clear that, according the CTC analyst who attended the June 2001 FBI-CIA meeting in New York City, an FBI employee brought the photos to New York and showed them to FBI agents at the meeting. I want to repeat that. An FBI employee brought the photos to New York. Furthermore, the CIA analyst was not able to provide all of the information FBI criminal investigators wanted because of laws and rules against contaminating criminal investigators with intelligence information. As your staff has pointed out, there are laws that complicate our work.

While his statement is technically correct, the impression it is trying to leave a false impression of what went on at that meeting on June 11, 2001. First the photographs were the photos the CIA had taken at the Kuala Lumpur al Qaeda planning meeting. How did a FBI agent even know about these photos if the CIA had not deliberately told this agent about these photos? Second if an FBI Agent knew about these photos and the fact they had been taken at Kuala Lumpur, it is clear this information was never official transferred over to the until August 23, when the photos of Mihdar and Hazmi were transferred over to the FBI and August 30 when the photo of Khallad was transferred over to the FBI. Since the FBI Cole investigators were focused heavily on Khallad, having known by the time the June 11, 2001 meeting that he had been the mastermind of the Cole bombing, it is clear that a photo of Khallad was not presented to these investigators at this meeting along with photos of other terrorists. If a photo of Khallad had been presented to the Cole investigators they would have known all of the people in these photos were directly connected to the planning of the Cole bombing, and they would have mounted a huge investigation of these people and have prevented the attacks on 9/11. It is now clear that the photos were of Mihdhar and Hazmi and other terrorists at the Kuala Lumpur meeting, but incredibly even after showing the Cole investigators these photos they must not have been given enough information to have watch listed or found the terrorists who we now know were inside of the US or about to return to the US. We now know that at the time of this meeting the CIA knew Hazmi was inside of the US, knew Mihdhar had a multi-entry visa for the US, even knew a huge attack was just about to occur in the US that would cause mass casualties, and yet the CIA and the CIA officer at this meeting did not give the FBI investigators any of this information, even when these investigator knowing something is not right, and ask who are these people, and what do they have to do with the Cole bombing?

Why did he not give the FBI *Cole* investigators this information? According to Black:

> *"...the CIA analyst was not able to provide all of the information FBI criminal investigators wanted because of*

laws and rules against contaminating criminal investigators with intelligence information. "

First, if the supervisor, Shannon, was worried about contaminating a FBI criminal investigation, and even if there were rules at that time against sharing intelligence information with criminal investi-gators from the *Cole* investigation until the information was officially passed over the wall, he could have asked the *Cole* criminal investigators to leave the room for a short time while this information was given to FBI intelligence investigators. Second, any prohibition preventing intelligence officers from passing information to criminal investigators was nullified if there is any indication this information was associated with any event resulting in loss of life, and everyone at this point knew about the numerous warnings that had been sent to both the CIA and FBI, indicating that a huge al Qaeda attack was about to take place inside of the US resulting in massive American casualties.

This meeting took place 90 days before 9/11 enough time to watchlist both Mihdhar and Hazmi and then locate al-Mihdhar when he returned to the US on July 4, 2001.

By late summer, I was growing more concerned about a potential attack on the United States. However, I knew that we needed very specific information about an attack if anyone was going to pay attention to us and facilitate action. Warning is one of our most important functions; translating warning into effective, specific homeland defense defensive action is hard. As an example, I concluded my briefing of 15 August 2001 to the Department of Defense's Annual Convention on Counter-terrorism that "...we are going to be struck soon, many Americans are going to die, and it could be in the US." However, the DCI and the President of the United States need exacting intelligence in order to take effective, selective defensive action. They need to know such things as – the attack is coming within the next few days and here is what they are going to hit. I regret that we did not have specific, actionable intelligence before the September 11, 2001 attacks as we had provided many times before.

The CIA knew that al-Hazmi had entered the US on January 15, 2000. By August 22, 2001, they knew that both Khalid al-Mihdhar and Nawaf al-Hazmi were in the US, and that they had left an al

Qaeda planning meeting, just prior to entering the US in January 2000. They also knew about a massive al Qaeda attack just about to occur inside of the US. Yet the Director of CIA's Counterterrorist Center, Cofer Black, claims they did not have "specific, actionable" intelligence before September 11.

The CIA had focused on both al-Mihdhar and al-Hazmi numerous times, even knew that Mihdhar had flown into and out of the US several times. And yet it was not until August 23, 2001 that these terrorists were first placed on a watchlist, almost 21 months after their names had first surfaced at the CIA. When they were watchlisted on August 23, 2001, they were not placed on a watchlist that would keep them off US airliners. Cofer Black's testimony never explains why this information was hidden for the FBI for 21 months, and then when it was finally sent to the FBI, it was not directly connected at that time to the huge al Qaeda attack the CIA was aware of, as described in the testimony above. And neither his testimony nor the questions from the Joint Inquiry Committee ever explain this?

The FBI's Handling of the Phoenix Electronic Communication and Investigation of Zacarias Moussaoui Prior to September 11, 2001
Eleanor Hill, Staff Director, Joint Inquiry Staff September 24, 2002
[As Supplemented October 17, 2002]

Introduction

Mr. Chairmen, members of this Joint Committee, good morning. I appreciate the opportunity to appear before the Committees once again. At our last hearing, we discussed information the Intelligence Community had available prior to September 11, 2001 regarding the September 11 hijackers. Today, I will discuss:

- The July 10, 2001 electronic communication (EC) from the FBI's Phoenix Field Office to FBI Headquarters," also known as the "Phoenix memo"

- The investigation, prior to September 11, 2001, of Zacarias Moussaoui

- The FBI Investigation of Zacarias Moussaoui, August 16 to September 11, 2001

Zacarias Moussaoui came to the attention of the FBI during a period of time when the Intelligence Community was detecting numerous indicators of an impending terrorist attack against US interests somewhere in the world. Moussaoui was in the custody of the INS on September 11, 2001. Our review has, in part, focused on whether information resulting from the FBI's investigation of Moussaoui could have alerted the US government to the scope and nature of the attacks that occurred on September 11, 2001.

Moussaoui has been indicted and faces a criminal trial this fall. In order to avoid affecting the course of that proceeding, the Joint Inquiry Staff originally limited the amount of detail in this presentation while attempting to provide a general under- standing of the facts of the investigation. Consistent with a September 23, 2002 order of the Court in the Moussaoui case that clarified the nature of the information that could be discussed in public, additional information has been included in this version of the Statement.

Our review of the FBI's investigation to date has identified three issues in particular to which I would draw Members' attention:

- Differences in the way the FBI's Field Offices and Headquarters components analyzed and perceived the danger posed by the facts uncovered during the FBI's investigation of Moussaoui prior to September 11, 2001;

- The tools available to the FBI under the Constitution and laws of the United States to investigate that danger, notably the Foreign Intelligence Surveillance Act (FISA), and whether FBI personnel were well organized and informed about the availability of those tools; and

- Whether the substance, clarity, and urgency of the threat warning provided by the FBI to other parts of the Intelligence Community corresponded to the danger that had been identified.

For purposes of this interim report, the American public should understand that, under FISA, the FBI can obtain a court order authorizing a physical search or electronic surveillance, such as a wiretap, if it can demonstrate that the subject: 1) is an agent of a foreign power, which can be a foreign country or an international terrorist group, and 2) was, among other things, engaged in international terrorism, or activities in preparation therefor, on behalf of that foreign power. Court orders issued under FISA are classified and are issued by the Foreign Intelligence Surveillance Court (FISC).

The FBI's focus at the time Moussaoui was taken into custody appears to the Joint Inquiry Staff to have been almost entirely on investigating specific crimes and not on identifying linkages between separate investigations or on sharing information with other US government agencies with counterterrorist responsebilities. No one at FBI Headquarters apparently connected Moussaoui, the Phoenix memo, the possible presence of Khalid al-Mihdhar and Nawaf al-Hazmi in the United States, or the flood of warnings about possible terrorist attacks during the summer of 2001.

Moussaoui was unhappy with the training at Airman and, at the end of May 2001, had contacted Pan American International Flight School in Minneapolis. While Airman Flight School provided flight lessons in piloting Cessnas and similar small aircraft, Pan Am provided ground training and access to a Boeing 747 flight simulator used by professional pilots.

Most of Pan Am's students are either newly hired airline pilots who use the flight simulator for initial training or are active airline pilots who use the equipment for an update or refresher training. Although anyone can sign up for lessons at Pan Am, the typical student has a pilot's license, is employed by an airline, and has several thousand flight hours. Moussaoui had none of these qualifications.

On August 11, 2001, Moussaoui and his roommate, Hussein al-Attas, arrived in Eagan, MN, and checked into a hotel. Moussaoui began classes at Pan Am on August 13, 2001. On Wednesday, August 15, 2001, an employee at Pan Am called the FBI's Minneapolis Field Office because the employee and other Pan Am employees were suspicious of Moussaoui.

The FBI determined that Moussaoui had paid $8,000 to $9,000 in cash for training on the Boeing 747 Model 400 aircraft simulator but met none of the usual criteria for students at the flight school. What set Moussaoui apart from all other students was that Moussaoui had no aviation background and, apparently, no pilot's license. It was also considered odd that Moussaoui indicated that he wished to learn to take off and land the 747 Model 400, which he referred to as an "ego boosting thing." It should be noted that this conflicts with published reports that he only wanted to pilot the plane in the air and did not want to land or take off.

Based on the information from the flight school, the FBI's Minneapolis Field Office opened an international terrorism investigation of Moussaoui. The Minneapolis Field Office reportedly viewed Moussaoui as a threat to national security.

The FBI's Minneapolis Field Office hosts and is part of a Joint Terrorism Task Force, or JTTF. Agents of the INS share space and work closely with the FBI in Minneapolis and were able to immediately determine that Moussaoui had been authorized to stay in the United States only until May 22, 2001. Thus, Moussaoui was "out of status" at the time – August – that the FBI began investigating him.

On the same day the Minneapolis Field Office learned about Moussaoui, it asked both the CIA and the FBI's legal attaché in Paris for any information they had or could get on Moussaoui. At the same time, they also informed FBI Headquarters of the investigation. The supervisory agent in Minneapolis told the Joint Inquiry Staff that FBI Headquarters had suggested that Moussaoui be put under surveillance, but that Minneapolis did not have enough agents to do that. Furthermore, the Minneapolis agents believed that it was more important to prevent Moussaoui from getting any additional flight training.

On Thursday, August 16, the FBI determined that Moussaoui was unlike any other student with whom his flight instructor had worked. Moussaoui began the ground school portion of the training with instruction in aircraft systems using a PowerPoint presentation. This portion of the instruction reportedly was useless for Moussaoui, who had no background in any type of sophisticated aircraft systems and, apparently, had only approximately 50 hours of flight training in light civil aircraft bearing no similarity to the 747-400. In addition, Moussaoui was extremely interested in the operation of the plane's doors and control panel, which Pan Am found suspicious. Further, Moussaoui reportedly said that he would "love" to fly a simulated flight from Heathrow Airport in England to John F. Kennedy Airport in New York. Moussaoui seemed to have a legitimate interest in aircraft and had asked for recommendations for schools to provide subsequent training.

After conducting flight school interviews, the FBI agents, along with two INS agents, went to Moussaoui's hotel. The INS agents temporarily detained Moussaoui and his roommate, Hussein al-Attas, while checking to determine if they were legally in the United States. Al-Attas showed the INS that he had a valid student visa and agreed to allow the agents to search his property in the hotel room.

[Al-Attas was recently convicted of making false statements to the FBI regarding statements by Moussaoui and the extent of his relationship with Moussaoui. He remains in custody as a material witness.]

Moussaoui showed the agents his passport case, which included his passport, a British driver's license, a bank statement showing a deposit of $32,000 in cash to an Oklahoma account, and an application to extend his stay in the United States. The INS agents determined that Moussaoui had not received an extension to allow him to stay in the United States beyond May 22, 2001, so they took him into custody.

Moussaoui declined to allow the agents to search his belongings. When the agents told Moussaoui that he would be deported, Moussaoui agreed to let the agents take his belongings to the INS office for safekeeping. The agents packed Moussaoui's belongings, noticing that he had a laptop computer among his possessions.

The agents interviewed Moussaoui at the INS office in Minneapolis. Moussaoui told them that he had traveled to Morocco, Malaysia, and Pakistan for business, although he could not provide any details of his employment. Nor could he convincingly explain the $32,000 bank balance.

After Moussaoui's detention, the Minneapolis supervisory agent called the office's legal counsel and asked if there was any way to search Moussaoui's possessions without his consent. He was told he had to obtain a search warrant.

Over the ensuing days, the Minneapolis agents considered several alternatives, including trying to obtain a criminal search warrant, seeking a search warrant under FISA, and deporting Moussaoui to France after arranging for the French authorities to search Moussaoui's possessions and share their findings with the FBI. Adding to the sense of urgency, a supervisor in the INS Minneapolis office told the FBI that INS typically does not hold visa waiver violators like Moussaoui for more than 24 hours before returning them to their home countries. Under the circumstances, however, the INS said it would hold Moussaoui for seven to ten days.

The FBI conducted no additional interviews of Moussaoui after August 17, 2001. On Saturday, August 18, Minneapolis sent a detailed memorandum to FBI Headquarters describing the Moussaoui investigation and stating that, based on Moussaoui's "possession of weapons and his preparation through physical training for violent confrontation," Minneapolis had reason to believe that Moussaoui, al-Attas "and others yet unknown" were conspiring to seize control of an airplane.

The Joint Inquiry Staff has been told in interviews with the Minneapolis agents that FBI Headquarters advised against trying to obtain a criminal search warrant as that might prejudice any subsequent efforts to get a search warrant under FISA. Under FISA, a search warrant could be obtained if they could show there was probable cause to believe Moussaoui was an agent of a foreign power and either engaged in terrorism or was preparing to engage in terrorism. FBI Headquarters was concerned that if a criminal warrant was denied and then the agents tried to get a warrant under FISA, the Court would think the agents were trying to use authority for an intelligence investigation to pursue a criminal case.

During this time-frame, an attorney in the National Security Law Unit at FBI Headquarters asked the counsel in the Minneapolis Field Office if she had considered trying to obtain a criminal warrant and she replied that a FISA warrant would be the safer course. Minneapolis also wanted to notify the Criminal Division about Moussaoui through the local US Attorney's Office, believing it was obligated to do so under Attorney General guidelines that required notification when there is a "reasonable indication" of a felony. FBI Headquarters advised that Minneapolis did not have enough evidence to warrant notifying the Criminal Division.

The FBI case agent in Minneapolis had become increasingly frustrated with what he perceived as a lack of assistance from the Radical Fundamentalist Unit (RFU) at FBI Headquarters. He had had previous conflicts with the RFU agent over FISA issues and believed Headquarters was not being responsive to the threat Minneapolis had identified. At the suggestion of a Minneapolis supervisor, the Minneapolis case agent contacted an FBI official who was detailed to the CTC. The Minneapolis agent shared the details of the Moussaoui investigation with him and provided the names of associates that had been connected to Moussaoui. The Minneapolis case agent has told the Joint Inquiry Staff that he was looking for any information that CTC could provide that would strengthen the case linking Moussaoui to international terrorism.

On August 21, 2001, the Minneapolis case agent sent an e-mail to the supervisory special agent in the RFU who was handling this matter, stating: "[It's] imperative that the [US Secret Service] be apprised of this threat potential indicated by the evidence... If [Moussaoui] seizes an aircraft flying from Heathrow to NYC, it will have the fuel on board to reach DC." In an interview with the Joint Inquiry Staff, the RFU agent to whom the message was addressed said that he told the Minneapolis agent that he was working on a notification to the entire Intelligence Community, including the Secret Service, about the threat presented by Moussaoui.

The RFU supervisory special agent sent a teletype on September 4, 2001, recounting the FBI's interviews of Moussaoui and al-Attas, and other information it had obtained in the meantime. The teletype, however, merely recounted the steps in the investigation. It did not place Moussaoui's actions in the context of the increased level of terrorist threats during the summer of 2001, nor did it provide its recipients with any analysis of Moussaoui's actions or plans, or information about what type of threat he may have presented.

A CIA officer detailed to FBI Headquarters learned of the Moussaoui investigation from CTC in the third week of August 2001. The officer was alarmed about Moussaoui for several reasons. First, Moussaoui had denied being a Muslim to the flight instructor, while al-Attas (Moussaoui's companion at the flight school) informed the FBI that Moussaoui was a fundamentalist. Further, the fact Moussaoui was interested in using the Minneapolis flight school simulator to learn to fly from Heathrow to JFK Airport made him concerned that Moussaoui was a hijacker. Others were similarly concerned. CIA stations were advised of the known facts regarding Moussaoui and al-Attas and were asked to provide any relevant information they might have. The two were described as "suspect 747 airline attackers" and "suspect airline suicide attacker," who might be "involved in a larger plot to target airlines traveling from Europe to the US..."

On Wednesday, August 22, the FBI legal attaché's office in Paris provided its report. That report started a series of discussions between Minneapolis and the RFU at FBI Headquarters focusing on whether a specific group of Chechen rebels was a "recognized" foreign power, i.e., one that was on the State Department's list of terrorist groups and for which the Foreign Intelligence Surveillance Court had previously granted orders. The RFU agent believed that the Chechen rebels were not a "recognized" foreign power and that, even if Moussaoui were to be linked to them, the FBI could not obtain a search order under FISA. Thus, the RFU agent told the Minneapolis agents that they needed to somehow connect Moussaoui to al Qaeda, which he believed was a "recognized" foreign power. This led the Minneapolis agents to attempt to gather information showing that the Chechen rebels were connected to al Qaeda.

Unfortunately this dialogue was based on a misunderstanding of FISA. The FBI's Deputy General Counsel told the Joint Inquiry Staff that the term "recognized foreign power" has no meaning under FISA and that the FBI can obtain a search warrant under FISA for an agent of an international terrorist group, including the Chechen rebels. But because of the misunderstanding, Minneapolis spent the better part of three weeks trying to connect the Chechen group to al Qaeda. The Minneapolis case agent contacted CTC, asking for additional information concerning connections between the group and al Qaeda; he also suggested that the RFU agent contact CTC for assistance on the issue. The RFU agent responded that he had all the information he needed and requested that Minneapolis work through FBI Headquarters when contacting CTC. Ultimately, the RFU agent agreed to submit Minneapolis' FISA request to the attorneys in the FBI's National Security Law Unit (NSLU) for review.

The Joint Inquiry Staff interviewed several FBI attorneys with whom the RFU agent consulted about Moussaoui. All have confirmed that they advised the RFU agent that the evidence was insufficient to link Moussaoui to a foreign power. One of the attorneys also told the RFU agent that the Chechen rebels were not a "recognized" foreign power. The attorneys also told the Staff that, if they had been aware of the Phoenix memo, they would have forwarded the FISA request to the Justice Department's Office of Intelligence Policy Review (OIPR). They reasoned that the particulars of the Phoenix memo changed the context of the Moussaoui investigation and made a stronger case for the FISA warrant. None of them saw the Phoenix memo before September 11.

During a conversation on August 27, 2001, the RFU agent told the Minneapolis supervisor that the supervisor was getting people "spun up" over Moussaoui. According to his notes and his statement to the Joint Inquiry Staff, the supervisor replied that he was trying to get people at FBI Headquarters "spun up" because he was trying to make sure that Moussaoui "did not take control of a plane and fly it into the World Trade Center." The Minneapolis agent said that the Headquarters agent told him, "[T]hat's not going to happen. We don't know he's a terrorist. You don't have enough to show he is a terrorist. You have a guy interested in this type of aircraft – that is it." The Headquarters agent does not remember this exchange. The Minneapolis supervisor told the Joint Inquiry Staff that he had no reason to believe that Moussaoui was planning an attack on the World Trade Center; he was merely trying to get Headquarters' attention.

In a subsequent conference call with FBI Headquarters, the chief of the RFU Unit told Minneapolis that a connection with a specific recognized foreign power, such as Hamas, was necessary to get a FISA search warrant.

On August 28, 2001, after reviewing the request for a search warrant, the RFU agent edited it and returned the request to Minneapolis for comment. The RFU agent says that it was not unusual for Headquarters agents to make changes to field submissions in addition to changes made by the NSLU and OIPR. The major substantive change that was made was the removal of information about connections between the Chechen rebels and al Qaeda. The RFU agent said he removed it because he believed this information was insufficient and that, if he received approval from the NSLU to use the Chechen rebels as a foreign power, he would have added it back to an expanded section about Chechnya.

After the edit was complete, the RFU agent briefed the FBI Deputy General Counsel. The Deputy General Counsel told the Joint Inquiry Staff that he agreed with the RFU agent that there was insufficient information to show that Moussaoui was an agent of a foreign power, but that the issue of a "recognized" foreign power did not come up. After that briefing, the RFU agent sent an e-mail to Minneapolis saying that the information was even less sufficient than he had previously thought because Moussaoui would actually have to be shown to be a part of a movement or organization.

Subsequent to concluding that there was insufficient information to show that Moussaoui was an agent of any foreign power, the FBI's focus shifted to arranging for Moussaoui's planned deportation to France on September 17. French officials would search his belongings and provide the results to the FBI. Although the FBI was no longer considering a search warrant under FISA, no one revisited the idea of attempting to obtain a criminal search warrant, even though the only reason for not attempting to obtain a criminal search warrant – the concern that it would prejudice a request under FISA – no longer existed.

On Thursday, September 4, 2001, FBI Headquarters sent a teletype to the Intelligence Community and other US government agencies, including the Federal Aviation Administration (FAA), providing information about the Moussaoui investigation. The teletype noted that Moussaoui was being held in custody but did not describe any particular threat that the FBI thought he posed, for example, whether he might be connected to a larger plot. The teletype also did not recommend that the addressees take any action or look for any additional indicators of a terrorist attack, nor did it provide any analysis of a possible hijacking threat or provide any specific warnings. The following day the Minneapolis case agent hand-carried the teletype to two employees of the FAA's Bloomington, MN, office and orally briefed them on the status of the investigation. The two FAA employees told the Joint Inquiry Staff that the FBI agent did not convey any sense of urgency about the teletype and did not ask them to take any specific action regarding Moussaoui. He just wanted to be sure the FAA had received the cable.

The final preparations for Moussaoui's deportation were underway when the September 11 attacks occurred.

Prior to September 11, 2001, no one at the FBI canvassed other individuals in the custody of and cooperating with the US government in connection with past terrorism cases to see if any of those individuals knew Moussaoui.

Conclusion

The staff has described three series of events – pertaining to al-Mihdhar and al-Hazmi, the Phoenix EC, and Zacarias Moussaoui – each of which raises significant questions in their own right. In the wake of the September 11 attacks, they also illustrate the danger of seeing events in isolation from each other. In our view, taken together, they clearly demonstrate how our counterterrorist efforts must be based on a comprehensive and current understanding of the overall context in which terrorist networks like al Qaeda operate.

The first matter involved Khalid al-Mihdhar and Nawaf al-Hazmi, the two hijackers who came to the attention of the Intelligence Community in early 2000 but subsequently entered the United States unobserved and undetected later. The Intelligence Community succeeded in determining that these bin Laden operatives were traveling in January 2000 to Malaysia and in collecting important information about them. The system broke down, however, in making the best use of that information and in ensuring that it was effectively and fully shared with agencies, like the FBI, the State Department and the INS, that could have acted on it to either prevent them from entering the United States or surveil them and uncover their activities while in the United States.

In addition, the FBI and the CIA had responsibilities to respond to the October 2000 attack on *USS Cole*. Each had information that the other needed to carry out those responsibilities. But, at a key meeting in New York on June 11, 2001, the CIA did not provide to the FBI information about the Malaysian meeting and its participants that could have assisted the FBI in its investigation. These events reflect misunderstandings that have developed over the last several years about the use of information derived from intelligence-gathering activities in criminal investigations.

The problem of communication demonstrated by the al-Mihdhar/al-Hazmi story existed not only between the CIA and FBI, but also within the FBI itself. Once it was determined in late August 2001 that Khalid al-Mihdhar was in the United States, the search to determine his whereabouts was constrained by FBI policies and practices regarding the use of intelligence information in FBI criminal investigations. This limited the resources that were made available for the FBI to conduct the search during a time in which al-Mihdhar and al-Hazmi were purchasing their September 11 tickets and traveling to their last rallying points.

The second matter – the Phoenix EC – also illustrates the Intelligence Community's strength and weaknesses. An FBI field agent perceived, amidst a profusion of cases, that terrorists could use the well-developed system of flight training education in the United States to prepare an attack against us. The field agent understood that it was necessary to go beyond individual cases and to undertake an empirical analysis broader than the geographic limits of a single field office. The idea was submitted to FBI Headquarters, where, for a variety of reasons, it generated almost no interest. First, no one gleaned from the FBI's own records that others at the Bureau had previously expressed concerns about possible terrorists at US flight education institutions. Second, anticipating future threats has not been a significant part of the FBI's general approach to its work. Third, the highest levels of the Intelligence Community had not communicated effectively to its personnel the critical importance of analyzing information in light of the growing awareness of an impending terrorist attack in the summer of 2001. Finally, FBI management did not perceive it would be useful to simply alert others at the FBI to the danger that one of its field offices perceived.

As for the third matter, one can see in the pre-September 11 handling of the case of Zacarias Moussaoui a myopic focus within both the FBI and the DCI's CTC on the case at hand. An FBI field agent and his supervisor saw a potential threat, were concerned about the possibility of a larger plot to target airlines, and reported their concerns to FBI Headquarters. The Moussaoui information was also shared with the DCI's CTC. But neither FBI Headquarters nor the DCI's CTC linked this information to warnings emanating from the CTC in the summer of 2001 about an impending terrorist attack, nor did they see a possible connection to information available on August 23, 2001 (this date was actually August 21, 2001) that bin Laden operatives had entered the United States. The same unit at FBI Headquarters also had the Phoenix EC, but still did not sound any alarm bells.

No one will ever know whether a greater focus on the connection between these events would have led to the unraveling of the September 11 plot. But clearly, it might have drawn greater attention to the possibility of a terrorist attack in the United States, generated a heightened state of alert regarding such attacks, and prompted more aggressive investigation and intelligence gathering regarding the information our government did possess prior to September 11.

Mr. Chairman, members of these two Committees, this completes my statement for today's hearing. Thank you.

The Joint Inquiry Staff statement on the FBI's handling of the Phoenix Memo and investigation of Zacarias Moussaoui prior to September 11, 2001

From this staff report it appears no one at the upper levels of the intelligence agencies or the US government connected the entering into the US of Khalid al-Mihdhar and Nawaf al-Hazmi, the arrest of Zacarias Moussaoui, or the Phoenix memo detailing the apparent increase in the number of radical Muslims to the warnings of a pending terrorist attack in the summer of 2001.

"On August 28, 2001, after reviewing the request for a search warrant, the RFU agent edited it and returned the request to

Minneapolis for comment. The RFU agent says that it was not unusual for Headquarters agents to make changes to field submissions in addition to changes made by the NSLU and OIPR. The major substantive change that was made was the removal of information about connections between the Chechen rebels and al Qaeda. The RFU agent said he removed it because he believed this information was insufficient..."

According to this testimony, the investigation of Zacarias Moussaoui was repeatedly delayed and finally sabotaged by agents in the RFU at the FBI Headquarters. Information was even removed from a FISA search warrant after Minneapolis FBI agents had painstakingly spent three weeks obtaining this information from French intelligence. This information described the connection between the Chechen rebels and al Qaeda, in order to show that Zacarias Moussaoui was part of al Qaeda, material that had been requested by the RFU unit at FBI Headquarters so the Minnesota FBI agents could obtain this FISA search warrant. According to later testimony, this information was deemed to be insufficient, by the RFU agents and therefore was removed prior to the RFU giving this FISA request for a warrant to the FBI General Counsel. The FBI General Counsel immediately rejected this FISA application as insufficient. Since the FISA Court had been set up in 1978 only five out of over 18,300 applications had ever been turned down.

Rather than attempting to speed this FISA application along and help in the investigation of Zacarias Moussaoui, agents at the RFU did everything they could to slow down and effectively sabotage the investigation of Zacarias Moussaoui. They misinterpreted FBI rules, and then removed critical information from the FISA application for a search warrant for the personal computer and duffel bag in the possession of Zacarias Moussaoui.

These FBI RFU agents were also the agents who refused to do anything with the Williams memo detailing the many radical Muslims getting training at Phoenix flight schools. Not only did this group effectively impede the Zacarias Moussaoui investigation and never start an investigation based on the Williams memo, they did not allow this information to go past their place in the FBI hierarchy at FBI Headquarters. No one at the top of the FBI heard about this until after 9/11.

It was not until August 28, 2001, the FBI started a search for the two al Qaeda terrorists, al-Hazmi and al-Mihdhar. In spite of the fact that the investigation of these terrorists had been delayed for 21 months, this still should have been more than sufficient time for the FBI to track down and put surveillance on them. In spite of then fact the FBI knew about the huge al Qaeda attack inside of the US, the assignment for this investigation to find these two al Qaeda terrorists who were clearly going to take part in this attack, went to an inexperienced agent who was given 30 days to complete an unspecified investigation. He did not even start this search until September 4. This investigation had basically gone nowhere and was in progress on 9/11.

Joint Congressional Inquiry
Part One: Findings and Conclusions
Report of the Joint Inquiry into
The Terrorist Attacks of September 11, 2001
By the House Permanent Select Committee on Intelligence
and the Senate Select Committee on Intelligence

A. Factual Findings

B.
1. Finding: While the Intelligence Community had amassed a great deal of valuable intelligence regarding Usama bin Laden and his terrorist activities, none of it identified the time, place, and specific nature of the attacks that were planned for September 11, 2001. Nonetheless, the Community did have information that was clearly relevant to the September 11 attacks, particularly when considered for its collective significance.

2. Finding: During the spring and summer of 2001, the Intelligence Community experienced a significant increase in information indicating that bin Laden and al Qaeda intended to strike against US interests in the very near future.

3. Finding: Beginning in 1998 and continuing into the summer of 2001, the Intelligence Community received a modest, but relatively steady, stream of intelligence reporting that indicated the possibility of terrorist attacks within the United States. Nonetheless, testimony and interviews confirm that it was the general view of the Intelligence Community, in the spring and summer of 2001, that the threatened bin Laden attacks would most likely occur

against US interests overseas, despite indications of plans and intentions to attack in the domestic United States.

4. Finding: From at least 1994, and continuing into the summer of 2001, the Intelligence Community received information indicating that terrorists were contemplating, among other means of attack, the use of aircraft as weapons. This information did not stimulate any specific Intelligence Community assessment of, or collective US government reaction to, this form of threat.

*National Security Advisor Condoleezza Rice stated in a May 16, 2002 press briefing that, on August 6, 2001, the President's Daily Brief (PDB) included information about bin Laden´s methods of operation from a historical perspective dating back to 1997. One of the methods was that bin Laden might choose to highjack an airliner in order to hold passengers hostage to gain release of one of their operatives. She stated, however, that the report did not contain specific warning information, but only a generalized warning, and did not contain information that al Qaeda was discussing a particular planned attack against a specific target at any specific time, place, or by any specific method.

However the PDB given to the President on August 6, 2001 had stated that:

> *"Nevertheless, FBI information since that time (1998) indicates a pattern of suspicious activity in this country consistent with preparation for hijackings or other types of attacks, including recent surveillance of Federal buildings in New York."*

This statement indicates that suspicious activity had taken place in the US consistent with hijackings and targeting buildings in lower Manhattan. This PDB was sent to the President right after an unprecedented number of unmistakable warnings were received by US intelligence sources indicating a massive terrorist attack possibly about to occur in the US. We now know that by the time of this PDB, Tenet and Black had given Rice, Clarke, Rumsfeld, and Ashcroft urgent warnings of a huge al Qaeda attack inside of the US that would cause mass casualties.

1. Finding: Although relevant information that is significant in retrospect regarding the attacks was available to the Intelligence Community prior to September 11, 2001, the

Community too often failed to focus on that information and consider and appreciate its collective significance in terms of a probable terrorist attack. Neither did the Intelligence Community demonstrate sufficient initiative in coming to grips with the new transnational threats. Some significant pieces of information in the vast stream of data being collected were overlooked, some were not recognized as potentially significant at the time and therefore not disseminated, and some required additional action on the part of foreign governments before a direct connection to the hijackers could have been established. For all those reasons, the Intelligence Community failed to capitalize fully on available, and potentially important, information. The sub-findings below identify each category of this information.

5b. The Intelligence Community acquired additional, and highly significant, information regarding Khalid al-Mihdhar and Nawaf al-Hazmi in early 2000. Critical parts of the information concerning al-Mihdhar and al-Hazmi lay dormant within the Intelligence Community for as long as 18 months, at the very time when plans for the September 11 attacks were proceeding. The CIA missed repeated opportunities to act based on the information in its possession that these two bin Laden-associated terrorists were traveling to the United States, and to add their names to watchlists.

5d. [This Joint Inquiry confirmed that these same two future hijackers, Khalid al-Mihdhar and Nawaf al-Hazmi, had numerous contacts with a long-time FBI counterterrorism informant in California and that a third future hijacker, Hani Hanjour, apparently had more limited contact with the same informant. In mid to late 2000, the CIA already had information indicating that al-Mihdhar had a multiple-entry US visa and that al-Hazmi had in fact traveled to Los Angeles, but the two had not been watchlisted and information suggesting that two suspected terrorists could well be in the United States had not yet been given to the FBI. The San Diego FBI Field Office, which handled the informant in question, did not receive that information or any of the other intelligence information pertaining to al-Mihdhar and al-Hazmi prior to September 11, 2001. As a result, the FBI missed the opportunity to task a uniquely well-positioned informant – who denies having any advance knowledge of the plot – to collect information about the hijackers and their plans within the United States.]

The large US intelligence agencies missed their best opportunity when they failed to investigate Mihdhar and Hazmi with sufficient urgency. It appears that they still could have stopped this plot had they put sufficient focus on finding and watchlisting these two terrorists.

On July 10, 2001, an FBI Phoenix Field Office agent sent an "Electronic Communication" to four individuals in the Radical Fundamentalist Unit (RFU) and two individuals in the Usama Bin Laden Unit (UBLU) at FBI Headquarters, and to two agents on International Terrorism squads in the FBI New York Field Office. In the communication, the agent expressed his concerns, based on his first-hand knowledge, that there was a coordinated effort underway by bin Laden to send students to the United States for civil aviation-related training. He noted that there was an "inordinate number of individuals of investigative interest" in this type of training in Arizona and expressed his suspicion that this was an effort to establish a cadre of individuals in civil aviation who would conduct future terrorist activity.

5f. In August 2001, the FBI's Minneapolis Field Office, in conjunction with the INS, detained Zacarias Moussaoui, a French national who had enrolled in flight training in Minnesota. FBI agents there also suspected that Moussaoui was involved in a hijacking plot. FBI Headquarters attorneys determined that there was not probable cause to obtain a court order to search Moussaoui's belongings under the Foreign Intelligence Surveillance Act (FISA). However, personnel at FBI Headquarters, including the Radical Fundamentalist Unit and the National Security Law Unit, as well as agents in the Minneapolis Field Office, misunderstood the legal standard for obtaining an order under FISA. As a result, FBI Minneapolis Field Office personnel wasted valuable investigative resources trying to connect the Chechen rebels to al Qaeda.

No one at the FBI apparently connected the Moussaoui investigation with the heightened threat environment [page 24] in the summer of 2001, the Phoenix communication, or the entry of al-Mihdhar and al-Hazmi into the United States.

5. Finding: Prior to September 11, the Intelligence Community's understanding of al Qaeda was hampered by insufficient analytic focus and quality, particularly in terms of strategic analysis. Analysis and analysts were not always used effectively because of the perception in some quarters of the Intelligence Community that they were less important to agency counterterrorism missions than were operations personnel.

11. Finding: Prior to September 11, 2001, the Intelligence Community did not effectively develop and use human sources to penetrate the al Qaeda inner circle. This lack of reliable and knowledgeable human sources significantly limited the Community's ability to acquire intelligence that could be acted upon before the September 11 attacks. In part, at least, the lack of unilateral (i.e., US-recruited) counterterrorism sources was of a product an excessive reliance on foreign liaison services.

The probability of the CIA or FBI doing this was extremely remote. Instead of analyzing the information they already had, they were focused (or so they claim) on trying to discover the secret by penetrating the al Qaeda inner circle. This could have been done with the extreme secrecy and the multi-decade vetting process the al Qaeda terrorists used for people in their inner circle. Both the CIA and the FBI actually had the secret right in their hands and failed to recognize it.

17. Finding: Despite intelligence reporting from 1998 through the summer of 2001 indicating that Usama bin Laden's terrorist network intended to strike inside the United States, the United States government did not undertake a comprehensive effort to implement defensive measures in the United States.

19. Finding: Prior to September 11, the Intelligence Community and the US government labored to prevent attacks by Usama bin Laden and his terrorist network against the United States, but largely without the benefit of an alert, mobilized and committed American public. Despite intelligence information on the immediacy of the threat level in the spring and summer of 2001, the assumption prevailed in the US government that attacks of the magnitude of September 11 could not happen here. As

a result, there was insufficient effort to alert the American public to the reality and gravity of the threat.

Why did the FBI and CIA not alert the US public to this massive danger? What was the reason for keeping this so secret?

Conclusion – Factual Findings

In short, for a variety of reasons, the Intelligence Community failed to capitalize on both the individual and collective significance of available information that appears relevant to the events of September 11. As a result, the Community missed opportunities to disrupt the September 11 plot by denying entry to or detaining would-be hijackers; to at least try to unravel the plot through surveillance and other investigative work within the United States; [page 35] and, finally, to generate a heightened state of alert and thus harden the homeland against attack. No one will ever know what might have happened had more connections been drawn between these disparate pieces of information. We will never definitively know to what extent the Community would have been able and willing to exploit fully all the opportunities that may have emerged. The important point is that the Intelligence Community, for a variety of reasons, did not bring together and fully appreciate a range of information that could have greatly enhanced its chances of uncovering and preventing Usama bin Laden´s plan to attack the United States on September 11, 2001.

Still remaining questions

There remained many questions after this testimony. The 9/11 Commission was going to take the information gathered from this investigation as a starting point and answer all of the questions that came out of the Joint Inquiry Committee hearings and investigations. The issues remaining from this investigation were:

Why was the information on Mihdhar and Hazmi hidden from the FBI for 21 months?

Why were Mihdhar and Hazmi never connected by the CIA or the FBI to the huge al Qaeda attack everyone it seems at the top of these agencies and even the US government was aware of?

Why was the investigation of Zacarias Moussaoui delayed and then finally sabotaged by the FBI mangers at the RFU section at FBI headquaters?

Chapter 16

9/11 Commission testimony

The 9/11 Commission reviewed more than 2.5 million documents, held interviews with 1,200 individuals, and heard 19 days of public testimony from 160 witnesses. They interviewed in many cases the same people who had been interviewed by the Joint Inquiry Committee, and who had been in charge of the various security functions on September 11. The same people who had failed the country on 9/11 and had already been interviewed by the Joint Inquiry Committee were interviewed again as to why they failed to protect the US on 9/11 and what could be done to protect the US from future terrorist attacks.

Most of the managers at the US intelligence agencies blamed their failure on insufficient resources, claiming they were significantly under funded and undermanned.

These agencies, however, appeared to have had significant information prior to 9/11, which if analyzed properly could have been used to prevent these events. The following testimony and staff reports describe the information these intelligence agencies had, and how this information had been analyzed.

Testimony to the 9/11 Commission from the administration and the NSC

Condoleezza Rice, testimony in March 2004

> *"There was no silver bullet that could have stopped this attack."*

One very simple silver bullet would have been to have the US government generate security measures, which would be designed to keep al Qaeda terrorists with dangerous weapons off US airliners. The August 6 PDB had already stated that al Qaeda was determined to attack inside the US, and that the terrorists might use hijacked aircraft against buildings in lower Manhattan. This warning, combined with the warnings of a huge catastrophic attack by al Qaeda in the summer of 2001, should have been enough to have the NSC request new security measures for the US airline industry.

Dangerous al Qaeda terrorists could have been kept off US airliners.

One of the most basic steps would have been to not allow anyone to carry a dangerous weapon on board a US airliner. This would have rescinded the change to the FAA ruling that allowed passengers to carry a knife with a four-inch blade on board US aircraft.

Condoleezza Rice further testified at the 9/11 hearings on the magnitude of the warnings that were coming into the NSC in the summer of 2001:

> *Let me read you some of the chatter that was picked up in that spring and summer.*
>
> • *"Big Event – there will be a very very very very big uproar.*
>
> • *Unbelievable news coming in weeks."*
>
> • *"There will be attacks in the near future."*
>
> Troubling yes, but they don't tell us when, they don't tell us where, they don't tell us who and they don't tell us how.

What would a prudent person have done in the shoes of Condoleezza Rice and Stephan Hadley? Would they have done nothing to mobilize the rest of the government and the US public, in the face of this massive intelligence that a huge al Qaeda attack was coming that would cause mass US casualties?

Donald Rumsfeld, for the Defense Department, testifying before the 9/11 Commission

> *That by the time the new administration had come into office, almost all of the hijackers were already in the country so nothing could have been done to stop this attack.*

First this is not true. The terrorists did not all arrive in the US until August 5, 2001, only the pilots and Hazmi were in the US prior to the Bush administration taking office. Second, the most obvious point to have stopped this attack was as the hijackers boarded the airliners carrying their weapons. The fact some were in the country already is irrelevant; they likely could not have been stopped at the entry points, and even if they were, other hijackers would have been sent in to replace the ones that could not get in.

Summary of warnings to top administration officials in summer of 2001

The following is a short summary of the warnings specifically addressed to the NSC and the people in the administration, as reported by the 9/11 Commission during their many public hearing and numerous staff reports:

In the spring of 2001, the level of reporting on terrorist threats and planned attacks increased dramatically.

In response to these threats, the FBI sent a message to all of its Field Offices on April 13, summarizing reporting to date.

In May 2001, the drumbeat of reporting grew loader, with reports to top officials that "Bin Laden's public profile may presage attack" and "Bin Laden network's plan advancing."

On My 29, Clarke suggested that Rice ask DCI Tenet what more the United States could do to stop Abu Zubaydah from launching "a series of major terrorists attacks," probably on Israeli targets, but possibly on US facilities. Clarke wrote to Rice, and her deputy Stephan Hadley, "When these attacks occur, as they likely will, we will wonder what more we could have done to stop them."

The reporting noted that operatives might opt to hijack an aircraft or storm an embassy.

Reports similar to these were made available to President Bush in morning intelligence briefings with DCI Tenet usually attended by Vice President Dick Cheney, and National Security Advisor Rice.

Threat reports surged in June and July, reaching an even higher peak of urgency.

A June 12 CIA report passing along biographical on several terrorists mentioned, in commenting on Khalid Shaikh Mohammed, that he was recruiting people to travel to the United States to meet with colleagues already there so they might conduct terrorist attacks on bin Laden's behalf.

Probably this is the most significant statement in the entire 9/11 Commission. This information is presented to the 9/11 Commission in terms of, "passing along biographical.... in commenting on Khalid Shaikh Mohammed. The significance of this information went unnoticed by the 9/11

Commissioners and mainstream news media, and remain buried deep within the 9/11 Commission report. In 1998 the FBI had posted a $2,000,000 reward for Khalid Shaikh Mohammed, and the FAA had issued an advisory saying he should be arrested if he ever attempted to board a US flight.

If the CIA was aware Khalid Shaikh Mohammed was bringing al Qaeda terrorists into the US in the summer of 2001, and knew he was so dangerous that he had to be kept off all US aircraft, why did they not notify the FAA immediately that these terrorists he was sending into the US would be just as dangerous as Khalid Shaikh Mohammed himself, and they should also be kept off US airliners?

A terrorist threat advisory distributed in late June indicated a high probability of near-term "spectacular" terrorist attacks resulting in numerous casualties.

On June 25, Clarke warned Rice and Hadley that six separate intelligence reports showed al Qaeda personnel warning of a pending attack.

The intelligence reporting consistently described the upcoming attacks as occurring on a calamitous level, indicating they would cause the world to be in turmoil and that they would consist of possible multiple – but not necessarily simultaneous – attacks.

On June 28, Clarke wrote to Rice that the pattern of al Qaeda activity indicating attack planning over the past six weeks "had reached a crescendo."

One al Qaeda intelligence report warned that something "very, very, very" big was about to happen, and most of bin Laden's network was reportedly anticipating the attack.

The headline of a June 30 briefing to top officials was stark; "Bin Laden Planning High-Profile Attacks." The report stated that bin Laden operatives expected near-term attacks to have dramatic consequences of catastrophic proportions.

On July 2, the FBI Counterterrorism Division sent a message to federal and state and local law enforcement agencies summarizing threats regarding bin Laden.

The same day, (July 5 sic), the CIA briefed Attorney General Ashcroft on the al Qaeda threat, warning that a significant terrorist attack was imminent. Ashcroft was told that preparations for multiple attacks were in late stages or already completed and that little additional warning could be expected.

The next day, the CIA representative told the CSG that the al Qaeda members believed the upcoming attack would be "spectacular," qualitatively different from anything they had done to date.

Rice and Hadley told us that before September 11th they did not feel they had the job of handling domestic security. They felt Clarke and the CSG were the National Security Council's bridge between foreign and domestic threats.

Information a huge attack was to take place against the US and it appears that only one person at the NSC or in the administration, Richard Clarke, asked that a request be sent to the CIA for a prioritized list of the possible targets the al Qaeda terrorists might attack. On September 4, 2001, Clarke had even written Rice and Hadley a memo with the following statement:

"When these attacks occur, as they likely will, we will wonder what more we could have done to stop them."

While the 9/11 Commission had held nine hearing prior to April 2004, the hearings on April 13, 14 were focused on testimony on why the intelligence agencies failed to prevent the attacks on 9/11.

TENTH PUBLIC HEARINGS • APRIL 13-14, 2004

LAW ENFORCEMENT AND THE INTELLIGENCE COMMUNITY

9:00 a.m. TUESDAY, APRIL 13

Opening Statement by Chairman Thomas H. KEAN: Good morning. As chair of the National Commission on Terrorist Attacks on the United States, I hereby convene this commission's 10th public hearing. The hearing will run all of today and tomorrow.

Our focus for the next two days will be law enforcement and the intelligence community.

As we did with our two prior sets of hearings this calendar year, we receive each series of witnesses with a statement from the commission staff. These statements are informed by the work of the commissioners as well as the staff, and they represent the staff's best efforts to reconstruct the factual record of what happened.

Judgments and recommendations are for commissioners and the commission to make, because we'll do that in the course of our work and most definitively and finally in our final report.

Viewers, by the way, who are watching at home can obtain staff statements at www.911commission.gov.

KEAN: Before we begin, let me make just a brief request to members of the audience who have taken the time to be with us today.

We are going to be hearing from a lot of witnesses in the course of the next two days. As a courtesy to them and the commissioners, I ask you if you could refrain from any loud demonstrations of approval or disapproval, because that simply takes time away from the witnesses and takes time away from the commission members who are questioning. There are ample other ways which you can inform the commission of your opinions and I encourage you to avail yourselves of them.

On behalf of the witnesses, on behalf of the staff and the commission, thank you very much for your cooperation.

We will now hear our first staff statement. It is entitled, "Law Enforcement, Counterterrorism and Intelligence Collection in the United States Prior to 9/11."

It will be read by our executive director, Phil Zelikow, of the commission staff.

9:05 – 9:30 a.m. TUESDAY, APRIL, 13

STAFF STATEMENT NO.9

ZELIKOW: Members of the commission, with your help your staff has developed initial findings regarding law enforcement and intelligence collection in the United States prior to the 9/11 attacks.

These findings may help frame some of the issues to be discussed during this hearing and inform the development of your judgments and recommendations.

This statement reflects the results of our work so far....

We were fortunate in being able to build upon strong investigative work done by the congressional joint inquiry and by the Department of Justice's Office of the Inspector

General. We've obtained excellent cooperation from the FBI and the Department of Justice, both in Washington and in six FBI field offices across the United States.

The role of the FBI: The FBI played the lead role in the government's domestic counterterrorism strategy before September 11th.

ZELIKOW: In the 1990s most of the FBI's energy was devoted to after-the-fact investigations of major terrorist attacks in order to develop criminal cases. Investigating these attacks always required an enormous amount of resources. As most of these attacks occurred overseas, many of the FBI's top terrorism investigators were deployed abroad for long periods of time.

New York was the office of origin for the Al Qaida program and consequently where most of the FBI's institutional knowledge on Al Qaida resided. Working closely with the U.S. attorney for the Southern District of New York, the Justice Department and the U.S. intelligence community, the FBI's New York field office was often successful in these investigations; many of the perpetrators of these plots were identified, arrested, prosecuted and convicted. These were episodes such as the World Trade Center bombing, the landmarks plot, the Manila Airlines plot, the Khobar Towers bombing, the East Africa embassy bombings, the millennium plot and the USS Cole bombing.

Going to the top of page three of the statement, the approach to counterterrorism, the FBI took a traditional law enforcement approach to counterterrorism. Its agents were trained to build cases. Its management was deliberately decentralized to empower the individual field offices and the agents on the street. The bureau rewarded agents based on statistics reflecting arrests, indictments and prosecutions. As a result, fields such as counterterrorism and counterintelligence, where investigations generally result in fewer prosecutions, were viewed as backwaters.

Agents developed information in support of their own cases, not as part of a broader, more strategic effort. Given the poor state of the FBI's information systems, field agents usually did not know what investigations agents in their own office, let alone in other field offices, were working on. Nor did analysts have easy access to this information. As a result, it was almost impossible to develop an understanding of the threat from a particular international terrorist group.

Agents also investigated their individual cases with the knowledge that any case information recorded on paper and stored in case files was potentially discoverable in court.

ZELIKOW: Thus there was a disincentive to share information, even with other FBI agents and analysts. Analysts were discouraged from producing written assessments which could be discoverable and used to attack the prosecution's case at trial.

In the investigative arena, the field office had primacy. Counterterrorism investigations were run by the field, not headquarters. Moreover, the field office that initiated a case maintained control over it, an approach the FBI called the office of origin model. This decentralized management structure allowed field offices to set their own priorities with little direction from headquarters.

Management priorities and challenges: The FBI determined early on the 1990s that a preventive posture was a better way to counter the growing threat from international terrorism. In its first budget request to Congress after the 1993 World Trade Center bombing, the FBI stated that, "merely solving this type of crime is not enough; it is equally important that the FBI thwart terrorism before such acts can be perpetrated."

By the late 1990s, the FBI recognized that certain limitations undermined a preventive counterterrorism strategy. It initiated several significant reforms.

Yet the FBI's leadership confronted two fundamental challenges in countering terrorism.

First, the FBI had to reconcile this new priority with its existing agenda. This immediately required choices about whether to divert experienced agents or scarce resources from criminal or other intelligence work to terrorism. As the terrorism danger grew, Director Freeh faced the choice of whether to lower the priority the FBI attached to work on general crime, including the war on drugs, and allocate these resources to terrorism.

The Department of Justice inspector general found that when the FBI designated national and economic security as its top priority in 1998, it did not shift its human resources accordingly.

Although the FBI's counterterrorism budget tripled during the mid-1990s, FBI counterterrorism spending remained relatively constant between fiscal years 1998 and 2001. The inspector general stated that before 9/11, "the bureau devoted significantly more special agent resources to traditional law enforcement activities such as white- collar crime, organized crime, drug and violent crime investigations, than to domestic and international terrorism issues."

ZELIKOW: According to another external review, there were twice as many agents devoted to drug enforcement matters as to counterterrorism. On September 11, 2001, only about 6 percent of the FBI's total personnel worked on counterterrorism.

Former FBI officials told us that prior to 9/11 there was not sufficient national commitment or political will to dedicate the necessary resources to counterterrorism. Specifically, they believed that neither Congress nor the Office of Management and Budget fully understood the FBI's counterterrorism resource needs.

Nor did the FBI receive all it requested from the Department of Justice under Attorney General Janet Reno. Reno told us that the bureau never seemed to have sufficient resources given the broad scope of its responsibilities. She said, in light of the appropriations FBI received, it needed to prioritize and put counterterrorism first. She also said that Director Freeh seemed unwilling to shift resources to terrorism from other areas, such as violent crime. Freeh said it was difficult to tell field executives that they needed to do additional counterterrorism work without additional resources.

Finally, even though the number of agents devoted to counterterrorism was limited, they were not always fully utilized in the field offices. We learned through our interviews that prior to 9/11, field agents often were diverted from counterterrorism or other intelligence work in order to cover major criminal cases.

The second core challenge was a legal issue that became a management challenge as well. Certain provisions of federal law had been interpreted to limit communication between agents conducting intelligence investigations and the criminal prosecution units of the Department of Justice. This was done so that the broad powers for gathering intelligence would not be seized upon by prosecutors trying to make a criminal case. The separation of intelligence from criminal investigations became known as the wall.

New procedures issued by Attorney General Reno in 1995 required the FBI to notify prosecutors when facts and circumstances are developed in a foreign intelligence or counterintelligence investigation that reasonably indicate a significant federal crime has been, is being or may be committed.

ZELIKOW: The procedures, however, prohibited the prosecutors from, quote, "directing or controlling," close quote, the intelligence investigation.

Over time, the wall requirement came to be interpreted by the Justice Department, and particularly the Foreign Intelligence Surveillance Court, as imposing an increasingly stringent barrier to communications between FBI intelligence agents and criminal prosecutors.

Despite additional guidance on information sharing issued by Attorney General Reno in February 2000 and by Deputy Attorney General Larry Thompson in August 2001, the wall remained a source of considerable frustration and concern within the Justice Department.

Justice Department prosecutors and FBI criminal agents were responsible for large criminal cases, like the embassy bombings. The intelligence side of the FBI, though, had the legal tools essential for domestic intelligence work, such as FISA surveillance. In this environment, domestic counterterrorism efforts were impaired.

Attempts at reform: There were attempts at reform. Start with the 1998 strategic plan.

The FBI issued a five-year strategic plan in May 1998 spearheaded by Deputy Director Robert Bryant. The plan mandated development of a strong intelligence base, including human sources, intelligence collection and reporting requirements.

As a result of the strategic plan, the FBI created an Office of Intelligence that was superseded by a new Investigative Services Division created in 1999. That division was intended to strengthen the FBI's strategic analysis capability across the spectrum of traditional criminal, counterintelligence and counterterrorism cases.

Thus for the first time, the strategic analysis function was made independent of the operational divisions. The

Investigative Services Division also was intended to increase the professional stature of analysts.

An internal review of the FBI's intelligence analysis function at the time found that 66 percent of the bureau's analysts were not qualified to perform analytical duties. The review made recommendations for improvements. It appears that these recommendations were either not implemented or not enforced.

ZELIKOW: The new division did not succeed. FBI officials told us that it did not receive sufficient resources, and there was ongoing resistance to its creation from the senior managers in the FBI's operational divisions. Those managers feared losing control. They feared losing resources. They feared they would be unable to get the assistance they wanted from the new division's analysts.

Director Robert Mueller dismantled the division soon after the 9/11 attacks. We will discuss his changes in Staff Statement No. 12.

The Counterterrorism Division and MAXCAP 05: In 1999, the FBI also created separate Counterterrorism and Counterintelligence Divisions to ensure enough focus on these missions.

By late 1999, Dale Watson, the first head of the new Counterterrorism Division, recognized the urgent need to elevate the counterterrorism capacity of the FBI organization-wide. He developed a strategy he called MAXCAP 05. His goal was that the bureau reach its maximum feasible capacity in counterterrorism by 2005 through a strategy focused on intelligence gathering, valid and straightforward reporting and tracking mechanisms, effective interagency liaison and cooperation, and accountable program management.

During July and August of 2000, at four regional conferences, Counterterrorism Division leadership presented the new strategy to all of the FBI's assistant directors and special agents in charge of the FBI's 56 field offices.

Field executives told Watson that they did not have the analysts, linguists or technically trained experts to carry out the strategy. Watson asked for help from the Training Division and the new Investigative Services Division. Watson told us that trying to implement this strategy was the hardest thing he had ever done in his life.

One year after the regional conferences, almost every FBI field office's counterterrorism program was assessed to be operating at far below maximum capacity. Watson thought the FBI had to step up to a major choice of mission, perhaps turning over a significant share of narcotics enforcement to the DEA in order to free up resources for countering terrorism.

Although he thought FBI Director Freeh was sympathetic, most FBI managers opposed such a fundamental change before 9/11, and none of the pre-9/11 budgets made that choice.

The FBI's new counterterrorism strategy was not a focus of the Justice Department in 2001....On May 9, 2001, Attorney General John Ashcroft testified at a hearing on U.S. efforts to combat terrorism. He testified that the Justice Department had no higher priority than to protect citizens from terrorist attacks.

On May 10, the department issued guidance for developing the fiscal year 2003 budget that made reducing the incidence of gun violence and reducing the trafficking of illegal drugs priority objectives.

Watson told us that he almost fell out of his chair when he saw the memo because it made no mention of counterterrorism.

The department prepared a budget for fiscal year 2003 that did not increase counterterrorism funding over its pending proposal for fiscal year 2002. It did include an enhancement for the FBI's information technology program, intended to support the collection, analysis and rapid dissemination of information pertinent to FBI investigations.

Acting FBI Director Thomas Pickard told us he made an appeal to Attorney General Ashcroft for further counterterrorism enhancements not included in this budget proposal. On September 10th, the attorney general rejected that appeal.

Despite recognition by the FBI of the growing terrorist threat, it was still hobbled by significant deficiencies. Some of those deficiencies were, for instance, in intelligence collection.

Intelligence collection efforts should begin with a strategy to comprehend what is being collected, identify the gaps, and push efforts toward meeting requirements identified by strategic analysis.

Prior to 9/11, the FBI did not have a process in place to manage its collection efforts effectively. It did not identify intelligence gaps.

Collection of useful intelligence from human sources was limited. By the mid-1990s, senior managers were concerned the bureau's statistically-driven performance system was resulting in a roster of mediocre sources.

ZELIKOW: The wall between criminal and intelligence investigation apparently caused agents to be less aggressive than they might otherwise have been in pursuing Foreign Intelligence Surveillance Act, FISA, surveillance powers in counterterrorism investigations. Moreover, the FISA approval process involved multiple levels of review, which also discouraged agents from using such surveillance.

Many agents also told us that the process for getting FISA packages approved was incredibly lengthy and inefficient. Several FBI agents added that, prior to 9/11, FISA-derived intelligence information was not fully exploited anyway but was collected primarily to justify continuing the surveillance.

The FBI did not dedicate sufficient resources to the surveillance or translation needs of counterterrorism agents. Surveillance personnel were more focused on counterintelligence and drug cases. Many field offices did not have surveillance squads before 9/11. Similarly, the FBI did not have a sufficient number of translators proficient in Arabic and other languages useful in counterterrorism investigations, and that resulted in a significant backlog of untranslated FISA intercepts by early '01.

FBI agents received very little formalized training in the counterterrorism discipline. Only three days of the 16-week new agents course were devoted to national security matters of any kind, counterterrorism or counterintelligence, and most subsequent counterterrorism training was received on an ad hoc basis or on the job.

Additionally, the career path for agents necessitated rotations between headquarters and the field in a variety of work areas, making it difficult for agents to develop expertise in any particular area, especially counterterrorism or counterintelligence. We were told that very few field managers of the FBI had any counterterrorism experience, and thus either were not focused on the issue or did not have the expertise to run an effective program.

Finally, agents' investigative activities were governed by attorney general guidelines, first put in place in 1976, the so-called Levi guidelines, and revised in 1995, to guard against misuse of government power.

The guidelines limited the investigative methods and techniques available to agents conducting preliminary investigations of potential terrorist activities or connections. They prohibited the use of publicly available source information, such as that found on the Internet, unless specified criteria were present.

ZELIKOW: These restrictions may have had the unintended consequence of causing agents to even avoid legitimate investigative activity that might conceivably be viewed as infringing on religious liberties or lawful political protest.

Agents we interviewed believed these limitations were too restrictive and adversely affected their intelligence investigations.

Strategic analysis

It is the role of the strategic analyst to look across individual operations and cases to identify trends in terrorist activity and develop broad assessments of the terrorist threat to US interests. The goal is not abstract. Such analysis drives collection efforts. It is the only way to evaluate what the institution does not know. The FBI had little understanding of, or appreciation for, the role of strategic analysis in driving investigations or allocating resources.

The role of the tactical analyst, on the other hand, is geared toward providing direct support to investigations. Agents viewed tactical analysts as performing duties that advanced their cases. They failed to see the value of strategic analysis, finding it too academic and therefore irrelevant. Creation of the ill-fated Investigative Services Division may even have worsened this attitude by distancing strategic analysts from agents in the operational divisions.

Moreover, strategic analysts had difficulty getting access to the FBI and Intelligence Community information they were expected to analyze. The poor state of the FBI's information systems meant that analysts' access to information depended in large part on their personal relationships with individuals in the units or squads where the information resided. In short, analysts didn't know what they didn't know. As a result, prior to 9/11 relatively few strategic counterterrorism analytical products had been completed. Indeed, the FBI had never completed an assessment of the terrorist threat to the US homeland.

According to the Department of Justice inspector general, FBI officials were comfortable relying on their individual professional judgment regarding the terrorist threat and, quote, "did not value a formal written assessment that uses a structured methodology," close quote.

Information comes to intelligence agencies from many sources. These sources include the reports from other US government agencies such as the State Department, from counterparts in foreign security agencies, from human agents, from signals intelligence such as communications, from imagery and from open sources like foreign newspapers. The CIA was originally created in large part to sort through all such sources and offer unbiased assessments to the nation's leaders. In other words, although the CIA became and remains a principal collector and operator in its own right, its first duty was to provide integrated analysis.

Analysis is more than a news report. A tactical analysis studies a particular case involving an individual or group as a guide to specific operations. Strategic analysis looks beyond the particular in order to see patterns, notice gaps, or assemble a larger picture on a wider time-frame to guide the development of national policy.

The most impressive piece of analysis on the emerging transnational terrorist threat was the 1995 National Intelligence Estimate entitled, "The Foreign Terrorist Threat to the United States." It judged at the time that: "[T]he most likely threat of an attack in the United States would be from transient groupings of individuals similar to those drawn together by Ramzi Yousef. Such groupings lack strong organization but rather are loose affiliations."

The NIE warned of terrorist attacks in the United States over the following two years. It was updated in 1997. As we mentioned in Staff Statement No. 5, by early 1997 the United States had received dramatic new information about the organization of al Qaeda and its efforts to mount catastrophic attacks against the United States.

The 1997 update failed to reflect this new information. No comprehensive National Estimates were subsequently produced on terrorism prior to the attacks on 9/11.

Thousands of particular reports were circulated. A number of very good analytical papers were distributed on specific topics, such as bin Laden's political philosophy, his command of a global network, analysis of information from terrorists captured in Jordan in December '99, al Qaeda's operational style, and on the evolving goals of the international extremist movement.

Hundreds of articles for morning briefings were prepared for the highest officials in the government with titles such as "Bin Laden Threatening to Attack US Aircraft," 1998; "UBL Plans for Reprisals against US Targets, Possibly in US," 1998; "Strains Surface between Taliban and Bin Laden," 1999; "Terrorist Threats to US Interests in Caucasus," 1999; "Bin Laden to Exploit Looser Security during Holidays," 1999; "Bin Laden Evading Sanctions," 2000; "Bin Laden's Interest in Biological and Radiological Weapons," February 2001; "Taliban Holding Firm on Bin Laden for Now," 2001; "Terrorist Groups Said Cooperating on US Hostage Plot," May 2001; and "Bin Laden Determined to Strike in US," August 2001.

Despite such reports, and a 1999 paper on bin Laden's command structure for al Qaeda, there were no complete authoritative portraits of his strategy and the extent of his organization's involvement in past terrorist attacks. Nor had the Community provided an authoritative depiction of his organization's relationships with other governments, or the scale of the threat his organization posed to the United States.

The head of analysis at the Counterterrorist Center until 1999 regarded the bin Laden danger as still in the realm of past experience, discounting the alarms about a catastrophic threat as relating only to the danger of chemical, biological or nuclear attack, which he downplayed, referring in 2001 before 9/11 to the overheated rhetoric on the subject. In other words, before the attack we found uncertainty among senior officials about whether this was just a new and especially venomous version of the ordinary terrorist threat America had lived with for decades or was radically new, posing a threat beyond any yet experienced.

In the Counterterrorist Center, priority was given to tactical analysis to support operations. Although the Counterterrorist Center formally reports to the DCI, the center is effectively embedded in the CIA's Directorate of Operations, or was. The center had difficulty attracting talented analysts from their traditional billets in the agency's Directorate of Intelligence.

The Counterterrorist Center also was especially vulnerable to the pressures that placed reporting ahead of research and analysis. Strategic analysis was a luxury that the strained cadres of analysts in the center could rarely indulge.

In late 2000, DCI Tenet recognized the deficiency of strategic analysis against al Qaeda. He appointed a senior manager to tackle the problem with in the Counterterrorist Center. In March 2001, this manager briefed DCI Tenet on creating a strategic assessment capability. The CTC established a new Strategic Assessments Branch during July 2001. The decision to add about 10 analysts to this effort was seen at the time as a major bureaucratic victory. The CTC labored to find analysts to serve in that office. The new chief of that branch reported for duty on September 10, 2001.

Warning and the case of aircraft as weapons

Since the Pearl Harbor attack of 1941, the Intelligence Community has devoted generations of effort to understanding the problem of warning against surprise attack. Rigorous analytic methods were developed, focused in particular on the Soviet Union. Several leading practitioners within the Intelligence Community discussed them with us. They have been articulated in many ways, but almost all seem to have about four elements in common: one, think about how surprise attacks might be launched; two, identify telltale indicators connected to the most dangerous possibilities; three, where feasible, collect intelligence against these indicators; and four, adopt defenses to deflect the most dangerous possibilities or at least get more warning.

With the important exception of al Qaeda efforts in chemical, biological, radiological, and nuclear weapons, we did not find evidence that this process regularly applied the methods to avoid surprise attack that had been so laboriously developed over the years. There was, for example, no evident Intelligence Community analysis of the danger of boat bombs before the attack on the *USS Cole* in October 2000, although expertise about such means of attack existed within the Community, especially at the Office of Naval Intelligence.

These past episodes suggest possibilities. Alone, they are not warnings. But returning to the four elements mentioned above:

The CTC did not analyze how a hijacked aircraft or other explosives-laden aircraft might be used as a weapon. If it had done so, it could have identified that a critical obstacle would be to find a suicide terrorist able to fly large jet aircraft. This had never happened before 9/11.

The CTC did not develop a set of telltale indicators for this means of attack. For example, one such indicator might be the

232

discovery of terrorists seeking or taking flight training to fly large jet aircraft, or seeking to buy advanced flight simulators. The CTC did not propose, and the Intelligence Community collection management process did not set, collection requirements against such telltale indicators. Therefore, the warning system was not looking for information such as the July 2001 FBI report of terrorist interest in various kinds of aircraft training in Arizona, or the August 2001 arrest of Zacarias Moussaoui because of his suspicious behavior in a Minnesota flight school. In late August, the Moussaoui arrest was briefed to the DCI and other top CIA officials under the heading, quote, "Islamic Extremist Learns to Fly," close quote. The news had no evident effect on warning.

Neither the Intelligence Community nor the NSC policy process analyzed systemic defenses of aircraft or against suicide aircraft. The many threat reports mentioning aircraft were passed to the FAA. We discussed the problems at that agency in Staff Statements 3 and 4.

Richard Clarke told us that he was concerned about this threat in the context of protecting the Atlanta Olympics in June 1996, the White House complex, and the 2001 G-8 summit in Genoa.

But he attributed his awareness to novels more than any warnings from the Intelligence Community. He did not pursue the systemic issues of defending aircraft from suicide hijackers or bolstering wider air defenses.

Strategic collection management depends upon strategic analysis to define the baseline of what is known, what is not known, and to guide the setting of clear, agreed requirements. This process did not occur. Assistant DCI Allen concentrated on day-to-day collection challenges with enormous energy and dedication. However, there was no comprehensive collection strategy to pull human – pull together human sources, imagery, signals intelligence and open sources. Even "The Plan" was essentially a CIA plan, not one for the Intelligence Community as a whole.

DCI Tenet and his predecessors had not developed the management and administrative tools to run the Intelligence Community that most federal departments use to monitor and rationalize their resources against priorities. The Intelligence Community did not have a financial accounting system, a chief financial officer or a comptroller. The CIA had these tools for its own operations; the Intelligence Community did not. Instead, to manage the Community as a whole, the DCI relied on a variety of financial systems maintained by different agencies and without standardized definitions for expenditures.

Lacking a management strategy for the war on terrorism or ways to see how funds were being spent across the Community, it was difficult for DCI Tenet and his aides to develop an overall Intelligence Community budget for the war on terrorism.

Finally, the Community had not institutionalized a process for learning from its successes and failures. We did not find any after-action reviews sponsored by the Intelligence Community after surprise terrorist attacks such as the embassy bombings of August 1998 or the USS Cole attack in October 2000. The Community participated in Inspector General inquiries conducted by individual agencies, but these reviews were perceived as fault-finding, without enough constructive emphasis on learning lessons and discovering best practices. What we did not find was anything between the extremes of no investigation at all, and an adversarial inquiry triggered by a public outcry. We did not find an institution or culture that provided a safe outlet for admitting errors and improving procedures.

MR. ZELIKOW: In conclusion, our investigation so far has found the Intelligence Community struggling to collect on and analyze the phenomena of transnational terrorism through the mid to late 1990s. While many dedicated officers worked day and night for years to piece together the growing body of evidence on al Qaeda and to understand the threats, in the end it was not enough to gain the advantage before the 9/11 attacks.

While there were many reports on bin Laden and his growing al Qaeda organization, there was no comprehensive estimate of the enemy either to build consensus or clarify differences.

With the important exception of attacks with chemical, biological, radiological or nuclear weapons, the methods developed for decades to warn of surprise attacks were not applied to the problem of warning against terrorist attacks. In intelligence collection, despite many excellent efforts, there was not a comprehensive review of what the Community knew, what it did not know, followed by the development of a Community-wide plan to close those gaps.

Analysis of the 9/11 Commission Staff report on strategic analysis.

The lack of analysis doomed CIA and the FBI to fail even before they started. The CIA did have "rigorous analytic methods," in effect a formal process to assess and react to threats coming from terrorist organizations such as al Qaeda, and to produce not only a written strategic analysis, but to identify and adopt defensive measure to deflect the most dangerous possibilities, or at least provide a warning of the danger, but never did carry out this formal process to produce an analysis. From testimony on the CIA at the 9/11 hearings:

> Rigorous analytic methods were developed, focused in particular on the Soviet Union. Several leading practitioners within the Intelligence Community discussed them with us. They have been articulated in many ways, but almost all seem to have about four elements in common: one, think about how surprise attacks might be launched; two, identify telltale indicators connected to the most dangerous possibilities; three, where feasible, collect intelligence against these indicators; and four, adopt defenses to deflect the most dangerous possibilities or at least get more warning.

The CIA never applied this process to analyzing the al Qaeda terrorists, even when they were warned of a huge imminent attack by these terrorists in the summer of 2001.

When this analysis was not completed, why didn't the other agencies or Congress demand that this be done? The 9/11 Commission itself never came to a final conclusion on why this analysis was never completed. A partial explanation for this failure comes from testimony given to the 9/11 Commission on October 13, 2003, by John Gannon, Manager of Analysis at the CIA:

From the testimony of Mr. John Gannon of the CIA testifying 7 months earlier, on October 13, 2003 before the 9/11 Commission

> MR. TIM ROEMER: I'm still not sure I understand how that's going to be helpful post-9/11 in terms of getting warning out and fixing a system that had some real problems in it, but John can you – Mr. Gannon, can you help at all in explaining why that officer was not responsible for terrorism and if it in fact has been fixed at this point?

MR. GANNON: Well, I think there were – prior to 9/11 I think there were – there was more than one officer who was responsible for articulating the terrorist threat. If you will pardon me, if I could go back to that point, and I left the Intelligence Community about that time and I think the major problem we were having and those officers were having was prioritizing the various threats we had. I recall going to the I think it was the Armed Services Committee with Director Tenet and Senator Levin at the time, did what he does so well, he said okay, you have laid out for us, a very rich and diverse threat assessment here. We were talking about the ballistic missile threat, a growing threat now from Iran, Iraq, North Korea, a residual threat from China and Russia, we're worried about the military modernization in China, you're talking about more regional threats like in Bosnia, Africa, we just went through the crisis in East Timor. Terrorism in all its dimensions, so it wasn't just conventional, that we were talking about chemical, biological and biological was a major concern, because we didn't know what we needed to know about the biological threat. But radiological, nuclear and then you know, humanitarian disasters and refugee flows and all those other issues that intelligence officers are being required to deal with, how did you put – Senator Levin said, well tell me one to 10, what are the real threats, what are the most important ones? And the Director responded, if any of those happens, I'm accountable, I can't prioritize. I went back and got some analysts together and tried to prioritize and what we came up with was a terrorist threat, probably abroad. And this was just very close to the eve of 9/11. But I would also say that we were dealing with a stretch at the time of our resources to deal with what I would call conventional kinds of threats and then the new technology-based threats. We talked for example, about terrorists or adversaries who might be able to get hold of laser technology and do damage to our satellites.

So here we had a Community that was being forced to deal with the new technological threats, but at the same time, while we worried about lasers we still had to worry about the Palestinian who would throw a rock. Because of the political implications of that. So, we couldn't prioritize, the Congress could not prioritize either, and we were hit by a terrorist incident that we would not have ruled out, in any of the exercises we would not have ruled out that that could have happened, or it might even be probable, but what we would have needed was hard intelligence that it was about to happen. So we –

MR. LEE H. HAMILTON: Mr. Gannon, I was struck by your comment a moment ago about prioritization. And it always seemed to me that this was one of the key problems. And you're all from the Intelligence Community. Who has the responsibility to prioritize and how does it work? I mean, you have all of these threats out here that when we listen to the intelligence people, scare you to death. And any one of them could cause great damage to the country. Is it the intelligence people that have the responsibility to prioritize, or is it the policymaker that has that responsibility, or is it some interaction between the two? You have to prioritize threats. There are dozens of threats against the United States and it makes an awful difference how you allocate resources as to how you prioritize those threats. You have thousands and thousands of targets in the United States. It makes a huge difference how you prioritize those targets. Now, the tendency, I can tell you, of the policymaker is not to make the decision, because it's too tough and because you could be wrong. And therefore you want to do everything, but you can't do everything, because you don't have the resources to do it. How do we get a better sense of prioritization of threats and targets in this system?

MR. GANNON: When it comes to actually doing something about a threat or developing policy, I think that is on the political side. But I think the development of an integrated threat assessment, which explains what we know and what we don't know, is I think, the responsibility, and should be, of the Director of Central Intelligence. He has been –

MR. HAMILTON: When you were ticking off all of those threats a moment ago, I think, with regard to Senator Levin's question, did the Intelligence Community at that time respond to the Senator and say, these are the threats and these are the priorities of the threats?

MR. GANNON: I believe it is the responsibility of the Director of Central Intelligence to bring the analysts together and to prioritize to the extent you can, and also to explain why you can't prioritize with regard to the intelligence issue.

In a reply to Tim Roemer's question on a different topic, it is clear why the CIA failed to analyze the al Qaeda organization in such a way they could have anticipated and prevented the tragedy of 9/11. The CIA's top people and midlevel managers testified that it was not possible to "prioritize" the possible targets al Qaeda was interested in attacking. From Mr. Gannon's testimony:

"So here we had a Community that was being forced to deal with the new technological threats, but at the same time, while we worried about lasers we still had to worry about the Palestinian who would throw a rock. Because of the political implications of that. So, we couldn't prioritize, the Congress could not prioritize either, and we were hit by a terrorist incident that we would not have ruled out, in any of the exercises we would not have ruled out that that could have happened, or it might even be probable, but what we would have needed was hard intelligence that it was about to happen."

There is no way to produce any meaningful strategic analysis if you are not going to prioritize a list of targets that the al Qaeda terrorists might attack?

Without this list, and without examining possible methods of attack, the rest of the US government would not know what security points were vulnerable and what extra security measures were required at these points, particularly the transportation systems in the US?

9:30 – 11:00 a.m. TUESDAY, APRIL 13

The Honorable Louis Freeh

Former Director, Federal Bureau of Investigation

KEAN: We will now hear from our first witness, the Honorable Louis J. Freeh, who served as director of the Federal Bureau of Investigation from 1993 to 2001.

KEAN: Director Freeh, we're very pleased to welcome you this morning. Will you please rise and raise your right hand?

Do you swear or affirm to tell the truth, the whole truth and nothing but the truth?

FREEH: I do.

KEAN: Please be seated.

Director Freeh, a prepared statement will be entered into the record in full. As you know, we've got an agreement that your statement summarized will be about 10 minutes long. And so please proceed.

FREEH: Thank you, Mr. Chairman, members of the commission.

Let me just begin by, again, expressing publicly my condolences to the families of the 9/11 attack and to extend my prayers and support for them, and my wishes that this commission, as the joint Intelligence Committees before it, does not only find some answers but certainly recommendations for change and improvement, many of which have already been undertaken, so that this type of awful, horrific human and personal tragedy never affects anyone else.

I want to just make a couple of points. I certainly appreciate the work of the staff and the report of the executive director. And maybe not addressing all of the details of what has been a very careful review of the FBI operations, certainly prior to September 11th and thereafter, and a very good audit with respect to many of the programs and operations.

FREEH: I would like to talk about some larger general issues, and certainly then engage in whatever questions you want.

I think the point that I would like to make is that it is imperative, in my view, that the commission distinguish between the period before September 11 and the period after September 11; that this is, I would respectfully suggest, a central question for the commission and for the American people. And I think the inability to focus on that question leaves not only a lot of speculation, but I think a lot of misinformation about some of the activities and some of the dynamics here involved.

I guess my view is that Al Qaida declared war on the United States in 1996. That's when bin Laden issued his first fatwa.

The 1998 fatwa was much more specific. It directed his followers to kill Americans anywhere.

That was followed by attacks against American soldiers in Yemen in 1992, which was actually the subject of a Southern District of New York FBI indictment returned in June of 1998 prior to the attacks against the embassies in East Africa.

The attacks upon the American soldiers in Somali, Project Restore Hope, was an activity sponsored by and directed by Al Qaida soldiers. That, as you know, was one of the overt acts publicly identified in the New York City indictment with respect to bin Laden.

The attacks against the embassies in 1998: acts of war against the United States. The attacks against our warship in 2000: acts of war against the United States.

FREEH: I remember briefing Senator Kerrey and Senator Shelby after one of these attacks -- it was the embassy attacks

239

-- and he asked me a very good question, a question that I think is maybe more relevant today than it was then. And he said, "Why is the FBI over in East Africa, hundreds of FBI agents sifting through a crime scene maintaining chain of custody, talking to people and giving them their Miranda rights, when this is an act of war against the United States?"

And my response then, as it would be now, is that, absent a declaration of war backed by the United States against Al Qaida, against this very competent and very dangerous terrorist organization, we were left with the tools that were available to fight terrorism and to neutralize and incapacitate, not just bin Laden, but many of his operatives and allied organizations.

The point there is not that anybody in the FBI or anybody in the United States thought that investigating these cases was the best response to a war that was declared against the United States. You could poll any FBI agent, any jury that tried and convicted many of the people in these cases and they would tell you absolutely not. An arrest warrant, two of them for bin Laden in the Southern District of New York, was not going to deter him from what happened on September 11th.

FREEH: But the point of these investigations was in the absence of invading Afghanistan, in the absence of armed Predator missiles seeking out our enemies, in the absence of all the things that were appropriately done after September 11th, when the United States declared war back on Al Qaida, we were left with alternatives which were better than no alternatives. And as I said in my statement, sometimes they worked.

And the investigations were not investigations that dealt with individuals. When the FBI investigated La Cosa Nostra, it wasn't investigating a particular person or group of people; it was investigating the organization and the enterprise. The purpose there was to get as much information as possible to incapacitate the leadership and dissolve the organization. The Watergate investigation would be the same example of that. These investigations were not cases; they were initiatives that were designed to gather information.

So before September 11th most of the information that was residing in the United States government with respect to Al Qaida came from FBI investigations, not from intelligence operations, not from collection. It came from the cooperating witnesses that we found in 1993, after the World Trade bombing in February. The FBI conducting an investigation but an investigation that went to the identification of the people who might have been involved in supporting that attack led to, if you recall, the prevention -- and I stress that word -- the prevention of a second major terrorist attack against the United States in New York City which was called the day of terror. And the organization was going to blow up tunnels and bridges and the United Nations and federal office buildings, killing potentially thousands and thousands of Americans.

FREEH: It was the investigation of the World Trade tower that prevented that and also gave us an arrest warrant for one Ramzi Yousef. Ramzi Yousef, related to Sheikh Khalid Mohammed, one of the architects of the September 11th attack.

He was found in Pakistan, staying in an Al Qaida guest house, by FBI agents who had an arrest warrant, and without that arrest warrant, he would never have been brought back to the United States.

Why was it important to have an arrest warrant? Because incapacitating him would prevent him from further attacks against the United States.

As you know, in 1995, he and others -- Sheikh Khalid Mohammed being one of them -- were planning to blow up 12 U.S. airliners over the Pacific Ocean, killing hundreds of Americans. That was aborted due to a series of events, but precisely the FBI criminal investigation served to prevent that from happening.

My point is that these investigations or projects that seek to gather maximum amount of information so the organization can be stopped from committing future acts of terrorism.

It was never our notion in the FBI that criminal prosecutions of terrorists and investigations of their organizations was a substitute for military action, for foreign policy action, for the United States doing what it did on September 11th, declaring war on an enemy that had declared war on us many years ago.

The point of it is that these investigations, as they existed, prevented acts of terrorism.

FREEH: With very limited resources, the FBI, as you know, before September 11, had 3.5 percent of the federal government's anti- terrorism budget. And it's no news to anybody that for many, many years, as your executive director recounted, the resource issue and the legal authority issue certainly limited what we were able to do before September 11th.

In the budget years 2000, 2001, 2002, we asked for 1,895 people: agents, linguists, analysts. We got a total of 76 people during that period. That's not to criticize the Congress, it's not to criticize the Department of Justice, it is to focus on the fact that that was not a national priority.

It's to repeat what we saw in the 2000 presidential election. Terrorism was not discussed. This was not an issue that candidates talked about, that the American people talked about during that period. And this was right after the attack on the USS Cole.

For many, many years, a lack of these resources and, maybe more importantly, a lack of legal authority, prevented us from doing what was easily done after September 11th. The Patriot Act, the November 18, 2002 decision by the court of review, which threw out a 20-year interpretation of the FISA statue. The court said to the judges, to the Department of Justice, to the FBI, to the intelligence community, "You've been misreading the statute for 20 years." Not only does the Patriot Act provide for this, but the actual statute provides for that.

So this wall that had been erected was a self-erected wall by the United States government, confirmed by interpretations, by the FISA court.

FREEH: But when challenged for the first time in 20 years, it was found by the court of review to be inconsistent with the statute, as well as inconsistent with the Constitution.

All of these things being said, the point I guess I want to make to you this morning and which I tried to make in my statement, is that we had a very effective program with respect to counterterrorism before September 11th given the resources in my view and given the authorities that we had.

Bin Laden was indicted in June of 1998. He was indicted again after the African bombings. He was put on our top 10 list. George Tenet and I reviewed plans to have him arrested and taken into custody in Afghanistan and brought back to the United States. I went over to see then-Chief Executive Musharraf in 2002 and made the case for him that this person be thrown out of Afghanistan; that he help us take him into custody so we could bring him back to the United States.

All of the other things that were being done were being done in a limited framework, given, again, lack of resources and, maybe more importantly, the legal authorities that we had to live with.

KEAN: If you could wrap up now. Time's up.

FREEH: Thank you, Mr. Chairman.

The final point I think I want to make then is that we could change the law, we can pass new statutes, we can add billions of dollars to the fight. We need to keep in perspective, however, what was the reality before September 11th and what was the reality thereafter.

FREEH: And at the end of the day, the FBI, as a part of the Department of Justice, has to obey the law. And whatever that law is, it's one that protects us, it protects our Constitution, it also protects our people. And that law can change but I think we have to keep in mind that when that changes, we can't judge what happened in the past by different standards.

Thank you.

KEAN: Thank you.

MR. FRED FIELDING: Morning, Mr. Director. Thank you very much for being here today and for all the cooperation you've provided to the Commission and its staff in closed sessions heretofore and for your very fulsome statement that you gave us. And, also, thank you on behalf of the whole commission for your public service, both in the Executive and Judicial branch.

I am sure it's no surprise to you or anybody here that there's a lot of interest in today's hearings and there's a lot of interest simply because on September 11th we were totally beaten. We were beaten and all our systems failed. Our systems to stop hijackings failed. Our intelligence – domestic and foreign apparatus – failed. We had 19 people who were able to – some of whom were known by the CIA to be terrorists – entered our country, got visas, were living under their own names in this country, took flight lessons, beat the security screening with knives to get into the aircraft, and turned four aircraft into missiles. And they had to have – it was interesting, they had to have a 100 percent success in order to do this and they did.

So we've now found in our discovery that there have been some clues; some dots, as we say, might have been connected were not. We're not passing judgment on that at this point, but what we're trying to determine here is how this intelligence failure occurred so that we can deny it from occurring again, if at all possible. And quite frankly, we're also trying to determine whether the FBI should continue to have its counterterrorism responsibility, whether it's capable of carrying out the new mission of counterterrorism and the enhanced mission and the enhanced responsibilities. So we appreciate your being here.

MR. FIELDING: Let me switch gears for a second. In September of 1999, the GAO issued a report that recommended that the FBI develop a national-level terrorist threat and risk assessment, so it could be used how – to determine how to allocate resources and budget in dealing with domestic threats, plus the – analyzing the likelihood of such a threat, and to identify any potential intelligence gaps, I believe, was part of the charter.

And it was my understanding that the department and you agreed to do that. And that's September – or the end of '99, and that wasn't completed until January of 2003.

And when we were talking to people that were involved in that, a senior CIA official that was detailed to the FBI after 9/11 told the Commission that the assessment was completed actually by CIA analysts that had been detailed to the FBI, since the FBI analysts were not capable of producing such a product.

Now, I'd like your comment on that and even the deeper question of was the FBI unwilling to do an analysis or was it unable to do an analysis from '99 at least until you left?

MR. FREEH: Well, I don't think it was incapable of doing that. In fact, there were analyses that were made with respect to assessments, which were done in the context of the Counterterrorism Division, which was set up at about the same time.

Did we have a deficiency with respect to analytical capability? Absolutely. I talked about that at appropriation hearings over many years. Most of the non-agent resources in our three-year request for 1,895 people were analysts. They were people who could perform strategic, as opposed to tactical, analysis for us and give us the type of strategy plans and disruption plans that we began to see actually in the spring and summer of 2001 in the FBI with respect to al Qaeda. But that capability was not there when I was Director. You know, we're in the process now of hiring 900 analysts, but that's 2004. It doesn't cover the gaps over many, many years, particularly the years that you cite.

MR. KERREY: In an otherwise, I thought, exceptional staff report, the staff I think [sic] miscorrectly describes the seven cases that you were involved with, saying that most of those were overseas. In truth, three of them were domestic and four of them were overseas; World Trade Center number one, Landmarks plot number one, the Millennium, and indeed, if you include the threats against the city of New York during the 2001 trial, there were four domestic attacks and/or efforts.

Did the FBI ever produce an evaluation of the threat to the homeland during this period to the President? Or was there one requested of you?

MR. FREEH: There was none requested, that I'm aware of. I don't think we ever furnished a national threat report to the President with respect to homeland security.

This is a clear misstatement of the facts. Congress itself, in 1999, had asked for a National Threat Analysis from the FBI and this was not produced until 2003, well after the events of 9/11.

MR. KERREY: I mean, of all the facts in this whole process that have just caused scales to fall from my eyes was listening to Betty Ong, flight attendant on Flight 11, talk to the ground and hear the ground surprised by a hijacking. I mean, not only were we not at a high state of alert in our airports, we were at ease. We stacked arms. I mean, we weren't prepared at all. And it's baffling to me why some alert wasn't given to the airlines to alter their preparedness and to go to a much higher state of alert. It seems to me that a lot of things would have changed if that would have happened. And I would respectfully disagree with your assessment of the Williams memo coming out of Phoenix, because I think had it gotten into the works up to the highest possible level, at the very least 19 guys wouldn't have got on to these airplanes with room to spare.

MR. FREEH: Well, Senator, I served on the Gore Commission, as your staff may know. And, you know, I thought the leadership, first of all, by the Vice President there was outstanding. I think the recommendations were outstanding. We spent many, many months writing detailed recommendations that asked for passenger screening, asked for many, many things which were never implemented.

The whole purpose and the conclusions of that report, if you read it, was that the airline industry and operations were vulnerable at multi points with respect to hijackings and terrorist attack. So I agree with you, there was no –

MR. KEAN: – of 10 seconds.

MR. BEN-VENISTE: (Laughs.) I think I can do it in 10 seconds, Tom.

My good friend and former mentor Jim Thompson, I think, has misinterpreted the question put to you about the recognition by the Intelligence Community of the potential for planes being used as missiles. My question to you was – given the substantial state of information, whether by rumor or by actual intelligence, relating to the use of kamikazes, suicide pilots, to crash planes into buildings, my question was, was it a failure in thinking not to reposition our domestic air defense, led by NORAD, to protect the Capitol and elsewhere against the possibility of attack on the United States by air, and particularly during time of heightened threat? You understood that that way.

MR. FREEH: Yes.

MR. HAMILTON: I appreciate that approach and I've listened to a lot of reports from commissions when I served in the Congress.

And one of the advantages a commission always has over the Congress is, we don't have to worry about raising the money. We can just make the recommendations to spend it. And there's a big difference, of course.

Final question relates to the broader responsibility. Director Mueller has made the pitch over and over again, and he's done it very effectively, that the FBI is changing its focus from law enforcement to the prevention of terrorism. And everybody of course nods their head in agreement – that's exactly what ought to be done. This question goes a little outside the Commission's responsibility, but you mentioned a moment ago that we really have not had a large increase in agents. So what's happening is, we're shifting a lot of resources, money and agents, from law enforcement, from criminal prosecution to terrorist prevention. And in the environment of today's world, that makes a lot of sense to most of us. But do you worry then that the FBI is going to lose its effectiveness in law enforcement and criminal prosecution?

MR. FREEH: Well, that's an excellent question. I guess I don't believe that investigations are inconsistent with prevention. I subscribe to the theory that Mary Jo White and I testified to before the Joint Intelligence Committee, and which actually the court of review, in its November 18th opinion, noted, investigations do lead to prevention. I don't think there's a dichotomy between them. Manila Air, the Millennium, the Day of Terror in New York were all preventions as a result of good investigations.

So I think that's a false dichotomy between investigations and prevention. If you're doing good investigations, you're developing informants, cooperating defendants, like Omar in the trade bombing case. You're creating a database. You're sharing intelligence with other people.

I do think there's a great danger in taking people off investigations that aren't, again, case- or [sic] defendant-specific, but are enterprise-specific, and, you know, when agents are off the streets, this is my bias, perhaps, as a street agent, they're not making informants, they're not developing sources. September 11th, had we had the right sources overseas or in the United States, could have been prevented. We did not have those sources. We did not have that telephone call. We didn't have that e-mail intercept that could've done the job. You get that by having sources, and you get sources by good investigations. You also prevent terrorism in that regard.

MR. HAMILTON: Thank you, Mr. Chairman.

Analyzing the testimony of Louis Freeh

The explanation of why the FBI failed to prevent the events on 9/11 was pointed out at the 9/11 Commission hearings.

> *"September 11th, had we had the right sources overseas or in the United States, could have been prevented. We did not have those sources. We did not have that telephone call. We didn't have that e-mail intercept that could've done the job. You get that by having sources, and you get sources by good investigations. You also prevent terrorism in that regard."*

The person responsible for the operation of the FBI, who had led this agency for the many years prior to 9/11, thought by having the right sources in place they could have prevented this event. But this massive failure had been mostly due to the lack of a strategic analysis by the FBI and the CIA The information that could not be obtained directly from the al Qaeda organization could be obtained with nothing more than a simple process of analysis, using the material the terrorists had actually written themselves using plain common sense with the information the FBI had already possessed.

1:30 – 2:00 p.m. TUESDAY, APRIL 13

STAFF STATEMNT NO. 10

Threats and Responses in 2001

MR. PHILIP ZELIKOW: Members of the Commission, with your help, your Staff has developed preliminary findings regarding awareness of the threat of terrorist attack in the months leading up to September 11th, 2001, and some aspects of the immediate response. This report reflects the results of our work so far. We remain ready to revise our understanding as our work continues.

I'd like to draw you now to page 2 of the statement, beginning with the spring of 2001, and turn the floor over to Chris Kojm, my deputy.

MR. CHRIS KOJM: In spring 2001, the level of reporting on terrorist threats and planned attacks began to increase dramatically, representing the most significant spike in activity since the millennium. At the end of March, the Intelligence Community disseminated a terrorist threat advisory indicating there was a heightened threat of Sunni extremist terrorist attacks against US facilities, personnel and other interests in the coming weeks.

In April and May 2001, the drumbeat of reporting increased. Articles presented to top officials contained headlines such as: "Bin Laden planning multiple operations;" "Bin Laden public profile may presage attack;" "Bin Laden network's plans advancing."

By late May, there were reports of a hostage plot against Americans to force the release of prisoners, including Sheikh Omar Abdel Rahman, "the blind sheik," who was serving a life sentence for his role in the 1993 plot to blow up sites in New York City. The reporting noted that the operatives may opt to hijack an aircraft or storm a US embassy.

The reporting also mentioned that Abu Zubaydah was planning an attack and expected to carry out more if things went well.

The US government redoubled efforts, ongoing since late 1999, to capture Abu Zubaydah. National Counterterrorism

Coordinator Clarke also called National Security Advisor Condoleezza Rice's attention to possible plots in Yemen and Italy and by an alleged cell in Canada that might be planning an attack against the United States.

Reports similar to these were made available to President Bush in morning meetings with DCI Tenet, usually attended by Vice President Cheney and National Security Advisor Rice as well. None of these reports mentioned that the attacks might occur in the United States. At the end of May, Counterterrorist Center Chief Cofer Black told Rice that the current threat level was a seven on a scale of 10, as compared to an eight during the Millennium.

The threat reports surged again in June and July, reaching an even higher peak of urgency. A terrorist threat advisory in late June indicated that there was a high probability of near-term spectacular terrorist attacks resulting in numerous casualties. Headlines from intelligence reports were stark. Quote, "Bin Laden threats are real," close quote. Quote, "Bin Laden planning high-profile attacks," close quote. The intelligence reporting consistently described the upcoming attacks as occurring on a catastrophic level, indicating that they would cause the world to be in turmoil, consisting of possible multiple, but not necessarily simultaneous, attacks. A late June report stated that bin Laden operatives expect near-term attacks to have dramatic consequences of catastrophic proportion.

Rice told us Clarke and his Counterterrorism and Security Group were the nerve center in coordinating responses but that principals were also involved. In addition to his daily meetings with President Bush and weekly meetings to go over other issues with National Security Advisor Rice, Tenet continued his regular meetings with Secretary Powell and Secretary Rumsfeld. The foreign policy principals talked on the phone every day on a variety of subjects, including the threat.

At Rice's request, on July 5 the CIA briefed Attorney General John Ashcroft on the al Qaeda threat, warning that a significant terrorist attack was imminent, and a strike could occur at any time. That same day officials from domestic agencies, including the Federal Aviation Administration, met with Clarke to discuss the current threat. Rice worked directly with Tenet on security issues for the G-8 summit. In addition to the individual reports, on July 11 top officials received a summary recapitulating the mass of al Qaeda-related threat reporting on several continents. Tenet told us that in his world, quote, "the system was blinking red," close quote, and by late July it could not

249

have been any worse. Tenet told us he felt that President Bush and other officials grasped the urgency of what they were being told.

On July 27 Clarke informed Rice and Hadley that the spike in signals intelligence about a near-term attack had stopped. He urged keeping readiness high during the August vacation period, warning that another report suggested an attack had just been postponed for a few months.

On August 3, the Intelligence Community issued a threat advisory warning that the threat of impending al Qaeda attacks would likely continue indefinitely. The advisory cited threats in the Arabian Peninsula, Jordan, Israel and Europe, and suggested that al Qaeda was lying in wait and searching for gaps in security before moving forward with the planned attacks.

During the spring and summer of 2001 President Bush had occasionally asked his briefers whether any of the threats pointed to the United States. Reflecting on these questions, the CIA decided to write a briefing article summarizing its under-standing of this danger. The article, which the President received on August 6, is attached to the Staff statement.

Despite the large number of threats received, there were no specifics regarding time, place, method or target.

Analyzing this testimony

The reporting also mentioned that Abu Zubaydah was planning an attack and expected to carry out more if things went well.

The threat reports surged again in June and July, reaching an even higher peak of urgency. A terrorist threat advisory in late June indicated that there was a high probability of near-term spectacular terrorist attacks resulting in numerous casualties.

The CIA getting reports of spectacular terrorist attacks involving Abu Zubaydah, a very high-level al Qaeda operative (in fact he was number four in the al Qaeda hierarchy), meant that the attack would be focused only on a major target inside of the US.

The search for al-Mihdhar

MS. BARBARA GREWE: It is in this context that we return to the story of al-Mihdhar and al-Hazmi. While top officials in Washington were receiving and reacting to various threat reports, we need to step further down in the bureaucracy to trace a now significant story of how particular al Qaeda associates were addressed by lower-level officials.

In Staff Statement No. 2, presented at our January hearing, we discussed the complex story of successes and failures in tracking and identifying hijackers Khalid al-Mihdhar, Nawaf al-Hazmi, Nawaf's brother Salem al-Hazmi, and the *Cole* bomber, Khallad.

Those efforts had trailed off in January 2000. No one at CIA Headquarters reacted to the March 2000 cable from Bangkok that someone named Nawaf al-Hazmi had traveled to the United States. But there were three episodes in 2001 when the CIA and/or the FBI had apparent opportunities to refocus on the significance of al-Hazmi and al-Mihdhar and reinvigorate the search for them. As in the 2000 story, the details are complex. We turn to the first episode, which is in January 2001, the identification of Khallad.

Almost one year after the original trail had been lost in Bangkok, the January 2000 rendezvous of suspected terrorists in Kuala Lumpur resurfaced. The FBI and the CIA learned from a conspirator in the *USS Cole* attack in Yemen that a person he knew as Khallad had helped direct the *Cole* bombing. One of the members of the FBI's investigative team in Yemen realized he had previously heard of Khallad from a joint FBI-CIA source who had said Khallad was close to bin Laden. Khallad was also linked to the East African bombings in 1998. The FBI agent obtained from a foreign government a photo of the person believed to have directed the *Cole* bombing.

We later learn that the "FBI agent", identified here, as "one of the members of the FBI investigative team in Yemen" is actually FBI Special Agent Ali Soufan, lead investigator on the Cole bombing. We also learn that Ali Soufan had obtained the passport photo of Khallad bin Attash in November, 1999, from the Yemen police and had sent this back to the FBI through the email services of the CIA, which also gave the CIA this passport photo of Khallad

The joint source confirmed the man in that photograph was the same Khallad he had described.

In December 2000, based on some analysis of information associated with Khalid al-Mihdhar, the CIA's bin Laden station speculated that Khallad and Khalid al-Mihdhar might be one and the same. So, the CIA asked that a Kuala Lumpur surveillance photo of al-Mihdhar be shown to the joint source who had already identified an official photograph of Khallad.

251

This has never been explained. The CIA had the passport photo of Khallad and also has the photo copied passport of Khalid al-Mihdhar with his photograph, which they obtained late December 1999. So how is it even conceivable that they might think that these people are the same when they have photos of each, and they do not look at all a like?

In early January 2001 two photographs from the Kuala Lumpur meeting were shown to the joint source. One was a known photograph of al-Mihdhar; the other a photograph of an unknown subject. The joint source did not recognize al-Mihdhar, but he indicated he was 90 percent certain that the other individual was Khallad. This meant that Khallad and al-Mihdhar were two different people. But the fact that both had attended the meeting in Kuala Lumpur also meant there was a link between Khallad, a suspected leader in the *Cole* bombing, the Kuala Lumpur meeting, and al-Mihdhar. Despite this new information, we found no effort by the CIA to renew the long-abandoned search for al-Mihdhar or his travel companions.

In addition, we found that the CIA did not notify the FBI of this identification until late August.

Khallad had been photographed at the Kuala Lumpur meeting with Khalid al-Mihdhar. We also know that Nawaf al-Hazmi and his brother, Salem al-Hazmi, were at the Kuala Lumpur meeting and they along with Khalid al-Mihdhar were on the plane that crashed into the Pentagon on 9/11.

In January 2001, the CIA knew that one of the people identified as having attended the Kuala Lumpur meeting (Khallad) had also been in charge of the *Cole* bombing. They also knew both Khalid al-Mihdhar and Nawaf al-Hazmi had been photographed together at this meeting with Khallad. The CIA at this point has to know that the Cole bombing was planned at this meeting, and that Khallad, Khalid al-Midhar, Nawaf al-Hazmi and Salem al-Hazmi were all complicit in this attack. Hence these people along with the fact that they were together at the planning meeting for the Cole bombing would be of immense importance to the FBI Cole investigators, headed by Ali Soufan. Despite this, the CIA inexplicably did not even inform the FBI of the link between al-Mihdhar and Khallad, the person who directed the *Cole* bombing, until August 30, 2001. They did not ask the FBI, to even start a search for either al-Mihdhar or al-Hazmi until August 22, 2001, in spite of the fact they had known about both terrorists since January 5, 2000. The 9/11 Commission was never able to provide a reasonable explaination for this.

DCI Tenet and Cofer Black testified before the Joint Inquiry that the FBI had access to this identification from the beginning. But based on an extensive record, including documents that were not available to CIA personnel who drafted that testimony, we conclude they were in error. The FBI's primary Cole investigators had no knowledge of Khallad's possible participation in the Kuala Lumpur meeting until after the September 11 attacks.

This is an example of how day-to-day gaps in information sharing can emerge even in a situation of goodwill on all sides. The information was from a joint FBI/CIA source. The source spoke essentially no English. The FBI person on the scene overseas did not speak the languages the source spoke. Due to travel and security issues, the amount of time spent with the source was necessarily kept short. As a result, the CIA officer usually did not simultaneously translate either the questions or the answers for his accompanying FBI colleague, and friend.

For interviews without such simultaneous translation, the FBI agent on the scene received copies of the reports that the CIA disseminated to other agencies, but he was not given access to the CIA's internal operational traffic that contained more detail. The information regarding the January 2001 identification of Khallad was only reported in operational traffic to which the relevant FBI investigators did not have access. The CIA officer does not recall this particular identification and thus cannot say why it was not shared with his FBI colleague. But he may have misunderstood the possible significance of the new identification.

This shows that Tenet and Black had lied to the Joint Inquiry Committee and to Congress. Information that Khallad was identified in the Kuala Lumpur photos along with Khalid al-Mihdhar and Nawaf al-Hazmi was with held from the FBI until August 30, 2001, although this information was widely known within the Bin Laden unit at the CIA and by the management of the CIA above this level. At the time it became known at the CIA that Khallad had masterminded the Cole bombing and had been at the Kuala Lumpur meeting, the CIA would have known that

253

they had photographed this terrorist at this meeting and then allowed him walk away to carry out the Cole bombing.

Hence the CIA knew they were now culpable in the attack on the Cole, an attack that had killed 17 US sailors.

We find out later, that the CIA had hidden this same or similar information from the FBI on at least 10 separate occasions. Yet we are told in the 9/11 Commission staff statement that this one case where this information was withheld from the FBI was due to the following reason: "This is an example of how day-to-day gaps in information sharing can emerge even in a situation of goodwill on all sides." No proof is ever provided "of good will on all sides", no further examination of why this information was never shared with the FBI, just an unsupportable statement to gloss over the real reasons this information was never shared with the FBI.

Al-Mihdhar left the United States in June 2000. It is possible that if in January 2001, agencies had resumed their search for him or placed him on the TIPOFF watchlist, they might have found him before or at the time al-Mihdhar applied for a new visa in June 2001 or they might have been alerted to him when he returned to the United States the following month. We cannot know.

The second opportunity is in the spring of 2001, looking again at Kuala Lumpur. By mid-May 2001, as the threat reports were surging again, a CIA official detailed to the International Terrorism Operations Section at the FBI wondered where the attacks might occur.

We will call him John. John recalled the Kuala Lumpur travel of al-Mihdhar and his associates around the Millennium. He searched the CIA's databases for information regarding the travel. On May 15th, he and another official at CIA reexamined many of the old cables from early 2000, including the information that al-Mihdhar had a US visa and that al-Hazmi had come to Los Angeles on January 15, 2000.

John, however, began a lengthy exchange with a CIA analyst to figure out what these cables meant. He recognized the relationship to the bombing case, and he was aware that

254

someone had identified Khallad in one of the surveillance photographs from the Malaysia meetings. He concluded that something bad was definitely up. Despite the US links evident in this traffic, John did not raise that aspect with his FBI counterparts. He was focused on Malaysia.

From this staff statement we are told that "By mid-May 2001, as the threat reports were surging again, a CIA official detailed to the International Terrorism Operations Section at the FBI (John) wondered where the attacks might occur. We are told that; "He searched the CIA's databases for information regarding the travel. On May 15th, he and another official at CIA reexamined many of the old cables from early 2000, including the information that al-Mihdhar had a US visa and that al-Hazmi had come to Los Angeles on January 15, 2000. He recognized the relationship to the (Cole) bombing case, and he was aware that Khallad had been identified in one of the surveillance photographs from the Malaysia meetings..." So John knows that Khallad, the mastermind of the Cole bombing was at the Kuala Lumpur meeting where the attack on the Cole was planned, knows with Mihdhar and Hazmi. He even knows that Hazmi is in the US and Mihdhar has a multi-entry visa for the US. But we are told; "Despite the US links evident in this traffic, John did not raise that aspect with his FBI counterparts. He was focused on Malaysia." But we are even told; " by mid-May2001 and threat reports were surging again, a CIA official detained to the ITOS section of the FBI wondered where the attacks might occur" so John knowing Hazmi is in the US and that Mihdhar has a US, visa, clearly indicating this attack will take place inside of the US, says nothing to his FBI counterparts, knowing now that it is highly likely that both Mihdhar and Hazmi will be part of this huge attack. This is in spite of his job at the FBI, liaison to Michael Rolince, head of the ITOS section of the FBI. The job of liaison is to provide CIA information to the FBI so the FBI can explode this information for investigation purposes. Instead of providing this CIA information he does not give any of this information to the FBI. He hides this information from the FBI until August 22, 2001. And we are told this is because "he was focused on Malaysia". The 9/11 staff statement tells us John is going to allow thousands of Americans to die in an al Qaeda attack he and the CIA are aware of because he is now focused on Malaysia? The 9/11 Staff statement says this in order to justify the inexplicable actions of John, but this explaination is clearly absurd!

This staff statement goes on to justify this in the following way:

> John's focus on the overseas target area might be understood from his description of the CIA as an agency that tended to play a "zone defense." In contrast, he said, the FBI tends to play "man-to-man." Desk officers at the CIA's Bin Ladin Station did not have "cases" in the same sense as an FBI agent who works something beginning to end. Thus, when the trail went cold after the Kuala Lumpur meeting in January 2000, the desk officer moved on to different things. By the time the March 2000 cable arrived with information that one of the travelers had flown to Los Angeles, the case officer was not responsible for following up that information. While several individuals at the Bin Ladin Station opened the cable when it arrived in March 2000, it was no one's concern, and no action was taken. We discussed some of the management issues raised by this in January, in Staff Statement No. 2.

August 2001: The search for Mihdhar and Hazmi Begins and Fails

During the summer of 2001, John asked an FBI official detailed to the CIA to review all of the Kuala Lumpur materials one more time. We will call her Mary. [Note: She was actually given this assignment on May 15, 2001 according to the FBI IG report.] John asked her to do the research in her free time. She began her work on July 24th.

That day she found the cable reporting that al-Mihdhar had a visa to the United States. A week later she found the cable reporting that al-Mihdhar's visa application – what was later discovered to be his first application – listed New York as his destination. On August 21st she located the March 2000 cable that "noted with interest" that al-Hazmi had flown to Los Angeles in January 2000. She grasped the significance of this information.

She did not find these cables until August 21, 2001 despite the fact that John (who had given her this assignment) already had read these cables on May 15, 2001:

So the FBI detailee assigned to the CIA spent over two months finding the exact same cables that John, the CIA officer detailed to ITOS at the FBI, already had in his possession, and then spent another month finding the cable on al-Hazmi. It was on August 21, she found the cable that stated that al-Hazmi had entered the US on January 15, 2000, another cable John already had in his possession on May 15, 2001, three months earlier. Mary had accidentally stumbled onto the cable that stated that Nawaf al-Hazmi had enetered the US on January 15, 2000. When she took this information to the INS she found out that Mihdhar had also entered the US on January 15, 2000, had left the US on June 2000, but had finally re-enetered the US again on July 4, 2001.

> Mary and an FBI analyst working the case, whom we will call Jane, promptly met with an INS representative at FBI Headquarters. On August 22nd INS told them that al-Mihdhar had entered the United States on January 15, 2000, and again on July 4th, 2001. Jane and Mary also learned that there was no record that al-Hazmi had left since January 2000, but they were not certain if he was still here and assumed that he had left with al-Mihdhar in June 2000. They decided that if al-Mihdhar was in the United States, he should be found.

On August 22, 2001 the FBI was finally notified that al-Mihdhar he had flown into Los Angeles with al-Hazmi on January 15, 2000, had left the US in June 2001, and then had entered the US on July 4, 2001.

> They divided up the work. Mary asked the bin Laden station to draft a cable requesting that al-Mihdhar and al-Hazmi be put on the TIPOFF watchlist.

> Jane took responsibility for the search effort inside the United States. As the information indicated that al-Mihdhar had last arrived in New York, and this was determined to be related to the bin Laden case in New York, she began drafting a lead for the FBI's New York Field Office.

> She called an agent in New York to give him a heads-up on the matter, but her draft lead was not sent until August 28th. Her e-mail told the New York agent that she wanted to get him started on this as soon as possible, but she labeled the lead as "routine." A "routine" designation informs the receiving office it has 30 days to respond to the lead.

> The agent who received the lead forwarded it to his squad supervisor. That same day the supervisor forwarded the lead to an intelligence agent to open an intelligence case. He also sent

it to the *Cole* case agents and an agent who had spent significant time in Malaysia searching for another Khalid, Khalid Shaikh Mohammed.

The suggested goal of the investigation was to locate al-Mihdhar, determine his contacts and reasons for being in the United States, and possibly conduct an interview.

Before sending the lead, Jane had discussed it with John, the CIA official on detail to the FBI, and with the acting head of the FBI's Bin Laden Unit.

Jane, "Before sending the lead, Jane, had discussed this with John". But from earlier information to the 9/11 Commission, we know that John is aware of the huge attack just about to occur inside of the US, and he knows that Mihdhar and Hazmi now that they arte found inside of the US are going to take part in this attack. John is the same CIA official who had blocked the original CIR written by a FBI desk officer at the CIA on Khalid al-Mihdhar almost 21 months earlier on January 5, 2000 and who had obtained the three photos of Khalid al Mihdhar to be shown to the FBI Cole investigators at a meeting in New York on June 11, 2001. Further more "Her e-mail told the New York agent that she wanted to get him started on this as soon as possible, but she labeled the lead as "routine." A 'routine' designation informs the receiving office it has 30 days to respond to the lead." So Jane sent the lead as routine after consulting with former CIA deputy chief, John! It is clear now that John had involved in hiding the information on Mihdhar from the FBI from January 2000 to August 2001. It clearly looks like he influences Jane to mark the lead "Routine" a designation that would effectively lower the sense of urgency on the search for Mihdhar to such an extent Mihdhar would not be found in time to prevent the attacks on 9/11. While all of this information attempts to justify the actions at the CIA, it only reinforces the notion that the CIA had been hiding information from the FBI and then even effectively sabotaging the final investigation and search for Mihdhar. But why did the 9/11 Commission not investigate this further instead of offering absurd reasons why the information on Mihdhar and Hazmi were kept hidden from the FBI.

The discussion apparently was limited to whether the search should be classified as an intelligence investigation or as a criminal one, a legally important distinction for reasons we explained earlier today in Staff Statement Number 9. Neither of these individuals apparently disagreed with the analyst's proposed plan. No one apparently felt they needed to inform higher levels of management in either the FBI or the CIA about the case.

One of the *Cole* case agents read the lead with interest and contacted Jane to obtain more information. Jane took the position, however, that because the agent was a designated "criminal" agent, the "wall" kept him from participating in any search for al-Mihdhar. In fact, she felt he had to destroy his copy of the lead because it contained information she believed could not be shared with any criminal agents.

The Joint Inquiry covered the details of their heated exchanges, and we will not repeat them here.

The result was that criminal agents who were knowledgeable about the *Cole* and experienced with criminal investigative techniques, including finding suspects and possible criminal charges, were excluded from the search.

Many witnesses have suggested that even if al-Mihdhar had been found, there was nothing the agents could have done except follow him onto the plane. We believe this is incorrect. Both al-Hazmi and al-Mihdhar could have been held for various immigration violations or as material witnesses in the *Cole* bombing case. Investigation or interrogation of these individuals and their travel and financial activities also may have yielded evidence of connections to other participants in the 9/11 plot. In any case, the opportunity did not arise.

Notably, the lead did not draw any connections between the threat reporting that had been coming in for months and the presence of two possible al Qaeda operatives in the United States.

Moreover, there is no evidence that the issue was substantively discussed at any level above a deputy chief of a section within the Counterterrorism Division at FBI Headquarters.

The search was assigned to one FBI agent for whom this was his very first counterterrorism lead. By the terms of the lead, he was given 30 days to open an intelligence case and make some unspecified efforts to locate al-Mihdhar. He started the process a week later. He checked local New York indices for criminal record and driver's license information and checked the hotel listed on al-Mihdhar's US entry form. On September

11 the agent sent a lead to Los Angeles based on the fact that al-Mihdhar had initially arrived in Los Angeles in January 2000. Time had run out on the search.

The CIA had identified and focused on al-Mihdhar no less than five times, according to the 9/11 Commission staff reports. The first time Khalid al-Mihdhar had come to the attention of the CIA was in January 2000, in the meeting in Kuala Lumpur. Then again, for a second time in January of 2001, while assisting the FBI in the *Cole* investigation, when in a review of the meeting in January 2000, al-Mihdhar was identified together in a photograph from this meeting with Khallad, the person who was known to be the leader of the *Cole* attack.

The third time was, according to the 9/11 staff statements, in May 15, 2001, in a review of cables from January 2000 due to a CIA official, John, at the FBI's ITOS group wondering, because of the surge on threat reports in the spring of 2001, where an attack would take place and whether al-Mihdhar was involved in this attack. The fourth time was at the June 11 meeting with the New York field agents on the *Cole* investigation. And finally, a fifth time, on August 22, 2001, when an inquiry to the immigration services indicated that al-Mihdhar had reentered the US on July 4, 2001, and that al-Hazmi had never left the US after having entered the country on January 15, 2000.

There is no explaination from the 9/11 Commission why John, who we now know had connected the warnings of an huge al Qaeda attack to Mihdhar and Hazmi never tells anyone at the FBI of this connection even though this was his job. In fact he does just the opposite, he hides this very information from the FBI on numerous occasions, information that could have prevented the attacks on 9/11. And the 9/11 Commission inexplicably never uncovers the reasons he hides this information from the FBI when that was exactly his job!

The FBI and investigation of Moussaoui

We want to briefly mention two other incidents in the summer of 2001. The first, the Phoenix Memo.

The Phoenix Memo was investigated at length by the Joint Inquiry. We recap it briefly in the statement that's provided to you. I just want to mention now – as its author told us, the Phoenix Memo was not an alert about suicide pilots. His worry was more about a Pan Am 103 scenario in which explosives were placed on an aircraft. The memo's references to aviation training were broad, including electronics and aircraft maintenance.

And lastly, Moussaoui. On August 15, 2001, the Minneapolis FBI Field Office initiated an intelligence investigation on Zacarias Moussaoui. He had entered the country on February 23, 2001, and began flight lessons at Airman Flight School in Oklahoma City. He began flight training at the Pan American flight training school in Minneapolis on August 13. Moussaoui had none of the usual qualifications for flight training on Pan Am's Boeing 747 flight simulators. Contrary to popular belief, Moussaoui did not say he was not interested in learning how to take off or land. Instead, he stood out because, with little knowledge of flying, he wanted to learn how to take off and land a Boeing 747.

The FBI agent who handled the case in conjunction with the INS representative on the Minneapolis Joint Terrorism Task Force suspected Moussaoui of wanting to hijack planes. Because Moussaoui was a French national who had over-stayed his visa, he was detained by the INS.

The FBI agent sent a summary of his investigation to FBI Headquarters on August 18. In his message he requested assistance from the FBI Field Office in Oklahoma City and from the FBI legal attaché in Paris. Each of these offices responded quickly. By August 24 the Minneapolis agent had also contacted a detailee from the FBI and a CIA analyst at the Counterterrorist Center about the case. DCI Tenet was briefed about the Moussaoui case. He told us that no connection to al Qaeda was apparent to him before 9/11.

Moussaoui had lived in London, so the Minneapolis agent also requested assistance from the legal attaché in London.

The legal attaché promptly prepared a written request of the British government for information concerning Moussaoui and hand-delivered the request on August 21st. He informed the British of developments in the case on September 4th. The case, although handled expeditiously at the American end, was not handled by the British as a priority amid a large number of other terrorist-related inquiries. On September 11th, after the attacks, the legal attaché renewed his request for information.

After 9/11 the British government, in response to US requests, supplied some basic biographical information about

Moussaoui. The British government has informed us that it also tasked intelligence collection facilities for information potentially relating to Moussaoui. On September 13, the British received new, sensitive intelligence that Moussaoui had attended an al Qaeda training camp in Afghanistan. It passed this intelligence to the United States that same day.

Had this information been available in late August 2001, the Moussaoui case would almost certainly have received intense and much higher-level attention. Prior to 9/11, there was a continuing dispute between FBI agents in Minneapolis and supervisors at Headquarters about whether evidence had been sufficient to seek a FISA warrant to search Moussaoui's computer hard drive and belongings. After 9/11, the FBI learned that Millennium terrorist Ressam, who was cooperating with investigators, could have recognized Moussaoui from the Afghan camps.

Either the British information or the Ressam identification would have broken that logjam. A maximum US effort to investigate Moussaoui could conceivably have unearthed his connections to the Hamburg cell, though this might have required an extensive effort with help from foreign governments. The publicity about the threat also might have disrupted the plot, but this would have been a race against time.

When a Supervisory Special Agent (SSA) at FBI Headquarters was told by FBI field agents in the Minneapolis office that Zacarias Moussaoui was possibly a terrorist who wanted to learn to fly large aircraft in preparation to use a large airliner to attack the World Trade Center Towers, the field agents were told, "that will never happen," and were dismissed as spinning this into a much larger issue than it really was.

After the events of 9/11, the Minnesota agents urged that FISA search warrants be granted in light of the attack on the World Trade Center Towers. They were told by FBI Headquarters, that there was no connection between Zacarias Moussaoui and the attacks on the World Trade Center Towers, that these two events were nothing but a coincidence.

2:00 – 3:30 p.m. TUESDAY, APRIL 13

PANEL: SUMMER 2001

Mr. Thomas J. Pickard
Former Acting Director, Federal Bureau of Investigation

In my view, the tragedy of 9/11 clearly demonstrates the high cost for the collective failure of the US government to penetrate the inner workings of or to deal with terrorism, as it was then and is now a war against the United States intended to inflict as many American casualties as possible. For many and very deep – for many complex reasons, we did not develop the necessary intelligence, either through our own resources or through foreign resources, to sufficiently understand and react to their planning, communications, control and capacity to do us harm.

I was the acting director of the FBI in the summer of 2001. The intelligence and the experience I had available to me at the time were what I acted upon. As I recall, during the period January to September 2001, the FBI received over 1,000 threats. Many of these threats had great specificity and others were very general in nature. All were taken seriously, but the volume was daunting. The increase in the chatter was by far the most serious, but it was also the most difficult to deal with. There was no specificity as to what, where and when. We knew the who, but only that it was al Qaeda.

I had regular conversations with the director of CIA and his deputy, and the Attorney General and his deputy about the threats we were receiving and to learn if there was anything more that would help us understand the fragmentary information we had. The only news I received was that the chatter subsided in August 2001.

Dick Clarke before this Commission stated that he – if he had known about these two individuals, al-Mihdhar and al-Hazmi, he would have put them on "America's Most Wanted." However, on September 10 all we knew was that they were to be put on the visa watchlist and we should attempt to locate them. The FBI did not know whether they had departed the United States, and we certainly had no information – none – that they were here to carry out an act of terrorism.

That there was no actionable intelligence that would indicate that such an attack was underway and hence no way of stopping this attack from happening.

*That there was no information as to the time, place,
method of attack or target so nothing could be done.*

Top CIA and FBI officials claimed there was no actionable
intelligence. This was excuse from virtually every manager at
both agencies as to why they did not anticipate and prevent al
Qaeda from carrying out the attacks of 9/11.

Any organization charged with preventing terrorist attacks on the
US should not have relied on or waited for actionable
intelligence. This type of intelligence would never have been
possible to obtain anyway. Suggesting nothing could be done
without actionable intelligence was to guarantee that a terrorist
attack based on the use of extreme secrecy would ultimately be
successful.

This was the type of thinking at the FBI, which meant they were
doomed to fail even before they started. They would not start an
investigation without some real evidence that could be
corroborated, and they would never get real evidence that could
be corroborated without an investigation.

*The FBI did not know whether they (al-Mihdhar and al-
Hazmi) had departed the United States, and we certainly
had no information – none – that they were here to carry
out an act of terrorism.*

The FBI knew of a huge al Qaeda attack inside of the US. Tenet
and Black had given Attorney General Ashcroft this warning of
this attack in mid-July. The FBI knew that these two al Qaeda
terrorists were inside of the US after attending an al Qaeda
planning meeting with terrorists who had carried out the
embassy attacks and *Cole* bombing. To say "we certainly had no
information – none – that they were here to carry out an act of
terrorism" is incomprehensible.

MR. ROEMER: Thank you, Mr. Chairman.

You two are certainly squarely in the hot seat. We have staff
statements and the Joint Inquiry report that has roundly and
deeply systemically criticized the FBI and the CIA for their
performances leading up to 9/11. They have cited problems in
sharing communication, connecting the dots, over-classifying
documents, and glitches and failures to protect the seams. I
have a question for both of you to just go at maybe one of the
problems.

I asked Director Freeh, Mr. Pickard, earlier about the active informant who had engaged two of the 19 hijackers, and he said, "Quite frankly, the FBI should have done better." Let me give you a case and get your response from it.

You have said in your remarks that that was the most chatter in the summer of 2001. When we have talked to some of the people that should have heard this serious chatter in your communication with them leading into the spring and the summer, when a BIG event was going to happen, an experienced terrorism supervisor in the Washington office six blocks from Headquarters, six blocks away, says he was not aware of any heightened terrorist threat, his squad took no special action leading up to 9/11. A supervisor in the Miami Field Office, a Special Agent in Charge, said, this was inside-the-beltway-kind of thing, never heard of that chatter until after 9/11. What happened?

MR. PICKARD: Your staff has put together some of the communications we sent out. I was concerned making sure that we were at maximum capacity, maximum effort on that. I personally had a conference call with all 56 SACs and all the assistant directors on July 19th just to make sure that – I know some people don't read everything that comes out. But just to reinforce that, I had all 56 SACs – I can't account for the SAC in Miami as to whether he was actually on the call, but whoever was in charge of the office that day was on that call, because I did not get on it until they were all on it. During that call I reiterated the issue of the threat level and also to make sure they were at their maximum effort on that. I don't know –

MR. ROEMER: Do you recall your precise words that you recently told the 9/11 Commission on that conversation?

Your words to the 9/11 Commission were "Evidence Response Teams ready." Evidence Response. That's reactive, that's not proactive saying here's the threat, here's what you need to do about it. You're saying, if we get hit, have the Evidence Response Teams ready.

That's what you told the 9/11 Commission staff.

MR. PICKARD: I also – I had a very brief conversation with them about that. I was surprised at the brevity of it.

MR. ROEMER: Well, it sounds like it was pretty brief to the Field Offices as well – response, not active threat.

265

Tom Pickard stated in his testimony that he had personally said to all 56 Joint Terrorism Task Force supervisors in a phone call in the summer of 2001:

"Have your Evidence Teams ready to go, (to collect evidence after the huge attack the FBI had been warned about in the summer of 2001).

This was the statement that Tim Roemer found so puzzling. What exactly were these response teams going to do? Pick up the little bits of DNA that were going to be all that was left from thousands of people after a huge attack? Why was there not more thought given to preventing this attack in the first place?

MR. PICKARD: But I also had – I spoke to each of the 56 SACs during the month of July, between July 9th and July 31st, each of them individually. I had them on the phone, secure conference call with the assistant directors from Counterterrorism, Dale Watson; Counterintelligence, Neil Gallagher; and the assistant director of the Criminal Division, Rubin Garcia. We discussed their performance, and in addition to that hour-and-a-half discussion of their performance in their Field Office and their commitment to the counterintelligence and counterterrorism efforts, we also discussed during that phone call the threat level. I don't know why the SAC in Miami did not get it. I spoke to him on July 18th.

MR. ROEMER: Six blocks away – your supervisor six blocks away didn't get it.

MR. PICKARD: I spoke to the SACs. They should have been working that information down. I don't –

MR. ROEMER: So could you have done a better job, or are you just saying, "I don't know why they didn't hear it." Did you task them again after the 19th?

MR. PICKARD: I don't understand why they didn't hear it. I spoke to each of them individually, as I said. And in addition, I had the communications out to them. I don't know what more I could have done. Some people, I don't understand whether they can't recall it or not. But if you talk to – for example, I know the staff, the New York office agents, they got it; they were always on top of it, and many of the other agents that I spoke to over the last week.

MR. ROEMER: When we – as you read in the staff statement, when we tasked out to the field if all those offices were on high alert and doing their maximum effort, I think we got nine out of

266

10 back saying they weren't at maximum effort, they weren't at war footing.

MR. KEAN: The New York office began searching for al-Hazmi and al-Mihdhar, knew that they were in the country and were searching for them that same summer. Were you aware of that?

MR. PICKARD: No, I was not before September 11th.

MR. KEAN: Do you think if those two matters from those different offices had been brought to your attention, do you think you might have thought a little differently about the plot or whether there was a plot, or you might have acted differently based on those pieces of information?

MR. PICKARD: I've thought long and hard about that, Governor. And it's a frightening thought to think that that could have been on my desk on September 10th, and would I have done something differently or not? And I can't answer that. I go back and forth on that constantly. It keeps me up at night, thinking: if I had that information, would I have had the intuitiveness to recognize, to go to the President, to do something different?

MR. KEAN: What bothers me is just the fact it didn't get to you –

MR. PICKARD: That –

MR. KEAN: – you know, that something in the FBI stopped those very two important pieces of information, one from – from different parts of the country, from rising to the kind of level where you might have seen them and might have acted on them.

MR. PICKARD: Governor, in defense of the employees there, they were getting – one of unit chiefs – at least 100 pieces of information a day. They were getting fed from a fire hydrant and trying to sort through those things.

I spoke recently with the individual who was in charge of the Minneapolis office, and he said – I asked him. I said, "Why didn't you call me?" I said, "You know me." I send a – once a year out an e-mail to all FBI employees to tell them to come to me with any issue that you have, whether it's investigative, administrative, your pay or some other problem. And I'd heard frequently from individuals who said, "I can't get a group on undercover operation through," or "I'm not getting my annual leave corrected," or whatever it might be. And my secretary used to kid me about it, because she'd print it out each night and say, "Here's your homework. Do it tonight and bring it back tomorrow morning" – because I don't type.

Those things bothered me, but those employees working down in the Counterterrorism Division were working very hard. They were trying to do the best they could with the hundreds of pieces of information they could.

And as we sit here with 20-20 hindsight, picking out three or four pieces of information, I think it is a disservice to them to recognize what pieces, in light of 9/11, were relevant.

What were the three or four pieces of information that could not be picked out from the hundreds of pieces of information that the Counterterrorism Division received? The fact two al Qaeda terrorists, al-Mihdhar and al-Hazmi, had entered the US after attending an al Qaeda planning meeting in Kuala Lumpur. The arrest of Zacarias Moussaoui by FBI agents in Minnesota attempting to get flight training on a large airline simulator when he was clearly an al Qaeda terrorist.

Information that three al Qaeda terrorists had entered the US to carry out a terrorist attack apparently are the three or four pieces of information that could not be recognized as relevant, according to Tom Pickard, even after the FBI had been warned of a massive al Qaeda attack inside of the US.

This testimony also indicates that there was virtually no communication either up or down the hierarchy of the FBI. Information on Zacarias Moussaoui, al-Mihdhar, al-Hazmi, and even the Phoenix memo never made it to the upper echelon of the FBI. This information was blocked somewhere in the bureaucratic maze at the FBI. It appears the information on Moussaoui and the Phoenix memo never even got off the first desk at FBI Headquarters it came to.

Information that should have gone down into the FBI organization also never went anywhere. The information in the spring of 2001 indicating a huge attack on the US was going to come without warning, and kill possibly thousands of Americans, information that reasonably should have generated a huge increase in the alert level, never went down to even the Field Office executive level much less to the level of the field agents. All information in the FBI had to pass through each level of hierarchy, as it went both up and down this organization. At each level, the person or supervisor at this position could block the information from going any further. Attempts to go around this block were met with threats of bureaucratic retaliation, and career ending reprimands.

FBI field agents in Minneapolis were in a panic due to the lack of progress in obtaining a search warrant for the computer that Zacarias Moussaoui had in his possession. When a Supervisory Special Agent (SSA) at the FBI Headquarters blocked their attempt to get a search warrant through the FISA Courts, they were powerless to go around this agent. They were even reprimanded when they went to the CIA to get information they thought they needed in order to complete an application for the FISA Court for this search warrant.

With information on terrorists entering the US or taking flight lessons, and information on a terrorist arrested because his flight instructor was suspicious, the FBI was not able to act on this information with enough urgency to forestall the attack that occurred on 9/11. When the FBI knew a massive al Qaeda attack was about to occur inside of the US, and knew that two al Qaeda terrorists were inside of the US, they treated this information with no sense of urgency.

2:00 – 3:30 p.m. TUESDAY, APRIL 13

PANEL: Summer 2001

Ambassador J. Cofer Black

Former Director, Counterterrorism Center, Central Intelligence Agency

Overshadowing all this was the rising volume of threat reporting. By the summer of 2001 we were seeing an increased amount of so-called "chatter" alluding to a massive terrorist strike. We were receiving this intelligence not only from our own sources, but also from liaison. Human intelligence was providing the same kinds of insights. Disruption efforts and detentions were also corroborating our concerns about a coming attack. None of this, unfortunately, specified method, time or place. Where we had clues, it looked like planning was underway for an attack in the Middle East or Europe.

More broadly, I also want to emphasize that CTC and the Intelligence Community produced significant strategic analysis that examined the growing threat from international jihadist networks and al Qaeda. I believe that the record shows that the US government understood the nature of the threat. This understanding was the result of a range of products we produced or contributed to, including: personal interaction via participation in the Counterterrorism Security Group; periodic stand-back assessments on UBL and Sunni extremist-related topics; contributing to the annual "Patterns of Global Terrorism."

But ultimately, we were not able to stop what happened on 9/11, despite our actions and our warnings.

Prior to this hearing I contacted former Counterterrorist Center colleagues at our Headquarters here in Virginia and those that are overseas and now in harm's way. I asked them the question, what am I going to tell these people? It should not be my words alone, but it should be ours. And hauntingly, all of my CTC friends independently said exactly the same thing, they used the same words, and they said them in the same order. We are profoundly sorry. We did all we could. We did our best. And they said, make them understand how few we were and what we had to deal with. The shortage of money and people seriously hurt our operations and analysis.

In CTC we heard our director's call. I've heard some people say this country wasn't at war. I want to tell you, Mr. Chairman, the Counterterrorist Center was at war, we conducted ourselves at war. And that's the way it is. We did the best we could under the law and with the resources provided and under our defined rules of engagement.

MR. JOHN LEHMAN: Thank you, and welcome, Mr. Pickard, Mr. Black. The reason you're both here and the reason your testimony carries special weight with us is that both of you are career professionals, that both of you are seen as role models in your particular professional fields. And your prepared statements reflect that. And please understand that the questions I am posing to you have nothing to do with the blame game or finger-pointing. Our high responsibility is to draw the right lessons and to make real achievable recommendations for change.

So that's what we need to find out.

Now let's start with the Presidential Daily Briefing that was just released at our request over the weekend. To me the most significant sentence in that PDB is that, after summarizing the history of the reporting from '98 forward, essentially, of growing alarm and threat in the Intelligence Community, the summary to the President was, quote, "We have not been able to corroborate some of the more sensational threat reporting," such as bin Laden wanting to hijack US aircraft, et cetera. Well, the more sensational threat reporting was right. Why didn't the combined Intelligence Community – why weren't they able to corroborate something as essential as that, Mr. Black?

MR. BLACK: Sir, looking at the PDB article, I would like to reflect upon the time of that. Clearly this was a period of heightened threat. We had a global collection network out. We were receiving significant amounts of intelligence. It certainly was spiking, and all the indications that we had were clearly pointing at the Saudi Arabia Peninsula, Saudi Arabia, to a lesser extent Israel and Europe. So the focus, the tactical focus of the threat was certainly in that area.

The strategic piece is that by Osama bin Laden's own words – has stated he has a war against the United States, he wishes to strike the United States. In fact, he declared that American civilians should be considered as combatants. I think that PDB piece is basically a place marker that is a reminder to the principals that read these materials that, whereas the tactical intelligence is pointing to locations overseas, that it is good to be mindful of what his ultimate objective is, that it is to strike hard against the United States. And I think that's essentially the balance between the two, sir.

271

MR. LEHMAN: Thank you.

MR. KEAN: "Hindsight" is a word we've used. We've all got to be careful to look at the world as it was before 9/11.

Ambassador Black, using hindsight now, if we were able to recognize the kind of tragedy that was going to happen, what would you have done differently? What did we do wrong?

MR. BLACK: Well, I'll tell you, I would start from the standpoint that when I started this job in 1999, I thought there was a good chance I was going to be sitting right here in front of you. And I was mentally prepared for it all along.

The enemy we're up against is one that I've been operating against since the early '90s.

I know these guys. I know what they want to do. I know how dedicated they are. And they were coming at us hard. And, you know, we did all that we could at our level to engage these guys to try and produce the kinds of intelligence, to kind of produce the kinds of leads. And the men and women that did this, Governor, that served this country in war out front did a fantastic job, you know? So on the one side you have catastrophic failure, more than 3,000 people dead; no one's more bothered by this than us. But we engaged these targets. You'll never hear from us, oh, you know, we didn't get it. "Oh, we got it, all right." We knew what we were up against. We gave it all we had. The big bottom line here – you know, people come up with these grand ideas for improvement, you know: big computers, or whatever. The bottom line here, I got to tell you – and I'll take part of the blame on this – I kind of failed my people despite doing everything I could. We didn't have enough people to do the job, and we didn't have enough money by magnitudes. And I could give you comparisons you, like, wouldn't believe.

We used to talk about it in the Counterterrorist Center. You know, this goes into the '90s. I mean, this has been so hard-wired that, you know, by the time we get up in the recent past, I mean, this train is on this track and this is where it's going. Hell, I don't know if we ever COULD have got it off without some kind of catastrophe. I will tell you, you know, going back to the '90s, doing the terrorist target, the only way we ever got more money essentially was we would spend ahead of the curve and run out.

You know, people talk about the millennium threat? I can remember we were spending money on the millennium threat, went to the director. I said, "Mr. Tenet, you know, we're spending money here; we're not going to make it to the end of the fiscal year. We're going to be three months short. We're going to have to stop and – you know, we won't be able to operate." He said – well, he sighed and he said, "Well, you know, do what's right for the country; blow it out." So we did. So we spent – you know, after the money threat was over, we spend our time trying to get the money to make up for that which we spent, OR – and I'm just not going to go into the exact kind of language I used, which is very graphic. But unfortunately, when Americans get killed, it would translate into additional resources. It's a constant track: either you run out, or people die, when people die you get more money.

And, you know, it would have been better if we as a country had made the commitment to provide our counterterrorist warriors the resources and the numbers so they could do the best job they could. But what I want to leave you with – I mean, that's all I want to leave with. The people that did this are heroes, and we didn't give them what they needed to fight and win. It's that simple. Thank you.

Analyzing the testimony of Cofer Black

"We did all that we could at our level to engage these guys to try and produce the kinds of intelligence, to kind of produce the kinds of leads..."

Cofer Black is blaming the failure to prevent the attacks on 9/11 on not having enough of the right intelligence. But they had been aware of the names of three of the al Qaeda terrorists who took part in these attacks for 21 months before 9/11, when these terrorists, Khalid al-Mihdhar, Nawaf al-Hazmi and Salem al-Hamzi were identified at the Kuala Lumpur al Qaeda planning meeting in January 2000. The CIA had extensive photographs of these terrorists when they attended this very meeting where the *Cole* bombing and the 9/11 attacks were planned. One of the terrorists photographed at this meeting was Tawfiq Bin Attash, Khallad, who was identified as the mastermind of the Cole bombing in January 2001 from his photograph at this same meeting. For still unexplained reasons, they hid this information from the FBI, for over 21 months

In the summer of 2001, that Khalid Shaikh Mohammed had chaired the al Qaeda planning meeting in Kuala Lumpur in January 2000, and was sending into the US at this time, al

Qaeda terrorists to carry out a horrific attack inside the US, an attack the CIA was already aware of. In August 2001 the CIA was aware that Zacarias Moussaoui, a suspected al Qaeda terrorist had been aresseted by the FBI attempting to take lesions on a Boeing 747 simulator. From April 2001, the CIA had been getting unmistakable warnings that a huge catastrophic and imminent terrorist attack was going to take place in the summer or fall of 2001. But according to this testimony, none of this information appeared to the CIA to be specific enough to indicate where and when this attack would come. In their testimony to the 9/11 Commission, the director and managers at the CIA said this agency, with thousands of highly paid employees and multi-billion-dollar budgets, had been outwitted by 19 terrorists, most of whom had just a high school education. All the management at the CIA could only say in the end, was the reason for their failure was that they had been understaffed and under funded.

9:00 – 9:30 a.m. WEDNESDAY, APRIL 14, 2004

STAFF STATMENT NO. 11

The Performance of the Intelligence Community

MR. ZELIKOW: Members of the Commission, with your help, your staff has developed initial findings on the performance of the Intelligence Community against the danger of Islamic extremist terrorism before the September 11th attacks on the United States. These findings may help frame some of the issues for this hearing and inform your work.

In Staff Statement Number 7, we discussed our initial findings on the work of the CIA as an instrument of national policy in the areas of clandestine and covert action. Today we focus on intelligence analysis and warning, the collection of intelligence and the overall management of the Intelligence Community before September 11th, 2001.

Information comes to intelligence agencies...

see pages 260 - 263 ...

...especially at the Office of Naval Intelligence.

Amid the thousands of threat reports, some mentioned aircraft in the years before 9/11. The most prominent hijacking threat report came from a foreign government source in late 1998 and discussed a plan for hijacking a plane in order to gain hostages and bargain for the release of prisoners, such as the "blind sheikh."

As we mentioned yesterday in Staff Statement Number 10, this 1998 report was the source of the allusion to hijacking in the President's Daily Brief article provided to President Bush in August 2001.

Other threat reports mentioned the possibility of using an aircraft laden with explosives. Of these the most prominent asserted a possible plot to fly an explosives-laden aircraft into a US city. This report was circulated in September 1998 and originated from a source who walked into an American consulate in East Asia. Neither the source's reliability nor the information could be corroborated.

The CTC did not analyze how a hijacked aircraft or other explosives-laden aircraft might be used as a weapon. If it had done so, it could have identified that a critical obstacle would be to find a suicide terrorist able to fly large jet aircraft. This had never happened before 9/11.

The CTC did not develop a set of telltale indicators for this means of attack. For example, one such indicator might be the discovery of terrorists seeking or taking flight training to fly large jet aircraft, or seeking to buy advanced flight simulators.

The CTC did not propose, and the Intelligence Community collection management process did not set, collection requirements against such telltale indicators. Therefore, the warning system was not looking for information such as the July 2001 FBI report of terrorist interest in various kinds of aircraft training in Arizona, or the August 2001 arrest of Zacarias Moussaoui because of his suspicious behavior in a Minnesota flight school. In late August, the Moussaoui arrest was briefed to the DCI and other top CIA officials under the heading, quote, "Islamic Extremist Learns to Fly," close quote. The news had no evident effect on warning.

Neither the Intelligence Community nor the NSC policy process analyzed systemic defenses of aircraft or against suicide aircraft. The many threat reports mentioning aircraft were passed to the FAA. We discussed the problems at that agency in Staff Statements 3 and 4.

Richard Clarke told us that he was concerned about this threat in the context of protecting the Atlanta Olympics in June 1996, the White House complex, and the 2001 G-8 summit in Genoa.

But he attributed his awareness to novels more than any warnings from the Intelligence Community. He did not pursue the systemic issues of defending aircraft from suicide hijackers or bolstering wider air defenses.

MR. KEVIN SCHEID: Mr. Chairman, the Counterterrorist Center and the larger Intelligence Community tried to understand the emerging terrorist threat with their traditional collection methods of human source collection, or the use of informants; information provided by foreign intelligence services; signals collection, or the intercept of communications; and open sources, or the systematic collection of print, broadcast and, in the late 1990s, Internet information.

The German government provided the US government information on an individual named "Marwan" who was acquainted with the target of a German investigation. The common first name and a phone number in the United Arab Emirates were provided as a possible lead in 1999. The CTC pursued this lead for a short time, but with the scant information provided, the CTC found nothing to provoke a special effort on this lead. The CIA did not ask any other agency in the Intelligence Community for assistance. We now know that "Marwan" was Marwan al-Shehhi, who later piloted United Airlines Flight 175 into the South Tower of the World Trade Center. He used the UAE telephone number in the period prior to the 9/11 attacks. We're continuing to investigate this episode.

Strategic collection management depends upon strategic analysis to define the baseline of what is known, what is not known, and to guide the setting of clear, agreed requirements. This process did not occur.

DCI Tenet's war

On December 4, 1998 DCI Tenet issued a directive to several CIA officials and the DDCI for Community Management stating: "We are at war. I want no resources or people spared in this effort, either inside CIA or the Community." Unfortunately, we found the memorandum had little overall effect on mobilizing the CIA or the Intelligence Community.

The memo was addressed only to CIA officials and the Deputy DCI for Community Management, Joan Dempsey. She faxed the memo to the heads of the major agencies of the Intelligence Community. Almost all our interviewees had never seen the memo or only learned of it after 9/11.

The DCI did not develop a management strategy for a war against terrorism before 9/11. Such a management strategy would define the capabilities – the capabilities the Intelligence Community must acquire for such a war, from language training to collection systems to analysts. Such a management strategy would necessarily extend beyond the CTC to the components that feed its expertise and support its operations, linked transparently to counterterrorism objectives. It would then detail the proposed expenditures and organizational changes required to implement these capabilities.

DCI Tenet and the CIA's deputy director for operations told us they did have a management strategy for war on terrorism. It was called "Rebuilding the CIA."

As some officials pointed out to us, the tradeoff of this management approach is that by attempting to rebuild everything, the highest priority efforts might get only an average share, not maximum support.

Lacking a management strategy for the war on terrorism or ways to see how funds were being spent across the Community, it was difficult for DCI Tenet and his aides to develop an overall Intelligence Community budget for the war on terrorism.

Finally, the Community had not institutionalized a process for learning from its successes and failures. We did not find any after-action reviews sponsored by the Intelligence Community after surprise terrorist attacks such as the embassy bombings of August 1998 or the USS Cole attack in October 2000. The Community participated in Inspector General inquiries conducted by individual agencies, but these reviews were perceived as fault-finding, without enough constructive emphasis on learning lessons and discovering best practices. What we did not find was anything between the extremes of no investigation at all, and an adversarial inquiry triggered by a public outcry. We did not find an institution or culture that provided a safe outlet for admitting errors and improving procedures.

While there were many reports on bin Laden and his growing al Qaeda organization, there was no comprehensive estimate of the enemy either to build consensus or clarify differences.

With the important exception of attacks with chemical, biological, radiological or nuclear weapons, the methods developed for decades to warn of surprise attacks were not applied to the problem of warning against terrorist attacks. In intelligence collection, despite many excellent efforts, there was not a comprehensive review of what the Community knew, what it did not know, followed by the development of a Community-wide plan to close those gaps.

The DCI labored within and was accountable for a Community of loosely associated agencies and departmental offices that lacked the incentives to cooperate, collaborate and share information. Like his predecessors, he focused his energies on where he could add the greatest value, the CIA, which is a fraction of the nation's overall intelligence capability. And as a result, the question remains: Who is in charge of intelligence?

Analysis of staff statement;

The 9/11 Commission was able to see what had gone wrong at the CIA, a lack of analysis, as described in their staff statement:

Despite such reports, and a 1999 paper on bin Laden's command structure for al Qaeda, there were no complete authoritative portraits of his strategy and the extent of his organization's involvement in past terrorist attacks. In the Counterterrorist Center, priority was given to tactical analysis to support operations.

9:30 – 11:00 a.m. WEDNESDAY, APRIL 14, 2004

The Honorable George J. Tenet
Director Central Intelligence Agency

"We never had the texture that said the date, time and place of the event inside the United States would result in September 11th. It was not the result of the failure of attention and discipline and focus and consistent effort, and the American people need to understand that."

MR. KEAN: Thank you very much. Please be seated.

Director Tenet, if you'd like to proceed with your opening remarks.

MR. TENET: Thank you, Mr. Chairman. I welcome the opportunity to be here again. On March 24th, I expressed my personal feelings for the loss I felt for the families who lost loved ones.

My colleagues at CIA and throughout our Intelligence Community feel the same sense of loss. That we did not stop these attacks haunts all of us to this day. And what we're doing here is essential not only because we have to be open and honest about the past, but also because we have to be clear-minded about the future.

In 1998, after the East Africa bombings, I directed the assistant director of Central Intelligence for Collection to ensure that all elements of intelligence in the Community had the right assets focused on the right problem with respect to al Qaeda and bin Laden. He convened frequent meetings of the most senior collection specialists in the Community to develop a comprehensive approach to support the Counterterrorist Center's operations against bin Laden. He told me that, despite progress, we needed a sustained, longer-term effort if the Community was to penetrate deeply into the Afghan sanctuary.

All of this collection recognizes the primacy of human and technical penetration of the al Qaeda leadership and network and the necessity to get inside the sanctuary in Afghanistan...

Mr. Chairman, I've outlined in my statement our analytical product. I don't mean to short-shrift it, but I know you want me to stay within 10 minutes. I think that there was depth and clarity across a range of products and a range of venues. I believe that that product got to our policymakers, including the most senior policymakers, in many forms.

How do I assess our performance? The intelligence that we provided our senior policymakers about the threat al Qaeda posed, its leadership and its operational span across over 60 countries, and the use of Afghanistan as a sanctuary was clear and direct. Warning was well understood, even if the timing and method of attacks were not. *The Intelligence Community had the right strategy and was making the right investments to position itself for the future against al Qaeda. We made good progress across intelligence disciplines. Disruptions, renditions and sensitive collection activities no doubt saved lives.*

However, we never penetrated the 9/11 plot overseas. While we positioned ourselves very well, with extensive human and technical penetrations, to facilitate the take-down of the Afghan sanctuary, we did not discern the specific nature of the plot.

We made mistakes. Our failure to watchlist al-Hazmi and al-Mihdhar in a timely manner, or the FBI's inability to find them in the narrow window at the time afforded them showed systemic weaknesses and the lack of redundancy. There were at least four separate terrorist identity databases at

State, CIA, the Department of Defense and the FBI. None were interoperable or broadly accessible. There were dozens of watchlists, many haphazardly maintained. There were legal impediments to cooperation across the continuum of criminal intelligence operations. It was not a secret at all that we understood it, but in truth, all of us took little action to create a common arena of criminal and intelligence data that we could all access.

We all understood bin Laden's attempt to strike the homeland, but we never translated this knowledge into an effective defense of the country. Doing so would have complicated the terrorists' calculation of the difficulty in succeeding in a vast, open society that, in effect, was unprotected on September 11.

During periods of heightened threat, we undertook smart, disciplined actions, but ultimately all of us acknowledge that we did not have the data, the span of control, the redundancy, the fusion or the laws in place to give us the chance to compensate for the mistakes that will always be made in any human endeavor.

This is not a clinical excuse. Three thousand people died. It was not – no matter how hard we worked or how desperately we tried, it was not enough. The victims and the families of 9/11 deserve better.

Analyzing the testimony of George Tenet

The CIA became aware in December 1999 that most of the important al Qaeda terrorists were coming together for a planning meeting in Kuala Lumpur. They knew that this was an extremely important meeting for the purpose of planning future terrorists attacks, possibly directed at the US. If they bugged just this one meeting they would have discovered the al Qaeda plans for the Cole bombing and the attack on 9/11. The CIA had all of the people who attended this meeting photographed. Many of the people at this meeting were identified as long time al Qaeda terrorists.

It has never been explained why they let all of these known terrorists proceed unimpeded from this meeting with their plans to bomb the *USS Cole* 10 months later and carry out the attacks of 9/11 almost 21 months later. At least two of the terrorists at this meeting took part in the *Cole* attack. As many as five of the participants at this meeting went on to take part in or oversee the attacks on 9/11. Several of the terrorists at this meeting who were involved with the attacks of 9/11 came into direct contact with the pilots who went on to hijack aircraft on 9/11.

We made mistakes. Our failure to watchlist al-Hazmi and al-Mihdhar in a timely manner, or the FBI's inability to find them in the narrow window at the time afforded them, showed systemic weaknesses and the lack of redundancy.

They had al-Hazmi or al-Mihdhar in their sights numerous times. They knew that they had been connected to the *Cole* bombing, and that at least two of them had flown into the US yet not once were they put on any airline watchlist that would have kept them off domestic flights. According to George Tenet's testimony, "we made mistakes."

In the situations that are documented, the failure of the CIA to inform the FBI and to watchlist these terrorists appears not to be due to simple mistakes, the CIA intentionally hiding this information from the FBI.

Mihdhar and Hazmi were not watchlisted until August 23, 2001. On this same day, the photographs taken at Kuala Lumpur 21 months earlier were given to the FBI. Inexplicably the photograph of Tawfiq Bin Attash, Khallad, the known mastermind of the Cole bombing was still hidden from the FBI for another 8 days and was not turned over to the FBI until August 30, 2001, one day after the FBI had opened the search and investigation for Mihdhar as an intelligence investigation. According to the FBI, this apparently was not enough time for a search to find them.

While, George Tenet said in this testimony said that, "we made mistakes" it now clear that information had been deliberately hidden from the FBI. The 9/11 Commission investigation could never explain why this information had been hidden from the FBI for over 21 months, when that was exactly the job the Commission had been chartered to do. They never asked George Tenet why the CIA had hidden this information from the FBI and received a credible response. .

According to the testimony given here, the American people need to understand about the events of 9/11:

"It was not the result of the failure of attention and discipline and focus and consistent effort, and the American people need to understand that. "

Tenet makes a good point, none of these reasons can account for the failure of the CIA to prevent the attacks on 9/11. This was due to their deliberate actions to hide information from the FBI.

9/11 Commissioners question George Tenet

MR. LEHMAN: But that report that you heard this morning was a damning report, not of your actions or the actions of any of the really superb and dedicated people that you have, but it was a damning evaluation of a system that is broken, that doesn't function.

And all I have to do is re-read the PDB which the agency resisted so strongly our declassifying, and the key line is, "We have not been able to corroborate some of the more sensational threat reporting, like the intention of bin Laden to hijack US aircraft." All the king's horses and all the king's men in the CIA could not corroborate what turned out to be true and told the President of the United States almost a month before the attack that they couldn't corroborate these reports. That's institutional failure.

And I'm here to tell you – and I'm sure you've heard it before – there is a train coming down the track. There are going to be very real changes made. And you are an invaluable part of helping us come to the right conclusions on that. Everybody talks about military capability, or law enforcement capability. Well, we sit behind the green door. And for the bang for the buck, the American taxpayer gets a hell of a lot for what we give them.

And you know, we had to find a way to talk to the American people about it as well, because I think they'd be supportive.

MR. RICHARD BEN-VENISTE: Let me first say that I have enormous respect for your dedication and the dedication of CIA officers who I have met in their desire to complete the mission.

The people at Alec Station – and that has come out earlier, that name has come out earlier in these hearings, not by us – who I have interacted with are heroes and dedicated individuals who I sense died that day on September 11th in a way that many Americans did, but perhaps more particularly because of their efforts over a long period of time to deal with these committed, brutal, inhuman enemies of the United States.

I want to talk about the PDB briefly. I think the individual who produced this PDB and her supervisor are entitled to a debt of gratitude for attempting to bring to the attention of the President of the United States the possibility – given all the information we knew – that despite indications leading to the notion that this incredible threat level that we were experiencing in the summer of 2001, leading to the horrific, dramatic, horrendous – whatever adjective you want to use, because there were many employed – spectacular attack by bin Laden, might well occur in the United States to me is extraordinary. She was prescient. She was right.

Subsequently, you wrote to us, "The PDB article was in response to a series of events. Throughout the spring and summer the President was shown a number of pieces outlining intelligence indicating that al Qaeda was planning a large attack. During these discussions, the President raised questions about whether the intelligence pointed to threats inside the United States. Although there was no formal tasking, the President's questions were discussed at a PDB planning session. At that time it was decided to do a piece laying out what we knew about Osama bin Laden's interest in striking inside the United States.

When this item was presented in the PDB on August 6th, with Dr. Rice present, the briefer introduced the piece by referring to the President's earlier questions. In summary, although the August 6th PDB piece was technically self-initiated, it was prompted by the President's questions and interest."

We know that the Italians closed the airspace over Genoa, and indeed they closed it over Naples for the pre-planning session, and then over Genoa. I don't think that was noise control. I think that had to do more with a threat of a use of airplanes used by suicide pilots. But even a couple of months before September 11th, we know that there was a planning session by NORAD where military officials considered a scenario in which a hijacked foreign commercial airliner flew into the Pentagon. Months before. And so people clearly were thinking about this possibility.

You had information in August that came through the FBI regarding an Islamic jihadist in the United States named Zacarias Moussaoui, who had been in a flight school in Minnesota and he had been trying to learn to fly a 747, despite the fact he had absolutely no background in aviation, he could not explain a bank account of 30-odd-thousand dollars deposited in cash, he could not explain his presence in the United States, he could not explain why he was trying to learn to fly a 747.

Now, this information came to you via the FBI because the FBI could not, in their interpretation, use the information to get a warrant to search Moussaoui's computer, et cetera, under FISA according to their thinking.

So they looked to CIA to get that information. The FISA Court protects against improper prosecution, violating laws with respect to the potential of prosecuting this man. My question is this –

MR. HAMILTON: Mr. – go ahead –

MR. BEN-VENISTE: My question is this: Given the threat level, given the knowledge about planes as weapons, given the fact of Moussaoui's arrest, why was it that you didn't put the question of prosecuting Moussaoui to the side and go after the information, which may well have led to unraveling this plot?

MR. TENET: I'd have to go back and look at all the – when we've talked in private session, we wanted to come back to Moussaoui. I have not gone back and reviewed all of that data at the time as to why I would make a decision to forego prosecution. It's not a call I could make, but I – Commissioner, I want to go back and prepare and look at all of the things that were on the table at the time. And I'd be happy to sit down with the Commission and walk through everything that was happening at the time. And I'm not trying to duck, but we need to sit down and go through this. And we've said we would when we last –

MR. BEN-VENISTE: And I'll tell you parenthetically, the FBI agent was criticized for going directly to the CIA, instead of going and running this through Headquarters, which would have taken even more time.

MR. ROEMER: Let's see. In the Woodward book, you say immediately upon learning of the 9/11 attacks that it's al Qaeda, and you mention somebody in a flight school. I assume that's Moussaoui. Is that correct?

MR. TENET: These are words attributed to me. I don't recall that piece of it. But I know I got up immediately and said it's got to be al Qaeda.

MR. ROEMER: And you have the information at that point on Moussaoui?

MR. TENET: Yes, I was briefed on Moussaoui in late August.

MR. ROEMER: August what?

MR. TENET: I believe it's the 23rd or the 24th.

MR. ROEMER: August 23rd or 24th. Is Mr. Pavitt or Mr. McLaughlin briefed on that as well?

MR. JOHN McLAUGHLIN: Yes, sir. I was briefed I think several days before.

MR. ROEMER: What was the date that you were briefed?

MR. McLAUGHLIN: I can't recall.

MR. ROEMER: Middle of August? August 15th? Earlier?

MR. McLAUGHLIN: No. I just don't recall. It was some time in August. It was just a couple of days before the director.

MR. ROEMER: Now, do you all share this information then with other people at CTC and FBI and other places? What do you do with this information?

MR. TENET: I believe that the context of the information – and again, I've got to go back and review all of this carefully – the context of this information is that it came to us from one of our domestic field stations who was asked to provide some assistance in dealing with this FISA request.

So that's the context it came to us. And I believe in that time period we immediately tried to undertake a way to figure out how to help the FBI get data and deal with this particular problem. But I'd really want to go back and check records.

MR. ROEMER: With this interesting, curious, fascinating piece of data, do share this data at the September 4th Principals' meeting with other people in the room at that point, when you're discussing this policy that has taken seven months to make its way through the process on al Qaeda?

MR. TENET: It wasn't discussed at the Principals' meeting, since we're having a separate agenda. My assumption at the time was, Mr. Roemer, that this was something that would be laid down in front of the CSG and people working this at the time. All terrorist –

MR. ROEMER: Why not bring it up to the principals? This is the first Principals' meeting in seven months on terrorism. Why wouldn't that be something that you would think would be interesting to this discussion?

MR. TENET: The nature of the discussion we had that morning was on the Predator, how we would fly it, whether we would –

MR. ROEMER: But it's an overall policy discussion about al Qaeda and how we fight al Qaeda –

MR. TENET: Well, it just wasn't – for whatever reason, all I can tell you is, it wasn't the appropriate place. I just can't take you any farther than that.

MR. ROEMER: Would it – made any difference if you had mentioned – did you ever mention it, for instance, to the President – you're briefing the President from August 6th on –

MR. TENET: I didn't see the President. I was not in briefings with him during this time. He was on vacation. I was here.

MR. ROEMER: You didn't see the President between August 6th, 2001, and September 10th?

MR. TENET: Well, no, but before – saw him after Labor Day, to be sure.

MR. ROEMER: So you saw him September 4th, at the Principals' meeting.

MR. TENET: He was not at the Principals' meeting.

MR. ROEMER: Well, you don't see him –

MR. TENET: Condoleezza Rice – I saw him in this time-frame, to be sure.

MR. ROEMER: Okay. You're not the – when do you see him in August?

MR. TENET: I don't believe I do.

MR. ROEMER: You don't see the President of the United States once in the month of August?

MR. TENET: He's in Texas, and I'm either here or on leave for some of that time. So I'm not here.

MR. ROEMER: So who's briefing him on the PDBs?

MR. TENET: The briefer himself. We have a presidential briefer.

MR. ROEMER: So – but you never get on the phone or in any kind of conference with him to talk, at this level of high chatter and huge warnings during the spring and summer, to talk to him, through the whole month of August?

MR. TENET: Talked to – we talked to him directly throughout the spring and early summer, almost every day –

MR. ROEMER: But not in August?

MR. TENET: In this time period, I'm not talking to him, no.

(Pause.)

MR. ROEMER: Does he ever say to Dr. Rice or somebody else, "I want to talk to Tenet; Tenet is the guy that knows this situation, has been briefing me all through the spring and the summer; Tenet understands this stuff; his hair's been on fire; he's been worried about this stuff?" Is that ever asked, or are you ever called on to –

MR. TENET: I don't have a recollection of being called, Mr. Roemer, but I'm sure that if I wanted to make a phone call because I had my hair on fire, I would have picked up the phone and talked to the President.

MR. ROEMER: It was just never made?

MR. TENET: No.

In reviewing this testimony, the most probing questions from the 9/11 Commissioners were the following:

> **Bob Kerrey; Given the threat level, given the knowledge about planes as weapons, given the fact of Moussaoui's arrest "given all the information we knew – that despite indications leading to the notion that this incredible threat level that we were experiencing in the summer of 2001, leading to the horrific, dramatic, horrendous – whatever adjective you want to use, because there were many employed – spectacular attack by bin Laden, might well occur in the United States to me is extraordinary."**

It is clear that Commissioner Bob Kerrey could not understand why Tenet claimed he did not know the attacks were going to occur inside of the US. Tenet had given extraordinary warnings to Rice, Clarke, Ashcroft and Rumsfeld in July of 2001, on just such an attack inside of the US.

> **Tim Roemer: Why not bring it up to the principals? (At the September 4, 2001 meeting of the principals.) This is the first Principals' meeting in seven months on terrorism. Why wouldn't that be something that you would think would be interesting to this discussion?**

> **MR. TENET: Well, it just wasn't – for whatever reason, all I can tell you is, it wasn't the appropriate place. I just can't take you any farther than that.**

When asked why he did not bring this information up to the principals at this meeting on September 4, Mr. Tenet says, "it wasn't – for whatever reason, the appropriate place, I can't take you any father than that."

I was at this 9/11 Commission hearing on April 14, 2004, sitting not more than 15 feet behind George Tenet when he made that statement that he had not told the President of the horrific nature of the threats and the threat reporting during the summer of 2001, because he had not been in contact with the President at all in August 2001.

Then he announced, in an unusually loud voice, just to make sure everyone could hear, that he would go back and recheck his calendar to insure this information was correct. Everyone at that hearing was puzzled that the head of the Central Intelligence Agency would not accurately remember if he had visited and talked to the President of the United States in August 2001.

After the hearings of April 13-14 were over, Bill Harlow told reporters that the CIA had found after "checking the records", that indeed Tenet had talked to the President at least twice in August. He had flown down to Crawford, TX, for a meeting on August 17, 2001, and then again, he had talked to the President on August 31, 2001 in Washington DC. Bill Harlow explained that George Tenet must have misspoken, or temporarily forgotten about these meetings. When you go back and review the questions Tim Roemer asks George Tenet, he asked Tenet, did he talk to the President in August, multiple times, and each time Tenet clearly states that he had not talked to the President in August. It is clear that Tenet is providing misleading testimony to the 9/11 Commission.

It turns out however, that Bill Harlow left out the fact that George Tenet had also flown down to Crawford, TX, for a meeting on August 24, a meeting described right on the White House website. This is one day after the CIA issued a worldwide alert for al-Mihdhar and al-Hazmi, knowing now that these two al Qaeda terrorists were in the US. Tenet also found out on August 23 that FBI agents in Minneapolis had arrested Zacarias Moussaoui. The CIA was told that Moussaoui had been arrested on August 17, because FBI agents suspected he might be a terrorist learning how to fly a large airliner without the ordinary experience.

MR. ROEMER: ... you say immediately upon learning of the 9/11 attacks that it's al Qaeda, and you mention somebody in a flight school. I assume that's Moussaoui. Is that correct?

MR. TENET: These are words attributed to me. I don't recall that piece of it. But I know I got up immediately and said it's got to be al Qaeda.

MR. ROEMER: And you have the information at that point on Moussaoui?

MR. TENET: Yes, I was briefed on Moussaoui in late August.

MR. ROEMER: August what?

MR. TENET: I believe it's the 23rd or the 24th.

If George Tenet was not able to remember any these meetings, as he claimed, then what about the President of the United States, or his Chief of Staff Andy Card, or Condoleezza Rice, or even the Secret Service? The question that comes to mind is "what were they all trying to hide?"

Tenet and the CIA knew at the time he was giving his testimony before the 9/11 Commission, that in the summer of 2001, when they were getting massive warnings of a huge al Qaeda attack inside of the US, that Khalid Shaikh Mohammed had been recruiting and sending al Qaeda terrorists into the United States at the very same time. This appears to be information Tenet did not disclose in public testimony to the 9/11 Commission. The CIA knew that Khalid Shaikh Mohammed had been behind the 1995 Bojinka plot to hijack US airliners and crash them into buildings in the US, and also knew that he had been involved in the original attack on the World Trade Center Towers in 1993 with his nephew, Ramzi Yousef, information that should have alerted them to the fact that the target of the attack was the World Trade Center Towers using multiple hijacked aircraft.

11:00 – 1:00 p.m. WEDNESDAY, APRIL 14, 2004

Panel: Preventing Future Attacks Inside The United States

Mr. James Pavitt
Deputy Director of Operations, Central Intelligence Agency

MR. JAMES PAVITT: Good morning. It's a privilege for me to be here before the Commission on an issue of such incredible, vital importance to our nation.

By virtue of my position in the CIA, I am not a public person. Indeed, in the history of the CIA, no one in my position has ever testified publicly before.

And like my colleagues here at the table, I'm a public servant, dedicated to defending the security of our nation. The last five years of my 30-year career in intelligence, I've had the honor of leading a unique organization, the Directorate of Operations, known to some of you as the clandestine service of America.

I'm remarkably proud of this extraordinary group of dedicated professionals, their commitment and their accomplishments. Many of the men and women of my organization operate abroad in dangerous locales and always in secret. They cannot publicly appear before this Commission. I'm here to represent all of them.

The threat posed by terrorists prior to 9/11 was unambiguous. The threat was not just outlined in sensitive intelligence documents. Two highly regarded commissions, the Bremer Commission, the Hart-Rudman Commission, were prophetic in laying out in unclassified context the terrorist threats that we faced, including the possibility of terrorists inflicting mass casualties both overseas and on American soil.

Two and a half years ago, that adversary shattered the sense of security the people of this country have come to cherish. We fought this enemy through the 1990s, but it was the tragedy of September 11th that unified and focused this country and allowed us to counter this threat as never before.

MR. KEAN: You're wrapping up, right, Mr. Pavitt?

MR. PAVITT: Yes sir.

Well, let me wrap up by simply making a personal comment. Seated behind me are family members of the victims of the terrible attacks. I told you that I represented the men and women of the Directorate of Operations, those people who cannot be with me today, who cannot come before a camera and have their faces shown if they're going to do their jobs. But I want everyone to know, and I particularly want the families to know, that those men and women were working ceaselessly, day in and day out, in a frenetic pace that I personally observed, doing all they could to stop what we knew was coming. We extend to all of the family members our genuine and our heartfelt condolences for the extraordinary loss that this nation and they suffered on the 11th.

We sounded an alarm. We knew the threat was lethal, unambiguous, and we knew it was coming at us. We put our hearts and our souls into disrupting and preventing those attacks. We did all we knew how to do, and we failed. We are committed to doing everything we can do, as intelligence officers, as Americans, and to work with this Commission, to ensure that we do our best to never let that failure happen again. In my business there is no perfection, but we will do everything we can to be as perfect as we can. Thank you.

MR. KEAN: Thank you, sir.

MR. LEHMAN: Thank you.

I have one last question of Mr. Pavitt. In 1986, the CTC was set up precisely to fuse what was going on in the terrorist threat world. On September 11th, what went wrong?

MR. PAVITT: Well, as I said in my statement, Commissioner, we simply failed to uncover the necessary intelligence, penetrate al Qaeda at the appropriate level, at the leadership level, to stop the attacks. In 1986, I think in truly a bureaucratic, raking way, the Intelligence Community, the CIA in particular, looked at something, took a Vice Presidential Commission recommendation and created a center.

It caused all sorts of issues. People fought it. People did not want to be a part of it. But what it did was merge analyst and operator in a way never merged before. It put operational traffic in the hands of the analyst. It brought in by 1989 a host of people from outside of CIA: FBI, Secret Service, FAA, NSA, and many, many others. And it was a very significant step forward in doing something against what was perceived in 1986 as an extraordinarily important target, better than we were doing it. And it set the standard, if you will, and became the model for other creations: proliferation, counterintelligence.

I cannot in public session give you the number, although I think, Commissioner, you know the number of people we had in CTC on the 10th of September: WOEFULLY – WOEFULLY inadequate to the threat that was out there. As I said, it has tripled. It's more than tripled, if you count people who are not actually staff officers of CIA or other agencies. We're still – we're still – struggling to deal with the volume of information that we're receiving. There's nobody who would like to be able to answer your question more definitively than I just have than me, that the reason we failed is because we didn't care, the reason we failed is because we weren't working hard, the reason we failed is because we were not recruiting spies overseas, the reason we failed is because we did not have good tactical operations. We were doing all those things. But 19 people, as Commissioner Fielding has said repeatedly, and I think most appropriately, simply beat us, all of us.

I believe that CTC was the right model. Given its staffing today, given the kind of dynamic operations and the kind of product that we're producing today – and I mean analytic product as well – we are making significant headway. The 11th was a terrible tragedy. Prior to the 11th, other terrible tragedies were stopped because of CTC. American lives were unambiguously saved because of what they did.

And let me make sure that I don't just put this on CTC's shoulders. CTC is an operational-slash-with analytic capability organization. But it is also something which all of my stations and bases around the world support. My chief of station in country X or country Y is driving counterterrorist operations today – and was prior to the 11th. We tried to put the right focus on this. It was an incredibly difficult target.

Remember that absolutely chilling video that we all saw, with Osama bin Laden sitting with some of those who murdered our citizens, laughing and talking about – some of those people that were in the 19 did not know what was going to happen. That's not an excuse, sir. It's not an excuse. But it does give you some sense of just how damn difficult it was to get in there and do it.

I would like to promise this Commission, I'd like to promise the people who are listening to what we're saying today that I have now in place, because of the largesse of Congress or the largesse of the Executive, I have in place what's necessary to stop this from happening again. I can't say that. I know that we have in place vastly better capability, and as a result we will do much better. But the threat is absolutely ominous, it's constant, it's changing, it's evolving.

And to make sure that we don't have it happen again is something I can't stand before this Commission and say I'm able to do.

MR. SLADE GORTON: On another subject, perhaps starting with you but asking each of you to comment on it, let's take the specific al-Mihdhar case. You know, picked up, lost, had a visa to the United States, came back here early in 2001; knowledge that he was a matter of any interest didn't get to the FBI until

August, and then got there in a fairly routine, non-emergency fashion.

If an identical situation took place today, how would it be handled differently? How would it have been managed?

What role would each of you have had in it? Would it have been done more efficiently? Might we well have picked him up before 9/11?

And I think probably the greatest burden of that is on you, Mr. Pavitt, but I want everyone to comment on it.

MR. PAVITT: Senator, your second question actually relates back to your first.

MR. GORTON: Okay.

MR. PAVITT: I do not believe that additional resources, which I argued for vigorously to Congressman Roemer and to Senator Kerrey and a whole host of other people, I do not believe that at the end of the day that would have allowed me to have a different answer than the one I gave you, which is no.

However, additional resources, particularly people, particularly people, I believe could have had a different impact on how the al-Hazmi and al-Mihdhar information was handled and dealt with. It was a mistake that certain things were not done. It was the intention not to make that mistake; it was the intention to do the right thing. It was the intention and the understanding of those who played, as I believe staff has stated to the Commission, that they thought they had done the right thing. But they can't, if you will, demonstrate that by producing a piece of paper.

I used the concept of triage in describing some of the things we were doing. Back in August of 2001, in CTC alone there were 19,000 CIA-generated messages — 19,000, and a handful — and I mean a handful of people dealing with them. Is that something we're proud of? Absolutely not. Is it something that contributed to the error? Yes, it did. It wasn't done the way we would do it today. We have put in safeguards. We have created training programs. We have indoctrinated. We are in lockstep with the FBI and others in the Community on what we need to do when we have that kind of information. But at the time it initially surfaced, it was a blip on a very, very complex radar screen. Not an excuse, again. We actually mounted very sophisticated operations, as you know, to figure out what this was. And then the next blip came up and the focus wasn't as complete as it could have been.

MR. GORTON: Would the name have gotten to the FBI earlier, under your present set of circumstances?

MR. PAVITT: Absolutely, sir. I believe absolutely. Yes, sir.

This shows that the CIA knew the attacks on September 11 were coming and they said that they did all they could think of to do to stop them, but that they had failed.

We sounded an alarm. We knew the threat was lethal, unambiguous, and we knew it was coming at us. We put our hearts and our souls into disrupting and preventing those attacks. We did all we knew how to do, and we failed.

We knew that the attack was coming, we did all we could think of to do and we failed.

MR. LEHMAN: Thank you.

I have one last question of Mr. Pavitt. In 1986, the CTC was set up precisely to fuse what was going on in the terrorist threat world. On September 11th, what went wrong?

MR. PAVITT: Well, as I said in my statement, Commissioner, we simply failed to uncover the necessary intelligence, penetrate al Qaeda at the appropriate level, at the leadership level, to stop the attacks.

James Pavitt was second in command at the CIA. He said they failed to uncover the necessary intelligence to penetrate al Qaeda at the appropriate level, the leadership level, to stop the attack. If they did "all they could think of to do," where in fact was their analysis on al Qaeda and the priority list of targets in the US they might be interested in attacking along with possible methods of attack?

Exactly what did we get for the $44 billion spent each year on the CIA and the other intelligence agencies?

According to James Pavitt in his testimony to the 9/11 Commission:

However, additional resources, particularly people, particularly people, I believe could have had a different impact on how the al-Hazmi and al-Mihdhar information was handled and dealt with. It was a mistake that certain things were not done.

The CIA had thousands of employees and a multi-billion-dollar budget; how many people and how many billions of dollars does it take to keep track of only two al Qaeda terrorists, Mihdhar and Hazmi, who were hiding in plain sight?

Had the FBI been given this information in March 2000, the events of 9/11 would most likely have been prevented. Had the CIA added the names of these terrorists to the State Department watchlist, or to a watchlist designed to keep al Qaeda terrorists off US airliners, the events on 9/11 could most likely have been prevented. There is no explanation as to why this was not done.

2:00 - 2:30 p.m. WEDNESDAY, APRIL 14, 2004

Staff Statement No. 12:

Reforming Law Enforcement, Counterterrorism and Intelligence Collection in the U.S.

MR. ZELIKOW: Members of the Commission, with your help, your staff has developed initial findings to present to the public on the FBI's current capacity to detect and prevent terrorist attacks upon the United States. This is the statement on the FBI today. These findings may help frame some of the issues for this hearing and inform the development of your judgments and recommendations.

We divide our discussion of these reforms and the FBI's current capacity to detect and prevent terrorist attacks in the United States into the following four broad areas, tracking the critiques in Staff Statement number 9: management priorities and strategy; intelligence collection and processing; strategic analysis; and knowledge management. Chris?

MS. CHRIS HEALEY: However, improvements have been slow. Many current officials told us the FBI still does not know what information is in its files. Furthermore, the Department of Justice's Inspector General reported in December 2003 that the FBI has not established adequate policies and procedures for sharing intelligence.

The FBI has had a long-standing plan to upgrade its information technology systems. The FBI has upgraded desktop terminals, established new networks, and consolidated data-bases. However, the replacement of the antiquated Automated Case Support system has been delayed once again. The director recently told us that the new Virtual Case File system, which is supposed to enhance internal FBI information sharing, should be ready by the end of the year.

Despite all these efforts, it is clear that gaps in intelligence sharing still exist. Michael Rolince, the Acting Assistant Director of the Office of Intelligence, put it more bluntly, "We are kidding ourselves if we think that there is seamless integration among all of the agencies." Former Acting FBI Director Thomas Pickard told us that the most difficult thing about information sharing is trying to figure out what information will actually be important to someone else. John Brennan, the Director of the Terrorist Threat Integration Center, told us that he is seeing a "cacophony of activities" within the Intelligence Community but no strategy and planning. Coordination and collaboration are insufficient, he told us. A fundamental strategy for joint work, for integration, is key. This is a problem neither the FBI nor the CIA nor any other agency can solve on its own. We found there is no national strategy for sharing information to counter terrorism.

Basic connectivity is still a problem for some FBI Field Offices. The then-Acting Director of the Washington Field Office told us last August that he still could not e-mail anyone at the Department of Justice from his desk. He said that the Washington Field Office, which is the second largest Field Office in the country, still has only one Internet terminal on each floor.

9/11 Commission Conclusions

Richard Ben-Veniste

We recognized that secrecy has often acted as the handmaiden of complacency, arrogance and incompetence. By conducting open hearings in the bright sunshine of public view rather than behind closed doors, and through open discussion of what we had learned, we earned the confidence of our fellow Americans and established our credibility as a Commission willing to ask hard questions of public officials and go the extra mile when requiring production of essential documents.

Our report provides a penetrating account of missed opportunities, failures of communication, lack of focus and the failure of imagination, all of which contributed to our government's failure to prevent the 9/11 catastrophe.

Slade Gorton

On September 4, 2001, Richard Clarke, the head of the Counterterrorism Security Group in the White House during both the Clinton and Bush administrations, handed a note to Condoleezza Rice, the head of the National Security Council, that read like this: "Decision makers should imagine themselves on a future day when the CSG has not succeeded in stopping an al Qaeda attack, and hundreds of Americans lie dead in several countries, including the United States." Earlier that year, in the first week of the Bush administration, Clarke had pressed Rice with a blue-sky plan developed in the last months of the Clinton administration and designed to, and I quote, "roll back al Qaeda over a period of three to five years." It was to this plan that I referred when I asked Richard Clarke at our hearing whether, had all his recommendations been adopted by the new administration on the day on which he presented them, would 9/11 have been prevented?," to which his honest answer was "no."

And so, with that marvelous clarity of 20-20 hindsight, the 9/11 Commission first concluded that our number one failure in the United States was the failure of imagination. No one in authority inside our government imagined an attack of this nature or of this size, so no one prepared for it.

The security directives of the FAA were directed almost solely at explosives, and thus it checked luggage. Four-inch knives were allowed as carry-on items and finally, on 9/11 itself, the first notice provided by the FAA to the Air Force took place nine minutes before the first hijacked airplane, Flight 11, impacted on World Trade Center number one. But notice that the Air Force received of the second hijacking was zero minutes before impact, of the third hijacking, zero minutes before impact, and of the fourth hijacking, zero minutes before Flight 93 crashed in the fields in Pennsylvania.

However, the Air Force was also at fault. It looked outward only for attacks or threats coming from overseas and never contemplated the possibility of suicide hijackings. It had only four fighters on standby alert at two bases on the East Coast and the President's shoot-down order, itself communicated to the Air Force after all four impacts, never got to the scrambled fighters at all. Only two Maryland International Guard fighters had such orders issued outside the normal chain of command.

The CIA. The CIA never developed intelligence precise enough to encourage either president to act decisively against al

Qaeda. The FBI. The FBI provided little information to the White House on counterterrorism at all. In fact, FBI Director Louis Freeh had such poor relations with the White House that he never met with President Clinton, nor did he provide useful information to President Bush. The FBI regarded terrorism as a law enforcement challenge. It went after terrorists after the fact, seeking to build cases that could be prosecuted successfully in court. And so, after these spectacular failures, in which 19 individuals with a total budget of less than half a million dollars defeated every defense of the United States against terrorism and inflicted on us the most costly surprise attack in our history, we were faced with a new and different challenge.

This sums up in a few sentences the conclusion of the 9/11 Commission. The conclusion that "our number one failure in the United States was a failure of imagination" is strange at best. This implies that the security of the US depends on the imagination of people working in huge bureaucracies.

How do you measure "imagination," to know when you are safe? Speculation based on imagination would never pass up through any organization; it would be filtered out with the kind of credibility analysis applied at each hierarchical level to this analysis.

The number one failure was not a failure of imagination, but a failure to do the job these agencies had been hired to do in the first place. The CIA had information that should have been provided to the FBI in a timely fashion, the FBI had started investigations that should have proceeded with the urgency requested by the field agents doing the investigations.

Chapter 17

Hiding the secret,

Khalid al-Mihdhar and Nawaf al-Hazmi

It is apparent that the most important information the CIA and FBI could have used to prevent the events of 9/11 was the information they had obtained on al-Mihdhar and al-Hazmi. The CIA had been aware of these two al Qaeda terrorists as early as 1995 and had refocused on them in December 1999, almost 21 months prior to the attacks of 9/11.

In order to understand exactly what took place in their search for these two terrorists, the following time-line is a chronology of the information on these terrorists as it passed through the intelligence agencies. This complete review of the information is important because it brings together in one place the complete story on the search for these two terrorists, using information from the Joint Inquiry Committee Report, the 9/11 Commission reports, the FBI Inspector General's report and mainline media news sources.

The first indication that the terrorists who had carried out the attack on 9/11 had been under surveillance for a considerable period of time prior to September 11, 2001 was chillingly described in a German magazine article, "The Deadly Mistakes of the US Intelligence Agency (Part 1)," by Oliver Schröm and Dirk Laabs in *Stern*, a German magazine on August 13, 2003, [translation into English by Gandalf].

> After the disaster of the East Africa bombings, George Tenet had stated: "With our efforts against bin Laden, we have to enter a new stage. Up to now, our work was noteworthy and in some cases even heroic; up to the day that we have to recognize as the day on which we had to suffer an inevitable blow, the consequences of which might be bigger than we expected," writes Tenet. "We are now at war, and I will not save personnel and resources."

> In December 11, 1999, a CIA field officer sent an urgent cable to the CIA Headquarters and recommended that not only the CIA but the other agencies, such as the Sate Department, the Immigration Bureau and the FBI to put all persons suspected as terrorists on a watchlist, "even if only their first names or

alias names were known." The CIA issued a cable to all CIA officers just after this, reemphasizing this message later in December 1999.

At this time, an intelligence service know as the Hamburg LfV located near the Hamburg central train station, not far from the al-Kuds mosque, had been investigating a radical Islamist in Hamburg who frequented this mosque, a man by the name of Mohammed Haydar Zammer. He had been a German citizen since 1982, and lived off of social welfare with his wife and six children. They were aware that Zammer had been an important contact person for al Qaeda, and was even recruiting in Germany other Islamic radicals for al Qaeda. Zammer is known to have recruited new members for al Qaeda who would be sent to terrorist training camps in Afghanistan.

It was well known that he was a religious fanatic who openly professed his admiration for Usama bin Laden at the al-Kuds mosque. It was known that he had called upon many of the young visitors to this mosque that they show join the holy war and fight the infidels, just as he had done in Afghanistan and Bosnia.

In 1998 the Italians had tipped off the German after they had raided an apartment and had found a large cache of weapons and ammunition, along with Zammer's mobile telephone number and address. At this time they started an intense surveillance of his apartment and phone calls. On January 31, 1999, Zammer receives a call from a person named Marwan, a person who would be later identified as Marwan al-Shehhi, from his cell phone in the UAE. Marwan talked about his studies at a university in Bonn, and was asked by Zammer to come to Hamburg after he had completed his exams. The German intelligence felt that this call was important enough to inform the CIA. In a database at the CIA is an entry "Marwan," student in Germany, citizen of the UAE, important contact person of Zammer and Darkazani, another al Qaeda member living in Germany. Marwan al-Shehhi would pilot United 175 into the WTC South Tower almost 30 months later.

Some short time later this German agency made note of a call from Zammer to the number 76 75 18 39 in Hamburg, the number for an apartment at 54 Marienstrasse, shared by a number of Arab students. While this extension was registered to Said Bahaji, a German-Moroccan who was majoring in electrical engineering, also living at this apartment and registered with the police were an Egyptian, Mohammed Atta, majoring in urban planning at the Hamburg Technical Institute and Ramzi bin al-Shibh, a Yemenite who was a part-time student. The German intelligence noted that two other people regularly visited this apartment, a Lebanese, Ziad Jarrah, a student studying airplane construction and a Moroccan, Mounir el-Motassadeq, a student of electrical engineering. The investigators set up what is called "boarder control," which adds their names, residence, and passport numbers to a police information system. This checks when they travel anywhere outside of Germany. When el-Motassadeq traveled from Hamburg to Istanbul, German intelligence knew immediately that this was not his real destination, but just a stopover on his way to al Qaeda training camps in Afghanistan run by Usama bin Laden.

On September 21, 1999, while the Hamburg agents are monitoring his telephone, Zammer calls 54 Marienstrasse, and reaches Marwan al-Shehhi. This confirmed the information that these agents had received nine months earlier that Marwan would be moving to Hamburg. From this call these agents become aware that Marwan, Atta, and Jarrah are planning to travel to Afghanistan shortly. "Don't forget us in your prayers," asks Marwan.

Shortly after October 9, 1999, Atta, Jarrah and al-Shehhi fly to Afghanistan to start their training. Ramzi bin al-Shibh, leader of the Hamburg cell, flies two months later to an important meeting in Kuala Lumpur, Malaysia.

The other part of the student group flies over later. Only Ramzi bin al-Shibh doesn't go to Afghanistan. The charismatic head of the Hamburg cell has an important appointment in Kuala Lumpur, the capital of Malaysia.

One of the people who would also attend this meeting was also well known to the CIA, but they only knew his first name, Khalid. The CIA had known that he was a visitor to an apartment of an important al Qaeda suspect. The CIA uncovers his full name when as he passes through Dubai, from Yemen to Kuala Lumpur, and the CIA obtain a copy of his passport. Al-Mihdhar's father-in-law, Ahmad Muhammad al-Hada, has an apartment in Yemen, where the phone had been monitored since shortly after the East Africa bombings, in 1998. The CIA knows that his 967-1-200578 in Sanaa in used as an important coordination point to manage meetings for al Qaeda.

This number had been traced to a fax that had been sent to London just after the East Africa bombings that claimed responsibility for this attack. This fax was traced to a number in

Baku, Azerbaijan, and from there, to al-Mihdhar's father-in-law in Sanaa, Yemen. It was noted that a call had even been placed to the phone in Yemen shortly after the bombings that was identified to a phone used by bin Laden.

The CIA found out that al-Mihdhar's father-in-law is closely connected to the East Africa bombings and had even sworn "Bayat," or total loyalty, to bin Laden and his organization. It turns out that Ramzi bin al-Shibh is actually a cousin of al-Mihdhar's wife, and had spent the prior five years putting together the al Qaeda cell in Hamburg.

When al-Mihdhar arrives in Kuala Lumpur, he is driven by another al Qaeda terrorist to Sungai Long, a suburb of Kuala Lumpur. There on January 6-8 he meets with bin al-Shibh and Tawfiq bin Attash, aka Khallad, who is part of bin Laden's personal bodyguards and one of the highest-ranking people in al Qaeda. Bin Attash is also known as "the single legged," having lost a leg in Afghanistan fighting for bin Laden.

Since leaving Saudi Arabia, al-Mihdhar has been under constant surveillance worked by the CIA. Agents at eight CIA stations in the Arabian and Asian areas had worked together to monitor al-Mihdhar.

In the December 1999 time-frame, the CIA became aware that recorded phone calls made it clear that a very important meeting was being set up so that a high-ranking member of al Qaeda could meet with other members of the al Qaeda organization.

The phone call revealed that a "Khalid," a "Nawaf" and Nawaf's younger brother would be attending this meeting. At CIA Headquarters, it was assumed that al-Mihdhar and Nawaf were important members of al Qaeda who were meeting with their commander to prepare for an upcoming al Qaeda attack.

When al-Mihdhar traveled to Malaysia, the CIA found out his complete identity.

His passport was copied when he passed through the Dubai airport. His complete name was noted as Khalid bin Muhammad bin Abdallah al-Mihdhar, and he was born in 1975 in Saudi Arabia. The CIA also noticed, with some degree of horror, that he possessed a valid US multi-entry visa. It was obvious to the CIA that he only possessed this type of visa in order to enter the US to carry out another attack, but this time inside of the US.

When al-Midhar's arrived in Kuala Lumpur, the local CIA officer sent a cable to CIA Headquarters, "Khalid identified. Arrived in Malaysia." This information was sent immediately to the Counterterrorist Center. The CTC maintained a huge database containing every relevant piece of information on the topic "terror" from the last 20 years.

Both Cofer Black and George Tenet and even CIA headquaters is kept informed of the surveillance operation in Kuala Lumpur.

Both Cofer Black and George Tenet were informed that some of the terrorists in Kuala Lumpur have valid visas for the US. But this information is not given to the FBI at this time.

The Malaysian intelligence photographed al-Mihdhar, al-Hazmi, Khallad the other al Qaeda terrorists when they go shopping in Kuala Lumpur. All of the photos of the al Qaeda terrorists are turned over to the CIA when they leave Kuala Lumpur on January 8, 2000. Some of the photos show Khallad together in photos of bin al-Shibh. By January 9, 2000 the CIA Headquarters has all of the information from the al Qaeda planning meeting, including then names of all of the participants. One of the terrorists is identified as a Saudi, Nawaf al-Hazmi (when he flies to Bangkok from Kuala Lumpur). It was discovered later that he had pledged an oath of "Bayat" to Usama bin Laden at an Afghan training camp.

By January 8, 2000 all of these terrorists have dispersed to all points in the world. These terrorists 10 months later attack the *USS Cole* in Yemen, and then take part in the attacks of 9/11, 20 months later. Malaysian intelligence is astounded when these terrorists disperse with no follow-up surveillance or arrests [*Stern*, August 13, 2003].

The al Qaeda planning meeting in Kuala Lumpur in January 2000 was extensively described in news articles from numerous mainstream news sources, and organized by Paul Thompson:

December 1999, NSA learns that an important al Qaeda planning meeting will be held in a condominium in Kuala Lumpur in January of 2000, and forwards this information to the CIA. Al Qaeda terrorists that have been at an al Qaeda safe house frequented by the East Africa al Qaeda bombing suspects are known to be going to this meeting. It is assumed at the CIA that this will be a very important planning meeting for the members of the al Qaeda terrorist organization in planning future terrorist attacks.

Malaysian Intelligence officers, at the request of the CIA, photograph al Qaeda terrorists gong to this meeting and send photographs to the CIA. Included in these photographs are photographs of al-Hazmi, al-Mihdhar, Khalid Shaikh Mohammed and Ramzi bin al-Shibh. Three of the September 11 hijackers – Khalid al-Mihdhar, Nawaf al-Hazmi and his brother Saleem al-Hazmi – were photographed and videotaped by Malaysian intelligence officials at this January 5, 2000, meeting in the company of suspected bin Laden lieutenants who 10 months later are suspects in the October 2000 bombing of the *USS Cole* in Yemen – Tawfiq bin Attash (aka Khallad) and Fahad al-Quso.

Present and actually presiding over the Kuala Lumpur meeting was Khalid Shaikh Mohammed, a high-level al Qaeda operative who helped finance the 1993 attack on New York's World Trade Center, which killed six people. He was also involved in the Bojinka plot (the foiled 1995 plan to blow up US passenger jets over the Pacific, and fly a large US airliner into the CIA Headquarters), and later in October 2000, the *USS Cole* attack, as well as September 11.

The FBI believes there were 11 people who attended the meeting in Kuala Lumpur. These are the only confirmed individuals, listed with their known involvement in certain al Qaeda attacks:

Tawfiq bin Attash (Khallad) – Suspect 10 months later in the *USS Cole* attack, better known by his alias "Khallad." Bin Attash is a "trusted member of bin Laden's inner circle," was in charge of bin Laden's bodyguards, and served as bin Laden's personal intermediary at least for the *USS Cole* attack [*Newsweek*, 9/20/01].

Fahad al-Quso – *USS Cole* and East African embassies, a top al Qaeda operative [*Newsweek*, 9/20/01]. Fahad al-Quso says when he is arrested in Yemen, in January 2001, that he had not attended this meeting due to problems with his passport, but that he had $7,000 to deliver to Khallad, which he did later that week in Bangkok, Thailand.

Khalid Shaikh Mohammed – 1993 World Trade Center Bombing, Bojinka Plot 1995, *USS Cole* – a top al-Qaeda leader and the alleged "mastermind" of the 9/11 attacks. The US has known Mohammed is an Islamic militant since the exposure of Operation Bojinka in January 1995 (see January 6, 1995), and knows what he looks like. US officials have stated that they only realized the meeting was important in the summer of

2001, but the presence of Mohammed should have proved the meeting's importance [*Los Angeles Times*, 2/2/02]. Although the possible presence of Mohammed at this meeting is highly disputed by US officials, one terrorism expert testifies before the 9/11 Commission in 2003 that he has access to transcripts of Mohammed's interrogations since his capture, and that Mohammed admits leading this meeting [*New York Post*, 7/10/03; *Newsweek*, 7/9/03]. Many media reports identify him there as well [*Independent*, 6/6/02; *CNN*, 11/7/02; *Canadian Broadcasting Corp.*, 10/29/03; *CNN*, 8/30/02]. For instance, according to *Newsweek*, "Mohammed's presence would make the intelligence failure of the CIA even greater. It would mean the agency literally watched as the 9/11 scheme was hatched – and had photographs of the attack's mastermind...doing the plotting." [*Newsweek*, 7/9/03]

Ramzi Bin al-Shibh – *USS Cole* and September 11 – Investigators believe he wanted to be the 20th hijacker. His presence at the meeting may not have been realized until after 9/11, despite the fact that US intelligence had a picture of him next to bin Attash, and had video footage of him [*CNN*, 11/7/02; *Newsweek*, 11/26/01; *Die Zeit*, 10/1/02; *Time*, 9/15/02; *Washington Post*, 7/14/02]. German police have credit card receipts indicating bin al-Shibh is in Malaysia at the same time [*Los Angeles Times*, 9/1/02]. Another account noting he was photographed at the meeting further notes that he entered and left Thailand three times in the first three weeks of January 2000 [*Los Angeles Times*, 10/17/01]. Anonymous Malaysian officials claim he is there, but US officials deny it [*Associated Press*, 9/20/02]. One account says he is recognized at the time of the meeting, which makes it hard to understand why he is not tracked back to Germany and the Hamburg cell with Mohamed Atta and other hijackers [*Der Spiegel*, 10/1//02]. Another opportunity to expose the 9/11 plot through bin al-Shibh's presence at this meeting will be missed in June. It appears bin al-Shibh and al-Mihdhar are directly involved in the attack on the *USS Cole* in October 2000 [*Washington Post*, 7/14/02; *Newsweek*, 9/4/02; *Guardian*, 10/15/01], so better surveillance or follow-up from this meeting could have prevented that attack as well. Al-Shibh wired $US6200 ($11,000) to Marwan al-Shehhi and $US14,000 to Zacarias Moussaoui, the French Moroccan, to pay for his flight training.

Khalid al-Mihdhar – *USS Cole* and September 11.

Nawaf al-Hazmi – September 11.

Saleem al-Hazmi – September 11.

Ahmad Hikmat Shakir – After 9/11, he will be linked to the 1993 World Trade Center bombing and 1995 Bojinka plot.

Riduan Isamuddin (Hambali) – an Indonesian terrorist better known as Hambali [*BBC,* 8/15/03]. He was the main financier of Operation Bojinka.

Yazid Sufaat – a Malaysian man who owned the condominium where the meeting was held [*New York Times*, 1/31/02; *Newsweek*, 6/2/02].

This meeting was meant to plan the *USS Cole* bombing, the September 11 attacks and to review the failed operations to bomb Los Angeles International Airport and targets in Jordan during the millennium celebrations. Two co-conspirators in the *USS Cole* attack delivered money to Khallad at the Kuala Lumpur meeting for the operation.

[Note: The actual CNN article from August 29, 2002, http://edition.cnn.com/2002/WORLD/asiapcf/southeast/07/30/s easia.state/, says the following:

US officials say the planning for the bombing of the USS Cole (in October 2000 that killed 17 US sailors) and September 11 took place in this condominium complex on the outskirts of Malaysia's capital, Kuala Lumpur.

In January of 2000, about a dozen of Osama bin Laden's trusted followers met here. The host was Hambali.

Among those who attended: Tawfiq bin Attash, (a.k.a Khallad), a key suspect in the bombing of the USS Cole nine months later; Khalid al-Midhar and Nawaf al-Hazmi, who nearly two years later crashed a plane into the Pentagon, and Khalid Shaikh Mohammed, Osama bin Laden's lieutenant, a key planner, US officials say, of September 11.

Eight months after that al Qaeda meeting, another guest would stay here – Zacarias Moussaoui, now on trial in the United States for September 11 related charges.

The operatives believed Malaysia to be a secure place to hold a high-level meeting of at least five very senior bin Laden lieutenants with vast knowledge of al Qaeda operations, over the course of three days, from January 6-8.

The CIA already knew many details about two of these attendees, al-Hazmi, al-Mihdhar, by the time the meeting begins.

CIA learns in January 4, 2000 that one on the attendees is named Khalid al-Mihdhar and has a multiple-entry visa to the US, after looking at his passport, as he enters Malaysia for this meeting.

At this one meeting, according to many press reports, were the terrorists and leadership of the al Qaeda organization who took part in the East African bombings in August of 1998, killing over 200 people and about 20 Americans. These terrorists went on to successfully bomb the USS Cole 10 months later in October 2000, killing 17 sailors. The terrorists at this meeting included the masterminds of these attacks and some of the al Qaeda terrorists who actually took part in the attack, 21 months later, on 9/11.

The CIA had all of these people in their sights with numerous photographs and even video footage of every person who attended this meeting.

Even to this day, the CIA has never publicly identified Khalid Shaikh Mohammed, or Ramzi bin al-Shibh as having been at this meeting. The CIA had photographs of Khalid Shaikh Mohammed and knew what he looked like, and had been aware of him from information obtained in the investigation of the Bojinka operation in the Philippines in 1995 to blow up 12 airliners going to the US from the Philippines. It turns out, the second phase of the Bojinka plan was to hijack large US airliners and crash them into large buildings in the US.

Drafting of the CIR at Bin Laden Unit of the CTC at CIA HQCIR is drafted to pass al-Mihdhar's visa information to the FBI

January 5, 2000:

Dwight, the Special Agent detailed to the CIA's Bin Laden Unit from the FBI's Washington Field Office, also read the cables discussing al-Mihdhar's US visa within hours of each cable being disseminated. CIA records also show that Dwight's immediate supervisor in the Bin Laden Unit opened one of the cables soon after Dwight.

Dwight opened one of the cables, which reported that al-Mihdhar's visa application had been verified and that he had listed New York as his intended destination.

Around 9:30 am on the same morning (January 5, 2000), Dwight began drafting in the CIA's computer system a CIR addressed to the UBL Unit Chief at FBI Headquarters and an SSA in the UBL Unit at FBI Headquarters who we call "Bob." Dwight's CIR also was addressed to the FBI's New York Field Office. The CIR first described the NSA information that had been received about al-Mihdhar, including the planned travel to Kuala Lumpur, Malaysia, in early January. The CIR also discussed the potential links between the suspected terrorist facility in the Middle East and the 1998 East Africa embassy bombings. The CIR stated that photographs of al-Mihdhar had been obtained and would be sent to the FBI under separate cover. The CIR detailed al-Mihdhar's passport and visa information, including that al-Mihdhar had listed on his visa application his intended destination as New York and that he planned to stay three months. Dwight also wrote that the CTC was requesting "feedback" on "any intelligence uncovered in FBI's investigation" resulting from the information in the CIR.

Michelle, the Bin Laden Unit desk officer who originally had taken notice of the information about al-Mihdhar and his connections to al Qaeda, accessed Dwight's draft CIR less than an hour after Dwight drafted it at approximately 9:30 am. Around 4:00 pm on the same day, Michelle added a note to the CIR in the CIA's computer system: "please hold off on CIR for now per [the CIA Deputy Chief of Bin Laden Unit]."

CIA records show that the same morning, the CIA Deputy Chief of Bin Laden Unit, who we will call "John," also had read the cable indicating that al-Mihdhar's visa was valid and that New York had been listed as his intended destination. Around 6:30 pm on the same day, John again accessed this cable and then another cable, the same two CIA cables about al-Hazmi and al-Mihdhar in the CIA's computer system that Dwight had used in drafting the CIR. CIA records do not indicate that John accessed Dwight's draft CIR. Eric, the other Deputy Chief of the Bin Laden Unit, accessed it two hours after Dwight began writing it, and Malcolm, the New York Field Office's detailee to the Bin Laden Unit, accessed it two days later.

CIA records show that as of eight days later, the CIR had not been disseminated to the FBI. In an e-mail to John in mid-January, Dwight had attached the draft CIR and wrote, "Is this a no go or should I remake it in some way?" The CIA was unable to locate any response to this e-mail.

By mid-February, the CIR had not been sent to the FBI and was still in draft form in the CIA's computer system.

When we interviewed all of the individuals involved with the CIR, they asserted that they recalled nothing about it. Dwight told the OIG that he did not recall being aware of the information about al-Mihdhar, did not recall drafting the CIR, did not recall whether he drafted the CIR on his own initiative or at the direction of his supervisor, and did not recall any discussions about the reasons for delaying completion and dissemination of the CIR. Malcolm said he did not recall reviewing any of the cable traffic or any information regarding al-Hazmi and al-Mihdhar. Eric told the OIG that he did not recall the CIR.

The CIA employees also stated that they did not recall the CIR. Although James, the CIA employee detailed to FBI Headquarters, declined to be interviewed by us, he told the CIA OIG that he did not recall the CIR. John (the Deputy Chief of the Bin Laden Unit) and Michelle, the desk officer who was following this issue, also stated that they did not recall the CIR, any discussions about putting it on hold, or why it was not sent.

CIA cable stating that al-Mihdhar's visa and passport information had been passed to FBI

Also on the same day that Dwight was preparing the CIR, Michelle, the Bin Laden Unit desk officer who was following the issue of al-Mihdhar, prepared a lengthy cable to several stations summarizing the information that had been collected at that point on al-Mihdhar and three other individuals who also were possibly traveling to Malaysia. The cable began, "After following the various reports, some much more credible than others, regarding a possible [bin Laden]-associated threat against US interests in East Asia, we wish to note that there indeed appears to be a disturbing trend of [bin Laden] associates traveling to Malaysia, perhaps not for benign reasons."

This cable then summarized the CIA's information that indicated several individuals were planning to travel to Malaysia. In the paragraph describing al-Mihdhar, Michelle stated that al-Mihdhar's travel documents, including a multiple-entry US visa, had been copied and passed "to the FBI for further investigation."

This cable – the fifth CIA cable to discuss al-Mihdhar's US visa – did not state by whom or to whom al-Mihdhar's travel documents were passed. It also did not indicate how they had been passed, or provide any other reference to the passage of the documents. Because this cable was an internal, operational cable, it was not forwarded to or copied to the FBI.

This cable was disseminated to various CIA stations approximately three hours after Michelle had noted in the cable system that Dwight was directed to hold off on sending his draft CIR to the FBI "for now per [the CIA Deputy Chief of the Bin Laden Unit]."

When we interviewed Michelle, she stated that she had no recollection of who told her that al-Mihdhar's travel documents had been passed to the FBI or how they had been passed. She said she would not have been the person responsible for passing the documents. According to Michelle, the language in the cable stating "[the documents] had been passed" suggested to her that someone else told her that they had already been passed, but she did not know who it was. The CIA Deputy Chief of the Bin Laden Unit also said he had no recollection of this cable, and he did not know whether the information had been passed to the FBI. Neither we nor the CIA OIG was able to locate any other witness who said they remembered anything about al-Mihdhar's travel documents being passed to the FBI, or any other documents that corroborated the statement that the documents were in fact passed to the FBI.

One interesting note: The Justice Department Inspector General in a report (FBI Inspector General's Report), released on June 2005, stated that the CIA had blocked a key cable (reporting that one of the two hijackers, Khalid al-Mihdhar, had obtained a multiple-entry visa to enter the United States) from being forwarded to the FBI in January 2000. The report says the Justice IG was "unable to determine" why the cable was not sent and who should be held responsible; that is the job of the CIA's Inspector General, which has been conducting its own congressionally mandated "accountability" review of 9/11 matters for more than two years. In a new disclosure, the report also states that a copy of the actual critical al-Mihdhar visa cable had not been turned over to any 9/11 investigators until February 2004 – when it was belatedly discovered in the files of the CIA by Justice IG investigators.

January 6, 2000

On January 6, the CIA office in Malaysia begins passing details of the meeting to the CIA Counterterrorist Center (CTC). Cofer Black, head of the CTC, orders that he be continually informed about the meeting, and CIA Director Tenet is frequently informed as well.

The al Qaeda terror summit in Malaysia ends and the participants leave. Hijackers Nawaf al-Hazmi and Khalid al-Mihdhar fly to Bangkok, Thailand, traveling under their real names. Al Qaeda leader Khallad bin Attash also travels with them and the three sit side by side in the airplane, but bin Attash travels under the false name "Salah Said" [Associated Press, 9/20/02; *9/11 Congressional Inquiry*, 7/24/03]. The CIA knows that a "Nawaf" has attended the meeting, but (at this time) does not know his last name. Shortly afterwards, the CIA is told of this airplane flight, and the fact that the person sitting next to al-Mihdhar on the plane is named "Nawaf al-Hazmi."

However, neither al-Hazmi nor al-Mihdhar, nor Khallad are placed on a terror watchlist. The CIA still fails to tell the FBI that al-Mihdhar has a valid US visa, and fails to give them al-Hazmi's last name.

The failure, which allowed the events on 9/11 to take place and the attack on the *USS Cole* to occur, was the failure of the CIA to watchlist the people at this al Qaeda meeting and share this information with the FBI.

Why the CIA blocked this information from going to the FBI has never been explained by any investigation. Investigations of this incident by the Joint Inquiry Committee and the FBI Inspector General's office have been stymied by the refusal of CIA personnel to accurately describe why they blocked this information from going to the FBI, or even who had actually ordered this information blocked.

The CIA loses track of these terrorists in Thailand.

A week after the meeting in Malaysia, hijackers Nawaf al-Hazmi and Khalid al-Mihdhar fly together from Bangkok, Thailand, to Los Angeles, California. The CIA receives a cable in March of 2000 that says that al-Hazmi has left Thailand and had flown to Los Angeles on January 15, 2000. It is not explained why Khalid al-Mihdhar is also not mentioned in this cable as he was on the same flight as Nawaf al-Hazmi, and they had traveled together to Thailand. Simply checking the flight manifest for the flight Nawaf al-Hazmi was on would have identified that al-Mihdhar had also entered the US. Checking these names with the INS would have also verified that both of these terrorists had entered the US.

The cable is marked "Action Required: None, FYI [For Your Information]." CIA Director Tenet later claims, "Nobody read that cable in the March time-frame" [9/11 Commission in open testimony on April 13, 2004]. Yet the day after the cable is received, "another overseas CIA station note[s], in a cable to the Bin Laden Unit at CIA Headquarters, that it had 'read with interest' the March cable, 'particularly the information that a member of this group traveled to the US...'" [*9/11 Congressional Inquiry*, 9/20/02]. Yet again, CIA fails to put their names on a watchlist, and again fails to alert the FBI so they can be tracked [*9/11 Congressional Inquiry*, 9/20/02]. Senior CIA counterterrorism official Cofer Black later says, "I think that month we watchlisted about 150 people. [The watchlisting] should have been done. It wasn't" [*9/11 Congressional Inquiry*, 7/24/03].

Two al Qaeda terrorists leave an important al Qaeda planning meeting, and fly to Thailand, and then one of these terrorists is noted in a cable as having flown to the US, which can only be to carry out terrorist attacks planned at the meeting in Kuala Lumpur. At the 9/11 Commission hearings on April 13-14, 2004, George Tenet stated publicly in front of this Commission, that no one in the CIA read the March 2000 cable indicating that al-Hazmi had flown into the US on January 15, 2000. On this same flight was Khalid al-Mihdhar who had also entered the US with Hazmi on January 15, 2000.

These two al Qaeda terrorists lived openly in San Diego at the house of an FBI informant, and enrolled in a San Diego area flight school, using their real names. In May 2000, they started flight training at a flight school in San Diego, registering with the FAA in their own names prior to starting their flight training.

During these months, May 2000 through May 2001, Hamburg al Qaeda cell member Ramzi bin al-Shibh, one of the participants of the *Cole* bombing, tries five times to get a US visa. He is turned down five times. Specifically, it appears the US has suspicions he has ties to terrorism, and especially ties to the *USS Cole* bombing plot. The *Los Angeles Times* similarly notes that "FBI agents [tell] officials of the Florida flight school" that bin al-Shibh wants to attend that he is "rejected because of unspecified involvement 'with the bombing of the *USS Cole...*'"

Hijacker Ziad Jarrah assists bin al-Shibh with his last two visa applications, and vouches for him. Not only is there the obvious visa connection to Ziad Jarrah while he is training at a US flight school, but also during this same time period bin al-Shibh wires money to Marwan al-Shehhi, Zacarias Moussaoui, and others, usually using his own name [CBS, 6/6/02].

Ramzi bin al-Shibh, who was known to have attended the Kuala Lumpur meeting, is connected to three of the 9/11 pilots who carried out this attack: Ziad Jarrah, pilot of United 93 (who vouches for bin al-Shibh); Mohammed Atta, pilot of American 11; and Marwan al-Shehhi, pilot of United 175.

Hijackers Nawaf al-Hazmi and Khalid al-Mihdhar move to the house of Abdussattar Shaikh in Lemon Grove, outside of San Diego, CA in the summer of 2000 [San Diego Union-Tribune, 9/16/01]. Shaikh is later revealed to be a "tested" undercover "asset" working with the local FBI [Newsweek, 9/9/02].

While hijackers Nawaf al-Hazmi and Khalid al-Mihdhar live in the house of an FBI informant, Abdussattar Shaikh, the informant continues to have contact with his FBI handler. The handler, Steven Butler, later claims that during summer Shaikh mentions the names "Nawaf" and "Khalid" in passing and that they are renting rooms from him [Newsweek, 9/9/02; Associated Press, 7/25/03 (B); 9/11 Congressional Inquiry, 7/24/03]. Shaikh tells Butler they are good, religious Muslims who are legally in the US to visit and attend school. Butler asks Shaikh for their last names, but Shaikh refuses to provide them. Butler is not told that they are pursuing flight training. Shaikh tells Butler that they are apolitical and have done nothing to arouse suspicion. However, according to the 9/11 Congressional Inquiry, he later admits that al-Hazmi has "contacts with at least four individuals [he] knew were of interest to the FBI and about whom [he] had previously reported to the FBI."

Two al Qaeda terrorists lived openly at the house of a paid FBI informant. The FBI handler for Abdussattar Shaikh, the informant, never got suspicious when the person who had never before met these boarders vouches for their character? He refused to give his FBI handler their last names, a tip-off that something was wrong.

When the Joint Inquiry Committee tries to interview Abdussattar Shaikh, the FBI refuses to provide access to him and makes sure that Abdussattar Shaikh is moved to a position so that the Joint Inquiry Committee is not able to contact him in order to find out what he knew about hijackers Nawaf al-Hazmi and Khalid al-Mihdhar prior to the events of 9/11.

It seems the FBI informant, Shaikh, will only talk to the FBI if he is given immunity; now this is definitely a bad sign. When investigators for the FBI Inspector General's office attempt to contact Steve Butler, he refuses to speak to them. It seems the "bona fides" that Steve has prepared each year for his informants are a bit perfunctory, in that each year. It always says the same thing but does not say how he actually checks the informant's bona fides. Checking the informant's bona fides means confirming that they are who they say they are and that they do not work for a foreign government or power (such as al Qaeda, for example).

On June 10, 2000, hijacker Khalid al-Mihdhar flies from San Diego to Frankfurt, Germany [*9/11 Congressional Inquiry*, 9/20/02]. Authorities later believe that al-Mihdhar visits his cousin-in-law Ramzi bin al-Shibh and bin al-Shibh's roommate Mohamed Atta and other al Qaeda members in bin al-Shibh's terrorist cell. However, since the CIA fails to notify Germany about their suspicions of either al-Mihdhar or bin al-Shibh, both of whom were seen attending the al Qaeda summit in Malaysia in January, German police fail to monitor them and another chance to uncover the 9/11 plot is missed.

Zacarias Moussaoui visits Malaysia twice, September 2000, and October 2000, and stays at the very same condominium where the January 2000 al Qaeda meeting was held [CNN, 8/30/02; *Los Angeles Times*, 2/2/02; *Washington Post*, 2/3/02]. After that meeting, Malaysian intelligence keeps watch on the condominium at the request of the CIA. However, the CIA stops the surveillance before Moussaoui arrives, spoiling a chance to expose the 9/11 plot by monitoring Moussaoui's later travels.

While Moussaoui is in Malaysia, Yazid Sufaat, the owner of the condominium, signs letters falsely identifying Moussaoui as a representative of his wife's company [*Reuters*, 9/20/02; *Washington Post*, 2/3/02]. When Moussaoui is later arrested in the US about one month before the 9/11 attacks, this letter in his possession could have led investigators back to the condominium and the connections with the January 2000 meeting attended by two of the hijackers [*USA Today*, 1/30/02]. Moussaoui's personal computer also contained the phone number of Ramzi bin al-Shibh in Germany, that would have linked him to Ramzi bin al-Shibh (and his roommate, Mohamed Atta), another participant in the Malaysian meeting.

October 2000

Following the attack on the USS Cole in October of 2000, Khallad was under intense investigation and on January 4, 2001, he was named as a key planner of the attacks.

The FBI's investigation into the USS Cole bombing reveals that terrorist Khallad bin Attash had been a principal planner of the bombing [Associated Press, 9/21/02 (B)], and that two other participants in the bombing, one of them a Fahad al-Quso, had delivered money to bin Attash "at the time of the January 2000 al Qaeda meeting in Malaysia." The FBI shares this information with the CIA.

Based on a description of bin Attash from an informant, CIA analysts reexamine pictures from the Malaysian meeting with this informant, and he identifies bin Attash as the mastermind of the Cole bombing, with both hijackers Nawaf al-Hazmi and Khalid al-Mihdhar. CIA Director Tenet later testifies that the presence of bin Attash, a known, important al Qaeda operative, gives the Malaysian meetings "greater significance" [9/11 Commission Report, 1/26/04]. At this point the CIA is now aware that both Nawaf al-Hazmi and Khalid al-Mihdhar have been associated with al Qaeda terrorists that had carried out the Cole bombings.

The day after the photo identification by the joint CIA-FBI human source in January 2001, the asset's identification of Khallad in the photo was reported to CIA Headquarters. However, the Joint Inquiry found no information showing that the FBI representative on the scene, who also worked with that source, was told about the identification or that the information was provided to FBI Headquarters. To the contrary, contemporary documents over the next month strongly suggest that the FBI did not know of this development. It was not until August 30, 2001 that CIA Headquarters transmitted to the FBI a memorandum stating, "We wish to advise you that, during a previously scheduled meeting with our joint source," Khallad was identified in a surveillance photo. [9/11 Commission Report, 1/26/04

February 2001

On February 1, 2001, the New York Cole case agent and another agent who spoke one of the source's languages interviewed the source overseas. The CIA case officer who had shown the Kuala Lumpur photographs to the source in early January was also present at the interview. During the interview, they showed the source the Yemeni-provided photograph of Khallad, which previously had been shown to the source by the CIA officer on December 16, 2000. The source again identified Khallad in the photograph.

As discussed above, the agents had received information indicating that al-Quso, who was in custody for his participation in the *Cole* attack, had traveled to Bangkok and met Khallad in January 2000. The New York agents were investigating the circumstances of that trip. The agents knew that al-Quso previously had claimed that he had intended to meet Khallad in Malaysia. The agents were concerned about al-Quso's veracity and whether al-Quso, as well as Khallad, had actually traveled to Malaysia. Therefore, an identification of Khallad in Malaysia during this period would have been very significant to the agents.

Both FBI agents who participated in the February 1 debriefing of the source told the OIG that they were not informed about surveillance photographs of the Malaysia meetings, that they did not know such photographs existed, and that they did not show any such Kuala Lumpur photographs to the source. They stated that they were not told that the source had identified Khallad from a Kuala Lumpur surveillance photograph in early January. They added that if they had been aware of any such identification of Khallad, they would have wanted to have the source repeat the identification for them since Khallad was a subject in the *Cole* criminal investigation. However, they stated that they were never informed of such identification.

In numerous CIA and FBI documents discussing the source and the early January debriefing, other important information from the source is described, but the source's identification of Khallad in the Kuala Lumpur photograph is never mentioned. Given the importance of that identification and the other details reported in the documents, we believe such information would have been included had the FBI been made aware of the identification.

For example, as described above, in the CIA case officer's cable reporting the December 16 debriefing of the source during which the source had identified Khallad in the Yemeni photograph, the CIA officer specifically noted that ALAT heard the identification and that the identification was repeated for the benefit of him. Max said he recalled this debriefing and the identification of Khallad being brought to his attention by the CIA case officer.

By contrast, in his cable reporting the early January source debriefing, the CIA case officer did not state that he brought to the attention of Max the identification of Khallad in the Kuala Lumpur photographs. Likewise in his cable describing the logistics of the debriefing, the CIA case officer provided a description of what was discussed with the source and stated that Max was present for a significant portion of the meeting with the source, but did not mention any Kuala Lumpur photographs or that the CIA case officer had brought the identification of Khallad to the attention of Max.

Because the agents (New York FBI agents), were keenly interested in Khallad and had asked the source to confirm his identification of Khallad from the Yemeni photograph, we believe the agents would have noted, remembered, and acted upon any information regarding another Khallad identification. We also believe that had the FBI known about the identification of Khallad in the Kuala Lumpur photographs, they would likely have sought information about the other participants in the meeting, including al-Mihdhar and al-Hazmi, which could have increased the FBI's chances of locating them before the September 11 attacks. [FBI IG Report]

The CIA had all of this information on Khallad who by this time was known to be the mastermind of the Cole bombing, but kept this information secret from the FBI. The FBI was unaware that Khallad had been at this meeting in January 2000, and unaware that future hijackers al-Hazmi and al-Mihdhar had been seen together with him at this meeting, the very meeting where the Cole bombing had been planned. The FBI did not get this information from the CIA until late August 2001.

The CIA has already been informed that al-Hazmi has entered the US in January 15, 2000, yet once again, in January 2001, when they now know that these three are extremely dangerous al Qaeda terrorists, that have been at an al Qaeda planning meeting and that one of them al-Hazmi, and entered the United States, they again fail to watchlist any of them, Khallad, al-Hazmi or al-Mihdhar [9/11 Congressional Inquiry, 7/24/03].

The Joint Inquiry Committee and the 9/11 Commission reports indicated the information and photographs of Mihdhar and Hazmi were not forwarded to the FBI until August 23, and the photograph of Khallad was not forwarded to the FBI until August

30, 2001, over 21 months after the they all were seen together at the al Qaeda planning meeting in Kuala Lumpur. Even after the CIA realized in January 2001 that all of these terrorists had been associated with the *Cole* bombing, they were still not watchlisted and this information was withheld form the FBI investigation of the Cole bombing on numerous occasions. No government investigation has explained why the CIA withheld this information from the FBI, or why the CIA did not connect Mihdhar and Hazmi to the huge al Qaeda attack the CIA knew was about to occur inside of the US.

Why did the 9/11 Commission not get to the bottom of this?

Clearly the 9/11 Commission had all of this information but failed to find the reasons the CIA had deliberately withheld this information from the FBI for 21 months.

On May 15, 2001, a supervisor at the CIA's Counterterrorist Center sends a request to CIA Headquarters for the surveillance photos of the January 2000 al Qaeda meeting in Malaysia. Three days later, the supervisor explains the reason for his interest in an e-mail to a CIA analyst: "I'm interested because Khalid al-Mihdhar's two companions also were couriers of a sort, who traveled between [the Far East] and Los Angeles at the same time ([H]azmi and [S]alah)." Hazmi refers to hijacker Nawaf al-Hazmi, and Salah Said is the alias al Qaeda leader Khallad bin Attash traveled under during the meeting. Apparently, the supervisor receives the photos.

Toward the end of May, this CIA supervisor contacts a FBI specialist working at FBI Headquarters about the photographs. The CIA wants the FBI analyst, who had been assigned to the *Cole* investigation, to review the photographs and determine if a person, Fahad al-Quso, who had carried money to Southeast Asia for bin Attash in January 2000, could be identified. The FBI analyst had known that Fahad al-Quso had carried money to Kuala Lumpur to give to Khallad in January 2000. Both this FBI analysis and another CIA analyst had been working together on the *Cole* investigation. This CIA analysis suggested to the FBI analyst that photographs of al-Quso be shown to FBI agents in New York, who were also working on the *Cole* bombings and who had interviewed Fahad al-Quso.

The CIA supervisor gave three Kuala Lumpur photographs to the FBI agent to take to New York to show to the New York agents. She was also told that one of the individuals in the photographs was named Khalid al-Mihdhar. The CIA (analyst) fails to tell the FBI analyst anything else about al-Mihdhar or al-Hazmi. When this FBI agent did some research in a NSA database, Interlink, she found the original NSA reports on the meeting in Kuala Lumpur. There was no information however on al-Mihdhar's US visa or his travel to the US. *[Joint Inquiry Final Report, December 2002].*

The account of the June 11 meeting and what took place prior to this meeting is described in much more detail in the FBI Inspector General's report.

June 11, 2001 meeting in New York City with (the FBI) *Cole* investigators

John's inquiries about Khallad

May 2001

Between the early January 2001 debriefing of the source and May 2001, the CIA's focus on whether Khallad, the suspected mastermind behind the *Cole* attack, had attended the Malaysia meetings appears to have subsided. In May 2001, John, a former Deputy Chief of the Bin Laden Unit, who by that time was detailed to ITOS in FBI Headquarters, had continuing concerns about the Malaysia meetings, especially whether they had any nexus to the *Cole* attack. [219]

[219] John told the OIG that in this detail to the FBI he acted as the CIA's chief intelligence representative to ITOS Section Chief Michael Rolince. John stated that he did not have line authority over anyone at the FBI and that his primary role was to assist the FBI in exploiting information for intelligence purposes, responsible for the *Cole* attack. He completed his report in January 2001, finding that UBL/al Qaeda was circumstantially tied to the attack.

John also noted to the OIG that during this period there were heightened concerns in the Intelligence Community about the threat of an imminent terrorist attack in Southeast Asia.

May 15, 2001

CIA records show that on May 15, 2001, John accessed the March 2000 cable stating that al-Mihdhar, al-Hazmi, and another person had traveled to Bangkok from Malaysia on January 8, 2000. The cable also stated that al-Hazmi had left Bangkok on January 15, 2000, flying from Bangkok to Hong Kong and then to Los Angeles.

Around this same time in May, John began inquiring about the Malaysia meetings with a CTC analyst, who we call "Peter," at

CIA Headquarters. John said he knew that Peter had been "down in the weeds" and knew the "nuts and bolts" of the *Cole* investigation because Peter had been assigned to prepare a CTC report on who was responsible for the *Cole* attack.

Peter told the OIG that his area of expertise and focus since August 1999 was the Arabian Peninsula. He said that because the *Cole* attack took place in Yemen, he was assigned to develop an intelligence report on who was responsible for the *Cole* attack. He completed his report in January 2001, finding that UBL/al Qaeda was circumstantially tied to the attack.[220] Peter stated that while working on the *Cole* report he regularly interacted with the IOSs in the FBI's UBL Unit. By the spring 2001, he was no longer working directly on the *Cole* attack, and had moved on to potential threats in Saudi Arabia and Yemen. However, Peter said he had a continued interest in the *Cole* information and continued to gather information on an *ad hoc* basis.

[220] The report did not mention al-Mihdhar's visa, al-Hazmi's travel to the United States or the Khallad identification from the Kuala Lumpur photographs.

According to John, he and Peter discussed the Malaysia meetings, and Peter provided him with a copy of the time-line of events related to the *Cole* investigation that Peter had compiled as part of his work on the *Cole* attack. [221]

[221] The time-line did not mention the Kuala Lumpur photographs, al-Mihdhar's US visa, or al-Hazmi's subsequent travel to the United States.

In addition, John said they discussed al-Quso, a *Cole* perpetrator in Yemeni custody, and any connections al-Quso may have had with the individuals in Malaysia. John and Peter were aware that al-Quso had stated that he was supposed to take money to a person named "Khallad" in Malaysia but had met him in Bangkok instead in January 2000. John told the OIG that Peter had posited that perhaps al-Quso had gone to Malaysia and met with the others who had been observed there in January 2000, and therefore al-Quso might have been in one of the Kuala Lumpur photographs.

In an e-mail to Peter in mid-May 2001, John noted that al-Mihdhar had arranged his travel to Malaysia and was associated with "[another terrorist organization] courier travel at the same time." John also noted in the e-mail that al-Quso, who was believed to be a courier since he had stated he had traveled to take money to Khallad, had traveled a few days earlier than al-Mihdhar. [222] In addition, John wrote that he was interested because al-Mihdhar was traveling with two "companions" who had left Malaysia and gone to Bangkok, Los Angeles, and Hong Kong and "also were couriers of a sort."

[222] As previously discussed, after al-Quso was detained in Yemen, he acknowledged that he had received $7,000 from someone named Ibrahim, which al-Quso asserted he took to Bangkok, Thailand on January 6, 2000, to deliver to "Khallad," a friend of Ibrahim's. Al-Mihdhar had traveled to Bangkok on January 8.

John noted in the e-mail that "something bad was definitely up." Peter replied in an e-mail dated May 18, "My head is spinning over this East Asia travel. Do you know if anyone in [the CIA's Bin Laden Unit] or FBI mapped this?"

b. Discussions among FBI and CIA employees

Around this same time, FBI IOS Donna and other FBI IOSs working on the *Cole* investigation were focusing on al-Quso's connection to Bangkok and his trip to deliver money to Khallad. The FBI, like the CIA, was aware that in January 2000 al-Quso had planned to travel to Malaysia to take money to Khallad. According to an FBI document drafted by Donna in May 2001, al-Quso had claimed that on January 6, 2000, he and Ibrahim al-Nibras went to Bangkok first but were unable to travel on to Kuala Lumpur because of problems with their travel documents, and Khallad had traveled to Bangkok to meet them there instead.

The FBI began researching telephone numbers that appeared to be connected to al-Quso's trip and requested that several Legat Offices contact local law enforcement authorities to obtain subscriber information.

Donna told the OIG that she and others were tracking the information related to the telephone numbers associated with al-Quso in an attempt to determine the truth of his statements. In addition, she said that she was focused on the identity and whereabouts of Khallad, since he was the purported mastermind of the *Cole* attack.

At some point before the end of May 2001, John discussed with Donna the East Asian travel of al-Quso. In response to Peter's May 18 e-mail that asked whether anyone had "mapped" the East Asia travel, John replied in an undated e-mail that "key travel still needs to be mapped" and stated "[Donna] sounds really interested in comparing notes in a small forum expert to expert so both sides can shake this thing and see what gaps are common."

John obtains three photographs of Mihdhar from the CIA

In addition to reviewing the East Asia travel of several bin Laden operatives in January 2000, John also began looking in CIA records for the Kuala Lumpur photographs. John obtained three of them. John told the OIG that he had not read the cable stating that the joint source had identified Khallad in the photographs, but he was aware that an identification of Khallad in the photographs had been made. At the end of his e-mail to Peter, John stated that he had obtained three surveillance photographs of al-Mihdhar in Malaysia, but he did not see "Khallad" in any of the photographs, and he believed he was "missing something" or "someone saw something that wasn't there." John also questioned whether there was a cable some-where that documented the identification of Khallad. [223]

[223] As noted above, John was correct – Khallad was not in any of these three photographs. After September 11 it was learned that the person the source had identified, as Khallad was actually al-Hazmi. It was also learned after September 11, however, that Khallad was in another Kuala Lumpur surveillance photograph that had not been shown to the source.

May 24, 2001

In response to John's e-mail, Peter wrote in an e-mail dated May 24 that he had thought one of the Kuala Lumpur photos was of Khallad. Peter added that Donna and another FBI IOS in the UBL Unit, who we call "Kathy," were meeting with Peter on May 29 to discuss the *Cole* investigation. Peter suggested that he could raise the issue of the Kuala Lumpur photographs and the possible identification of Khallad with the FBI IOSs. Peter told the OIG that he had learned about the source's identification of Khallad in the Kuala Lumpur photographs when it had occurred, but by May of 2001 it had been several months since he had worked on the *Cole* matter and he could not recall whether Khallad had been identified in the photographs.

On May 24, Donna sent John an e-mail stating that a meeting with Peter and others was "tentatively scheduled" for May 29 for "an in depth discussion about the *Cole*."

We were unable to determine with certainty whether a meeting with Peter, Donna, and Kathy actually took place on May 29. None of the witnesses had notes of any such meeting, nor were there any e-mails discussing the meeting after it would have taken place.

The witnesses told the OIG that they could not recall whether a meeting took place on May 29. For example, when asked whether she knew Peter, Kathy told the OIG that his name sounded familiar and that she may have met him, but she did not recall a meeting on May 29, 2001, about the *Cole* investigation. A May 29 e-mail from Peter to Mary indicates that he met with Mary earlier in the day, but it does not identify the other participants or what was discussed.

However, it is clear that at some point before the end of May 2001, Donna became aware of the existence of the Kuala Lumpur photographs in January 2000. Donna told the OIG that she recalled John printing one of the CIA photographs on the printer in his office at FBI Headquarters, and Donna acknowledged that she obtained two other Kuala Lumpur photographs from him. According to Donna, Peter had raised the photographs in a discussion with her prior to her obtaining the photographs from John, although she said that she did not recall the details of their discussion about the photographs. Donna said she did recall that, at the time, Peter had posited that one of the photographs could relate to al-Quso, which if true would contradict al-Quso's statements about going only to Bangkok and not going to Malaysia. According to Donna, the FBI was attempting to determine the veracity of al-Quso's information, so the photographs potentially were connected to the *Cole* investigation. She stated, however, that outside of this potential connection, the photographs were "another piece of a thousand things coming in" at the time. She said that if al-Quso were determined to be in the photographs, then the photographs would have become significant to the *Cole* investigation.

Donna also told the OIG that she did not recall a "substantive conversation" with John about the photographs or the Malaysia meetings. Donna told the OIG that she wrote on the back of the photographs what John told her about the photographs, which included that "Khalid Al-Midar" traveled from Sanna, Yemen, via Dubai, to Kuala Lumpur on January 5, 2000, and he was in Kuala Lumpur between January 6 and 8. She also wrote Khalid al-Mihdhar's name on the back of the photograph in which he had been identified.

According to Donna, neither John nor Peter discussed with her the fact that Khallad had been identified in these photographs. Donna told the OIG that she believes she would have noted being told that Khallad was in the photographs because she was interested in identifying Khallad and because it would have meant that the photographs had a definite connection to the *Cole* investigation. Donna also said that no one told her that al-Mihdhar had a US visa or that al-Hazmi had traveled to the United States.

John told the OIG that he did not recall anything about his discussion with Donna when he printed the Kuala Lumpur photographs for her. John said he recalled that at the time the FBI was trying to "nail down al-Quso's story." He said that he did not recall ever discussing the Khallad identification from the Kuala Lumpur photographs with Donna or anyone else at the FBI.

John emphasized that the FBI was focused on the *Cole* investigation, not the Malaysia meetings. He stated that while he had begun to theorize that Khallad had been in Malaysia, it was only "speculative" and he had not confirmed any of the information about a source identifying Khallad in the Kuala Lumpur photographs. Therefore, according to John, he would not have discussed the identification of Khallad with Donna. John emphasized that a significant impetus for the CIA's interest in Khallad's activities revolved around concerns that Khallad was planning a future terrorist operation in Malaysia.

Peter told the OIG that he recalled talking to FBI IOSs, including Donna, about mapping the telephone number information based on information provided by al-Quso. But he said that he did not recall discussions with Donna about the Kuala Lumpur photographs or the Khallad identification.

June 11, 2001, meeting

a. Planning for the meeting

Around the same time that Donna was discussing al-Quso and the *Cole* investigation with Peter and John, she also was planning a meeting at the New York FBI Office to discuss the *Cole* investigation. The planned participants for the New York meeting included personnel from FBI Headquarters, the CIA's CTC, and the New York FBI agents working on the *Cole* investigation. FBI documents show that Donna began organizing the meeting as early as May 24.

There was no record of an agenda for the meeting, and no supervisors were involved in the preparation for this meeting or were consulted regarding what should be accomplished at the meeting. Donna told the OIG that she organized the meeting in an effort to consolidate information and determine what further action was warranted on the *Cole* investigation. She stated that the purpose of the meeting at the New York FBI Office was to address unresolved issues and produce additional leads or other activities focusing on the *Cole* investigation. According to a May 24 e-mail by Donna, the meeting was "to discuss our direction, particularly as it relates to Nashiri." [224]

[224] Abdul Rahim al-Nashiri was al Qaeda's chief of operations in the Persian Gulf and was suspected to have been involved in the attack on the *Cole*. According to Donna, at the time he was believed to be the "on-scene commander" for the *Cole* attack, and the IOSs had been assigned the task of trying to locate him based on the intelligence reporting on him. He has since been arrested outside the United States.

Donna stated that she planned to take the Kuala Lumpur photographs with her to New York to find out whether the New York FBI *Cole* agents, who had met and debriefed al-Quso, could identify him in the photographs. She said that if al-Quso was in the photographs, the FBI would have reason to question al-Quso's statement that he had not gone to Malaysia but had met Khallad in Bangkok instead.

Sometime after obtaining the Kuala Lumpur photographs from John, Donna queried CTLink for the name Khalid al-Midhar [sic], which John had provided to her and which she had noted on the back of one of the photographs.[225] In CTLink she discovered the NSA information from late 1999 and early 2000 referencing al-Mihdhar's planned travel to Malaysia and al-Mihdhar's association with a suspected terrorist facility in the Middle East linked to al Qaeda activities.

[225] CTLink is a database administered by the CIA and used to disseminate information within the Intelligence Community.

Mary, an FBI detailee to the Bin Laden Unit who worked as a CTC desk officer, also attended the June 11 meeting, as did Peter, the CTC analyst. According to Mary, Donna invited her to the meeting and told her the meeting was intended for information sharing and as a "brainstorming session" concerning the *Cole* investigation. Mary told the OIG she had recently been given the assignment by CTC management of "getting up to speed" in her spare time on the Malaysia meetings and determining any potential connections between the Malaysia meetings and the *Cole* attack. Mary said that she had not yet begun reviewing the Malaysia meetings at the time of Donna's invitation.

According to Peter, the meeting was also described to him as an "information sharing and brainstorming session" to determine whether any further leads should be pursued. Peter said that he heard about the meeting from Mary and contacted Donna about attending because he was interested in learning what the New York FBI agents had uncovered in their investigation of the *Cole* attack.

According to FBI personnel in New York, Donna told them that FBI Headquarters and CIA personnel had indicated they had "information to share" regarding the *Cole* investigation. The FBI New York personnel anticipated the meeting would be a mutual exchange of information. Scott, one of the New York case agents on the *Cole* investigation, said he was told that the CIA representatives who would be attending the meeting wanted a briefing on the *Cole* investigation. On his own initiative, Scott arranged for David Kelley, an AUSA from the SDNY who was assigned to the *Cole* matter, to discuss with the CIA representatives other issues related to the *Cole* investigation, one of which was the impact on the prosecution if some of the targets of the *Cole* investigation were captured or detained outside the United States.

b. The June 11 meeting

On June 11, the meeting was held in a conference room at the FBI's New York Field Office. We could not determine with certainty all the participants at the meeting. There was no list of attendees, and the witnesses could not recall exactly who was there. However, we confirmed that Donna, Mary, Peter, Scott, and another New York agent assigned to the *Cole* investigation who we call "Randall," attended. AUSA Kelley attended for part of the meeting. Although it was unclear exactly how long the meeting lasted, the witnesses said it lasted between two and four hours.

In interviews with the OIG, the attendees said they did not recall the specifics of what was discussed at the meeting. The only contemporaneous notes from the meeting that we were able to obtain were Donna's. Her notes indicate that the latest developments in the *Cole* investigation were discussed. The second page of the notes is labeled "to do" and referenced several items.

Toward the end of the meeting, Donna produced the three Kuala Lumpur surveillance photographs and asked the agents if they recognized al-Quso in any of the photographs. Donna said she told the agents that the photographs had been taken in Malaysia around the Millennium. Donna said she provided Khalid al-Mihdhar's name to at least some of the agents.

A New York agent tentatively identified one of the pictured individuals as al-Quso, but he could not make a definitive identification. [226] The witnesses' accounts of what happened next differ.

[226] Only a limited number of New York agents had actually met al-Quso. The others had only seen photographs of him.

Scott told the OIG that after reviewing the Kuala Lumpur photographs, the FBI agents began to ask questions, such as whether there were additional photographs or information concerning the background on the photographs, including questions about al-Mihdhar, who was in the photographs. According to Scott, he pressed Donna and Peter for details of the Malaysia meetings. Scott told the OIG he was interested in the fact that the photographs were from Malaysia because from the al-Quso's debriefings he knew that Khallad had planned to meet al-Quso in Malaysia, and any information linking Khallad to Malaysia was "directly related" to the *Cole* investigation.

Scott contended that Donna "refused" to provide any further information about the photographs or the Malaysia meetings due to "the wall." Scott told the OIG that he previously had numerous conversations about the wall with Donna, which had been an issue between them. He stated that during this June 11 meeting, he disputed that the wall was applicable to the information at hand because the photographs had not been obtained as the result of a FISA Court order, and he continued to press Donna for more information. Scott said the meeting degenerated into an argument about the wall.

Donna, Mary, and Peter described the showing of the Kuala Lumpur photographs as a sidebar to the main meeting and generally inconsequential. All three asserted that neither the display of the surveillance photographs nor the meeting overall was contentious. Although Donna agreed that the FBI agents asked further questions regarding the origin of the photographs and asked for additional information regarding the Malaysia meetings, she contended that she responded simply by saying she did not know anything further. She told the OIG that these questions made sense to her when they were asked, but she did not know the answers.

In his initial OIG interview, Scott described the meeting as very contentious and combative.

In a second OIG interview, although Scott did not characterize the meeting as having the same level of combativeness, he contended that he pressed Donna for more information but none was forthcoming. Scott stated he had heated telephone conversations and e-mail exchanges with Donna over this issue after the June 11 meeting.

She stated that someone asked what kind of passport al-Mihdhar was traveling on, and Peter responded that it was a Saudi passport. [228] According to Donna, she had not known this information prior to Peter stating it. Donna told us that this was the only information volunteered by Peter, and she believed he would have provided additional information if he knew it.

[228] Donna's contemporaneous notes reflect this information. It appears as the last entry on the notes, indicating that this was discussed at the end of the meeting.

Peter told the OIG that he was not asked any questions at the June 11 meeting, he had no formal role, and he did not brief anyone on anything at the June 11 meeting. Peter explained that it is not within his purview or authority as an analyst to share CIA information. He said he did not recall the meeting becoming heated or contentious. He said he did not recall any time during the meeting where Donna said, "I can't answer that question" or directly refused to answer a question. [229]

[229] As described earlier, Peter and John had exchanged several e-mails about the Malaysia meetings and the photographs. However, it is unclear based upon the information available to us exactly what Peter knew at this point. He said he was unable to remember exactly what additional information he had on June 11, 2001.

Mary stated that she had not been "up to speed" on the case at this time, so she was not in a position to provide information at the meeting. She stated that she and Peter were not asked any questions during the meeting. She said that she did not recall any serious disagreements arising during the meeting.

When we asked Scott whether an intelligence-designated agent could have been provided the information outside the presence of the criminal agents, Scott agreed that could have been done, but he did not think of it at the time and no one else suggested it. During his subsequent testimony before the

Joint Intelligence Committee, however, Scott said that the wall must not have been at issue because the criminal agents could have just left the room and any information could have been related to an intelligence agent.

According to Donna, she remained in New York after the meeting, without Peter and Mary, and she continued the discussions with the New York agents regarding the photographs after the meeting. She said that these subsequent conversations became fairly "heated," as the agents pressed her with questions such as whether there were additional photographs and any documentation about the photographs. [230]

[230] We believe it likely that the agents were confusing the post-meeting discussions with the showing of the photographs at the meeting.

Donna told the OIG she had provided to the agents all the information she had received from the CIA regarding the photographs. She told us that all she knew was that these three photographs were taken in Malaysia around the Millennium, and one of the persons in the photographs was someone named Khalid al-Mihdhar. Donna stated she advised the agents of this and told them that efforts would be made to obtain the requested information. She said she was not aware that there would have been additional information to provide. She added that she recalled having the impression that the agents did not believe her when she said that she did not have the information about the photographs that the agents were requesting.

As discussed earlier, however, Donna had additional NSA information about al-Mihdhar that she had discovered through her CTLink query. The information related to the planned travel to Malaysia of several members of an "operational cadre" and al-Mihdhar's association with a suspected terrorist facility in the Middle East linked to al Qaeda activities. Donna told us that she could not provide this information directly to the agents working the *Cole* criminal investigation due to the caveat, which prevented all NSA counterterrorism-related intelligence information from being provided to FBI criminal agents without approval from the NSA. [231] Donna told us that the New York FBI primarily worked criminal terrorism investigations and the sharing of intelligence information with the criminal agents was often an issue. She said that some of the New York agents had become "overly sensitive" about a perceived lack of information sharing.

[231] It is important to note, however, that this NSA information originally had been routed not only to FBI Headquarters but also to the New York FBI Office in late 1999 and early 2000.

Donna emphasized that any information could be shared but often a process had to be followed before certain intelligence information could be shared with agents working criminal investigations. She added that it was not her job to keep information from the agents but instead to ensure they had the tools necessary to do their job.

According to Donna, the only issue regarding the Kuala Lumpur photographs would have been obtaining permission from the CIA to allow individuals outside of the FBI to see the photographs in furtherance of the *Cole* investigation, such as in interviews conducted in Yemen. [232] Donna said at some point while she was in New York, she and the agents discussed providing the photographs to the agents working in Yemen in order to get a positive identification of al-Quso in the photographs and to conduct further investigation. [233] She stated that she told the agents that she would attempt to obtain the requisite permission to provide the photographs to the agents working the *Cole* investigation in Yemen.

[232] A policy in the intelligence Community, which is designed to protect intelligence sources and methods, is that the originator of intelligence information controls the further dissemination of the information. This policy is described as originator controlled, or "ORCON." Dissemination of ORCON information requires permission from the originating agency to further disseminate the information outside the receiving agency.

[233] Apparently unbeknownst to the involved FBI and CIA personnel, the Yemeni authorities already had been given the photographs on January 3, 2001, six months before anyone at the FBI received the photographs.

Although she had no explicit discussion with John regarding the use of the photographs, Donna stated she understood that the photographs were "not formally passed" to the FBI when John gave them to her, but only provided for limited use in the meeting. Therefore, Donna said she did not believe that she could leave the photographs with the New York agents until the requisite permission to show the photographs outside of the FBI had been obtained.

However, John told the OIG that that since the photographs had been given to Donna, an FBI employee, they could be further distributed within the FBI. John agreed that the photographs could not be used by the FBI in any manner where they would be disclosed to a foreign government.

For example, he said that without approval from the CIA, the FBI agents could not keep the photographs and show them to al-Quso, who was in Yemeni custody, because Yemeni officials also would see the photographs.

c. Follow-up after the June 11 meeting

We looked for evidence as to whether Donna or the New York agents conducted any follow-up efforts about the Kuala Lumpur photographs or obtaining permission from the NSA to pass the intelligence information to the New York agents. Donna said that she "probably" had follow-up conversations with John, Peter, and Mary about the photographs, but she did not specifically recall the conversations or obtaining additional information. Mary told the OIG that she recalled conversations with Donna about obtaining permission for the FBI to use the photographs of the Malaysia meetings in their investigation.

Donna stated she was not contacted by Scott after the meeting, although she was working with another agent on the squad, who we call "Glenn," in connection with tracking telephone toll records. Those records related to the *Cole* participants, the travel of al-Quso to Bangkok, and al-Quso's potential travel to Malaysia.

According to Scott, over the course of the summer, he had several more conversations with FBI Headquarters asking about any additional information on the Kuala Lumpur photographs, but he was not provided any additional information. He stated that he did not seek assistance from any supervisor in obtaining additional information. He told us that he and the rest of the New York Field Office had been fighting a battle with FBI Headquarters over information sharing for months, and he was "dumbfounded" that he could not obtain the information about the Kuala Lumpur photographs. He stated that in hindsight he probably should have sought the intervention of a supervisor.

Documentary evidence shows that, as a result of the June 11 meeting, Donna and the New York agents discussed the Kuala Lumpur photographs in several follow-up conversations. In an e-mail dated August 22 from Donna to Glenn, she wrote that there were additional photographs of the Malaysia meetings and that the reason that al-Mihdhar was of interest at the time was because of some threat information that led to the CIA looking at all persons named "Khalid." In addition, she wrote that she had received assurances that the FBI would be able to use the Kuala Lumpur photographs outside the FBI. We discuss this e-mail in further detail in the next section.

Documents also show that on August 27 Donna requested permission from the NSA to provide the intelligence information about al-Mihdhar to the New York *Cole* criminal agents. However, this request came after the FBI had discovered on August 22 that al-Mihdhar might be in the United States and had opened an investigation to determine whether he was in the country. We discuss the events that led to that investigation and the investigative efforts of the FBI in the next section of the report.

OIG conclusions on May and June discussions

While there were several interactions between FBI and CIA personnel in May and June 2001 that could have resulted in the FBI learning more about the Kuala Lumpur photographs and al-Mihdhar, the FBI personnel did not become aware of significant intelligence information about al-Mihdhar and al-Mihdhar's connections to Khallad. The fact that al-Mihdhar had possessed a United States visa was not disclosed at this time by the CIA to Donna or the FBI. The fact that al-Hazmi had been at the Malaysia meeting and then traveled to Los Angeles also was not disclosed by the CIA. In addition, the fact that the source had identified Khallad, the purported master-mind of the *Cole* bombing, from the Kuala Lumpur surveillance photographs was not disclosed during these interactions.

Although Donna knew about the Kuala Lumpur surveillance photographs, we do not believe that she was informed that al-Mihdhar had a US visa or that Khallad had been identified in the photographs. Donna's contemporaneous notes on the back of the Kuala Lumpur photographs reflect the limited information that she had obtained about the photographs and the Malaysia meetings. The notes do not mention anything about al-Mihdhar's possession of a US visa. In addition, Donna stated that she was aware of the significance of Khallad to the *Cole* investigation, but the notes on the photographs also do not mention Khallad. Moreover, John, who provided the photographs to Donna, told the OIG he did not recall discussing the Kuala Lumpur photographs with her, and he did not believe that he would have discussed with Donna that Khallad had been identified in the photographs, because at the time he was not sure that this was true and he thought the information was "speculative." Although an e-mail message indicated that Peter was planning to discuss the Khallad identification with Donna in a meeting on May 29, we were unable to determine that this meeting actually occurred.

It was impossible for us to determine exactly what happened at the June 11 meeting with respect to the Kuala Lumpur photographs because the witnesses cannot recall the specifics of the discussions and there is little documentary evidence. It is clear, however, that the information regarding al-Mihdhar's US visa and the fact that Khallad had been identified in the Kuala Lumpur photographs was not discussed at the June 11 meeting.

Donna told the agents about the photographs and provided them limited information that she had obtained from the CIA about the photographs. Most of the questioning about the photographs took place after the meeting, when Peter and Mary had left. We believe those interactions after the meeting became very contentious, with the New York FBI wanting more information. Donna did not provide the New York agents with the NSA intelligence information about al-Mihdhar's association with a suspected terrorist facility in the Middle East linked with al Qaeda activities, which she obtained through her research. She said she did not because of the restrictions placed on sharing such NSA information. As we discuss further in the next section, Donna subsequently contacted the NSA in reference to having the NSA information passed to the agents, but this did not occur until much later, on August 27, 2001.

We found little attempt by either the FBI agents or Donna after June 11 to follow up on the information about the photographs that was discussed at the meeting. There is little evidence of follow-up until some time in August 2001, when, as we discuss in the next section, the FBI learned that al-Mihdhar had recently entered the United States, and the FBI opened an investigation to locate him.

The interaction between the CIA and the FBI in May and June 2001 was another failed opportunity for the FBI to obtain the critical information about al-Mihdhar and Khallad. The failure of the FBI to learn about al-Mihdhar, his connection to Khallad, and his travel to the United States at that time demonstrated significant problems in the flow of information between the CIA and the FBI. We discuss these deficiencies in the analysis section of this chapter. [FBI Inspector General's Report]

The CIA at this time knew Tawfiq Bin Attash, Khalid al-Mihdhar and Nawaf al-Hazmi were at the Kuala Lumpur meeting where Cole bombing had been planned, directly connecting all of these terrorists to the Cole bombing. They CIA even knew Hazmi had already entered the US, and would most likely be a part of the huge attack they had been getting numerous warning about since April 2001. Yet we are told instead of giving this information to the FBI Cole investigators, they give the three photos of Mihdhar to a FBI agent to take to New York to show to the Cole investigators to see if they can identify Fahad al-Quso in these photos? Since Fahad al-Quso had just a minor role in tie Cole bombing and the FBI already had interviewed his several times, this reason the CIA gives for setting up this meeting is absurd, a fact that had to be known from the investigations of this meeting.

Around the same time, the CIA analyst receives an e-mail mentioning al-Hazmi's travel to the US. These two analysts, the FBI and the CIA analyst, travel to New York the next month, June 11, 2001, and to talk to New York FBI agents that were working on the Cole bombings. Again the CIA analyst fails to divulge what he knows [9/11 Congressional Inquiry, 7/24/03].

In New York, the FBI and CIA analysts and another CIA analyst who had been detailed to the CIA's Bin Laden Unit met with the New York FBI Cole investigators and showed them the pictures from the Kuala Lumpur meeting to see if they could identify Fahad al-Quso. The New York agents wanted to know where and why these photographs had been taken, why were these people being followed, and where were additional photographs? What was the reason behind this?"

In addition to not being told why al-Mihdhar was being surveyed, the New York agents were not told about his US visa, Nawaf al-Hazmi's entry into the United States, the January 2001 photo identification of Khallad, or the fact that the analyst had come upon material in a CIA database that led him to conclude that "al-Hazmi was an experienced [Mujahadeen]."

The FBI IOS had none of that information, but the CIA analyst from the Bin Laden Unit, who attended the New York meeting, acknowledged to the Joint Inquiry that he had seen all of it. In fact, he had received an e-mail just three weeks earlier that referred to al-Hazmi's travel to the United States. That information, he related in a Joint Inquiry interview, "did not mean anything to him," since he was interested in terrorist connections to Yemen. The CIA analyst explained to the Joint Inquiry that the information was operational in nature and he would not disclose it outside CIA unless he had prior authority to do so. Because no one at this (sic) meeting asked the CIA agent from the Bin Laden Unit what he knew, he did not volunteer anything. He told investigators that as a CIA agent he was not authorized to answer FBI questions regarding CIA information. Nonetheless, the CIA agent said, "at the end of the day we knew the name Khalid al-Mihdhar but nothing else." The *Cole* criminal investigator testified that he was told that "the information could not be passed" at that time, but might be "in the days and weeks to come." However, no additional information was transmitted for use in a criminal case until after September 11 [*Joint Inquiry Final Report*, December 2002].

The statement "at the end of the day we knew the name Khalid al-Mihdhar but nothing else" is false. They knew that Mihdhar and Hazmi had been seen together with Khallad, mastermind of the Cole bombing and tying them all directly to the planning of the Cole bombing. Yet the CIA officer we are told withheld this information from the FBI Cole investigators even when asked. This CIA officer even knew Hazmi was inside of the US, and would have known about the many warning of a huge al Qaeda attack inside of the US. He would also have known by keeping the identity of the people in the photographs secret, the FBI would not be able to stop this huge attack and thousand of Americans would die. This meeting was held on June 11, 2001, over 90 days prior to the attacks on 9/11. Had the FBI been given this information at this time, the events on 9/11 would have been prevented.

After this meeting ended, the FBI agent sent by the CIA with the photographs continued to have a discussion with the FBI criminal agents on the *Cole* investigation. She said she knew the identity of the person in the photographs, one of them being Khalid al-Mihdhar, but was not allowed to share this information with the New York agents due to the warning attached to this information in the NSA database. No investigation has ever explained why did she not have this information officially passed over the wall when she knew this was required in order to share this material with the *Cole* investigators?

July 2001 – September 11, 2001 Joint Inquiry Committee Final Report

In early July 2001, the same CTC Supervisor (on detail to the FBI ITOS) located in a CIA database the cable for which he had been searching that contained information the CIA had acquired in January 2001 about Khallad's attending the Malaysia meeting. He told the Joint Inquiry that Khallad's presence at the meeting deeply troubled him and he immediately sent an e-mail from FBI Headquarters to CTC stating, "[Khallad] is a major league killer, who orchestrated the *Cole* attack and possibly the Africa bombings."

[Page 159] [*Joint Inquiry Final Report*, December 2002]

A review was (had already been) launched at CIA of all cables regarding the Malaysia meeting. The task fell largely to an FBI analyst assigned to CTC. [*Joint Inquiry Final Report*, December 2002].

Because the FBI analyst had other assignments she does not even get to this task until July 24. It was only on August 21, 2001, that the analyst put together two key pieces of information: the intelligence the CIA received in January 2000 that al-Mihdhar had a multiple-entry visa to the United States, and the information it received in March 2000 that al-Hazmi had traveled to the United States.]

This is the exact same information the CIA had on Khalid al-Mihdhar's multiple-entry visa in December 1999, and the information they received in a cable in March 2000 on the fact al-Hazmi had entered the US on January 15, 2000. In fact this is the exact same information this CIA supervisor who was now working at the FBI ITOS unit already had on al-Hazmi and al-Mihdhar on May 15, 2001. She had spent over three months finding information we now know was already well known at the Bin Laden unit of the CIA. This has never been explained.

Working with an INS representative assigned to CTC, the analyst learned that al-Mihdhar had entered the United States on January 15, 2000, had departed on June 10, and had reentered the United States on July 4, 2001. Suspicions were further aroused by the fact that al-Mihdhar and al-Hazmi had arrived in Los Angeles in January 2000, when Ahmed Ressam would have been in Los Angeles to conduct terrorist operations at Los Angeles Airport, but for his apprehension at the US-Canada border in December 1999. She alerts FBI intelligence on August 21, 2001 about this information [*Joint Inquiry Final Report*, December 2002].

Yet when this FBI analysis finds the information that Hazmi is inside of the US she contacts the INS and finds out that Mihdhar is also inside of the US. There is no explaination why when she finds the same information well known by many people at the CIA she contacts the INS when no one else did. The mystery deepens!

On August 23, 2001, the CIA sent a cable to the State Department, INS, Customs, and FBI requesting that "Bin Laden-related individuals," al-Mihdhar, al-Hazmi, Khallad, and one other person at the Malaysia meeting, be watchlisted immediately and denied entry into the United States "due to their confirmed links to Egyptian Islamic Jihad operatives and suspicious activities while traveling in East Asia." Although the CIA believed that al-Mihdhar was already in the United States, placing him on the watchlist would enable authorities to detain him if he attempted to leave. The CIA cable stated that al-Hazmi had arrived in Los Angeles on January 15, 2000 on the same flight as al-Mihdhar and that there was no record of al-Hazmi's departure. On August 24, the State Department watchlisted al-Mihdhar, al-Hazmi, and the others listed in the CIA cable. On August 27, it revoked the visa that al-Mihdhar had obtained in June [*Joint Inquiry Final Report*, December 2002].

The Search for Khalid al-Mihdhar

FBI Headquarters promptly sent to the FBI New York Field Office a draft communication recommending the opening of "an intelligence investigation to determine if al-Mihdhar is still in the United States." It stated that al-Mihdhar's "confirmed association" with various elements of bin Laden's terrorist network, including potential association with two individuals involved in the attack on *USS Cole*, "make him a risk to the national security of the United States." The goal of the intelligence [p. 160] investigation was to "locate al-Mihdhar and determine his contacts and reasons for being in the United States."

That communication precipitated a debate between FBI Headquarters and New York Field Office personnel as to whether to open an intelligence or criminal investigation on al-Mihdhar. A New York FBI agent tried to convince Headquarters to open a criminal investigation, given the importance of the search and the limited resources available in intelligence investigations, but Headquarters declined to do so. An e-mail exchange between Headquarters and the New York agent described the debate.

From FBI Headquarters:

"If al-Mihdhar is located, the interview must be conducted by an intel [intelligence] agent. A criminal agent CANNOT be present at the interview. This case, in its entirety, is based on intel. If at such time as information is developed indicating the existence of a substantial federal crime, that information will be passed over the wall according to the proper procedures and turned over for follow-up criminal investigation. (Emphasis in original.)

From the New York agent: Whatever has happened to this – someday someone will die – and wall or not – the public will not understand why we were not more effective and throwing every resource we had at certain 'problems.' Let's hope the [FBI's] National Security Law Unit (NSLU) will stand behind their decisions [about the "wall"] then, especially since the biggest threat to us now, UBL, is getting the most 'protection.'"

The agent was told in response: "we (at Headquarters) are all frustrated with this issue," but "[t]hese are the rules. NSLU does not make them up." The former head of the FBI's International Terrorism Operations Section explained to the Joint Inquiry why the search for al-Mihdhar was conducted as an intelligence, rather than a criminal matter: "Although we certainly suspect, and rightfully so, that they were probably engaged in... criminal acts, the information brought to us came essentially in total in the intelligence channel, so an intelligence investigation was opened." [Page 161, *Joint Inquiry Final Report*, December 2002].

On August 22 once the FBI was aware of the intelligence information about al-Mihdhar, the FBI took steps to open an intelligence investigation to locate him. Yet the FBI did not pursue this as an urgent matter or assign many resources to it.

One of the FBI detailees to the CTC section of the CIA sent a request in a EC, entitled Khalid M. al-Mihdhar, request to [sic] poem an intelligence investigation" The EC outlined al-Mihdhar's travel to the United States, in July 2001, his previous travel to the United States with al-Hazmi, in January 2000, and the background of his attendance at the Malaysia meetings. As to the identification of Khallad [in the Kuala Lumpur photographs] by the source, this was not included due to the fact that this information had not yet been officially passed to the FBI (over the wall). While the CTC detailee had called the New York office to indicate a sense of urgency to opening the investigation, she designated the EC precedence as routine. The EC in draft form was received in the New York office on August 28. This EC is marked "routine." The precedence designations can be listed as "routine," "priority," connotation some sense of urgency, and "immediate," connotation the highest sense of urgency [Page 298, *FBI Inspector General's Report*].

On the 28th of August this EC is forwarded to various agents on the Bin Laden squad, including the *Cole* Criminal case agent. In the cover letter the Supervisory Special Agent on the JTTF New York Field Office directs the Relief Supervisor to open an intelligence investigation and assign a particular Special Agent. On August 29, 2001, the FBI New York Office opened a full field investigation to locate al-Mihdhar. The investigation was assigned to a Special Agent... This agent was a relatively inexperienced agent who had recently transferred to the Bin Laden squad (in the FBI). This was this agent's first intelligence investigation. On August 30 the Special Agent (assigned to find al-Mihdhar) receives a telephone call from the agent who had initiated the EC) in reference to the investigation. He said (that the agent who has initiated this investigation told him that) the goal of this investigation was to locate and identify al-Mihdhar for a potential interview. According to the investigating Special Agent, (the intelligence agent that initiated the EC) did not indicate the investigation was an emergency or identify any other exigent circumstance [P. 302, *FBI Inspector General's Report*].

On August 30, the information that the CIA and the NSA has on Khallad is passed in a CIR from the CIA to the FBI.

September 4. The agent assigned to find al-Mihdhar told the OIG that he began work on locating al-Mihdhar on September 4. On this date, this agent completed a lookout request for the INS, identifying al-Mihdhar as a potential witness in a terrorist investigation. The INS lookout form has a box indicating whether the individual was wanted for "security/terrorism" reasons. (This agent did not check this box; he said in later questioning that "another agent" had told him that he should identify the subject on the form as a witness not a potential terrorist to prevent overzealous immigration officials from overreacting.) When the OIG contact this "other agent" after 9/11, he said he did not provide this advice to this Special

Agent and that he always checked security/terrorism box when he completed this form for a potential witness in a terrorism investigation. In spite of what he said, when this "other agent" reviewed the INS form with the box incorrectly checked he did not change it. He said that he only checked to see if this application was complete, and that he had not seen the other predicting material on al-Mihdhar's travel, or al-Mihdhar's visa.

Both agents acknowledged that they did not notice the false statements on al-Mihdhar's visa application. (This was the statement on his visa application, for his trip to the US on July 4, 2001, and (it) failed to mention that he had never entered the US before. It was known at this time that he had traveled to the US on January 15, 2001.) On this date the investigating agent requested an NCIC criminal history check, credit card check and motor vehicle records be searched for al-Mihdhar and al-Hazmi.

An FBI agent determined on September 5 that al-Mihdhar had not registered at a New York Marriott. The agent checked computerized national and New York criminal and motor vehicle indices on al-Mihdhar and al-Hazmi, but those checks were negative.

The Special Agent also conducted Choicepoint™ searches on al-Hazmi and al-Mihdhar. (The results were negative in spite of the fact that there were records in this system on al-Hazmi, which were not found until after 9/11). Page 304, FBI Inspector General's report.

Al-Hazmi and al-Mihdhar had traveled to Los Angeles, California on January 15, 2000, via United Airlines, and the INS records indicated that they claimed to be destined for a "Sheraton hotel" in Los Angeles. Therefore on September 10, 2001, the investigating Special Agent drafted an investigation lead for the FBI Los Angeles Field Office. The lead was not transmitted until the next day, September 11, 2001. By the morning of September 11, when American Airlines Flight 77, that al-Mihdhar and al-Hazmi hijacked crashed into the Pentagon, the investigating Special Agent had not uncovered any information regarding al-Mihdhar's or al-Hazmi's location... [Joint Inquiry Final Report, December 2002].

The period from July – September 11, 2001 from the FBI Inspector General's report is the account of this time period that is much more detailed and provides many details not in the Joint Inquiry Committee final report.

The FBI's efforts to locate al-Mihdhar in August and September 2001

The fifth and final opportunity for the FBI to locate al-Mihdhar and al-Hazmi occurred in late August 2001, when it was informed that al-Mihdhar and al-Hazmi had traveled to the United States. The FBI learned in August 2001 that al-Mihdhar had entered the United States in July 2001 and that al-Mihdhar and al-Hazmi had previously traveled together to the United States in January 2000. On August 29, the FBI began an investigation to locate al-Mihdhar, but it did not assign great urgency or priority to the investigation. The New York FBI criminal agents who wanted to participate in the investigation were specifically prohibited from doing so because of concerns about the wall and the procedures to keep criminal and intelligence investigations separate. The FBI did not locate al-Mihdhar before the September 11 attacks.

We review the facts surrounding the FBI's discovery of this information about al-Mihdhar and al-Hazmi and what the FBI did with this information in August. We also examine the FBI's unsuccessful efforts to locate al-Mihdhar before the September 11 attacks.

Continuing review of the Malaysia meetings in July and August 2001

As discussed above, John, the CIA Bin Laden Unit Deputy Chief, was detailed to the FBI's ITOS in May 2001. Shortly before assuming his duties at the FBI, John had asked CTC management to assign a CTC desk officer with "getting up to speed" on the Malaysia meetings and determining any potential connections between the Malaysia meetings and the *Cole* attack. This assignment was given to Mary. She told the OIG that "getting up to speed," meant she would have to research and read the pertinent cable traffic as her schedule permitted. She emphasized that her priority assignment during this period was the credible threats of an imminent attack on US personnel in Yemen, and she said that she worked the Malaysia meetings connections to the *Cole* attack whenever she had an opportunity.

In early July 2001, based on recent intelligence information, the CIA had concerns about the possibility of a terrorist attack in Southeast Asia. On July 5, 2001, John sent an e-mail to managers at the CTC's Bin Laden Unit noting, "how bad things look in Malaysia." He wrote that there was a potential connection between the recent threat information and information developed about the Malaysia meetings in January 2000. In addition, he noted that in January 2000, when al-Mihdhar was traveling to Malaysia, key figures in the failed attack against the *USS The Sullivans* and the subsequent successful attack against the *USS Cole* also were attempting to meet in Malaysia, and that one or more of these persons could have been in Malaysia at that time. Therefore, he recommended that the *Cole* and Malaysia meetings be reexamined for potential connections to the current threat information involving Malaysia. He wrote, "I know your resources are strained, but if we can prevent something in SE Asia, this would seem to be a productive place to start." He ended the e-mail by stating that "all the indicators are of a massively bad infrastructure being readily completed with just one purpose in mind."

July 13, 2001:

On July 13, John wrote another e-mail to CTC managers stating that he had discovered the CIA cable relating to the source's identification of "Khallad" from the Kuala Lumpur surveillance photographs in early January 2001. John began the e-mail by announcing "OK. This is important." He then described Khallad as a "major league killer who orchestrated the *Cole* attack and possibly the Africa bombings." The e-mail recommended revisiting the Malaysia meetings, especially in relation to any potential information on Khallad. Significantly, John ended the e-mail asking, "can this [information] be sent via CIR to [the FBI]?"

Despite John's recommendation that this information be forwarded to the FBI in a CIR, we found no evidence indicating that the CIA provided this information to the FBI until August 30, 2001, which, as we describe below, was after the FBI learned about al-Mihdhar's presence in the United States.

In a response e-mail dated July 13, 2001, a CTC Bin Laden Unit supervisor stated that Mary had been assigned to handle the request for additional information on the Malaysia meetings. In addition, the e-mail stated that another FBI detailee to the CTC, Dwight, who was out of the office at the time, would be assigned to assist Mary upon his return.

Later in July, Mary drafted a cable to another CIA office requesting follow-up information about the Malaysia meetings. The cable included a reference to the source's identification of Khallad in one of the Kuala Lumpur photographs and that

Khallad and al-Mihdhar had been in Malaysia at the same time, possibly together. A week later, the CTC supervisor forwarded the cable to John for his review prior to release, and the cable was sent to the office to which it was addressed three days after that.

On the same day she drafted the cable referencing the source's identification of Khallad, Mary located one of the CIA cables referencing al-Mihdhar's possession of a US visa. On the same date, Mary also reviewed the CIA cable that stated this visa information had been passed to the FBI in January 2000. [234]

[234] As discussed above, we found no evidence that this information had, in fact, been provided to the FBI.

In early August, Mary and Donna continued to discuss the Kuala Lumpur photographs. In an e-mail on August 7 from Donna to Mary, Donna requested a copy of the flight manifest for al-Mihdhar's January 2000 trip to Malaysia in order to determine whether al-Quso had traveled with al-Mihdhar.

She also asked, "if we could get the pictures cleared to show al-Quso." [235] She continued, "the reasoning behind this would be that first, we do not have a concensous [sic] that the individual with Midhar [sic] is in fact al-Quso ... [second] to determine if al-Quso can identify al-Mihdhar by an other [sic] name." Donna then discussed her continuing efforts to track telephone number information developed in the investigation. At the close of the e-mail, Donna wrote, "I plan to write something up, but perhaps we should schedule another sit down to compare notes on both sides. Let me know."

[235] Apparently the desk officer was unaware that clearance had been received and that the photographs had been shared with Yemeni officials.

In a response e-mail on the same date, Mary wrote, "Okay, all sounds good." Mary also wrote that she thought Donna had al-Mihdhar's flight manifest because John had mentioned it, but Mary indicated she would find the manifest. She wrote, "I think we will be able to clear the pictures, they are for passage to al-Quso, right?" Mary also asked whether the FBI would be able to meet with al-Quso again. Mary ended the e-mail, "I think a sit down again would be great" and mentioned the potential logistics of arranging the meeting.

In another e-mail exchange on August 7, Donna thanked Mary and advised her that the FBI would again have access to al-

Quso. Donna continued by stating that the Kuala Lumpur photographs also would be passed to a foreign government because al-Quso was currently in its custody. She stated that John could call if he had any questions. Donna tentatively scheduled a meeting with Mary at FBI Headquarters on August 15, 2001. However, it appears that the meeting did not take place.[236]

[236] Mary told the OIG that she took a week of annual leave during August, which she thought was during that week, and she thought that the meeting therefore had not occurred.

2. Discovery of al-Mihdhar's entry into the United States

August 21:

On August 21, Mary located the CIA cables referencing al-Hazmi's travel to the United States on January 15, 2000. [237] Mary checked with a US Customs Service representative to the CTC about al-Hazmi's and al-Mihdhar's travel. She discovered that al-Mihdhar had entered the United States on July 4, 2001, and had not departed. In addition, she confirmed that al-Hazmi had traveled to the United States in January 2000.

[237] Mary was copied on an e-mail from John to Peter in mid-May, 2001, in which John discussed the travel of al-Mihdhar and others who appeared to be "couriers on a sort." In this e-mail John stated, among other things, that "Nawaf' [al-Hazmi] had traveled with someone from Bangkok to Los Angeles to Hong Kong. Mary stated to the OIG that she received this e-mail before she was "up to speed" on the Malaysia meetings.

Mary immediately relayed to Donna in a voicemail message on August 21 that Mary had something important to discuss with her. Donna was on annual leave on August 21. Mary told the OIG she did not have an opportunity to focus on the Malaysia meetings until August, but upon discovering on August 21 that al-Hazmi had traveled to the United States "it [the importance of the information] all clicks for me."

On August 22, Mary met with Donna at FBI Headquarters and informed her of al-Mihdhar's July 4 entry and al-Hazmi's travel to the United States in March 2000. [238] Donna verified in INS indices al-Mihdhar's recent entry. She also learned that both al-Mihdhar and al-Hazmi had entered the United States on January 15, 2000, and that they were allegedly destined for the Sheraton Hotel in Los Angeles, California. The INS records showed al-Mihdhar had departed the United States from Los

Angeles on June 10, 2000, on Lufthansa Airlines. No departure record could be located for al-Hazmi. An INS representative advised Donna that departure information often was not captured in INS indices. [239] Therefore, she incorrectly surmised al-Hazmi had also departed on June 10, 2000. [240]

[238] There is some discrepancy in witness statements on whether this meeting occurred on August 22 or August 23. Although it is unclear on which date this meeting occurred, we believe the meeting occurred on August 22, 2001.

[239] The problem of INS departure records not being complete or accurate is described in an August 2001 OIG report entitled "The Immigration and Naturalization Service's Automated 1-94 System."

[240] Investigation conducted after September 11 found that al-Hazmi had remained in the United States.

Further INS indices checks confirmed al-Mihdhar had reentered the US on July 4, 2001, at the JFK Airport in New York, allegedly destined for the "Marriott hotel" in New York City. By the terms of his entry, al-Mihdhar was authorized to remain in the United States until October 3, 2001.

Mary and Donna met with John on August 22 in his office at FBI Headquarters to discuss their discovery that al-Mihdhar recently had entered the United States and there was no record of his departure. All of them said they could not recall the specifics of the conversation, but all agreed that they realized it was important to initiate an investigation to determine whether al-Mihdhar was still in the United States and locate him if he was.

On August 22, 2001, Donna sent an e-mail to the New York FBI Special Agent who we call "Glenn." He was one of the agents assigned to the Cole investigation. In the e-mail, Donna advised Glenn that she had obtained al-Mihdhar's flight manifest. Donna also wrote, "The reason they [the Intelligence Community] were looking at Midhar [sic] is relatively general – basically they were looking at all individuals using the name Khalid because of some threat information." Significantly, the e-mail also advised that the CIA had additional surveillance photographs beyond those she had taken to New York, and the source had identified one of the individuals in these additional photographs as Khallad. Donna said that she was "requesting the details on that [Khallad's identification]." Donna also stated in her e-mail that the clearance to show the Kuala

Lumpur surveillance photographs to al-Quso should not be a problem. [241]

[241] Donna was unable to recall how she first discovered the information on the Khallad identification. We were unable to find any documents or other evidence clarifying this issue.

This e-mail was the first reference we identified that the FBI had been informed of additional Kuala Lumpur surveillance photographs in the CIA's possession. It is also the first reference in any FBI document to the identification of Khallad in the Kuala Lumpur photographs. After her meeting with Donna on August 22, 2001, Mary asked another CTC officer to draft a CIR to the State Department, INS, US Customs Service, and FBI requesting the placement of al-Mihdhar and his travel companions, al-Hazmi and Salah Saeed Muhammed bin Yousaf, on US watchlists. [242]

[242] At this time, several agencies maintained separate watchlists. The State Department watchlist was the VISA/VIPER system. Within VISA/VIPER, the TIPOFF system focused on suspected terrorists. The INS maintained the LOOKOUT system, which was also available to the Customs Service through TECS.

The CIR briefly outlined al-Mihdhar's attendance at the Malaysia meetings and his subsequent travel to the US in January 2000 and July 2001. On August 24, the State Department placed al-Mihdhar and his travel companions on its terrorism watchlist. This is the first record of the placement of al-Mihdhar or al-Hazmi on any US watchlist.

On August 23, 2001, Donna contacted the State Department and requested a copy of al-Mihdhar's most recent visa application from the US Consulate in Jeddah, Saudi Arabia.

3. The FBI's intelligence investigation on al-Mihdhar

a. Steps to open the investigation

On August 23, Donna contacted her supervisor, an SSA who we call "Rob," regarding the information about al-Mihdhar's travel to the United States. As discussed in Chapter Three, Rob was the acting Unit Chief of the UBLU at the time. [243]

[243] He was the acting Unit Chief of the UBL from June 28, 2001, until September 10, 2001.

After reviewing the information, Rob concurred with Donna that the appropriate course of action would be to open an intelligence investigation in New York, al-Mihdhar's last known destination in the United States, to locate al-Mihdhar.

To expedite the investigative process and provide a "heads up [alert]" to the New York Field Office that the information was coming, on August 23 Donna telephoned an agent on the Bin Laden squad in the New York Field Office who we call "Chad." To comply with the wall, the New York Field Office had designated agents as either "criminal" or "intelligence," and Chad was an intelligence agent. Donna discussed with Chad al-Mihdhar's most recent entry into the United States and FBI Headquarters' request for the New York office to open a full field intelligence investigation to locate al-Mihdhar. Donna told the OIG that she did not normally telephonically contact the field on these types of issues, but there was some urgency to her request because the FBI did not want to lose the opportunity to locate al-Mihdhar before he left the United States. She told us, however, that al-Mihdhar's significance continued to be his potential connection to Khallad and the Cole attack – not that he was operational in the US.

Chad told the OIG that although he routinely worked with Donna, this was the first time that Donna had relayed a need for urgency in an intelligence investigation. Chad told us, however, that he questioned both the urgency and the need for a separate intelligence investigation. Chad explained that the attempt to locate al-Mihdhar seemed to relate to the criminal investigation of the Cole attack, and efforts to locate an individual normally would be handled through a sub-file to the main investigation and not as a separate full field investigation. Nevertheless, he told Donna that New York would open an intelligence investigation.

On August 23, Donna sent an e-mail to John concerning her telephone conversation with Chad. She advised in the e-mail that "[Chad] will open an intelligence case." In the e-mail she also discussed a connection that had been made between al-Mihdhar in Malaysia to another suspect in the Cole attack. She wrote, "I am still looking at intel, but I think we have more of a definitive connection to the Cole here than we thought." She ended by stating that she was working on the EC requesting a full field investigation, but doubted that it would be completed that day.

On August 27, Donna requested permission through the NSA representative to the FBI to pass to the FBI agents working on the Cole investigation the information associating al-Mihdhar with a suspected terrorist facility in the Middle East linked to al

Qaeda activities. Donna told the OIG that she thought that the NSA information on al-Mihdhar could be useful to the *Cole* criminal investigators, even if the al-Mihdhar search remained an intelligence investigation.

On the morning of August 28, Donna sent Chad a draft copy of an EC requesting the intelligence investigation to locate al-Mihdhar. In the cover e-mail, Donna stated, "here is a draft" and that the EC had not been uploaded due to some tear line information that was not yet approved for passage. [244] She concluded, "I do want to get this going as soon as possible."

[244] According to the NSA, the request was approved later that same day.

The EC, entitled "Khalid M. Al-Mihdhar" with various aliases, stated in the synopsis, "Request to open an intelligence investigation." The EC outlined al-Mihdhar's travel to the United States in July 2001, his previous travel to the United States with al-Hazmi in January 2000, the background on and his attendance at the Malaysia meetings, his association with a suspected terrorist facility in the Middle East linked to al Qaeda activities, and similarities between al-Mihdhar's travel and that of *Cole* suspects al-Quso, Ibrahim al-Nibras, and Khallad. As to the identification of Khallad in the Kuala Lumpur photographs by the source, Donna told the OIG that she did not include this information because it had not yet been officially passed to the FBI, although she had requested the passage from a CTC Representative to the FBI. [245] While Donna had relayed urgency to opening the investigation in her telephone conversation with Chad and in her cover e-mail, she designated the EC precedence as "routine," the lowest precedence level. [246] She explained this by saying this case was "no bigger" than any other intelligence case. She also told us, however, that there was a time consideration because al-Mihdhar could be leaving the United States at any time and that is why she had personally contacted Chad.

[245] This information officially was passed to the FBI in a CIR on August 30, 2001.

[246] As discussed in Chapter Three, ECs are marked with a precedence level based on an escalating scale beginning at "routine;" "priority," connoting some urgency; and "immediate," connoting the highest level of urgency.

b.   **The FBI opens the intelligence investigation**

On August 28, Chad forwarded Donna's draft EC to his immediate supervisor, a Supervisory Special Agent who we call "Jason." Jason became a supervisor on the JTTF in the New York Field Office in 1996. He had been on the New York JTTF since 1985.

At approximately 2:00 pm on August 28, Jason forwarded the EC to various agents on the Bin Laden squad, including the *Cole* criminal case agent who we call "Scott." In the cover e-mail, Jason directed the Relief Supervisor, who we call "Jay," to open an intelligence investigation and assign it to a Special Agent who we call "Richard." Jason also directed another agent to check on an investigative lead related to al-Mihdhar while the agent was in Malaysia. [247]

[247] Jason told the OIG that he did not specifically recall this e-mail. He said he was out of the office the majority of the time from June until September 11, 2001, due to a serious medical condition, and he did not return to work full-time until September 11, 2001.

Scott received the EC on August 28. Scott, who had been at the June 11 meeting and had discussions with Donna about the Kuala Lumpur photographs, contacted Donna to discuss the appropriateness of opening an intelligence investigation as opposed to a criminal investigation. Donna told the OIG that when she realized that the EC had been disseminated to Scott, she asked Scott to delete it because it contained NSA information and therefore required approval for review by criminal agents. Scott told the OIG that he deleted the EC as she requested.

Shortly thereafter, Scott, Donna, and Rob engaged in a conference call to discuss whether the case should be opened as a criminal instead of an intelligence investigation. Scott told the OIG that he argued that the investigation should be opened as a criminal investigation due to the nexus to the *Cole* investigation and the greater investigative resources that could be brought to bear in a criminal investigation. Scott explained that more agents could be assigned to a criminal investigation due to the squad designations. He also asserted that criminal investigation tools, such as grand jury subpoenas, were far quicker and easier to obtain than the tools available in an intelligence investigation, such as a national security letter.

Donna told the OIG that the information on al-Mihdhar was received through intelligence channels and, because of restrictions on using intelligence information, could not be provided directly to the criminal agents working the *Cole* investigation. The only information that could be provided directly to them was the limited INS information. She stated that without the intelligence information on al-Mihdhar, there would have been no potential nexus to the *Cole* investigation and no basis for a criminal investigation. Rob told the OIG he had concurred with Donna's assessment that the matter should be an intelligence investigation. He added that there was also a process through which the information could potentially be shared with the criminal agents in the future. [248]

Scott was not satisfied with that response, and he asked for a legal opinion from the FBI's National Security Law Unit (NSLU) whether the investigation should be opened as a criminal matter relating to the *Cole* criminal investigation. Additionally, Scott wanted a legal opinion on whether a criminal agent could accompany an intelligence agent to interview al-Mihdhar if he was located.

[248] Rob told the OIG that the squad's Supervisory Special Agent acted as "the wall" between intelligence and criminal investigations during this period, and Jason could subsequently open a criminal investigation if warranted.

According to Donna, she subsequently contacted the NSLU attorney who we call "Susan" on August 28, and she and Rob discussed the issue with Susan. It is unclear how she presented the matter to Susan because there were no documents about the conversation and she and Susan had little or no recollection of the specific conversation. Donna told the OIG that she provided the EC to Susan. According to Donna, Susan agreed with her that the matter should be opened as an intelligence investigation. Donna said Susan also advised that a criminal agent should not be present for an interview of al-Mihdhar if he was located. During an OIG interview, Susan said she could not specifically recall this matter or the advice she gave. Rob told the OIG that he did not recall the specifics of this consultation, but he stated that the NSLU opinion was supportive of FBI Headquarters' determination that the case should be opened as an intelligence investigation.

At approximately 7:30 am on August 29, Donna sent an e-mail to Jason, which stated:

I think I might have caused some unnecessary confusion. I sent the EC on Al-Midhar [sic] to [Chad] via e-mail, marking it as DRAFT so he could read it before he went on vacation. There is material in the EC, which is not cleared for criminal investigators. [Scott] called and [Rob] and I spoke with him and tried to explain why this case had to stay on the intel side of the house. In order to be confident for this case to be a 199, and to answer some questions that [Scott] had, [Rob] and I spoke with the NSLU yesterday afternoon. [249] The opinion is as follows: Al-Mihdar [sic] can be opened directly as a FFI [Full Field Investigation]. The EC is still not cleared for criminal investigators... Per NSLU, if Al-Mihdar [sic] is located, the interview must be conducted by an intel agent. A criminal agent CAN NOT be present at the interview. This case, in its entirety, is based on intel. If information is developed indicating the existence of a substantial federal crime, that information will be passed over the wall according to the proper procedures and turned over for follow-up criminal investigation. [250]

[249] Rob told the OIG that he could not recall whether he had talked to anyone from the NSLU about this issue.

[250] Rob told the OIG that the New York Field Office technically could have ignored Headquarters' recommendation and opened a criminal investigation. However as a practical matter, the field would not normally ignore Headquarters' decision.

Approximately 15 minutes after sending the e-mail to Jason, Donna sent an e-mail to Scott with the same language advising that the NSLU agreed the investigation should be an intelligence investigation and a criminal agent could not attend the interview if al-Mihdhar was located. That same morning, Scott responded in an e-mail to Donna stating:

...where is the wall defined? Isn't it dealing with FISA information? I think everyone is still confusing this issue ... someday someone will die – and wall or not – the public will not understand why we were not more effective and throwing every resource we had at certain 'problems.' Let's hope the National Security Law Unit will stand by their decisions then, especially since the biggest threat to us now, UBL, is getting the most 'protection.'

Later that morning, Donna replied in an e-mail:

I don't think you understand that we (FBI HQ) are all frustrated with this issue. I don't know what to tell you. I don't know how many other ways I can tell this to you. These are the rules.

NSLU does not make them up and neither does UBLU. They are in the MIOG [251] and ordered by the [FISA] Court and every office of the FBI is required to follow them including FBI NY...

[251] The MIOG is the FBI operational manual – Manual of Investigative Operations and Guidelines. Donna asserted this reference actually related to the Attorney General's FBI Guidelines that are contained in the MIOG.

4. The New York Field Office's investigation

On August 29, 2001, the FBI's New York Field Office opened a full field intelligence investigation to locate al-Mihdhar. The investigation was assigned to a Special Agent who we call "Richard." Richard was a relatively inexperienced agent, who had recently been transferred to the Bin Laden squad. [252] This was Richard's first intelligence investigation.

[252] Richard began working in the New York Field Office after graduating from the FBI Academy in June 2000. After serving briefly on an applicant squad, a drug squad, and a surveillance squad, Richard was assigned to the UBL squad in July 2001.

On August 29, Donna received al-Mihdhar's visa application from the US Consulate in Jeddah. The application indicated that al-Mihdhar planned to travel as a tourist to the United States on July 1, 2001, for a purported month-long stay. On the application, al-Mihdhar falsely claimed that he had not previously applied for a US non-immigrant visa or been in the United States. [253]

[253] Donna said she did not notice this discrepancy. As we discuss below, neither did the New York FBI.

On August 30, 2001, Donna sent an e-mail to Richard. After a paragraph introducing herself, Donna advised she was attaching al-Mihdhar's visa application form, which included al-Mihdhar's photograph, and that she would be faxing the remaining documents. Donna stated she would send a couple of pages from the Attorney General Guidelines "which apply to your case" and then she would mail the documents.

Richard told the OIG that on August 30, he received a telephone call from Donna in reference to the investigation. He said that Donna said the goal of the intelligence investigation was to locate and identify al-Mihdhar for a potential interview. According to Richard, Donna did not indicate the investigation was an emergency or identify any other exigent circumstance. On August 30, 2001, the CIA sent a CIR to the FBI outlining the identification of "Khallad" from one of the Kuala Lumpur surveillance photographs in January 2001 by the source. The first line of the text stated the information should be passed to Rob. The CIA cable stated the FBI should advise the CIA if the FBI did not have the Kuala Lumpur photographs so they may be provided. This is the first record documenting that the source's identification of Khallad in the Kuala Lumpur photographs was provided by the CIA to the FBI.

Richard told the OIG that he began to work on locating al-Mihdhar on September 4. He stated that he had received the assignment on Thursday, August 30, but he worked all weekend and Monday on another exigent investigative matter involving a Canadian hijacking. As a result, he said he did not have the opportunity to begin work on the al-Mihdhar investigation until Tuesday, September 4.

On September 4, Richard completed a lookout request for the INS, identifying al-Mihdhar as a potential witness in a terrorist investigation. Due to his unfamiliarity with completing the lookout form, Richard contacted an INS Special Agent who was assigned to the FBI's JTTF in New York. We call this Special Agent "Patrick." The INS lookout form has a box indicating whether the individual was wanted for "security/terrorism" reasons.

Richard did not check this box. He said that he thought Patrick told him to identify the subject on the form as a witness, not a potential terrorist, to prevent overzealous immigration officials from overreacting.

By contrast, Patrick, who was assigned to the JTTF since September 1996, told us that he did not provide this advice to Richard and he always checked the security/terrorism box whenever he completed the lookout form for a potential witness in a terrorism investigation. However, Richard asked Patrick to review the lookout request form for completeness, and Patrick sent the form to INS Inspections for inclusion in the INS lookout system, without making any changes. [254] During his initial interview with the OIG, Richard asserted that he also asked Patrick to review and explain al-Mihdhar's travel documents, including the INS indices printouts and the visa application. In a follow-up interview, Richard said he could not definitively recall whether he had actually provided the predicating materials to Patrick or whether he merely had Patrick review the INS lookout request form.

Patrick told the OIG that he recalled this request because it was the first one from Richard and because of al-Mihdhar's subsequent involvement in the September 11 attacks. Patrick stated that he had not reviewed the predicating materials, but had only checked the request form for completeness. He added that if he had been shown any of the predicating materials on al-Mihdhar's travel, the review would only have been cursory. Patrick and Richard both acknowledged that they did not notice the false statements on al-Mihdhar's visa application.

Richard also contacted a US Customs Service representative assigned to the JTTF and verified that a TECS lookout was in place for al-Mihdhar. Richard conducted other administrative tasks such as uploading the initial information about al-Mihdhar into ACS.

On September 4, Richard requested a local criminal history check on al-Mihdhar through the New York City Police Department. Richard told the OIG that he initially focused on al-Mihdhar, since he was captioned as the subject of the investigation in the predicating EC. After reviewing the EC several times, Richard noted the connection to al-Hazmi, so he conducted the same record checks on al-Hazmi as he had on al-Mihdhar. On September 5, Richard requested an NCIC criminal history check, credit checks, and motor vehicle records be searched in reference to al-Mihdhar and al-Hazmi.

On September 5, Richard and another JTTF agent contacted the loss prevention personnel for the New York area Marriott hotels, since al-Mihdhar had indicated when he entered the United States in July 2001 that his destination was the Marriott hotel in New York. Richard learned that al-Mihdhar had not registered as a guest at six New York City Marriotts.

Richard stated he also conducted Choicepoint™ searches on al-Hazmi and al-Mihdhar. 255 Richard said he recalled he had another JTTF officer assist him with the searches because he was not familiar with the system. Richard did not locate any records on either al-Hazmi or al-Mihdhar in Choicepoint™. 256

255 Choicepoint™ is a commercial service that mines information such as names, addresses, phone numbers, and

other identifying information from public sources (such as telephone directories, local taxing authorities, and court records), as well as purchase information from merchants or other companies. The information is then consolidated into a large database and is accessible to law enforcement and other subscribers for a fee. [256] After September 11, however, the FBI located records on al-Hazmi in this commercial database.

Richard told the OIG that it was not uncommon not to find a record because of variations in spelling of names or other identifying information.

Al-Hazmi and al-Mihdhar had traveled to Los Angeles, CA, on January 15, 2000, via United Airlines, and INS records indicated that they claimed to be destined for a "Sheraton hotel" in Los Angeles. Therefore, on September 10, 2001, Richard drafted an investigative lead for the FBI Los Angeles Field Office. He asked that office to request a search of the Sheraton hotel records concerning any stays by al-Mihdhar and al-Hazmi in early 2000. He also requested that the Los Angeles office check United Airlines and Lufthansa Airlines records for any payment or other information concerning al-Mihdhar and al-Hazmi. However, the lead was not transmitted to Los Angeles until the next day, September 11, 2001.

By the morning of September 11, when the American Airlines Flight 77 that al-Mihdhar and al-Hazmi hijacked and crashed into the Pentagon, Richard had not uncovered any information regarding al-Mihdhar's or al-Hazmi's location in the United States.

From *Stern* [German magazine], "The Deadly Mistakes of the US Intelligence Agency (Part 1)," August 13, 2003:

Washington, September 11, 2001

At 8:50 am, CIA director George Tenet is sitting at his breakfast table in the St. Regis Hotel, only a few blocks away from the White House. He is together with David L. Boren, former senator of Oklahoma, an old friend and supporter.

Their talk was abruptly interrupted: Security personnel enters the room. "Mr. Director," one of them says, "there is a serious problem."

"What's the matter?" Tenet asked. The security officer hesitates. Tenet indicates that he should speak freely even in the presence of Boren. "A tower of the WTC has been attacked." Another guard offers Tenet a mobile phone. Tenet at once calls the CIA [sic] Headquarter in Langley and asks for details.

"They steered the plane directly into the building?" he asks incredulously. He orders his closest employees to the conference room and wants to be there himself within 15 minutes. "That looks like bin Laden," Tenet said to Boren. Without waiting for a reaction Tenet thinks aloud: "I wonder if this has something to do with the guy who trained for a pilot's license."

After reviewing all of this information, there are many unanswered questions.

Why had the CIA known about Mihdhar and Hazmi for 21 months and then not provide this information to the FBI, and not even watchlist these terrorists until August 23, 2001? Why did the CIA not connect these al Qaeda terrorists to the huge al Qaeda attack the CIA knew was just about to occur inside of the US? Why did the CIA not connect the fact that Khalid Sheikh Mohammed was sending a large number of al Qaeda terrorists into the US in June of 2001 to link up with other al Qaeda terrorists already inside of the US to the huge attack the CIA knew was imminent?

In order to better understand what went on, a time-line from May 2001 to September 11, 2001 is listed below:

Summary of FBI IG time-line, May - September 11, 2001
(Pages 284-311 FBI IG Report)

May - June 11, 2001

From the FBI IG report: "While there were several interactions between FBI and CIA personnel in May and June 2001 that could have resulted in the FBI learning more about the Kuala Lumpur photographs and al-Mihdhar, the FBI personnel did not become aware of significant intelligence information about al-Mihdhar and his connections to Khallad at any point during this period. The fact that al-Mihdhar had possessed a United States visa was not disclosed at this time by the CIA to Donna or the FBI. The CIA also did not disclose the fact that al-Hazmi had been at the Malaysia meeting and then traveled to Los Angeles. In addition, the fact that the source had identified Khallad, the purported mastermind of the *Cole* bombing, from the Kuala

Lumpur surveillance photographs was not disclosed to the FBI by the CIA during these interactions.

Mid May 2001

Around the same time that Donna was discussing al-Quso and the *Cole* investigation with Peter and John, she also was planning a meeting at the New York FBI Office to discuss the *Cole* investigation. The planned participants for the New York meeting included personnel from FBI Headquarters, the CIA's CTC, and the New York FBI agents working on the *Cole* investigation. FBI documents show that Donna began organizing the meeting as early as May 24.

Attendees of June 11, 2001 meeting in FBI IG report included a number of people.

- CIA Supervisor "Peter." who told the FBI IG investigators he was just tagging along to this meeting.

- FBI IOS "Donna", working at FBI Headquaters, in the UBL unit.

- FBI analyst Mary working at Alec Station, the Bin Laden Unit of the CIA.

- FBI New York *Cole* investigator "Scott" in FBI IG report.

- Former CIA Bin Laden Deputy Chief working at the ITOS section of FBI, "John." While he was not actually at this meeting in New York, he was the one who had obtained three photographs of Mihdhar taken at the Kula Lumpur meeting and gave these to Donna to take to the meeting. After 9/11, investigators found out that one photograph had only Mihdhar and Hazmi in it. John had transferred to the FBI ITOS unit in May 2001.

Summarizing the story of the June 11 meeting in New York with the Cole investigators:

The following is the description of the meeting between the CIA and the FBI in New York on June 11, 2001. While several government investigations looked at this meeting and what had taken place just prior to this meeting, no investigation figured out why this meeting had been called in the first place and what exactly went on at this meeting.

Information to share

"According to FBI personnel in New York, Donna told them that FBI Headquarters and CIA personnel had indicated they had "information to share" regarding the *Cole* investigation. The FBI New York personnel anticipated the meeting would be a mutual exchange of information. Scott, one of the New York case agents on the *Cole* investigation, said he was told that the CIA representatives who would be attending the meeting wanted a briefing on the *Cole* investigation."

There is no record of what was the "information to share" regarding the *Cole* investigation that FBI Headquarters and CIA personnel had. It turns out that the information at this meeting went almost exclusively in one direction, from the FBI *Cole* investigators and the *Cole* investigation, to the CIA. Virtually no information went back to the *Cole* investigators from the CIA. Although the CIA showed photographs of Khalid al-Mihdhar and Nawaf al-Hazmi together at the Kuala Lumpur meeting, and did give them the name Khalid al-Mihdhar and the fact he had a Saudi passport, they refused to give the *Cole* investigators any more information, in particular the passport number of al-Mihdhar.

According to the account by the FBI IG, the CIA claimed they did ask if the *Cole* investigators could identify al-Quso in any of the photographs they were shown. But when asked by the *Cole* investigators, the CIA refused to say why they were interested in the people in the photographs, and refused to tell the *Cole* investigators that there were more photographs from the Kuala Lumpur meeting and that the person the Cole investigators were most interested in, Khallad bin Attash had been at the Kuala Lumpur planning meeting with Mihdhar and Hazmi.

> Scott told the OIG that after reviewing the Kuala Lumpur photographs, the FBI agents began to ask questions, such as whether there were additional photographs or information concerning the background on the photographs, including questions about al-Mihdhar, who was in the photographs. According to Scott, he pressed Donna and Peter for details of the Malaysia meetings. Scott told the OIG he was interested in the fact that the photographs were from Malaysia because from the al-Quso's debriefings he knew that Khallad had planned to meet al-Quso in Malaysia, and any information

linking Khallad to Malaysia was "directly related" to the *Cole* investigation.

Scott contended that Donna "refused" to provide any further information about the photographs or the Malaysia meetings due to "the wall."

Clearly the *Cole* investigators were not interested in knowing if al-Quso had traveled to Malaysia, but in the fact that al-Quso had said he was going to meet Khallad in Malaysia. If the photos were of a meeting in Malaysia that occurred about the same time Khallad had been in Kuala Lumpur, and they showed a number of other people, then these people must also have been linked to Khallad and the *Cole* bombing. Even though the CIA supervisor, Peter, who attended the meeting knew about Khallad and the photograph of Khallad at the Kuala Lumpur meeting, knew that al-Mihdhar and Nawaf had been at this same meeting and even knew that Nawaf was inside of the US, he said nothing. John also had this same information, yet he did not provide this information to Donna, or allowed this information to be passed to the FBI *Cole* investigators. This is not only a criminal felony, obstructing an on going criminal investigation into the murder of 17 US sailors by the al Qaeda terrorists, but allowed 3000 people to be murdered by these same al Qaeda terrorist on 9/11, and no one to this day has provided any even a semi-reasonable explaination for this.

Around this same time, FBI IOS Donna and other FBI IOSs working on the *Cole* investigation were focusing on al-Quso's connection to Bangkok and his trip to deliver money to Khallad. The FBI, like the CIA, was aware that in January 2000 al-Quso had planned to travel to Malaysia to take money to Khallad. According to an FBI document drafted by Donna in May 2001, al-Quso had claimed that on January 6, 2000, he and Ibrahim al-Nibras went to Bangkok first but were unable to travel on to Kuala Lumpur because of problems with their travel documents, and Khallad had traveled to Bangkok to meet them there instead.

Donna told the OIG that she and others were tracking the information related to the telephone numbers associated with al-Quso in an attempt to determine the truth of his statements. In addition, she said that she was focused on the identity and whereabouts of Khallad, since he was the purported mastermind of the *Cole* attack.

But how did Donna find out about the telephone numbers associated with al-Quso, in her attempt to determine the truth of his statements?

She clearly found out about the telephone numbers from the FBI investigation of al-Quso. CIA Supervisor, Peter had given her this phone number to a phone in Kuala Lumpur, as is described in the following FBI IG testimony:

> Peter told the OIG that he recalled talking to FBI IOSs, including Donna, about mapping the telephone number information based on information provided by Quso. But he said that he did not recall discussions with Donna about the Kuala Lumpur photographs or the Khallad identification.

Malaysian intelligence had given the CIA a log that had this exact number. And Donna further states that she was focused on the identity and whereabouts of Khallad, since he was the mastermind of the *Cole* attack. According to Donna's own words, she sets up a meeting with the *Cole* investigator to ask if they could identify al-Quso in three photographs she was given. The only other name she was given of people in these photos was the name Khalid al-Mihdhar.

> Donna told the OIG she had provided to the agents all the information she had received from the CIA regarding the photographs. She told us that all she knew was that these three photographs were taken in Malaysia around the Millennium, and one of the persons in the photographs was someone named Khalid al-Mihdhar.

She states that she writes on the back of one of the photographs, that these are of Mihdhar at meeting in Kuala Lumpur. From the FBI's investigation of al-Quso, Donna knows that Khallad had been in Kuala Lumpur at exactly the same time, and now knows that Khalid al-Mihdhar had been at the same location. She knows that Khallad had been identified as the mastermind of the *Cole* bombing. When she goes to the June 11, 2001 meeting with the FBI, she states that she provided all of the information she had obtained from the CIA regarding the photographs, but she does not tell the *Cole* investigators that Khalid al-Mihdhar and Khallad had been at the same meeting. She is clearly not telling the FBI IG the whole story.

> "It was impossible for us to determine exactly what happened at the June 11 meeting with respect to the Kuala Lumpur

photographs because the witnesses cannot recall the specifics of the discussions and there is little documentary evidence. It is clear, however, that the information regarding al-Mihdhar's US visa and the fact that Khallad had been identified in the Kuala Lumpur photographs was not discussed at the June 11 meeting."

Reason given for setting up the meeting on June 11, 2001

This testimony by Donna and Peter appears to be complete nonsense.

"According to Donna, Peter had raised the photographs in a discussion with her prior to her obtaining the photographs from John, although she said that she did not recall the details of their discussion about the photographs. Donna said she did recall that, at the time, Peter had posited that one of the photographs could relate to al-Quso, which if true would contradict Quso's statements about going only to Bangkok and not going to Malaysia. According to Donna, the FBI was attempting to determine the veracity of al-Quso's information, so the photographs potentially were connected to the Cole investigation."

Al-Quso had no reason to lie about not being allowed to travel to Kuala Lumpur, and having to go to Bangkok instead to deliver the money he was bringing from Yemen to Khallad, and both the CIA and the FBI was aware of this.

Al-Quso had been in jail in Yemen for six months by the time of this meeting took place, and had been interviewed many times by the FBI. It would have made little difference to the Cole investigators if the money al-Quso delivered to Khallad were delivered to him in Kuala Lumpur or in Bangkok. Either way Khallad would have had his money.

If the CIA wanted to identify al-Quso in these photographs they could also have had the CIA station in Yemen wire back pictures of him, since he was in a Yemeni jail, or they could have just e-mailed these photos to the Cole investigators in New York, instead of having two CIA employees and a FBI UBL unit employee travel from Washington DC to New York for this identification. It is clear, however, that they did not want to give these photographs to the FBI Cole investigators. They only wanted the Cole investigators to have them look at these photos briefly and not take possession of them.

Real reason for New York meeting with *Cole* investigators

So if the CIA was not actually interested in knowing if the *Cole* investigators could identify al-Quso at the Kuala Lumpur meeting, what then was the real reason the CIA requested a meeting in New York with the *Cole* investigators?

When John requested photographs from the CIA he asked for photos of al-Mihdhar from the Kuala Lumpur meeting.

Twelve people had been photographed at the Malaysia meeting but John only gets photographs of al-Mihdhar.

Then John says that he does not see Khallad in any of the three photographs of Mihdhar, the photos he requested from the CIA, but then asks if there is a cable that documented the identification of Khallad.

> "In addition to reviewing the East Asia travel of several bin Laden operatives in January 2000, John also began looking in CIA records for the Kuala Lumpur photographs. John obtained three of them. John told the OIG that he had not read the cable stating that the joint source had identified Khallad in the photographs, but he was aware that an identification of Khallad in the photographs had been made. At the end of his e-mail to Peter, John stated that he had obtained three surveillance photographs of al-Mihdhar in Malaysia, but he did not see "Khallad" in any of the photographs, and he believed he was "missing something" or "someone saw something that wasn't there." John also questioned whether there was a cable somewhere that documented the identification of Khallad... [223]
>
> [223] As noted above, John was correct – Khallad was not in any of these three photographs. After September 11 it was learned that the person the source had identified as Khallad was actually Hazmi. It was also learned after September 11, however, that Khallad was in another Kuala Lumpur surveillance photograph that had not been shown to the source.

How would John know if Khallad were not in any of the three photos if he did not know what Khallad already looked like in the first place? If John did not actually have the cable that identified Khallad at the Kuala Lumpur meeting, where did he get the photograph of Khallad that he used to identify Khallad in the photos? John could not have had the photo of Khallad taken at the Kuala Lumpur meeting; the photograph the CIA gave the FBI on August 30, 2001. If he had he would had immediately known that Khallad was not in the same photograph with Khalid al-Mihdhar but in a completely different photograph. So exactly where did John get the photo he was using to identify Khallad? With each unanswered question, the mystery surrounding this meeting deepens.

And why was John looking for Khallad in the photographs of Mihdhar in the first place? What had triggered this search, the FBI IG report never provides the reason for John's search for Khallad in these photographs.

When John gave these photos to Donna to show to the *Cole* investigators, she was only told the name of one person in the photos, Khalid al-Mihdhar, and that the photos had been taken at a meeting in Kuala Lumpur.

Even though she must have known that Khallad had been at this same meeting, she was given no photos of Khallad. But the CIA, including both John and Peter, were aware that Khallad had directed the *Cole* bombing, so not giving Donna a photo of Khallad from the Kuala Lumpur meeting, with photos of al-Mihdhar at this same meeting, makes no sense.

Providing photos to the *Cole* investigators with Khallad along with Khalid al-Mihdhar and Nawaf al-Hazmi would have been important to the *Cole* investigation. It would have made a huge difference for the *Cole* investigation to know that Khallad had been in one of the Kuala Lumpur photos taken at the Kuala Lumpur meeting along with Khalid al-Midhar and Nawaf al-Hazmi, and it would have been extremely important for the FBI to know that al-Hazmi was already in the US. The *Cole* investigators would have focused an immense amount on energy on these two terrorists, Mihdhar and Hazmi since they would now be directly connected to the person who had masterminded the *Cole* bombing and the planning of this attack.

In spite of the fact that Donna knew that Khallad must have been at the Kuala Lumpur meeting with Khalid al-Mihdhar, when asked about the photos and the people in these photos and if there are other photos, she only gives them the name Khalid al-Mihdhar but nothing else. She says the "wall" prevented her from passing any additional information to the FBI Cole investigators.

In addition, both John and Peter knew this same information as well as knowing that al-Mihdhar had a multi-entry visa for the US, and that Nawaf al-Hazmi had traveled to the US on January 15, 2000, just after the Kuala Lumpur meeting. In fact, it appears all of this was common knowledge at the Bin Laden Unit, the Alec Station at the CIA at least amongst the CIA supervisors.

When asked about these photos by the Cole investigators, Peter, a CIA supervisor who later tells the FBI IG that he had no official role at this meeting and was just tagging along, gives them the fact that Mihdhar had a Saudi passport but then gives them nothing else.

Since the only persons known to be in one these photos were Khalid al-Mihdhar and Nawaf al-Hazmi, it seems like the only reason this meeting was set up in the first place was to see if the Cole investigators could identify al-Mihdhar and al-Hazmi. Had the FBI Cole investigators uncovered information that the CIA had kept secret up to this point, the identity of these two terrorists and the fact that they had been seen together with Khallad at the al Qaeda planning meeting in Kuala Lumpur?

After the meeting on June 11, 2001

"There was no record of an agenda for the meeting, and no supervisors were involved in the preparation for this meeting or were consulted regarding what should be accomplished at the meeting. Donna told the OIG that she organized the meeting in an effort to consolidate information and determine what further action was warranted on the *Cole* investigation." FBI IG Report

From reviewing the information given to the FBI IG investigators prior to this meeting, both Peter and John deliberately did not give all of the information they had on the Kuala Lumpur meeting to either Mary or Donna, the fact that Khallad was seen with al-Mihdhar and Nawaf and the fact that Nawaf was in the US. This makes it clear that senior CIA managers just did not trust this information with FBI IOSs.

Later in July, estimated to be July 24, 2001

Later in July, Mary drafted a cable to another CIA office requesting follow-up information about the Malaysia meetings. The cable included a reference to the source's identification of Khallad in one of the Kuala Lumpur photographs and that Khallad and al-Mihdhar had been in Malaysia at the same time, possibly together. A week later, the CTC supervisor forwarded the cable to John for his review prior to release, and the cable was sent to the office to which it was addressed three days after that. On the same day she drafted the cable referencing the source's identification of Khallad, Mary located one of the CIA cables referencing al-Mihdhar's possession of a US visa. On the same date, Mary also reviewed the CIA cable that stated this visa information had been passed to the FBI in January 2000...

Mary knows by July 24, 2001, that Khallad and al-Mihdhar were both at the Kuala Lumpur meetings; information that John, Peter, and Donna had been aware of at the time of the New York meeting on June 11, 2001 that al-Mihdhar has a multi-entry visa for the US. She also knows that this information had been hidden from the Cole investigators at the June 11, 2001 meeting.

August 21

On August 21, Mary located the CIA cables referencing al-Hazmi's travel to the United States on January 15, 2000. Mary checked with a US Customs Service representative to the CTC about al-Hazmi's and al-Mihdhar's travel. She discovered that al-Mihdhar had entered the United States on July 4, 2001, and had not departed. In addition, she confirmed that al-Hazmi had traveled to the United States in January 2000.

On August 21, 2001, Mary finds out that al-Hazmi had entered the US on January 15, 2000. This information, along with the information that Khallad and al-Mihdhar were seen together in the Kuala Lumpur meeting is the exact same information that John, and Peter were aware of on May 15, 2001. This is the information in fact that John had when he asked the CIA to have Mary come up to speed on that date, and the exact same information that the CIA, the Bin Laden Unit including almost all of the CIA's upper management had from information received in early January 2000 and on March 15, 2001. Yet she is alarmed enough to contact a US Customs Service representative at the CTC, to find out about al-Hazmi's and al-Mihdhar's travel. She finds out that al-Hazmi entered the US on January 15, 2000 and had never left and that al-Mihdhar had originally enetered the US on January 15, 2000, left the US in June 2000, and had then reentered the US on July 4, 2001.

August 22, 2001

Mary met with Donna, at FBI Headquarters and informed her of al-Mihdhar's July 4 entry and al-Hazmi's travel to the United States in March 2000. Donna verified in INS indices al-Mihdhar's recent entry. She also learned that both al-Mihdhar and al-Hazmi had entered the United States on January 15, 2000, and that they were allegedly destined for the Sheraton Hotel in Los Angeles, California.

....

Mary and Donna met with John on August 22 in his office at FBI Headquarters to discuss their discovery that al-Mihdhar recently had entered the United States and there was no record of his departure. All of them said they could not recall the specifics of the conversation, but all agreed that they realized it was important to initiate an investigation to determine whether al-Mihdhar was still in the United States and locate him if he was.

Donna sent an e-mail to the New York FBI Special Agent who we call "Glenn." He was one of the agents assigned to the *Cole* investigation. In the e-mail, Donna advised Glenn that she had obtained al-Mihdhar's flight manifest. Donna also wrote, "The reason they [the Intelligence Community] were looking at Midhar [sic] is relatively general – basically they were looking at all individuals using the name Khalid because of some threat information." Significantly, the e-mail also advised that the CIA had additional surveillance photographs beyond those she had taken to New York, and the source had identified one of the individuals in these additional photographs as Khallad. .. This e-mail was the first reference we identified that the FBI had been informed of additional Kuala Lumpur surveillance photographs in the CIA's possession. It is also the first reference in any FBI document to the identification of Khallad in the Kuala Lumpur photographs.

After her meeting with Donna on August 22, 2001, Mary asked another CTC officer to draft a CIR to the State Department, INS, US Customs Service, and FBI requesting the placement of al-Mihdhar and his travel companions, al-Hazmi and Salah Saeed Muhammed bin Yousaf, on US watchlists... The CIR briefly outlined al-Mihdhar's attendance at the Malaysia meetings and his subsequent travel to the US in January 2000 and July 2001. On August 24, the State Department placed al-Mihdhar and his travel companions on its terrorism watchlist.

This is the first record of the placement of al-Mihdhar or al-Hazmi on any US watchlist.

August 23, 2001

....

To expedite the investigative process and provide a "heads up [alert]" to the New York Field Office that the information was coming, on August 23 Donna telephoned an agent on the Bin Laden squad in the New York Field Office who we call "Chad." To comply with the wall, the New York Field Office had designated agents as either "criminal" or "intelligence," and Chad was an intelligence agent. Donna discussed with Chad al-Mihdhar's most recent entry into the United States and FBI Headquarters' request for the New York office to open a full field intelligence investigation to locate al-Mihdhar. Donna told the OIG that she did not normally telephonically contact the field on these types of issues, but there was some urgency to her request because the FBI did not want to lose the opportunity to locate al-Mihdhar before he left the United States. She told us, however, that al-Mihdhar's significance continued to be his potential connection to Khallad and the *Cole* attack – not that he was operational in the US.

Chad told the OIG that although he routinely worked with Donna, this was the first time that Donna had relayed a need for urgency in an intelligence investigation. On August 23, Donna sent an e-mail to John concerning her telephone conversation with Chad. She advised in the e-mail that "[Chad] will open an intelligence case." In the e-mail she also discussed a connection that had been made between al-Mihdhar in Malaysia to another suspect in the *Cole* attack. She wrote, "I am still looking at intel, but I think we have more of a definitive connection to the *Cole* here than we thought." She ended by stating that she was working on the EC requesting a full field investigation, but doubted that it would be completed that day.

August 27, 2001

On August 27, Donna requested permission through the NSA representative to the FBI to pass to the FBI agents working on the *Cole* investigation the information associating al-Mihdhar with a suspected terrorist facility in the Middle East linked to al Qaeda activities. Donna told the OIG that she thought that the NSA information on al-Mihdhar could be useful to the *Cole* criminal investigators, even if the al-Mihdhar search remained an intelligence investigation.

On the morning of August 28, Donna sent Chad a draft copy of an EC requesting the intelligence investigation to locate al-Mihdhar. In the cover e-mail, Donna stated, "here is a draft" and that the EC had not been uploaded due to some tear line information that was not yet approved for passage... She concluded, "I do want to get this going as soon as possible."

The EC, entitled "Khalid M. Al-Mihdhar" with various aliases, stated in the synopsis, "Request to open an intelligence investigation." The EC outlined al-Mihdhar's travel to the United States in July 2001, his previous travel to the United States with al-Hazmi in January 2000, the background on and his attendance at the Malaysia meetings, his association with a suspected terrorist facility in the Middle East linked to al Qaeda activities, and similarities between al-Mihdhar's travel and that of *Cole* suspects al-Quso, Ibrahim al-Nibras, and Khallad. As to the identification of Khallad in the Kuala Lumpur photographs by the source, Donna told the OIG that she did not include this information because it had not yet been officially passed to the FBI, although she had requested the passage from a CTC Representative to the FBI...

On August 21, 2001 Mary found the cable that said al-Hazmi had entered the US on January 15, 2000. When she contacted US Customs and she found out that al-Mihdhar had entered the US on July 4, 2001, she contacts Donna and they both visit John in his office at the FBI.

While the CIA transferred over to the FBI the photographs of Mihdhar and Hamzi from the Kuala Lumpur meeting on the very next day August 23, 2001, no one could explain why this information had not been sent to the FBI prior to this date. And still unexplained is why the photograph of Khallad, taken at the Kuala Lumpur meeting remained hidden from the FBI for eight more days, and was not sent to the FBI until August 30, 2001. This photograph remained hidden from the FBI until one day after the FBI had opened this search and investigation for Mihdhar as an intelligence investigation. This does not look at all like just a simple coincidence!

Donna had promised Scott at the June 11, 2001 meeting in New York between the FBI and the CIA to provide additional information that the CIA had on Khalid al-Mihdhar, the person who was identified as one of the people in at the Kuala Lumpur meeting photographs. When the EC was sent over to the FBI New York field office, written by Donna, Scott was sent a copy of this EC and requested that the investigation and search for Mihdhar be given to his team of experienced FBI investigators already investigating the Cole bombing. This EC did it not say that Khallad had been at the Kuala Lumpur meeting with Mihdhar or that the CIA had photographed them both at this meeting. In what can only be called an act of absolute treachery, when Donna found out her EC had gone to Scott with the very information on Mihdhar she had promised to give him at the Kuala Lumpur meeting, she tells Scott he has to destroy the information he has on Mihdhar and that he would not even be allowed to be present when Mihdhar was arrested and interviewed! When she had told Scott at the June 11, 2001 meeting she would give him additional information on Mihdhar she was clearly lying. This was treachery that cost the lives of 3000 innocent Americans on 9/11!

Chapter 18
The arrest of Zacariuos Moussaoui

On August 15, two long-time flight instructors at Pam Am Aviation in Eagan, MN, became suspicious of one of their flight students, a Zacarias Moussaoui. He was in the process of obtaining training on a Boeing 747 flight simulator although he did not posses a private pilot's license. After several attempts to convince the Minneapolis FBI Field Office that Zacarias Moussaoui might be a terrorist attempting to get flight training in order to carry out a horrific terrorist attack, the FBI became convinced that a field investigation should be started, and on August 16, 2001 initiated an investigation of Zacarias Moussaoui.

The field agent in charge of this investigation was Agent Harry Samit, aka "Henry" in the FBI Inspector General's report. The information FBI Agent Harry Samit had obtained from his investigation of Zacarias Moussaoui was the following:

- Zacarias Moussaoui was attempting to get training on how to fly a Boeing 747 with no apparent reason for getting this training and with no qualifications that were the normal prerequisites for this type of training, which included a private license, and commercial license, an instrument rating, and even in most cases a multi-engine rating.

- Zacarias Moussaoui could not explain the $32,000 in his bank account, where it came from, or why he was spending considerable sums on this training for which he had no use.

- Zacarias Moussaoui had concealed his connection to radical Muslim ideologies. His travel companion, however, told FBI investigators that Moussaoui believed in radical Muslim causes and hated Americans. Zacarias had even mentioned that it was easy to conceal a folding knife so it could be brought on board a US airliner. The two of them had also taken physical training together. Moussaoui's travel

371

companion, aka Attas, could not understand why Moussaoui had wanted to go from no real flight skills to training on the largest US airliner in a single step.

- The instructors at Pan Am Aviation, who had been instructors for Zacarias Moussaoui, and who had many years of flight training and flight instruction experience, had both become convinced that Zacarias Moussaoui was a terrorist attempting to get training on a Boeing 747 in order to carry out a terrorist attack, possibly hijacking a large US airliner in flight and crashing this type of aircraft into a building. They had even told the FBI that a large Boeing 747 loaded with fuel could be, in effect, a huge bomb.

- When question by FBI Agent Harry Samit, Zacarias Moussaoui had no reasonable explanation why he was taking training on a Boeing 747 flight simulator.

- During the FBI investigation of Moussaoui, two four-inch folding knives were found in his possession, one on his person and one in his car.

- Harry Samit had found a will for Al-Attas and asked an Arabic speaker to translate the will and a conversation in Arabic between Al-Attas, and Ahmed, the imam from a mosque that Al-Attas attended. According to this translation the conversation went as follows:

Imam; "I heard you guys wanted to go on Jihad."

In reply, Al-Attas said, "Don't talk about that now."

When Al-Attas informed the imam that Moussaoui was to be deported to France, the imam became very upset.

The translation of the will of Al-Attas reads; "death is near and "those who anticipate in Jihad can expect to see God."

Agent Harry Samit became convinced that these facts indicated strongly that that Zacarias Moussaoui was a radical Muslim terrorist who was taking flight lessons on a Boeing 747, even when he was not qualified for a private pilot's license, as part of a larger terrorist organization that was in the process of preparing for a terrorist attack using hijacked aircraft. From the information gathered in his investigation, this was the only logical scenario that Harry Samit could put together that would explain where the money in his bank account came from and why Zacarias was reluctant to explain many of the facts that had been uncovered. Where had the money come from, the $32,000 in his bank account? Why had Zacarias Moussaoui been so evasive during the interview process of the investigation? Why was he getting training on a large commercial airliner when he no rational reason for doing this? From this information Harry Samit concluded that the organization Zacarias Moussaoui was associated with and must have been funding his flight training was still in place. He had also concluded that the confederates of Zacarias Moussaoui were still likely to carry out an attack using hijacked large airliners without Moussaoui.

Harry Samit also knew from the information developed about Moussaoui that Moussaoui had been in a big hurry to finish his flight simulation training, and that he was in fact scheduled to complete his flight training by August 20, 2001.

Hence his suspicions that there was a very high probability of a horrific attack by the other people who Moussaoui was collaborating with would likely happen within a few weeks of August 20, 2001. He felt that it was highly probable that there would be a terrorist attack using hijacked aircraft flown into a major building is the US, and that the World Trade Center Towers or the White House was the likely target.

From the FBI Inspector General's Report

On August 20, Harry Samit after his investigation of Moussaoui wrote a 26-page report and e-mailed it to over 70 people in the FBI outlining the facts and issues with the Moussaoui investigation. This 26-page report included, "statements received from the flight school representatives that Moussaoui was arrested as an overstay on his visa and that deportation was pending and that he was in possession of two knives when he was arrested." Moussaoui had absolutely no comprehensible reason to be trying to obtain training on a large commercial airliner when he did not even qualify for a private pilot's license, and he further had no rational explanation where the $32,000 that was in his bank account came from. This report clearly laid out all of the information obtained in this short investigation with what appeared to be the only possible explanation, that Moussaoui was part of a larger terrorist organization that was financing his training, and that he clearly appeared to be

373

preparing himself for the hijacking of a large commercial aircraft, and even that his confederates were still in place ready to carry out this attack with him.

The RFU's assessment of Minneapolis FBI's FISA request

At FBI Headquarters, Martin and Robin began looking into the merits of the Minneapolis FBI's FISA request, based on the information about Moussaoui that the Minneapolis FBI had provided, primarily in the 26-page EC Henry had sent to FBI Headquarters about the Moussaoui investigation.

Martin told the OIG that his reaction upon reading the 26-page EC with respect to obtaining a FISA warrant was that while he believed Moussaoui was "a dirty bird" and was probably "up to something," there was no evidence linking Moussaoui to a foreign power of any kind. Martin said that based upon what was in the EC, his opinion was that "there was no way" that a FISA warrant could be obtained because of the lack of evidence linking Moussaoui to a foreign power.

Robin told the OIG that Martin informed her that Minneapolis was seeking a FISA search warrant and Martin provided her with a copy of the 26-page EC to read. She said that after reading the EC, she also believed that Moussaoui was "up to something." However, she said that after reading the EC she asked Martin, "Where's the foreign power?" In her view there was no evidence of a terrorist organization's involvement with Moussaoui. According to Robin, Martin agreed with her assessment that the FISA request lacked a connection to a foreign power.

To page 133 FBI IG Report

The process at FBI Headquarters was to review information that came from the field agents, decide if there was enough information to open either a criminal investigation or an intelligence investigation.

- For a criminal investigation, probable cause was needed to show that the individual being investigated had committed a crime.

- To open an intelligence investigation, probable cause was needed to show that an individual being investigated was a foreign power or an agent of a foreign power.

Two or more people who were foreigners could be considered a foreign power. This requirement to show the target of an intelligence investigation had to be a foreign power or an agent of a foreign power was because of a law Congress had passed in the late 1970s, in reaction to abuses of the Nixon presidency, where numerous investigations of Americans had been carried out by the CIA of people who were considered enemies of his administration. Congress had made a law that created a special court, the FISA Court, to independently review each application for a search warrant, to ensure that the target of any investigation was not an American being investigated for political reasons but was either an agent of a foreign power or a foreign power. While the law only states "foreign power," it appears the FBI managers whose job was to submit field request for search warrants to the FISA Court would only submit requests when the "foreign power" that was identified on the FISA application had been brought before the FISA Court in a prior application. They routinely referred to a foreign power that had been submitted to the FISA Court in a prior search warrant request as a "recognized foreign power."

From discussions with David Frasca (aka "Don" in the FBI IG report), head of the RFU at FBI Headquarters, Harry Samit had been told that there was not enough evidence to obtain a criminal search warrant, and the investigation should be opened as an intelligence investigation using the FISA process.

Minneapolis seeks to expedite the FISA process (FBI IG report)

When Gary first discussed seeking a FISA search warrant for Moussaoui's belongings with Martin on August 22, Gary indicated that Minneapolis wanted to expedite the process. As noted above, Gary told the OIG that the Minneapolis FBI had been informed by INS officials that the INS could only hold Moussaoui for seven to 10 days before deporting him; Gary said that he was aware that FISA requests normally took a long time and that the Minneapolis FBI was concerned about expediting the process to ensure that the FISA warrant was obtained and executed before Moussaoui's deportation. Gary said that he explained to Martin that the INS said it could only hold Moussaoui for seven to 10 days.

[FBI IG Report, p158]

375

Consulting with NSLU attorneys

The NSLU is part of the FBI's Office of General Counsel in FBI Headquarters. The NSLU provided advice to FBI Headquarters and field offices on counterterrorism and counter-intelligence matters. NSLU attorneys usually were consulted when a question arose whether there was sufficient information to support the FISA request. However, NSLU attorneys were not "assigned" to work on a particular FISA request or to work with specific SSAs, The consultations with NSLU attorneys typically consisted of oral briefings by the SSA and the IOS who were handling the particular FISA request. In connection with these consultations, NSLU attorneys did not normally receive and review the documents prepared by the field office or initial drafts of the LHM prepared by the SSA and IOS. After questioning the SSA and IOS, and based on the information provided by the SSA and the IOS, the NSLU attorney typically would provide verbal guidance about what was needed to support the FISA request... Field offices did not normally participate in these consultations with the NSLU attorneys.

As noted above, the Minneapolis FBI's first contact with FBI Headquarters was with SSA Jack. On August 21, Jack made an appointment with NSLU attorney Howard to discuss the Moussaoui matter the following morning. Jack said that even though the case was in the process of being reassigned to Martin in the RFU, Jack kept his appointment with Howard because he was "curious" and wanted to discuss the Minneapolis FBI's options for obtaining authority to search Moussaoui's laptop and other belongings.

During the meeting on August 22, Jack orally briefed Howard on the facts, as reported in Henry's EC. Jack did not provide Howard with a copy of the EC. According to Howard's notes from the meeting, they discussed whether there was sufficient information to obtain either a criminal search warrant or a FISA search warrant. With respect to the FISA warrant, Howard told the OIG that he advised Jack that he did not believe that there was sufficient information to obtain a FISA warrant, primarily because Minneapolis lacked the necessary information to articulate a foreign power. Howard's notes indicate that he advised Jack that obtaining the FISA warrant also would be difficult because Moussaoui was already in custody. Howard told the OIG that at the time, OIPR viewed anyone in custody as a target of criminal investigation by the FBI, even if the person was being held on administrative charges, and therefore OIPR would question whether the FBI's "primary purpose" was to collect intelligence information.

With respect to approaching the USAO to obtain a criminal warrant, Howard's notes reflect that he did not believe that there was sufficient information to obtain a criminal search warrant. His notes state that he advised Jack that a decision needed to be made quickly and that if the Minneapolis FBI decided to pursue the criminal case, then it would be difficult to later pursue the FISA warrant. Howard told the OIG, however, that whether to pursue the FISA warrant or the criminal warrant was a "judgment call" for Minneapolis to make and that he considered the matter to be a "work in progress."

Jack confirmed that he received this advice from Howard. He told the OIG that Howard advised him that he did not see evidence of a foreign power and that Howard concurred that there was no evidence of a criminal act. Jack told the OIG that he and Howard were "brainstorming" about the possible ways to proceed. Howard's notes indicate that he told Jack that it looked as if Minneapolis had several "good leads" and that Minneapolis needed to follow up on those leads.

Martin's meeting with Howard

As noted above, on August 20 the Moussaoui case was transferred from Joseph to the RFU and assigned to Martin and Robin. On approximately August 22, Martin and Robin consulted with Howard for legal advice on Minneapolis' chances for obtaining a FISA warrant.

Martin said that when he began explaining to Howard the facts of the Moussaoui matter, Howard said that he was aware of the matter already because he had recently been consulted by Jack... Howard reiterated the same advice to Martin as he told Jack – that he did not believe that there was sufficient evidence to tie Moussaoui to a foreign power and therefore a FISA warrant was not possible absent further investigation by Minneapolis.

Martin told the OIG that he recalled Howard advising him that there was not sufficient evidence to support a link to a foreign power. Like Jack, Martin did not provide Howard with a copy of the 26-page EC, although Martin had the document with him.

Howard's e-mail exchange with Rowley

After his meeting with Martin and Robin, Howard sent an e-mail dated August 22 to Minneapolis CDC Rowley. In the e-mail, he asked whether she had been asked for her "assessment of [Minneapolis'] chances of getting a [criminal] warrant" for Moussaoui's computer. Howard told the OIG that he did this because he wanted to make sure that the CDC was "engaged in the thought process." He stated that the decision on which type of warrant to seek was the field office's decision, and he wanted to make sure that the CDC was "part of the process."

In an e-mail response later the same day, Rowley wrote, "Although I think there's a decent chance of being able to get a judge to sign a criminal search warrant, our USAO seems to have an even higher standard much of the time, so rather than risk it, I advised that they should try the other route." Rowley told the OIG that in retrospect she wished that she had made it clear in her e-mail that she believed that, in fact, there was sufficient evidence to support probable cause for a criminal warrant.

Howard told the OIG that he recalled having the following reaction to Rowley's e-mail: "Good Lord, Coleen, we don't use FISA because we don't have probable cause for a criminal warrant. That plays right into the hands of those people who think FISA is subterfuge." Howard did not respond to the e-mail, nor did he and Rowley discuss the matter on the telephone.

French information about Moussaoui

Around the same time that Martin consulted with Howard, the Minneapolis FBI obtained additional information about Moussaoui from the French government. As noted above, because Moussaoui had entered the United States with a French passport, Henry had sent a lead to the FBI's Paris Legat to obtain any relevant information on Moussaoui from the French authorities. On August 22, the FBI's Paris Legat reported to the Minneapolis FBI and FBI Headquarters that the French government had reported that Moussaoui was purportedly associated with a man who was born in France and died in 2000 in Chechnya fighting with "the Mujahideen." We call this person "Amnay." The Legat's EC stated that while in Chechnya, Amnay worked for Emir Al-Khattab Ibn (Ibn Khattab), the leader of a group of Chechen rebels. According to the EC, the French authorities, after Amnay's death, had interviewed a person who we call "Tufitri" who had known

Amnay. That person stated that Amnay was recruited to go to Chechnya by Moussaoui and that Moussaoui was "the dangerous one."

Martin advises Minneapolis FBI that French information is not sufficient to connect Moussaoui to a foreign power

After Martin received and reviewed the French information, he still did not believe there was sufficient information to identify a foreign power in the Minneapolis FISA request. Martin discussed the French information with Gary and stated that it provided little help to Minneapolis in connecting Moussaoui to a foreign power. Martin explained that Ibn Khattab and the Chechen rebel group he led were not an identified terrorist organization. Gary's notes of the conversation indicate that Martin explained that Minneapolis needed evidence linking Moussaoui to a "recognized" foreign power. Martin told the OIG that by "recognized" he meant a foreign power that previously had been pled before the FISA Court. Martin told the OIG that he believed that the Chechen rebels had never previously been pled to the FISA Court as a foreign power.

Rather, Martin described the situation in Chechnya as dissidents engaged in a "civil war." He acknowledged, however, that it may have been possible to develop the intelligence to support the position that Khattab's Chechen rebels were a terrorist group. But he said that he was not aware of any insurgency/rebel group ever being pled as a foreign power.

In addition, Martin stated that even if the Intelligence Community had developed the intelligence that Khattab's Chechen rebels were a terrorist organization and could therefore constitute a foreign power under FISA, this could not be completed in a short time, which was what the FBI believed at the time was necessary in the Moussaoui case. Martin said he there-fore advised the Minneapolis FBI that, to obtain a FISA war-rant, it needed to develop information linking Moussaoui to a recognized or previously-pled, identifiable foreign power.

Robin also told the OIG that she did not believe that the French information was sufficient to connect Moussaoui to a foreign power. She said that she understood that the Chechen rebels had never been pled as a foreign power to the FISA Court and that the Intelligence Community had never developed sufficient intelligence that the conflict in Chechnya was more than a civil war. In one case she was familiar with, she understood that the FBI had previously attempted to obtain a FISA warrant using Khattab and the Chechen rebels as the foreign power but that it was "turned down" by OIPR. She stated that "building a foreign power" was "not an overnight thing" and would have required months to collect the required intelligence information, as had been the case when one particular terrorist group was first put forth as a foreign power.

Gary told the OIG that during the conversation between him and Martin on August 22 about the French information, he raised with Martin the issue of the mandatory notification of the Criminal Division when there was a reasonable indication of a crime, as set forth in Deputy Attorney General Thompson's August 6 memorandum, which Charles had faxed to Gary. According to Gary, Martin said that he did not see any evidence of a federal felony, that the FISA route was easier, and that going the criminal route first would be relevant to whether they were able to obtain a FISA warrant. Gary's notes indicate that Martin stated, "Don't see federal crime." Gary told the OIG he deferred to Martin but faxed him a copy of the Thompson memorandum.

Martin told the OIG that he did not remember a specific conversation with Gary about whether there was probable cause to obtain a search warrant. However, he said that he recalled a conversation in which he asked Gary, "What would the crime be?" Martin told the OIG he believed that the Minneapolis FBI did not have any evidence of a crime and only had "gut feelings."

7. Robin's research to link Moussaoui to recognized foreign power of terrorist organization

Robin conducted additional research on Moussaoui to try to bolster Moussaoui's connection to a recognized foreign power. Robin sought to find a direct link between Moussaoui or any of the other names or organizations that had surfaced in the investigation and foreign powers that she was aware had previously been pled to the FISA Court.

According to Robin, the Moussaoui FISA request was different from the typical FISA request because the Minneapolis FBI had not conducted a lengthy investigation on Moussaoui before he was arrested; As a result, Robin said, the FBI lacked information about Moussaoui that would have been gathered if the FBI had conducted physical surveillance and trash covers and obtained phone records and financial records, which was how intelligence investigations typically proceeded before a FISA warrant was requested. Moreover, Minneapolis was seeking an emergency FISA warrant, which meant that there was little time to develop more information to support the FISA request.

...One of the documents that Robin retrieved in her search using the name Ibn Khattab was the Phoenix EC... Williams stated his belief that there were an "inordinate number" of persons of interest to the FBI who also were receiving training in aviation-related fields of study and that there was a possibility that bin Laden was coordinating an effort to train people in the US in order to conduct terrorist activity in the future.

ACS records show that Robin printed the Phoenix EC on August 22. Robin told the OIG that her usual practice was to read the documents that she printed, but she said she did not have a recollection of reading the Phoenix EC at the time.

Robin did not provide the EC to anyone else or discuss its contents with anyone, including Martin or the Minneapolis FBI. Robin told the OIG that when she read the Phoenix EC after the Joint Intelligence Committee Inquiry staff informed her that ACS showed that she had printed the EC, she concluded that nothing in the EC would have bolstered Moussaoui's connection to a foreign power for FISA. She also asserted that the Phoenix EC's reporting of information about individuals who were of interest to the FBI – that they were Middle Eastern and were in flight school – was not significant at the time because there were thousands of Middle Eastern men in US flight schools at the time.

Martin and Robin consult with NSLU attorney Tim

Around August 23, Don directed Martin and Robin to consult with another NSLU attorney, Tim, about the Moussaoui case. According to Martin, Don thought that Tim should be consulted because he handled counterterrorism matters full-time and therefore may have had more expertise than Howard.

Tim told the OIG that while in theory the Chechen rebels could have been a foreign power, because "anything could be a foreign power," it was his understanding that this did not happen in practice before September 11, 2001. He added that even if the Chechen rebels were considered a foreign power under FISA, the FBI still would have had to show that Moussaoui was an agent of that foreign power.

Both Martin and Tim told the OIG that Tim's advice was that the Minneapolis FBI lacked sufficient evidence of a foreign power to obtain a FISA warrant. Tim advised Martin that Minneapolis would have to collect more information supporting Moussaoui's connection to a foreign power in order to obtain a FISA warrant.

Tim told the OIG that Martin's "attitude" in presenting the case was that "he didn't think [Minneapolis] should get the FISA" but that Minneapolis "wanted one."

Martin tells Minneapolis its FISA request was not an emergency

On August 24, Martin and Gary discussed the options for the Minneapolis FBI in pursuing a FISA warrant for Moussaoui. Martin asserted that the Moussaoui situation did not qualify as an emergency, which required information that an "imminent act of terrorism" was about to take place, and he added the FISA request lacked sufficient evidence of a connection to a known foreign power.[130] Gary's notes from the conversation indicate that Martin stated that Minneapolis could write a Letterhead Memorandum (LHM) for the FISA request, have its CDC approve it, and that Martin would try to push it "up [the] food chain" at FBI Headquarters. However, according to Gary's notes, Martin advised him that the: FISA request could "take a few months" to complete, that there were " hundreds of these FISA requests," and that the FBI had to prioritize them.[131] The notes also indicate that Martin said that he had showed the FISA request to an NSLU attorney and that office was not supportive of the application.

---

[130] As discussed in Chapter Two, the SSAs and NSLU attorneys we interviewed told us that what rose to the level of an expedited FISA request depended on what the field office and ITOS management deemed to be an immediate priority, but the final decision would be made by the ITOS Section Chief, Michael Rolince. According to these witnesses, in the summer of 2001 expedited FISA requests normally involved reports of a suspected imminent attack or other imminent danger.

[131] Rolince and others told the OIG that there were always more FISA requests than ITOS resources and OIPR attorneys to complete all of them and have them heard before the FISA Court in the amount of time desired by the

field office. Rolince stated that he instituted a policy that only the Section Chief was permitted to determine what constituted a priority and would be pushed to OIPR. He said that this arose out of the OIPR Counsel expressing to him that his attorneys were being called by SSAs and analysts making demands about what cases were priorities and had to be completed for presentation to the FISA Court... He also stated that al Qaeda FISA requests were generally the priority, although there were times when another foreign power was the priority for a certain period of time because of a specific set of circumstances.

Martin seeks information from FAA

During this same time period, Martin initiated additional requests for information about Moussaoui. Martin advised the Federal Aviation Administration (FAA) representative at FBI Headquarters about the Moussaoui investigation and provided him with a copy of Henry's 26-page EC. The FAA employee checked FAA databases for information about Moussaoui and obtained records indicating that he had registered for a student pilot's certificate at the flight school in Norman, OK. The FAA employee e-mailed this information to the Minneapolis FBI and the RFU.

According to the FAA employee, he, Martin, and Robin met with Don when the Moussaoui matter first came to the RFU, and they discussed what the FBI could tell the FAA about Moussaoui. The FAA employee stated that they decided that since Moussaoui and Al-Attas were in custody and no other individuals were known to be working with them, the Minneapolis FBI would continue its investigation, but the FBI would not advise the FAA about the investigation at that point.

Minneapolis FBI seeks assistance from the CIA and London Legit

On August 24, after the Minneapolis FBI was told by Martin that the French information was not sufficient to link Moussaoui to a foreign power, the Minneapolis FBI sought assistance from other agencies to connect Moussaoui to al Qaeda or another foreign power.

Henry e-mailed an FBI manager detailed to the CIA to ask him to determine whether the CIA had any information linking Moussaoui to a foreign power. A CIA counterterrorism employee e-mailed the FBI manager detailed to the CIA, who forwarded the message to Henry that Ibn Khattab was "a close buddy with bin Laden from their earlier fighting days and that the CIA employee's interpretation of the French information that Moussaoui was a "recruiter for Khattab."

Also on August 24, the same day that Henry was exchanging e-mails with the CIA employee about obtaining information to connect Moussaoui to a foreign power, a CIA manager who was working in ITOS at FBI Headquarters as a "consultant" on intelligence issues e-mailed Martin about the Moussaoui case. The CIA manager asked whether leads had been sent out to obtain additional biographical information, including any overseas numbers, and whether the FBI had obtained photographs and could provide them to the CIA. Martin responded to the e-mail and provided an update stating that requests for information and photographs already had been sent to the appropriate foreign intelligence agencies and to the CIA, and that the Minneapolis FBI had sent telephone numbers and addresses from Moussaoui's and Al-Attas' "pocket litter" to the CIA. Martin concluded the e-mail by writing, "[p]lease bear in mind that there is no indication that either of these two had plans for nefarious activity as was apparently indicated in an earlier communication."

Also on August 24, Henry e-mailed the FBI's London ALAT, providing him with an update on the Moussaoui investigation and asking for assistance in establishing that Moussaoui was acting on behalf of a foreign power. Although the London ALAT contacted the British authorities twice in writing, made several telephone calls, and indicated the urgency of the Moussaoui matter, the British government did not provide the FBI any information about Moussaoui until September 12. We discuss the information and the ALAT's efforts to obtain this information from the British authorities in Section J below.

Minneapolis prepares emergency FISA request

On the morning of Saturday, August 25, Henry completed the Minneapolis FBI's formal FISA request, which consisted of a (5-page LHM) and e-mailed it to FBI Headquarters. The LHM stated that the Minneapolis FBI was requesting a FISA search warrant on an emergency basis and that Minneapolis "wish[ed] to emphasize the urgency of this matter in reminding recipients that Moussaoui is in INS custody pending deportation."

The LHM summarized Henry's 26-page EC, including the statements received from the flight school representatives, that Moussaoui was arrested as an overstay on his visa, that deportation was pending and that he was in possession; of two knives when he was arrested. The LHM also summarized Al-Attas' statements about Moussaoui's radical Islamic fundamentalist beliefs, including that Moussaoui believed that it was acceptable to kill civilians who harm Muslims. The LHM noted inconsistencies in Moussaoui's statements, such as his unconvincing explanation for the large sums of money in his possession while he was in the United States and his inability to convincingly explain the reasons for his recent trip to Pakistan. With respect to information linking Moussaoui to a foreign power, the LHM contained three paragraphs. The LHM included the information provided by French authorities. The LHM also included the statement from the CIA employee that Ibn Khattab was "known to be an associate of Usama bin Laden from past shared involvement in combat."

Both Gary and Henry told the OIG that they believed that based on the information they provided in the LHM, the Minneapolis FBI could support that Moussaoui was connected to Ibn Khattab and that because Khattab was connected to Usama bin Laden, al Qaeda could be used as the foreign power in the FISA application.

Martin told the OIG, however, that he believed the information provided by the Minneapolis FBI to support a link between Ibn Khattab and bin Laden was not sufficient to support a FISA request. According to Martin, it was "common knowledge" that there was a "purported" link between Khattab and bin Laden. But he said that the most recent intelligence indicated that Khattab and bin Laden were not connected.

Robin told the OIG that she believed that trying to link Moussaoui to al Qaeda by arguing that Moussaoui was linked to Khattab, and Khattab was linked to bin Laden, was "too far removed" to obtain a FISA warrant. She stated that based on intelligence information, it was known that Khattab and bin Laden were "contemporaries" but were not connected to each other; she said that Khattab was not working for bin Laden.

Analysis

At this point in the FISA search warrant application process, both Harry Samit and his supervisor had been trying to connect Moussaoui to bin Laden, because of statements made by Michael Maltbie that Moussaoui had to be shown to be an agent of a "recognized foreign power." Clearly al Qaeda was by this time a recognized foreign power, a foreign power that had been used in a prior FISA warrant application. While there were indications the group that he had been part of in Chechnya, was headed by Ibn Khattab, and Khattab had once been part of bin Laden's organization, there was no recent evidence that these two were still part of the same organization.

What can be said is that the logic of Michael Maltbie, Robin, and David Frasca at this point borders on the absurd. There is no way their logic could pass the test of what would a prudent person do in the same circumstances!

Everyone knew that the primary weapon of terrorists was secrecy, and that obtaining much significant information at all prior to any request for a search warrant would be difficult if not downright impossible. The 26 page e-mail by Harry Samit and his FISA request clearly laid out the case that there was probable cause to show that Moussaoui was an agent of a foreign power. How else could you explain the $32,000 in Moussaoui's bank account or his training on a Boeing 747 when he had absolutely no reason to be doing this? Harry Samit's application should have been submitted to the FISA Court, and if there was not evidence that Moussaoui was connected to a foreign power that had been used in a prior FISA application, it could have been argued that Ibn Khattab's organization or an unknown foreign power was behind Moussaoui.

At that point if the application had been turned down by the FISA Court, it would have made the FISA Court culpable for the deaths of the 3,000 people murdered by the al Qaeda terrorists on 9/11. It turns out (and this fact is deliberately left out of the FBI Inspector General's report) that from 1978 when this FISA Court was set up by Congress, only five applications had ever been turned down by this Court, in over 18,300 applications). So the chance that Harry Samit's application would have been turned down was less than one in 3,000. Had Harry Samit's application be prefaced with:

"We request an emergency grant of this FISA warrant application request due to the fact that evidence so far uncovered by this investigation indicates a very high likelihood of an imminent terrorist attack that could kill thousands of American citizens. Because this investigation has shown that the individual being investigated is in an unexplained hurry to return to his training on a Boeing 747 while he was not qualified to be taking this training, and because we have at this time no specific information on exactly when a possible attack will actually be carried out, we request this application be considered with the absolute highest possible urgency."

In addition, all this application had to show was "probable cause," a prudent person believing because of evidence collected during an investigation or interview the individual being investigated is likely to be an agent of a foreign power, not *prima facie* evidence that they actually were an agent of a foreign power. The search warrant was being requested to establish evidence that the person is or is not an actual agent of a foreign power and then to find out exactly what that person is up to.

At this point, when Michael Maltbie and Robin say they do not believe there is enough evidence to show Moussaoui is part of a recognized foreign power, they are imposing on this application a requirement that the FISA Court had NEVER imposed on any application, that the foreign power had to be one that had been argued in a prior application, and that the request for the search warrant show *prima facie* evidence that this person was indeed an agent of a foreign power.

If a huge terrorist attack is about to occur, then what if it was not possible to collect enough evidence to show that the organization that the person under investigation was an agent of has come before the FISA Court in a prior warrant application?

Terrorist organizations are secret; that is their main weapon. If you cannot collect the necessary information, which in most cases you won't be able to, do you just allow thousands of Americans to be killed by terrorists? Do you just allow thousands of Americans be killed because the al Qaeda terrorist organization uses secrecy, when everyone at the FBI knew that the al Qaeda organization used secrecy?

As for the argument that Harry Samit did not have enough information to show that there was probable cause that Moussaoui was an agent for a foreign power, how much information did you need for probable cause? To the average "prudent" American, it appears there was indeed more than enough evidence to show probable cause that Moussaoui was an agent of a foreign power. How else could you explain the huge sum of money in his bank account, which he had absolutely no explanation for, and his desire to train on a Boeing 747 flight simulator, again for which he had no reason to be taking this kind of training? The only logical explanation was that he was an agent of a foreign power and he was training in order to hijack a large commercial airliner, and that his confederates were still out there about to commit this terrorist act.

Even from a superficial look at the evidence, if Maltbie and Robin denied Harry Samit even a chance to request from the Court a search warrant, and he could not continue his investigation and search of Moussaoui's duffel bag, they had to know that literally thousands on Americans would be killed in this horrific attack if Samit were correct in his analysis. They were sabotaging his investigation with spurious arguments and had to know exactly what they were doing and the horrific possible outcome!

Dispute between Minneapolis and Martin (FBI IG report)

Around this time, Gary and Henry were becoming increasingly frustrated with the advice from Martin that they lacked sufficient information linking Moussaoui to a foreign power. On Monday, August 27, in a telephone call between Martin arid Gary, the tension surfaced.

According to Gary's notes of the conversation, Martin told them that "what you have done is couched it in such a way that people get spun up." Gary told the OIG that after Martin made this statement, Gary said "good" and then stated that Minneapolis was trying to keep Moussaoui from crashing an airplane into the World Trade Center. Gary's notes of the conversation indicate that Gary stated, "We want to make sure he doesn't get control of an airplane and crash it into the [World Trade Center] or something like that." According to Gary's notes, Martin responded by stating that Minneapolis did not have the evidence to support that Moussaoui was a terrorist. Gary's notes indicate that Martin also stated, "You have a guy interested in this type of aircraft. That is it."

Martin told the OIG that he did not recall making any statement about Minneapolis getting "spun up" about the Moussaoui investigation. When asked whether he spoke with Minneapolis about whether they were overreacting, Martin stated that he "could have." Martin told the OIG that he never heard Gary make a statement that he thought that Moussaoui was going to hijack an airplane and crash it into the World Trade Center. He said that the first time that he heard that statement was in October 2001 at a meeting in FBI Headquarters involving several Minneapolis agents and FBI Headquarters employees to discuss the Moussaoui investigation. He said that during the meeting Gary made a reference to having made this statement to Martin some time in August 2001, but that Martin had never before heard Gary make the statement.

Gary's notes also indicate that the Minneapolis FBI asked Martin whether the FISA request, which had been e-mailed on Saturday, August 25, had been presented to Section Chief Rolince for approval as an emergency FISA. Martin stated that it had not been presented to Rolince.

Gary's frustration with Martin can be seen in an e-mail Gary sent to Martin on August 27 after their telephone conversation. In the e-mail, Gary advised Martin to contact the CIA employee for more information about Khattab and his connections to bin Laden in order to support the foreign power portion of the FISA application. Martin responded in an e-mail on August 28 that FBI Headquarters had the latest information on Ibn Khattab and Chechnya, "as this program is administered by our unit," and that the matter had been discussed with the CIA employee. Martin also wrote, "I need to ask you guys to do me a favor. In the future, please contact and pass info to me and allow me to talk with [an FBI detailee to the CIA] and [the CIA]. Things work much better when our agencies are communicating HQ to HQ."[133] Henry told the OIG that he was frustrated with the advice that the Minneapolis FBI was receiving from FBI Headquarters and that he expressed this in a conversation with Martin. Henry said he told Martin that he disagreed with Don's arguments for not pursuing the criminal warrant. He told the OIG that he had said to Martin:

...if you're not going to advance this the FISA route, or if you don't believe we have enough for a FISA, I shudder to think – and that's all I got out. And [Martin] cut me off and said, you will not question the unit chief and you will not question me. We've been through a lot. We know what's going on. You will not question us. And that could be the mantra for FBI supervisors.

[133] Martin told the OIG that normally contacts with other agencies are made by the SSAs at FBI Headquarters. He stated that he was concerned about the Minneapolis FBI

communicating directly with the CIA because it was "not conducive to good information flow" and that FBI Headquarters needed to be "apprised of what's going on." He also asserted that since FBI Headquarters was responsible for putting the FISA request together, it was necessary for FBI Headquarters to ensure that it had all of the available information from outside agencies, and that this was more likely to occur when the agencies were communicating at the Headquarters level.

Analysis

Throughout the FBI inspector General's report, the reader is confronted with apparently conflicting testimony, which is never resolved – in this case testimony about conversations between Harry Samit and his boss and Michael Maltbie. The testimony of Michael Maltbie is riddled with "do not recall" and "never heard."

Harry Samit's testimony and the testimony of his boss are consistent with their investigation, and with their testimony under oath in the trial of Zacarias Moussaoui. Not once does Harry Samit or his boss say, "do not recall." At this trial, the spokesman for the FBI said Michael Maltbie and David Frasca would make no comment, and the FBI would make no comment. At this point it would appear that the testimony of both David Frasca and Michael Maltbie have no credibility, and the preponderance of credibility would have to be placed on the statements of Harry Samit and his supervisor. What is so incomprehensible is after Harry Samit and his supervisor make it absolutely clear that this is an emergency and that a horrific terrorist attack could take place in the very near future, Michael Maltbie stated that it "had not been presented to Rolince." The reasons behind not requesting an emergency FISA are utterly incomprehensible and have never been explained by the FBI in any way. Both the reasons this emergency request was never submitted to Rolince and the complete lack of the FBI IG to find out why it was not done need to be explained in complete detail. This failure had allowed 3,000 people to be murdered by the al Qaeda terrorists. The American people should have some explanation of this incomprehensible behavior. It appears that the FBI IG in fact went out of his way in an attempt to absolve Michael Maltbie, David Frasca and even Michael Rolince of culpability in this matter. This is unacceptable; the Al Qaeda terrorists murdered

3,000 Americans and the American people should be told why this happened.

Minneapolis contacts RFU unit chief
(FBI IG report)

Because of Gary's and Henry's frustrations in dealing with Martin, Gary told the OIG that he approached Roy, the Minneapolis Acting SAC, and asked Roy to call Don to "find out what [Martin]'s problem was." On August 27, Gary and Roy together placed a call to Don to discuss the Moussaoui FISA request.

According to Gary, Don was "immediately defensive" and asked Martin to join the call. Gary's notes of the conversation do not indicate that Martin's performance was discussed.

Gary told the OIG, and his notes reflect, that Martin and Don discussed the lack of a foreign power and stressed that more direct connections were needed to establish the required link. Gary told the OIG that he recalled asking, "What is the mechanism?" to address the Moussaoui situation. He said that he asked Martin and Don if "they won't let us go criminal" and if there was insufficient information for a FISA, "what can we do?"

Gary's notes indicate that he was advised that if Moussaoui could not be connected to a terrorist organization, there was "no mechanism to address on a case-by-case basis." Gary's notes also reflect that the question, "What is being done to address the loophole (if he isn't part of a known group)?" was asked. Gary told the OIG that he posed this question. The reply is noted in quotation marks as "That isn't something for you to worry about." Gary told the OIG that he recalled that Don gave this reply. Don, however, told the OIG that he did not make this statement.

Roy told the OIG that he recalled having the telephone call but said he did not recall the substance of the conversation. He told the OIG, however, that he recalled that at some point he spoke to Don about Martin and expressed his belief that Martin was "hindering" the process or trying to "submarine" Minneapolis' case.

Don told the OIG that he recalled speaking on the telephone with Roy and Gary and discussing the foreign power issue. He said that his response to the disagreement was to have Susan – another NSLU attorney – weigh in on the merits of the FISA request. Don asserted that at no time did Roy or anyone else from Minneapolis raise any concerns to him about how Martin, Robin, or anyone else at FBI Headquarters was handling the case.

Martin also told the OIG that he did not recall the specifics of this telephone conversation. However, with respect to the issue of ensuring the identity of Moussaoui, he stated that his concern was that the Minneapolis FBI practice "due diligence" and ensure that the information that the FBI had received was for the same person. Martin told the OIG that he was aware that the name "Moussaoui" had resulted in multiple hits in the FBI's computer system when the Minneapolis FBI had first checked Moussaoui's name.

On August 30, the (French) ALAT provided additional information obtained from the French authorities that confirmed Moussaoui's identity to Minneapolis and FBI Headquarters.

Henry told the OIG that he thought that Martin's suggestion that the Minneapolis FBI do more to confirm that Moussaoui was the same Moussaoui as reported by the French was "another arbitrary roadblock." He said that he believed that they should trust the professionalism of the French, although he also said that he was not aware of the specific information that the French authorities were relying on to assert that the Moussaoui in custody was the same Moussaoui as in their report.

Rolince told the OIG that some time in August 2001, Don stopped briefly at his office to give him a "heads up" on a case in the Minneapolis Field Office. Rolince said that the conversation lasted approximately 20 seconds. Rolince said he did not recall if Don mentioned the name Moussaoui or not. According to Rolince, Don indicated there was an issue with a FISA and Rolince might receive a call from FBI management in Minneapolis. Rolince said Don told him the subject of the investigation was in jail on an immigration charge and me logical leads had been sent out. Rolince told the OIG he did not receive any further details from Don about the issue in Minneapolis, but this type of heads up was not atypical. Rolince stated that he received this type of brief notification as often as 10-15 times a week from his subordinates about potential contacts from the field.

Analysis

This testimony by Rolince is contrary to basic common sense. Michael Rolince is over David Frasca and Michael Maltbie. David Frasca heads the unit called the Radical Fundamentalist Unit, a unit in the FBI that is specially charged to investigate radical terrorists in order to prevent terrorist attacks on Americans. Here for the first time the FBI has actually arrested a terrorist who is trying to train to fly a huge commercial airliner and who most likely is connected with other terrorists who will carry out a horrific attack in the near future that could result in the deaths of thousands on Americans, and did. And yet he says that he spends 20 seconds on the issue of obtaining a search warrant to continue this investigation in order to prevent this attack. Why would he spend only 20 seconds on an issue that was so important? He says in his testimony that he gets these types of briefings 10-15 times a week. Is he saying that there were 10-15 terrorists a week who the FBI was obtaining search warrants for? He had even sent out a warning in April that bin Laden was planning to attack inside of the US.

FBI IG Report cont.

> Rolince told the OIG that he never received a telephone call or other contact from the Minneapolis FBI about the Moussaoui matter. He said that he did not raise the limited information he received from Don about the Moussaoui investigation with anyone else in the FBI.

Testimony of Rolince to the FBI IG

Not only do Rolince, Maltbie and Frasca sabotage Harry Samit's investigation, they did not send any of the information on his investigation to anyone above them at the FBI. When the CIA had been asked to provide information on Moussaoui, and was given the basic facts on the investigation, this information shot right to the very top of the CIA, right to John McLaughlin and George Tenet in just a few days.

They were aware of how deadly Moussaoui and his confederates could be. They had even titled their cable, "Terrorists Learning to Fly." And yet at the same time, the FBI inexplicably shuts down their only investigation, and even blocks this information from going past them in the FBI hierarchy, ultimately allowing the attacks on 9/11 to take place, and to this day there has been no explanation.

15. Martin and Robin's consultation with NSLU attorney Susan (FBI IG report)

After the call with Minneapolis on August 27, Martin and Robin met with NSLU attorney Susan to discuss the Moussaoui FISA request. Martin told the OIG that he orally briefed Susan about the facts of the case. He did not provide her with any of the documentation that had been generated, such as the 26-page EC or the 6-page LHM, although he had the documents with him at the meeting. Martin told the OIG that while he did not recall specifically what was discussed with Susan, he recalled that she did not believe that there was sufficient evidence of a connection to a foreign power. Martin added that he recalled informing Susan of the facts that related to the issue of the foreign power, which was the information received from the French authorities.

According to Susan, the meeting lasted approximately 45 minutes. She said she was made aware of a handful of other facts, such as that Moussaoui was an Arab, was in flight school and had been asking some weird questions, and had paid cash for flight school. Susan told the OIG that Martin and Robin downplayed the Khattab information to her. She stated, however, that she believed the evidence of a link between Moussaoui and Khattab was very "tangential" since it was based on the statement of Tufitri, who had no direct knowledge of a connection between Moussaoui and Khattab. In addition, Susan told the OIG that based on her experiences in ITOS, the Chechen rebels would not have been accepted by OIPR as a foreign power. Susan told the OIG that based on the facts that she was presented, she told Martin and Robin that the FISA request lacked the necessary connection of Moussaoui to a foreign power.

Susan told the OIG that attempting to argue that Khattab was part of al Qaeda was not feasible, because at the time the FBI's position was that Khattab did not take direction from bin Laden but rather was the leader of the rebels in Chechnya. She said that it was her understanding at the time that the CIA and the FBI did not agree about Khattab's role and relationship to bin Laden.[136] Susan also stated that in her experience it would not have been feasible to get an emergency FISA through

OIPR if a new foreign power that had never been pled before was presented.

[136] The FBI IOSs we interviewed told the OIG that the CIA, not the FBI, collected intelligence information on the Chechen rebels and Khattab. According to the IOS who was responsible for targets in Chechnya, by the spring of 2001 both the CIA and the FBI took the position that Khattab did not take direction from bin Laden.

Susan told the OIG that she asked Martin and Robin whether the FBI had any information indicating anyone was sending people to the United States for flight training, but that she was told no. She said that Robin did not mention the Phoenix EC to her. Martin told the OIG that he did not recall any such question from Susan. Robin also told the OIG that Susan never brought up the issue of whether Middle Easterners were training in US flight schools.

[Note: We know Robin had read the now-famous Phoenix EC that pointed out the fact that a large number of radical Muslims, and people possibly connected to bin Laden, were getting flight training in Phoenix. In this interview Susan asks if either Robin or Maltbie had such information and Robin says nothing. Even if Susan had not asked this question, this information is so horrific with respect to the Moussaoui investigation that it should have been brought up without any questions from Robin. Robin has all of the information about the Moussaoui investigation and we find out she is aware of the now-famous Phoenix EC. Yet, she does not connect this together, or as she claims tell anyone else, or even bring it up when she is directly asked about this information. And again the FBI IG can get no explanation.]

We asked Susan whether she had read the Phoenix EC since September 11 and whether it would have made a difference to her opinion about the Moussaoui FISA request. Susan said that she first read the Phoenix EC several months after September 11. She said that if she had read the Phoenix EC at the time, she would have been concerned enough about Moussaoui to bring the matter to an OIPR attorney's attention...

After the consultation with Susan on August 27, Don instructed Martin to have the matter reviewed again by the head of NSLU, Spike Bowman, because of the level of concern raised by the Minneapolis FBI about Moussaoui and the FISA request.

Martin arranged for a meeting with Bowman the next afternoon, August 28.

Martin's edits to Minneapolis' FISA request

Prior to the meeting with Bowman, Martin began reviewing and editing the Minneapolis FBI's 6-page LHM, in case the FISA request was approved by Bowman. Martin e-mailed an edited draft of the LHM to Gary and stated that he had made some refinements and wanted comments from Minneapolis. Martin noted that he had removed the paragraph reflecting that a CIA employee had stated that Khattab was an associate of bin Laden, but that Martin would "add the foreign power info re Al-Khattab/UBL later, when we get an [attorney] to buy this argument."

Gary responded with a lengthy e-mail setting forth his concerns about Martin's edits. First, Gary expressed concern about the removal of the statement connecting Khattab to bin Laden. Gary wrote, "It seems that we are setting this up for failure if we don't have the foreign power connection firmly established for the initial review." Gary also raised questions about the following made by Martin:

- Change from the statement about Moussaoui "preparing himself to fight" to a statement that Moussaoui and Al-Attas "train together in defensive tactics." Gary wrote, "During the interview neither Al-Attas nor [Moussaoui] used the term 'defensive tactics.' I think that softens our argument and misrepresents the statements of Al-Attas."

- Change to the statement "Al-Attas was also asked if he had ever heard Moussaoui make a plan to kill those who harm Muslims and in so doing become a martyr himself. Al-Attas admitted that he may have heard him do so, but that because it is not in his own heart to carry out acts of this nature, he claimed that he kept himself from actually hearing and understanding." Martin changed this section to read: "Al-Attas was also asked if Moussaoui has a plan to kill those who harm Muslims and/or to martyr himself while conducting an act of terrorism. Al-Attas indicated that Moussaoui may have such a plan, but that he does not know for certain if this is the case." Gary acknowledged that Martin had changed the statement based on a previous telephone conversation with Gary, but Gary wrote "now that I see it in print I think we might be misstating Al-Attas' response" to the question.

- Change from the statement that "Moussaoui was unable to give a convincing explanation for his paying $8,300 for 747-400 training" to "Moussaoui would [sic] give an explanation for his paying $8,300 k cash for 747-700 flight simulation training." After noting that Martin had left out the "not," Gary stated that he did not think that this statement was accurate because Moussaoui gave an explanation "but it was not convincing."

- Change from the statement that Moussaoui had no convincing explanation for the large sums of money known to have been in his possession during his time in the United States" to "Moussaoui would not explain the large sums of money known to have been in his possession during his time in the United States." Gary noted here again that Moussaoui had offered an explanation but that "his explanation fell short."

- Change from the statement that "Tufitri stated that Moussaoui was 'the dangerous one'" to Tufitri "described him as being dangerous." Gary pointed out that Tufitri "did not describe him as being dangerous in general terms, Tufitri specifically referred to him as 'the dangerous one.'" Gary added, "I think this is significant – and it accurately reflects the information as it was provided by [the French authorities].

Martin responded by e-mail to Gary the same day. With regard to Gary's concerns about the foreign power information, Martin explained that Robin would be pulling together the information required for the foreign power section of the FISA application and that it would be added to the LHM once it was ready to be sent to OIPR. Martin added, "Don't worry about this part."

Gary told the OIG that he believed Martin's edits "softened" the FBI's position. He said that he questioned why Martin had taken out the foreign power information when it was legally required to obtain the FISA warrant, and claimed he was given "no real explanation" for why Martin omitted the foreign power information. Henry told the OIG that he believed that Martin's edits appeared to be "dumbing [the LHM] down" and that the edits "would definitely cause [the FISA request] to fail."

It is clear that Don believes that Michael Maltbie's edits are going to cause the FISA request to fail. There is no evidence that either Maltbie or Robin put together a foreign power section, as they claimed they were going to do, and without it this application would certainly not be approved and a FISA warrant granted. It looks exactly like Michael Maltbie was deliberately torpedoing the investigation. Both Maltbie and Robin knew that if they did not get a search warrant prior to Moussaoui being extradited to France, there was no chance that his duffel bag could be searched in the US. And multiple times they deliberately slant the information in NSLU hearings for FISA warrant approval to effectively block this search warrant application from being approved by the NSLU.]

> In response, Martin told the OIG while he believed that the LHM was generally well-written, the three paragraphs for the foreign power section of the LHM were not adequate to establish the foreign power element, and he intended, along with Robin, to compile a "real" foreign power section when an NSLU attorney gave approval to move forward with the FISA request. Martin said that handling the request this way was common and denied that he was attempting to "torpedo" the case.

> Robin also told the OIG that, as they did with other cases, she and Martin were preparing to create a new foreign power section for the Moussaoui LHM that would be comprehensive. She said that Martin's edits were normal and that the changes were designed to create "a logical, intelligent package that we thought would get to court" and to make the LHM less "inflammatory." She explained that by "inflammatory" she meant that the Minneapolis LHM was not focused, but rather used terms that were geared toward getting someone's attention without providing any evidentiary support. Robin asserted that Martin was streamlining the document and adding the "buzzwords" that he knew from experience OIPR would require in order to get the package to the FISA Court. Robin stated that the RFU wanted FISA requests to get OIPR's attention but did not want the RFU to seem like "maniacs."

The FISA application did not get to a FISA Court in over 17 days from the original request, it never even made it to the FBI OIPR section that had to approve it prior to it being submitted to the FISA Court. It never made it past the NSLU unit at the FBI Headquarters, which had to approve it prior to it being submitted to the OIPR unit. In not one of any of these many discussions at FBI Headquarters is there any talk at all that if this search warrant application is not approved quickly, thousands on

Americans might be killed. Saving the lives of thousands of Americans is never considered, not even once. The lives of thousands of Americans meant nothing to the people at FBI Headquarters.]

17. Consultation with NSLU chief Spike Bowman

On the afternoon of August 28, Martin and Robin met with Bowman to discuss the Moussaoui FISA request. Don told the OIG that he had planned to attend the meeting but that on his way to Bowman's office he was called into a meeting with Section Chief Rolince. No one from Minneapolis was asked to participate in the meeting.

Bowman told the OIG that it was "quite unusual" for him to be consulted about a particular FISA request. He said that it also was unusual for the field office to be so adamant that it had sufficient evidence to obtain a FISA warrant and for the Headquarters SSA to be as adamant that the FISA warrant was not sufficiently supported.

Martin orally briefed Bowman about the facts of the Moussaoui case but did not provide him with any of the documentation that he had with him. Robin told the OIG that she thought that Bowman was very familiar with the facts because he had been briefed by other attorneys who had been involved in the matter.

Martin said that Bowman advised that even if everyone were to agree that the Chechen rebels could be pled as a foreign power, the Minneapolis FBI lacked sufficient evidence to establish that Moussaoui was an agent of that foreign power. Martin told the OIG that Bowman said that Tufitri stating that Moussaoui told Amnay how to serve Allah by fighting with the Chechen rebels did not meet the standard of an agent of a foreign power. According to Bowman, Martin conveyed the opinion that he did not believe there was sufficient information for a FISA. Bowman said he was aware that Moussaoui was a French citizen who had overstayed his visa, that he was a bad flight school student who paid in cash and who could not satisfactorily explain how he was being supported in the United States, that he was asking odd questions about the airplane (such as whether you could open the doors during flight), that he was more interested in learning how to take off and land the airplane than flying it, that he was traveling with a friend who did not seem to share his interest in aviation, and that the French authorities had reported that Tufitri was blaming

Moussaoui for recruiting Amnay to fight in Chechnya on behalf of the rebels there.

Bowman told the OIG that he did not believe, based upon the facts, that there was sufficient evidence of a link to a foreign power. He said that he was aware that the Minneapolis FBI wanted to argue that because there was some connection between Moussaoui and Khattab and because there was a relationship between Khattab and bin Laden, Moussaoui was an agent of al Qaeda. Bowman said that it was his under- standing that it was common knowledge that Khattab and bin Laden had "some kind of relationship," but in his opinion this was not a close enough link to argue that Moussaoui was an agent of al Qaeda. Bowman also stated that one Muslim encouraging another Muslim to fight in a Muslim cause was not sufficient to meet the requirements of an agent of a foreign power under FISA.[137]

[137] As discussed in Chapter Two, the legislative history of FISA provides that to meet the definition of an agent of a foreign power, there must be "a nexus between the individual and the foreign power that suggests that the person is likely to do the bidding of the foreign power" and that there must be a "knowing connection" between the individual and the foreign power.

We asked Bowman whether he had read the Phoenix EC and whether it would have made a difference in his advice. Bowman stated that he read the Phoenix EC only after September 11, but that he believed for several reasons it would not have made any difference if he had read it at the time. He asserted that the Phoenix EC was a routine communication pointing out what a field office believed was an "anomaly" and that it was not an "alarmist" communication. In addition, he said that the Phoenix EC did not connect any of the people referenced in the Moussaoui case with any foreign power. He said that it did not "associate Moussaoui with anything."

According to this testimony, had Bowman read the Phoenix EC, that terrorists were apparently training in aviation in Phoenix and then reviewed the information that Moussaoui appeared to also be a terrorist attempting to train on a huge commercial aircraft, he would have still ruled that the FBI could not apply for a search warrant to stop a possible horrific terrorist attack that might kill thousands of Americans. The FBI went each year before Congress asking for billions of dollars and justified this by saying they were going to protect Americans from any terrorist attacks, and then when the evidence is right in front of them that a huge attack might be in the works, they do everything they can to block any investigation that could have prevented this attack with what can only be described as the stupidest of arguments.

After the events of September 11, the FBI made the case that in spite of the horrific failure they should continue to be the organization that would protect Americans, that they had now added additional safeguards to their organization that would be foolproof. The problem with this argument is that as clearly indicated above, there is always going to be a fool that is going to be bigger than the proof!]

> After meeting with Bowman, in an e-mail to Gary and Acting SAC Roy, Martin informed the Minneapolis FBI of Bowman's opinion that there was insufficient evidence of a connection to a foreign power. Martin wrote:
>
> "We just left a meeting with Spike Bowman, #1 in NSLU. He says we have even less than I thought. Apparently, even if we could show that the ZM that recruited [the person] in France is the one you have locked up in INS detention, we still don't have a connection to a foreign power. We would need intel to indicate the guy was actually a part of the group, an integral part of the movement or organization, and not just an individual [redacted]."
>
> In the e-mail, Martin advised Gary to call him to discuss the next course of action. Roy responded by e-mail and wrote, "Thanks for your help and continued support." Gary's notes indicate that Martin and Gary also spoke on the telephone after the Bowman meeting and Martin explained that the FBI needed more information linking Moussaoui to a foreign power. The notes state that Martin told Gary, "We need [Moussaoui] to be an integral part of a terrorist organization." [138] The notes also indicate that Martin conveyed that more intelligence information was needed on "how he is acting on behalf of a foreign power." The notes state: "Bottom Line – You don't have a foreign power." The notes also state that Martin advised Gary to ensure that Moussaoui was entered on a watch list and that the FBI's Paris Legat was contacted about deportation arrangements for Moussaoui (which we discuss below).

[138] Bowman told the OIG that Martin accurately conveyed his advice that even assuming that there was a foreign power to which the FBI could attempt to connect Moussaoui, the Minneapolis FBI lacked sufficient evidence to establish that Moussaoui was acting as an agent on behalf of a foreign power. He stated, however, that Martin's interpretation of his advice that agency law requires a showing that the target was an "integral part" of the terrorist organization was not correct. He opined that the agency standard required a showing that the target was "serving the interest" of the foreign power.

b. Translations of recorded conversation between Al-Attas and "Ahmed" and Al-Attas' will

With regard to Al-Attas, Henry asked an Arabic speaker who was not employed by the FBI to translate Al-Attas' will, and to translate and transcribe the tape of a nine-minute conversation between Al-Attas and the individual we call "Ahmed," the imam from Al-Attas' mosque whom Al-Attas called while he was in custody. According to an e-mail from Gary to Roy on August 29, the translation by the translator stated Ahmed had said on the tape, "I heard you guys wanted to go on Jihad." Gary's e-mail also stated that the translator reported that Al-Attas immediately responded on the tape, "Don't talk about that now." In addition, Gary's e-mail stated that the translator informed the Minneapolis FBI that Ahmed became very upset when he heard that Moussaoui was going to be deported.

Gary's e-mail added that, according to the translator, the translation of the will that Al-Attas had with him stated that "death is near" and that "those who participate in Jihad can expect to see God."[139]

[139] The will and the tape also were sent to the FBI's Chicago Field Office for translation and transcription by an FBI linguist, which was completed around September 6, 2001. The Chicago translation of the tape was the same as that of the initial translator: "Sheikh do not talk about it now. Do not talk about it now sheikh." The Chicago translation said the will stated that "death has approached" and expressed Al-Attas' hope that "Allah will award him with paradise and keep him with the prophets, martyrs and pious." Henry forwarded these translations to FBI Headquarters in an e-mail dated September 6, 2001, with a lead that stated "For information."

On August 29, Roy transmitted the information from the will to Don by e-mail, stating, "I obtained some additional information this afternoon and I am forwarding that to you. Please understand that this is only preliminary and we realize the interpretation was not done by a certified linguist." Roy did not ask that Don do anything in particular with the information.

Don responded by e-mail, writing, "The 'will' is interesting; The Jihad comment doesn't concern me by itself in that this word can mean many things in various Muslim [sic] cultures and is frequently taken out of context." Don told the OIG that the term "Jihad" often was used and had many different meanings.

Failure to reconsider seeking a criminal warrant

After Martin conveyed to the Minneapolis FBI that FBI Headquarters believed that the FISA warrant was not feasible, the Minneapolis FBI and FBI Headquarters began taking steps to finalize Moussaoui's deportation. Yet, neither FBI Headquarters nor the Minneapolis FBI reconsidered the criminal search warrant issue or trying to contact the Minneapolis US Attorney's Office (USAO) about a criminal search warrant, even after the legal decision was made that insufficient evidence existed to obtain a FISA warrant.

Don told the OIG that he did not know why he, Martin, or the Minneapolis agents did not raise the issue again about seeking a criminal search warrant, once a decision was made not to pursue the FISA warrant. He suggested that it did not happen because no one thought to raise the matter again.

Don said that looking back on the matter now, he wished that there had been a discussion about seeking a criminal warrant once the FISA route was exhausted. Martin told the OIG that if the Minneapolis FBI believed that it had sufficient evidence to obtain a criminal search warrant, then the Minneapolis FBI should have raised the issue. He said, however, that he did not believe that there was sufficient evidence of a crime to obtain a criminal search warrant.

When Henry was asked why he did not propose seeking a criminal warrant once the FISA route was exhausted, he responded, "I never thought about it." He stated that he "could have done that but it did not occur to [him]." Gary told the OIG that he did not pursue a criminal search warrant because FBI Headquarters would not obtain the requisite authorization from the Department of Justice.

20. Additional French information received about Moussaoui

On August 30, the FBI's Paris ALAT provided additional French information to the Minneapolis FBI and FBI Headquarters about Moussaoui. The ALAT's report included information from a person who we call "Idir" who knew Moussaoui. Idir confirmed the relationship between Moussaoui and Amnay. Upon learning of Amnay's death, Idir had accused Moussaoui of causing the death. Idir explained that Moussaoui had become a radical fundamentalist and that he had brought Amnay to these beliefs. He said that Moussaoui and Amnay "were inseparable, one was the head and the other was the armed hand of the same monster." Amnay states that when Moussaoui had come to his Community, Idir had warned the local Muslim community of the moral danger Moussaoui posed to young Muslims and that Moussaoui was "driven from at-risk urban areas by his co-religionists for propagating his message of intolerance and hatred."

The report from the Paris ALAT also stated that Idir recalled that Moussaoui had traveled to Kuwait, Turkey, and Afghanistan. Idir said Moussaoui was a "strategist" who was potentially very dangerous and was devoted to Wahabbism, the Saudi Arabian sect of the Islamic religion adhered to by bin Laden. Idir also described Moussaoui as "extremely cynical" and "a cold stubborn man, capable of nurturing a plan over several months, or even years and of committing himself to this task in all elements of his life." The date of birth Idir provided for Moussaoui was the same as the one in Moussaoui's passport, which had been seized upon his arrest in Minneapolis.

The Paris ALAT's report also stated that the ALAT had inquired with the French authorities about deporting Moussaoui to France and that the French authorities were interested in pursuing the matter. In the lead portion of the EC, the Paris ALAT wrote a lead for the Minneapolis FBI that stated, "With FBI HQ concurrence and assistance, advise Legat Paris of interest in further exploring the possibility of deporting [Moussaoui] by US law enforcement escort to France as described in the text of this EC." The lead for the RFU was a "read and clear" lead.

Gary's notes indicate that Martin brought this new information to Gary's attention in a telephone call on August 30.

Deportation plans

Martin and the Minneapolis FBI coordinated with the INS to finalize plans for Moussaoui's deportation. Under the law, Moussaoui could be deported to either France, his country-of citizenship, or England, his country of last residence. The French advised that they could hold Moussaoui and search his belongings, and on approximately August 30, it was decided to deport Moussaoui to France.

Don initially was opposed to sending FBI agents to escort Moussaoui. He sent a reply e-mail to Roy on August 31 stating that he believed that the deportation of Moussaoui should "remain an INS issue." (Emphasis in original.) Don wrote in the e-mail the Minneapolis FBI should ensure that the FAA was involved and noted that FAA sky marshals were armed.

Section Chief Rolince told the OIG that he also was "initially opposed" to sending a Minneapolis agent with Moussaoui to France. His said that at first he thought it was unnecessary because, based on his past experience, the agent would have accompanied Moussaoui in an attempt to obtain information. He said that he changed his mind when it later was explained to him that the Minneapolis agent was going to accompany Moussaoui as part of an overall strategy to ensure that Minneapolis obtained all of the information from the search and further investigation.

On September 4, Don, Martin, and Roy received an e-mail from the Paris ALAT in which he stated that he wanted to confirm the deportation plans. He wrote that it was his understanding that the proposal was to send Moussaoui to Paris with an INS escort and the FBI case agent.

Martin replied by e-mail that Don "still [held] the position that [Moussaoui] will be escorted by INS, and that no FBI personnel is needed." Martin also wrote that because the case had been opened only two weeks and because the interviews were well documented, the ALAT and the French authorities should be able to handle the case without the FBI sending the case agent.

Gary also told the OIG that he had suggested at some point that Roy "go up" the chain of command about Minneapolis' FISA request, but that Roy did not. Gary told the OIG that he believed that Roy was "not aggressive enough" because he did not appeal to anyone in upper management at FBI Headquarters, but that Roy may have decided to focus on the deportation issue and "drop" the FISA issue. Gary told the OIG that he believed that part of the reason that Roy did not contact anyone above Don about the Moussaoui FISA request was because he was an acting SAC, and also possibly because Roy did not have any international terrorism experience. Gary also said that Gary himself was "on a learning curve too," and that if he had more experience, he would have sought assistance from someone above Don with trying to get FBI Headquarters to submit the Moussaoui FISA request to OIPR.

Roy responded to this issue by stating that he did not go above Don because, before the September 11 attacks, there was no apparent "urgency" to the Moussaoui matter, and he believed that the Minneapolis FBI had taken the matter through the appropriate channels, since the head of the NSLU also had given his opinion on the FISA request. Roy added that shortly after Bowman's opinion was received, the deportation plan was in place and that plan was going to result in Moussaoui's belongings being searched, which was what Minneapolis was attempting to achieve.

Dissemination of information about Moussaoui

On August 28, Don received an e-mail from the FBI detailee to the CIA who we call Craig, which indicated that the CIA had not yet received a formal communication from the FBI about the FBI's requests in the Moussaoui investigation. Don e-mailed Martin and Robin on August 31 to request that they prepare a "comprehensive teletype" to the CIA about Moussaoui.

Henry told the OIG that he began drafting an LHM to the FAA and that he thought it was important to inform the FAA that Minneapolis believed that Moussaoui wanted to seize control of an airplane and that he might be released soon after he was back in France. Henry prepared a 7-page LHM in which he summarized the FBI's investigation, including what the FBI had learned from the flight school employees about Moussaoui and his interest in and ability to use the mode control panel. Henry noted, "While it is not known if his physical training and study of martial arts are also connected to this plan, such preparations are consistent with facilitating the violent takeover of a commercial aircraft."

Henry also included a section at the end of the LHM labeled "threat assessment" in which he wrote:

Minneapolis believes that Moussaoui, Al-Attas, and others not yet known were engaged in preparing to seize a Boeing 747-

400 in commission of a terrorist act. As Moussaoui denied requests for consent to search his belongings and was arrested before sufficient evidence of criminal activity was revealed, it is not known how far advanced were his plans to do so.

Henry wrote that the French authorities were planning to receive Moussaoui into custody when he was deported and would search his belongings, but that it was not known whether he could be detained over the long term.

On September 4, Gary discussed this LHM with Martin. According to Gary's notes of the conversation, Martin told him not to provide the LHM to the FAA because FBI Headquarters was issuing a teletype that day to all agencies. Martin instructed Gary to provide the local FAA office with a copy of the teletype once it was received in Minneapolis.

Martin's 11-page teletype was issued on September 4. It was addressed to the FBI Minneapolis and Oklahoma City offices, six FBI Legat offices, the CIA, FAA, Department of State, INS, US Secret Service, and US Customs Service. The teletype consisted of a summary portion and the details of the Moussaoui investigation. In the summary portion of the teletype, Martin wrote that Moussaoui had been detained on a visa waiver overstay violation after he was brought to the attention of the FBI by instructors at the Minneapolis flight school, who had become suspicious of him because he was taking flight simulation training for a 747-400 aircraft. The teletype stated that this training is normally given to airline pilots, and that Moussaoui had no prior experience and had paid $8,300 in cash for the course. The teletype included the information received from the French authorities about Moussaoui, including that he adhered to radical Islamic fundamentalist beliefs and he had recruited a person to join the Jihad against Russian forces in Chechnya. It also included the later information received from the French, such as the description of him as "full of hatred and intolerance and completely devoted to the Wahabite cause" and that he was "considered to be potentially very dangerous because of his beliefs and the nature of his character." The teletype added that Moussaoui had traveled to Pakistan for two months prior to his arrival in the United States and that "it is noted that Islamic extremists often use Pakistan as a transit point enroute to receiving training at terrorist camps in Afghanistan."

After the summary portion of the teletype, Martin included specifics from the investigation, most of which were taken from the 26-page EC prepared by Henry at the initiation of the investigation. Unlike the LHM Henry had prepared to give to the FAA, however, the teletype did not contain a threat assessment or any indication that the Minneapolis FBI believed that Moussaoui, Al-Attas, and others not yet known were engaged in preparing to seize an airplane in commission of a terrorist act.

On September 5, Henry and an INS agent provided Martin's teletype to the FAA office in Minneapolis and briefed FAA employees on the threat that the Minneapolis FBI believed Moussaoui posed. Henry told the OIG that while the teletype contained most of the facts of the investigation, it lacked conclusions and analysis and had "no statement of opinion as to the threat that this represents."

Martin told the OIG that at the time that he was preparing the teletype, he was not aware that the Minneapolis FBI was preparing an LHM to provide to the local FAA office. He stated that he discussed to whom to address his teletype with the IOS at FBI Headquarters who prepared teletypes for the FBI when it disseminated threat information, and he also discussed the contents of the teletype with an FAA employee detailed to FBI Headquarters. Martin told the OIG that he included in the teletype what he believed was supported by the facts of the investigation. He asserted that Minneapolis had a "gut feeling" that Moussaoui was "up to no good," but did not have intelligence information of an ongoing plot or plan to hijack an airplane.

Don told the OIG that the FBI used teletypes to disseminate facts gathered from an investigation and to disseminate information about threats. He said that Martin's teletype was a compilation of the facts and did not "speculate as to what Moussaoui was up to." Don said that the FBI anticipated that the recipient agencies would provide the FBI with their reactions to the teletype or information that was relevant to the teletype.

September 11 attacks

On September 10, Henry received an e-mail from Carol, the FBI Headquarters employee whom he had contacted for more information about Khattab's connections to Al Qaeda. She asked whether Henry had ever received anything that he could use in support of a search warrant for Moussaoui's belongings. Henry responded that the RFU had determined that Minneapolis had insufficient evidence to pursue either a FISA or a criminal warrant. He noted that Minneapolis "did not pursue this further because [FBI Headquarters has] directed that this is an INS matter." He added that he "strongly disagree[d]." He also wrote that Moussaoui was being deported to France and that his "big fear" was that Moussaoui would be released following his deportation. He concluded by thanking Carol for her assistance.

Carol responded a few minutes later by e-mail in which she wrote, "Thanks for the update. Very sorry that this matter was handled the way it was, but you fought the good fight. God Help [sic] us all if the next terrorist incident involves the same type of plane."

On the morning of September 11, at 8:34 am Eastern Standard Time, Martin sent an e-mail to Gary finalizing plans for Moussaoui's deportation, which the FBI believed would occur within several days. Just 12 minutes later, the first hijacked airplane hit the North Tower of the World Trade Center.

After the first airplane hit, Martin tried to call Minneapolis ASAC Charles but reached Rowley instead. According to Rowley, she told Martin that it was essential to get a criminal search warrant for Moussaoui's belongings. Rowley said that Martin instructed her that Minneapolis should not take any action without FBI Headquarters approval because it could have an impact on matters of which she was not aware. In her May 20, 2002, letter to the FBI Director, Rowley wrote that in this conversation with Martin she had said "in light of what just happened in New York, it would have to be the 'hugest coincidence' at this point if Moussaoui was not involved with the terrorists." Rowley wrote that Martin replied "something to the effect that I had used the right term 'coincidence' and that this was probably all just a coincidence." Rowley told the OIG that she agreed to follow Martin's directive not to immediately seek a criminal warrant, and she was told that FBI Headquarters would call her back.

Martin told the OIG that he recalled that there was a lot of confusion when he spoke to Rowley. Martin said that he did not recall making the statement about a coincidence to Rowley. He explained to the OIG that he did not feel comfortable giving legal advice about seeking a criminal warrant, so he went to the NSLU attorney who we call Tim, who advised that the Minneapolis FBI should seek the criminal search warrant.

While Rowley was waiting for a return call from FBI Headquarters, Minneapolis ASAC Charles was on the telephone with Don. Because Acting SAC Roy was out of the office, Charles was responsible for the Minneapolis office and had called FBI Headquarters immediately after the first airplane hit the World Trade Center. Charles had reached Don and asked him for permission to seek a criminal search warrant for Moussaoui's belongings. According to Charles, Don responded that he still did not believe that there was enough evidence to support a criminal search warrant. Charles stated that, during the course of this conversation the Pentagon was hit by another hijacked airplane, and that Don then told Charles to go to the USAO for a criminal warrant.

Don confirmed that he spoke to Charles on the morning of September 11. He asserted that he immediately told Charles that the Minneapolis FBI could seek a criminal warrant. Don told the OIG that it was a brief conversation that lasted several seconds at the most.

Once Don authorized contact between the Minneapolis FBI and the Minneapolis USAO, Henry and Rowley went to the USAO to obtain a criminal search warrant for Moussaoui's belongings. They consulted with several senior Assistant United States Attorneys, and drafted an affidavit in support of the search warrant. The affidavit stated that there was probable cause to believe that the laptop computer and other items seized from Moussaoui would contain evidence of a violation of 18 USC § 32 – destruction of aircraft or aircraft facilities. The affidavit contained much of the information reported in Henry's 26-page EC about Moussaoui's interactions with the flight school and interviews with the Minneapolis FBI, as well as the information from Al-Attas' will and from the transcribed conversation of Al-Attas while he was in custody. The affidavit also included information about the September 11 attacks on the World Trade Center and the Pentagon. The search warrant was granted that day.

The FBI searched Moussaoui's belongings that were being held at the INS offices in Minnesota, including the laptop computer, associated computer software such as diskettes, spiral-bound notebooks, clothes, and a cellular telephone. The return from the search warrant stated that the following items, among other things, were found: a pair of shin-guards; a

Northwest Airlines 747 cockpit operating manual; two 747 training videos; seven spiral notebooks containing handwritten notes about aviation; a Microsoft flight simulator book; a PowerPoint compact disc; a cell phone; binoculars; headphones; a skullcap; a cassette recorder; European coins; eyeglasses; disposable razors; and several documents, including financial records, blank checks, and identification papers from France.

Moussaoui's belongings did not reveal anything that specifically provided a warning or an indication of an imminent terrorist attack. There were no plans, correspondence, or names or addresses in his computer or notebooks that linked him directly to the September 11 terrorist attacks. However, information was obtained in the search that, through further traces, was used by the government to indict Moussaoui for conspiring in the September 11 terrorist attacks.

(J) Information received from British authorities on September 12-1 3

On September 11, after the attacks, the London Legat again requested information about Moussaoui from the British. According to British reports that the FBI reviewed on September 12 and 13, Moussaoui had attended an al Qaeda training camp in Afghanistan... The ALAT told the OIG that he did not know why the British authorities failed to provide the information about Moussaoui sooner. However, he said that 10 to 15 days to respond to a request for information from the FBI was normal.

OIG Analysis

We concluded that there were significant problems in how the FBI handled the Moussaoui case. In our view, these problems were attributable to both systemic issues in how the FBI handled intelligence and counterterrorism issues at the time, as well as to individual failings on the part of some of the individuals involved in the Moussaoui case.

A. No intentional misconduct

At the outset of our analysis, we believe it is important to state that we did not conclude that any FBI employee committed intentional misconduct, or that anyone attempted to deliberately "sabotage" the Minneapolis FBI's request for a FISA warrant, as Rowley wrote in her letter to FBI Director Mueller. For example, Rowley argued that Martin edited the initial FISA request submitted by the Minneapolis FBI and omitted information to "deliberately further undercut the FISA effort." Rowley also suggested that as part of the alleged sabotage, FBI Headquarters personnel failed to make Minneapolis aware of the two Phoenix ECs.

As we discuss below, we believe that Rowley's letter raised significant problems in the way the Moussaoui investigation was handled, and we criticize some of the actions of FBI employees. Her letter also alluded to broader problems that existed in how the FBI handled intelligence matters and FISA requests. But contrary to her assertions, we found no evidence, and we do not believe, that any FBI employee deliberately sabotaged the Moussaoui FISA request or committed intentional misconduct.

Summary of the FBI Inspector General's report

The process: applying for the FISA search warrant

The process to obtain a search warrant was for the field agent, in this case, Agent Harry Samit as the primary investigating field agent, to do the investigation, present this information to Headquarters, to the RFU at FBI Headquarters in Washington DC. A recommendation from FBI Headquarters would be issued to start either a criminal or an intelligence investigation, and obtain either criminal or FISA search warrants, or additional information would be requested to ensure the FISA Court would approve the warrant.

Harry Samit was convinced that Moussaoui was a possible terrorist and that he was part of a larger operation that was about to carry out a horrific attack inside of the US. If a terrorist attack was actually going to take place and in fact was imminent, as the Minneapolis FBI investigators thought, and in fact turned out to be the correct analysis of the evidence they had, it would have been imperative for everyone involved in this investigation to prevent this attack.

Everyone at the FBI connected with this investigation had to have been aware that every minute of delay in getting search warrants and not proceeding with the investigation potentially could result in a delay long enough that it would allow a horrific terrorist attack to be carried out with the most horrific of consequences.

All of this information made it highly likely, according to FBI Agent Harry Samit, that Moussaoui was a terrorist, who with other confederates was planning to hijack a large US airliner and fly it into the World Trade Center Towers or the White House." Even to an ordinary American, no other explanation seemed reasonable.

Samit had even stated in a LSH prepared for the FAA that says; "Minneapolis believes that Moussaoui, Al-Attas, and others not yet known were engaged in preparing to seize a Boeing 747-400 in commission of a terrorist act. As Moussaoui denied requests for consent to search his belongings and was arrested before sufficient evidence of criminal activity was revealed, it is not known how far advanced were his plans to do so."

In spite of all of this evidence, Harry Samit was never given permission to even request a criminal or a FISA search warrant. Michael Maltbie and David Frasca went to numerous attorneys at the FBI NSLU to seek an opinion on the evidence that Harry Samit had obtained, but these attorneys rendered the same opinion over and over; that there was insufficient evidence to show that Moussaoui was an agent of a foreign power, or to even show that the foreign power being proposed in the FISA search warrant request was a "recognized foreign power," shorthand for a foreign power that had been used in a FISA application before.

The FBI IG report states:

> At the outset of our analysis, we believe it is important to state that we did not conclude that any FBI employee committed intentional misconduct, or that anyone attempted to deliberately "sabotage" the Minneapolis FBI's request for a FISA warrant, as Rowley wrote in her letter to FBI Director Mueller. For example, Rowley argued that Martin edited the initial FISA request submitted by the Minneapolis FBI and omitted information to "deliberately further undercut the FISA effort." Rowley also suggested that as part of the alleged sabotage, FBI Headquarters personnel failed to make Minneapolis aware of the Phoenix EC.

But contrary to her assertions, we found no evidence, and we do not believe, that any FBI employee deliberately sabotaged the Moussaoui FISA request or committed intentional misconduct.

But then they go on to say:

"Although it is impossible to reconstruct Martin's exact conversations with the NSLU attorneys, the evidence shows that Martin provided a brief recitation of the facts that contained less than all of the available information about Moussaoui. At the start of the briefings Martin also conveyed to the NSLU attorneys his belief that there was insufficient evidence for a FISA. He did not present the request to NSLU attorneys neutrally or convey the Minneapolis FBI's strong concerns that Moussaoui was likely to commit a terrorist act. Martin under-sold the case to the attorneys and conveyed it in a way that did not fully present the field's views."

"In addition, when presenting the case to NSLU attorneys, Martin made clear that he did not think there was sufficient evidence for a FISA warrant and orally provided some facts of the case."

"NSLU chief Bowman told the OIG that it was unusual for a field office to be so adamant that there was sufficient information to support a FISA warrant and for the SSA to be so adamant that there was not... Because Moussaoui was going to be deported shortly, the opinion that there was insufficient evidence to seek a FISA warrant was, in effect, a denial of the FISA request. In light of the unusual circumstances of this case, it would have been a better practice for the NSLU attorneys to inquire about available documentation and review it before rendering an opinion. In this case, however, a comprehensive legal review of the documentation in the Moussaoui investigation did not take place."

"It is impossible to determine for certain whether any of the NSLU attorneys would have provided a different recommendation concerning the Moussaoui FISA request if they had read all the documentation, including the 6-page LHM or the 26-page EC."

"We believe that the RFU failed to appreciate the significance of these individual facts and failed to analyze their effect on the totality of the circumstances. Instead, it treated each fact individually and too readily discounted their significance. The end result of this approach was that all of the facts were never

414

fully considered in their totality or fully presented to anyone for a legal sufficiency review – whether by the NSLU or OIPR."

So from the FBI IG report, it appears that because of the way this information was presented for review to the attorneys at the NSLU, they all recommended that that no request for a FISA warrant be submitted to the OIPR unit, which had to approve the request before it could be submitted to the Court. But according to this very report, Maltbie undersold the case and did not present the case neutrally.

Maltbie did not indicate the concerns of the Minneapolis FBI agents to the NSLU attorneys in spite of the fact that these FBI agents were convinced that it was possible a huge terrorist attack might take place against a massive target in the US, resulting in thousands of US civilian deaths. And Maltbie did this multiple times, with each review of the information given to the attorneys at the NSLU resulting in a determination that there was not enough evidence to request a search warrant. It might be argued if he had only done this once it might be unintentional, but it is hard to see how when this is done many times it can be claimed he could have been doing this unintentionally.

When the search warrant review process indicated that no search warrant request should be submitted to the OIPR, it meant, according to the FBI IG report, that no search of Moussaoui's possessions would take place before he was deported to France, effectively shutting down the investigation in the US. According to the information that came out of the Moussaoui trial, there was enough information in his duffel bag to allow the FBI in a few days to find almost all of the hijackers who took part in the attack on 9/11.

In addition to underselling each review with the NSLU attorneys, Maltbie gave information back to FBI agent Harry Samit that would create an impossible burden to overcome.

Harry Samit had to show that Moussaoui was an agent of a "recognized" foreign power, without explaining that this meant that this group had been used in a prior FISA warrant request.

Then Maltbie said that Harry had to prove that this Moussaoui was the one referred to in information the FBI had obtained from French intelligence.

Finally Maltbie said that Harry had to show that Moussaoui was an "integral part of this foreign power," instead of "agent" of a foreign power" when even the NSALU lawyers said this was a completely incorrect interpretation of their advice.

Even after thousands of people had been killed in the attack on the World Trade Center Towers on 9/11, Maltbie would not allow Harry Samit to request permission to seek a search warrant. It is clear that there was nothing Harry Samit could have done that would have gotten Maltbie to agree to allow him to submit a request to the OIPR prior to the attacks on 9/11.

Maltbie's boss, David Frasca, would not even allow Minneapolis to submit a request to the OIPR, even after the attack on the WTC Towers. It was only after this attack was followed by the attack on the Pentagon that Frasca allowed Minneapolis to submit a search warrant request to the FBI OIPR. The search warrant was approved in hours by OIPR, submitted to the FISA Court and granted in hours on 9/11 with no more evidence than the evidence that had been turned down many times in the weeks prior to 9/11. Since there was absolutely nothing that tied Moussaoui to the events on 9/11, the fact that a criminal search warrant was approved in hours shows that there had been enough evidence all along to get a search warrant, had it been pursued by FBI Headquarters with sufficient diligence.

This appears to substantiate the charges by Coleen Rowley that FBI Headquarters deliberately sabotaged Harry Samit's investigation, and Harry Samit's statement under oath at the Moussaoui trial that both Maltbie and Frasca were guilty of criminal negligence for blocking an investigation that could have prevented the deaths of 3,000 Americans.

Rowley had written a letter to both FBI Director Mueller and the *New York Times*, when Mueller had appeared before Congress and said that the FBI never had enough evidence that could have allowed them to prevent the attack on 9/11, information she knew was wrong. Not only had these two FBI managers allowed terrorists to murder many Americans but also it was quite clear from the information in Rowley's letter that the very top leadership of the FBI was covering this up. And as this analysis on the FBI IG report shows, because of clear inconsistencies between the information brought out at the Moussaoui trial and the FBI IG report, even the FBI IG report appears to be a cover-up for culpability of FBI managers at FBI Headquarters.

The credibility of the FBI IG report is further diminished by the fact that it never even once pointed out that only five FISA applications had ever been turned down in over 18,300 FISA applications. While the FBI IG report dwells on the fact than Maltbie and Frasca required significantly more information than Harry Samit had or was ever going to get, and even lent an air of credibility to these requests when by all accounts that were totally bogus. Not once does the FBI IG report point out that the chance for any FISA request being turned down was only one chance in over 3,000 applications.

This report never even hints at what should have been the main concern by the managers at FBI Headquarters. A basic common-sense view of the evidence suggested that if Harry Samit were right, and the FBI blocked his investigation; thousands of Americans would perish in a huge terrorist attack.

The two instructors who had been training Moussaoui had the opinion that Moussaoui was a terrorist, FBI agent Harry Samit and his boss had this opinion, even the CIA, where this information was deemed so significant it went right to very top of this organization in just a few days, came to this opinion.

Not once in all of this testimony is it noted where people at FBI Headquarters consider that thousands of Americans might perish if Harry Samit's investigation did not go forward. Michael Maltbie and David Frasca never came to this opinion until it was too late, after the events of 9/11, while their boss Michael Rolince further ensured that no one else at the FBI would take action that could have prevented the events on 9/11 by blocking this information from going to anyone else at the FBI. And to this day, why this happened has not been explained in any way!

The FBI inspector General's investigation of the events on 9/11 was undertaken under orders from Congress to find out what individuals at the FBI were culpable in not preventing the events on 9/11, either by negligence or deliberate action.

The Moussaoui Trial

The Moussaoui trial is important to the investigation of 9/11 and the finding the truth behind the events on that day because this is the first time information regarding the issues surrounding the events on 9/11 have been brought into a US Federal Court and testimony given under oath with cross-examination to test the accuracy of the statements made.

The critical information that the whole country expected to come out of this trial was not whether Moussaoui was going to get the death penalty or not, but what the testimony of several of the government witnesses would disclose about what exactly did the government know about the events on 9/11 prior to September 11, 2001. What were Michael Maltbie and David Frasca going to say was the reason they had sabotaged the investigation of Moussaoui in the weeks just prior to September 11? What was the role of Khalid Shaikh Mohammed in the 9/11 attacks, a role that the CIA had carefully tried to minimize in their testimony before the Joint Inquiry Committee and the 9/11 Commission, in order to obfuscate their culpability in allowing 9/11 to occur?

While testimony at both the Joint Inquiry Committee and the 9/11 Commission was riddled with misleading testimony, half-truths and even out-and-out lies, as has been shown by the publicly available information that has come out after these investigations, the Federal Court setting made it much harder to obfuscate or provide untruthful testimony. Even if prosecution witnesses dissembled in their testimony over the events on 9/11, the defense attorneys had an obligation to test every single one of their statements to ensure they were true.

Zacarias Moussaoui had pleaded guilty in April 2005 to six charges, some of which carried a penalty of capital punishment. The issue that was to be decided by this court trial that had started March 6, 2006 was whether the government could sentence him to death for the events that occurred on 9/11. Moussaoui had admitted to US authorities prior to this trial that he had been part of another plan to fly a commercial airliner into the White House, although he claimed this plot was separate from the 2001 attacks. He had vowed to fight against being sentenced to the death penalty. Moussaoui is the only person who has been charged in the US in connection with the attacks on 9/11, even though the US government is holding almost all of the leaders who directed this attack including Khalid Shaikh Mohammed, mastermind of the 9/11 attack, Abu Zubaydah, al Qaeda commander outside of Afghanistan, and Ramzi bin al-Shibh, one of the key planners of the 9/11 attack, and roommate to several of the pilots who carried out the attack on 9/11.

From news accounts of the trail of Moussaoui

Prosecution opening statements

For the prosecutors to obtain a sentence of death, they had to prove that Moussaoui's actions caused the death of at least one person on 9/11. Their argument was that Moussaoui could have prevented the attacks if he had not lied to the FBI, but had told the FBI what he knew about the plot on 9/11. In a novel twist, and to counter the argument that Moussaoui was not required to give testimony that could incriminate himself because of the US Constitution, prosecutors have argued that once Moussaoui decided to talk to FBI, he was then obliged from that point to tell what he knew and to tell the truth. They have further argued that the jury should also consider in the deliberations what might have happened if Moussaoui had told what he knew about the plot on 9/11 [AP, March 23, 2006].

Defense opening statements

The defense attorneys for Moussaoui argued that regardless of what Moussaoui said to the FBI, it would have made no difference anyway. They argued that because of bureaucratic inertia and intransigence inherent at the FBI, the FBI had been rendered dysfunctional and incapable of reacting to any information Moussaoui might have had in his possession fast enough to have stopped the events of 9/11.

Defense attorney McMahon said during opening statements on March 6 that even if Moussaoui had told authorities what he knew in August 2001 about the plot for 9/11, officials wouldn't have had sufficient time to stop these events from taking place [Bloomberg, March 20, 2006].

After opening statements, Judge Brinkema warned the prosecution they might have a very weak case because of the right guaranteed in the Constitution, the right not to testify against one's self. Remaining silent cannot be used to sentence a defendant to death.

Prosecution witness, FBI Agent Harry Samit
Monday, March 20, 2006

In testimony for the prosecution, FBI Agent Harry Samit told a federal jury on March 20, 2006 that he had Zacarias Moussaoui arrested by the INS for immigration violations on August 16, 2001 at the Residence Inn located in Eagan, MN. He had been convinced after a short investigation that it was extremely likely that Moussaoui was a terrorist attempting to get flight training on large US airliners in order to fly a large US airliner into a building in the US. Samit said he had been first alerted to Moussaoui from a phone call from two concerned instructors at an Eagan, MN flight school, who had been convinced Zacarias Moussaoui was possibly a terrorist attempting to get flight training on a large US aircraft.

Agent Harry Samit testified that he tried numerous times to get his superiors in Washington to help with the investigation of Moussaoui and to confirm what he felt were good reasons to believe that Moussaoui was going to be part of an imminent terrorist airline-hijacking.

However, in court he stated his FBI managers at FBI Headquarters had blocked his investigation on numerous occasions. He had described this obstruction to Justice Department investigators as "criminal negligence." He told the jury that they were motivated by a desire to protect their careers [*NY Times*, March 21, 2006].

Once the INS arrested Moussaoui, he and his possessions were in the custody of the INS. On August 17, 2001, his INS-appointed lawyer no longer allowed the FBI to interview him. Agent Samit sent e-mail to his FBI superiors about Moussaoui marked urgent starting on August 18, 2001. He eventually would send over 70 e-mails as FBI Headquarters repeatedly blocked his requests for search warrants required to search Moussaoui's duffel bag, notebook and laptop computer [CNN Friday, March 24, 2006].

During the two days of interviews he had with Moussaoui, FBI Agent Samit testified to the jury that he felt he had "uncovered enough facts to be suspicious Moussaoui was a terrorist" and was convinced Moussaoui was planning to hijack a large US aircraft. At first, Samit said he initially had not linked Moussaoui to Usama bin Laden, because there were many other terrorist groups that also had very similar if not the same beliefs [Bloomberg, March 20,2006].

Mr. Samit confirmed that he had later told Justice Department investigators during the FBI Inspector General's investigation of the FBI that he felt that his superiors in Washington "took a calculated risk not to advance the investigation" by blocking his requests for search warrants for Mr. Moussaoui's belongings and computer. He further testified that he had come to believe that "the wager was a national tragedy." [NY Times, March 21, 2006].

Agent Harry Samit told jurors, "What I believed and what I could prove are two different things."

Samit had been able in two days of questions to get the following information from Moussaoui:

Moussaoui said, "He was in flight school for fun and intended to visit New York." Moussaoui also said he wanted to visit the White House." He further said that he spent two months in Pakistan just before his arrival in the United States in February 2001. He claimed he stayed in the Karachi area and had been looking for a wife. Although Pakistan is the gateway to Afghanistan, Samit said he never asked Moussaoui directly if he had been to Afghanistan or attended a terrorist training camp.

Samit interviews Hussein al-Attas

Samit said he believed Moussaoui was lying. His traveling companion, a friend from Oklahoma named Hussein al-Attas, had told agents Moussaoui talked about "Jihad," or holy war, and his approval of martyrdom. This directly contradicted what Moussaoui had told Agent Samit.

Samit composes e-mail

Samit said he considered Moussaoui "the most serious" matter and composed a 26-page e-mail on August 18, 2001, which he sent to over 50 people at the FBI Headquarters. In this e-mail he said Moussaoui's evasiveness, his religious views, his possession of knives and his bulking up at a gym gave the Minneapolis office "cause to believe" that Moussaoui and "others yet unknown were engaged in a "conspiracy to commit a terrorist act."

As a field agent in Minnesota, he said, he needed both help and approval from his superiors at Headquarters to get a criminal search warrant to continue his investigation. Samit needed to show on the search warrant application "probable cause" of a crime. To obtain a FISA intelligence search warrant he had to show there was "probable cause" that Moussaoui was a foreign power or an agent of a foreign power. A terrorist organization would qualify as a foreign power.

After sending this e-mail and a request for Headquarters to proceed with applying to a court for a criminal search warrant, David Frasca at FBI Headquarters rejected his request to apply for this warrant on August 21.

Samit focuses on getting a FISA search warrant

After having his request to apply for a criminal search warrant rejected, Samit said he did not request another criminal search warrant, even when he later became aware from statements Moussaoui's travel companion made that clearly indicated that Moussaoui had lied to Agent Samit during his investigation. Lying to an FBI agent is a federal crime that can initiate criminal charges and in fact be grounds to request a criminal search warrant.

Instead, he decided to focus on gathering enough information to get a FISA intelligence search warrant.

His first request for a FISA search warrant application, which he sent to Michael Maltbie who worked for David Frasca, was rejected. Michael Maltbie said he had to show that Zacarias Moussaoui was an agent of a "recognized foreign power;" an agent of a foreign power, i.e. any terrorist organization, was not good enough.

In order to get additional information to show that Zacarias Moussaoui was an agent of a recognized foreign power, Samit sent a request to the FBI offices in France, where Moussaoui said he was from.

Three weeks later, Agent Samit was able to get information from French intelligence that showed that Moussaoui had served under a terrorist leader in Chechnya, who had been connected to bin Laden and al Qaeda.

The communication sent to Samit and FBI Headquarters agent Mike Maltbie from a bureau agent in Paris stated that French intelligence thought that Moussaoui was "very dangerous," and had been indoctrinated in radical Islamic Fundamentalism at London's Finnsbury Park mosque, and was "completely devoted" to a variety of radical fundamentalism that Usama bin Laden believed in, and that he had traveled to Afghanistan. However Michael Maltbie, Agent Samit's superior at FBI Headquarters, stripped all of this information off of the FISA application linking Moussaoui to al Qaeda before handing the FISA warrant to the FBI General Counsel. The procedure at the FBI was that In order to obtain a FISA search warrant, the FISA application first had to be approved of by the FBI General Counsel prior to being submitted to a FISA Court.

This second application for a FISA search warrant was rejected by the General Counsel for the FBI because he said the application was not sufficient. In a later investigation by investigators for the FBI Inspector General's office, Michael Maltbie said he had stripped off all of the information linking Moussaoui to al Qaeda before handing the FISA warrant to the FBI General Counsel because he felt this information was not sufficient.

Mike Maltbie complained to the agents in Minnesota that the Minneapolis agents were getting people "spun up" for no good reason about Moussaoui.

Agent Samit testified that instead of requesting a search warrant in the US FISA Court, Maltbie wanted to deport Moussaoui to France where he and his possessions could be searched without the need for a US search warrant. According to Samit, this was because requesting a FISA search warrant could potentially have jeopardized Maltbie's career at the FBI.

Samit said his investigation was for all intents and purposes "shut down" by his managers at FBI Headquarters. According to his testimony, his investigation was "denied every tool at the division's disposal."

Agent Samit did not made any more requests for FISA intelligence search warrants after his second attempt to get one failed. He was even forbidden from contacting local federal prosecutors in order to obtain a criminal search warrant in Minneapolis [CNN, March 20, 2006; www.times.uk.com, March 25, 2006].

Defense cross-examination of FBI Agent Harry Samit
Monday, March 20, 2006

In a five-hour cross-examination, on Monday, Moussaoui defense attorney Edward MacMahon's questions about e-mails detailed a long and frantic series of attempts by Samit to obtain a warrant to search Moussaoui's personal belongings. The FBI agent Samit testified that he tried to do everything possible to warn his superiors of suspicions about a possible hijacking.

Prosecutors had already stated that had Moussaoui's possessions been searched before September 11, FBI agents would have found several small knives, jumbo-jet pilot manuals, two lists of flight schools that the other 9/11 pilots had attended, and other clues that might have helped them understand the Sept. 11 plot [CNN, March 20, 2006].

Under a well-constructed cross-examination of Agent Samit, MacMahon was able to show that the lies Moussaoui told had never fooled FBI Agent Samit. In the 26-page memo Agent Samit sent to FBI Headquarters on August 18, he accused Moussaoui of plotting international terrorism and air piracy over the United States. These are two of the six charges Moussaoui had pleaded guilty to last year, 2005 [AP, March 20, 2006].

FBI agents in the Minnesota FBI Field Office were appalled when their Washington supervisors denied their requests for search warrants. Samit in his testimony told the jury, "They obstructed it." He called the actions of Michael Maltbie and David Frasca a decision that ultimately "cost us the opportunity to stop the attacks."

Agent Harry Samit said he sent the warning on August 18, 2001 in an e-mail marked "**urgent**" to over 50 counterterrorism officials.

McMahon asked Samit. "You thought you had a terrorist planning terrorist attacks?" "Yes, sir," Samit responded.

French communication, August 22, 2001

Samit stated that on August 22 he learned from the French that Moussaoui had recruited someone to go to Chechnya in 2000 to fight with Islamic radicals under Emir Ibn al-Khattab. He reiterated a conversation he had with a CIA official who told him on August 22 or 23 that al-Khattab had fought with bin Laden in the past. This information was unfortunately not enough to convince either Maltbie or Frasca, his superiors at FBI Headquarters, to support his request for a FISA warrant to search Moussaoui's possessions.

French communication, August 30, 2001

MacMahon displayed a communication addressed to both Harry Samit and FBI Headquarters Agent Mike Maltbie from French intelligence that described Moussaoui as "very dangerous" and indoctrinated in radical Islamic fundamentalism at London's Finnsbury Park mosque. The report said that Moussaoui was "completely devoted" to the variety of radical fundamentalism that Osama bin Laden believed in. The French even pointed out that they had evidence that Moussaoui had traveled to Afghanistan.

From this Agent Samit correctly concluded that Moussaoui must have been at al Qaeda training camps based in Afghanistan.

Maltbie and Frasca blocked every attempt Samit made to get a search warrant. Because of this, Agent Samit repeated in court a remark he had made to FBI Inspector General investigators who were investigating FBI and the events on 9/11.

"I accuse the people in FBI Headquarters of criminal negligence."

No one from Washington called Samit to say this intelligence from France had changed the situation in any way in terms of obtaining a search warrant for Moussaoui possessions. Regardless of what information Samit provided FBI Headquarters, Maltbie and Frasca continued to say to Samit that he had not established a link between Moussaoui and al Qaeda terrorists. Samit told MacMahon he was never able to persuade Maltbie and Frasca or anyone at FBI Headquarters or the Justice Department to take his fears seriously.

Samit still works for the FBI and because of the possibility of retaliation, was extremely reluctant to say anything in open court that would come back and get him in trouble at the FBI. Samit acknowledged, under questioning from MacMahon, that he told FBI Inspector General investigators "obstructionism, criminal negligence and careerism" had prevented him from getting a warrant from Michael Maltbie and Maltbie's boss, David Frasca. He said it was that opposition that blocked "a serious opportunity to stop the 9/11 attacks."

Because Maltbie and Frasca blocked every attempt Agent Samit made to get search warrants to search Moussaoui's possessions and continue his investigation, an investigation that had a good chance of preventing the attacks on 9/11 was blocked. To this day, this has never been explained.

Coleen Rowley, an FBI lawyer, shared Samit's contempt for the people in Washington who were their superiors. In a letter she sent to both FBI Director Robert S. Mueller, and the *New York Times* in May 2002, she stated that FBI Washington managers Michael Maltbie and David Frasca had blocked the investigation of Moussaoui. After writing the letter, she was forced to retire from the FBI. She did not testify at the Moussaoui trial, and neither she nor Agent Samit, nor anyone else in the Minnesota FBI office, was ever contacted by the 9/11 Commission during their "what was supposed to be extensive" investigation of the events on 9/11 [*LA Times*, March 21, 2006].

Agent Samit explained in court that Mr. Frasca believed if a criminal warrant was applied for in the case of Moussaoui and turned down, and then a FISA warrant was requested, it might possibly arouse suspicion that agents were abusing the FISA Court in order to get information for a case they actually thought might be a criminal case.

Samit said senior bureau officials had once been told that he was trying to prevent Moussaoui from flying a large passenger airplane into the World Trade Center Towers.

Samit went on to describe how he took it upon himself to cable the Secret Service that the President's safety might be in jeopardy. He detailed in the cable that fact that Moussaoui, who at this time he was sure was an al Qaeda terrorist, had told him in an interview how he hoped to be able to fly a Boeing 747 from London's Heathrow Airport to New York, and how he also hoped to visit the White House. As Harry Samit explained it, it was obvious what this could mean. Moussaoui was a terrorist who wanted to take over a large US airliner, a Boeing 747 from a flight from London going to New York City, and either fly it into the World Trade Center Towers, or the White House. Samit stated in his communication to the Secret Service, "If he seizes an airplane from Heathrow to New York City it will have the fuel on board to reach DC." Samit said he never heard back from the Secret Service after he had contacted them over this threat [*LA Times*, March 21, 2006].

The White House and the Secret Service were clearly aware of Moussaoui and the fact that he was likely involved in a plan to hijack aircraft in order to attack the World Trade Center Towers or the White House. Since Moussaoui had been already arrested by the time FBI Agent Samit called the Secret Service at the White House, his role as a terrorist had been neutralized, and the only possible reason Samit had to call the White House after Moussaoui's arrest was to alert the Secret Service that persons in league with Moussaoui were still unknown and still posed significant threats to the US. At this point the White House knew the possible targets, the method of the attack and even the approximate timing for the attacks that were ultimately carried out on 9/11. What else did they need to have mounted a vigorous defense against this coming attack?

From the information that has come out since 9/11, it appears their reaction to this information was to do absolutely nothing to prevent the events that occurred on 9/11. Why this is so has never been explained.

Samit's letter to the FAA; August 31, 2001

MacMahon also presented in court an August 31 letter Samit was going to send to the FAA in order "to advise the FAA of a potential threat to security of commercial aircraft" from "whomever Moussaoui was conspiring with."

But inexplicably, and what only can be described as a continuing horror show, his boss Michael Maltbie barred him from sending his letter to FAA Headquarters, saying he would handle it [AP, March 20, 2006].

Samit said that when he had carefully prepared a long memo about Moussaoui for FAA officials, his Washington FBI superiors deleted key sections of the memo, including the part connecting Moussaoui with Al Qaeda and their leader Osama bin Laden.

Samit had become so frustrated with his managers at FBI Headquarters and was so sure attacks were imminent he went around his obstructionist FBI managers in Washington when they prevented him from sending his complete letter to FAA Headquarters. Instead he provided a copy of this memo to a FAA official he had known in Minnesota. The FAA official he sent the memo to never got back to him, and in fact never even asked to see the folding knives Samit had found in Moussaoui's pocket and his car, and which he had described in this memo to the FAA.

Samit overheard his boss, Agent Greg Jones, on the phone talking with FBI Headquarters, telling their FBI superiors that Minneapolis Agent Samit was trying to keep Zacarias Moussaoui "from flying an airplane into the World Trade Center." The FBI agent on the other end, replied to this statement with "that will never happen," and with unimaginable arrogance and ridicule completely discounted this dire prediction from the Minnesota FBI agents [LA Times, March 21, 2006].

On September 10, Samit had an e-mail exchange with a friend of his in the FBI, in which he had described his losing battle with superiors over proceeding with the Moussaoui investigation at all possible speed.

"Very sorry that this matter was handled the way it is, but you fought the good fight," she stated. "God help us all if the next terrorist incident involves the same type of plane."

The next day, terrorists hijacked four planes. Harry Samit's suspicions were right all along, but he was never able to convince his superiors that preventing the deaths of thousands of people was more important than their careers at the FBI.

The fact that Michael Maltbie was promoted at the FBI after the horrific events on 9/11 showed that Maltbie was indeed right; his career was much better served by obstructing Harry Samit's

428

investigation even if it resulted in the deaths of almost 3,000 people and traumatized almost every single person in the United States.

William Carter, an FBI spokesman, said after this horrific testimony on the deliberate obstruction of Agent Samit's investigation, an investigation that now even the FBI stated could have prevented the deaths of almost 3,000 people, that neither Mr. Maltbie nor Mr. Frasca, who are still employed there, nor the FBI itself would have any comment on this testimony [*NY Times*, March 21, 2006].

Essentially, it was not their business to have to explain why Maltbie or Frasca had sabotaged Agent Harry Samit's investigation, even if this investigation could have prevented the deaths of almost 3,000 people. It was simply not the responsibility of the FBI to have to explain this to anyone. The fact that 3,000 people had died due to the deliberate actions of Maltbie and Frasca was just tough luck!

The FBI said there would be no further comment or explanation on why Maltbie or Frasca had blocked Samit's investigation that now the prosecution is claiming could have prevented the events on 9/11 and prevented the deaths of the 3,000 lives lost in this horrific attack, or why Maltbie had been promoted after he obstructed this investigation in an act Harry Samit called criminal negligence.

Video deposition of al-Attas
Tuesday, March 21, 2006

When Samit had Moussaoui arrested in Minnesota in August 16, 2001, he was with al-Attas. Al-Attas spent over a year in jail for lying to 9/11 investigators. Al-Attas had originally gotten out of jail on bail when he was arrested with Moussaoui but was later re-arrested on September 11, 2001, when it became apparent both he and Moussaoui could be connected with the events on 9/11.

In a video testimony, al-Attas said Moussaoui talked about holy war every day when they had been roommates. Moussaoui had even taught him martial arts and had even suggested he should travel to Pakistan to learn how the Islamic militants were justifying a holy Jihad.

Moussaoui had told al-Attas, "Your obligation, like any other Muslim, is to be ready for Jihad... This is the only way for me (or you) to get to paradise."

Al-Attas met Moussaoui in a mosque in Norman, OK, called the Islamic Society.

They had been roommates in off-campus housing close to the University of Oklahoma. Al-Attas was a 24-year-old undergraduate at the University of Oklahoma and Moussaoui was a 33-year-old student at the Airman Flight School. Airman Flight School at one point had also given Mohammed Atta, pilot on American 11 that flew into World Trade Center North Tower, a quote for the same flight school training program that was later given to Moussaoui.

In August 2001 al-Attas drove Moussaoui to Eagan, MN, so he could start 747-jet simulator training, even though Moussaoui, after 50 hours of training, was still not able to fly a small, single-engine airplane.

Al-Attas told investigators that he found it unusual that Moussaoui would get flight training on a 747 when he was not able to even fly a small aircraft. Moussaoui had claimed that learning to fly a 747 would be "easy" because it had a computerized cockpit.

Before leaving Oklahoma for Minnesota, Moussaoui purchased binoculars and small folding knives at a sporting goods store in Oklahoma City.

Moussaoui told al-Attas that folding knives would be easy to conceal. Both al-Attas and Moussaoui stayed at the Residence Inn in Eagan, and were there when FBI agents took them into custody on August 16, 2001.

FBI agent Harry Samit testified that al-Attas told him that Moussaoui was a religious Muslim who talked about harming nonbelievers, preparing for Jihad and extolling martyrdom. Al-Attas had been given immunity in order to get him to provide a video testimony against Moussaoui [CNN, March 21, 2006].

Prosecution questioning of Michael Rolince
FBI Supervisor of International Terrorism Operations
Tuesday, March 21, 2006

On Tuesday, March 21, Rolince took the stand for the prosecution.

Rolince had been Supervisor of the FBI's International Terrorism Operations section at FBI Headquarters. In his testimony, he claimed he had spent only about 20 seconds discussing the Zacarias Moussaoui case prior to September 11, 2001. He acknowledged later, however, that he had additional discussions concerning Moussaoui. In fact he described two hallway conversations he had with his subordinate, David Frasca. These conversations, according to Rolince, dealt with a dispute Frasca and Maltbie were having with Minnesota FBI agent Samit over whether or not to proceed with getting a criminal or FISA search warrant in order to search Moussaoui's computer, notebook and duffel bag.

Defense cross-examination of Michael Rolince
Tuesday, March 21, 2006

On cross-examination by MacMahon, Rolince conceded that he discussed with both FBI and CIA officials a plan to have the French intelligence service search Moussaoui's possessions by deporting him to France.

When he heard about Moussaoui in a passing hallway conversation in August 2001, he had been informed that the "immediate threat" had been "neutralized."

According to Rolince, Frasca had warned him that Agent Samit was not satisfied with the reasons he and Maltbie had given to Samit to block his search warrant applications and that Agent Samit might be calling him to discuss this issue. It was well known in the FBI that anyone who went around official channels would be taking a big risk with their career from retaliation.

According to Rolince, "On any given day there were dozens" of debates at his level among the field offices, Headquarters and the Justice Department about whether they had enough information to get a search warrant [AP, March 21, 2006].

The now-retired Rolince stated that it was not until September 11, 2001 that he was informed about the Minneapolis Field Office's belief that Moussaoui was a terrorist intent on hijacking airliners.

Rolince said no one told him about the "hunches and suspicions" of the FBI agents at Minnesota. He further stressed, "The case was not anywhere near fully developed."

However, Rolince indicated he never read the urgent, lengthy memo sent that month by Samit to FBI Headquarters [CNN, March 21, 2006].

When MacMahon asked Rolince if he knew that when Moussaoui was arrested he was under suspicion of planning a hijacking, he replied: "No."

Then after a moment he asked, "Can I ask what document that's coming from?"

MacMahon replied; "That's Mr. Samit's communication to your office on August 18, 2001."

Rolince continued that Mr. Samit's "suppositions, hunches, and suspicions were one thing, and what we knew" was a different matter [NYTimes, March 22, 2006].

Rolince said that as many as 70 threats were under active investigation by the FBI in August. He went on to say that at least 100 buildings and structures in New York and Washington had been viewed as "logical targets" for terrorists. He even indicated that "there was concern throughout the law enforcement community, and we certainly anticipated an attack."

Rolince characterized Moussaoui's arrest in Minneapolis as one of these investigations. However, he suggested that the Samit investigation never produced enough details for the FBI to request search warrants to open Moussaoui's belongings. According to Rolince, It was easier to have him deported to France, where his possessions could be searched with fewer restrictions. Rolince admitted under cross-examination by the defense attorneys that had the FBI searched Moussaoui's possessions prior to 9/11, they could have had enough information to identify a number of the 9/11 hijackers. Using this information they could have gotten airport security officials to prevent the attacks on the World Trade Center and the Pentagon.

Rolince had concluded that there was simply not enough evidence uncovered by Minnesota Agent Samit in the three weeks prior to 9/11 to believe that Moussaoui was part of a larger suicide-hijacking mission [*LA Times*, March 22, 2006].

Under further cross-examination, Rolince conceded that he had never seen an April 2001 intelligence briefing paper warning that bin Laden was preparing to mount an attack, even though his signature was on it. MacMahon then produced an April 13, 2001, FBI communication, signed as approved by Rolince, that warned about a bin Laden terrorist attack inside the US. On the stand, Rolince said that he had never approved this document.

At this point the judge asked him; "Is it possible for a document to say you approved it if you have not approved it?"

When Rolince stated, "Absolutely," the jury, and the people who were in the courtroom attending this trial, broke out in laughter [www.timesonline.co.uk, March 25, 2006].

Prosecution questioning of Robert Cammaroto, a former top security official at the FAA
Wednesday, March 22, 2006

Robert Cammaroto, a former top security official at the Federal Aviation Administration, testified on Wednesday, March 22, 2006 that numerous security measures could have been implemented to protect against hijackings had officials known about Zacarias Moussaoui's terrorist plans, particularly if officials had known of a possible plot by Moussaoui to hijack airliners using small knives. Cammaroto was the FAA official most responsible for issuing security directives to air carriers in 2001 when officials became aware of various threats. According to Cammaroto, the FAA could have redeployed federal air marshals, tightened security checkpoints and directed flight crews to resist hijackers if the FAA officials had they known that al Qaida terrorists were training pilots to take over planes and fly them into buildings. Cammaroto also testified that security directives could be implemented almost immediately once the FAA learned of a threat and that these security measures could have been kept in place indefinitely.

Cammaroto stated that in 2001, "we (the FAA), believed airplane bombings would not involve suicide." The measures then in effect were designed to detect "Cubans" intending to hijack a plane to return to Cuba.

Prosecutors were using the testimony from Robert Cammaroto to show that the government could have prevented the attacks on 9/11 if Moussaoui had not lied about his terrorist plans when he was arrested on August 16, 2001 [AP, March 22, 2006].

Cammaroto described new FAA directives issued after Philippine authorities broke up what came to be known as the Bojinka plot by Ramzi Yousef, the person behind the World Trade Center bombing in 1993, and others to place liquid explosives with time-delayed fuses on US airliners. These bombs were designed to explode over the Pacific as the planes were flying to the US in 1995.

According to Cammaroto, he was still issuing directives related to this Bojinka plot five years after this plot had been discovered. He described a directive issued in 2000 that ordered US airliners to keep Ramzi Yousef's uncle, Khalid Shaikh Mohammed, and his baggage off any US airliner and for airport authorities to call law enforcement immediately if he ever showed up to board a flight. Mohammed was the mastermind behind the 9/11 attacks on the World Trade Center and the Pentagon.

Cammaroto said the details of the Bojinka plot, which were well known at the FAA, reinforced the view that attacks on passenger aircraft would most likely not be an attack involving suicide. According to Cammaroto, this was because prior to the Bojinka plot, the terrorists had set off a bomb they had left on a passenger airliner, using a delayed-action trigger, killing one Japanese passenger.

Defense cross-examination of Robert Cammaroto
Wednesday, March 22, 2006

Defense attorneys pointed out in cross-examination, however, that Yousef's roommate and co-conspirator, Abdul Hakim Murad, told Philippine authorities in 1995 that they had been planning to fly a plane into the CIA Headquarters as part of this plot. Defense attorneys stated to the jury that the government knew as much, if not more than Moussaoui did, about the events on 9/11 beforehand and had not been able to act on this information in time to prevent the attacks on 9/11 [*SF Chronicle*, AP, March 23, 2006].

Prosecution questioning of former FBI Agent Aaron Zebley
Friday, March 24, 2006

For three hours, in testimony from FBI Agent Aaron Zebley, jurors were given information that spelled out how the FBI was able to quickly uncover the connections between the terrorists and was able to identify the pilots of the four hijacked airplanes, and seven of the other hijackers, the terrorists who physically took over the airplanes.

The FBI demonstrated how they traced records of telephone calls between the US-based terrorists to Ramzi bin al-Shibh in Hamburg, Germany, and then to the overseas paymaster located in the UAE. They then traced these numbers to addresses where the hijackers lived in the US. From there, they were able to obtain bank and shopping records of the terrorists, and even track down the flight schools the terrorists attended.

This rapid detective work, unfortunately not done until well after the events on 9/11, used many of the 11,000 agents at the FBI. The prosecutors were attempting to show this investigation could have unraveled the plot of 9/11 in the time between Moussaoui's arrest and the attacks.

Testimony by FBI Agent Aaron Zebley, witness for the prosecution, was brought in to show that if Moussaoui had admitted to being a hijacker at the time of his arrest, and had told the FBI about the rest of the plot for the attacks on 9/11, FBI agents would have been able to find the other terrorists and prevent the attacks that took place on 9/11 [http://www.cnn.com March 24, 2006].

Zebley went over in detail how the FBI could have found 11 of the 19 hijackers by searching wire transfer and phone calling-card records in addition to investigating flight schools identified from the two lists of flight schools in Moussaoui's duffel bag.

According to Zebley, the FBI could then have warned the Federal Aviation Administration and the Secret Service [*Reuters*, Alexandria, March 24, 2006].

Defense cross-examination of Aaron Zebley
Friday, March 24, 2006

MacMahon, Moussaoui's defense attorney, tried to blunt this argument, that a major investigation would have been launched and would have found the other terrorists in time to stop the attacks on 9/11. He said the FBI had completely ignored warnings from FBI Agent Harry Samit. He also said the FBI Agent Samit had sent 70 messages to FBI Headquarters warning that he thought Moussaoui was a terrorist, but no one listened.

The defense even produced evidence the FBI had information by August 23, 2001 that two hijackers – Khalid al-Mihdhar and Nawaf al-Hazmi – both known to be al Qaeda terrorists who were associated with the East Africa embassy bombings and even the *Cole* attack, were in the United States to carry out a terrorist attack. Despite having this information, and the fact al-Mihdhar and al-Hazmi used their real names while in they lived in the United States, the FBI was not able to find them prior to 9/11 [*Reuters* Alexandria, March 24, 2006].

Does "The FBI needs a confession from a...terrorist to start an investigation?" MacMahon asked in court, a question that caused the prosecution to state an objection.

In reply, and somewhat rattled by the question, Zebley said, "Everyone would have been listening had Moussaoui admitted why he was rushing to complete a Boeing 747 flight simulator training, why he was buying folding knives with short blades and who was sending him money."

According to Zebley, if Moussaoui had allowed the agents who had arrested him to go through his belongings including his duffel bag, they certainly would have found the Western Union receipts for $14,000 in wire transfers from Germany from Ramzi bin al-Shibh, and bin al-Shibh's name and phone number written in Moussaoui 's notebook.

Zebley said that would have been "something you could run with."

Moussaoui's money transfers would have led the FBI right to one of the key coordinators of the plot – Ramzi bin al-Shibh. Ramzi bin al-Shibh, from Yemen, had tried four times to acquire a visa to come to the United States. Each time he had failed. One of the pilots of 9/11, Ziad Jarrah had even vouched for him on two of these visa applications. Ramzi bin al-Shibh not only had sent Moussaoui the money for his flight training, but had also helped facilitate the transfer of money for the flight training of three of the other hijacker-pilots, all of whom had once shared an apartment with him in Hamburg, Germany.

Using telephone records, Zebley demonstrated how a call made by bin al-Shibh was traced to an al Qaeda operative in the United Arab Emirates, a call made to have money wired to Moussaoui. The UAE number Moussaoui called could be traced to the other hijackers, who had called that number repeatedly in the summer of 2001. These phone calls could then have been traced back to the US, to home addresses and then flight schools and the other communications between the terrorists.

Robert Spencer asked Zebley; "Was that information available to the FBI in August 2001?"

Zebley, answered, "It could have been."

In the cross-examination of Zebley, he did concede that the FBI investigation never showed that Moussaoui had ever called the UAE telephone number that had been called by Ramzi bin al-Shibh. He also conceded that in fact Moussaoui had indeed never once contacted any of the other terrorists who took part in the hijacking on 9/11 [CNN, March 24, 2006].

The prosecution rested its case after FBI Agent Zebley's testimony concluded.

After Moussaoui was found eligible for the death sentence, the trial started the last phase, to determine if there was sufficient evidence to Moussaoui put to death, or were there mitigating circumstances that should be taken into account to preclude the death sentence.

At this point in the trial, many of the relatives of the victims presented testimony as to how this event affected them.

Thursday, April 6, 2006

On Thursday, April 6, 2006, former New York City Mayor Rudolph Giuliani described the scene he came upon the morning of September 11, 2001, stating that at first he just could not believe people were jumping to their deaths from the World

Trade Center. It was not until he actually saw people jumping that he began to believe what other people had been telling him.

When he had first arrived on the scene, his deputy told him about people jumping from the World Trade Center Towers.

He stated, "I saw several people, I can't remember how many, jumping. There were two people right near each other. It appeared to me they were holding hands. Of the many memories, that's one that comes to me every day."

In court he said that when the buildings collapsed, "It was horrid. The worst thing I've ever seen in my whole life... parts of human bodies... hands or legs."

Friday, April 7, 2006

On Friday, April 7, 2001, Tamar Rosbrook stated that he had made a video on September 11, 2001, which showed on video monitors in the court, person after person jumping from the World Trade Center and attempting to land on an awning located in the plaza at the bottom of these towers, in a mistaken belief this might prevent them from being killed.

From images in this video, prosecutors pointed out the body parts and the people on fire.

Jurors saw person after person choosing to jump, knowing they would be killed rather than stay in the towers and be killed by the fire.

"That was a man on fire as he fell through the canopy. Those are the remains of his body," Rosbrook stated in US District Court in Alexandria.

Monday, April 10, 2006

On Monday, the jury listened to audiotapes made from 9-1-1 phone conversations of two people who were trapped in the towers as they requested emergency help.

On the first tape, Melissa Doi, who worked for IQ Financial Services on the 83rd floor of the South Tower, told the 9-1-1 operator as her office filled with smoke.

"I'm going to die. I know I'm going to die,"

The operator replied, "No, no, no, no, no, no."

Doi: "Please, God, it's so hot. I'm burning up." "It's so hot; it's very, very hot. Are they going to be able to get somebody up here?"

The operator replied: "Of course, ma'am... We're coming up for you."

Doi: "Well, there's no one here yet, and the floor is completely engulfed."

Later, Doi stated to the operator: "I don't see any air anymore; all I see is smoke. I'm going to die."

Again the operator replied back to her: "No, no, no. Ma'am, say your prayers."

The last that is heard is Doi crying: "Help, help, help, help."

Tuesday April 11, 2006

In another tape, Kevin Cosgrove, who was a vice president at Aon Corporation, and worked 22 stories above Melissa Doi, called 9-1-1. He stated to the emergency operator.

"We're not ready to die, but it's getting bad." A minute later, he stated, "Oh, please hurry; I've got young kids." Then he said, "Smoke, really bad. 105, Two Tower... Can't see. It's really bad."

As the tape was played, scenes of the burning towers synchronized to the time of his call were shown to the jurors.

Cosgrove stayed connected to the operator up to the very instant the building collapsed. In the final second of his conversation he was obviously aware that the building was collapsing.

"Oh my God, ohhhhhhh," as the tower starting to collapse, and an image was shown on a video screen which had been synchronized in time with his phone call. His call ended abruptly at 9:58 am, the time the South Tower collapsed.

C. Lee Hanson, the grandfather of 2½-year-old Christine, the youngest person killed in these attacks, described talking to his son on United Flight 175 while he was watching on television, the North Tower on fire from the first attack by American Airlines Flight 11.

His son Peter had called him from the airplane and told him the plane he was on with his wife, Soo-Kim, and daughter had been hijacked. They were traveling Los Angeles for a visit to Disneyland. His son stated on the phone: "I think they are going to try to crash this plane into a building. Don't worry Dad. If it happens, it will be quick."

Mr. Hanson said, "as we were talking, all of a sudden he stopped and said very softly: 'Oh my God, oh my God, oh my God.' I looked over at the television set and saw a plane fly into the building."

Wednesday, April 12, 2006

On Wednesday, prosecutors played the cockpit voice recordings of the hijackers seizing control of United Airlines Flight 93.

According to The *New York Times*, the 31-minute recording – heard in public for the first time – illustrated the sounds of struggle and panic on the flight as hijackers took control of the airplane and struggled with passengers who attempted to save their own lives by fighting back.

A long silence on the tape was broken by the cries of the hijackers at the controls of the plane, as passengers tried to break down the cockpit door.

One of the flight attendants had entered the cockpit in an attempt to help the pilots. While in the cockpit, she was heard begging the hijacker, "Please, please, don't hurt me." And then a short time later she again pleads, "I don't want to die, I don't want to die." This was followed by one of the hijackers saying: "Everything is fine." Apparently the terrorists had killed her by slitting her throat, a technique they had practiced extensively prior to boarding these flights.

At one point, the hijacker pilot, Ziad Jarrah, was heard on the tape as he stated; "Here's the captain, I would like to tell you all to remain seated. We have a bomb aboard, and we are going back to the airport, and we have our demands. So, please remain quiet."

This was an obvious attempt to quiet the passengers so they would not storm the cockpit *en masse*. Several passengers had learned from cell phone calls that two the other planes had already crashed into the World Trade Center in New York.

In a recording of one of the phone calls by Todd Beamer to an operator, he tells of his plans to overpower the hijackers. He is heard encouraging the other passengers with, "Let's roll."

The cockpit recording finally ended with three minutes of noise. This apparently was when the passengers were just outside the cockpit door. One passenger shouts, "In the cockpit! If we don't, we'll die!"

While this was taking place, two of the hijackers can be heard talking about ending their hijacking attempt.

One is heard saying; "Is that it? I mean shall we pull it down?" The reply is, "Yes, put it in it and pull it down."

Passengers are heard apparently breaking through the cockpit door and fighting with hijackers. While shouting; "Go! Go! ... Move! Move!" In a final moment of desperation the hijackers flip the plane upside down, and send it into a final plunge into the ground, while shouting; "Allah is the greatest" nine times. The plane hit the ground in Shanksville, Pennsylvania, at more than 500 miles an hour at 10:03 am.

Everyone on Flight 93 was killed instantly, all 33 passengers, five flight attendants, two pilots and the four hijackers.

April 13, 2006

On April 13, 2006, Zacarias Moussaoui testified for the second time. He told the jury of his delight in hearing witnesses who testified about the pain and grief they felt over losing their loved ones in such a horrific way on 9/11.

"It make my day," Mr. Moussaoui said several times when he was asked about his reaction to the one witness who had testified earlier. He even went on to ridicule the testimony of family members who had told the jury how these attacks had changed their lives forever.

"I find it disgusting that some people will come here to share their grief," he stated. "Americans should know, that grief is precisely what he and fellow fighters in al Qaeda want to achieve. We want to inflict pain on your country."

When the prosecutor asked about the account of an employee at the Pentagon who had crawled to safety from a corridor that had been demolished on September 11, 2001, Moussaoui stated, "I was sorry that he survived."

He did, however, take the opportunity to say that he condemned America for her support for Israel, and predicted that the radical Islamic movement he was a part of would eventually overcome the United States.

Prosecutor Robert A. Spencer asked Moussaoui if he would try to kill Americans, even in prison, if he was allowed to live.

"Any time, anywhere," Moussaoui replied.

On flying planes into buildings occupied by American civilians, Mr. Spencer said, "You'd do it again tomorrow, wouldn't you?"

"Today," Moussaoui stated.

In commenting on his defense attorneys, he said; "I felt you did not have my best interest at heart, first, you are an American, second, you are Jewish."

Mr. Moussaoui said the defense team's idea "to portray me as crazy" would not succeed. He said his lawyers should have presented other arguments to the jury to save his life. He went on to say that "prison would be worse than death" for him, and that he would be more valuable as a "bargaining chip" to exchange for American soldiers taken hostage. He felt this "could work on even the most revengeful juror," he said.

What information from this trial answered questions America had regarding the events on 9/11?

In particular what were Michael Maltbie and David Frasca going to say was the reason they sabotaged the investigation of Moussaoui in the weeks just prior to September 11? And what was the testimony from Khalid Shaikh Mohammed going to say about his role in the 9/11 attacks?

What was the information that came from Michael Maltbie and David Frasca, or Khalid Shaikh Mohammed that everyone had waited over four years to hear? And how was the government going to present testimony from these key people without negating the very careful veil of secrecy they had maintained for 4½ years about the events on 9/11? Even many of the relatives of some of the 3,000 people killed on 9/11 felt that this trial would reveal the information about the events on 9/11 that they thought their government had kept secret up to this point.

In the end there was virtually no new information from Maltbie, Frasca, or Khalid Shaikh Mohammed. The FBI said Michael Maltbie and David Frasca would not comment. Instead they had Michael Rolince (David Frasca's boss) testify, and true to form he said he knew practically nothing about Moussaoui. He said he had only one 20-second conversation about Moussaoui. The big question everyone was asking was why did Michael Rolince testify when it was Maltbie and Frasca who had been involved with the Moussaoui investigation, not Rolince, and Rolince claimed complete ignorance about Moussaoui.

What new information came from the trial of Zacarias Moussaoui?

The following facts, some of which had never been revealed before, came out of the testimony at this trial.

In Zacarias Moussaoui's duffel bag were the following items:

- **Two lists of flight schools where the other pilots who hijacked airplanes on 9/11 had trained**

- **Western Union receipts for $14,000 in wire transfers from Germany, from Ramzi bin al-Shibh**

- **Two folding knives with blades that were approximately four inches**

In his notebook, Moussaoui had the name and phone number of the person who had sent the money through Western Union, Ramzi Bin al-Shibh, roommate of Mohamed Atta, Ziad Jarrah and Marwan al-Shehhi, three of the 9/11 pilots and all of whom at one time had lived with Ramzi bin al-Shibh at 54 Marienstrasse in Hamburg, Germany.

According to testimony at this trial, had the FBI chased down the phone records for Ramzi bin al-Shibh prior to 9/11, they would have found that he had called an al Qaeda operative in the United Arab Emirates to get the money for Moussaoui.

That UAE number would have led back to several phone calls from the US. These calls were made by the other terrorist hijackers already in the US, who had called this number repeatedly in the summer of 2001. The phone calls could have been traced back to home addresses for these terrorists, to the flight schools they had attended and to additional communications between the terrorists.

The FBI was aware that Zacarias Moussaoui had been in a big hurry to finish his training. In fact he was in such a hurry he told FBI agents who first investigated him to quickly get their investigation completed so he could hurry back to finish his flight training. FBI Agent Samit testified he had found out from the flight school Moussaoui attended that his training was due to be completed by August 20. 2001.

After talking to Moussaoui's travel mate, Agent Samit became aware that Zacarias Moussaoui had lied to him. He had asked if Moussaoui was a radical Muslim or part of a radical Muslim group, and Moussaoui said he was not. His travel mate, however, confirmed he was a radical Muslim who had a massive hatred for Americans and wanted to fight and kill them in a holy Jihad.

Zacarias Moussaoui had $32,000 in his bank account he could not explain to FBI investigators. And he could never come up with any reasonable explanation why he was getting very expensive flight training on a Boeing 747 flight simulator when he did not even posses a private pilot's license.

Zacarias Moussaoui had refused to cooperate with the FBI. He refused to allow FBI Agent Samit to look through his belongings, his duffel bag and his notebook or his motel room. He stopped cooperating with the FBI completely and would provide no interviews to FBI agents after August 17, 2001.

While this fact could never be used in a court of law, but in the minds the Minnesota FBI investigators, this had to be *prima facie* evidence he was in fact a terrorist intent on doing great harm to the US using hijacked aircraft.

The two flight instructors for the Pan Am flight school thought that Zacarias Moussaoui was for sure a terrorist trying to get flight training on a large airline simulator in order to use a large US airliner as a flying bomb. He could not speak French although he said he was from France. He asked questions about whether certain doors could be opened during flight. And he wanted to simulate on the Boeing 7476 simulator flying a 747 from Heathrow to JKF in New York, although he did not even have a pilot's license.

Agent Harry Samit was not at all fooled by Moussaoui's lies. He knew from the many many pieces of evidence that Zacarias Moussaoui must have been a terrorist who wanted to fly a large US airliner into a large building in the US, and quite possibly use small knives to take over the aircraft.

All of this information was carefully communicated to FBI Headquarters in e-mail marked URGENT! In fact FBI Agent Harry Samit had sent 70 e-mails to FBI Headquarters marked "URGENT", in order to get a search warrant to pursue an investigation of Zacarias Moussaoui.

David Frasca, head the RFU (Radical Fundamental Unit) at FBI Headquarters, originally turned down Samit's request for a criminal search warrant; and Michael Maltbie, who worked for David Frasca, then turned down Harry Samit two more times when he tried to get FISA search warrant. The first time his FISA warrant application was not submitted to the FISA Court was because Michael Maltbie said he had to show that Zacarias Moussaoui was an agent of a "recognized foreign power." Being an agent of a foreign power, i.e. terrorist organization, was not good enough (this was according to the FBI Inspector General's report). The FISA Court in subsequent investigations by the FBI Inspector General have said the FISA Court has no concept of an agent of a "recognized foreign power;" only an agent of a "foreign power." So this reason given to FBI Agent Harry Samit by Michael Maltbie was bogus.

After a delay of three weeks in order to obtain additional information, Agent Samit was able to get information from French intelligence to show that Moussaoui was indeed connected to bin Laden and al Qaeda. He resubmitted his FISA warrant application to Michael Maltbie in order to get it approved so it could be submitted to the FISA Court. Michael Maltbie, according to the FBI inspector General's report, stripped off all the information from this FISA application describing in detail how Zacarias Moussaoui was linked to al Qaeda. When this application with this information stripped off was sent to the FBI General Counsel to be approved prior to sending this on to the

FISA Court, the General Counsel said this application was inadequate, and rejected it immediately, sending it back to Minnesota.

What is so tragic is that only five FISA search warrants have ever been rejected by the FISA Court in over 18,300 applications since 1978, the date when this process was first set up. Had either of these applications been submitted to the FISA Court there was less than one chance in 3,000 it would have been rejected. Had the search warrant been approved, the FBI, according to sworn testimony in this trial by former FBI Agent Aaron Zebley, would have found the two lists of flight schools where the other pilots of 9/11 had trained, the Western Union receipts for $14,000 in wire transfers from Ramzi Bin al-Shibh in Germany, the folding knives with small blades, and in Moussaoui's notebook the name and phone number of Ramzi bin al-Shibh. According to Aaron Zebley, this could have been enough to find 11 of the terrorists quickly and stop the events on 9/11.

What is even more ironic is that the RFU, the same unit headed by David Frasca and where Michael Maltbie was an agent, had been given a now famous memo from FBI Agent Williams from an FBI office in Arizona in July 2001. It stated his investigation had uncovered radical Muslims, and even persons who he suspected were part of the bin Laden organization, getting flight training at flight schools in Arizona. So the RFU knew terrorists are getting training at US flight schools, knew that FBI field agents in Minnesota thought that Zacarias Moussaoui was a terrorist attempting to get training on large US airliners and had found a link from him to bin Laden, leader of al Qaeda, and even knew at this time that a huge al Qaeda terrorist attack was about to take place and they proceeded to do everything possible to block this investigation.

This FBI group was aware that a huge attack would take place in the summer of 2001, and knew it was connected with Usama bin Laden. Rolince, the Headquarters supervisor of the FBI's International Terrorism Operations section, under which were the RFU headed by David Frasca and the Bin Laden Unit, had signed an April 2001 intelligence briefing paper warning that bin Laden was preparing to mount an attack. On April 13, 2001, in a

FBI communication approved by Rolince, a warning was even issued about the threat bin Laden posed to some target inside the US. Rolince had even stated in court that the FBI and his group in particular had warning about attacks on 100 buildings in New York and Washington, and certainly the World Trade Center Towers, the Pentagon and the Congress would have had to be right at the top of this list of buildings. So now this unit at the FBI Headquarters knows by August 23, 2001:

- Bin Laden was planning a huge attack for the summer or fall 2001 inside of the US.

- Radical Muslims, some connected to bin Laden were taking flight training in Arizona.

- Zacarias Moussaoui is a terrorist connected to bin Laden, and is trying to learn how to fly a large US airliner.

- Two terrorists connected to bin Laden, Khalid al-Mihdhar and Nawaf al-Hazmi, were in the US about to carry out a terrorist attack.

While Rolince said there was not enough evidence in the three weeks before the September 11 attacks to believe that Moussaoui was part of any large suicide hijacking mission, it was the belief of FBI field agents in Minnesota that Moussaoui was indeed a terrorist attempting to get flight training on a large US airliner in order to crash it into a large building in the US. However every attempt to get additional information by the Minnesota FBI field agents had been inexplicably blocked by people who reported to Rolince.

From Agent Samit's testimony, David Frasca and Michael Maltbie threw up roadblock after roadblock. This unit knew there was an imminent attack by Usama bin Laden, knew the attack would be inside of the US, knew about the Williams memo, and knew Minnesota agents had the INS arrest a person who was thought to be a terrorist getting flight training on very large aircraft, and still they did everything they possibly could do to block the investigation of Moussaoui.

Michael Rolince had even stated in testimony at this trial that:

When he heard about Moussaoui in a passing hallway conversation in August 2001, he said he was informed that the "immediate threat" had been "neutralized."

So it obvious that Maltbie, Frasca, and Rolince viewed Moussaoui getting training on how to fly a Boeing 747 as a threat to the US, and that with his arrest this threat had been neutralized. Thus by his own testimony they were well aware Moussaoui was a huge threat to the US.

But when does one person take over a jumbo jet by himself? Samit's boss had told Maltbie that Samit thought Moussaoui was the type of person who could hijack a large airliner and fly it into the World Trade Center Towers. But there are two towers, which would have taken at least two hijacked airliners to destroy. And prior hijackings had used five to six terrorists to hijack one airplane, so there must have been at least 10 or 12 terrorists involved if they were going after the World Trade Center Towers. If you arrest one you still have at least nine to 11 more terrorists getting ready to hijack at least two planes. So the big question is: why did they not start an investigation to find these other terrorists?

[NOTE: In July of 2004 I flew out to Minneapolis and had a sit-down interview with Coleen Rowley and her boss, FBI Supervisory Agent (Joint Terrorism Task Force) Joseph Rivers, at the FBI Field Office in Minneapolis. I wanted to go over with them exactly how I had known about the attack on the World Trade Center Towers, in February 2001. I also told them that I had gone through Logan Airport on September 8, 2001 looking for the al Qaeda terrorists who I assumed could be found in front of the security checkpoints at this airport. I knew the week ahead of the attack that they would be at these checkpoints carefully surveying the security procedures in order to try to figure out how best to get their four-inch knives on board the aircraft they were going to hijack without being detected. Oddly enough, FBI Supervisory Agent Rivers asked me how I knew the terrorists would be at Logan Airport. It turns out I didn't know for sure, but I was passing through Logan airport on my way to business trip to an EDA software conference, SNUG, at the Marriott, in Newton, MA, to be held on September 10. I had assumed since they would hijack four airplanes from a several of the big eastern airports, Logan was right at the top of the list for being one of these airports.]

No one has been able to explain when they viewed Moussaoui as a threat why Harry Samit was denied his requests for search warrants multiple times. The official FBI statement made by William Carter, the FBI spokesman, was that neither the bureau nor Maltbie nor Frasca, who are still employed there, would have any comment after the trail of Moussaoui was finished.

Testimony by Agent Samit shows that in addition to blocking his attempt to get search warrants several times, Michael Maltbie blocked Agent Harry Samit from sending a lengthy memo, without first deleting references to al Qaeda and bin Laden to the FAA, warning them about a potential threat to security of commercial aircraft from "whomever Moussaoui was conspiring with" and "connecting Moussaoui to Al Qaeda leader Osama bin Laden." There is no explanation at all provided as to why he did this.

While Agent Samit had blamed Michael Maltbie's actions for blocking several of his attempts to obtain search warrants on careerism, what justification is there for blocking references to al Qaeda in memos being sent to the FAA, warning them about the facts of the Moussaoui arrest? According to Robert Cammaroto, a former top security official at the Federal Aviation Administration, numerous security measures could have been implemented immediately to protect against hijackings had they known of Zacarias Moussaoui's terrorist plans. Stricter security could have been put in place before September 11 if officials had known of a potential plot to hijack airliners using small folding knives. This was exactly the information Agent Samit had and had put in this lengthy memo he had drafted for the FAA, and which was modified before being sent to the FAA by Michael Maltbie.

Agent Harry Samit said in his testimony at the Moussaoui trial that he sent this information to the local office of the FAA. The question then remains, why didn't this office alert FAA Headquarters? What is so ironic is after the disaster on 9/11, the FBI agent at FBI Headquarters, Michael Maltbie, who sabotaged these warrants and the investigation of Moussaoui and who did not allow Samit's memo to be sent unaltered to the FAA.

In October 2002, FBI Director Robert Mueller sat before Congress and said that after the most extensive investigation in US history not one other person in the US knew about the events on 9/11. If this were true then why is the prosecutor, who works for the same Justice Department as the FBI, now saying Moussaoui knew enough about the events on 9/11 that they could have been prevented if he had told the FBI what he knew?

Both he and Louis Freeh stated in sworn testimony to Congress and the 9/11 Commission that the FBI never had enough information to have prevented the events of 9/11. But their testimony was given over one year after the events on 9/11, after they knew the information in Moussaoui's duffel bag and notebook led right back to the other terrorists.

The only thing that prevented the agents in Minnesota from getting to the information in Moussaoui's duffel bag was Maltbie and Frasca blocking Agent Samit's request for a warrant from even being submitted to the FISA Court or a criminal court.

Long-time professional FBI field agents were sure Moussaoui was a terrorist trying to get training on a large US airliner. They had his duffel bag and notebook until they turned them over to the INS on August 17, 2001. They had statements from his travel companion who said he was a radical Islamist who wanted to kill Americans in a holy Jihad, which contradicted what Moussaoui had told the FBI, so they had evidence he had lied to an FBI investigator.

They had all of the information they needed right in Moussaoui's duffel bag and his notebook, according to sworn testimony from former FBI Agent Zebley, to have prevented the events on 9/11. They even had all of the information they needed to obtain a FISA warrant, in order to find the items in his duffel bag and notebook that could have been used to unravel the plan for 9/11. All that prevented the FBI from getting this information were the actions of Michael Maltbie and David Frasca in blocking the investigation of Zacarias Moussaoui. So Mueller's and Freeh's statements that the FBI did not have all the information necessary was only because of deliberate actions taken by the FBI, actions of FBI managers at FBI Headquarters now well established at the Moussaoui trial.

Why is this information at the Moussaoui trial not come out until March and April of 2006?

The Justice Department presented the following facts at the Moussaoui trail; that Moussaoui had enough information to stop the events on 9/11, that there were two lists of flight training schools in his duffel bag along with the Western Union receipts for $14,000 wired to him by Ramzi Bin al Shibh, along with small knives. The Justice Department stated that had the FBI been able to view this information, they could have stopped the events on 9/11.

The 9/11 Commission knew about Zacarias Moussaoui, and knew the FBI investigation of him had been blocked at FBI Headquarters. And yet not one person from the 9/11 Commission ever talked to anyone at the Minnesota FBI Field Office to find out why this investigation had been sabotaged. No testimony was taken from Agent Samit, Agent Colleen Rowley or Agent Michael Maltbie or Supervising Agent David Frasca.

This entire incident appears to have been swept under the rug by the 9/11 Commission for unexplained and unknown reasons.

No one knows to this day why the investigation of Moussaoui was sabotaged. This is what the 9/11 Commission was chartered to do. Was the 9/11 Commission investigation deliberately spiked? Was this part of some a cover-up? And why have Michael Maltbie and David Frasca never been forced to testify under oath to explain their actions in blocking Harry Samit's investigation of Moussaoui?

After the trail of Moussaoui was over the FBI said neither of them would comment, the FBI will not have any comment.

And why has mainstream news media not asked that this information be forthcoming so it can be printed in all of the major newspapers?

In Moussaoui's trial a, "Substitution for the Testimony of Khalid Shaikh Mohammed," was presented that said that neither the prosecution attorneys nor the defense attorneys had ever interviewed Khalid Shaikh Mohammed, and stated that they would never be given any opportunity to do so due to matters of "National Security."

Neither Khalid Shaikh Mohammed nor Ramzi Bin al-Shibh have been brought to trial, five years after the events on 9/11, when they were clearly the ringleaders of this attack? What are the matters of "National Security" that the CIA was still trying to keep secret 6 years after 9/11? Ramzi Bin al-Shibh had already confessed the role he and Khalid Shaikh Mohammed played in the attacks on 9/11, in an interview to an Arab TV channel prior to his arrest, so this argument is completely absurd.

No one to this day knows why the FBI sabotaged their own investigation that could have prevented 9/11. And not the Congress, or mainstream media has called on this agency to explain this.

Chapter 19

The *Cole* Investigation

The Joint Inquiry Committee investigation of 9/11, along with the 9/11 Commission report and the FBI Inspector General's report noted that the CIA had hidden information from the FBI on numerous occasions but were never able to explain the reasons why this had been done. In July of 2006 new information was published that documented several more times information had been with held from the FBI by the CIA. An article in the *New Yorker* magazine, "The Agent, Did the CIA stop an FBI detective from preventing 9/11?" by Lawrence Wright, details several more times that FBI *Cole* investigators had requested information from the CIA without success. This information is important since it adds to the record from the Joint Inquiry Committee, the 9/11 Commission and the FBI IG report and starts to fill in the missing pieces and explain the actions at the CIA that previously made no sense. This information allowed for the first time the complete story on 9/11 to finally be put together and told.

From the article "The Agent, Did the CIA stop an FBI detective from preventing 9/11":

Just after the attack on the *USS Cole*, in October 2000, John O'Neill, head of the FBI's National Security Division, assigned a Special Agent from the FBI New York Manhattan office, Ali Soufan, to lead the *Cole* investigation. He was the only FBI agent in New York who spoke Arabic. Ali Soufan had written a report earlier that year on a fatwa bin Laden had issued in February 1998, declaring war on the US, which O'Neill distributed to his supervising agents.

[Note: This is a strange coincidence since it was this same February 1998 Fatwa that I had read on the United flight from San Francisco to Newark, NJ, on February 11, 2001. After reading this Fatwa, I had concluded that bin Laden had publicly declared war on the US, which could only mean that he was going to hit the US with a mammoth attack. I could think of no other reason why he would publicly declare war on the US 10 years after al Qaeda had been started. Knowing a huge attack was coming; it only took a relatively short time, about 45 minutes to one hour, to conclude that this attack had to be against the

454

World Trade Center Towers. There was no other way to attack these builds as simple as using four large US aircraft hijacked in flight. With just simple logic it was easy to conclude they would use four or five al Qaeda hijackers per plane armed with four-inch knives, just the same sort of knives that were deemed legal to bring on board US aircraft by the FAA. Simple logic determined the time for this attack would most likely be in the first two weeks of September. The *Cole* attack gave the clearest indication that the al Qaeda attack would be directed at the WTC Towers. Bin Laden had used as weapons against the Cole, suicide, secrecy, surprise and psychology, and it was clear he must have felt that using these weapons he could successfully attack any target anywhere in the world, and clearly the largest targets in the world were the two World Trade Center Towers.

I had conclusion that the FBI investigators had focused too much on the minutiae instead of on the strategic significance on this attack, and thus had overlooked the fact that this attack now meant the biggest buildings in the US were subject to horrific attacks.

If the al Qaeda terrorists thought they could destroy any target in the world, why would they waste they effort on any other target than the biggest buildings in the biggest US city.]

Within days of the *Cole* bombing, Yemeni authorities brought two known al Qaeda terrorists, Jamal Badawi and Fahad al-Quso, in for questioning. These terrorists quickly admitted they had been to Afghanistan, and had met there with the one-legged jihadist, Khallad bin Attash. Badawi also confessed that he had been the one who had bought the boat Khallad had used in bombing of the *Cole*. Fahad al-Quso was later found to be the person who was to photograph the bombing of the *Cole*, a task he failed to do when he overslept on the day of the bombing. When Soufan learned for the Yemen police that al-Quso had mentioned the name Khallad, and that Khallad had a metal leg, he knew immediately that Khallad had to be the person identified years earlier as one of bin Laden's top lieutenants.

While neither Soufan nor O'Neill were at first allowed to question al-Quso or Badawi, the person in Yemen in charge of the *Cole* investigation, General Qamish, provided them with the passport photograph of Khallad. This was sent to the CIA, and to intelligence sources in Afghanistan who identified the photograph of Khallad right away as a top al Qaeda lieutenant. Ultimately the Yemenis relented and allowed Soufan to interrogate al-Quso. Al-Quso admitted after several days of intensive interrogation that he had been the person assigned to photograph the actual bombing and had also been assigned to deliver $36,000 to Khallad, money he had been given in Yemen. Al-Quso also told Soufan that he had first traveled to Bangkok and from there he was supposed to go to Kuala Lumpur to meet with Khallad there. However, when he was prevented from delivering the money to Khallad in Kuala Lumpur, Malaysia, he remained in Bangkok and delivered the money to Khallad there.

Soufan knew almost immediately this just did not add up. Al Qaeda financed terrorist attacks. Why would money be sent out of Yemen to be given to the mastermind of the *Cole* bombing, when the actual bombing took place back in Yemen?

To Soufan, this added up to the financing for yet another unknown terrorist attack. He concluded that this money was clearly not intended for the *Cole* bombing, but intended for a new upcoming terrorist attack. Ali Soufan at this point was aware that another terrorist attack might in the works and that a planning meeting must have taken place for this new attack in Kuala Lumpur, Malaysia.

In November 2000, Soufan sends the CIA station in Yemen the first of several official requests for information on Khallad. The CIA Yemen station actually had the photos from the Kuala Lumpur meeting in their possession at this time, photos of Khallad, Khalid al-Mihdhar and Nawaf al-Hazmi, and other al Qaeda terrorists together at this meeting.

Just after this request received no response, Ali Soufan asked the Director of the FBI, Louis Freeh, to send CIA Director, George Tenet, an official request on his behalf, formally asking for information the CIA might have on Khallad and if there had been an al Qaeda planning meeting in Southeast Asia, a meeting indicated by al-Quso's travels to deliver money to Khallad in Kuala Lumpur.

While the FBI had supplied much information to the CIA, it turned out that in most cases the CIA did not reciprocate by giving back information it had. In 1998, the FBI had uncovered a phone number in Yemen during their investigation of the East Africa bombings that had been called many times by the embassy bombers, both before and after the bombings. It was discovered that this number had even been called by bin Laden himself. This number was connected to an al Qaeda terrorist named Ahmed al-Hada, Khalid al-Mihdhar's father-in-law.

In December 1999, the NSA passed on information from an overheard conversation on Ahmed al-Hada's phone to the CIA and the FBI that there would be an upcoming meeting in Kuala Lumpur, and that Khalid, Nawaf and Salem, believed to be Nawaf's brother, would be attending. When the CIA uncovered their full names and then passed this information on to Saudi Arabia, they were told that both Khalid al-Mihdhar and Nawaf al-Hazmi were Saudi citizens and were long-time al Qaeda terrorists.

The CIA broke into the hotel room of Khalid al-Mihdhar in Dubai, while he was traveling from Yemen to Kuala Lumpur, and photocopied his passport. This information was transmitted back to the US, to the Bin Laden Unit at the CIA devoted to tracking al Qaeda terrorists, Alec Station. The passport indicated that al-Mihdhar had a multi-entry visa for the US. On January 5, 2001, al-Mihdhar and al-Hazmi arrived in Kuala Lumpur to attend this al Qaeda planning meeting.

This meeting took place at a condominium owned by a Malaysian businessman connected to al Qaeda. On January 5-8, 2000, the CIA had the Malaysian intelligence photograph all of the al Qaeda terrorists who attended this meeting. The Special Branch of the Malaysian intelligence was able to photograph a dozen al Qaeda terrorists who took part in this meeting, both outside of the condo where the meeting actually took place, and at Internet cafes in Kuala Lumpur. It was only later that the CIA found out that this meeting is where both the *Cole* bombing and the 9/11 attacks had been planned.

On January 9, 2000, the CIA, including Black and Tenet, received all of these photographs and was given the identities of the participants at this meeting. They had already identified Khalid al-Midhar prior to this meeting, and later identified Nawaf al-Hazmi and Salem al-Hazmi, Nawaf's younger brother, in the photographs taken at this meeting. Also identified in photos at this same meeting was Khallad (Tawfig bin Attash). Khallad was later identified by the FBI as the mastermind of the *Cole* bombing. During his interrogation, al-Quso told Soufan that he had stayed in the Washington Hotel in Bangkok, when he delivered the money to Khallad. When Soufan checked the phone records al-Quso had called from the Washington Hotel, he found numerous calls to a pay phone in Kuala Lumpur.

In April 2001, Soufan sent another request, his third and last official request, asking the CIA asking for all of the information they had on Khallad, and the significance of the phone number al-Quso had called in Kuala Lumpur. Along with this request, Ali Soufan included Khallad's passport photo.

The CIA replied that that they had no information on Khallad, or the phone number in Kuala Lumpur, even though they had numerous photographs that had been taken of Khallad, Khalid al-Midhar and Nawaf al-Hazmi together at the meeting in Kuala Lumpur. The CIA also had in their possession a log from Malaysian intelligence that listed the number Soufan had given them, and the fact that it went to a phone booth right in front of the condominium where the Kuala Lumpur al Qaeda planning meeting had taken place.

On January 8, 2000, Malaysian intelligence informed the CIA that al-Mihdhar, al-Hazmi, and Khallad had left the meeting in Kuala Lumpur and were traveling together to Bangkok. It was in Bangkok where al-Quso was able to deliver the $36,000 he was carrying to Khallad. It is now clear that some this money went to al-Mihdhar and al-Hazmi, to pay for their living expenses and flight training in the US.

[NOTE: The FBI IG report and 9/11 Commission listed $7,000 as the amount of money al-Quso was carrying to Khallad.]

The CIA failed to put any of these terrorists on watchlists in the US after the Kuala Lumpur meeting, in direct violation of a CIA directive in late 1999, but they did not give this information to the FBI, even after they were informed on March 15, 2000, that al-Hazmi had left Bangkok and flown into the US.

There was never any explanation by the CIA why they did this. Lawrence, in this article suggested that the CIA was planning to recruit al-Mihdhar or al-Hazmi. This explanation is completely absurd. The CIA was specifically prohibited by law from ever conducting any investigation of anyone in the territory of the US. That by law was the exclusive purview of the FBI.

The meeting at FBI New York field office on June 11, 2001

As this article continued on we learn that a former head of the Bin Laden Unit at the CIA Tom Wilshire, had transferred over the FBI ITOS unit in May 2001. In early May 2001, Wilshire sent an e-mail to his supervisors at the Counterterrorist Center in the CIA, when he was alerted to Khallad. In his e-mail he stated, "OK this is important. This is a major league killer." Wilshire had been aware of a cable sent to the CIA Headquarters from Thailand on March 15, 2000, that stated that Nawaf al-Hazmi had entered the US on January 15, 2000. Wilshire had even concluded that it was quite possible Khalid al-Mihdhar had entered the US along with Nawaf since they had been traveling together after the January meeting in Kuala Lumpur. He sent in an e-mail to a colleague at the CIA that at about this same time period stating that definitely; "something bad was up."

Around May 15, 2001, Wilshire asked his CIA managers to get one of the FBI IOSs at the CIA, referred to as Mary in the FBI IG report, to "come up to speed" in her free time on the information surrounding the meeting in Kuala Lumpur, by going back and finding prior CIA cables. What is strange is even though Wilshire had the cable on al-Mihdhar's multi-entry visa and Nawaf's entry into the US, he did not share these with this FBI analyst and never even indicated that he even had such cables. He did not reveal that he knew that some the participants at the Kuala Lumpur meeting were already in the US. He also did not indicate the urgency he had stated in his e-mails to his colleagues at the CIA at exactly the same time.

[Note: According to the FBI IG report, because of her current work assignments, Mary did not have time to start on this assignment until July 24, two months after she had been first asked to find these cables.]

Tom Wilshire later told FBI IG investigators that he wanted to know what the FBI, in particular the *Cole* investigators, knew about the identity of some of the people who had been at the Kuala Lumpur meeting, in particular if the FBI *Cole* investigators could identify Fahad al-Quso. He gave three of the Kuala Lumpur surveillance photos to a FBI IOS agent at the FBI UBL unit, identified as Dina Corsi, aka Donna in the FBI IG report. After obtaining these photos, she set up a meeting in New York for June 11, 2001, to show these photos to the *Cole* investigators. According to statements she later made to the FBI IG, she said she wanted to check the veracity of al-Quso's story, and wanted to know if the FBI *Cole* investigators could identify him in the photographs taken at the Kuala Lumpur meeting.

All of the information on al-Quso that the CIA had came from the FBI, and Ali Soufan's investigation and interrogation of al-Quso. Al-Quso was already locked up in a Yemeni jail at the time the FBI interviewed him in November 2000, just after the *Cole* bombing. Why would the CIA want to know if the FBI could identify him in photos taken at the Kuala Lumpur meeting, when al-Quso told FBI Agent Ali Soufan that he could not get to this meeting in Kuala Lumpur due to his travel being blocked by visa issues. All of this information had already been given to the CIA. Al-Quso told Soufan that he had delivered the money to Khallad in Bangkok, and not Kuala Lumpur, Malaysia. There appeared no reason to not believe his story. What difference did it make to the CIA or the FBI if al-Quso had delivered the money to Khallad in Malaysia or in Bangkok, Thailand? Khallad would still have gotten his money in any case.

The photos Tom Wilshire asked for were photos that showed Khalid al-Mihdhar, since Wilshire had remembered a cable the CIA had received in January 2001 that had identified Khallad in the same photo with Khalid al-Mihdhar. The photos Wilshire gave Dina Corsi had Khalid al-Mihdhar, Nawaf al-Hazmi and an unknown third person. One of the photos had a picture of Khalid al-Mihdhar and Nawaf al-Hazmi standing next to a tree in Kuala Lumpur, Malaysia.

Tom Wilshire did not give Corsi any photos of Khallad from the Kuala Lumpur meeting, in spite of the fact that Ali Soufan had asked the CIA in April, just the month before, for all of the information the CIA had on Khallad. Khallad had been photographed at the Kuala Lumpur meeting and Wilshire knew the FBI would be interested if he were identified in photographs the CIA had from the meeting in Kuala Lumpur with several other terrorists.

The FBI *Cole* investigators knew what Khallad looked like and by the time of this meeting in New York knew that he had directed the *Cole* bombing. If they had been handed any photos of him along with photos of the other people who attended the same meeting, the *Cole* investigators would immediately know that these other people were also connected with the *Cole* bombing.

When Wilshire gave Corsi the photos, he also gave her one name, the name Khalid al-Mihdhar. But for some reason he did not tell her the fact that al-Mihdhar had been seen with Khallad at the Kuala Lumpur meeting or the fact that Nawaf al-Hazmi had also been seen with Khallad, and he knew that Hazmi had entered the US almost 1½ years earlier.

The 9/11 Commission and the FBI IG report both document that when she went to this meeting on June 11, 2006, a CIA Supervisor, Clark Shannon, accompanied her. Clark Shannon told the FBI IG investigators when they interviewed him that he was just "tagging along" with Dina Corsi to this meeting, and that he had no official function. Ali Soufan was in Yemen and was not able to attend.

At this meeting, the FBI **Cole** *investigators first briefed the CIA for three to four hours on the* **Cole** *investigation at the request of the CIA, and then Corsi showed the* **Cole** *investigators the three photographs that had been taken of al-Mihdhar at the Kuala Lumpur meeting.*

One photo was a photo of al-Mihdhar and al-Hazmi next to a tree in Malaysia. CIA Supervisor Shannon then asked the **Cole** *investigators if they could recognize anyone in the photographs.*

[Note: This differs slightly from the FBI IG report that says it was Corsi who asked the **Cole** *investigators if they could identify al-Quso in these photographs.]*

The *Cole* investigators immediately suspected that these people were connected to the *Cole* investigation. If they weren't, why was the CIA asking the FBI *Cole* investigators about these photos in the first place?

The FBI *Cole* investigators asked these CIA agents who these people were, and when and where the pictures had been taken. One of the *Cole* investigators even demanded, "Were there any other photographs of this meeting?" Shannon refused to say anything more about photographs at this point, and refused to identify the people in these photographs.

To the *Cole* investigators, it was obvious that for some reason, the CIA was deliberately withholding information critical to a criminal investigation into a terrorist act that had killed 17 sailors. When the meeting became heated, Corsi provided the name Khalid al-Mihdhar. Steve Bongardt, Soufan's assistant on the *Cole* investigation, then asked for additional information on al-Mihdhar, his birth date and passport number, so he could be tracked down. Because of numerous ways a Middle Eastern name can be spelled, it was often difficult to track down a person with just a name and no passport number to go along with the name.

Shannon did add that al-Mihdhar had a Saudi passport. However, he refused to provide any other additional information on these photos. No information was given to the Cole investigators that implied that al-Mihdhar was connected to the Cole bombing or to Khallad in any way. No information was given to the Cole investigators that indicated that al-Mihdhar was a long time al Qaeda terrorist that had a multi-entry visa for the US, or that Hazmi, who was seen with Mihdhar at the Kuala Lumpur meeting, was already in the US. According to his testimony to FBI IG investigators later, top CIA officials had forbidden him from disclosing any information on al-Mihdhar, or on Nawaf al-Hazmi, or the fact they had been seen together with Khallad at the meeting in Kuala Lumpur. Corsi promised that in the days and weeks to come she would try to get permission to pass along the information the *Cole* investigators were looking for. But she never did. Apparently, she was also forbidden from providing any additional information to the FBI by upper CIA management.

At the time of this meeting, Tom Wilshire, Clark Shannon and the CIA knew that Nawaf al-Hazmi had been in the United States for 18 months. The CIA Supervisor who had all of this information, Clark Shannon, told the FBI IG investigators later that he had just read the cable on Nawaf's entry into the US three weeks prior to this meeting. But, as the FBI IG investigation shows, he sat there at this meeting with the *Cole* investigators on June 11, 2001, three months prior to 9/11, when there was plenty of time available to have stopped the tragic events on 9/11, and even in the face a numerous angry questions from the *Cole* investigators, said absolutely nothing that could have helped the *Cole* investigation and prevented the disaster on 9/11.

The CIA response to the *New Yorker* article questioned the accuracy of this information, and further said, "Based on rigorous internal and external reviews of its shortcomings and successes before and after 9/11, the CIA has improved its processing and sharing of intelligence. CIA's focus is on learning and even closer cooperation with partners inside and outside government, not on public finger-pointing, which does not serve the American people well."

What new information beyond the information in the FBI IG report came out from Soufan's investigation and this article?

The CIA officers and FBI agents who attended this meeting and even the names of people who supervised some of those who attended were identified by their real names for the first time.

- Donna in the FBI IG report is identified as Dina Corsi. She is the FBI IOS working at the UBL unit at the FBI headquaters who claimed to have actually set the meeting up in New York for June 11, 2001.

- Mary, another FBI IOS, Mary worked at Alec Station at the CIA, the Bin Laden Unit, is never identified by her real name.

- John, the Bin Laden Unit Deputy Chief who had transferred to the ITOS unit at the FBI in May 2000, and is referred to as John in the FBI IG report, is identified as Tom Wilshire. He is the one who gave the three photos to Dina Corsi to take to the meeting in New York.

- Peter, the CIA supervisor who was in close communication with John, in the May 2001 time frame and who told the FBI IG investigators he was just tagging along when he attended the June 11, 29001 meeting in New York, is identified as Clark Shannon.

- Scott the FBI Cole investigator at this meeting and Ali Soufan's assistant is identified as Steve Bongardt.

The account of this meeting differs from the account in the FBI IG report. It is Dina Corsi in the FBI IG report who asks the *Cole* investigators if they can identify al-Quso in any of the photographs. In this account Clark Shannon is the one who asked if the *Cole* investigators could recognize anyone in these photos. It turns out it is FBI standard procedure when inquiring about the identity of people in photographs never to reveals the name of any person. It therefore would have been highly unlikely that Corsi would have asked could the Cole investigators identify Quso in these photographs.

We now know that one of the photos has only the images of Khalid al-Mihdhar and Nawaf al-Hazmi along side a tree in Malaysia. If the *Cole* investigators were asked if they could identify anyone in this photo, and the CIA already knew full well what al-Mihdhar and al-Hazmi looked like from their identification at the Kuala Lumpur meeting, what were they thinking when they said that this meeting had been set up to see if the *Cole* investigators could identify al-Quso in these photos? Surly the CIA must have known that their story on why this meeting had been set up would never hold up with later scrutiny.

This account describes three additional times the FBI asked for information from the CIA about Khallad and the meeting in Kuala Lumpur.

In November 2000, Soufan sent the CIA station in Yemen the first of several official requests for information on Khallad.

When this request received no response, FBI Director Louis Freeh even sent CIA Director George Tenet an official request on Ali Soufan's behalf, formally asking about information the CIA might have on Khallad and if there might have been an al Qaeda planning meeting somewhere in Southeast Asia, a meeting indicated by the al-Quso delivery of money to Khallad, just after January 8, 2000 in Bangkok. Again there was no response.

[NOTE, now this is all a bit bizarre since Louis Freeh had been told about the Kuala Lumpur meeting in January 2000, 10 months earlier, the fact that three al Qaeda terrorists, Khalid, Nawaf, and Salem were traveling to this meeting, and even that Khalid had been identified by the CIA as Khalid al-Mihdhar from his passport even before the meeting started.]

In April 2001, Soufan sent another request, the third official request, to the CIA, including Khallad's passport photo and asking if the CIA had any information on Khallad, or if they had any information on the significance of these phone numbers, numbers Soufan had received from al-Quso in Kuala Lumpur or to Khallad. He received no response to his request.

Fifth, the CIA Yemen station passed photos of Khallad, Khalid al-Mihdhar and Nawaf al-Hazmi at the Kuala Lumpur meeting to Ali Soufan just days after the attacks of 9/11, clearly indicating that they had these photos all along and could have given them to him in November 2000, when he had first requested this information. Had Ali Soufan gotten this information at that time, his investigating team would have had enough time to prevent the attacks on 9/11.

How does this information on the *Cole* Investigation square with the information from the FBI IG report?

When I went back to combine the time line of Ali Soufan with the time line from the FBI IG report, significant new information became apparent. Ali Soufan sent the CIA an official request in April 2001 asking for all of the information the CIA had on Khallad, and the significance of the phone number al-Quso had called in Kuala Lumpur. This request also included a passport photo of Khallad that Ali Soufan had obtained from the Yemeni authorities. Even though they never officially responded to his request and never gave him the information that they actually had on Khallad, according the FBI IG's report, this request generated significant activity at the CIA,

Tom Wilshire reads Ali's request for information

According to the FBI IG report, in May the following activity took place at the CIA:

FBI IG Report page 284:

"In addition to reviewing the East Asia travel of several bin Laden operatives in January 2000, John (aka Tom Wilshire) also began looking in CIA records for the Kuala Lumpur photographs. John obtained three of them. John told the OIG that he had not read the cable stating that the joint source had identified Khallad in the photographs, but he was aware that an identification of Khallad in the photographs had been made. At the end of his e-mail to Peter (aka Clark Shannon), John stated that he had obtained three surveillance photographs of al-Mihdhar in Malaysia, but he did not see "Khallad" in any of the photographs, and he believed he was "missing something" or "someone saw something that wasn't there." John also questioned whether there was a cable somewhere that documented the identification of Khallad. [223"]

[223] As noted above, John was correct – Khallad was not in any of these three photographs. After September 11 it was learned that the person the source had identified as Khallad was actually al-Hazmi. It was also learned after September 11, however, that Khallad was in another Kuala Lumpur surveillance photograph that had not been shown to the source.

How would Tom Wilshire, aka John, have known what Khallad looked like when he was looking through the photos with Khalid to identify him?

Since Wilshire had not located the CIA cable that had identified Khallad and al-Mihdhar together at the Kuala Lumpur meeting, the only possible way he knew what Khallad looked like was from the passport photo Ali Soufan sent with his April request for information on Khallad. If Wilshire had the photograph of Khallad taken at Kuala Lumpur, the photo they gave the FBI in August 30, 2001, he would have known immediately that Khallad was not in the same photograph as Mihdhar but in fact in an entirely different photograph. Since there were only two photographs of Khallad at the CIA, the Kuala Lumpur photo and the photo from Ali Soufan's request, he must have had the photo from Soufan's request.

As I was trying to square the information on Ali Soufan with the FBI IG report, it was becoming clear for the first time that while the CIA never officially responded to Ali's request, Wilshire had Ali's request. He used the passport photo that was sent with this request to see if Khallad was in any of the photographs with al-Mihdhar, and quickly found out he was not.

My first reaction to the fact Tom Wilshire, former Deputy Chief of the CIA Bin Laden Unit had Ali's request was,

OH MY GOD!

466

According to the FBI IG report, John thought that the source had identified Khallad in one of the photos with al-Mihdhar. This appeared to be a misidentification. Wilshire quickly saw that Khallad was in none of these photos with al-Mihdhar. Wilshire knows that Ali had asked for all of the information the CIA had on Khallad, and for any information the CIA had on the telephone number Quso had called in Kuala Lumpur. The CIA had already received a log that indicated this number was a number to a phone booth right in front of the condominium where the Kuala Lumpur al Qaeda meeting on January 6-8, 2000 had taken place. In spite of having Ali's request, and knowing Khallad had been seen with Khalid al-Mihdhar and Nawaf al-Hazmi at the Kuala Lumpur meeting, Wilshire never officially responds to Ali's request.

Clark Shannon also has Ali's request

From the information in the FBI IG investigation taken down, after the events of 9/11.

> FBI IG report, Pages 283-284:

> In an e-mail to Peter in mid-May 2001, John noted that al-Mihdhar had arranged his travel to Malaysia and was associated with "[another terrorist organization] courier travel at the same time." John also noted in the e-mail that al-Quso, who was believed to be a courier since he had stated he had traveled to take money to Khallad, had traveled a few days earlier than al-Mihdhar. In addition, John wrote that he was interested because al-Mihdhar was traveling with two "companions" who had left Malaysia and gone to Bangkok, Los Angeles, and Hong Kong and "also were couriers of a sort."

> Around this same time, FBI IOS Donna (aka Dina Corsi) and other FBI IOSs working on the *Cole* investigation were focusing on al-Quso's connection to Bangkok and his trip to deliver money to Khallad. The FBI, like the CIA, was aware that in January 2000 al-Quso had planned to travel to Malaysia to take money to Khallad. According to an FBI document drafted by Donna in May 2001, al-Quso had claimed that on January 6, 2000, he and Ibrahim al-Nibras went to Bangkok first but were unable to travel on to Kuala Lumpur because of problems with their travel documents, and Khallad had traveled to Bangkok to meet them there instead.

The FBI began researching telephone numbers that appeared to be connected to al-Quso's trip and requested that several Legat Offices contact local law enforcement authorities to obtain subscriber information.

Donna told the OIG that she and others were tracking the information related to the telephone numbers associated with al-Quso in an attempt to determine the truth of his statements. In addition, she said that she was focused on the identity and whereabouts of Khallad, since he was the purported mastermind of the *Cole* attack ....Peter told the OIG that he recalled talking to FBI IOSs, including Donna, about mapping the telephone number information based on information provided by al-Quso. But he said that he did not recall discussions with Donna about the Kuala Lumpur photographs or the Khallad identification.

So we know where Corsi obtained the telephone number Quso that had called in Malaysia. She was given this number by Clark Shannon who could only have obtained this number from Ali Soufan's request for information. The fact that Fahad al Quso had called this number appeared nowhere else except in Ali Soufan's request.

As I was for the first time placing this information together, my reaction was again another:

OH MY GOD!

Both Tom Wilshire and Clark Shannon had obtained, read and were aware of Ali Soufan's request for information on Khallad. Who else in the entire world was aware of this fact or is aware of this fact even today? No government investigation has ever uncovered this horrific fact

The FBI Cole investigators clearly were never made aware of this, even when they were all sitting together with the CIA officers in that meeting in June 11, 2001 in New York.

They were unaware that these CIA officers had Ali's request at the time of this June 11, 2001 meeting, and that this request must have triggered this meeting. They have never been made aware of this fact even to today. Had the Cole investigators been made aware of this information that had been carefully kept secret by the CIA, they would have known that the people in the photographs were directly connected to the planning of the Cole bombing and their investigation and would have demanded that the CIA turn over all of the information they had on these people. They would have demanded all of the information on Mihdhar and Hazmi, which would have allowed them to prevent the attacks on 9/11.

CIA sting operation on the FBI *Cole* Investigators

The CIA, Wilshire, Shannon and Corsi never did directly reply to Ali's request. They did not give him the information they had on either this telephone number, or any of the information the CIA had on Khallad. Instead, Corsi, at the request of Clark Shannon, did something, which at first seems almost incomprehensible. She scheduled a meeting, at the behest of Clark Shannon and Tom Wilshire, with the very *Cole* investigators who worked for Ali, for June 11, 2001, in New York, indicating to them that this meeting was being set up "to share" with them new information the CIA and FBI Headquarters had on the *Cole* investigation.

When the meeting took place, CIA Supervisor Clark Shannon asked if the Cole investigators could identify anyone in the three photos Corsi had placed in front of them, photographs Wilshire had obtained from the CIA that had the image of Mihdhar in them.

One photo had al-Mihdhar and al-Hazmi and no one else. But, the CIA knew what both of these terrorists look like.

So it is clear when the CIA supervisor Shannon made this request, he and the CIA only wanted to know if the Cole investigators could identify either al-Mihdhar or al-Hazmi in these photos.

It now clear that the CIA only wanted to know if the FBI *Cole* investigators had uncovered the information that the CIA had kept secret about these two terrorists for that past 19 months, the meeting in Kuala Lumpur, and the fact that al-Mihdhar and al-Hazmi had been seen together with Khallad at this meeting, and even the fact that al-Hazmi was in the US and Mihdhar had a US visa. The reason given to the FBI IG that the CIA wanted to know if the *Cole* investigators could identify al-Quso in these photos was nothing but a ruse.

Why was the CIA so worried when they received the request for information from Ali Soufan?

But why had the CIA become so worried about the FBI being aware of this information after they received the request for information on Khallad from Ali Soufan in April 2001? When I went back to see why the CIA had become so worried, I realized that all the FBI would have had to do to find the information the CIA was keeping secret was find the flight that Khallad had taken to Bangkok from Kuala Lumpur, on January 8, 2000, a flight the FBI was aware of, and see who was sitting next to him on that flight.

They would have found Khalid al-Mihdhar and Nawaf al-Hazmi sitting right next to Khallad bin Attash, in three adjacent seats on this flight.

The FBI could then have gone back to December 1999 and found the cable from the NSA that had been sent to FBI Headquarters, stating that Khalid, Nawaf and Salem, Nawaf's younger brother, were traveling from Sanaa, Yemen to Kuala Lumpur for an important al Qaeda planning meeting.

They would have already known that al-Mihdhar was Khalid al-Mihdhar, and Nawaf was Nawaf al-Hazmi from the flight manifest. Sending these names to INS would have told the FBI that both Khalid al-Mihdhar and Nawaf al-Hazmi had entered the US on January 15, 2000. The only piece of information that was missing would be fact that al-Mihdhar had a multi-entry visa for the US, but sending al-Mihdhar's name to the State Department would have given them this last piece of information.

It is now obvious why the CIA was so worried and in a panic when they received Ali Soufan's request for information on Khallad in April. They knew how close the FBI was getting to actually uncover the information they had kept secret since January 5, 2000.

Why reasons given to FBI IG investigators make no sense.

This meeting makes no sense after analyzing this material in the *New Yorker* and in the FBI IG report for a number of reasons.

Corsi told the FBI IG investigators that she had stated in her request to the *Cole* investigators when setting up this meeting that the CIA and FBI Headquarters had information to share with them. But when she and Clark Shannon were asked to share the information they had, Shannon did not share anything with the

Cole investigators, and Corsi told these investigators that she could not share this information due to the "wall." But Corsi knew about the "wall" before setting up the meeting. So it is obvious that there was never any real intent at the CIA or FBI Agent Corsi to share information at this meeting, only an attempt to find out what the FBI *Cole* investigators knew, and if they had found out about al-Mihdhar and al-Hazmi.

When asked later by FBI IG investigators why she had called this meeting, Corsi said because the CIA wanted to know if the FBI *Cole* investigators could identify al-Quso in any of the Kuala Lumpur photos.

Why had Corsi used the identity of al-Quso as the reason for this meeting in the first place, when it is obvious that this explanation made no sense?

The reason that Corsi gave to the FBI IG makes no sense for several reasons. If this meeting was to see if the *Cole* investigators could identify al-Quso, then why did one of the photos have only al-Mihdhar and al-Hazmi standing next to a tree in Kuala Lumpur? When this picture was given to the FBI *Cole* investigators and they were asked, did they recognize anyone in this photo, what were Corsi, Wilshire and Shannon thinking?

That Fahad al-Quso had turned into a tree!

Al-Quso was already in jail in Yemen, and had been since the October-November 2000 time frame. He already had been interviewed many times by the FBI. So why would the CIA be interested in him at this point?

Furthermore, the Yemen CIA station could have just wired the CIA Headquarters a photo of al-Quso in a few hours if the CIA needed to know what he looked like, since al-Quso was in jail.

Not once in any of the investigations could I find any record that the *Cole* investigators said they doubted the story al-Quso told Ali Soufan, that he stayed in Bangkok because he could not get into Kuala Lumpur. They knew the Khallad would have gotten his money under any circumstance.

These photos could also have been e-mailed electronically to the FBI *Cole* investigators in just a few seconds instead of giving them to Corsi, accompanied by two other CIA employees, Shannon and Mary, and having them travel to New York City from Washington DC for this meeting, if all they wanted was to have the *Cole* investigators identify al-Quso in these photos. It is now obvious that the CIA did not want the FBI to actually take possession of the photos under any circumstances, only to briefly look at them.

A bogus explanation for this was offered later, why the CIA did not want the FBI *Cole* investigators to actually take possession of these photos. The CIA said that they did not want to give the photos to the FBI, to prevent them from turning these photos over to Yemen authorities. However, it turns out that this explanation was completely absurd. The CIA had already given these photos to the Yemen authorities in January 2001, six months earlier.

Senior CIA managers knew that they had to come up with some even semi-plausible reason to explain why this meeting was to be held. They could not say that they were calling this meeting to find out if the FBI *Cole* investigators had uncovered the information on Khalid al-Mihdhar, Nawaf al-Hazmi, or the meeting in Kuala Lumpur.

The CIA also knew that the only names the FBI was aware of at the time of the June 11, 2001 meeting were the names Khallad and al-Quso. They clearly could not claim they wanted to have the FBI identify Khallad, since both the FBI and the CIA knew exactly what Khallad looked like. Had the CIA provided a picture of Khallad along with pictures of Khalid al-Mihdhar and Nawaf al-Hazmi from the Kuala Lumpur meeting, the FBI *Cole* investigators would have known immediately that Khalid al-Mihdhar and the other people in these photographs were connected to the *Cole* bombing. They would also know that the CIA was withholding critical information from an ongoing FBI criminal investigation.

The FBI investigators would have known immediately that CIA employees were committing a major criminal felony by withholding vital information from an ongoing criminal investigation. The CIA knew that the *Cole* investigators would then have demanded to know the identities of the other people in the photographs. The only reason the CIA could think of to hide from the FBI IG investigators what must have been their real reason for calling this meeting was the excuse that they wanted to know if the FBI could identify al-Quso in the Kuala Lumpur photos.

While using Quso was an excuse for setting this meeting up, one statement by Corsi to the FBI IG investigators was extremely revealing. From the FBI IG report:

> According to Donna, the FBI was attempting to determine the veracity of al-Quso's information, so the photographs potentially were connected to the *Cole* investigation. She stated, however, that outside of this potential connection, the photographs were "another piece of a thousand things coming in" at the time. She said that if al-Quso were determined to be in the photographs, then the photographs would have become significant to the *Cole* investigation.

Corsi says if Quso were determined to be in the photographs, the photographs showing al-Mihdhar and Hamzi and the other terrorists connected to Khallad and the Kuala Lumpur meeting during January 6-8, 2000 in Kuala Lumpur, then the photographs would be significant to the Cole investigation. But she knew al-Mihdhar was in these photos along with several other al Qaeda terrorists. She would have had to know that these terrorists were also significant to the Cole investigation since she knew that Khallad, the mastermind of the Cole bombing and another long time al Qaeda terrorist had been in Kuala Lumpur at exactly the same time. *If Corsi is aware how significant all of these people are to the Cole investigation, then all of the CIA officers familiar with these photographs were clearly aware of this also. Yet not one of these CIA employees sees fit to provide this information to the FBI until it is too late to prevent the events on 9/11.*

It is now clear after merging the information on Ali Soufan with the information in the FBI IG report, that it is impossible to come to any other conclusion than this meeting was set up because of Ali Soufan's request sent to the CIA in April, and not because the CIA wanted to share information with the FBI or find out if al-Quso was in any of the photos from Kuala Lumpur.

What did Clark Shannon know at this time?

It is also clear that Clark Shannon was fully aware of Ali Soufan's request for information at the time of this meeting. He is the one that asked Dina Corsi to check on the phone number in Kuala Lumpur, a number he could have gotten from no other source that Ali Soufan's request for information in April 2001. He was also the one who asked the *Cole* investigators in the June 11, 2001 New York meeting if they could identify anyone in the Kuala Lumpur photos. In what only can be described as almost defying all belief, he had actually read, according to his testimony to the FBI IG investigators, a cable three weeks prior to the June 11 meeting that stated that Nawaf al-Hazmi had traveled to the US on January 15, 2000.

Why was Clark Shannon at this meeting?

What was the real reason that CIA Supervisor Clark Shannon attended this meeting? According to the FBI IG report, he told them that he was "just tagging along." Yet it was Clark Shannon and not Dina Corsi who asked the question of the *Cole* investigators, "Do you recognize anyone in these photos?" (The FBI IG report differs on this account, and said it was Corsi who asked the *Cole* investigators if they could recognize al-Quso in the photos? Her statement to the FBI IG investigators makes no sense.)

When the Cole investigators asked Shannon who these people were and where they were photographed, Shannon said absolutely nothing. And even though Shannon knew about the Kuala Lumpur meeting, knew that Khalid al-Mihdhar and Nawaf al-Hazmi had been seen and photographed there together with Khallad, knew that al-Mihdhar had a multi-entry visa for the US, and knew that he was meeting with the very group who worked for the FBI supervisor who had requested the information the CIA had on Khallad in April, he said nothing. What is even more horrific, Shannon knew that al-Hazmi and possibly Mihdhar were already in the US, and even knew that these al Qaeda terrorists had to be connected to the massive warnings the CIA had about a huge attack inside of the US.

He offered no more additional information, other than the fact that Khalid had a Saudi passport. But he did not give them the passport number, or a birth date, an absolute requirement when tracking Middle Eastern people with many confusing names.

He told the FBI IG investigators that it was not his responsibility to give information to the FBI, and furthermore, there were restrictions on giving information to criminal investigators. But if Shannon thought the information should only go to intelligence investigators, all he had to do is ask the FBI criminal investigators to step out of the meeting for a few minutes while he gave the intelligence agents all of the information he had.

[Note: This statement that it was not his job to give information to the FBI is refuted by the testimony of Cofer Black to the Joint Inquiry Committee and the 9/11 Commission stating:

"We are in the business of providing information to the FBI, and not withholding it."

Giving information to the FBI was in fact their whole purpose in life; without this as their stated mission and actual mission, they had no other reason to exist.]

What was the real reason this meeting had been set up?

The only explanation that makes sense is that Shannon was there to find out what the *Cole* investigators knew about Khalid al-Mihdhar and Nawaf al-Hazmi. Had the FBI uncovered the information that the CIA had kept secret for 18 months prior to this meeting?

By deliberately hiding this information from the FBI at this meeting, the fate of almost 3,000 Americans was sealed. All of these people were now doomed. After this, there was nothing that would be able to save them from a horrific death. They were all going to die three months later in what has been described as the worst single attack on civilians in modern US history.

After going over the facts behind this meeting and concluding that the CIA had deliberately withheld information from the FBI in what must have been a secret criminal conspiracy.

If the CIA had deliberately withheld information from the FBI in a criminal conspiracy at this meeting on June 11, 2001, then all of the other times they withheld the exact same or similar information had to part of this same conspiracy.

The analysis of the June 11, 2001 meeting between the CIA and the FBI clearly points to what must have been a huge, wide-ranging carefully crafted conspiracy at the CIA, that started on January 5, 2000, and lasted until August 30, 2001, to deliberately hide from the FBI the very information that could have prevented the al Qaeda attacks on 9/11.

Chapter 20
The CIA Inspector General's Report

The CIA Inspector General's report was completed in 1995 but not released until August 21, 2007, almost 6 years after the events on 9/11. When Porter Goss took over for George Tenet, he said that this CIA IG report pinpointing the management and individual failures at the CIA would never be released since the people at this agency – an agency whose deliberate actions had allowed 3,000 Americans to be killed on 9/11, were "America's finest," and releasing this report would serve no purpose. But General Hayden, the new CIA director was forced to release an executive summary of this report by an act of Congress.

Unfortunately it had very little new information that was not already in the Joint Inquiry (JI) Committee report, and stated that it was focused only on answering questions raised in that report.

> The JI concluded that, before 9/11, neither the US Government nor the CIA had a comprehensive strategy for combating al-Qa'ida. It charged that the Director of Central Intelligence (DCI) was either unwilling or unable to marshal the full range of IC resources necessary to combat the growing threat to the United States. The OIG Team also found that the IC did not have a documented, comprehensive approach to al-Qa'ida and that the DCI did not use all of his authorities in leading the IC's strategic effort against UBL.

> December 1998, the DCI signed a memorandum in which he declared: "We are at war." ....

> The Team found that neither the DCI nor the DDCI followed up these warnings and admonitions by creating a documented, comprehensive plan to guide the counterterrorism effort at the Intelligence Community level....

> The Team recommends that an Accountability Board review the performance of the Executive Director, the Deputy Director for Operations, and the Chief of CTC during the years prior to 9/11 regarding their management of the Agency's counterterrorism financial resources, including specifically their redirection of funds from counterterrorism programs to other priorities....

> The Team found that certain units within CTC did not work effectively together to understand the structure and operations of al-Qa'ida. This situation had a particularly

negative impact on performance with respect to Khalid Shaykh Muhammad (KSM), the mastermind of the 9/11 attacks....

CTC considered KSM to be a high-priority target for apprehension and rendition, but did not recognize the significance of reporting from credible sources in 2000 and 2001 that portrayed him as a senior al-Qa'ida lieutenant and thus missed important indicators of terrorist planning. This intelligence reporting was not voluminous and its significance is obviously easier to determine in hindsight, but it was noteworthy even in the pre-9/11 period because it included the allegation that KSM was sending terrorists to the United States to engage in activities on behalf of Bin Ladin....

The Team also recommends that an Accountability Board review the performance of the Chief of CTC for failure to ensure that CTC units worked in a coordinated, effective manner against KSM...

Agency officers did not, on a timely basis, recommend to the Department of State the watchlisting of two suspected al-Qa'ida terrorists, Nawaf al-Hazmi and Khalid al-Mihdhar. These individuals, who later were among the hijackers of 9/11, were known by the Agency in early January 2000 to have traveled to Kuala Lumpur, Malaysia, to participate in a meeting of suspected terrorists. From Kuala Lumpur, they traveled to Bangkok. In January 2000, CTC officers received information that one of these suspected terrorists had a US visa; in March 2000, these officers had information that the other had flown from Bangkok to Los Angeles.

In the period January through March 2000, some 50 to 60 individuals read one or more of six Agency cables containing travel information related to these terrorists. These cables originated in four field locations and Headquarters. They were read by overseas officers and Headquarters personnel, operations officers and analysts, managers and junior employees, and CIA staff personnel as well as officers on rotation from NSA and FBI. Over an 18-month period, some of these officers had opportunities to review the information on multiple occasions, when they might have recognized its significance and shared it appropriately with other components and agencies. Ultimately, the two terrorists were watchlisted in late August 2001 as a result of questions raised in May 2001 by a CIA officer on assignment at the FBI.

In 1998, CTC assumed responsibility for communicating watchlisting guidance in the Agency. As recently as December 1999, less than a month before the events of early January 2000, CTC had sent to all field offices of the CIA a cable reminding them of their obligation to watchlist suspected terrorists and the procedures for doing so. Field components and Headquarters units had obligations related to watchlisting, but they varied widely in their performance. That so many individuals failed to act in this case reflects a systemic breakdown—a breakdown caused by excessive workload, ambiguities about responsibilities, and mismanagement of the program. Basically, there was no coherent, functioning watchlisting program…

Agency officers also failed to pass the travel information about the two terrorists to the FBI in the prescribed channels. The Team found that an FBI officer assigned to CTC on 5 January 2000 drafted a message about the terrorists' travel that was to be sent from CIA to the FBI in the proper channels. Apparently because it was in the wrong format or needed editing, the message was never sent. On the same date, another CTC officer sent a cable to several Agency addressees reporting that the information and al-Mihdhar's travel documents had been passed to the FBI. The officer who drafted this cable does not recall how this information was passed. The Team has not been able to confirm that the information was passed, or that it was not passed. Whatever the case, the Team found no indication that anyone in CTC checked to ensure FBI receipt of the information, which, a few UBL Station officers said, should have been routine practice.

Separately, in March 2000, two CIA field locations sent to a number of addressees cables reporting that al-Hazmi and another al-Qa'ida associate had traveled to the United States. They were clearly identified in the cables as "UBL associates." The Team has found no evidence, and heard no claim from any party, that this information was shared in any manner with the FBI or that anyone in UBL Station took other appropriate operational action at that time.

In the months following the Malaysia operation, the CIA missed several additional opportunities to nominate al-Hazmi and al-Mihdhar for watchlisting; to inform the FBI about their intended or actual travel to the United States; and to take appropriate operational action. These included a few occasions identified by the Joint Inquiry as well as several others.

The team recommends that an Accountability Board review the performance of _____, _____, _____, _____, for failing to insure that someone in the Station informed the FBI and took appropriate operational action regarding al-Hazmi in March 2000. In addition the Team recommended that the Accountability Board assess the performance of the later three managers for failing to ensure prompt action relevant to al-Hazmi and al-Mihdhar during several later opportunities between March 2000 and August 2001.

Strategic analysis

The Team, like the JI, found that the IC's understanding of al-Qa'ida was hampered by insufficient analytic focus, particularly regarding strategic analysis.... Most important, a number of important issues were covered insufficiently or not at all. The Team found:

• No comprehensive strategic assessment of al-Qa'ida by CTC or any other component.

• No comprehensive report focusing on UBL since 1993.

• No examination of the potential for terrorists to use aircraft as weapons, as distinguished from traditional hijackings.

• Limited analytic focus on the United States as a potential target.

• No comprehensive analysis that put into context the threats received in the spring and summer of 2001.

What is new in this report?

According to an ABC report, "There could be no charge more severe for a CIA chief than that he left his country vulnerable to terrorist attack, but that is the accusation in the US today against the former head of the CIA, George Tenet."

This report clearly states that Tenet was at fault for failing to provide any strategic analysis. It says by virtue of his position he bears ultimate responsibility for the fact "that no such

480

strategic plan was ever created". It goes on to say, CTC manger Cofer Black and other unnamed mangers in the CIC section of the CIA were guilty of misconduct for not informing the FBI of al Qaeda terrorist Hazmi and his entry into the US and for the missed opportunities to inform the FBI of both Mihdhar and Hazmi between March 2000 and August 2001.

Incredible as it seems this report states that; "In the period January through March 2000, some 50 to 60 individuals read one or more of six Agency cables containing travel information related to these terrorists" and yet not one of these people informed the FBI, they deliberately hid this information from the FBI for 21 months, even after April 2001 when the warnings of a massive and catastrophic attack inside of the US that would kill thousands of Americans permeated every part of the CIA. They continued to hide this information even after they knew by doing so thousands of Americans would perish. It says the fact "That so many individuals failed to act in this case reflects a systemic breakdown". [NOTE: this appears to be yet another CIA code word. "Rendition", a CIA code word meaning a kidnapping leading to torture and even murder now takes its place with "systemic breakdown", which is an excuse for deliberately hiding information while knowing thousands of Americans will perish!]

The report describes that the CIA had: "No comprehensive analysis that put into context the threats received in the spring and summer of 2001". It says little attention was paid to reports that "that KSM was sending terrorists to the United States to engage in activities on behalf of Bin Ladin"....

While it does recommend disciplinary reviews hearings for George Tenet, his Deputy Director of Operations Jim Pavitt, and CTC Director Cofer Black and many others it never has sufficient detail to explain why the CIA would know the names of two al Qaeda terrorists for 21 months, know they had entered the US, even know a huge al Qaeda attack inside of the US was imminent and then never raise the alarm by informing the FBI these terrorists were connected to the warnings of this attack.

Tenet disagreed with this report and said it was "flat wrong". He sited a August 2001 IG report that said "The DCI Counterterrorist Center (CTC) is a well-managed component that successfully carries out the Agency's responsibilities to collect and analyze intelligence on international terrorism and to undermine the capabilities of terrorist groups". The fact that this was issued in August 2001, just weeks prior to 9/11 says it all!

By not adequately describing why the CIA hid information from the FBI, it continues the cover up of out right criminal conduct at the CIA to keep secret from the FBI the information on Mihdhar and Hazmi for 21 months. What is worse it assigns credit for the ultimate watching listing of Hazmi and Mihdhar to the very people who actually were heavily involved with the conspiracy to keep this information secret. From this report:

> Ultimately, the two terrorists were watchlisted in late August 2001 as a result of questions raised in May 2001 by a CIA officer on assignment at the FBI.

This "CIA officer assigned to the FBI" is Tom Wilshire. In May Wilshire had asked Mary, a low level FBI IOS agent at the CIA to come up to speed on the Kuala Lumpur meeting, by going through past cables at the CIA. On August 21, she finds the cable that says Hazmi is inside of the US, the every same cable Wilshire already had in his possession in May when he gave her that assignment. When she has both Hazmi and Mihdhar watchlisted, Wilshire was forced to turn over the photos of Mihdhar and Hazmi taken at Kuala Lumpur to the FBI.

The very person praised by this report, Tom Wilshire, helped set up the June 11 meeting with the FBI Cole investigators just to see if the FBI had uncovered information on Mihdhar and Hazmi, and then effectively sabotaged the final FBI investigation and search for Mihdhar by withholding the photo of Khallad taken at Kuala Lumpur for 8 days after the photos of Mihdhar and Hazmi were given to the FBI. But what is even more horrific, the CIA IG knows Wilshire is a CIA liaison to Michael Rolince at the ITOS unit of the FBI, and that Wishire knew Hazmi was inside of the US and Mihdhar has a US visa, and knew that both had been at the Kuala Lumpur meeting with Khallad bin Attash. Why did the CIA IG investigators not ask him why he had never transferred all of this information to the FBI and Rolince, information that would have prevented the events on 9/11 when that was his job? This cover up by this CIA IG report is so blatant and obvious it is clear that they have nothing but tremendous contempt for the American people!

This report is not only a cover up of CIA criminal behavior, but attempts to turn conspirators into heroes! This report, however, does reconfirm the overall facts of what went on at the CIA, which are simply DAMMING!

While it never uncovered the reasons, it says that the CIA deliberately withheld critical information from the FBI knowing thousands of Americans would perish! And we now know from this CIA IG report that no one will never ever be held accountable!

GOOD GOD ALMIGHTY!

Chapter 21
What went wrong?

Conclusions from the Joint Inquiry Committee and the 9/11 Commission reports?

The CIA

On the afternoon of September 11, 2001, as I sat in my room at the Newton Marriott, and I had heard on the television there had been 6,500 people killed in the WTC Towers, I kept repeating over and over, "Oh My God, I am responsible for 6,500 people being killed. It's all my fault." But then I asked, "Why is this all my fault? Don't the CIA and FBI feel like it was partly their responsibility also? Why is this all my fault alone?" But how can you blame them, if they probably did not even know this huge attack was going to happen? How do you blame huge bureaucracies with layers and layers of clueless brain-dead bureaucrats as employees?

As I attempted to think in more depth about the CIA that day, the only concept I had for this organization could be summed up as "missing in action." If this huge organization could not anticipate and prevent the attacks on 9/11, then just what did they really do? Nothing, not one concrete thing they did, could I even bring to mind. They appear to have been just completely missing in the months and years prior to 9/11. While the investigations by the Joint Inquiry Committee and the 9/11 Commission after 9/11 have provided more detail on exactly what they did and what role they played prior to 9/11, in working to prevent the attacks on that day it was the combination of the FBI Inspector General's report combined with the account of FBI agent Ali Soufan that finally allowed the whole story on 9/11 to be put together for the first time.

The strategic information the CIA had

Prior to the attack of 9/11 the CIA knew that:

- The al Qaeda terrorist organization had declared war on the US, in the February 1998 Fatwa, and was now determined to mount attacks inside the US targeting American civilians.

- The methods and weapons al Qaeda had employed in several previous attacks consisted of secrecy, surprise, suicide, and psychology.

- The al Qaeda organization had a large supply of people willing to commit suicide in furthering their goals.

- The al Qaeda terrorists had wanted to attack large symbolic targets inside the US, which would result in a very large number of civilian casualties.

- The top people at the CIA testified to the Joint Inquiry Committee and the 9/11 Commission that they were convinced the al Qaeda terrorists were going to launch a huge spectacular attack in the summer or fall of 2001. They knew this attack might possibly be an attack inside the US that would result in thousands of American casualties.

Tactical information

The NSA had informed the CIA in December 1999 that information derived from a phone conversation to at a safe house in Yemen frequented by terrorists involved in the East Africa bombings indicated that three al Qaeda terrorists were traveling to an important planning meeting to be held in Kuala Lumpur, Malaysia, during the first week of January 2000.

The CIA contacted Malaysian intelligence and asked them to photograph the participants attending this meeting.

Photographs taken by Malaysian intelligence were used to identify several of the participants at this planning meeting, including Tawfiq bin Attash (Khallad), who directed the *Cole* attack, Khalid al-Mihdhar, Nawaf al-Hazmi and Salem al-Hazmi, who took active part in the attack on 9/11. This meeting took place in a condominium in Kuala Lumpur, later used by Zacarias Moussaoui, when he stayed in Kuala Lumpur.

Also, identified at this meeting, was Khalid Shaikh Mohammed, a high-ranking al Qaeda operative who chaired this meeting. The CIA knew what he looked like from his involvement in the investigation of the Bojinka plot. The Bojinka plan, discovered in the Philippines in 1995, was to place bombs on international flights into the US from Southeast Asia. The second part of this plan was to hijack several large American airliners and crash them into large buildings in the US.

Khallad went on to take part in the bombing of the USS Cole 10 months after the Kuala Lumpur meeting. Prior to this meeting even starting, the CIA had obtained a copy of Khalid al-Mihdhar's passport and knew he had a multiple-entry US visa. On March 15, 2000, the CIA learned that al-Hazmi had entered the US on a commercial air carrier on January 15, 2000. In December 2000, after learning from the FBI that Khallad had been involved with the Cole bombing, the CIA re-confirmed that he had been photographed at the Kuala Lumpur meeting.

In April 2001 through the end of July 2001 the CIA received numerous warnings that the al Qaeda terrorists were planning an enormous attack inside of the US to take place in the summer or fall of 2001. Warning of this attack indicated that it would come without warning, and cause mass casualties.

On June 12, 2001 the CIA received information that Khalid Shaikh Mohammed had recruited a number of terrorists for this attack, had already sent in some of these terrorists who were to link up with the rest of them during the summer of 2001.

While the CIA had been aware that Hazmi had been inside of the US since January 15, 2000, on August 22, 2001, they learned that both al-Hazmi and al-Mihdhar were inside the US.

The CIA's lack of strategic analysis

The CIA had organized the Counterterrorist Center (CTC), which had been focused on al Qaeda. They even had a complete procedure for doing this type of analysis. It appears from the information that came out of the Joint Inquiry report and the 9/11 Commission reports that they had never put together a complete strategic analysis of this organization, detailing the motivations of this group and what this group might do in the way of terrorist attacks against the US.

This analysis could have identified the targets al Qaeda would be most likely to attack, and perhaps even list possible methods that might be used against these targets. In an Armed Services Committee meeting in June 2001, Senator Levin had posed this very question to CIA Director George Tenet. Specifically, he asked: "Can you provide this committee a priority list of the targets the al Qaeda terrorists might attack?" George Tenet's statement at this hearing was that is was not possible to come up with a priority list of targets.

Even after this meeting, when John Gannon, head of the CIA analysis unit, attempted to answer this question, the CIA was unable to compile a prioritized list of targets the al Qaeda terrorists might attack. The CIA was never able to provide any explanation as to why they could not prioritize a list of targets.

The massive warnings in the spring and summer of 2001 of a huge attack in the final planning stages, which would kill thousands of Americans and come without warning, should have prompted the CIA to generate this analysis had it not been done earlier.

Because this analysis was not done, there was no road map, or direction that could be provided to the tactical side of the CIA alerting them to the meaning of al Qaeda terrorists coming into the United States.

By not producing this strategic analysis, the only remaining option the CIA had for the defense of the US, according to testimony from all of their top managers to three investigations, was to "obtain the secret," a difficult if not impossible task. It was well known at the CIA that the most important tactic employed by al Qaeda was maintaining extreme secrecy in their plans.

Tactical analysis at the CIA

In spite of being at an enormous disadvantage because no strategic analysis was ever produced at the CIA, they still ultimately had obtained much information.

However as revealed in the Joint Inquiry and 9/11 Commission reports and hearings, while the CIA had obtained much information that could have been used to prevent the attacks on 9/11, this information was inexplicably never given to the FBI until late August while it was too late for the FBI to prevent the attack that occurred on 9/11.

The information that a high level al Qaeda planning meeting was being held in Kuala Lumpur and that it had been attended by Khalid al-Mihdhar and Nawaf al-Hazmi was known by the CIA while the meeting was actually taking place, but the photos of Mihdhar and Hazmi taken at this meeting were not given to the FBI until August 23, 2001. The photo of Khallad bin Attash the mastermind of the Cole bombing was not given to the FBI until August 30, 2001, 8 days after the photos of Mihdhar and Hazmi were given to the FBI

The information that Hazmi had entered the US on January 15, 2000, information that the CIA learned on March 15, 2000, was kept secret from the FBI until August 23, 2001.

Not one of many government investigations could explain this. Some explanations raised by the investigators were that the CIA did not talk to the FBI or that the "wall" prevented information from being sent to the FBI from the CIA made no sense from a simple common sense point of view.

The CIA had been aware of a horrific al Qaeda attack inside of the US since April 2001 that would cause mass casualties. They knew that one al Qaeda terrorist, Hazmi, had been inside of the US preparing for this attack since January 15, 2000, and knew from August 22, 2001 that both Mihdhar and Hazmi were inside of the US in preparation for this attack. Why would a government agency allow thousands of Americans to die because they do not talk to another agency or because they cannot figure out how to pass information over a wall?

The CIA had issued a directive in December 1999 to add all terrorists to the appropriate watch list even if only their first name or alias were known. Yet the names Khalid al-Mihdhar and Nawaf al-Hazmi were not added to any watchlist until August 23, 2001, 21 months after the CIA first became aware of them. These investigations left this unexplained.

Perhaps the most bizarre event occurred on June 11, 2001 when three photographs taken at the Kuala Lumpur meeting were presented to the Cole investigators. A CIA Supervisor, Clark Shannon then asked if the Cole investigators could identify the people in these photographs. He knew one of the photographs had only the images of Mihdhar and Hazmi in it. He knew Hazmi was already inside of the US and that Mihdhar had a multiple-entry visa for the US. He also knew al-Mihdhar and Nawaf al-Hazmi had both been at the Kuala Lumpur meeting with Khallad, the mastermind of the *Cole* attack, directly connecting all of these terrorists to the planning of the Cole bombing. And yet even when asked by FBI Cole investigators, who are these people, and how are they connected to the Cole bombing, he says nothing!

Both Cofer Black and George Tenet stated to the Joint Inquiry Committee that all of the information on Mihdhar and Hazmi had been given to the FBI from the beginning. The 9/11 Commission found that this was a total and complete deviation from the truth.

George Tenet stated in his testimony to the 9/11 Commission hearings on April 14, 2004, that no one read the cable that came into the CIA describing the information al-Hazmi had left Thailand and flown to the United States. But this cable had been marked, "Read with interest" by Alec Station, the Bin Laden Unit at the CIA.

Had the information on Mihdhar and Hazmi and the meeting in Kuala Lumpur been sent to the FBI in a timely fashion, it is clear the events on 9/11 would have been prevented.

Nawaf al-Hazmi had numerous phone and Internet contacts with both Ramzi bin al-Shibh and Khalid Sheik Mohammed while he was in the US after leaving the meeting in Kuala Lumpur.

Khalid al-Mihdhar had contacted his father-in-law in Yemen on eight separate occasions when he was in the US from January 15, 2000 to June 2000. This information came from a NSA wiretap on the phone in his father-in-law's house placed there after the bombing of the embassies in East Africa.

Ramzi bin al-Shibh, identified as having attended the Kuala Lumpur meeting in January 2000 was the roommate of several of the pilots who took part in the attack on 9/11 – Mohammed Atta, pilot on American Flight 11 that crashed into the North WTC on 9/11; Marwan al-Shehhi, pilot of United Flight 175 that crashed into the South WTC; and Ziad Jarrah, the pilot that crashed into the Pentagon on American 77. Ziad Jarrah had vouched for Ramzi bin al-Shibh on several visa applications when bin al-Shibh attempted to enter the United States.

The criminal conspiracy to hide information from the FBI

It was only after almost five years after the events on 9/11 that new information finally surfaced which started to make sense of all of the CIA's bizarre, inexplicable behavior.

The information from the Joint Inquiry Committee, the 9/11 Commission and even the FBI IG report while more complete than then other reports still could not adequately explain this behavior at the CIA. The un-redacted version of the FBI Inspector General's report was finally released by May 2006. Then in July 2006 an article in the New Yorker by Lawrence Wright on FBI Agent Ali Soufan provided significant new information. This information for the first time combined with the FBI IG report explained what actually happened at the CIA that allowed the attacks on 9/11. It was clear from this information that the meeting between the FBI and the CIA had actually been a CIA sting on the FBI, to find out if the FBI had uncovered information in their search for Khallad on Mihdhar and Hazmi and the meeting in Kuala Lumpur. It was also clear that when the CIA withheld information form the FBI Cole investigators at this meeting that this had clearly become a criminal conspiracy to obstruct this FBI investigation.

From a time-line of all the instances where the CIA had hidden information from the FBI over a 21-month time period, along with the information on Ali Soufan's investigation of the Cole bombing, the only possibility that allowed this to make sense was that the CIA had deliberately hidden information from the FBI in a wide ranging criminal conspiracy. This information included the names Khalid al-Mihdhar and Nawaf al-Hazmi, the fact they attended an al Qaeda planning meeting in Kuala Lumpur with Khallad bin Attash, the fact that the CIA knew Khalid al-Mihdhar had a multi-entry visa for the US and that Nawaf al-Hazmi had entered the US on January 15, 2000.

This conspiracy to hide this information from the FBI involved the top leader-ship of the CIA an included lower-level managers and supervisors, particularly in the Bin Laden Unit, Alec Station.

Knowing there had been a criminal conspiracy at the CIA to withhold information form the FBI, I went back to re-examine all of the numerous times the CIA hid from the FBI they information they had on Khalid al-Mihdhar, the al Qaeda planning meeting in Kuala Lumpur of January 5-8, 2000, on Nawaf al-Hazmi, and on Khallad bin Attash, to see if this could more fully now finally explain this and ultimately find the reason the CIA kept this information secret.

Time line of the CIA interaction with the FBI

December 1999

In late December 1999, information from an over heard phone conversation at a al Qaeda safe house in Yemen was passed by the NSA to the CIA and FBI that three al-Qaeda terrorists were traveling to an important al Qaeda planning meeting in Kuala Lumpur. Identified were Khalid, traveling from Sanaa, Yemen through Dubai to Kuala Lumpur, Nawaf and Salem, Nawaf's younger brother, both were traveling from Pakistan to this meeting. At this time the NSA passed this information on Khalid to the CIA and the FBI, it did not pass the last name of Khalid or Nawaf or Salem, even these last names were in their system. The CIA obtained a photocopy of Khalid's passport when he passed through Dubai on his way to Kuala Lumpur and discovered Khalid's last name, al-Mihdhar.

January 5, 2000

On January 5, 2000 the passport information came into the Bin Laden unit of the CIA. Included was the information on Khalid-al-Mihdhar along with his passport photo. This was described in a CIR, written up by an FBI Agent Doug Miller working at this CIA unit. Miller requested that this information be forwarded to the FBI. This document listed Khalid al-Mihdhar's multi-entry visa and that he was going to a meeting in Kuala Lumpur, and "the potential links between the suspected terrorist facility in the Middle East and the 1998 East Africa embassy bombings." The CIR even detailed al-Mihdhar's passport and visa information. Records show that Tom Wishire had accessed this cable shortly after the FBI detailee wrote it. Before it could be sent to the FBI, Miller was required to get permission form the CIA supervisor in his unit for permission to send this CIR. Unexplained to today, one of the deputy chiefs at the Bin Laden Unit of the CTC section of the CIA, Tom Wilshire blocked this CIR from being forwarded over to the FBI. He had a CIA desk officer attach a notice to this CIR, "Blocked by Order of the Deputy Chief". The CIA Bin Laden Unit desk officer who had added this note, then issued a cable through out the CIA a few hours later that stated "that al-Mihdhar's travel documents, including a multiple-entry US visa, had been copied and passed to the FBI for further investigation." In spite of this cable stating that this information had been sent to the FBI, this information had not been forwarded to the FBI.

According to the FBI IG report:

> This cable (that stated that al-Mihdhar's travel documents, including a multiple-entry US visa, had been copied and passed to the FBI for further investigation) was disseminated to various CIA stations approximately three hours after Michelle had noted in the cable system that Dwight [the FBI detailee who drafted the CIR] was directed to hold off on sending his draft CIR to the FBI "for now per [the CIA Deputy Chief of the Bin Laden Unit]."

> When we (the FBI IG investigators) interviewed Michelle, she stated that she had no recollection of who told her that al-Mihdhar's travel documents had been passed to the FBI or how they had been passed. She said she would not have been the person responsible for passing the documents. According to Michelle, the language in the cable stating "[the documents] had been passed" suggested to her that someone else told her that they had already been passed, but she did not know who it was. The CIA Deputy Chief of the Bin Laden Unit also said he had no recollection of this cable, and he did not know whether the information had been passed to the FBI.

> Neither we nor the CIA OIG was able to locate any other witness who said they remembered anything about al-Mihdhar's travel documents being passed to the FBI, or any other documents that corroborated the statement that the documents were in fact passed to the FBI.

The day the cable on al-Mihdhar was blocked from being passed to the FBI, January 5, 2000 clearly was the start of the conspiracy to hide information on Mihdhar and the meeting in Kuala Lumpur from the FBI. This was also the day the al Qaeda planning meeting opened in Kuala Lumpur. *[FBI IG Report]*

January 5-8, 2000

The CIA asked the Special Branch of Malaysian intelligence to photograph all of the people at the Kuala Lumpur meeting, and identified them if possible. It was at this Kuala Lumpur meeting where the Cole and 9/11 attacks were planned and it is clear that these 12 al Qaeda terrorists had been directly involved in the planning of these attacks. The CIA realized in November 2000 that they were culpable in the Cole bombing when they found out that Tawfiq Bin Attash, aka Khallad, a al Qaeda terrorist who had attended this meeting was not only connected to the *Cole* bombing but was identified as the mastermind of this attack.

Tenet, Black and many other people in the Bin Laden Unit at the CIA were aware of Khalid's passport and the fact he had a multi-entry visa. *[Joint Inquiry Report, 9/11 Commission report]*

January 9, 2000

George Tenet and Cofer Black receive the photographs from the Kuala Lumpur al Qaeda planning meeting. Many if not all twelve people who attended were known to be long time al Qaeda terrorists and were identified.

Identified at this meeting were Khalid al-Mihdhar, Nawaf al-Hazmi, Salem al-Hazmi (Nawaf's younger brother), the al Qaeda terrorists on AA 77 that hit the Pentagon, Tawfiq bin Attash (Khallad), the mastermind of the Cole bombing, Hambali, a well know al Qaeda terrorist in southeast Asia, Khalid Sheik Mohammed (master mind of the attacks on 9/11), and Ramsey bin al-Shibh, roommate of three pilots on 9/11, along with 5 other long time al Qaeda terrorists known to the CIA.

None of this information was turned over to the FBI and no one at that meeting was watchlisted in the US, although al-Mihdhar was watchlisted in Thailand when it was discovered he was flying to Thailand on January 8, 2000 along with Khallad and Nawaf. In spite of the fact that the CIA had just issued a guideline in late 1999 that all known terrorists had to be placed on watch lists even if the CIA was only aware of their first name or their alias none of these terrorists were watch listed in the US until August 23, 2001 21 months later. At the time of this flight from Kuala Lumpur to Bangkok, the CIA did not have Nawaf's last name. When they reviewed the flight manifest they learned Nawaf's last name. The information on the Kuala Lumpur meeting was widely disseminated inside of the CIA and was forwarded to the CIA station in Yemen along with the photographs taken at that meeting. *[9/11 Commission, FBI Inspector General's report, Mainstream Media reports]*

March 15, 2000

A cable was sent to the CIA on March 15, 2000 from the CIA Thailand station stating Nawaf al-Hazmi had traveled to the US on January 15, 2000. This cable did not have Khalid al-Mihdhar's name on it, even though when al-Mihdhar left Malaysia for Bangkok, his name was the only name listed with Thailand, since the CIA did not find out Nawaf's last name until after the plane that carried Hazmi, Mihdhar and Khallad Bin Attash landed in Bangkok.

Mihdhar had been watchlisted with Thailand authorities but not soon enough to allow the Thailand authorities to alert the CIA in time so that they could have been followed in Thailand. Only after they entered Thailand and after the CIA found Hazmi's last name from the flight manifest, was he was added to the watchlist in Thailand.

Even though both Khalid al-Mihdhar and Nawaf al-Hazmi had been watchlisted with Thailand authorities, only Nawaf al-Hazmi's name was on the cable that was sent from the Thailand CIA station to CIA Headquarters on March 15, 2000. This cable had been inexplicably delayed by two months after Nawaf had left Thailand for the US. It is known that at least 50-60 people at the CIA were aware of the information that Hazmi had entered the US, and yet not one of these people informed the FBI or any other agency. *[9/11 Commission report, CIA IG Report]*

November 2000

In November of 2000, after learning about Fahad al-Quso's explanation that had delivered $36,000 to Khallad in Bangkok, New York FBI agent Ali Soufan asked CIA officials in Yemen if they knew anything about an al Qaeda planning meeting in Kuala Lumpur, or if they had any information on Khallad Bin Attash, or a new terrorist operation in Southeast Asia. Ali knew that al-Quso had traveled from Yemen to Bangkok, and stayed in Bangkok when he was not allowed to travel on to Kuala Lumpur for visa reasons. Ali quickly concluded that this made no sense. Why would al Qaeda send money out of Yemen to a person who would later direct the *Cole* bombing, when the *Cole* bombing took place in Yemen? Al Qaeda money to finance a terrorist attack flowed to the country where the attack was to take place, not away from it.

Soufan suspected almost immediately that an attack other than the *Cole* bombing was being financed with this money, and that there must have been a planning meeting in Kuala Lumpur, Malaysia, to plan this new attack. Ali Soufan received a reply that stated that the CIA had no information on any al Qaeda meeting that might have taken place in Southeast Asia, or on Khallad Bin Attash. [Note: At this time, the CIA station in Yemen had the photos from the Kuala Lumpur meeting, including photos of Khallad Bin Attash, Khalid al-Mihdhar, Nawaf al-Hazmi, and nine other al Qaeda terrorists who had attended this meeting and not only refused to give them to Ali, but did not disclose that this meeting in Kuala Lumpur had even taken place.]

When FBI Agent Ali Soufan informed the CIA in November 2000 that Khallad had been identified as the mastermind of the *Cole* bombing, they had already been aware that Khallad had been at the Kuala Lumpur meeting, and had been seen with Khalid al-Mihdhar and Nawaf al-Hazmi at this meeting. The CIA however did not provide this information to the FBI, even though the request for information was now coming from an official FBI criminal investigation. Withholding information at this point would be considered felony criminal obstruction of justice. The CIA clearly knew that by withholding this information from this FBI investigation they were committing numerous felonies. *[Account of Ali Soufan, by Lawrence Wright]*

Later in November 2000

Shortly after getting no response from his request to the CIA Yemen station, Ali Soufan requested that the Director of the FBI, Louis Freeh, send an official request directly to the Director of the CIA, George Tenet, asking if there had been an al Qaeda meeting somewhere in Southeast Asia before the *Cole* bombing and for all information the CIA had on Khallad bin Attash.

[NOTE: We know that Freeh had been given the cable from the NSA describing the meeting in Kuala Lumpur in January 2000 and the fact that Nawaf and Khalid were traveling to this important al Qaeda planning meeting. George Tenet had even briefed him on this meeting. The name Khalid al-Mihdhar was included right in one of his one page daily briefing papers in January 2001. So why did he not tell Soufan about the meeting in Kuala Lumpur when he must have known this was very information Soufan was asking the CIA about? This has never been explained.]

At this time, al-Quso had already provided information about Khallad and his role in the *Cole* bombing, and the Yemen police had provided a passport photo of Khallad to the FBI. This photo passed through the CIA on its way to FBI Headquarters, when sent by Soufan since the FBI did not have a system for sending photographs from Yemen. The CIA told Freeh that it had no information on Khallad or a planning meeting in Southeast Asia. It is now clear that this criminal conspiracy included even the Director of the CIA. George Tenet had been involved in hiding from the FBI the information the CIA had on Khallad, and the meeting in Kuala Lumpur obstructing a FBI criminal investigation. *[Account of Ali Soufan, by Lawrence Wright]*

December 2000

The Joint FBI/CIA source identifies Khallad from the passport photo Ali Soufan had obtained from Yemen authorities. Ali Soufan had sent this photograph through the CIA to the FBI, because the FBI did not have any e-mail capability that could transmit photographs in November 2000. While the CIA immediately knew from this identification that Khallad had been at the Kuala Lumpur meeting with Mihdhar and Hazmi, this information is kept secret from the FBI.

(9/11 Commission, FBI Inspector General's report)

January 2001

The Joint FBI/CIA source identifies Khallad from the photo taken of him at the Kuala Lumpur meeting, reconfirming for the second time that Khallad had been at the Kuala Lumpur meeting with Mihdhar and Hazmi. This information is sent to the CIA via a cable, a CIR. This information again not sent to the FBI at this time and in fact is not sent to the FBI until August 30, 2001. The CIA official who had talked to the Joint source tells the 9/11 Commission that he cannot recall this identification of Khallad from the Kuala Lumpur photographs and hence cannot explain why this information was not shared with the FBI. It is obvious however, that the CIA immediately knew that they were now culpable in the Cole bombing for having hidden the information on the Kuala Lumpur meetings for the prior 12 months from the FBI. *(9/11 Commission, FBI Inspector General's report)*

April -May 2001

In April 2001, both the FBI and the CIA learn that a huge al Qaeda terrorist attack is in the planning stages and this attack is aimed at the US, an attack that would come without warning and kill thousands of US civilians. Numerous warning of this attack came into the CIA and FBI headquaters, from April through the end of July. The CIA learns that Abu Zubayda, the number four in the al Qaeda hierarchy is connected with this attack, indicating that this attack has the full support of the very top leadership of al Qaeda. *(9/11 Commission report, Mainstream news media reports)*

April 2001

In April 2001 Ali Soufan sent a final request to the CIA for all of the information they had on Khallad. He asked if a telephone number he had obtained from phone records of calls al-Quso made from the Washington Hotel in Bangkok and his house in Yemen to a pay phone in Kuala Lumpur had any significance and whether there was a connection between these phone calls and Khallad. The CIA said that they could not help him or provide any information. At this time the CIA already had much information on Khallad and had logs from Malaysian intelligence that listed the phone number Ali gave the CIA in Kuala Lumpur, which was to a phone booth in front of the condominium where the al Qaeda planning meeting had taken place on January 5-8, 2000. *[Account of Ali Soufan, by Lawrence Wright]*

June 11, 2001

In late May FBI IOS Agent Dina Corsi at the behest of CIA Supervisor Clark Shannon makes an official request to the New York office of the FBI to hold a meeting in New York City FBI field office on June 11, 2001, with the FBI *Cole* investigators. An FBI IOS analyst working at the FBI Headquaters, Dina Corsi, along with another FBI detailee at the CIA Alec Station, the Bin Laden Unit, "Mary," and a CIA Supervisor from the Bin Laden Unit, Clark Shannon, attended this meeting with the FBI New York *Cole* investigators. One of these Cole investigators is FBI Special Agent Steve Bongardt, Ali Soufan's main assistant on the *Cole* bombing investigation.

From the information that was developed during the FBI IG investigation and the 9/11 Commission report, it appeared to make no sense as to why this meeting was called or what actually happened at this meeting. The FBI IG even directly criticized the FBI IOS agent, Dina Corsi, in their report, with a comment that this meeting had no clearly defined purpose.

By combining the information from the account of the lead *Cole* investigator FBI Agent Ali Soufan with the FBI IG report, this meeting for the very first time made sense.

It is now clear from the FBI IG report that this meeting had been set up at the request of Clarke Shannon to FBI IOS Agent Dina Corsi. He indicated to her the CIA wanted to know if Fahad al-Quso's story that he could not travel onto Kuala Lumpur was correct, was Quso in the photographs from the Kuala Lumpur meeting. Dina was told that she should obtain the three photographs that Tom Wilshire had obtained from the CIA of Mihdhar at the Kuala Lumpur meeting, show these to the FBI Cole investigators and see if they could recognize Quso in these photos.

We now know from Chapter 19, the Cole investigation that this reason used to set up this meeting was just a ruse. From the FBI IG report we are told that Wilshire had obtained these photographs in May 2001 and was looking to see if he could find Khallad bin Attash in these photos. It is clear in his attempt to identify Khallad in the photos Wilshire must have had the passport photograph of Khallad that had been attached to Ail Soufan's request for information on Khallad that came into the CIA headquaters in April 2001. Since there were only two photographs of Khallad at the CIA, the Kuala Lumpur photo and the passport photo from Ali Soufan, if Wilshire had the photo from Kuala Lumpur of Khallad he would have known immediately that Khallad was actually never in the same photos with Mihdhar but was in a separate photo. Since Wilshire never realized this, he clearly had Ali Soufan's passport photo of Khallad.

Note: We know that both Mihdhar and Khallad had been photographed at the Kuala Lumpur meeting because the CIA had passed the photos of Mihdhar over to the FBI on August 23, 2001 and a separate photo of Khallad on August 30, 2001.

This meant that Wishire had Ali Soufan's request for information on Khallad. We also know that Clark Shannon also had Ali Soufan's request, since he gave Dina Corsi a phone number that Quso had called in order to reach Khallad in Kuala Lumpur, and the significance of this number appears no where else but in Soufan's request.

The fact that both Clark Shannon and Tom Wilshire had FBI Agent Ali Soufan's request was never uncovered by any government investigations of the events on 9/11. It has been kept as one of if not the most the most heavily guarded secret at the CIA, a secret that had been uncovered by combining a time line from the FBI IG report (pages 283-4) with the account of FBI Agent Ali Soufan.

Instead of giving Soufan the information he asked for, Wilshire and Shannon requested that Corsi set up this meeting with the very people who worked for Soufan, in order to find out if the FBI in their search for Khallad had uncovered information about Mihdhar and Hazmi? Khallad bin Attash had been seen with Khalid al-Mihdhar and Nawaf al-Hazmi at the Kuala Lumpur meeting, and the CIA thought that because of this connection the FBI had uncovered information about Mihdhar and Hazmi.

The CIA was aware that the FBI Cole investigators knew about the flight Khallad had taken on January 8, 2000, from Kuala Lumpur to Bangkok. They knew if the FBI checked this flight manifest they would have found Khalid al-Mihdhar and Nawaf al-Hazmi were sitting right next Khallad in adjacent seats on this flight.

During this June 11 meeting just after the three photos of Mihdhar had been presented to the FBI Cole investigators, Clark Shannon asked them if they recognized anyone in the photos. One of the photos had only Khalid al-Mihdhar and Nawaf al-Hazmi standing next to a tree in Kuala Lumpur, Malaysia. The CIA knew exactly what al-Mihdhar and Nawaf looked like, from their identification at the January 2000 meeting in Kuala Lumpur, when the both of them and Khallad had all been seen together.

It is now clear that the CIA set this meeting only to find out if the FBI had uncovered information on Khalid al-Mihdhar or Nawaf al-Hazmi. This meeting was a CIA sting on the FBI, set up for the purpose of finding out if the FBI was aware of

al-Mihdhar or al-Hazmi. No other explanation seems even remotely possible!

None of the FBI agents involved with the Cole investigation attending this meeting were aware that Wilshire and Shannon had Ali's request for information on Khallad.

Both Wilshire and Shannon knew at the time of this meeting that a huge al Qaeda attack was aimed right at a target inside of the US, an attack that would kill thousands on Americans and knew that al-Hazmi was already in the US. They also knew that Mihdhar had a multi-entry visa for the US that it was quit likely that both Mihdhar and Hamzi were going to take part is this huge attack. They also knew by keeping this information secret it was going to be all but impossible for the FBI to prevent this attack, and that thousands of Americans were now going to die in this huge attack.

This meeting is important because it clearly shows in unmistakable terms the diabolical nature of this criminal conspiracy to hide the information on Mihdhar, Hazmi and their connection to Khallad at the Kuala Lumpur meeting, they were hiding the very information that the FBI could have used to prevent a horrific attack the CIA was aware of and they knowingly refused to give this information to the FBI. This meeting is also important since it makes clear that all of the other times the CIA inexplicably hid the exact same information from the FBI had to be part of this same conspiracy.

But an even bigger question is why did the FBI IG not find this out? Why did the FBI IG investigators not interview FBI Agent Ali Soufan and learn of his request sent to the CIA in April, for information on Khallad, and the significance of the phone number in Kuala Lumpur? They clearly must have known who Ali Soufan was; he had been lead investigator on the Cole bombing.

What did they think when Wilshire for no apparent reason is looking to see if he can identify Khallad in the photos of Mihdhar, or when Shannon gives a phone number to Corsi. Did they ask Wilshire why he was doing this or where Shannon got this phone number? Did they ask Wilshire where he had obtained the photo of Khallad he was using to identify him in the photos of Mihdhar, since it had to be obvious he could not have had the photo from

Kuala Lumpur? Clearly all of this would all have been quickly explained if they talked to Ali Soufan.

A description of Ali Soufan or any alias of him is never mentioned in the FBI IG report.

HOW IS THIS POSSIBLE?

The fate of almost 3,000 Americans was sealed at the June 11, 2001 meeting. They were now all going to die and nothing was going to stop this. [Joint Inquiry Committee Report, FBI IG Report, Account of Ali Soufan, by Lawrence Wright]

June 11 – August 22, 2001

Dina Corsi the FBI IOS Agent who had set up the June 11, meeting with the FBI Cole investigators promises to provide information to FBI Agent Steve Bongardt on Khalid al-Mihdhar, but never does. Apparently she is forbidden by the CIA from providing this information to Steve Bongardt and his team of Cole investigators.

June 12, 2001

On June 12, 2001, the CIA is informed that Khalid Sheikh Mohammed had recruited approximately 20 terrorists for the huge al Qaeada attack the CIA had already known about. It is learned that he had already sent some of these terrorists into the US, and that he was in the process of sending the rest of these al Qaeda terrorists into the US, to link up with the other terrorists already here to carry out the huge attack the CIA had been getting numerous warnings about.

The CIA knows that Khalid Sheikh Mohammed had helped finance the original attack on the World Trade Center Towers in 1993, and was behind the Bojinka plot. The first part of this plot was to blow up aircraft going to the US, the second part was to hijack multiple large aircraft in the US and fly these into major and important buildings in the US, the World Trade Center Towers, Capitol Building, Pentagon and CIA Headquaters. *(9/11 Commission report, Mainstream news media reports)*

July 10, 2001

Tenet and Black brief Condoleezza Rice in the White House on the unprecedented warning the CIA has received about a massive attack inside of the US that will come without warning and kill thousands of Americans. Rice requests the CIA to brief Donald Rumsfeld and John Ashcroft, but takes no further action to prevent these attacks. These briefings take place one week later.

From the 9/11 Commission report:

> "The attack will be spectacular and designed to inflict mass casualties against U.S. facilities or interests. Attack preparations have been made. Attack will occur with little or no warning."

> -CIA Intelligence Report for President Bush, July 2001

John Ashcroft is so disturbed by this information in the briefing of this massive impending al Qaeda attack that by the third week in July, he quits flying commercial aircraft. By July 25 the information that Ashcroft has quit flying commercial aircraft is so wide spread that it has reached main stream news media and they ask him directly the reasons he no longer uses commercial aircraft. He releases a press statement that said he would no longer going to fly commercial aircraft for the remainder of his term in office due to unspecified threats he had received from the FBI. He would add nothing further. No one is able to find out what this threat is. No one is aware that Tenet and Black had given Ashcroft a detailed briefing on a huge impending attack inside of the US that would kill thousands of American civilians or that this threat was so horrific and specific that Ashcroft would feel that the safety of US commercial aircraft had become so dangerous he had to discontinue the use f commercial aircraft.

(9/11 Commission report and documents given to this commission along with 9/11 Commission interviews with Richard Clarke, Condoleezza Rice, and George Tenet.

NOTE: The fact that these meetings occurred has been acknowledged by the 9/11 Commission, but were left out of the final 9/11 report, even though they show actions that were nothing less than criminal negligence in ignoring these clear warnings of horrific attacks that were to take place on 9/11.)

July 13, 2001

According to the FBI IG report Tom Wilshire makes a request to his CTC managers, (Cofer Black, and likely George Tenet) that the CIA provide the FBI with all of the information from the Kuala

Lumpur meeting including the information that Khallad, Khalid al-Mihdhar, and Nawaf al-Hazmi had been seen together at this meeting, in addition to the information that Nawaf al-Hazmi had entered the US on January 15, 2000 and that Khalid al-Mihdhar had a multi-entry visa for the US. CIA management turned down his request and forbid Wilshire from giving this information to the FBI. Wilshire is well aware that the CIA was receiving many warnings of a huge catastrophic attack inside of the US that would kill thousands of innocent Americans and was clearly having second thoughts about continuing to keep this information secret. He clearly was aware that continuing to hide this information from the FBI was going to make it all but impossible for them to prevent this attack, and that thousands of Americans would die as a result. *(FBI Inspector General's report)*

August 21, 2001

From the FBI IG report we learn that "Mary", a low level FBI IOS agent at the Bin Laden unit of the CIA found the cable at the CIA that states that Nawaf al–Hazmi had entered the US on January 15, 2000. This is the exact same information that both Shannon and Wilshire and 50-60 other people at the CIA have been aware of for 20 months, according to the CIA IG Report. She also finds the cable that details all of the information on Mihdhar written by FBI Agent Doug Miller and even finds the cable that states that the information in Miller's CIR on Mihdhar had been sent to the FBI when in fact it had not. The cable with all of the information on Mihdhar is marked on the bottom, "Blocked by order of the Deputy Chief", (Tom Wilshire).

[NOTE: Both George Tenet and Cofer Black lie to congress and the Joint Inquiry Committee investigation on this point. They claimed this information had been sent to the FBI from the beginning. They are never charged with perjury.]

"Mary" unaware that this is the same information had been hidden from the FBI for the past 21 months, and without getting permission from anyone at the CIA contacts the INS and is told that both Hazmi and Mihdhar had entered the US on January 15, 2000. INS tells her that Mihdhar had then left in June 2000 and had again re-entered the US on July 4, 2001. (It is now clear that Mary had been kept in the dark about the fact that the CIA had been hiding this information from the FBI. The CIA looked on some of the FBI IOS agents working at the CIA as spies for the FBI and they were not trusted.)

She next does something that will turn out to be catastrophic for thousands of Americans on 9/11. She contacts Dina Corsi and updates her on what she has found. Dina Corsi and Mary then meet with Tom Wilshire in his FBI office for advice, in spite of the fact that Wilshire is not their supervisor, and he claimed to the FBI IG investigators that he had no official role at FBI headquaters. (By this time Wilshire had already been involved in two prior occasions to hide this information from the FBI, the blocking of a cable with information on Mihdhar on January 5, 2000, and the meeting with the FBI Cole investigators, with the help of Dina Corsi, on June 11, 2001).

Both Corsi and Wilshire are aware that a paper trail has been established from the Bin Laden unit at the CIA to the INS connecting Mihdhar and Hazmi to this unit and the fact they are in the US. The CIA can no longer keep the names of these terrorists secret and is forced to turn over the photographs of Mihdhar and Hazmi from the Kuala Lumpur meeting to the FBI. In this meeting Wilshire and Corsi conspire to take the investigation of Mihdhar away from Mary and give this assignment to Corsi. Mary is unaware at this time that the meeting she had been at on June 11, 2001, with Corsi and Shannon and the FBI Cole investigators had actually been a CIA sting on the FBI carried out by Shannon, and Wilshire, and Corsi, although at this time Corsi may also have not been totally aware of why the CIA had requested this meeting.

In an August 22 e-mail message to FBI agent "Glenn" at the FBI New York office, Corsi indicates to him that she knows that in addition to the photographs of Mihdhar and Hazmi the CIA has from the Kuala Lumpur meeting, the CIA also has photographs of Khallad taken at the same Kuala Lumpur meeting. At this point in time Corsi is aware that the CIA had been hiding the photo of Khallad taken at the Kuala Lumpur meeting from the FBI. She knew this photo had been hidden from the FBI during the June 11 meeting in New York with the Cole investigators and knows that they are still continuing to hide this photo from the FBI.

[NOTE: At this point Corsi would have known that the search for Mihdhar should have been opened as a criminal investigation since the fact that Mihdhar and Khallad were seen together at the planning meeting for the Cole bombing directly connects Mihdhar to the planning of this attack.]

FBI IG investigators later cannot find out how Corsi got this information on Khallad. Wishire and Shannon, the two CIA officials who she had been working with, tell the FBI IG investigators, that they never gave her this information, and in fact claim they never told anyone at the FBI about Khallad or the fact he had been photographed at the Kuala Lumpur meeting, in spite of the fact they had known that Khallad had been the mastermind on the Cole bombing and in December 2000 had reconfirmed that Khallad had been at the Kuala Lumpur meeting.

Corsi never tells the FBI IG investigators where, how or even when she had obtained this information, that the CIA had photographs of Khallad from the Kuala Lumpur meetings or the fact that she knew the CIA had been keeping these hidden from the FBI.

It is now clear that it was just after Corsi met with Wishire, she wanted to insure that this investigation was opened as an intelligence investigation and not a criminal investigation, in spite of the fact that she knows both Khallad and Mihdhar had been seen together and both photographed at the Kuala Lumpur meeting, directly connecting both Mihdhar and Hazmi to the criminal acts in the Cole bombing.

It is not until the next day on August 23, Dina Corsi contacts her own supervisor, "Rob" about the fact that "Mary" had found the cable indicating that Hazmi was in the US and that the CIA had been forced to turned over the photos they had of Mihdhar and Hazmi from the Kuala Lumpur meeting to the FBI. It is not known exactly what Corsi told Rob, although the FBI IG report states he concurred with her that the search for Mihdhar should be opened as an intelligence investigation. But it is not know if Corsi told her supervisor about Khallad or the photos of Khallad that Corsi knows the CIA had kept secret from the FBI. Did Corsi give the information to Rob that Khallad had been identified with Mihdhar and Hazmi at the Kuala Lumpur meeting? It is difficult to believe that if Corsi had given this information to Rob, he would not have demanded that the photos of Khallad be turned over to the FBI immediately, and that investigation of Mihdhar be part of the Cole bombing criminal investigation since it would have then been clear that Mihdhar had been at the very meeting where the mastermind of the Cole bombing had planed this attack

On August 23, Corsi telephones "Chad", an intelligence agent at the New York field office Bin Laden unit and discussed with him FBI headquaters request (with a need for urgency) for a full field intelligence investigation of Mihdhar. Chad stated to Corsi that this investigation of Mihdhar seemed to relate to the criminal investigation of the Cole attack, and efforts to locate him would normally be handled through a sub-file to the main investigation (of the Cole bombing) and not as a separate investigation. However, because of her insistence to open this as an intelligence investigation, he tells Corsi, New York will open an intelligence investigation.

Just after talking with Chad, on August 23, Corsi sends an email to Wilshire advising, "Chad will open an intelligence case". It is clear from this email that Corsi is secretly coordinating her work with Wilshire, in spite of the fact that Wilshire has no official role at the FBI.

After consulting with Wilshire, on August 22, 2001, Corsi prepares the EC, the document that is to start the search for Mihdhar in the US. Since the photographs of Khallad had not been turned over to the FBI at the time the Mihdhar photos were, no one else at the FBI can not connect Mihdhar directly to the planning of the Cole bombing.

It is now clear that Corsi wrote up the EC to insure that this investigation was opened as an intelligence investigation and not a criminal investigation, in spite of the fact that she knows both Khallad and Mihdhar had been seen together and even photographed at the Kuala Lumpur meeting, directly connecting both Mihdhar and Hazmi to the criminal acts in the Cole bombing.

On the morning of August 28, Corsi finally sends the EC to Chad. This EC outlines Mihdhar's travel to the US, and similarities between al-Mihdhar's travels and that of Cole suspects al-Quso, Ibraiham al-Nibras, and Khallad. She does not include the identification of Khallad in the Kuala Lumpur photographs by the source. She later tells the FBI IG investigators that she did not include this information because it had not yet been officially passed to the FBI although she claims she had requested this from a CTC representative.

When she sends the EC over to the FBI it is marked "routine" urgency, in spite of the fact that Mihdhar and Hazmi are known to be extremely dangerous al Qaeda terrorists who are likely connected with the massive attack both the CIA and FBI have been getting numerous warnings about since April 2001. Marking the EC routine insures that the investigation of Mihdhar will be opened with no sense of urgency.

Corsi also wants this information on Mihdhar kept away from the Cole investigators. On August 28, this EC is forwarded to Steve Bongardt. He calls Dina Corsi and requests that this investigation be opened as a criminal investigation as part of the Cole bombing. She tells him that he must destroy the information on Mihdhar that he has since it contains NSA information.

In a conference call with Steve Bongardt, Dina Corsi and her boss, Rob, Steve argues that the search for Mihdhar is now connected to the Cole bombing and that the investigation should be opened as a criminal investigation, which would apply many more resources to this search.

Corsi later tells FBI IG investigators that "the information on Mihdhar was obtained through intelligence channels and because of restrictions on using intelligence information, could not be provided to the Cole investigators." She stated that the only information that could be provided to them was the limited INS information. She goes on to state, "that without the intelligence information there would have been no potential nexus to the Cole investigation and no basis for a criminal investigation." This is in spite of the fact that Khallad, the mastermind of the Cole bombing, had been clearly identified at the Kuala Lumpur meeting with Mihdhar and Hazmi, directly implicating both Mihdhar and Hazmi in the planning of these attacks. The photographs of Khallad had remained hidden from Bongardt and the rest of the Cole investigators at this time.

Steve requested that Corsi obtain an opinion from the NSLU unit at the FBI, the legal unit, to see if they feel this investigation can be opened as a criminal investigation. While Corsi did obtain an opinion from the NSLU unit at the FBI that this investigation should be opened as an intelligence investigation, it is clear from the FBI IG report that it was easy to get the NSLU unit at the FBI to render whatever opinion you wanted. By stating the conclusion the NSLU was suppose to reach, and then by giving the NSLU lawyers only the information that supported this side of the issue, they would consistently rule for whatever opinion was wanted.

On August 29, Corsi e-mails Steve that the NSLU agreed the investigation should be an intelligence investigation and that Steve and other FBI criminal agents could not be present when the intelligence FBI agents interview Mihdhar.

Steve Bongardt replies: "..where is the wall defined? Isn't it dealing with FISA information? I think everyone is still confusing this issue ...someday some one will die - and the wall or not - the public will not understand why we were not more effective and throwing every resource we had at certain problems."

There seems to be no legitimate reason all of the photographs from the Kuala Lumpur meeting were not immediately turned over to the Cole investigation, they had been taken by Malaysian intelligence, and had nothing to do with the FISA process. Knowledge that Mihdar and Hazmi had been connected to the Cole bombing and also the east Africa attacks, and were in the US preparing for the huge al Qaeda attack everyone at both the CIA and FBI knew about would immediately render the boiler plate FISA notice on any NSA traffic "null and void", and completely inoperable, and this was stated right in all NSA notices. The only NSA information associated with this information was the cable that was issued in December 1999, that stated that Khalid, Nawaf and Salem were traveling to Kuala Lumpur to attend a high level al Qaeda planning meeting, and while the NSA had a disclaimer on the front of this document stating this information could not be given to a criminal investigator, for fear of tainting a later criminal case in court, the statement said this notice was null and void if the information was possibly connected to a terrorist act inside of the US.

While the photos of Mihdar were turned over the FBI on August 23, 2001, the photos of Khallad remained hidden from the FBI for another eight days, not until August 30, 2001, one day after the FBI had opened the search for Mihdar as an intelligence investigation. An intelligence investigation opened with "Routine" urgency would in effect have meant that this investigation would have but a fraction of the resources given to a criminal investigation with the highest priority. The investigation was given to one of the least experienced FBI agents in the New York office, who had gotten no where by the time the attacks on 9/11 occur.

Had the photographs of Khallad been turned over to the FBI New York office and the Cole investigators at the time the photographs of Mihdhar and Hazmi were turned over, it is inconceivable that the Cole investigators would not have known immediately that the CIA had obstructed their investigation. Had they been part of the search for Mihdhar and Hazmi, it is inconceivable they could not have been located Mihdhar and Hazmi in the almost three weeks they would have had to locate them. Since the credit cards of Mihdhar and Hazmi were used to buy 10 of the airplane tickets used on 9/11, this alone would have prevented these attacks.

When the CIA withheld the photos of Khallad at the Kuala Lumpur meeting until August 30, 2001, they effectively sabotaged the investigation and search for Mihdhar. This was the 5th time the CIA had hidden information that Khallad had been at the Kuala Lumpur meeting with Mihdhar and Hazmi from an on going criminal investigation into the Cole bombing. This is clearly criminal obstruction of this FBI investigation.   *[FBI Inspector General's report]*

As I looked this information over for the first time and it was becoming clear what had happened I felt intensely sick, it was if ice water had suddenly filled my veins. It was now clear that the CIA had deliberately withheld critical information from the FBI on Mihdhar and Hazmi and the fact they had been seen at the Kuala Lumpur meeting with Khallad, even when it was known they were in then US, and were likely to take part in the attack the CIA was aware of. Just when it looked like there was a possibility that the attacks on 9/11 might have been stopped when Mary found the cable that stated that Hazmi was inside of the US, Corsi and Wilshire conspired to take this investigation away from her. It is clear they worked together to insure the EC to start the search for Mihdhar would specify an intelligence investigation with absolutely no sense of urgency by marking this EC "Routine". Both Corsi and Wilshire were aware that if the EC came over to the FBI office in New York, and they did not keep this investigation of Mihdhar away from Steve Bongardt and the rest of the Cole investigators, everyone including Wilshire, Shannon and Corsi would have been immediately arrested for criminally obstructing the Cole investigation multiple times.

What can explain all of this?

A big question is how was it possible that four official government investigations of 9/11 did not see this, particularly the FBI IG investigation, which had almost all of this information?

The Joint Inquiry Committee investigation, and the 9/11 Commission could never explain why the information on Mihdhar and Hazmi had been hidden from the FBI for 21 months, or why Mihdhar and Hazmi were never connected by the CIA to the huge al-Qaeda attack, the CIA had been getting numerous warnings about since April 2001, or why they had never been watch listed.

But is now clear the only possible explaination for the CIA deliberately hiding information from the FBI was a wide-ranging criminal conspiracy.

A conspiracy to hide information from the FBI would explain why information on Kahlid al-Mihdhar was blocked on January 5, 2000, why Khalid al-Mihdhar's name was left off the cable that came into CIA headquarters on March 15, 2000 even though we know his name had been on the watchlist when he entered Thailand.

This explains why Tenet stated at the April 14, 2004, public 9/11 Commission hearing that no one read the cable when it came into CIA headquaters even though it was noted right on the cable; "read with interest" by Alec Station, the Bin Laden Unit at the CIA. The CIA had clearly read this cable, but by this time they wanted to block any and all attention that might have led back to Khalid al-Mihdhar and his attendance at the Kuala Lumpur al Qaeda planning meeting.

The reasons behind this CIA criminal conspiracy to maintain this secrecy?

Why did the CIA hide the information on Khalid al-Mihdhar, the meeting in Kuala Lumpur, and finally over the names Nawaf al-Hazmi and Khallad?

In November 2000, shortly after FBI Agent Ali Soufan's investigation of the Cole bombing, the CIA found out that they had photographed Khallad at the Kuala Lumpur meeting in January 2000. The CIA inexplicably had let Khallad and 11 other well-known al-Qaeda terrorists walk away from this meeting. Then 10 months later these terrorists carried out the *Cole* bombing. The CIA had every reason, after this point, to keep the names Khalid al-Mihdhar, Nawaf al-Hazmi and the fact that Khallad had been at this meeting in Kuala Lumpur absolutely secret.

They were afraid they would be found culpable in the Cole bombing and the deaths of 17 US Navy sailors if this information ever came out.

This clearly explains why after October 2000, the CIA kept this information secret from the FBI, and which ultimately caused the CIA to hide the very information that could have prevented the attacks on 9/11.

But what explains why the CIA kept the information secret on Khalid al-Mihdhar and the meeting in Kuala Lumpur in January 2000, 10 months before the *Cole* bombing?

There are three important clues that help answer this question:

- Khalid al-Mihdhar was a known an al Qaeda terrorist the CIA had known about since 1995.

- Ali Mohammed was an al Qaeda spy that had infiltrated the Army Special Forces, the FBI and even the CIA. His first task at the CIA was working as a covert agent. He had instructed bin Laden's personal bodyguard and did the surveillance on the East Africa embassies in 1993, prior to the truck bombing in 1998. He had clearly come into contact with Khalid al-Mihdhar during the East Africa bombings.

- Khalid al-Mihdhar's father in law, Ahmad Muhammad al-Hada, a long-time al Qaeda member who was very active in bin Laden's organization. His name and phone number in Yemen were found in the possession of one of the East Africa bombers in 1998.

The CIA perhaps had Khalid al-Mihdhar under surveillance in Yemen, or in Tanzania or Kenya, and knew about the upcoming bombing and then failed to do anything to stop this huge terrorist attack on the East Africa embassies.

Khalid al-Mihdhar was clearly connected to Ali Mohammed from their work on the East Africa bombings. Clearly both had worked on this attack. Al-Mihdhar's father-in-law was a central planner in this attack. Ali Mohammed was the al Qaeda terrorist who had done surveillance of the target, and was present when bin Laden said, "the bomb should be placed here", while pointing to a spot in Ali's photograph of the East Africa embassies where the huge truck bomb would be detonated. Exposing al-Mihdhar would have exposed Ali Mohammed and the fact that Ali Mohamed had once been an al-Qaeda spy inside of the CIA. Ali Mohammed's first assignment at the CIA was to infiltrate a mosque in Hamburg, Germany. This connection would have proved highly embarrassing to the CIA.

While this is speculation, and there is little information to back this up, it is hard to find another explanation that comes close to explaining why the CIA was so concerned that they wanted to keep the name Khalid al-Mihdhar secret from the FBI, in a conspiracy that started on January 5, 2000, just before the al Qaeda terrorists first met in Kuala Lumpur.

A conspiracy theory explains why the CIA never watch-listed either al-Mihdhar or al-Hazmi on the numerous occasions that their names became the focus of attention.

In spite of the fact that the CIA had just issued a cable to all CIA officers in late 1999 to remind them to watchlist all dangerous terrorists even if they only had first names or aliases, when al-Hazmi first entered the US, on January 15, 2000, he was not watchlisted. The CIA was aware that had al-Hazmi been watchlisted, it would have alerted the FBI to him and led back the meeting in Kuala Lumpur and then to al-Mihdhar.

This explains why the CIA kept this information secret on numerous occasions from ongoing criminal investigations, going so far as to commit numerous felonies to keep this information secret, and in the *Cole* investigation "criminal obstruction of justice." If the CIA employees were willing to commit felonies to keep this information secret, it only stands to reason that CIA managers feared even greater criminal penalties if the information they were keeping secret got back to the FBI.

However after reviewing the CIA actions to hide the information from the Kuala Lumpur meeting and the names of the people who attended this meeting from the FBI, it is now clear that the attacks on 9/11 occurred not due to simple mistakes at the CIA, but because of a wide ranging conspiracy to hide the very information the FBI could have used to prevent this al Qaeda attack on 9/11, even when the CIA knew this would all but insure the success of the massive attack they were getting warnings about in the summer of 2001..

But did the CIA know in advance the exact nature of the attacks on 9/11? When the CIA allowed the al Qaeda attacks to take place, did they have "malice aforethought"?

What exactly did the CIA know prior to the 9/11 attacks?

According to testimony by George Tenet at the 9/11 hearings, the CIA never had the texture, the time, the place and the methods used by the terrorists in the attack on 9/11. They claimed they were unable to connect the different bits of information, the dots, to put this together. And yet it appears they did have significant information. When this information that the CIA had is examined closely, several events, which were downplayed by the CIA in testimony before the Joint Inquiry Committee and 9/11 Commission investigations, appear to be central to what the CIA must have known prior to 9/11.

The hijacking of Air India 814

Air India Flight 814 was hijacked on December 24, 1999, enroute from Katmandu to New Delhi, India, by six terrorists who used concealed weapons to take over the flight in midair. It is believed the terrorists used concealed pistols, hand grenades and folding knives.

"There is little question that, while the Indian airlines hijackers were 'Afghans,' they were directly tied to the Al-Muhajiroun in Pakistan and Usama bin Laden, who is currently living in Afghanistan," according to Alijandra Mogilner in statements to Asian newspapers. Alijandra Mogilner is an analyst who specializes in counterterrorism.

This hijacked aircraft was flown to the Indian city of Amritsa, then to Lahore, Pakistan, where it was refueled. It then took off and flew to Kabul, where it was refused clearance to land, and then flew on to Dubai, and then the United Arab Emirates, where it was allowed to refuel in exchange for the release of some passengers. From there it flew to Kabul where it again was refused clearance to land, and finally to Kandahar, on December 25, where it landed.

When it was obvious that the Taliban guards were setting up only low-key security and were not negotiating in good faith with outside parties, many analysts thought the Taliban's actions were not only inappropriate, but went so far as to accuse them of double-dealing. "This whole thing is an absolute con and the media is allowing the Taliban not only to get away with it, but to let them come out smelling like a rose," open-source intelligence analyst Ronald W. Lewis said in statements to Asian news-papers located in this region.

The hijacking was resolved on December 31, with the release of three terrorists held by Indian authorities and the escape of the remaining five hijackers, who went right through unchallenged by the Taliban security that completely ringed the aircraft. The released terrorists traveled to an audience with Usama Bin Laden just after this hijacking.

This hijacking had been described extensively in major newspaper during the last week of December 1999. It was even denounced in several speeches on the floor of the Congress. The details of this hijacking were well known not only throughout the world but also at all of the security agencies in the US. It was "front page news."

Not widely known at that time, but clearly known by the intelligence agencies, was the fact that the final destination of the hijacked flight, the airport at Kandahar, Afghanistan, was where Mohamed Atef, the military commander for al Qaeda, had his headquarters. Kandahar was also the city where al Qaeda had their administrative headquarters.

The al Qaeda planning meeting in Kuala Lumpur, Malaysia

Just one week after this successful hijacking, on January 5-8, 2000, the al Qaeda terrorists held a planning meeting in Kuala Lumpur, Malaysia. This meeting took place just days after the failed attempt to bomb the *USS The Sullivans*. This meeting was where the next attack on a US warship, the *USS Cole,* and the 9/11 attacks were planned.

For as yet unexplained reasons, the CIA did not bug this meeting, and instead of providing direct surveillance themselves, asked Malaysian intelligence to photograph the persons who attended this meeting and provide these photographs back to them.

Because this meeting came just one week after the Air India 814 hijacking, a hijacking that terminated right at the headquarters of the military commander of al Qaeda, the CIA would have known that the main topic of discussion at this meeting would be this hijacking.

It is clear that the al Qaeda terrorists had already been planning the attack on 9/11 using hijacked aircraft from about February, or March of 1999, but this meeting is important with respect to the use of hijacked aircraft.

Even if the al Qaeda terrorists were contemplating hijacking aircraft to carry out the attacks on 9/11, prior to the Air India 814 hijacking, this was the very first real confirmation for the al Qaeda leadership that a small group of armed terrorists could successfully hijack a large aircraft, and how it could be done.

Khalid Shaikh Mohammed

In 2000 the intelligence agencies of the US government were well aware of Khalid Shaikh Mohammed and how incredibly dangerous he was with respect to civil aviation. His involvement in the Bojinka plot, a plan to place liquid bombs on multiple aircraft going to the US, and in a later version of the same plot, to hijack multiple aircraft and crash them into buildings in the US, was well known throughout the upper levels of the US government. In 1998 the FBI posted a $2,000,000 reward for his capture.

It is widely believed that Khalid Shaikh Mohammed chaired the meeting in Kuala Lumpur on January 2000, where both the next attempt to bomb a US warship, the *USS Cole*, and the 9/11 attack were discussed and planned. But even to this day the CIA has never publicly acknowledged this fact. They would not even acknowledge that they were holding him in a secret overseas prison until September 2006.

From the photographs taken by Malaysian intelligence of the people who attended this meeting, the CIA would have known that Khalid Shaikh Mohammed attended this al Qaeda planning meeting with eleven other al Qaeda terrorists.

The CIA learns Khalid Shaikh Mohammed is sending 20 al Qaeda terrorists into the US for a huge terrorist attack

On June 12, 2001 according to the 9/11 Commission report, the CIA learned that Khalid Shaikh Mohammed had recruited 20 al Qaeda terrorists for an attack inside of the US. They learned that part of this group was being sent into the US to link up with some of the other terrorists who were already in the US to carry out this huge attack.

The FBI and CIA had not connected Khalid Shaikh Mohammed to al Qaeda during the time of the 1993 original attack on the World Trade Center or during the time of the Bojinka plot. However when Khalid Shaikh Mohammed was identified at the Kuala Lumpur al Qaeda planning meeting in January 2000, along with many other long-time al Qaeda terrorists, they would have known that he was now connected with al Qaeda. The arrest of his nephew, Ramzi Yousef in 1996 at an al Qaeda safe house in Pakistan where he had fled after the Bojinka plan was discovered, would have been more proof that both Khalid Shaikh Mohammed and his nephew, Ramzi Yousef, were involved with al Qaeda.

Once the FBI and CIA were aware Khalid Shaikh Mohammed and Ramzi Yousef were involved with the al Qaeda organization, they would have been aware that their involvement with the 1993 attack on the World Trade Center meant they would surely have been familiarizing al Qaeda with the original 1993 attack on the World Trade Center Towers.

Khalid Shaikh Mohammed came up with the plans for the attacks on 9/11 by combining the plan for the 1993 attack on the World Trade Center Towers with his Bojinka plan. The Bojinka plan was a plan to hijack several US airliners and fly them into important buildings in the US, the WTC Towers, Pentagon, Capital Building and the White House.

In October 2000, an attack that the FBI found out that the attack on the USS Cole had been preceded by a failed attack on the *USS The Sullivans*. This would have alerted US intelligence to one important fact. The al Qaeda terrorists do not give up on a target if they or other jihadists who join with them are unsuccessful in their first attack.

The CIA was also learned that Abu Zubaydah was involved with the al Qaeda attack coming in the summer or fall of 2001. Abu Zubaydah was number four in al Qaeda indicating that the leadership of al Qaeda must have been focused on this one huge attack.

Tenet, and perhaps many of the other top managers at the CIA and the Bin Laden Unit, Alec Station were some of the people who had this almost complete information concerning the attack on the US that virtually everyone was aware was about to take place.

Additional information the CIA had.

Just prior to July 4, 2001

NSA overheard a conversation between two al Qaeda terrorists in Yemen. People who worked at the White House as part of the NSC, and employed by the NSA, had focused on a conversation between two al Qaeda terrorists. In this phone conversation, the terrorists expressed disappointment over the fact that the US had not responded seriously to the *Cole* bombing. One of the al Qaeda terrorists was heard saying, "Don't worry; we're planning something so big now that the US will have to respond." This report was so widespread that it went to the *New York Times*, which never printed it. They felt there was not sufficient information to make it into a front-page story.

June - July 2001

A Pakistani journalist was granted an interview with Usama bin Laden in June 2001. He was told by bin Laden that the US should expect a big surprise in the next few weeks. He was also told that the targets would be Israeli and US interests. People around bin Laden told this same journalist that there would be a major increase in the coffin business in the US in the near future. This information was broadcast in the US in July 2001. The CIA was clearly aware of this interview.

August 21, 2001

On August 23, 2001 "Mary" the FBI IOS agent working at the CIA found the cable that stated that Hazmi had entered the US on

January 15, 2000. INS told her that Mihdhar had reentered the US on July 4, 2001.

Just prior to August 23, 2001

CIA manager John McLaughlin was informed that a possible al Qaeda terrorist, Zacarias Moussaoui, had been arrested getting training on large US airliners.

[Note: FBI investigators found that Zacarias Moussaoui was in a big hurry to complete his flight training, training, which was due to be finished by August 20, 2001, on a Boeing 747. FBI investigators also found two folding knives, each with a blade that was approximately four inches in length. One was on his person, and one was in his car. These knives are the size legally allowed on board US aircraft, by the FAA.

FBI investigators found out that Moussaoui had told his travel companion that these knives are easy to conceal when boarding passenger aircraft. Moussaoui's refusal to cooperate with the FBI investigation and refusal to allow FBI investigators to look inside his duffel bag and other possessions alerted these FBI agents immediately that it was highly likely that Moussaoui was a terrorist. The FBI investigators believed that Moussaoui was learning how to fly a large aircraft, in order to participate in an aircraft hijacking, in the not too distant future. They also surmised that the possible targets were the World Trade Center or the White House. FBI investigators alerted both the Secret Service at the White House and the FAA on this information.

This information on Mihdhar and Hazmi and Moussaoui was well known by George Tenet and the rest of the CIA hierarchy by August 23, 2001.

August 23, 2001

By August 23, Mary, the FBI IOS agent at the CIA had been instrumental in getting the CIA to issue a worldwide alert for Mihdhar and Hazmi. This information went quickly up the chain of command at the CIA. Tenet, Black, almost everyone in the chain of command was quickly aware of this information. It was now know at the FBI that both Mihdhar and Hazmi had been at the Kuala Lumpur planning meeting.

August 24, 2001

Tenet travels to Crawford, TX, for a six-hour meeting with the President, on August 24, 2001, a meeting that would later be kept secret, even though it was described right on the White House website.

August 30, 2001

The CIA notified the FBI that photographs of Khallad at the Kuala Lumpur meeting on January 2000 were being sent over to the FBI. This connected Khalid al-Mihdhar and Nawaf al-Hazmi directly to the al Qaeda terrorist known to be the mastermind of the *Cole* bombing.

In spite of all of this information, the CIA testified to the Joint Inquiry Committee and 9/11 Commission investigators, that they never knew the target, the method or the timing of the huge al Qaeda attack they were getting warnings about in the summer of 2001. When you look closely at what they did know this statement is all but incomprehensible.

Analyzing what the CIA knew

The CIA was aware that the al Qaeda planning meeting in Kuala Lumpur was held just one week after the hijacking of Air India 814.

When the CIA photographed the terrorists at the Kuala Lumpur meeting just after the hijacking of Air India 814, a hijacking that ended with the hijacked aircraft flown to the headquaters of the al Qaeda military commander, the CIA would have known that hijacking would have been the main focus of discussion at that meeting. The fact that Khalid al-Mihdhar and Nawaf al-Hazmi were identified at that meeting and then were known to have entered the US should have alerted the CIA to a possible aircraft hijacking inside of the US. The fact that Khalid Shaikh Mohammed was also identified at that meeting and then it was learning on June 12, 2001 he had recruited a number of al-Qaeda terrorists and that they were being sent into the US to carry out the attack the CIA was aware would have alerted the CIA to two important details:

First from his involvement in the Bojinka plot, the CIA knew that Khalid Shaikh Mohammed had proposed in this plan the use of several hijacked aircraft to be used as flying bombs directed at buildings in the US. The targets that they had focused on, from a plan found on a computer of Abdul Harkim Murrad, a confederate in this plan, were the World Trade Center Towers, the Pentagon, the Capital building and CIA headquaters.

Second his involvement and financing in the original attack on the World Trade Center Towers would clearly indicate his interest in these buildings as targets.

Since the CIA was clearly aware from the investigation of the attack on the *USS Cole* that this attack had been preceded in the very early part of January 2000 by an attack on the *USS The Sullivans*, this was clear evidence the al Qaeda terrorists were determined to go back after a target they or other jihadists who were closely associated with their cause, had missed in a previous attack.

It is inconceivable the CIA was not aware that Khalid al-Mihdhar, Nawaf al-Hazmi and Salem al-Hazmi were part of the group of al Qaeda terrorists the CIA knew Khalid Shaikh Mohammed was sending into the US. Summarizing at this point what the CIA knew:

They knew a huge al Qaeda attack was just about to occur inside of the US.

They knew Khalid Shaikh Mohammed was sending into the US and number of al Qaeda terrorists to link up with other terrorists already inside of the US.

The CIA and the entire CIA management were fully aware that Hazmi had entered the US in March 2000 and on August 23, 2001 that Mihdhar was also inside of the US. They clearly knew these two al Qaeda terrorists were part of the al Qaeda terrorists Khalid Shaikh Mohammed had sent into the US to carry out the huge attack the CIA was aware of.

For anyone to believe that the CIA did not know this boarders on pure insanity!

THIS IS JUST NOT POSSIBLE!

There is no possible way the CIA including almost all of top management were not aware of this!

They were aware that these terrorists had entered the US right after attending the al Qaeda planning meeting in Kuala Lumpur and had been discussing the hijacking of Air India 814. The fact that the CIA issued a worldwide alert for these terrorists on August 23, 2001, indicates how dangerous they were thought to be.

The CIA was informed several days prior to August 23 that Zacarias Moussaoui, who FBI agents thought was clearly a terrorist, had been arrested as he attempted to get training on a 747 airliner, when he was unqualified to even get a private pilot's license. George Tenet was informed about Zacarias Moussaoui on August 23, 2001. The CIA knew that the FBI investigators had found two folding knives with four-inch blades in Moussaoui's possession. The CIA was aware that the hijackers would likely use concealed folding knives, with blades no longer than those deemed legal by the FAA as their primary weapons to hijack the aircraft.

The CIA and the FBI had been aware for years that al Qaeda terrorists had attended US flight schools, a fact that was confirmed with the arrest of Zacarias Moussaoui.

Using about the number of hijackers that had been used on Air India 814 would have meant that the CIA could reasonably assume five or six hijackers would be employed to take over each airplane, armed with concealed folding knives, with blades no longer that four inches. With the knowledge that 20 terrorists were being sent to the US in the summer of 2001, the CIA could have assumed that three or four aircraft would be the likely number of aircraft hijacked.

The CIA had been getting numerous warnings of a huge attack inside of the US in the summer of 2001, when the summer passed with no attack, it was assumed that this attack had been delayed by a few months to the fall of 2001.

In June 2001, a Pakistani journalist was granted an interview with bin Laden in Afghanistan. At this interview bin Laden said that there would be a big surprise for the US in the next few weeks, and that the target would be Israeli or US interests. People around bin Laden told this journalist that the coffin business would increase significantly in the US in the near future. Clearly the CIA was aware of this forecast of an attack inside of the US, by Bin Laden himself.

The NSA told the CIA, just prior to July 4, 2001, that this attack was so large the al Qaeda terrorists were expecting a massive reaction from the US. This information came from the NSA, from an overheard conversation between two al Qaeda terrorists in Yemen expressing disappointment over the reaction of the US to the Cole bombing. One terrorist replied, that the next attack is going to be so big the US would be forced to react. The CIA knew this reaction would mean the US joining with and assisting the Northern Alliance. The leadership of the Northern Alliance was Sheik Massoud in Afghanistan. When two Al Qaeda terrorists posing as journalists on September 9, 2001 assassinated Massoud, the CIA would have known that this attack would likely take place within 1-2 weeks, if not days.

August 24, 2001 meeting with the President

On August 24, 2001 when George Tenet flew down to Crawford, TX, for a six-hour meeting with the President of the United States, a meeting that the CIA had tried to conceal, with the information the CIA had, it is inconceivable George Tenet did not know:

- The target of the huge al Qaeda terrorist attack they were getting warnings about in the summer of 2001, was an attack on the World Trade Center Towers, and perhaps the Pentagon and the Capital Building.

- The al Qaeda terrorists would hijack three or four large commercial aircraft to carry out this attack.

- They would use five or six al Qaeda terrorists to take over each aircraft in midair with the terrorists armed primarily with concealed four-inch folding knives, which were legal to bring on board commercial US aircraft.

- The names of three of the terrorists who were going to take part in this attack were Khalid al-Mihdhar, Nawaf al-Hazmi and Salem al-Hazmi.

- The terrorists who were going to pilot these hijacked aircraft had gotten flight training at US flight schools.

- The attack would take place shortly after August 20, 2001, the date Moussaoui was scheduled to complete his flight training.

- The assassination of Massoud would pinpoint the date of this attack to within a few days after September 9, 2001.

What did the CIA not know?

The CIA was apparently unaware of the exact date for the attack on 9/11, until after September 9, 2001 and only knew it would be within days of this date.

They did not know the exact flight numbers of the aircraft to be hijacked.

They did not know the names of the other terrorists outside of Nawaf al-Hazmi, Khalid al-Mihdhar and Salem al-Hazmi. However, all they had to do was search the FAA records to find that Hani Hanjour and al-Hazmi had trained together in Arizona in January 2001.

They could have given the information they had to the FAA, which would have prevented the attacks on 9/11 from succeeding. According to testimony by Robert Cammaroto of the FAA at the trial of Zacarias Moussaoui, had this information been sent to the FAA, that this attack would use folding knives with four-inch blades and use Nawaf al-Hazmi and Khalid al-Mihdhar as hijackers, the FAA would immediately have prevented these type of knives from coming on board US aircraft and would have stopped al-Hazmi and al-Mihdhar from boarding any US aircraft.

Had Nawaf al-Hazmi, Salem al-Hazmi, and Khalid al-Mihdhar been watchlisted for airline reservations, their flight could have been identified, and this would have pointed to other flights of this same type, 767 or 757 flights leaving eastern airports for California at around 8:00 am on Tuesday morning, September 11, 2001. Mihdhar and Hazmi, in fact, used their credit cards to buy tickets for 10 of the other terrorists who took part in the events on 9/11. Monitoring their credit card activity would have prevented the attacks on 9/11. The FAA stated that these measures did not need any specific time frame. These security measures could have been left on indefinitely.

According to Cofer Black, just prior to 9/11 the CIA knew that:

"We are going to be struck soon, many Americans are going to die, and it could be in the US. However, the DCI and the President of the United States need exacting intelligence in order to take effective, selective defensive action. They need

to know such things as – the attack is coming within the next few days and here is what they are going to hit. I regret that we did not have specific, actionable intelligence before September 11, 2001."

On that morning (September 11, 2001), National Public Radio (NPR) was presenting live coverage of the attacks on its show *Morning Edition*. Host Bob Edwards went to a reporter in the field – David Welna, NPR's Congressional correspondent – who was in the Capitol Building as it was being evacuated. Here is a portion of Welna's report:

"I spoke with Congressman Ike Skelton – a Democrat from Missouri and a member of the Armed Services Committee – who said that just recently the Director of the CIA warned that there could be an attack – an imminent attack – on the United States of this nature. So this is not entirely unexpected."

Exactly what did the DCI George Tenet tell the President during the daily briefings he had with the President in the month of July when we now know he told Condoleezza Rice, Richard Clarke, Donald Rumsfeld and John Ashcroft of a huge attack just about to occur in the US, or at the meetings he had with him and his staff in Crawford, TX, on August 17th, or 24th, or at the meeting he held with the President in Washington on August 31, or at the six other meeting he had with the President in early September prior to the events on 9/11?

[NOTE: While George Tenet testified public testimony on April 14, 2004 that he had not met with the President during the month of August 2001, Bill Harlow, spokesman for the CIA corrected this testimony only a few hours later and said he had met with the President in August. How would the Director of the CIA not know if he met with the President in the weeks before 9/11? What was Tenet trying to hide?}

Did Tenet tell the president the same thing he told Rice, Clarke, Ashcroft and Rumsfeld? If he did not why did he not tell the President?

George Tenet never explained why he did not bring this information up to all of the principals in the Principals' meeting on September 4, 2001, when he testified before the 9/11 Commission. His answer to their question was, "**for whatever reason, it was not appropriate.**" The September 4, 2001 meeting was, in fact, the very first Principals' meeting the Bush administration had held on the al Qaeda terrorists. Not made public before is the fact that at this September 4th meeting, Rice, Clarke, Ashcroft, Rumsfeld and Tenet all already were aware of this huge al Qaeda attack just about to occur

The FBI

The FBI is made up of two main groups, criminal investigation and intelligence. Information from criminal investigations generally has to be presented to a court in order to prove criminal intent or action.

Criminal investigators are almost completely focused on tactical investigations. Intelligence is made up of two parts, tactical operations and strategic analysis. Tactical investigations find clues and trace these clues back to follow a trail to a logical end point. All clues that are used must be verifiable and corroborated in order to be considered appropriate and relevant. Tracing clues from one to another has been the hallmark of the tactical investigations of the FBI intelligence unit.

Strategic analysis is done by analyzing the history of an organization, along with the attacks they have already carried out. This is combined with the analysis of their thinking obtained from materials the organization has actually written. This analysis is then used to anticipate what this organization is capable of doing and what their next move or plan might be. It would be incumbent on the tactical division to use the strategic analysis as much as possible not only to understand the full meaning of the clues they might encounter, but also to proactively monitor points during an investigation, in order to identify the activity the terrorists might employ prior to attempting some major terrorist attack.

The most important outcomes of strategic analysis at the FBI would be to provide a plan and an organized direction to what might otherwise be just a chaotic and random search of unconnected clues or dots at the tactical division of the FBI. The strategic analysis would provide a road map that the FBI tactical units could follow to guide their investigation.

The Strategic Analysis Unit at the FBI

From the FBI OIG office

"Since [sic] September the FBI has acknowledged that it lacked an effective strategic analysis program for international terrorism prior to September 11." Director Mueller acknowledged that the FBI analytical capabilities prior to September 11 were inadequate. He stated that the FBI's analytical capability "[was] not where it should be." Prior to September 11, the FBI's strategic analysis capabilities were extremely limited. The FBI did not regularly prepare analytical products that predicted trends, explained patterns, or identified national security vulnerabilities with respect to international terrorism [Note 84].

A striking example of the FBI's failing in this regard is documented in a September 2002 OIG audit report which found that the FBI had not performed a comprehensive national-level assessment of the threat and risk of terrorist attack, despite having promised Congress that it would do so following a September 1999 General Accounting Office (GAO) report. As of September 11, 2001 the FBI had developed a draft of a report that was purportedly the threat assessment. The OIG reviewed a draft of the report in May 2002; we concluded that it was not a threat assessment because it did not describe the nature of the terrorist threat, identify critical intelligence requirements, or make recommendations to any level of the FBI management [P. 84-85, FBI OIG report, November 2004].

This sums it up quit adequately, no strategic analysis. The difference between the type of analysis done at the FBI and the CIA would be the focus of the FBI on potential attacks inside the US. The CIA would be focused on areas outside the US.

With all of the information the FBI had, it appears that even a simple analysis was never completed. Congress had become so concerned over what the al Qaeda terrorists might ultimately do; they had ordered the FBI in 1999 to provide a complete National Threat Analysis. In spite of receiving this direct request, the FBI never completed this task.

The head of the counterterrorism unit at the FBI, Dale Watson, testified at the Joint Inquiry Committee hearings that a written analysis was not needed. He had all of this information right in his head, so no written analysis was necessary. The most important analysis affecting the safety of the people in the US, on the al Qaeda organization – at that time the most dangerous terrorist organization in the world was warning of a huge attack inside of the US – was never produced, ignoring the wishes of Congress and leaving the US exposed to attacks by al Qaeda.

These al Qaeda warnings, combined with a well-written analysis, could have even pinpointed not only the target of the attack, but also the method of this attack and even the approximate date for the attack. Even without any strategic analysis at all, these massive warnings in the summer of 2001 should have at least triggered the intelligence officials at the FBI to ask the simplest question of all:

What are the possible targets the al Qaeda terrorists might be interested in attacking?

Tactical operations at the FBI

While the tactical operations side of the FBI would have been at a serious disadvantage without the use of a well-constructed strategic analysis to guide its activities, the information the FBI received should have triggered serious investigations with a significant degree of urgency. FBI field people attempted to do aggressive and important investigations when they came across suspicious activity indicating possible terrorist attacks. However, FBI Headquarters placed roadblock after roadblock on these investigations. Investigations were either not started or were delayed, or were even sabotaged. Several of the ongoing investigations had been stalled or given so little urgency, they were still in progress when the events of 9/11 took place.

It was as if the FBI were two completely different organizations. One had insightful, intelligent and concerned agents in the FBI Field Offices, and the other, the FBI Headquarters, had agents who either did not want to start investigations or who tried to hamper and even sabotage field investigations. When field investigators had a sense of urgency with respect to furthering important investigations, agents at FBI Headquarters not only displayed no sense of urgency, but also often used ridicule to dissuade any sense of urgency.

The investigations that were either not started or were delayed, or were undertaken with no sense of urgency, were the Williams memo, the arrest of Zacarias Moussaoui in Minnesota, and finally in late August 2001, the search for al-Hazmi and al-Mihdhar.

The Williams memo, sent from a concerned agent in Arizona, detailing the fact that many radical Muslims were taking flight training at Arizona flight schools, went nowhere. It stated that radical Muslims, and perhaps even al Qaeda terrorists, were attending flight schools in Arizona and requested an investigation of other major flight schools in the US to see if more terrorists were attempting to get training in the US. This memo went to the RFU at FBI headquaters and died.

Investigation of Zacarias Moussaoui

The FBI had arrested Zacarias Moussaoui in Minnesota after his flight instructors became suspicious that he might be a terrorist learning to fly a large civilian airliner. In order to emphasize how urgent this investigation was, the FBI Minneapolis field agents told the Supervising Special Agent at the Radical Fundamentalist Unit (RFU) at FBI Headquarters that Zacarias Moussaoui was the type of person who might fly a large US aircraft into the World Trade Center Towers. The Minneapolis agents were dismissed with a "that will never happen, you do not know he is a terrorist, you are just trying to spin this into a bigger story than it is" reply.

All of the requests for a search warrant sent to the supervisors, Michael Maltbie and David Frasca were denied with what appears to be reasons that in most cases are just ludicrous, the primarily reason for denying these requests was that there was not enough evidence to show that Moussaoui was an agent of a foreign power.

The Minnesota agents considered request for more information as nothing but time-delaying tactics and even sabotage of their warrant request. These requests had the effect of blocking the FISA search warrant request from even going to the OIPR unit, the unit that had to approve the request prior to it being sent to the FISA Court itself.

The many requirements for additional information was bizarre since in over 18,300 FISA applications from the time the FISA Court had been set up, only five had ever been denied.

When looked at through the eyes of a prudent person it is clear that most of these additional requirements were bogus. The FISA application only had to show probable cause Zacarias Moussaoui was an agent of a foreign power. It did not have to show that he was integral to the foreign power being argued in the FISA warrant, as stated by Michael Maltbie, but merely an agent of a foreign power. And it did not have to show *prima facie* evidence, just probable cause.

The people making the requests for FISA search warrants were FBI agents who had been in the FBI doing field investigations for years. Their pleas to pursue the investigation of Moussaoui with extreme urgency fell on deaf ears. The duffel bag in Moussaoui's possession contained a Western Union receipt for $14,000 from Ramzi bin al Shibh, along with his phone number. Bin al Shibh had been the roommate of Mohamed Atta, Marwan al-Shehhi, and Ziad Jarrah. Evidence at the Moussaoui trial showed how the FBI in one to two weeks was able to exploit this information in the duffel bag and to quickly find and connect all of the terrorists who took part in the attacks on 9/11.

The Minneapolis Field Office agents were so completely baffled by this blatant obstruction of their investigation that they ultimately wrote a letter to Robert Mueller.

Coleen Rowley, the Minneapolis FBI agent who wrote the critical letter on May 12, 2002, to FBI Director Robert Mueller, stated: "The decision to take him (Moussaoui) into custody on August 15, 2001, on the INS 'overstay' charge was a deliberate one to counter that threat and was based on the agents' reasonable suspicions." These suspicions had been reinforced by the French intelligence. However the FBI HQ refused to give the Minneapolis agents the go-ahead on a search warrant. "The fact is that key FBI HQ personnel whose job it was to assist and coordinate with field division agents on terrorism investigations and the obtaining and use of FISA searches (and who theoretically were privy to many more sources of intelligence information than field division agents)," she told Mueller, "continued to, almost inexplicably throw up roadblocks and undermine Minneapolis' by-now desperate efforts to obtain a FISA search warrant, long after the French intelligence service provided its information and probable cause became clear. HQ personnel brought up almost ridiculous questions in their apparent efforts to undermine the probable cause. In all of their conversations and correspondence, HQ personnel never disclosed to the Minneapolis agents that the Phoenix Division had, only approximately three weeks earlier, warned of al Qaeda operatives in flight schools seeking flight training for terrorist purposes!" Because of these deliberate delays, this investigation had gone nowhere by 9/11.

On 9/11, once a warrant was submitted to the OIPR for a search warrant of Moussaoui's possessions, it was quickly approved, submitted to a court and approved again, the whole process taking just a few hours, with no more information prior to the events on 9/11. This is proof the reasons that were used to block the request for a FISA warrant in the first place were bogus.

It is now clear that Maltbie and Frasca were never going to approve the Harry Samit's warrant application going to the OIPR under any circumstances. Even after the World Trade Center Towers had been attacked, Maltbie would not approve the warrant, he said he did not feel comfortable in approving the application until it was first reviewed and approved by the NSLU, the legal unit at the FBI Headquarters.

But David Frasca, Maltbie's boss, who also had to approve the warrant refused to approve the warrant, even after the World Trade Center Towers were struck. He only approved sending the warrant to the OIPR after the Pentagon was also attacked.

But the warrant application carried no additional information than the information that Maltbie and Frasca had rejected many times before. On September 11, 2001. At the time there was no way to directly connect Moussaoui to the attacks in New York. The applications were approved in hours with the exact same information that Maltbie and Frasca had argued for weeks had been insufficient.

Several flight instructors think Moussaoui is a terrorist attempting to learn how to fly a large airliner since he had none of the normal qualifications, long time FBI field agents think the same thing, since the answers Moussaoui gave did not add up, but supervisors at FBI headquaters block any further investigation of Moussaoui by blocking the search warrant for his possessions including his duffle bag without any reasonable explaination. They do this even when the FBI field agents are pleading for urgency and when we now know the CIA and FBI had been getting massive warnings of a huge al Qaeda attack that will take place inside of the US. The head of the justice department had gotten a clear warning of a huge attack inside of the US by Tenet and Black weeks earlier and quit flying commercial aircraft because of this warning. And while the information that a terrorist was learning to fly a large US airliner goes right up to the very top of the CIA in days, this information however never makes it past Michael Rolince, the immediate supervisor for David Frasca and Michael Maltbie. And none of this has ever been explained.

While Corsi and Wishire, who both work for Michael Rolince, were busy sabotaging the investigation of Mihdar other people working directly for Rolance were busy criminally sabotaging the investigation of FBI Agent Harry Samit in Minneapolis, according to sworn testimony of FBI Agent Samit at Moussaoui's trail.

Sabotaging Harry Samit's investigation of Moussaoui, insured that this investigation of this al Qaeda terrorist trying to learn to fly a 747 airliner without a pilots license, will never go nowhere by the time the events on 9/11 take place.

Michael Maltbie and David Frasca, who reported to Michael Rolince, blocked Samit's investigation of Moussaoui, by refusing to allow a request for a FISA warrant for Moussaoui's duffle bag. In this bag was the receipt from Ramzi bin al-Shibh for $14,000, (plus aircraft manuals and two folding knives), which after 9/11 allowed the Minneapolis agents to connect all of the terrorists together in a few days. This request was denied even after the two WTC towers were attacked and was not allowed by Frasca until after American Airlines 77 had attacked the Pentagon.

After they obtained a search warrant on September 11, 2001, Minneapolis FBI agents traced the receipt to the phone records of Ramzi bin al-Shibh and from then quickly found the person in the UAE who was the paymaster for the attacks on 9/11. They quickly connected the phone records for the al Qaeda paymaster to most of the terrorists who took part in 9/11.

Samit, in sworn testimony at Moussaoui's trial accused Maltbie and Frasca of criminal conduct by arbitrarily blocking his FISA requests, even after they had been told that Moussaoui was the type of person that might hijack with the help of other confederates a large aircraft and fly it into the World Trade Center Towers or the White House.

Investigation of Khalid al-Mihdhar and Nawaf al-Hazmi

The final search for al-Mihdhar and al-Hazmi was another investigation that also had a high possibility of stopping the events of 9/11, had it been handled with sufficient urgency.

However, in spite of the fact the two terrorists who were to be the target of this investigation were known al Qaeda terrorists who had just left an al Qaeda planning meeting prior to entering the US, and the fact the FBI knew about the huge attack just about to occur inside of the US this investigation was assigned to one of the FBI's least-experienced intelligence agents, and he was given no sense of urgency for this investigation.

This intelligence agent had never done this type of investigation before. On August 28, 2001, he was given 30 days to do what was described as an unspecified investigation. No criminal investigation had been started to find Hazmi and Mihdhar, in spite of the fact that this would have brought a larger effort to bear on this investigation. Because the CIA continued to hide the photograph of Khallad bin Attash taken at Kuala Lumpur from the FBI, the FBI was not able to tie Mihdhar and Hazmi directly to the planning of the Cole bombing in Kuala Lumpur.

Even when Steve Bongardt, FBI Agent on the Cole bombing, found out Mihdhar was inside of the US and knew he was a dangerous terrorist that would be in the US for no other reason than to carry out a terrorist attack, he was told by FBI IOS Agent Dina Corsi from FBI headquaters to destroy the information he had on Mihdhar, and if Mihdhar was found he was not allowed to be in the same room where Mihdhar would be was interviewed.

We now know that Dina Corsi was aware on August 22, 2001 of the photograph the CIA had of Khallad Bin Attash taken at the Kuala Lumpur meeting, and the fact that the CIA had been hiding this photograph from the FBI since January 2000. This photograph alone would have immediately tied both Mihdhar and Hazmi to the planning of the Cole bombing, and ensured the search for Mihdhar went to Steve Bongardt and the other Cole investigators, and would almost surely have prevented the attacks that were carried out on 9/11.

By continuing to hide the photograph of Khallad for an additional 8 days, after the photos of Mihdar and Hazmi had been turned over to the FBI, the CIA effectively sabotaged the investigation the FBI had in their search for Mihdhar. The CIA did this knowing full well that the result would be the deaths of thousands of innocent Americans

The inexperienced FBI intelligence agent assigned to this case did not come close to locating these terrorists by 9/11.

AND NO OFFICIAL GOVERNMNET INVESTIGATION HAS BEEN ABLE TO EXPLAIN ANY PART OF THIS!

Assigning the FBI investigation of two al-Qaeda terrorists known to be inside of the US to an inexperienced FBI agent and give him no sense of urgency when at the same time the FBI was aware of a huge al Qaeda attack that would shortly take place inside of the US and cause mass casualties makes no sense!

An even bigger mystery;

What turns out to be an even bigger mystery is the fact that Corsi and Wishire, both worked for Michael Rolince and while they were busy sabotaging the investigation of Mihdar and Hazmi people who also work directly for Rolince were busy sabotaging the investigation of FBI Agent Harry Samit.

The fact that the exact same group inside of the FBI headed by the same FBI manger that sabotaged these two investigations that could have stopped the attacks on 9/11, is a coincidence that has never been explained.

Even to this day, after several full investigations by the Joint Inquiry Committee, the 9/11 Commission and the FBI Inspector General's office, and even the CIA Inspector General's report, why any of these failures occurred has never been explained.

The Joint Inquiry Committee had raised these questions months before the 9/11 Commission was formed, yet, none of this incomprehensible behavior by supervising agents at the FBI Headquarters or the New York office of the FBI was explained or further examined by the 9/11 Commission. The 9/11 Commission never even talked to the Minneapolis agents whose investigation, that could have prevented the

attacks on 9/11, was sabotaged by RFU FBI supervisors at FBI Headquarters.

The 9/11 Commission never came to any conclusion regarding whether the 9/11 attacks could have been prevented. From a careful reading of the testimony given to the 9/11 Commission, you can come to virtually no other conclusion, than the events of 9/11 could have been prevented had the CIA and the FBI done the job they were suppose to do. They had many opportunities to stop these attacks and at each point, analysis to anticipate and stop these attacks was not done, or information was kept secret from the very agencies that could have used it. Investigations were not started, or were inexplicably blocked, or were done with no sense of urgency. These huge agencies with thousands of employees and billions of dollars in funding failed to do the very jobs they were chartered to do, and this has been explained.

Chapter 22
Final Conclusions
From the 9/11 Commission hearings on April 13, 2004

I am sure it's no surprise to you or anybody here that there's a lot of interest in today's hearings and there's a lot of interest simply because on September 11th we were totally beaten. We were beaten and all our systems failed. Our systems to stop hijackings failed. Our intelligence – domestic and foreign apparatus – failed. We had 19 people who were able to – some of whom were known by the CIA to be terrorists – entered our country, got visas, were living under their own names in this country, took flight lessons, beat the security screening with knives to get into the aircraft, and turn four aircraft into missiles. And they had to have – it was interesting, they had to have a 100 percent success in order to do this and they did.

So we've now found in our discovery that there have been some clues; some dots, as we say, that might have been connected were not. We're not passing judgment on that at this point, but what we're trying to determine here is how this intelligence failure occurred so that we can deny it from occurring again, if at all possible. And quite frankly, we're also trying to determine whether the FBI should continue to have its counterterrorism responsibility, whether it's capable of carrying out the new mission of counterterrorism and the enhanced mission and the enhanced responsibilities.

This sums it up in words that leave absolutely no mistake as to where the fault for the events of 9/11 lay. No amount of secrecy or cover-up or delay or obfuscation can hide the brutal truth.

It is obvious from every perspective that many government agencies failed in doing even their basic job of protecting the US from these attacks. In most cases they failed to do the very job they had been tasked to do, and for which the US public had paid billions and billions of dollars for them to do.

The American public had been cheated. Not only had they paid billions and billions of dollars for this task to be done, but also when it was not done, these very agencies were in the position of making it impossible for any other government organization to do these same tasks.

The relatives of the people killed at the World Trade Center, the Pentagon and on the hijacked flights on 9/11 were cheated even more. The most important members of their families had been killed in a terrorist attack that could have been prevented.

When they desperately attempted to get answers as to why the intelligence agencies and the administration allowed this attack to take place, the administration did everything in its power to block any investigation, using excuses that America could not have an investigation in time of war and that the morale of the people at these intelligence agencies might be harmed.

The investigations

Joint Inquiry Committee of the House and the Senate

When the Joint Inquiry Committee was finally able to proceed, the investigators were denied many of needed documents from the administration and from the agencies that had been responsible for allowing the events of 9/11 to take place. In some cases, they were blocked completely from talking to witnesses who were aware of the reasons these agencies had not prevented these attacks. Much of the testimony that was presented to this investigation by these agencies was misleading.

CIA Director Tenet and Cofer Black, head of the CTC section of the CIA, stated in sworn testimony that the CIA had passed information over to the FBI on several occasions when they clearly had not.

The Joint Inquiry Committee never came to any conclusion to why the Deputy Chief at the Bin Laden Unit blocked the CIR written by the FBI detailee working at this unit describing Khalid al-Mihdhar, on January 5, 2000.

They never came to any conclusion as to why the information on the al Qaeda planning meeting in Kuala Lumpur on January 6-8, 2000 was not passed to the FBI.

They never found out why the information sent to the CIA on March 15, 2000 that Nawaf al-Hazmi, a known al Qaeda terrorist, who had entered the US on January 15, 2000, was never acted on.

They never found out why the information from the FBI-CIA joint source in December 2000, and January and February, 2001 that Khallad bin Attash had been identified in photos from the Kuala Lumpur meeting with Khalid al-Mihdhar had not been passed to the FBI.

They never uncovered the actual reasons why information that the CIA had on Khallad, Khalid al-Mihdhar and Nawaf al-Hazmi was not passed to the FBI *Cole* investigators at the meeting in New York on June 11, 2001.

Both Robert Mueller and Louis Freeh told the Joint Inquiry Committee that there was never enough information to allow the FBI to prevent the attacks of 9/11. But at the trial of Zacarias Moussaoui, the prosecutor showed how FBI investigators had located almost all of the hijackers from the information that they had found in Moussaoui's duffel bag. A Western Union receipt for $14,000, from Ramzi bin al-Shibh was found in this duffel bag and this led right to the al Qaeda paymaster in the UAE and then to the all of the hijackers.

This information remained hidden because Michael Maltbie and David Frasca had prevented FBI Agent Harry Samit from obtaining permission to even request a search warrant for Moussaoui's duffel bag. Mueller also said that after the most intensive investigation in US history, they had found no one else in the US who had known about the events on 9/11. Then the very same Justice Department turned around and later said Moussaoui should be executed at his trial because he knew about the upcoming attacks on 9/11. But never did the Joint Inquiry Committee explain why Maltbie or Frasca had blocked the search warrant for Moussaoui's duffel bag.

The Joint Inquiry Committee investigation was shown to have been obstructed by the administration when Senator Robert Graham, who co-chaired this investigation, stated in his book that the subpoena this committee had issued for the FBI informant in San Diego who had housed Khalid al-Mihdhar and Nawaf al-Hazmi was blocked directly by the administration.

The 9/11 Commission Investigation and Report

The 9/11 Commission fared even worse. The person picked by the White House to lead this investigation of the administration and the intelligence agencies, Phil Zelikow, had actually been part of the administration, and after the report was completed, he returned to be chief of staff for Condoleezza Rice. The 9/11 Commission relied heavily on the material gathered by the Joint Inquiry Committee investigation. However, questions, misleading testimony and outright attempts by the intelligence agencies to sabotage the Joint Inquiry investigation, were never followed up on or pursued by the 9/11 Commission investigation, leaving many unanswered questions even today.

All of the questions left unanswered by the Joint Inquiry Committee listed above were still unanswered by the 9/11 Commission. This Commission never even talked to FBI Agent Harry Samit or Coleen Rowley and never did find out why Maltbie and Frasca had sabotaged their investigation. Public testimony was never requested from CIA managers Tom Wishire or Clark Shannon or FBI IOS Agent Dina Corsi, CIA and FBI agents involved in hiding information from the FBI. There is no public testimony from Ali Soufan or Steve Bongardt, or Doug Miller, FBI agents who could have shed much light on what went on to allow the attacks on 9/11 to succeed.

They brought before the public hearings the mangers of the CIA and FBI who had all failed on 9/11 and asked them why they failed. Almost to a man these managers either lied why they had failed or said they were understaffed and lacked a large enough budget to have prevented the attacks on 9/11.

Almost all of the lies were immediately obvious to even a casual observer.

When Tenet and Black told the Joint Inquiry Committee investigating the attacks on 9/11 why they did not give the information on Mihdhar and Hazmi to the FBI right away, they both said they had. This turned out to be a lie, and their testimony was perjury.

Mueller and Freeh said there had never been enough evidence at the FBI that could have stopped the attacks on 9/11. Yet at the trail of Zacarias Moussaoui, FBI agents Samit and Zebley said after the had obtained a search warrant for Moussaoui's possessions they found enough information in Moussaoui's duffle bag that they were able to link all of the al Qaeda terrorists together in a few days.

Tenet was asked why he did not tell the President in August 2001 about the upcoming huge al Qaeda attack he and the CIA knew was just about to occur in the US and would kill thousands of Americans. He said that he had not talked to the President in August when in fact he had on the August 17th, 24th, and the 31st. He further met with the President six more times in September, just before 9/11.

When Rice and other administration officials were asked by mainstream news media and the 9/11 Commission why they did not do more to prevent the attacks on 9/11 when they had been told an al Qaeda attack was imminent, they said they thought the attack would be against a target outside of the US. We now know that was a lie. On July 10, 2001, Tenet and Black in unmistaken able terms told Rice and Clarke in the now famous White House meeting that the attack was going to take place inside of the US and cause mass American casualties. We also now know that Ashcroft and Rumsfeld were given the same information by Tenet and Black a week later.

When Tenet was asked why he did not bring this huge al Qaeda attack up when he met with the principals on September 4, 2001, for the very first Principals' meeting the administration had held on al Qaeda, he said that, "For whatever reason, it was not appropriate." It turns many people at that meeting already knew about this attack, Rice, Clarke, Ashcroft, Rumsfeld and Tenet.

Many CIA and FBI officials were brought in front of the 9/11 Commission and all said it was not their fault, and that the many simple mistakes that were made were due to lower level officials. This was accepted as the official view of what had taken place, in spite of the fact this made no sense.

The CIA did not give the information they had to the FBI on Mihdhar and Hazmi for 21 months, due to simple mistakes, even though withholding this information from the FBI Cole investigators was criminal? The CIA never connected Mihdhar and Hazmi to the massive and over whelming warnings of an attack inside of the US, which the CIA had received since April 2001, due to simple mistakes?

ALL OF THIS MADE NO SENSE!

It is now clear that the 9/11 Commission and report were a sham, a charade, political theater to show the American people that the CIA and FBI managers and directors had not been culpable in allowing the attacks on 9/11 to take place, even though information came out that they had taken many deliberate actions to allow the attacks on 9/11 to occur.

It is clear that the 9/11 Commission had but one purpose.

To cover up what actually happened!

The 9/11 Commission wanted to hide the culpability of the CIA and FBI managers in the eyes of the American people. These mangers had plenty of opportunity to prevent the attacks on 9/11 and did not. The 9/11 Commission never pursued their investigation to the point where they could understand why the CIA deliberately kept secret information from the FBI for 21 months, information that would have prevented the attacks on 9/11.

The 9/11 Commission members themselves later even said they had secret meetings where the testimony of the FAA and NORAD was considered for criminal referrals because it was found to be full of numerous and obvious lies. They decided to turn this information over to the inspectors general of each agency instead of telling the American people and making this public. Of course the inspector general investigation of each agency found there had been no deliberate attempt to obscure the truth, even though the FAA and NORAD had the exact record of events on 9/11 saved in second-by-second recordings, accounts that differed widely from the account these agencies had given to the 9/11 Commission in public testimony.

While the Commissioners seemed like good and decent people, it is inconceivable they were not aware of the misleading testimony, even at the moment it was given, and certainly later when the truth finally came out. Why did the Commissioners not speak out and let the American people know that this testimony that had been given in public was wrong and misleading?

When the 9/11 Commission said it was not in their charter to find anyone to blame, but said this was the duty of the American people and the Inspector General for each agency, it looked to

540

these relatives of those killed on 9/11, as if there would finally be accountability after all in these IG reports.

The FBI Inspector General's report

While the FBI Inspector General's report gave at the time it was published, the most complete picture of the events that lead up to 9/11, from a careful review of this report it is clear that it also included misleading testimony and inadequate follow-up in their investigation, seriously compromising this investigation. The FBI IG report has extremely important facts completely wrong.

From the trial of Zacarias Moussaoui, we were told that from the information obtained from his duffel bag and other possessions, the FBI was able to find connections to almost all of the hijackers of the 9/11 attacks in a few days. The most important clue was the name and telephone number of Ramzi bin al-Shibh on a Western Union receipt for $14,000.

Testimony at the Moussaoui trial

"For three hours, in testimony from FBI Agent Aaron Zebley, jurors were given information that spelled out how the FBI was able to quickly uncover the connections between the terrorists and was able to identify the pilots of the four hijacked airplanes, and seven of the other hijackers, the terrorists who physically took over the airplanes.

The FBI demonstrated how they traced records of telephone calls between the US-based terrorists to Ramzi bin al-Shibh in Hamburg, Germany, and then to the overseas paymaster located in the UAE. They then traced these numbers to addresses where the hijackers lived in the US. From there, they were able to obtain bank and shopping records of the terrorists, and even track down the flight schools the terrorists attended."

But the FBI IG report says:

"Moussaoui's belongings did not reveal anything that specifically provided a warning or an indication of an imminent terrorist attack. There were no plans, correspondence, or names or addresses in his computer or notebooks that linked him directly to the September 11 terrorist attacks."

This is now shown to be false and an attempt to ameliorate the culpability of FBI Supervisors Maltbie and Frasca in denying Samit a search warrant for Moussaoui's possessions.

The material in Moussaoui's duffel bag linked Moussaoui directly with Ramzi bi al-Shibh. He was the roommate of three of the pilots who hijacked airplanes on 9/11. Had Harry Samit obtained a search warrant, he could have tracked the information on Ramzi bin al-Shibh to phone calls to the paymaster in the UAE, and then to the other terrorists in the 9/11 attack. He already had told the FAA and FBI Headquarters and even the White House that Moussaoui was likely to hijack a large aircraft and fly it into the World Trade Center or the White House. He also knew that Moussaoui's other confederates were still out there ready to carry out this attack.

This calls into question the accuracy of the major facts in the FBI IG report and shows its clear intent to minimize what Harry Samit referred to in sworn testimony as the criminal conduct of Michael Maltbie and David Frasca at the RFU at FBI Headquarters in sabotaging his investigation. The intent for the FBI IG in doing this is readily apparent. If the search of Moussaoui's possessions could not have prevented the attacks on 9/11, then denying FBI Agent Samit's search warrant was not important. But as was clearly described in much detail at the trial of Moussaoui, had Samit obtained his search warrant, it is most likely he would have located the other terrorists quickly and prevented the attacks on 9/11.

The FBI IG investigation was never able to find the real reason for the CIA-FBI meeting in New York on June 11, 2001.

The FBI IG report criticized Dina Corsi, the FBI IOS working at the UBL unit of the FBI for setting up a meeting with no clearly defined purpose. But had the FBI IG investigators just interviewed New York FBI Agent Ali Soufan, lead FBI investigator on the *Cole* bombing, they would have found the real reason for this meeting. They would have found that Dina Corsi, who set up this meeting, Tom Wilshire, former Deputy Chief of the Bin Laden Unit at the CIA, and Clark Shannon, CIA supervisor at the CIA, were all aware of Ali Soufan's request, (or the information in this request), a request for the information the CIA had on Khallad, and for the significance of the phone number al-Quso had called in Kuala Lumpur.

***How could the FBI IG investigators not have talked to Ali Soufan? He was lead FBI investigator on the* Cole**

investigation, and the FBI IG was fully aware the Cole bombing and the attack on 9/11 had come together at the Kuala Lumpur al Qaeda meeting on January 6-8, 2000.

Had they interviewed Ali Soufan, they would have realized that this meeting in New York had not been set up to find out if the *Cole* investigators could identify al-Quso, but only for the CIA find out if the information they had kept secret from the FBI for 1 ½ years was still secret. This was the information that Khalid al-Mihdhar had attended the meeting in Kuala Lumpur with Nawaf al-Hazmi and Khallad, and the information that al-Hazmi had entered the US to carry out an attack with other terrorists connected to Khalid Sheikh Mohammed, an attack that the CIA was well aware of by the time of the New York meeting.

The FBI IG report also appears to be written with intent to obfuscate the facts surrounding the FBI and even CIA investigations.

The FBI IG report did not list what everyone knew, time lines of when they knew it, where they had obtained this information, and then ask what each person who was interviewed should have done to prevent the attacks on 9/11

Instead it dwells on random dialog between many of the people at the FBI and CIA and has much hearsay testimony from many witnesses. There is never any attempt to resolve conflicting testimony, when this would have been reasonably easy to do.

Much of this testimony has "unable to recall," "have no recollection," "don't remember," and many other obvious attempts hide culpability. [Note: One benefit to have raw testimony with items such as "can't recall" is that it is readily apparent who is telling the truth and who is not telling the truth.] This report is filled with endless discussions of mindless FBI procedures, in an attempt to justify these mindless procedures. There is never any attempt to interject even so much as a hint of common sense into the activities at FBI Headquarters.

When it is obvious a huge terrorist attack that could kill thousands of Americans is about to take place, endlessly talking about whether a foreign power is a recognized foreign power or not is nothing short of asinine, total lunacy, and absolutely absurd.

543

All issues should have been resolved by asking, "What would a prudent person have done in the same situation".

What this investigation should have done is ask each person involved with the events on 9/11, what did you know and when did you know it, and then why did you not act to prevent the events on 9/11? Did you act the way a prudent person would have acted? If you did not, then tell us why you did not?

The CIA Inspector General's Report

While originally looked on as the report that would reveal the most information on why the CIA deliberately withheld information from the FBI, the very information that could have prevented the attacks on 9/11, this report was yet another attempt to cover up what actually went on at the CIA. Very few additional details were released that were not already known from the Joint Inquiry Committee report on 9/11.

There was clearly no attempt what so ever to find the truth on why the CIA had kept information secret from the FBI. Ironically the CIA IG report had much of the general out line of what went on:

> Agency officers did not, on a timely basis, recommend to the Department of State the watchlisting of two suspected al-Qa'ida terrorists, Nawaf al-Hazmi and Khalid al-Mihdhar. These individuals, who later were among the hijackers of 9/11, were known by the Agency in early January 2000 to have traveled to Kuala Lumpur, Malaysia, to participate in a meeting of suspected terrorists. Agency officers did not, on a timely basis, recommend to the Department of State the watchlisting of two suspected al-Qa'ida terrorists, Nawaf al-Hazmi and Khalid al-Mihdhar.

> The Team found that an FBI officer assigned to CTC on 5 January 2000 drafted a message about the terrorists' travel that was to be sent from CIA to the FBI in the proper channels. Apparently because it was in the wrong format or needed editing, the message was never sent. On the same date, another CTC officer sent a cable to several Agency addressees reporting that the information and al-Mihdhar's travel documents had been passed to the FBI. The officer who drafted this cable does not recall how this information was passed. The Team has not been able to confirm that the information was passed, or that it was not passed.

In January 2000, CTC officers received information that one of these suspected terrorists had a US visa; in March 2000, these officers had information that the other had flown from Bangkok to Los Angeles. In the period January through March 2000, some 50 to 60 individuals read one or more of six Agency cables containing travel information related to these terrorists. These cables originated in four field locations and Headquarters. They were read by overseas officers and Headquarters personnel, operations officers and analysts, managers and junior employees, and CIA staff personnel as well as officers on rotation from NSA and FBI. Over an 18-month period, some of these officers had opportunities to review the information on multiple occasions, when they might have recognized its significance and shared it appropriately with other components and agencies. Ultimately, the two terrorists were watchlisted in late August 2001 as a result of questions raised in May 2001 by a CIA officer on assignment at the FBI.

Separately, in March 2000, two CIA field locations sent to a number of addressees cables reporting that al-Hazmi and another al-Qa'ida associate had traveled to the United States. They were clearly identified in the cables as "UBL associates." The Team has found no evidence, and heard no claim from any party, that this information was shared in any manner with the FBI or that anyone in UBL Station took other appropriate operational action at that time.

In the months following the Malaysia operation, the CIA missed several additional opportunities to nominate al-Hazmi and al-Mihdhar for watchlisting; to inform the FBI about their intended or actual travel to the United States; and to take appropriate operational action. These included a few occasions identified by the Joint Inquiry as well as several others.

While this is the outline of what went on, this report could have but never did try to find out why Tom Wilshire blocked the original CIR on Mihdhar from being sent to the FBI or why a CIA desk officer sent a cable saying this information on Mihdhar had been sent to the FBI, when it had not been sent. The FBI IG lacked subpoena power for CIA officers, but this was not the case for the CIA IG investigators. There was no investigation of the June 11, 2001 meeting in New York between the CIA and the FBI to find out the real reason Tom Wilshire, Clark Shannon and Dina Corsi set up this meeting in the first place, or an investigation to find out why Wilshire continued to hide the photograph of Khallad from the FBI for 8 days after he was forced to turn over the photos to the FBI of Mihdhar and Hazmi attending the Kuala Lumpur meeting with Khallad.

This report evens describes the actions of Tom Wilshire, perhaps the main conspirator in hiding information from the FBI, which ultimately caused 3000 innocent Americans to perish on 9/11, as a hero for initiation the search in May that eventually lead to the watchlisting of Mihdhar and Hazmi. This was the search started by a request from Wilshire in May to Mary, a FBI IOS agent at the CIA that eventually found cables on August 21, 2001 stating that Hazmi was inside of the US, cables that Wishire already had back in May.

While it stated that is was clearly the failure of George Tenet for having no strategic analysis of the al Qaeda organization it turns out this was only one factor, which allowed the attacks on 9/11 to succeed. This report never looked deep enough into the details to uncover the criminal conspiracy behind the CIA deliberately hiding this information on Mihdhar and Hazmi from the FBI.

Why did the CIA IG investigation not explain this? They had access to all of the people who were involved with hiding this information from the FBI. They could have asked everyone these people, what did they know and what did they do with this information? Since they had everything at their disposal to be able to answer all of these questions and they did not, it is clear they never had any intention of finding out what actually happened at the CIA that had allowed the attacks on 9/11. It is clear this was nothing a continuation of the cover up of the criminal actions of people at the CIA that resulted in the deaths on almost 3000 people.

Since we learn from this report no one will ever be held accountable, they now assume they are above the law. They have gotten away with deliberately hiding of information from the FBI even when they knew by hiding this information thousands of Americans would perish.

When the anger of the American people finally boils over, let's hope this criminal and evil organization will no longer exist!

Major print media

What was ultimately perhaps the biggest failure, which led to the horrific events of 9/11, was the failure on the part of the mainstream US news media to alert the US public to the growing danger of the al Qaeda organization.

The media in a society as large as the US serves as our eyes and ears. When a danger is starting to manifest itself, its first and foremost role should be to alert all of us to this danger and what can done about it. This quite simply is their most important job.

Why had the major US print media done nothing at all to warn the US population to the growing danger of al Qaeda? After the Fatwa had been published worldwide in 1998, and this was followed by several horrific attacks on US interests abroad, why did not one of the journalists who work at these organizations come forward and say we have to get a warning to the American public? If these terrorists attack the US directly, it will cause thousands of American casualties. This was exactly what would have been required to fire up the big US intelligence agencies so they would proactively do something about this threat.

This was my very first reaction when I first read the Fatwa on that flight of February 11, 2001. Why hadn't the major mainstream media and newspapers in the largest cities in the US print eight-inch headlines?

WAR

The most maniacal and radical terrorist group in the world publicly declares war on the US.

With such a headline, it is inconceivable that the intelligence agencies would not have known that this warning was a precursor for an attack directly inside of the US.

Only one news organization even came close to describing the al Qaeda organization and its threat. CNN had televised interviews with bin Laden in the late 1990s. In a chilling forecast bin Laden had said, when asked what they were planning next, "Watch the headlines, what we do next will appear in the headlines."

He had even given a press interview in the summer of 2001, shown widely in the US, declaring his intention to bring his war in the form of "a big surprise" directly to the US.

How could so many people have let down the US public so completely?

They were our eyes and ears, and instead of giving us a warning, they left the US blind to the dangers of the al Qaeda terrorist organization. The whole country paid a dreadful price for this failure.

Not publishing these warnings was perhaps the last opportunity to put enough attention on this issue so these agencies would do what was required to protect the American public. The big security agencies, and even the FAA, were never going to proactively look for and disrupt attacks by al Qaeda without a concerned population that would apply pressure to ultimately ensure that these agencies would protect them.

It appears mainstream journalism had become just a cacophony of recent or daily events, trivial and unimportant events. News was described in a way that made it impossible for the reader to put events together and see the bigger picture.

Tragically, while much information on an impending terrorist attack had been kept secret by the current administration, one clear signal that the US was just about to be attacked did manage to reach the *New York Times* just before the July 4 holiday. The NYTimes had learned from the NSA from a conversation between two al Qaeda terrorists in Yemen who were complaining about the lack of response by the US to the *Cole* attack. They reassured themselves that the next attack would be so big and horrific the US was bound to respond.

No discussion was held at the *NYTimes* over the fact that if they did not publish this story thousands of Americans lives would be at extreme risk. No, the only discussion that took place was whether to run this story or not, since there appeared to be too little information to make this into a front-page story! A good front-page story was more important then saving the lives of thousands of Americans!

The failure of mainstream news media to warn America about 9/11 was further compounded into an even more horrific failure to ensure that the investigations of 9/11 were complete and accurate, and to hold accountable those who failed America on 9/11.

The mainstream media failed to hold the current administration and the intelligence agencies accountable for their failure to prevent the attacks on 9/11. This administration and the CIA had clear warnings that a huge al Qaeda attack was coming in the summer of 2001, and knew that bin Laden was determined to attack targets inside of the US. The administration and CIA inexplicably did nothing to prevent these attacks. Many investigations took place but the facts just never made any sense. In spite of this, mainstream media never attempted to find the real reasons the CIA did not allow information to go to the FBI that would have prevented the attacks on 9/11 or the reasons the FBI sabotaged its own investigations.

When the CIA was aware of two names two al Qaeda terrorists that took part in these attacks for 21 months the mainstream news media never asked them why they never connected these two al Qaeda terrorists known to be inside of the US to this huge al Qaeda attack we know the CIA was aware of, or why they never gave these names to the FBI during this time. This doesn't begin to pass the smell test!

Was mainstream media deliberately covering up the actions of the CIA?

No one in mainstream news media ever questioned why 44 billion dollars a year and 80,000 people was not enough to allow the CIA to connect these two al Qaeda terrorists to this huge al Qaeda attack?

When Tenet testified at the April 14, 2004 9/11 Commission hearing that he had not talk to the president in August, Bill Harlow, CIA spokesman said he had, just after the 9/11 Commission adjourned. While some in the mainstream media wrote this off as George Tenet must just have a bad memory or had misspoken, Tim Roemer had asked him about this at least 15-20 times. It is clear he had lied to the 9/11 Commission, everyone at these hearings knew it, including all of the reporters for the mainstream news media, but they said nothing!

Mainstream media hiding the CIA's culpability in the Cole bombing lead to the attacks on 9/11. This allowed the

549

administration to use this agency in the run up for war and the catastrophic situation we now have in Iraq. But by not holding the CIA accountable for the failures that led to 9/11, the administration was able to use this agency to construct intelligence out of thin air to make the case for war with a country that not only had no part in the attacks on 9/11, but also wanted no war with the US.

After 9/11 we learn there are two types of people in the world, the good guys and the evildoers. And where are the evildoers. When you turn on your TV at night and watch national news, or the news on cable, you are looking right at them!

In the end, the whole country paid a massive penalty for the horrific failure of the mainstream news media.

It is now abundantly clear, mainstream news media in deed has blood on their hands.

The FAA

There appears to be more emphasis placed at the FAA on not offending foreign passengers than on maintaining a safe environment for the US flying public.

The FAA issued numerous rules without regard to passenger safety. They clearly had either not taken into account that their rules would allow dangerous al Qaeda terrorists to board US aircraft with weapons and hijack these aircraft, or they just did not care enough to make sure that their rules would protect the American flying public.

The FAA had even made a rule that allowed passengers to carry four-inch knives on board US aircraft. The FAA never had a program to do sufficient security checks on people who fit the profile of an al Qaeda terrorist. In fact they did just the opposite. They levied huge fines on airlines that might question two or more passengers on the same flight who looked suspicious and were from the Middle East.

After 9/11, several items appeared describing the FAA and the rules they had made with respect to passengers getting on US airliners. Newspaper accounts appeared reporting that Norman Mineta had issued a ruling stating that no radical-looking Muslim passenger could ever be treated any differently than any ordinary-looking American passenger. These passengers had to be treated exactly like everyone else. No additional security measures were allowed at all, no additional questions could be asked of them under any circumstance. Nothing could be done to treat them any different from American passengers.

The ultimate effect of these rules was to absolutely ensure that determined al Qaeda terrorists could get onto almost any US airliner carrying four-inch knives, unchallenged in any way. What however, is so remarkable, when it became known in the late 1990s, that bin Laden's' al Qaeda organization was attacking US interests around the world, and even wanted to attack inside the US, why were rules specifically created that made it impossible to prevent dangerous al Qaeda terrorists from getting on US airlines?

What were the people at the top of the FAA thinking? Their first priority should have been to protect the US airliners from terrorists, not making it easier for the terrorists to carry out aircraft hijackings. The 9/11 Commission never even attempted to explain this. Another large government organization had completely failed to carry out its mission and there has never been any official explanation.

The Congress

It was the job of Congress to oversee the intelligence agencies, both the CIA and the FBI. In 1999, the Intelligence Committee of the US Congress had sent a formal request to the FBI, asking for a National Security Assessment, and in particular, an assessment of the al Qaeda terrorist organization and what this group might do to the US.

Dale Watson, head of the Counterterrorism Center at the FBI, said that he did not have to write down the information, because this information was all in his head. When this analysis was not forthcoming, why did Congress not demand this report be produced in a timely manner? When they specially asked for this report, why did they not follow up when it was not produced? This is a classic example of extremely poor oversight of the intelligence agencies by Congress, and unfortunately 3,000 Americans paid with their lives for this horrific failure.

What could have been the outcome had such a report been produced? We will never know the answer to this question. We do know the ultimate outcome could not have been more disastrous than it was. The best tool the US government had that could have stopped this attack was a written and complete strategic analysis on al Qaeda. Without this analysis, the US was totally blind to the threat of al Qaeda and totally exposed to horrific consequences that a huge attack from this organization could inflict.

The NSC, the administration and the Office of the President

The National Security Council and almost all of the top administration officials were warned about the threat of an imminent terrorist attack during the spring and summer of 2001.

In now famous July 10 White House meeting, Tenet and Black desribed to Rice and Clarke a massive al Qaeda attack just about to occur inside of the US the would kill thousands on Americans. A week later Tenet and Black gave the same information to Rumsfeld and Ashcroft. The intelligence reporting described this upcoming attack as occurring on a calamitous level, killing thousands of Americans, and coming without warning. All during July when Tenet knew about this attack what did he tell the President? Mr. Tenet was asked this in an interview on CBS why he did not tell the President since he met with him every morning, Tenet said;

"Because the United States Government doesn't work that way." "The President is not the action officer, you bring the action to the national security adviser and people who set the table for the President to decide on policies they're going to implement." "You thought you might have time - you can second guess me until the cows come home - that's the way I did my job."

This basically does not make any sense, we are told by the administration that the President is the chief decider, but here he is portrayed as the chief idiot! In any case we are now told it was either Tenet or Rice, who informed the President of this massive attack in July 2001. So why did the President not do something to prevent this attack?

No one at the NSC (aside from Richard Clarke) ever bothered to ask Tenet for a written strategic analysis of al Qaeda with a prioritized list of the targets these terrorists might be interested in attacking?

According to public testimony, Richard Clarke had asked Condoleezza Rice if she could get a prioritized list of targets al Qaeda might attack from Tenet. However, no further mention is made in all of the subsequent testimony on what happened with this request. It appears this request had been simply ignored.

Just before the September 4, 2001 Principals' meeting Clarke made a comment to Condoleezza Rice that, "the American people will wonder if we could not have done more" to prevent the horrific attack on the US that the top officials in the administration had been warned about and were all aware of.

In the August 6 PBD, the President was told that surveillance indicated a possible attack using hijacked aircraft against buildings in lower Manhattan, and neither the administration nor the NSC did anything to effectively prevent this attack. Even the President was given the information the FBI had that al Qaeda had put been engaged in the surveillance of buildings in lower Manhattan, and concluded this was consistent with an attack on these building with hijacked aircraft.

With unmistakable warnings of a huge al Qaeda attack about to occur in the summer of 2001, no effective action was ever taken by the administration or the leadership of the NSC to anticipate and prevent this attack from taking place.

While the NSC did hold meetings with many other government agencies in the summer of 2001, and provided warnings of a possible imminent attack, there obviously was no effective coordination or follow-up to ensure that these agencies had indeed taken the necessary effective action that would have prevented a terrorist attack from occurring.

While the FAA issued 52 warnings that contained the words "al Qaeda" or "bin Laden," over half of the warnings they had issued, in the months just before 9/11, these warnings did not cause the airlines to increase aircraft security or anticipate aircraft hijackings. The FBI did not alert their employees to this warning and to be extra vigilant for any signs of an al Qaeda attack, particularly signs indicating that al Qaeda terrorists were entering the US or training on US flight simulators. Had the NSC effectively alerted the other government agencies to this danger and then followed up to ensure effective action was taken, the actions at these agencies could have prevented the attacks that occurred on 9/11. In spite of the unmistakable warnings in the summer of 2001, not only were no effective actions taken to prevent the events that took place on 9/11.

Even to this day, it still remains incomprehensible why, when warnings were given to the NSC and the administration that a huge al Qaeda directed attack would take place inside of the US that would kill thousands of Americans, they took no action to prevent this from occurring.

They did not even bother to alert the American people!

For reasons that have never been explained even to this day, they allowed 3,000 Americans to be murdered by a group of religious fanatics from a far-off country, even when it is clear they had all of the information that would have been needed to have prevented this from happening.

What is even worse, it would seem that the administration had a hand in compromising the Joint Inquiry Committee investigation, the 9/11 Commission investigation, the FBI IG investigation and even the CIA IG investigation and report. While they claim that they are the people and party who would do the most to protect American against terrorism, this activity has made us all significantly less safe. Without knowing all of the details behind the horrific failures that led to 9/11, America is now at significant risk from the same sort of attack that occurred on 9/11.

New York City officials

As I was standing in front of the World Trade Center Towers at midnight of February 14, 2001, and knew the al Qaeda terrorists were going to attack these building with large hijacked airliners, I kept asking over and over:

"How could the New York city officials allow these structures to stand as they did?"

"What were they thinking to permit this?"

"Hadn't they considered the safety of the people who worked in these buildings and what would happen if these building collapsed due to a catastrophic terrorist event?"

I had come to the conclusion that these huge structures might have been practical and justified in the late '60s and early '70s when they were built, when the threat from international terrorists was low, but not in the late 1990s when the threat from the al Qaeda organization had become well known worldwide. The information on all of the prior attacks this organization had carried out had been reported in most major newspapers in the US.

Even the simplest analysis of these buildings indicated that any attack directed against them would be catastrophic. They were simply much too tall for their cross-section dimensions. This fact alone would mean huge stress loads were being applied to the support columns that visibly ran down the outside of these buildings. In the case of a terrorist attack or other catastrophic event, the occupants would have a very difficult time getting to the ground floors to safety from the upper floors.

[Note: According to the people who designed these buildings, they were designed to withstand a collision with a 707 that had no fuel on board. We were told this was the case of an aircraft lost in the fog trying to find the airport. However, no plane can fly on empty. Any plane without fuel is essentially a rock, and goes straight down. Any aircraft that is landing, even in the fog, by regulation, must have 45 minutes of fuel remaining in case of a missed approach so they can get to the alternate airport. (The pilot must be able to see the runway at the inner marker, when they are at 400 feet above the end of the runway, or they are required to execute a missed approach). So it is obvious that the example chosen by the designers of this building was not a realistic situation. Since it is now obvious these building collapsed when hit by planes carrying fuel, it is also obvious the way they were designed had made them deathtraps from day one. This raises an even more horrific question, was an unrealistic scenario chosen to validate this design, because every real scenario showed the building would collapse?]

It should have been obvious to almost everyone, that the World Trade Center Towers' height and worldwide symbolic importance made these buildings attractive targets for the al Qaeda terrorists.

Terrorists who were later found to be linked with al Qaeda had attacked these very it structures once before. The al Qaeda attack on the *USS The Sullivans* and later on the *USS Cole* indicated that once these terrorists miss a target, they never give up. They go right back and attack the same target again until it is destroyed.

Even when New York City officials were contemplating an emergency command center in the World Trade Center Building Seven, one of their main concerns was the fact that all of these buildings might again become terrorist targets. How could they have had this kind of concern and then have taken so little action to protect these buildings? Even from a superficial analysis, it must have been obvious to almost everyone that these towers were still the most important targets in the world. When this was so obvious, why hadn't any of the New York City officials considered this?

It looks as if the administration and officials running New York City had not given this any thought at all when that was the very job they were supposed to do. They apparently had done nothing to minimize the danger to the people who worked at these towers. It is still totally incomprehensible why this was so. Clearly these towers were the most visible buildings in all of Manhattan. You could literally see these buildings from almost anyplace where you had a clear view in Manhattan. With so many people depending on their very lives with keeping the integrity of these structures intact, why was it that there had been no advance planning in the event a hijacked airplane was heading for New York City? It appears there was no plan, no thought given to any of this.

FBI and CIA

Neither the FBI nor the CIA produced a well thought out, written strategic analysis on the al Qaeda terrorists prior to 9/11. A strategic analysis was apparently never created on how this terrorist organization might mount an attack on the US, or even a prioritized list of the targets they might be interested in attacking. As clues came in from the operations on the tactical side of these agencies, the relevance of these clues was not fully appreciated, at least at certain levels of the government, for the information they represented or how they might fit into a larger picture. There was no analysis to alert the US airline industry to increase aircraft security, or have air traffic control and the military carry out exercises that could have prevented massive damage from hijacked aircraft.

The CIA

While the CIA would have been hampered by not having a strategic analysis, even without this analysis to guide tactical operations, it appears (or it was made to appear) from the many investigations and public testimony, that there was no coherent direction or management for tactical operations at CIA Headquarters. The impression created by testimony given to the Joint Inquiry Committee and the 9/11 Commission was of a bumbling agency that had just made numerous simple mistakes.

However, from information found in the FBI IG report with the account of FBI Agent Ali Soufan, the lead FBI investigator on the Cole bombing, the many times the CIA withheld information from the FBI was no accident or bureaucratic foul-up, but a deliberate and carefully crafted criminal conspiracy to hide information from the FBI.

The CIA hid vital information from the FBI on at least nine separate occasions documented right in government reports. NOTE: While the account of FBI Agent Ali Soufan is not an official government report, it was vetted and approved by John Miller, information officer at the FBI.

But what is even more horrific when their conspiracy to hid the information of Mihdhar and Hazmi from the FBI fell apart on August 21, 2001, when Mary a low level IOS FBI agent working at the CIA found the cable that stated that Hazmi had entered the US, the CIA effectively sabotaged the search and investigation of Mihdhar.

Two well-known terrorists attend an important al Qaeda planning meeting in Kuala Lumpur, with Khallad Bin Attash, later to be identified as the mastermind of the Cole bombing, one is known to have flown into the US right after this meeting by the CIA, and this information was hidden from the FBI on 9 separate occasions for 21 months, from January 5, 2000, to August 22, 2001, with no explanation from the CIA why this was done even to this day.

What is even more horrific that after April 2001, the CIA was aware a massive al Qaeda attack was just about to occur inside of the US, and knew by withholding the information on Mihdhar and Hazmi, it was going to make it impossible for the FBI to stop this attack and as a result, thousands of Americans would perish.

The CIA knowingly took actions that lead to the deaths of thousands of Americans.

People at the very top of the CIA under took these actions. We know this because in 2006 almost 5 years after the events on 9/11, the world learned that Tenet and Black had briefed the top people in the administration on July 10, 2001 Rice, Clarke, and a week later Rumsfeld, Ashcroft on the coming attacks on 9/11.

The 9/11 Commission had been given this information and then inexplicably left this out of their final report.

On July 13, 2001, Tom Wilshire, former head of the Bin Laden Unit at CIA, working for Michael Rolince at FBI ITOS unit, requested from the CTC mangers at the CIA the transfer to the FBI of all of the information the CIA had on Khallad, Khalid al-Mihdhar, and Nawaf al-Hazmi, including the information that Nawaf had entered the US on January 15, 2000. This request was not allowed. This information was given to the 9/11 Commission but they chose to keep it secret from the American people, and it is only found in the FBI IG report.

When the conspiracy to hide this information on Mihdhar and Hazmi fell apart on August 21, 2001, and the CIA was forced to turn over to the FBI the photos of Mihdhar and Hazmi taken at the Kuala Lumpur meeting on August 23, 2001, they continued to hide the photograph of Khallad from the Kuala Lumpur meeting for eight more days until August 30, 2001, effectively sabotaging the FBI investigation and search for Mihdhar.

The fact that both Dina Corsi and Tom Wilshire were involved in the CIA meeting on June 11, 2001 we now know was a CIA sting on the FBI, and that Wilshire had been part of this conspiracy to hide information back on January 5, 2000, is a connection that was never made by any of these government investigations.

When the totality of this is looked at the only conclusion that can draw is withholding of this information was deliberate, widespread, and was a criminal conspiracy to hide information from the FBI. This information was the name Khalid al-Mihdhar, and Nawaf al-Hazmi the meeting in Kuala Lumpur, and the fact that Khallad (Tawfig bin Attash) the mastermind of the Cole *bombing, had been seen with al-Mihdhar and al-Hazmi at this Kuala Lumpur al Qaeda planning meeting.*

It is now clear that deliberate actions by many CIA employees to hide information from the FBI allowed the events of 9/11 to occur. This conspiracy extended into the Bin Laden unit, many levels of the CIA hierarchy including many of the top managers, the head of the CIA station in Yemen, and the head of the CIA station in Thailand.

But why would the CIA engage in this type of criminal behavior? It looks like the CIA had become a criminal organization decades ago. Several administrations had allowed them to continue to operate as long as they confined their criminal activities outside the US and to activities that would not negatively affect US interests. At some point they blurred the line between criminal activities outside of the US not affecting US interests and criminal activities that could ultimately and profoundly affect the US.

This criminality had gotten so blatant at the CIA it had become a major issue straining relations between European countries and the US. Both German and Italian government officials have either banned the CIA outright or have asked for the arrest of CIA officials. According to a recent article (October 13, 2006) in the *San Francisco Chronicle*:

> German prosecutors had asked German federal officials to forbid the CIA agents who were involved in the kidnapping of Khaled Masri, a German citizen who was held in an Afghanistan prison for five months, from ever entering Germany again. Masri stated on a German television program that he had been kidnapped in a CIA program euphemistically referred to by the CIA as rendition. The Munich state prosecutor, August Stern, passed the names and aliases of CIA operatives to the German Federal Criminal Police Office, requesting that these CIA agents never be allowed into Germany. He stated that he was afraid that they might continue to commit additional crimes in Germany. Just the year before the Italian authorities had issued 26 arrest warrants for CIA agents and US military personnel allegedly involved in the rendition of Hassan Osama, who was seized right on a street in Italy and sent to Egypt, where it is known torture was routinely used on these types of captives.

Without this criminal conspiracy, this al Qaeda attack would never have succeeded. Money was spent to insure that the FBI did not have the information they needed, ensuring that this huge al Qaeda attack would succeed, an attack that the entire upper echelon of the US government was aware of.

Numerous times information that could have stopped this attack, and could have been passed to the FBI in sufficient time to prevent this attack, was blocked by mid-level and high-level CIA managers.

While the CIA was engaged in this deception, people who were part of these investigations and the mainstream news media were well aware of the deception and they all said nothing.

The FBI

The FBI had never produced a strategic analysis and in uncovering the plan for the attack of 9/11 prior to this attack? It is now clear that they in spite of a request from Congress to do exactly this, had gotten anywhere in producing this analysis.

While the FBI would have been hampered by not having a complete written strategic analysis, even without this analysis to guide tactical operations, it appears there was no direction, no systematic procedures or no coherent management of tactical investigations to ensure the proper focus and attention to important tactical information at FBI Headquarters.

In general, the FBI had:

- No systematic way to ensure all information held by the CIA had been accurately communicated to the FBI and was accurately filed in the proper database at the FBI.

- No systematic procedures to establish priority for information coming from the CIA or other organizations to the FBI.

- No defined job descriptions for FBI detailees to the CIA to ensure all relevant information in the CIA was properly communicated to the FBI.

- Had agreed to the requirement that FBI agents working at the CIA had to get permission from the CIA prior to passing critical information over to the FBI.

Specifically, FBI Headquarters, ignored the Williams memo calling for an investigation of radical Muslims training at US airline schools, delayed and then finally sabotaged the investigation of Zacarias Moussaoui, and gave no sense of urgency to the investigation of Khalid al-Mihdhar and Nawaf al-Hazmi when the FBI knew they were al Qaeda terrorists, knew both were in the US, and even knew that a huge attack was about to take place inside of the US. Information on Moussaoui and Mihdhar never went up the chain of command at the FBI headquaters until after the attacks on 9/11.

The 9/11 Commission could never find out why the FBI sabotaged its own investigation of Moussaoui, or gave the search for Mihdhar such low priority that no effective effort was made that would have stopped the attacks on 9/11.

In both investigations long time very experienced FBI field agents were extremely concerned they were confronting extremely dangerous al Qaeda terrorist who were just about to cause massive damage to the US.

FBI Agent Harry Samit and his supervisor thought Moussaoui might hijack a large aircraft and fly it into the World Trade Center Towers. When FBI Agent Steve Bongardt found out on August 28, 2001 that Mihdhar was inside of the US, called Dina Corsi and said, "Dina, You have to be kidding me!" Mihdhar is in the country?" The next day he called her and said "If this guy is in the country, it's not because he's going to fucking Disneyland!" In email he wrote, "Someday somebody will die – and, Wall or not, the public will not understand why we were not more effective."

In both cases their investigations were blocked by agents from FBI headquaters, using what were absurd reasons why their investigations should not go forward or go forward with no urgency. In both cases FBI agents at FBI headquaters used opinions from the NSLU attorneys to block these investigations, opinions that were rendered after hearing only one side of the issue.

What turns out to be the coincidence of the century is that Maltbie, Frasca, and Wilshire, perhaps even Corsi, all worked for the same person at FBI headquaters, Michael Rolince the FBI ITOS manger. Rolince is also the FBI manger that prevented this information from going past his position at the FBI? What did the American people get for the $44 billion a year spent on intelligence? It is clear some of this money was spent by these two agencies, the CIA and FBI to actually ensure that the events on 9/11 would not be prevented.

The salaries of people at the CIA were paid for with US tax dollars. The information they had obtained was paid for with US tax dollars, and this information was entrusted to them to use to protect America and Americans from attack. Instead the CIA withheld this information from the FBI until it was too late.

The 9/11 Commission: the unanswered questions

The four investigations of this event had much information, in the end, but they failed to put the pieces together in enough detail to be able to correctly see the whole picture. Because in the end the story of 9/11 is so simple, and the information that could have provided the big picture on what happened on 9/11 was so obvious, it is not possible to conclude any thing other that these four investigations were deliberately sabotaged. Several questions were obvious and should have been answered but were not:

Exactly why did Maltbie and Frasca sabotage FBI Agent Harry Samit's investigation of Zacarias Moussaoui?

Why was this investigation by the Minneapolis FBI agents delayed by what were nonexistent and bogus rules for the FISA Court? What exactly had motivated the FBI supervisors at the RFU to do this, and in effect allow the al Qaeda terrorists to murder 3,000 Americans?

Why did the CIA hide information from the FBI for 21 months in a criminal conspiracy?

What were the managers of the CIA so afraid of they would commit criminal felonies numerous times to hide information they were trying to keep secret? It is clear after October 2000, they were hiding their culpability in the Cole bombing but why did they hide this information from the FBI starting in January 2000? We still don't know. Were they afraid of CIA criminal culpability in the East Africa bombing, or of al-Mihdhar's connection to Ali Mohammed?

Tom Wilshire's job as liaison to Michael Rolince was to provide CIA information to the FBI to use in FBI investigations Wilshire did just the opposite and hid information from the FBI? Why did not one of the many government investigation ever ask him why he did this?

Instead of providing critical information to the FBI, the fact that Mihdhar and Hazmi had been at the Kuala Lumpur meeting with Khallad bin Attash, Wilshire did everything he could to keep this information secret from the FBI. Why did no one from any of these investigations ask him why he did this? This renders all of these investigations nothing but crude blatant cover-ups!

How do you explain George Tenet's absurd testimony to the 9/11 Commission on April 14, 2004?

He stated that he had not talked to the President in August when we know now he had on at least three occasions. And what did he tell the President on these occasions or the six other times he talked to the President in September, just before 9/11? What exactly did the President know prior to 9/11? We still don't know.

When asked why he did not bring up warnings of an imminent terrorist attack at the September 4 Principals' meeting at the White House, he said, "For whatever reason, it was not appropriate." These answers were absurd. Everyone at the time knew they were absurd. He emphasized that he talked directly with the President every day, apparently except for the month of August 2001.

How do you explain that is was the exact same section inside of the FBI that sabotaged both the investigation of Moussaoui and the investigation of Mihdhar?

When I was mulling over this question I realized that there was one scenario could explain all of this, and while it is based in part on sheer speculation that has no corroboration, it is presented here for the sake of completeness.

We know in mid May Tom Wilshire moved to the FBI to become liaison to Michael Rolince at the ITOS section of the FBI. It is clear he moved to this new job just after getting the request for information from FBI Agent Ali Soufan.

We also now know that Wilshire was horrified that the criminal agents on the Cole investigation had uncovered information on Mihdhar in their search for Khallad. What if Wilshire moving over to the FBI was no accident but a well constructed conspiracy to find out if the FBI criminal agents on the Cole investigation had uncovered information on Mihdhar and Hazmi, in addition to convince Rolince that he should join this CIA conspiracy and shut down any FBI investigation that might lead back to Mihdhar. This clearly explains why the Moussaoui investigation was shut down, and why the William's memo never went anywhere and why the Mihdhar investigation was taken away from the FBI Cole investigators and given no priority.

Why would Rolince not want Mihdhar found and arrested? For the same reason the CIA did not want Mihdhar arrested and exposed, Mihdhar would lead back to some major embarrassment for the FBI much like the CIA, perhaps exposing Ali Mohammed. Mohamed had not only been working at the CIA, while a high level al Qaeda terrorist but also worked at the FBI. It was clear neither the FBI nor the CIA wanted him exposed.

It would also explain why Rolince never let any of the information on Moussaoui or Mihdhar go past his position at the FBI to higher levels of the FBI.

It also makes clear what everyone is now aware of just prior to the events on 9/11. Powerful groups within the CIA and FBI headquaters were literally at war with the FBI criminal investigation teams at the FBI. FBI headquaters did everything they could to hide information from these teams, block their search warrants with no reasonable explaination shutting down investigations, take away and destroy information they already had, even keeping them away from taking part in investigations of al Qaeda terrorists who were to carry out attacks on 9/11. It appears the FBI field agents trying desperately to carry out investigations of terrorists, which would have prevented the attacks on 9/11, never had a chance. The full weight of FBI Headquaters was used to block their investigations at every turn, and they never knew why.

Did this conspiracy to shut down criminal investigations that could have lead back to Mihdhar go above Rolince at FBI Headquaters, perhaps to include even FBI directors?

How else can you explain the actions of Tom Pickard, who took over for Louis Freeh as FBI Director, in the summer of 2001? In his testimony to the 9/11 Commission, he said to the 56 JTTFs in the summer of 2001, "have your evidence teams ready to go", he never said help us prevent this huge attack. And, why did he fire John O'Neill just before the attacks on 9/11? Had O'Neill been in charge of the FBI Field headquarters in New York when FBI HQ agent Dina Corsi told Steve Bongardt that he had to destroy the information he had on Mihdhar, and not be part of the search for Mihdhar, O'Neill never would have allowed this. It is inconceivable that had the Cole investigators been given this investigation of Mihdhar that they could not have prevented the attacks on 9/11.

Why did long time FBI Director Louis Freeh not give Ali Soufan information that Mihdhar and Hazmi had been at a meeting in Kuala Lumpur with Khallad bin Attash, when Soufan sent this very request in November 2000 through the FBI Director to the George Tenet? Freeh had been given all of this information in January 2000, just 10 months earlier.

While they is absolutely no evidence to support the fact that Rolince, and the FBI ITOS unit, and FBI directors had joined with the CIA in this conspiracy to keep information away from the FBI criminal investigation teams, and I would not suggest this scenario were true without evidence, the absolute horror story of horror stories is this scenario can explain virtually every action taken at the FBI headquaters that could never be explained before.

How do you square the fact that Tenet and Black told Rice and Clarke about this huge al Qaeda attack on July 10, 2001 but then would not allow Tom Wilshire to pass information on Mihdhar to the FBI on July 13, 2001, just 3 days later?

I asked Bob Woodward on October 24, 2006, when he was in San Francisco to be interviewed at the Commonwealth Club, how he squared the fact that Tenet and Black warned Rice on July 10, 2001, but when Tom Wilshire, former head of the Bin Laden Unit at the CIA asked his managers (Black and Tenet) three days later, on July 13, 2001, according to the FBI Inspector General's report, if he could provide the information the CIA had on al-Mihdhar and al-Hazmi to the FBI and the fact that both were at the Kuala Lumpur meeting on January 5-8, 2000 with Khallad bin Attash, and the fact that al-Hazmi had been in the US since January 15, 2000, and that al-Mihdhar had a multi-entry visa, he was not given permission to do so. How did Woodward answer this? He said that every time you look at the events on 9/11 you could peel back another layer on the onion that can be peeled back.

Why have no photos of al Qaeda terrorists at the Kuala Lumpur meeting ever been released by the CIA outside of the four photos of Mihdhar, Hazmi and Khallad.

There were 12 al Qaeda terrorists who attended the Kuala Lumpur meeting. The photos of only four have ever been released. What deep dark secret is the CIA still hiding almost 6 years after the events on 9/11? Why has no one been allowed to even come into contact with these high value terrorists outside of the Red Cross, who are sworn to secrecy about their contact with these terrorists?

Why has the administration asked for secret military tribunals for the high value terrorists, particularly Khalid Shaikh Mohammed, Ramzi bin al-Shibh, and Abu Zubaydah?

The information that will be used to convict and execute these al Qaeda members will be given to the military jury, but when this information is given to the defendants or the American people, it will be only in an unclassified form?

These terrorists will be told that they are to be executed for what they did, but they will not be told what it is exactly that they did. So they will have no way to defend themselves. They will be told whatever it was that they did, that it was bad. What secrets at the CIA are so horrific that the American people will be kept in the dark forever about the information that might emerge from these terrorists? The current administration argues that if you are against changing the rules – rules that have been in place since the United States was formed over 200 years ago – you are in effect protecting the terrorists. However if anyone can be subject to these new rules by a simple order by an un-elected official, you are not protecting the terrorists; they will be tried and convicted under any circumstance in a fair trial, but protecting everyone in the US. You are in effect protecting yourself from being charged and convicted without a fair trial.

It is clear a new investigation is needed that will get to the truth. This investigation must be free from partisan or administration manipulation, free from misleading and false testimony, free from agencies covering up their culpability, and free from administrators who block important information even before it gets to the investigators.

Chapter 23

Where do we go from here?
The lessons of 9/11

Testimony by George Tenet on April 14, 2004 before the 9/11 Commission:

> *During periods of heightened threat, we undertook smart, disciplined actions, but ultimately all of us acknowledge that we did not have the data, the span of control, the redundancy, the fusion, or the laws in place to give us the chance to compensate for the mistakes that will always be made in any human endeavor.*
>
> *This is not a clinical excuse. Three thousand people died. It was not – no matter how hard we worked or how desperately we tried, it was not enough. The victims and the families of 9/11 deserve better.*

What are the ultimate lessons that can be learned from the 9/11 Commission hearings, the Joint Inquiry Committee hearings and the FBI Inspector General's report? And ultimately, what can be learned from the experience I had and from the analysis done on the flight on February 11, 2001?

First, fire all of the criminals at the FBI and the CIA. This ought to be self-evident, but out most of the criminals have been promoted, and given awards, even large cash bonuses. The American people deserve better than to have the people who allowed 9/11 to happen still working at these agencies. It does not make us safer to have these people who allowed 9/11 to happen to be looking out for our safety.

After the events on 9/11 and my accidental involvement in this, it is clear that there are important observations about analysis and how to predict terrorist attacks before they occur.

To understand your enemy, you have to get inside of their head.

You have to see the world through their eyes, and what is even more important even feel their same emotions. This has to be the first and most important rule in intelligence

The attacks on 9/11 were completely predictable.

To uncover almost every detail of the attacks on 9/11, all you had to do was believe that the terrorists meant what they said when they wrote the Fatwa, a document published in newspapers worldwide. At the press conference on May 28, 1998, where bin Laden issued this Fatwa, not only were the sons of Sheikh Rahman, the al Qaeda terrorist who had masterminded the 1993 attack on the WTC Towers, sitting just to the left of bin Laden, but this Fatwa had been written by Sheikh Rahman himself, the mastermind of the original 1993 attack on the World Trade Center Towers, an obvious clue as to what they were going to do next.

Analysis done by one person can be as valuable as analysis done by a large number of people. Analysis done by large groups with very large budgets does not guarantee success.

In analysis, the smallest detail may give the most important insights.

One of the most important clues in understanding the al Qaeda terrorists and their thinking was in the *USS Cole* bombing, when the two suicide bombers stood up in their boat and waved at the Americans on the deck of the *Cole*. This one simple fact revealed an enormous amount of information about how the al Qaeda terrorists actually planned and carried out their attacks.

This revealed that the al Qaeda terrorists were meticulous in their planning, and did not overlook even the smallest of details.

Nothing in this world happens in isolation. Everything that happens is connected to everything else. Analysis is finding those connections.

Finding these connections is the key to intelligence.

No event or action in this world happens without some comprehensible reason.

Understanding the reason for example why the al Qaeda terrorists published the Fatwa, allowed an untrained person in just a few hours to uncover almost every detail for the events that took place on 9/11

Where do we go from here?

Build a small, focused intelligence organization modeled after the MI5 in England.

After the disaster of 9/11, and the horrendous failures at both the CIA and FBI Headquarters, it is obvious that another solution is needed to provide security against determined terrorist organizations such as al Qaeda.

The obvious solution would be to build an entirely new smaller and better-focused intelligence service modeled on the MI5 in England. Throughout much of the testimony at the 9/11 Commission, the underlying undercurrent appeared to be that this small focused group of terrorists had outwitted these bureaucracies, at virtually every turn. This small group succeeded due to their quick reaction, entrepreneurial leadership, and extremely well focused attention. None of this is found in a large bureaucracy and never will be.

As George Tenet clearly stated publicly: "The victims and families of 9/11 deserve better."

A better approach would be to create a small, focused, dedicated and well-organized intelligence organization. This organization would focus primarily on Muslim extremists and al Qaeda in particular, primarily to prevent attacks in the future.

Since these terrorist organizations use extreme secrecy and surprise as their main weapons, it should focus on generating carefully crafted strategic analysis, starting with an understanding of the thinking of people at the very top of these organizations. They should never rely solely on hard intelligence. Perhaps this organization could provide insight on how the US can win the war against this type of adversary outside of using military force. In the end this war can only be won if it is realized this is war is really about ideas, and not about military power.

Are these sorts of changes ever going to happen? These changes are not going to happen in our lifetime. Too many entrenched bureaucracies with well-vested interests and their corrupt friends in Congress will prevent any change whatsoever. Too many bureaucracies with a desire to perpetuate their dysfunctional and criminal organizations even when this means the safety and security of the American people will continue to remain at horrendous risk. They really could care less that they were unable to protect the American people on 9/11 and will be unable to protect them in the future. The misleading testimony that was almost universally presented by the managers of these agencies testifies to this. To them the only thing that matters is their continued dysfunctional existence and the preservation of their huge and failed bureaucracies, regardless of the fact they will continue to fail in the future as they had failed in the past and as they failed on 9/11.

The same corrupt politicians keep returning to Congress, to continue their corrupt policies and perpetuate dysfunctional agencies. There is virtually no chance to remove even a small percentage these politicians in Congress.

What to do next? Who are we fighting and why? How do we win this war?

It is as important to know exactly who you are fighting in a war as to actually wage the war itself. If it is defined as a war on terror, then we have already lost. This is analogous to saying we can win a war on crime. You can minimize crime but you can never eliminate it.

To define a mission that is even doable, you first have to define the adversary you are fighting. In this case, this is a war against Sunni Muslim extremists, and those who are part of this group that use terrorist attacks in order to further their agendas. At this point this is al Qaeda.

In the end, this war will be won or lost as a war of ideas not a war in military terms.

These organizations have attacked the US, not for what we stand for and not for our freedom, but because they see the US as standing in the way of their ultimate goal of uniting all of the Muslim lands under a single caliphate, and returning the Muslim law of the Shariah as the law over all of these lands. The US just happens to be perceived at the most obvious impediment to allowing this to happen.

They see the only way to win this war is to get the moderate Muslims on their side. In order to do this, they have repeatedly attacked the US in an effort to provoke the US into invading Muslim countries. Without the moderate Muslims on their side, al

Qaeda has perceived that they will never be able to achieve their ultimate goal.

Due to an almost unimaginable lack of understanding of this group or their thinking, apparently due to naivety, old-fashioned stupidity or complete incompetence, we have inadvertently blundered into doing exactly what they wanted us to do. We have stepped right directly into their trap.

By attacking Muslim countries, in a way that inflamed Arabs and Muslim nationalistic feelings, we have caused thousands, if not hundreds of thousands, of moderate Muslims to join with the al Qaeda terrorists and actively oppose us.

Muslims worldwide have a cultural phenomenon that is not well understood in the West. This is best summed up in the phrase, "in the defense of Islam." Muslims worldwide easily become outraged at attacks on other Muslim countries especially by countries inhabited by people they consider to be infidels and see activity to stop these attacks as serving "in the defense of Islam."

What is so ironic is these moderate Muslims had initially opposed bin Laden and were even at one time largely friendly toward the US.

The irony is that the al Qaeda organization perceives moderate Muslims as their real enemy. They are, however, cleverly manipulating them in order to turn these moderate Muslims against the US and the West and to force the US out of the Middle East. Bin Laden is using the complete lack of sensitivity in the US for the issues that affect the minds of Muslim peoples against us in this war.

In spite of all of the very smart people in the US and the West, bin Laden is completely outsmarting us and even at this late date we are not even aware of it.

Appendix
The 9/11 Letters

Correspondence and Summaries of FBI reports, from September 11, 2001 to the current time

The following letters and summaries of FBI reports details the process that had been used to analyze the thinking of the top leadership of the al Qaeda organization, and the subsequent steps that were used to come to the conclusions that they were, in February 11, 2001, in the planning stages for a huge attack on the World Trade Center Towers that would culminate with the destruction of these towers prior to the end of October, 2001. Not only could you conclude that this attack would happen with a high degree of probability, you could conclude that there was absolutely no possible way that this attack would not take place. Included is the information sent to the Joint Inquiry Committee, Eleanor Hill Staff Director describing how this analysis was done. The following material is based on correspondence that has taken place over the last 2½ years, starting from September 11, 2001. Every single point presented in this correspondence can be reiterated and/or backed up with testimony, either public or private, under oath or not.

Robert Schopmeyer/Veritools, Inc

Letter to the 9/11 Commission

From Robert Schopmeyer
To Members of the 9/11 Commission
April 11, 2004

Prior Knowledge of the Events of 9/11, from conclusions reached on February 11, 2001 from a careful analysis of the thinking of the leadership of the al Qaeda organization.

On a flight from San Francisco to Newark, NJ on February 11, 2001, after reading and analyzing material on the history and writings of the al Qaeda organization, I came to the following conclusions:

That the February 1998 Fatwa published worldwide by the al Qaeda organization, had to be nothing less that an open public declaration of war on the United States.

That this declaration of war, coming 10 years after the founding of this organization had to mean that the al Qaeda organization was now determined to mount titanic sized attacks inside of the US.

On the attack on the *Cole* in October, the al Qaeda organization had use as weapons, secrecy, suicide surprise and psychology. An analysis of this attacked indicated that the leadership of the al Qaeda organization, thought that by using these weapons they could successfully attack any target anywhere in the world, even large building in New York and Washington DC.

Based on this information and also the fact that a huge attack had to be in the planning stages, the target had to be the World Trade Center Towers. No other target even came close to matching this target from a measure of the magnification factor for these buildings. Magnification refers to the total amount and duration of newsprint coverage in newspapers primarily in Europe and the Middle East

The method of attack had to be the use of four large aircraft that would be hijacked in midair using four or five Arab member of the al Qaeda organization, carrying knives with four-inch blades, knives that were deemed legal by the FAA.

An analysis of the timing for this plan indicated that this plan most likely had started around February 2000, and was in place ready to go by around August 1, 2001, this allowed 1½ years to bring in and train four teams of pilots, and bring in the remaining hijackers. The final phase of the attack would be during the month of August to train the hijacking teams as whole teams, and then a completion date to be decided at the last minute somewhere in September or October.

I further concluded that the FBI and FAA would do nothing to preemptively stop this plan and would never consider accepting or acting on any input of this speculative nature, information that this plan was in progress.

A reexamination of the information and analysis used to reach these conclusions, indicated that not only was this attack plan highly probable, but that there was absolutely no possible way it would not take place.

On the 19th of February I came back to California and informed virtually every single employee at Veritools, 11-12 employees, of this information. That a huge attack would take place against the WTC Towers, that it would involve the use of four hijacked airliners and that both WTC Towers would be totally obliterated by the end of October at the latest.

This information has been given to FBI offices, in Boston, San Francisco, Minneapolis, and San Jose and to the Joint Senate-House Committee, Eleanor Hill Staff Director.

All of these conclusions were based on an analysis of the history of this organization and material that their top leadership had actually written and published worldwide in Muslim newspapers. All of these conclusions were derived using a very careful analysis of the thinking of the top leadership of al Qaeda, which could be obtained from these written statements, combined with a history of their attacks previously on overseas US targets and applying to this analysis a very simple logic along with just very basic common sense. This analysis was in effect a strategic analysis of what most likely the al Qaeda organization could do, with an analysis of what security was in place to prevent them from carrying out an attack using US aircraft.

In the light of this information, it is possible to review and reach conclusions on several of the statements recently made by various witnesses at the 9/11 Commission hearings.

That there was no "silver bullet that could have stopped this attack."

That by the time the new administration had come into office, almost all of the hijackers were in the US already and so nothing could have been done to stop this attack.

That there was no actionable intelligence that would indicated such an attack was under way, and hence no way to stop this attack from happening.

That there was no information as to the time, place, the method of attack or the target so nothing could be done.

That everything that could be done, was done.

On the first point, an obvious silver bullet would have been to have the US government generate a secret policy with steps that should be taken to ensure that al Qaeda terrorists with dangerous weapons be prevented from ever getting onto US airliners. This would seem to be almost too obvious, but apparently was never done. This could have been done with the following steps; all airliners should have been required to know exactly who was getting on their aircraft, this is simple common sense. Passenger lists could have been reviewed for those exact types that fit the profile of the al Qaeda terrorists, four or five Arab males between 18-32 years in age, sitting in first class or business class all going one way. This group could have been checked to see if one or more were pilots registered with the FAA, with almost all of this being done using computers scanning passenger reservations lists. Requirements should have been added so that pilot in command was informed if any passengers were carrying four-inch knives on board, pilots should have been warned that such an attack by the al Qaeda terrorists was possible and likely. Security cameras should have been placed at baggage security check in points at major airports to detect any suspicious surveillance of these security points by young Arab males. This alone could have stopped this attack dead in its traces.

That by the time the new administration had come into office, almost all of the hijackers were in the US already and so nothing could have been done to stop this attack.

One of the most obvious times to have stopped this attack was as the hijackers boarded the airliners carrying their weapons. The fact they were in the country already is irrelevant, they most likely never could have been stopped at the entry points, and even if they were, other hijackers would have been sent in to replace the ones that could not get in.

That there was no actionable intelligence that would indicated such an attack was under way, and hence no way to stop this attack from happening. Since it was well known that the al Qaeda terrorist keep their planning extremely secret, it would be highly doubtful that and rare that any real actionable intelligence would ever be obtained prior to a well panned attack. It would have been incumbent on any organization that was charged with preventing terrorist attacks on the US, to not rely or wait for actionable intelligence, which they most likely would never get anyway, but preemptively do the type of strategic analysis listed above and then add monitors, which would indicate that some type of attack was in progress. Almost all al Qaeda terrorist plans involve surveillance, estimating what is going to be surveyed and carefully adding security cameras would be perhaps one of the best ways to thwart attacks in the future. To suggest nothing can be done without actionable intelligence is to literally ensure that terrorist attacks would be successful at great lose to those subject to the attack itself.

That there was no information as to the time, place, method of attack or target so nothing could be done. Again, from the prior attacks by the al Qaeda terrorists, it was well known that their main weapon was extreme secrecy, it is highly conceivable that no information of any kind would have ever have been obtained on these areas. Yet this plan could still have been easily stopped using the methods as listed above. Even when only a range of dates was known or estimated, the extra security measures that were listed before could have been kept in place over the range of dates that were of concern, or even left in place indefinitely. Obviously making the cockpit doors much more solid and having armed guards on major airliners are important longer term goals, these steps would have taken time, added an extra layer of security to the system, but because these steps might not have gotten done in the 231 days of the new administration, the steps mentioned previously would have had to have been employed to ensure that this attack was not going to be successful.

That everything that could be done was done. Obviously from the previous discussion, this appears not to be the case, none of the steps mentioned previously appears to have been done. So not everything that could have been done was done. In fact it looks like none of these very common-sense obvious steps were done at all.

The initiation of the steps listed above to increase aircraft security would have logically followed and been done after a through review of the al Qaeda organization, their thinking especially the thinking of the top leadership, and then a strategic analysis generated of all of the things this organization could do to attack targets in the US itself.

Without this strategic analysis as a starting point and guide, there would have been no real single coherent picture of the steps that needed to be done and how each step fit with each other step to provide a comprehensive approach to completely stop any possible terrorist attack using US aircraft. It looks like none of these steps were done, and it also looks like no strategic analysis was ever done. This one single fact left the US open to horrific attacks with the resulting obvious terribly tragic consequences.

The review mentioned above would have been done generally when it was perceived that the threat level on the US had changed in some significant way. The events that should have triggered this review were the publishing the Fatwa and the Declaration of Jihad, even a simple reading of these indicated that al Qaeda was now sending a public and open signal that they intended to mount attacks against the US in a major way. The attack on the embassies and the *Cole* should also have triggered these types of reviews. Finally, even if these reviews had not taken place, the massive amount of information that was received in the summer of 2001 an impending attack should have triggered an immediate review of what the threat from al Qaeda could mean. It is a major mystery as to why this was not done. Indications are received that al Qaeda wanted to attack in the US, it was going to be a spectacular attack possibly using hijacked airliners that could kill thousands of Americans and would come without warning and no major review was done. How is this even remotely possible? This makes no sense.

Robert Schopmeyer/Veritools, Inc.

Summary of the interview given to Special Agent Vince Tagleari, FBI Field Office, San Jose, CA, on September 19, 2001 on having prior knowledge of the events of 9/11

The information below was given in an interview at the San Jose FBI office to Agent Vincent Tagleari. This information concerns the World Trade Center attack of 9/11/2001. All of this information is true and accurate to the best of my ability. I am providing this information because of my duty to be a responsible American citizen.

My name is Robert Schopmeyer, I am the president of a software company in Palo Alto, that develops and sells software for the electronic design automation market, primarily design and verification software for visualizing and analyzing the results from both HDL simulators and analog simulators, HDL stands for High Level Design language. Veritools software is currently running in almost every single major electronic company in the world. Veritools has an excellent reputation in this industry.

On a trip to New York in February of this year I became aware of the following information:

That Usama Bin Laden was currently planning a huge attack on the continental US

That these attacks would involve an attack on the World Trade Center Towers

That he and his people had been working on this plan already for at least one year and that at this time, February, 2001 he had at least 100 people already working on this plan, many of these already in the US.

That their plan was to hijack at least four airliners and crash these in the Word Trade Center Towers.

That they intended to hijack these airliners using four or five persons per plane from Middle East countries using small knives that were legal to bring aboard aircraft per FAA rules.

That their ultimate goal was to collapse these structures and kill everyone in these buildings.

That their goal was to kill 30,000 Americans in this single attack

That this plan was to be completed in no more than nine months from February.

That given the nature of this plan, it would have been very hard if not totally impossible to stop.

That the only way I could see that this plan could be stopped in February, was to have the airlines make the cockpit doors so they could not be penetrated, in addition to having armed guards on board. I could see no way this was going to be done in sufficient time to stop this attack. I could not see any way the FBI was going to be able to do any investigation since they do not start any investigation without verifiable information, which I did not have.

That given that I could see no way this plan could be stopped; I gave these buildings one chance in one billion of not being smashed completely to the ground in nine months.

Agent Vincent Tagleari has already informed me verbally that I am not responsible in any way for the World Trade Center attack, and that I should not feel that I am to blame for these events. He has said that had I come in February with this information, they would have been unable to have stopped these attacks with this information, since I did not have any specific date or flight number for these attacks.

Since I believe all of this information in this letter to be true and accurate, to the best of my ability, I will willingly agree to submit to a polygraph test given by any official government agency, with their own people, to answer any questions, to eliminate any doubt whatsoever as to the truth of what I believed to be the facts with regard to the information concerning this event.

Robert Schopmeyer/President Veritools, Inc.

Summary of the analysis of the thinking of Usama bin Laden and the conclusions that an attack was coming on the WTC Towers

Analysis was done on February 11, 2001 on a United Airlines flight to New York from magazine articles describing history and writings of al Qaeda

Transcribed on 9/19/01

Sent to the FBI Field Office at San Jose, attention Vince Tagleari, September 19, 2001

About nine (seven) months ago, I had an occasion to be on a United flight, traveling to New York City. I was reading an article on Usama Bin Laden on the flight; the article not only had a detailed description of his background, but also had a section, a translation of his "Declaration of the World Islamic Front for the Jihad Against the Jews and the Crusaders." The printed text for this Declaration what been printed in three sections, but it was the last or third section, that was totally stunning in its effect;

"To kill Americans and their Allies, both civil and military, is an individual duty of every Muslim, who is able, in any country where this is possible.... By Gods leave, we call on every Muslim who believes in God and hopes for reward to obey God's command to kill Americans and plunder their possessions wherever he finds them and whenever he can."

I was vaguely aware that some in the Middle East were not our friends, but was totally unaware anyone could feel this way with this much intensity toward the people in the US.

As I was sitting on this flight after reading this, I felt that if he had really felt this way, how was it possible that we had had so very few real problems in the US up to this point. All of the attacks by these people had been mostly some where in the Middle East. How lucky the US had been up to now to have had no major attacks, but then also how vulnerable we were if he/they had "really" decided to go after Americans in the continental US, particularly, with the openness of the US. They could have literally done many bad things, almost at will.

The next sequence of events was the sequence that put everything together. After reading over this section of this stunning Declaration several times, and still having a very hard time trying to figure out why anyone would think this way, I picked up a travel magazine in the seat pocket in front of my seat to try to find a different and less intense subject. On the cover of this magazine was a picture of Manhattan, looking down from a position just above the Statue of Liberty. In this photograph, almost all of the buildings show up in the back ground, except for two huge towers standing higher than everything else, sticking out of the very end of Manhattan, the World Trade Center Towers.

After reading the Declaration, and then viewing this photograph of these huge buildings, I almost immediately came to a totally stunning conclusion, it might be called, an emotional lighting bolt, I was so totally stunned, I was virtually paralyzed a few seconds. I had come to the conclusion that Bin Laden and his groups next target had to be these huge buildings, nothing else that I could think of stood out like two enormous targets, nothing else made any sense in view of his Declaration, no other target any where in the rest of the US else even came close. If he had decided that it was the goal of his followers to kill Americans and destroy American possessions, these had to be his next prime targets, no other event could possibly do as much damage to either property and people in the US or the psyche of the American people, nothing else made any sense. Since I had come to this realization while I was actually sitting on a flight to New York City, it became almost immediately obvious how he was going to do this, he was going to instigate several his followers to capture several airliners while in flight, take over these airplanes and then crash these planes into these buildings.

What I put together over the duration about of this flight and how it came from what I knew, was the following sequence:

He had a net worth of several hundred million dollars, he had thousands of completely devoted and fanatical followers, he had terrorist training camps all over the Middle East with literally thousands of recruits.

His printed and published "Declaration" said that he not only wanted to kill Americans and destroy our possessions where ever they could be found, in any country, but had issued a commandment to all in his faith to do the same.

The biggest and most obvious targets in the US were these World Trade Center Towers; no other structure even came close.

It seemed that, he must have had at this very time; over 100 people, right then, working on the completion of this plan. If he believed in the truth of his own printed writings, nothing else made sense.

If I had just become aware of what must have been his plan, he must have been working on this plan for at least a year or more prior to this.

Given that these people did not seem to have infinite patience and that a plan of this sort did not seem to require more than two years to set up and complete, I gave this plan at best no more than the next nine months to be completed.

Given the lack of security of American airliners, and especially the FAA rule, which allows four-inch knives legally on airliners, I could think of no possible way that this plan would fail. The hijackers could walk onto any airliner, right through security, they did not even have to hide these knives, get on the airliner, and capture it in flight, with very little opposition from the terrified passengers.

After going through all of the above, I gave the chance of these building still being there after another nine months, a chance of one in a 100 billion. How could they still be there with at least 100 fanatical people already at this time working on the completion of this plan?

Other people in our government had to be aware of this plan, it was just too obvious and too inconceivable they were not.

When I was in New York after the flight, I went down to see these two huge buildings up close, and had a terrifying image of what was going to happen. I was totally sick over the fact that perhaps no one else seemed to be aware of what was about to happen. I could see no way to stop this plan, I could see no possible way I could convince the necessary authorities of what I thought that I knew, and how I could get then to stop this.

As I stood in front of these towers, looking up at these buildings, I felt these towers never should have been built in the first place, or once these types of threats became known, they should have been dismantled and rebuilt with many fewer stories, and then blended into the rest of the city so they would not stand out, and would never become a target.

I had absolutely no real evidence of any kind, about this plan, none whatsoever, I had just put two and two together, from an accidental sequence of events, and had then following my thoughts to what I thought at the time was a logical conclusion.

Without any hard verifiable evidence, no one would ever have taken this information seriously, at that time, and taken real action to prevent this from taking place. If I had gone to the authorities at this time, with all that I had was a gut feeling about a general plan, with no tangible independently verifiable evidence of any kind, there would have been nothing they could have done, given the process of starting investigations, only when facts can be independently verified in some way. This is the current American process, and with the secrecy of the groups from the Middle East, almost ensures that the plans of this type will never be anticipated, or seriously looked into until after the fact. This is unfortunately the sad truth of our current legal investigation processes and agencies.

With a few simple steps, at the time, it seemed to be even possible to stop these types of attacks. What should have been done and should be done now is the following:

All airliners must, I mean MUST, have penetration proof cockpit doors to prevent any unauthorized persons from ever, the word is "EVER" being able to come thorough the cockpit door, this is an absolute must. No passenger cabin personnel can be allowed to have any cockpit door keys. No pilot should be able to open the cockpit door once in the air, even under the threat of a bomb on board.

All airliners must have personnel with firearms, this is an absolute requirement, and there is absolutely is no other way. At a minimum, the pilots must be firearm trained. As a minimum, they should also have a video view of what is going on just outside of the cockpit area.

As a backup, each airliner must have multiple persons armed with firearms, at the front of each airliner, with seats facing backward to allow them see everyone in the passenger cabin. Airline personnel would have guns; the attackers would only ever have knives. No air craft should ever be given up in the face of a bomb threat, any action based on this type of threat only places even more people in jeopardy.

To prevent bombs from coming on board, all passengers, flight crew, service personnel, their clothes, their shoes, their carry on must be checked with some nitrogen detection device, to prevent any explosives from every coming a board an airplane.

UNTIL THIS IS DONE, THERE IS ABSOLUTELY NO SECURITY FOR ANYONE ON ANY CURRENT AMERICAN AIRLINER!!!!!

OUR CURRENT SECURITY AS HAS BEEN SHOWN, IS ABSOLUTELY NO GOOD.

Unfortunately, the steps listed above that would have been effective for the World Trade Center attack, will not be good enough for the next attack. These people keep getting smarter and smarter all of the time, on how to over come the last set of security measures.

The US seems to be unable to prepare for the new realities of a coming war, we always seems to be fighting the last war, with tragic results. The US only acts when provided with absolute positive and verifiable proof that some criminal or military activity is about to happen, and what proof are you ever going to get when these people will never trust even their phone number to anyone who has not been a blood relative for years.

The US agencies today, are totally and completely unable to put themselves into the mind of our enemies, which is what they must do, and anticipate what destructive activities they are planning next. Can this be changed, I hope and pray it can and will, but given the recent events, I hold out little hope.

In tragic hindsight I think, all America would like answers to these questions:

When will American airliners be rendered safe with effective armed guards?

Why did the US official agencies and officials not know what was patently obvious, that people from the Middle East were willing to die for their cause, and that the biggest and most obvious target in the world was the World Trade Center? To say they could not conceive of this type of event ever happening, almost defies all logic.

Why were there no red flags when four or five Middle East persons, age 20-30, many registered with the FAA as pilots and even some registered as having 757 training, were sitting in first class, or business class, on four different flights leaving at almost the exact same time in the morning.

Why did these buildings exist without a plan for protection against destruction by hijacked airliners? Sprinklers attached directly on the steel beams to keep them cool, and allow more time prior to collapse would have been a start.

Why was there no notification by ATC to all security persons of large buildings when aircraft are obviously off course, combined with rapid evacuation plans, and notification to the military?

Where were the instruction and training to pilots to never open any cabin doors for any reason, and did passenger cabin personnel have keys to the cockpit?

Where were the firearms for the flight crew for use as a last resort?

What about crew training, so when passengers threaten to take over the aircraft, crew could perhaps depressurize the passenger cabins as a last resort? The measures in place had been designed for Cuban hijackers last seen over 20 years ago.

Why is there no explosive checking for all passenger, their cloths and shoes, and carry-ons going onto the aircraft?

We knew about Bin Laden, we knew of his Declaration, he had written it down, and it had been published for all to see. We knew he was capable, motivated and rich enough to do these kind of deeds, we know these deeds could happen and then did nothing to protect our buildings and cities from him or other like him from doing this.

What will his next plan be, and what measures will be needed in order that his next plans can be completely and effectively stopped?

Bob Schopmeyer/Veritools, Inc.

P.S. After these events and after having given this much thought, it is becoming a little clearer of how I had come to the conclusions I did.

#1. I knew he had huge financial resources at his use and had many very devout followers, who could and would be able to do any action toward anyone or state that they felt were an enemy of Islam.

584

#2. After reading his "Declaration," I was amazed that we had to this point been free of major attacks by his group and found this to be very puzzling, it made no sense.

#3. It was actually not seeing the photograph of the towers that caused me to believe his plan was to attack these two towers, but seeing the photograph of these towers and realizing that if he really believed in the truth of what he had written, and if he had had these enormous resources, the only logical conclusion was that he must be planning some type of attack on the continental US. Then that these towers had to have been the most obvious targets, in effect target number one, and target number two, nothing else made any sense.

#4. There was absolutely no security on US airliners, in particular since the FAA ruling on the legality of carrying small knives on board.

#5. His followers could easily take over several planes using multiple persons aboard each flight who had enough religious fervor that they were willing to be sacrificed in this plan, and who would then force these captured air planes to crash into these structures an attempt to collapse these buildings.

#7. If I had come to be aware of his plan, it then must have been in place at least a year or more prior to my knowing about it, it did not make sense that I had discover this plan just after it started. I assumed this plan had to be completed in much less that another year.

#8. In an earlier part of this letter I asked why the FBI did not know, I now know why and also why, even at the time that I was on this flight, it would have done no good even if they did know about this plan.

The persons behind these groups were sworn to a secrecy that would never have allowed an anyone outside this group from knowing about the plan, no information would even have gotten out unless by some accident. There is no known sum of funding large enough that can ever correct this.

The FBI is trained never to react or use its time unless they have detailed evidence that they can independently verify, which would not have been possible, with the type of secrecy found in these groups.

The worst part is, even if the FBI had known the identity of the hijackers, known the exact flight numbers of the hijacked airliners, and known even the dates of the flights, had known about the real plan, which never would have been possible, nothing even then could ever have been done to stop this plan.

If the people who were just about to hijack the airliner had been stopped and then arrested, even in the single second just prior to their starting the aircraft take over, they all would have denied they were part of any plan and said carrying knives of the type they had was completely legal. No search warrants could have even been issued, to search for proof, because there would never have been any "PROBABLE CAUSE" of any kind. Then they would then just have waited to execute this plan some other day. Our entire system was unfortunately designed to ensure this horrible plan could not fail. The FBI cannot be blamed in any way.

Only on board security, with security people carrying firearms could have stopped this from happening, and after this, the passengers could only have been saved only if explosives would have been kept completely off of any of these aircraft. Neither of these security steps was in place at this time, and there was no known way of making these steps happens in sufficient time.

#8. The World Trade Center in 1993, the embassy bombings, and the World Trade Center, September 11, are not the end results of this group but only the steps along the way as part of their much bigger plan.

The main goal of this group is to get the US to blindly react militarily, to one of these attacks in order to start the polarization of the Islam world with its one billion Muslim followers, with the west and in particular the US, with tragic results for the interests of the US in all of these Muslim countries.

That this is the ultimate goal is almost too obvious, and that the US is now stepping directly into Bin Laden trap, as is now happening is a forgone conclusion, once again which no one can stop, it is already too late. We are doing exactly what he wants us to do, with the exact consequences that he trying to achieve. He is leading us down this deadly path without us even knowing it, we are now following into his trap and are not even aware that what we are about to do is exactly what he wants us to do, I repeat, we are doing exactly the very thing he wants us to do.

The only words that can be used to describe Bin Laden are, "EVIL GENIIS." We are still, even today, not aware of how incredibly smart are the person/persons that the US is up against, but we are just beginning find out with the absolute most tragic of consequences.

May 7, 2002

Dear Senator Patrick Leahy, Senator Chuck Grassley,
and Senator Dianne Feinstein:

Attached is the FBI report, (FBI FINAL_TRIP_TO_NY.doc), that was
the culmination of several FBI interviews, starting on September 11,
2001 on the events of 9/11. The following letter helps to explain this
report in more detail.

In a recent newspaper article, Senator Grassley, you were quoted as
saying with respect to the FBI, "why did they not connect the dots," in
reference to the disclosure that the FBI was warned about Middle
Eastern persons attending US flight schools.

On February 4, 2001, I had been able all of the dots, and do this with a
whole lot less dots than the FBI had, even though I had no connection
to any US intelligence organization or their information.

I had come to the following conclusions on this date on a flight from
San Francisco to New York City.

*That Osama Bin Laden's group had to be planning at this time, a
huge attack directly on the continental US*

*That this huge attack had to be against some target in the US, that
would result in massive physiological damage to the US, and generate
"massive media coverage," that was their goal.*

*That this target without any doubt had to be the World Trade Center
Towers in New York City, no other target even came close to
matching these huge buildings in terms impact and physiological
value.*

*That the terrorists would hijack at least four very large US airliners,
using four or five members on each hijacking team, and drive these
planes into the sides of these building in order to collapse these
structures.*

*That this plan had to have been in active operation in the US for at
least one year prior to February 4, 2001. From prior operations that
they had carried out in the past, and an estimate of the steps required
for this plan, I had estimated that the plan would take between one
year and six months at the earliest to about one year and nine months
at the latest to complete, starting from the February, 2000 date. This
is the date that I had assumed they had seriously started this plan,
this was just a best guess on my part. From this time estimate, I had*

587

concluded that they would be ready and able to carry out this attack by around the first of August, 2001 and would have completed the execution of this plan by no later than by the end of October, 2001. I had actually picked the third week of October as the most likely time period for this attack.

The only way I could see that this plan could be stopped in February, 4, 2001, was to have the FAA require the airlines to provide solid, penetration proof doors on aircraft cockpits and armed guards on US aircraft. Since I did not see how this was going to happen prior to August 1, 2001, I could see no way these building were not going to be completely flattened by this massive attack, at the very latest, by the end of October.

I was able to connect the dots primarily because I had one very important dot the FBI may not have, I had come to a basic understanding of how the terrorist actually thought. It turns out that was not as hard to do as might be first imagined.

Bin Laden and the al Qaeda terrorist organization had published in 1998, a document called the "**Declaration of Jihad**." Understanding their thinking essentially required answering to two very important questions with regards to this document:

#1. What was the sequence of thought that had lead these author/authors to have come to the ideas or conclusions expressed in this declaration, and in particular, the one sentence in the "Fatwa:"

"To kill Americans and their Allies, both civil and military, is an individual duty of every Muslim, who is able, in any country where this is possible... By God's leave, we call on every Muslim who believes in God and hopes for reward to obey God's command to kill Americans and plunder their possessions wherever he finds them and whenever he can."

#2. And, what was the motivation of the author/authors for writing down and then publishing this Declaration in publications that even the people of the United States would see.

Answering the first question, just required the reader to actually place themselves in the shoes of the author, and then ask, what actual thinking or thought sequence would it have taken for the reader themselves to personally have come to the exact same conclusions and opinions as the author of this Declaration. After knowing how they thought, I had analyzed their thinking to see if the attacks on the overseas targets to this point seemed to fit this thinking.

Osama Bin Laden in his mind, had decided that the leadership of Saudi Arabia should be replaced with a Islam based "caliph," and in fact all of the Muslim countries should be ruled by a single "caliph" made up of Muslim scholars, and that all western person and influence should be removed or expelled from the Middle East.

The attack on the Khobar Towers made perfect sense, he was sending a message to the US, to get out of Saudi Arabia.

The attack on the embassies made less sense or no sense, these in my opinion, these were out of the area that was to be governed by this single caliph. This meant that UBL now was going to attack the US interests anywhere they were located, even outside of the area where he wanted them expelled from. This could only mean that he had an enormous enmity for the US and its people, unrelated to the reasons in the "Declaration."

This could only mean that the US could expect an attack anywhere in the world. He really did mean what he wrote in the "Fatwa." What is the difference between attacking Tanzania and Kenya and the continental US, just a couple more hours on an airplane.

The attack on the *Cole* made sense with one huge question, if he felt he could attack the *Cole* armed with large guns, what did this really imply. This could only mean that UBL felt he literally could hit ant target or any building that he wanted to, anywhere in the world. What building for example comes with a four-inch gun mounted on the roof, I cannot think of any. If he could hit the *Cole*, he could attack "any" building anywhere in the world. The Americans after every attack seemed almost completely oblivious to these attacks and what they meant.

Why had there been no investigation after every single one of these attacks to see what in the world went wrong with our intelligence and security agencies. We just sat there, completely and totally oblivious, doing absolutely nothing until the next attack happened. Why did we not have a review after every attack of what went wrong, this made no sense to me at all? UBL must have also seen this almost unimaginable lack of awareness on the part of the US to his continuing threats and attacks. We almost seemed to be just sitting there waiting for the eventual slather

In order to answer the second question, just imagine you are the head of a large terrorist organization and ask, what would motivate you to publish this, especially when the Americans would be able to see it. The answer to the second question was absolutely stunning. When the terrorists had this Declaration published, it could only mean one absolutely terrifying thing in my opinion. That they were announcing to the world that they had declared unrestricted war against the US and its citizens. Not directly attacking the US after publishing this would have made them look like complete fools to their own organization. This meant that they would now be expected to do the worst, meanest, most horrendous acts against the US and our citizens.

This simple and basic understanding of how these people thought was in effect the "dot" that the FBI did not have, although the FBI had access to the same generally available information that I had. They apparently had never bothered to think completely through this process to understand what these people were thinking and why, and then what impact on the US this would imply.

It was at this point that I became completely puzzled, why with this tremendous negative feeling toward the US and our citizens, had we not been directly attacked with some mammoth attack before now by this group. This made no sense at all. That is when, quite by accident, I picked up a travel brochure with the picture of the Manhattan, and in the middle of this picture, in a very prominent way, was the World Trade Centers Towers. From, knowing basically at this point how the leadership of the al Qaeda thought, it was obvious that this had to be their next target, and that no other target would come anywhere close in giving them the massive impact than the destruction of this one single target would.

From knowing that this had to be their main focus, it was straight forward to deduce how they were going to attack this structure, they were going to hijack several large US airliners in flight, I had assumed at least four, and then drive these aircraft into the sides of these huge building. Why, because there is simply no other way that is as simple as this approach.

How were they going to capture these airlines? By the use of force, with four or five of their al Qaeda terrorists carrying onto the airliners, small knives that had been deemed perfectly legal by the FAA. Why, because again, there is just no other way to do this that is as simple as this.

Basically, from looking at all of their past operations, almost all of their plans are carried out over huge distances, over a period of months or years, with almost no communications for months between team members and their hierarchy. It was obvious that all of their plans had to be extremely simple, essentially simple enough to be a level no higher than just a third grade level in terms of simplicity and understanding. This meant that when you were trying to figure out what they were going to do, you just had to come up the very simplest plan that you could think of, that would demolish the target you had assume they wanted to attack.

I had connected all of the dots with almost no dots, and certainly no dots that were not in general publications. The question is not how did I figured this out, but with many more dots, and dots that had come from real information about the terrorists, why was the other government agencies not able to figure this out by connecting the dots that they had. Were all of their dots in one place or were they scattered among different groups at for example, the FBI?

What dots did they have that I did not have:

They had the names of two of the terrorists. Robert Mueller said in a speech to the Common wealth Club in San Francisco, on April 19, that they were not able to locate these two people with their extensive FBI search. But one these persons had their name listed right in the San Diego phone book, and both had reservations on the flights for the September 11 attack, under the exact spelling of their names that was in the FBI database.

They had been informed by a flight instructor, that a student at a Minnesota flight school, Zacarias Moussaoui, had to be a terrorist, and then after several FBI agents had dismissed this information, had arrested this person, instead of watching him to see if he could lead them to the other terrorists. When does a single terrorist hijack a very large airliner by themselves??

They had the report from pilot of American Flight 11, on August 1, that one of the passengers, a James Wood had come to the stunning conclusion that four of the passengers had to be terrorists, and they had been informed by the pilot of this information. Apparently, these were four of the pilots from 9/11, on a training flight.

Why did I not come forward to the FBI and report what I thought I knew prior to 9/11. I did not think that with absolutely no real credible and verifiable information, my input would taken and used at all, and in

591

fact thought it would create such a very negative impression with the FBI such that if and when I were able to find credible information later on, I would no longer have enough credibility to be taken seriously at all. Think of yourself going down to an FBI office and in a FBI interview, saying to them; "terrorists are going to capture four large aircraft, crash these into the World Trade Center, and do this between August 1 and October 31." The very first question they would ask, "How do you know this," and you would say, I simply put two and two together and connected the dots. Can you even imagine the expression on the FBI agents face at this point? Everyone knows that the FBI never works from speculation, but only starts an investigation from cold hard evidence.

I thought I had one chance and only one chance to convince them of what I knew. I thought I could only attempt to do this after I was able to get some verifiable information that would corroborate my thinking. Every day I would look in the newspapers for this information. Had they put the story on Zacarias Moussaoui in the paper, I would have immediately gone down and said, "That's it, you now have one of the terrorists, this confirms my thinking." Had they reported the James Wood story, or the story of the two al Qaeda terrorists that had slipped into the country, I could have gone down to the FBI office and said, "here is how you connect the dots."

I never had any of this. I could not figure out how to approach the FBI, and be believed at all until after the events of 9/11. And then I went down to tell them of my thinking only because I felt that I was totally and completely responsible for all the deaths of those people that were killed in the World Trade Center, and to ask them if they thought I was at fault also. At the end of the FBI interview, I asked Agent Tagleari, "was this huge disaster all my fault, for not coming in before 9/11, was I to blame. Would my information have been able to stop this attack had I come in February when I first found out"?

Even though the FBI said they felt it was not may fault, I still cannot get over the fact that I was not able to alert someone to this huge attack even though I was completely sure and in fact had absolutely no doubt that this huge attack was going to happen. In fact, after I went back to rethink this several times, I could see no way it was not going to happen. Given the lack of security on airliners, could see no way they could fail in this attack.

To this day, I cannot figure out who I could have told that would have believed me and then started the process to stop this attack. Who in the world would have believed me? Who could I have talked to that would have been able to stop this horrendous attack? For this failure on my part, I am just so terrible sorry. I to this day cannot get over the fact that I could not stop this attack. How is it possible to know about a plan like this in almost every important detail, and then not be able to stop it? What a terrible tragedy!

I hope the experience that I had and the description of the thinking that lead me to understand what was going on, will in some way, be able to help some US government agency in the US, in understanding the thinking of these people and perhaps help to stop the next attack. If you would like me to come down and discuss this information in any, I would be more than happy to help you in any way I could.

Best regards,
Robert Schopmeyer/ President Veritools, Inc.

Phone 650 462 XXXX
Cell Phone 650 533 XXXX
Email schop@veritools.com

Correspondence between myself and the Joint Inquiry Committee of the House and the Senate from October 18, 2003, and October 22, 2002

From: Robert Schopmeyer
Date: Friday, October 18, 2002 2:15 PM
To: rick.cinq@mail.house
Cc: Robert Schopmeyer
Subject: WORLD TRADE CENTER FBI RTEPORT
            FOR THE JOINT INQUIRY COMMITTEE
Attn: ALL JOINT INQUIRY COMMITTEE MEMBERS
Attn: JOINT INQUIRY COMMITTEE,
            STAFF DIRECTOR Eleanor Hill
Attn: JOINT INQUIRY COMMITTEE
            STAFF INVESTIGATOR, Michel Jacobson
Attn: JOINT INQUIRY COMMITTEE
            STAFF INVESTIGATOR, Rich Cinquegrana

I am Robert Schopmeyer, President of a software company in Pal Alto, CA, Veritools, Inc. I am president of a small software company located in Palo Alto, CA.

Here is the information I had promised I would send to this Joint Inquiry Committee after having had a phone conversation with Michel

Jacobson, Joint Inquiry Committee, Staff Investigator on October 11, 2002. I had gone over the content of this material with Michel on the phone in much greater detail then is possible in a written report, and with questions and answers and with a further detailed explanation of how I had come to the conclusions I did on the World Trade Center attacks seven months before it actually happened, and how I had known in almost every important detail about this attack months before it actually took place. I would like to request that this information be added to the record of this committee if at all possible.

In view of Robert Mueller's statement "that after one of the most extensive inquires ever undertaken by the FBI, the bureau had not been able to identify anyone in the United States besides the hijackers themselves who had prior knowledge of the "plot," I felt I had to set the record straight. The FBI has at least four complete phone reports starting on September 11, 2001, and has at least three complete written reports with face to face interviews, the first on September 19, 2001, and the latest with Agent Dan Reynolds, San Jose office on September 24, 2002, on the fact that I been aware of most of the important details of this plot from February, 2001, even to the timing of this event. These interview summaries are attached to this e-mail message. Apparently even after all of this time, none of this information is getting to the top of this organization. I again, would like to request that this information be added to the record of this committee. If any member of this committee would like to go over any part of this information in more detail here or in Washington DC, I would be more than willing to travel to Washington DC and answer any question whatsoever in sworn testimony or not, or provide additional information to clarify anything in this report. I can be reached at 650 462 XXXX, or 650 533 XXXX.

This is a summary of the conclusions I had come to after reading and analyzing nothing more than publicly available information on a flight from San Francisco to New York, to Newark Airport, in early February, 2001.

That Osama Bin Laden's group had to be planning at this time, February 2001, a huge attack directly on the continental US

That this huge attack had to be against some target in the US, that would result in massive physiological damage to the US, and generate "massive media coverage," that was their goal.

That this target without any doubt had to be the World Trade Center Towers in New York City, no other target even came close to matching these huge buildings in terms impact and physiological value.

That the terrorists would hijack at least four very large US airliners, using four or five members on each hijacking team, using small knives, and after taking over these aircraft, drive these planes into the sides of these building in order to collapse these structures.

That this plan had to have been in active operation in the US for at least one year prior to February, 2001. From prior operations that they had carried out in the past, and an estimate of the steps required for this plan, I had estimated that the plan would take between one year and six months to about one year and nine months to complete, starting from the February, 2000 date. While this is the date that I had assumed they had seriously started this plan, this was just a best guess on my part. The year and a half I had calculated from an estimate of three months to bring in the pilots, 12 months to get them trained as private pilots with multi-engine and instrument training, from my own experience as a pilot, and then three months to bring the rest of the hijackers. From this time estimate, I had concluded that they would be, then ready and able to carry out this attack by around the first of August, 2001, which would give them time to practice, and then they would have completed the execution of this plan by no later than by the end of October, 2001. I had actually picked the second to third week of October 2001, as the most likely time period for this attack. I was completely and totally convinced that the two World Trade Center Towers would be completely destroyed by the end of October.

I had also come to the conclusion that the FBI would literally let this huge attack happen right under their noses. If the hijackers keep their plans secret, which I assumed they would, then they and their plan would remain effectively and completely undetected by the FBI, since the FBI does not proactively look for these types of people planning these sorts of attacks. The FBI only starts a serious investigation after some law has been broken in a major way triggering the opening of a field investigation. .

The only way I could see that this plan could be stopped in February, 2001, while on this flight, was to have the FAA require the airlines to provide solid, penetration proof doors on aircraft cockpits and armed guards on US aircraft. Since I did not see how this was going to happen prior to August 1, 2001, I could see no way these building were not going to be completely flattened by this massive attack by the end of October at the very latest.

My conclusions were in fact that not only was this attack probable, once I had understood the thinking of UBL, I could see absolutely no way it would not happen. The World Trade Center Towers had no chance, no chance at all to still remain standing after October 31, 2001.

After going down to see these building up close during this trip in order to see if I could come to the conclusion that they would not collapse, I concluded that, the if the force of the collision with several large aircraft did not bring these building down, the resulting fire from the jet fuel would for sure disturb the integrity of these structures enough to cause these building to collapse. These building at even a cursory glance appeared to be way too tall for their overall size, in order to remain standing in the event of a collision with large aircraft loaded with thousands of pounds of jet fuel.

What information did I have that no one else had?

Absolutely nothing at all, just the same publicly available information that everyone else also had. Every single person, including all of the people at the FBI, the CIA, all the reporters for every newspaper in the US, even all of the members of the US Congress and this committee, that had access to this public information could have come to almost the exact same conclusions that I did, using nothing else but this same publicly available information. Contained with this information was one single but absolutely monumentally important piece of information, one key fact, that when analyzer in the proper fashion, and then from this first step, followed in a very simple step by step logical progression, lead exactly to each and every conclusion that I had come up with on that fight in February, 2001.

This vital piece of information that was part of this public information was the text of the "Declaration of Jihad, the companion "Fatwa," and the fact that these documents had been "published in a newspaper."

On this flight from San Francisco to Newark, I was totally and completely puzzled over how anyone could first think these thoughts, and then totally and completely puzzled over why anyone would ever allow these thoughts to have been written down and published in a newspaper or magazine that Americans would be able to read. This totally made no sense, in view of the fact that terrorists are secretive by nature and now they and their whole organization would be exposed to potentially massive bombing by the Americans for no valid purpose that I could see.

It was this last question that became the actual "key," to figuring out that an attack was coming on the World Trade Center, this was the "KEY." On this flight, at this time, I was doing nothing more than just trying to figure out this very strange puzzle, and had in fact, absolutely no thought at all of trying to figure out what target the al Qaeda terrorists were planning to attack next.

The "Fatwa" says:

"To kill Americans and their Allies, both civil and military, is an individual duty of every Muslim, who is able, in any country where this is possible... By Gods leave, we call on every Muslim who believes in God and hopes for reward to obey God's command to kill Americans and plunder their possessions wherever he finds them and whenever he can."

I had come to the conclusion, being totally unable to figure this out after 20 minutes, that the best way to understand why these terrorists had allowed this material to be published was to treat this puzzle as two different questions.

I figured that the easiest way to answer the second question, why did they allow this material to be published, was to first answer the question, what was the actual thinking of the authors of these documents that had allowed them to come up with the thoughts in the Declaration and the Fatwa. I figured this was absolutely essential in order to answer; why they had allowed this material to be published.

I figured to would be easy to answer the second question, why they had allowed the Declaration and Fatwa to even have been published, after I figured out the answer to the first question. Without figuring out the first question, I assumed that I would have no hope of ever being able to answer the second question in any reasonable time period.

To understand the actual thinking of the people that had written and were behind these documents, and completely understand how anyone could have come up with these thoughts was not as hard as one would imagine. All you had to do is pretend you were, if you can imagine this, Osama Bin Laden himself, in Saudi Arabia and a young person, and then imagine all of the life experiences that would have been required for you personally to come up with this thinking. Some might described this as a process of putting yourself in his mind, but in fact it is more of

597

a process of building another persons thought process in your mind, and then letting this thought processes take over your thinking temporarily, in such a way so you will be able to answer any question on the motivations of this other person. This allows you to see the world from their point of view.

This process went like this: as a young person in Saudi Arabia, UBL was extremely devout and "pious" as a Muslim, and understanding his thinking first starts with understanding the meaning this word "pious." To understand this thinking and the meaning of the word, pious, you become in your mind a very devout and pious Muslim in Saudi Arabia, as a young person. When a very impressionable young person is pious, they invariably have varying degrees of contempt for those who are not as pious. This contempt actually turns to hatred for those who are in a higher social or political status, but clearly are not as a pious. Hence after a few years, UBL grew to hate all of the ruling class of Saudi Arabia since he perceived them to be totally non-pious Muslims. UBL came to believe that this leader ship had to be in fact, replaced by a Caliph of very esteemed mullahs, or imams, that would then rule Saudi Arabia as a Muslim country, under the laws of the Shariah.

Even the Saudi Arabian leaders had concluded the same thing after the major shrines in Saudi Arabia had been taken over by force by very radical Muslims, who felt that theses shrines should no longer be controlled by the leaders of Saudi Arabia since they were not devout enough Muslims. After this take over was put down, the Saudi leaders decided they would move to as far right as possible on religious matters, in fact to the right of every other religious group in Saudi Arabia.

The Iraq conflict with the US and putting troops directly into Saudi Arabia, added another element to this hatred. Now the very corrupt Saudi leaders were being protected by infidels, who also were in fact despoiling the holy ground of Saudi Arabia by even being there. At some point UBL realized that to ultimately get rid of the Saudi leaders would require the expulsion of the US forces who by now were in essence giving protection to the leaders of Saudi Arabia. Hence at some point this immense hated for the Saudi leaders transferred itself to the even more immense hatred of US itself and then ultimately to an immense hatred the people of the US, whom UBL assumed was financing these troops on the Saudi peninsula through the payments of their taxes. Hence in his thinking, he had come to the conclusion that in this Jihad, even innocent US civilians should become the targets of his attacks.

His thinking then progressed to the point, after he meet Amen Al-Zawahiri, that he felt that not only Saudi Arabia, but all of the Muslim areas should ultimately be governed by this single Caliph, establishing strict Muslim rule over all of these Middle East countries.

What was most obvious after this process, was that you could begin to see that the depth of his hatred for the United States and its citizens was absolutely monumental. Anyone who had not gone through the process I had just described would never have been able to even begin to understand this thinking. Without having gone through this process, it would been just like trying to explain what the color purple was to a blind person, without them ever having seen it for themselves in person.

Next, I wanted to refine my image of his thought process by running all of the attacks that had already occurred up to this point, by this thought process, to see if they made sense once you understood his thinking. The attack on the Khobar Towers made perfect sense, he was sending a message to the US, to get out of Saudi Arabia. The attack on the embassies made less sense or no sense, these in my opinion, since these were out of the area that was to be governed by this single Caliph. This meant that UBL now was going to attack the US interests anywhere they were located, even outside of the area where he wanted them expelled from. This could only mean that he had an enormous enmity for the US and its people, unrelated to the reasons in the "Declaration." This could only mean that the US could expect an attack anywhere in the world. "He really did mean what he wrote in the Fatwa." What is the difference between attacking Tanzania and Kenya and the continental US, just a couple more hours on an airplane.

The attack on the *Cole* made sense with one huge question, if he felt he could attack the *Cole* armed with large guns mounted on the deck of this ship, what did this really imply. This could only mean that UBL felt he literally could hit ant target or any building that he wanted to, anywhere in the world. What building for example comes with a four-inch gun mounted on the roof. If he could hit the *Cole*, he could attack "any" building anywhere in the world. This meant very clearly, that no structure anywhere in the world was going to be immune from an attack by al Qaeda, even building in the US. The Americans after every attack seemed almost completely oblivious to these attacks and what they meant.

Next I went back to the original question why had he allowed this Declaration and Fatwa to be published? Think of it, he had already hit the Khobar Towers with a huge attack without any Declaration all, now he had issued and published this Declaration for all of the world to see. Issuing this Declaration in my opinion had to signify something entirely new. Again at this point I tried one final time to answer this as an American and could make no sense out of this. That is when I decided that the only approach was to again think this through with UBL's thought process. I again, imagined myself in his place, at the front of hundreds of screaming terrorists, all heavily armed, and in my mind imagined myself issuing this Declaration, and then asked the question, why am I doing this?

The answer was instantly and completely obvious. Proclaiming and then publishing this Declaration could absolutely only mean one thing, that Osama Bin Laden was now at this point openly declaring total war against the US, and that he now was going to plan and then mount the biggest attack he could possible imagine directly against the "continental" United States. I could think of absolutely no other reason for issuing this Declaration. It had to signify now the coming of attacks directly against the US on US soil. In fact I felt that if he did not do this, after making this widely disseminated Declaration, in front of his own followers, it would have made him look like a complete fool. Notice as an American, Osama proclaiming and publishing this Declaration made no sense at all, when you actually became Osama Bin Laden himself your mind, it started to make perfect sense.

Hadn't anyone else noticed this event and then tried to analyze what exactly it meant, this information was available for everyone to see and analyze. Did the FBI and CIA just think that publicly available information had no real value since everyone knew it anyway, and that nothing could be gained by very carefully analyzing what certain publicly available facts could ultimately mean. Did they think that only secret information had any real value in trying to analyze what the terrorist were going to do next.

It was at this point, I went back to see exactly when this Fatwa had actually been published, and discovered that it had actually been published in February of 1998, three years earlier. This was in fact the very next puzzle that solving of the first two puzzles next lead to. At this point, I could not for the life of me, figure out why this huge attack had not already taken. How was this even possible, how long for Gods sake, would it take to mount a large an attack on the US and then next what was the target of this attack going to be? As I was trying to figure this out, I figured that what ever the actual plan for the attack was, it had to be incredibly simple, on the order of a plan that a third grader would be able to understand and remember. This is because these plans take place over long periods of time and at great distance from Afghanistan, and with no contact or very little contact at all during this time with the leaders of this group for either secrecy or logistical reasons.

I was not able to figure this last puzzle out, and in fact after 20-25 minutes of intense thinking, I completely gave up even trying to solve this puzzle. No answer was even close to becoming obvious, nothing was coming out, and I had actually become exhausted over the mental energy I had put into trying to figure this puzzle out.

It was then, when I laid down this magazine that I had been reading and picked out a travel brochure from the seat pocket in front of me, in order to get some material that had less intense subject matter. The picture right on the front cover was of lower Manhattan, looking down from a point high above the Statue of Liberty. The picture of the WTC Towers was prominently displayed right dead center on this front cover. As soon as I saw this picture, I was just completely and totally stunned. Looking at this one picture just completely knocked the wind right out of me. When I got my breathing back, I realized that this one picture answered both questions completely and almost perfectly.

This attack had not yet happened yet because it was going to be such a huge attack, that it simply had to be taking a significantly long time to prepare for. Without any doubt whatsoever, these building had to be the focus of Osama Bin Laden and the al Qaeda organizations next attack. He was just going to obliterate these building. I concluded that if these buildings were his targets, he would use the simplest plan possible to collapse these structures. The simplest plan I could think of was for his group to hijack four large airliners and then drive these aircraft into the walls of these buildings. He could hijack these aircraft very easily by just using four or five members of his terrorist organization to capture each plan in flight, carrying right through security perfectly legal knives with blades that were no longer than four inches as weapons. With four or five terrorists on board armed with knives, no passenger would want to stand up to them knowing they would be immediately killed, as long as the passengers were not organized.

Next, I asked the question, when is this attack going to happen? Much of the material on the al Qaeda organization that I had read on this flight was completely new to me, even though I frequently read many newspapers and magazines. Because of this I, concluded that when it came to knowledge of terrorists or their activities, I was in fact a complete and total idiot. Hence, I figured that if I had just discovered their plan they had to have been working on it for quit a while already, I had estimated that they must have been actively working on this plan for at least one year prior to this flight in February, 2001. By actively working on it I mean the date they had first come to the US with actual terrorist team members, I did not see any way I could estimate how long they had worked on their plans outside of the US. If they started in January or February of 2000, and this plan took 1½ years, then they would be ready to go by some time around the first of August. I had estimated it would take about one year to train the pilots, with three months on the front end to select the schools, and get the pilot training started, and the another back three months after the training to bring in the other team members into the US and get ready.

After the first part of August they would practice and then pick a date and it was over. The attack on the *Cole*, basically showed that these people do not wait, they plan, they survey the target, they pick a date and it is over. I assumed then that this would imply that by the end of October this plan would have been completed for sure, although no one could forecast the actual date. This was going to be decided at the last minute based on when the terrorists thought they were completely ready and when they thought that further delay would only expose them to possible detection.

For the rest of the flight I keep going over and over this thinking that allowed me to think that these huge building were going to be completely destroyed, hoping against hope that I could find a flaw in this thinking. I did not want in any way to see these huge buildings destroyed and all of these people killed, but nothing else I could think of then or for the rest of this flight even came close to matching these buildings as a potential target.

Once I came to a realization of what the publishing of the Declaration and Fatwa really meant, and that a huge attack was in the planning stages, I knew that the leadership of al Qaeda had to be 100 percent focused on these buildings as their target and that nothing else even came close. I could see no way that these huge building were not going to be obliterated, especially with the total lack of any real security that existed on the major airliners. Once I had thoroughly understood the thinking of the leadership of al Qaeda, I could come to no other

602

conclusion. If you had not first understand their thinking, these conclusions would never have made any sense at all, they would appear to be in fact almost bizarre.

Needless to say when I came back to California and told my employees at Veritools in February 2001, they were totally completely stunned, I had originally assumed they would have been more supportive, but that was not the case. I recently just found out that some of them felt I must have lost my mind, after I had told them that the World Trade Center Tower were doomed and would be completely destroyed by al Qaeda terrorists using four large hijacked airliners before the end of October 2001. I told them that I had concluded that these hijackers were going hijack and then drive these airliners right into the walls of the WTC Towers in order to collapse these structures, and that there absolutely was no way in world this attack was not going to happen.

You have my permission to talk to the people at Veritools who also knew of this coming attack in February 2001. I had told almost all of them of this just as soon as I had returned from New York. They are all still, one year later very scared and still greatly disturbed over this in particular since they had known it was coming for several months. When I had told one of our sales persons, Alina, of this huge attack on February 12, 2001, she stood there absolutely motionless for at least two minutes with her mouth wide open, just staring at me. When (I) had asked if I should go to the FBI, Alina said that there was absolutely no way anyone at the FBI would take this information seriously, and sadly after listing to her I came to the same conclusion she did.

The employees of Veritools were so scared of the hijackers, that in June 2001, when the entire sales force was getting ready to fly to Las Vegas for the DAC (Design Automation), one of the sales persons, Tina, asked me what they should do if the World Trade Center hijackers were on her flight from San Francisco to Las Vegas. I told her that if she or anyone spotted any of World Trade Center terrorists on their flight, to get the hell off immediately, say nothing to anybody, throw away their ticket and I would buy them a new ticket no questions asked. That their life was worth far more then the price of an airline ticket. I also made the same announcement to the rest of the company employees, all of the sales people that were going to Las Vegas, about 10 people. This was in spite of the fact at the time I did not think in any way that the terrorists would be going to Las Vegas, it was only after 9/11 that I learned they had been in Las Vegas four times, from May to August and had most likely flown in from flight originating from West Coast cities.

The rest of this story is explained in the following attachments I have added to this letter. The attached FBI report is the information I gave to The FBI on September 19, 2001 along with signed affidavits at that time from employees of Veritools on the information concerning the fact that I had informed them of this huge attack along with the conclusion that the WTC Towers would be totally and completely destroyed by the end of October, 2001. That these building had absolutely no chance to with stand this huge attack

In retrospect I have come to believe that this approach was literally "the one and only approach" that could have been used by any intelligence organization to, understand the thinking of the top people at the al Qaeda organization, and then to be able to anticipate what activities they must have been planning next. Without this framework of what their next plans might be, even critical information that the FBI had, was then not appreciated for its importance and not adequately followed up on. For example when they had arrested Zacarias Moussaoui, instead of trying to look on his computer, and then giving up when the search warrant was not forth coming, why did they not ask;

How many other hijackers does it take to take over a huge airliner, four or five at the least?

If it takes more than one, then where are the other four or five terrorists now?

If several terrorists are really trying to plan a airliner high jacking, would it not be the prudent thing to do, to ask all of the airline companies to look at their passenger reservation lists in order to see if these other terrorists are on their flights just as soon as they could, in order to prevent any hijacking from taking place?

All you would have had to do is have the airlines look for four or five young terrorists, all carrying small knives through security onto these airliners, and then see if this pattern fit for two to four airliners all taking off at the same time, a completely logical thing to do. Since no one at the FBI seems to have even anticipated the WTC attack, or even that such an attack was possible, all the information the FBI received was just a bunch disconnected dots with no framework whatsoever to allow the FBI to fill in the holes and finally connect the dots together.

I also think that it is important that this story get out, if for no other reason that to alert the top officials of the US government that when they have vital information they should share it immediately with the US population. During July and August of 2001, almost all of the NSC and the Central Intelligence Agency top officials were getting signals of a huge attack on the US by al Qaeda, and in fact were almost in a panic over what the target this attack could be.

Why had they not put their concerns on the front page of every newspaper in the US with a request for anyone with any possible information at all on these attacks to come forth? Why had they kept this information so secret? Had they done this, I would have immediately come forward with what I was convinced were the conclusions I had come to about this attack. Maybe this would have made no difference, but at least I would have had a chance to present what I thought I knew about the plan at this time. Let's hope the next time they will do this, but I have my doubts. You can start, by letting the top officials of our government know that it can be vitally important to ask the US public to help out in these types of situations.

From: Cinquegrana, Rick Rick.Cinquegrana@mail.house.gov
Date: Saturday, October 19, 2002 7:20 AM
To: 'Robert Schopmeyer' schop@veritools.com
Subject: RE: WORLD TRADE CENTER FBI REPORT
          FOR THE JOINT INQUIRY COMMITTEE

Mr. Schopmeyer – Thank you very much for the information regarding your thought process prior to the September 11 attacks. I will ensure that it is provided to Mike Jacobson, with whom you say you have already spoken. He will evaluate your report and how it fits into our work regarding what the U. S. government knew or should have known about those attacks. Thank you again for your assistance to the Joint Inquiry.

Rick Cinquegrana

Cinquegrana, Rick Rick.Cinquegrana@mail.house.gov

Date: Saturday, October 19, 2002 2:25 PM

To: 'Robert Schopmeyer' schop@veritools.com
Subject: RE: WORLD TRADE CENTER FBI REPORT FOR THE
              JOINT INQUIRY COMMITTEE

I would have to agree with the FBI that you bear no personal responsibility for the attacks on September 11. There was other information, including the 1993 bombing of the World Trade Center garage, indicating that the towers were a continuing target of terrorists because of their symbolic value. As you report the FBI has told you, your report, without specific details that you could not have known, would likely not have been sufficient to change the outcome. I can assure you that the point you are making about the need to better inform the American public has not been lost on us – in fact, I am attaching the last in a series of public statements that the Staff has released in which that very point is made.

Best of luck in your endeavors.

----- Original Message -----
From: Robert Schopmeyer [mailto:schop@veritools.com]
To: Cinquegrana, Rick
Sent: Saturday, October 19, 2002 5:16 PM
Subject: RE: WORLD TRADE CENTER FBI REPORT FOR THE
              JOINT INQUIRY COMMITTEE REPLY

Rick,

Thank you very much for your reply, if there is anything I can do to help you and your committee out, please let me know what else I can do.

One issue that may not have come through, I went down to the FBI and made a report, starting in 9/11/2001, I was in Boston at this time, because I felt, at this time, that I was personally completely and totally responsible for all of the lives that were lost at the World Trade Center and to ask the FBI, did they feel that I was to blame for not preventing this disaster. They said that in their view I was not to blame in any way, and had I come in to the FBI in February 2001, with these conclusions, they would have done nothing at that time, since I did not have a specific date, or specific flight number or any specific name, just some general dates and conclusions based on speculation.

I had decided that without some credible specific information, my conclusions would never have been given serious consideration by the FBI. I looked every day in the papers in order to see if I could find just exactly that type of information. The arrest of Zacarias Moussaoui, the listing of the names of the two al Qaeda members, Nawaf al-Hazmi and Khalid al-Mihdhar, even the feeling of panic felt by the top leadership of the CIA, FBI, NSC and even the Senate Intelligence Committee that a huge attack against US interests was imminent, if any of this information had been published in the newspapers I could have gone to the FBI and said, here it is, this is how I think you can now connect all of these dots together. Unfortunately, I never had any of this information. HOW SAD.

I would hope in the future, that the leaders of our country will start to realize how vitally important it is to let this type of information be widely disseminated, so that the citizens of this country can be enlisted in order to provide additional help or insight in these situations, and possibly prevent these types of disasters. Do I think that the information that I had along with the information that these agencies had could have prevented the disaster of 9/11? I don't know, and I don't know if anyone will ever know for sure, but it could not have made it any worse.

Robert Schopmeyer/President Veritools, Inc.

----- Original Message -----
From: Cinquegrana, Rick <Rick.Cinquegrana@mail.house.gov>
To: 'Robert Schopmeyer' <schop@veritools.com>
Sent: Saturday, October 19, 2002 8:20 AM
Subject: RE: WORLD TRADE CENTER FBI REPORT FOR THE
            JOINT INQUIRY COMMITTEE

> Mr. Schopmeyer – Thank you very much for the information
> regarding your thought process prior to the September 11 attacks. I
> will ensure that it is provided to Mike Jacobson, with whom you say
> you have already spoken. He will evaluate your report and how it fits
> into our work regarding what the U. S. government knew or should
> have known about those attacks.
>
> Thank you
> again for your assistance to the Joint Inquiry.
>
> Rick Cinquegrana

From: Cinquegrana, Rick Rick.Cinquegrana@mail.house.gov
Date: Saturday, October 22, 2002 1:15 PM
To: 'Robert Schopmeyer' schop@veritools.com
Subject: RE: WORLD TRADE CENTER FBI REPORT FOR THE
           JOINT INQUIRY COMMITTEE

Thanks very much for your follow-up thoughts. I will ensure they are fully considered by the staff here as we write our final report.

Email to Robert Kerrey just prior to the April 13-14, 2004 9/11 Commission Public Hearings

Dear Mr. Robert Kerrey,   **April 11, 2004**

This is a summary what I and my company's employees knew about on the events of 9/11, seven months prior to this attack on the World Trade Center, and how we found out this information;

On February 11, 2001 on a flight from San Francisco to New York City, I came upon the following statement in the material I was reading on this flight on the al Qaeda organization;

"It is the duty of every Muslim in the world to kill Americans, both military and civilian in what ever country they are found, and destroy their possessions."

After being totally puzzled over why anyone would ever be associated with the release of this information to worldwide distribution in Muslim newspapers, this is a summary of the conclusions that I came up with, after analyzing the thinking and motivation of the top people for issuing this statement;

That this statement, had to be a public and open declaration of war against the US by the top leadership of al Qaeda.

Note; Mr. Kerrey, in your statement on March 24, that the terrorists had declared war on the US in a press conference in February 1998, I am not sure you were referring to this same statement, but if you were, you appear to be the only person in the US government that I have ever seen that had figured out the importance of this statement and what it really meant up to now.

That this declaration of war had to mean, since it had come 10 years after the start of al Qaeda, that they now were going to mount a titanic sized attack directly inside of the US against some target of major psychological and symbolic value, in fact publishing this statement had to be the "Go Signal" for this attack.

After much analysis, that the target of this attack had to be the two twin towers of the World Trade Center, no other target even came close in terms of "magnification factor" as this target. Magnification factor refers to the degree of magnification that this attack by a small team of terrorists would get "magnified" in the mainstream news media.

That the method of attack had to be the use of four hijacked large aircraft that would be hijacked in flight, using four or five al Qaeda terrorists per plane armed with small knives that had blades no longer than four inches.

That their goal was to kill at least 30,000 people, who would be in these buildings at the time of their attack.

That this plan had to have been in active operation in the US for at least one year prior to February, 2001, with the approximate time-line; three months to bring in the pilots, 12 months to get them trained as pilots, then they would be ready and able to carry out this attack by around the first of August, 2001. This would give them time to practice, during August, and then they would have completed the execution of this plan by no later than by the end of October 2001. I was completely and totally convinced that the two World Trade Center Towers would be completely destroyed, obliterated is a better term, by the no later than end of October.

I had also come to the conclusion that the FBI would literally let this huge attack happen right under their noses. If the hijackers keep their plans secret, which I assumed they would, then they and their plan would remain effectively and completely undetected by the FBI, since the FBI does not proactively look for these types of people planning these sorts of attacks. The FBI only starts a serious investigation after some law has been broken in a major way triggering the opening of a field investigation. The only way I could see that this plan could be stopped in February, 2001, while on this flight, was to have the FAA require the airlines to provide solid, penetration proof doors on aircraft cockpits and armed guards on US aircraft. Since I did not see how this was going to happen prior to August 1, 2001, I could see no way these building were not going to be completely flattened by this massive attack by the end of October at the very latest.

My conclusions were in fact that not only was this attack probable, once I had understood the thinking of UBL, I could see absolutely no way it would not happen. The World Trade Center Towers had no chance, no chance at all to remain standing after October 31, 2001.

I came back to my company, Veritools, Inc. in Palo Alto, California, on February 19, 2001 and told every single person at my company, around 11-12 employees this information. That this huge attack was in progress, that these huge building would be completely destroyed before the end of October 2001, killing everyone inside of these structures, and that I had to go to the FBI with this information.

I have given this information to the following FBI offices:

Boston FBI Field Office, on September 11, 2001, phone interview

San Francisco, CA Agent Robert Stow, September 19, 2001, phone interview

San Jose, CA, Agent Vince Tagleari, September 19, 2001, in person interview, written report

San Francisco, CA, Agent Marior Remaro, April 19, 2002, in person interview and written report

San Jose, Ca, Agent Dan Reynolds, Oct 2002, written report

Joint House Senate Inquiry Committee, Members, Staff Director, Eleanor Hill, written report, Staff Investigator, Michel Jacobson, written report, Staff Rick Cinquegrana, phone interview and written report

I had volunteered in writing to the FBI and to the Joint Inquiry Committee, to testify "under oath in a sworn statement" backed up with poly graph tests of any kind, any where, at any time, with any question to establish beyond any doubt the truth of all of these facts as I know them, and also to allow my employees to do the same.

I would be willing to do the same with the 9/11 Committee in Washington DC, with you personally in person, or over the phone.

The process I used to figure this out that this huge attack was going to occur is explained in much more detail in the attached documentation below.

Best regards,
Robert Schopmeyer/President Veritools, Inc.
Phone number 650 462 XXXX